Core 3 & 4

Core 3 & 4

Hugh Neill and Douglas Quadling

Series editor Hugh Neill

CAMBRIDGE
UNIVERSITY PRESS

CAMBRIDGE UNIVERSITY PRESS
Cambridge, New York, Melbourne, Madrid, Cape Town,
Singapore, São Paulo, Delhi, Tokyo, Mexico City

Cambridge University Press
The Edinburgh Building, Cambridge CB2 8RU, UK

www.cambridge.org
Information on this title: www.cambridge.org/9780521548977

First published 2005
7th printing 2011

Printed in Dubai by Oriental Press

A catalogue record for this publication is available from the British Library

ISBN 978-0-521-54897-7 Paperback

Contents

Introduction   *page* vii

Module C3   Core 3

  0   Some preliminaries   3

  1   Successive transformations   10

  2   Functions   16

  3   Exponential growth and decay   39

  4   Extending differentiation and integration   54

  5   Differentiating exponentials and logarithms   65

  6   Trigonometry   90

  7   The modulus function   113

    Revision exercise 1   129

  8   Solving equations numerically   135

  9   The chain rule   150

 10   Differentiating products   163

 11   Volumes of revolution   173

 12   Simpson's rule   182

    Revision exercise 2   192

    Practice examinations for C3   197

Module C4   Core 4

  1   Differentiating trigonometric functions   203

  2   Integration   224

  3   Parametric equations   241

  4   Vectors   254

  5   The binomial expansion   275

    Revision exercise 3   284

  6   Rational functions   289

  7   Differential equations   314

  8   Curves defined implicitly   328

  9   Scalar products of vectors   346

Revision exercise 4   362

Practice examinations for C4   366

Answers to C3   371

Answers to C4   385

Index   399

Introduction

Cambridge Advanced Mathematics has been written especially for the OCR modular examinations. Each book or half-book in the series corresponds to one module. This book covers the third and fourth core mathematics modules, C3 and C4.

The book opens with an unusual chapter entitled 'Some preliminaries'. The purpose of this chapter is to introduce some notation and ideas concerned with sets of numbers, and proof. The chapter is meant for reference when it is needed: there are no exercises.

The remainder of the book is divided into chapters roughly corresponding to specification headings. Occasionally a section includes an important result that is difficult to prove or outside the specification. These sections are marked with an asterisk (*) in the section heading, and there is usually a sentence early on explaining precisely what it is that the student needs to know.

Occasionally within the text paragraphs appear in a grey box. These paragraphs are usually outside the main stream of the mathematical argument, but may help to give insight, or suggest extra work or different approaches.

The authors have assumed that the students have access to graphic calculators and that students will use them throughout the course to assist their learning of mathematics.

Numerical work is presented in a form intended to discourage premature approximation. In ongoing calculations inexact numbers appear in decimal form like 3.456..., signifying that the number is held in a calculator to more places than are given. Numbers are not rounded at this stage; the full display could be, for example, 3.456 123 or 3.456 789. Final answers are then stated with some indication that they are approximate, for example '3.46 correct to 3 significant figures'.

There are plenty of exercises, and each chapter contains a miscellaneous exercise which includes some questions of examination standard. The authors thank Charles Parker, Lawrence Jarrett and Tim Cross, the OCR examiners who contributed to these exercises. In each module there are also two revision exercises, with many questions taken from OCR examination papers, and two practice examination papers.

The authors also thank Peter Thomas and Clive Johnson, who read the book very carefully and made many useful comments, and OCR and Cambridge University Press for their help in producing this book. However, the responsibility for the text, and for any errors, remains with the authors.

Module C3

Core 3

0 Some preliminaries

The reason for this unusual chapter number and title is that this is not a chapter in the usual sense of this book. It contains a number of things which you might well have seen before, in which case you can skip it and go straight to Chapter 1, and use this for occasional reference.

If you haven't seen the material before, skim it quickly, go on to Chapter 1 and come back to it when you need to.

So this chapter consists of

- some new notation
- some details about methods of proof and disproof.

0.1 Notation for numbers

When you have been working with functions, an expression which occurs frequently is 'where x is a real number'.

There is a special notation for this, which is '$x \in \mathbb{R}$'.

The symbol '$\in$' stands for 'belongs to' or 'is a member of', and the symbol '$\mathbb{R}$' stands for 'the set of real nunmbers'.

In a similar way, when you are dealing with sequences, such as an arithmetic or a geometric sequence, the sequence is often called u_1, u_2, u_3 etc. In this case the subscripts 1, 2, 3, ... are natural numbers which are denoted by the symbol $\mathbb{N}$.

Thus, to say that $n \in \mathbb{N}$ means that n can be a whole number greater than 0. (Some authors allow $\mathbb{N}$ to include the number 0, but this will never be the case in these books.)

0.2 Modulus notation

Suppose that you want to find the difference between the heights of two people. With numerical information, the answer is quite straightforward: if their heights are 90 cm and 100 cm, you would answer 10 cm; and if their heights were 100 cm and 90 cm, you would still answer 10 cm.

But how would you answer the question if their heights were H cm and h cm? The answer is, it depends which is bigger: if $H > h$, you would answer $(H - h)$ cm; if $h > H$ you would answer $(h - H)$ cm; and if $h = H$ you would answer 0 cm, which is either $(H - h)$ cm or $(h - H)$ cm.

Questions like this, in which you want an answer which is always positive or zero, lead to the idea of the modulus.

> The **modulus** of x, written $|x|$ and pronounced 'mod x', is defined by
>
> $$|x| = x \qquad \text{if } x \geqslant 0,$$
> $$|x| = -x \qquad \text{if } x < 0.$$

Using the modulus notation, you can now write the difference in heights as $|H - h|$ whether $H > h, h > H$ or $h = H$.

Another situation when the modulus is useful is when you talk about numbers which are large numerically, but which are negative, such as -1000 or $-1\,000\,000$. These are 'negative numbers with large modulus'.

For example, for large positive values of x, the value of $\dfrac{1}{x}$ approaches 0. The same is true for negative values of x with large modulus. So you can say that, when $|x|$ is large, $\left|\dfrac{1}{x}\right|$ is close to zero; or in a numerical example, when $|x| > 1000$, $\left|\dfrac{1}{x}\right| < 0.001$. (See Fig. 0.1.)

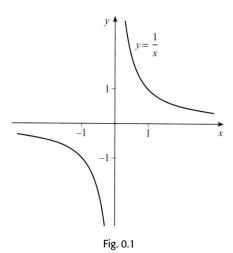

Fig. 0.1

0.3   Implication

It is extremely useful to have a way of shortening the argument 'If A, then B', where A and B are mathematical statements. Examples of such arguments with statements A and B might be

'If $x = 5$, then $x^2 = 25$',

and

'If XYZ is a triangle and angle $X = 90°$, then $XY^2 + XZ^2 = YZ^2$'.

These statements can be rewritten using the symbol $\Rightarrow$ as

$$x = 5 \quad \Rightarrow \quad x^2 = 25,$$

and

$$XYZ \text{ is a triangle and } X = 90° \quad \Rightarrow \quad XY^2 + XZ^2 = YZ^2.$$

The $\Rightarrow$ sign is read as 'implies'. If the statement on the left is true, then the statement on the right is true.

> Notice that if the statement on the left is not true, nothing is said about the statement on the right. The use of $\Rightarrow$ in the statement $0 = 1 \quad \Rightarrow \quad 1 = 2$ is perfectly correct. If the statement on the left is true, the statement on the right follows logically. This is not a particularly helpful piece of deduction, because $0 = 1$ is false!

If you link several statements together by a chain of implications, as

$$A \quad \Rightarrow \quad B \quad \Rightarrow \quad C \quad \Rightarrow \quad \ldots \quad \Rightarrow \quad K,$$

then you can deduce that $A \Rightarrow K$. In this way you can sometimes prove a whole theorem through a number of small steps.

Sometimes the sign is reversed, as $\Leftarrow$, which is read as 'is implied by'. So $A \Rightarrow B$ can also be written as $B \Leftarrow A$.

It sometimes happens that $A \Rightarrow B$ and $A \Leftarrow B$. You can then combine $\Rightarrow$ and $\Leftarrow$, to write

$$A \quad \Leftrightarrow \quad B$$

where the symbol $\Leftrightarrow$ means 'implies and is implied by'. This means that the two statements are completely equivalent; if either one is known to be true, so is the other. So $\Leftrightarrow$ is often read as 'is logically equivalent to' or as 'if and only if'.

For example, when doing algebra, you can add the same number to both sides of an equation, so that

$$x = y \quad \Rightarrow \quad x + z = y + z.$$

It is also true that

$$x = y \quad \Leftarrow \quad x + z = y + z, \quad \text{or} \quad x + z = y + z \quad \Rightarrow \quad x = y.$$

So you can write

$$x = y \quad \Leftrightarrow \quad x + z = y + z.$$

But there are some important algebraic steps which cannot be reversed in this way. For example, the step

$$x = y \quad \Rightarrow \quad xz = yz$$

is valid, but it is not true that

$$x = y \quad \Leftarrow \quad xz = yz, \quad \text{or} \quad xz = yz \quad \Rightarrow \quad x = y,$$

since z could be zero, and then x and y need not be equal.

Another non-reversible step is squaring both sides of an equation. You can write

$$x = y \quad \Rightarrow \quad x^2 = y^2, \quad \text{but not} \quad x = y \quad \Leftarrow \quad x^2 = y^2.$$

The correct reverse implication is

$$
\begin{aligned}
x^2 = y^2 \quad &\Rightarrow \quad x^2 - y^2 = 0 \\
&\Rightarrow \quad (x - y)(x + y) = 0 \\
&\Rightarrow \quad \text{either } x - y = 0 \text{ or } x + y = 0 \\
&\Rightarrow \quad \text{either } x = y \text{ or } x = -y.
\end{aligned}
$$

These points are important when you solve equations. It is very tempting to join up the steps in a solution with $\Leftrightarrow$ signs without thinking. But you can easily reach a wrong conclusion if one of the implications is not reversible.

Example 0.3.1

Solve the equation $\sqrt{2x + 1} = \sqrt{x} - 5$.

$$
\begin{aligned}
\sqrt{2x + 1} = \sqrt{x} - 5 \quad &\Rightarrow \quad 2x + 1 = (\sqrt{x} - 5)^2 \\
&\Leftrightarrow \quad 2x + 1 = x - 10\sqrt{x} + 25 \\
&\Leftrightarrow \quad 10\sqrt{x} = 24 - x \\
&\Rightarrow \quad 100x = (24 - x)^2 \\
&\Leftrightarrow \quad 100x = 576 - 48x + x^2 \\
&\Leftrightarrow \quad x^2 - 148x + 576 = 0 \\
&\Leftrightarrow \quad (x - 4)(x - 144) = 0 \\
&\Leftrightarrow \quad \text{either } x = 4 \text{ or } x = 144.
\end{aligned}
$$

But in fact, neither $x = 4$ nor $x = 144$ satisfies the equation. With $x = 4$ the left side is $\sqrt{9} = 3$ and the right side is $\sqrt{4} - 5 = -3$. With $x = 144$ the left side is $\sqrt{289} = 17$, and the right side is $\sqrt{144} - 5 = 7$. It follows that the equation has no solution.

The point is that solving equations is a two-way process. You need to show both that

If x satisfies the equation, then x would have certain values

and that

If x has one of these values, then it satisfies the equation.

With a simple equation such as

$$2x + 3 = 7 - 3x \quad \Leftrightarrow \quad 3x + 2x = 7 - 3 \quad \Leftrightarrow \quad x = 0.8,$$

all the steps are equivalence steps, so that both parts of the solution are included in the single chain of reasoning. (But it is still a good idea to check that $x = 0.8$ does satisfy the original equation, to make sure you haven't made a mistake.)

But in Example 0.3.1 above there are two non-reversible steps,

$$\text{(a) } \sqrt{2x + 1} = \sqrt{x} - 5 \quad \Rightarrow \quad 2x + 1 = (\sqrt{x} - 5)^2$$
$$\text{and} \quad \text{(b) } 10\sqrt{x} = 24 - x \quad \Rightarrow \quad 100x = (24 - x)^2.$$

You can easily check that when $x = 4$ the equation on the right of (a) is satisfied, but the equation on the left is not; and when $x = 144$ the equation on the right of (b) is satisfied, but the equation on the left is not.

There are actually four different equations,

$$\text{(i)} \quad \sqrt{2x+1} = \sqrt{x} - 5$$
$$\text{(ii)} \quad -\sqrt{2x+1} = \sqrt{x} - 5$$
$$\text{(iii)} \quad \sqrt{2x+1} = -\sqrt{x} - 5$$
$$\text{(iv)} \quad -\sqrt{2x+1} = -\sqrt{x} - 5$$

all of which after two squarings lead to $100x = (24 - x)^2$, and thence to $x = 4$ or $x = 144$. Equation (ii) has $x = 4$ as a root; (iv) has $x = 144$; and (i) and (iii) have no solution.

Example 0.3.2
Solve the simultaneous equations $2x - 5y = 3$, $10y - 4x = -5$.

$$2x - 5y = 3 \text{ and } 10y - 4x = -5 \quad \Rightarrow \quad 2(2x - 5y) + (10y - 4x) = 2 \times 3 + (-5)$$
$$\Rightarrow \quad 4x - 10y + 10y - 4x = 6 - 5$$
$$\Rightarrow \quad 0 = 1.$$

This is *not* a 'proof' that $0 = 1$. It would have been wrong to write down a sequence of equations ending with the statement 'Therefore $0 = 1$'. The advantage of the $\Rightarrow$ notation is that nowhere in the chain of reasoning is it asserted that any of the statements are true; only that *if* the first statement is true, then so is the last.

The correct interpretation of this example is that if there were numbers x and y such that $2x - 5y = 3$ and $10y - 4x = -5$, then 0 would equal 1. Since you know that 0 does not equal 1, the conclusion is that there are no numbers x and y satisfying these simultaneous equations. That is, the equations have no solution. This is an example of proof by contradiction which you will see more about in the next section.

Solving equations is an act of faith. You begin by assuming that there is a solution, and use the rules of algebra to find out what it must be. If you end up with an answer (or answers), you must check that it does (or they do) satisfy the equation. You do this either by making sure that all the steps can be joined by $\Leftrightarrow$ and not just $\Rightarrow$, or by direct substitution. If you end up with a false statement, then the equation has no solution.

0.4   Proof by contradiction

Sometimes it is not possible to find a way of proving a theorem by deduction, and a more roundabout method of proof has to be used.

A typical form for such an argument is:

> $A, B, C, \ldots$ are already known to be true.
> If K were not true, one of $A, B, C, \ldots$ would not be true.
> Therefore K is true.

That is, you look at what you want to prove, and investigate the effect of assuming the opposite. If this leads you to a contradiction, then it follows that the conclusion is true. This technique is known as **proof by contradiction**.

Example 0.4.1
(a) Prove that the square of an odd number is odd.
(b) Prove that, if the square of a natural number is odd, the number itself is odd.

(a) This can be proved deductively. Denote the set $\{0, 1, 2, 3, \ldots\}$ by S. (That is S consists of the natural numbers $\mathbb{N}$ together with 0.) Any odd number can be written as $2m + 1$, where $m \in S$. Then

$$(2m + 1)^2 = (2m)^2 + 2(2m) + 1$$
$$= 4m^2 + 4m + 1$$
$$= 2(2m^2 + 2m) + 1.$$

Since $m \in S$, $2m^2 + 2m \in S$, so that $(2m + 1)^2$ can be written as $2k + 1$, where $k \in S$. Therefore $(2m + 1)^2$ is an odd number.

(b) The argument in part (a) cannot be reversed, so an indirect approach (proof by contradiction) is used.

Let n be a natural number whose square is odd. Then, if n were not odd, it would be even, so you could write n as $2m$, where $m \in \mathbb{N}$. But

$$n = 2m \quad \Rightarrow \quad n^2 = 4m^2 = 2(2m^2),$$
$$\Rightarrow \quad n^2 = 2k, \text{ where } k = 2m^2.$$

So if n were even, n^2 would be even, which contradicts the definition of n^2. It follows that n is not even, so n is odd.

0.5 Counterexamples

The previous two sections were about methods of proving that a statement is true, but occasionally you might want to show that a statement is false. A particularly good way to do this is by using a **counterexample**.

Here are some examples (of a counterexample!).

Example 0.5.1
Disprove the statement 'All prime numbers are odd'.

All you need to say is

'2 is a prime number and 2 is even'.

The counterexample is 2, and this one counterexample (in this case the only one) shows that the statement is false.

Example 0.5.2

Is the statement 'The lowest common multiple (LCM) of two positive integers m and n is mn', true or false?

The statement is false.

Let $m = 2$ and $n = 4$. Then the LCM of m and n is 4, but $mn = 8$.

Example 0.5.3

For all positive integers n, $n^2 + n + 41$ is prime. Prove that this statement is untrue.

When $n = 41$, $n^2 + n + 41 = 41^2 + 41 + 41 = 41(41 + 1 + 1) = 41 \times 43$.

Hence when $n = 41$, $n^2 + n + 41$ is not prime, and the statement is untrue.

1 Successive transformations

In C1 you learned how translating, stretching and reflecting graphs modify the equations of the graphs. In this chapter you will see how the equation of a graph changes when two such transformations are carried out successively. When you have completed it, you should

- be able to find the result of carrying out two transformations in succession.

1.1 Combining transformations

In C1 Chapter 10 three pairs of rules are given for transforming graphs, starting from an equation $y = f(x)$. In this summary, 'x-translation' is used for a translation in the x-direction; 'x-stretch' for a stretch parallel to the x-axis; and 'x-reflection' for reflection in $x = 0$ (but note that this is reflection in the y-axis!).

$$\text{Replace} \begin{Bmatrix} x \text{ by } x - k \\ y \text{ by } y - k \end{Bmatrix} \text{ to get } \begin{Bmatrix} x\text{-translation} \\ y\text{-translation} \end{Bmatrix} \text{ of displacement } k, \text{ giving } \begin{Bmatrix} y = f(x - k) \\ y = f(x) + k \end{Bmatrix}.$$

$$\text{Replace} \begin{Bmatrix} x \text{ by } x/c \\ y \text{ by } y/c \end{Bmatrix} \text{ to get } \begin{Bmatrix} x\text{-stretch} \\ y\text{-stretch} \end{Bmatrix} \text{ with factor } c, \text{ giving } \begin{Bmatrix} y = f(x/c) \\ y = cf(x) \end{Bmatrix}.$$

$$\text{Replace} \begin{Bmatrix} x \text{ by } -x \\ y \text{ by } -y \end{Bmatrix} \text{ to get } \begin{Bmatrix} x\text{-reflection} \\ y\text{-reflection} \end{Bmatrix}, \text{ giving } \begin{Bmatrix} y = f(-x) \\ y = -f(x) \end{Bmatrix}.$$

Sometimes you want to transform a graph with a combination of two or more of these.

Example 1.1.1

The graph $y = \dfrac{1}{x}$ is translated by 3 in the x-direction and stretched by a factor 2 in the y-direction. What is the new equation? Draw a sketch to illustrate the situation.

After the x-translation of 3, $y = \dfrac{1}{x}$ becomes $y = \dfrac{1}{x - 3}$.

After the y-stretch of factor 2, $y = \dfrac{1}{x - 3}$ becomes $\dfrac{y}{2} = \dfrac{1}{x - 3}$, which is $y = \dfrac{2}{x - 3}$.

Fig. 1.1 shows sketches of the three graphs.

In this example the order of the two transformations makes no difference. If you do the y-stretch first, $y = \dfrac{1}{x}$ becomes $y = \dfrac{2}{x}$. Then the x-translation transforms this to $y = \dfrac{2}{x - 3}$. The answer is the same either way.

In the next example this doesn't happen. You get different answers by carrying out the transformations in different orders.

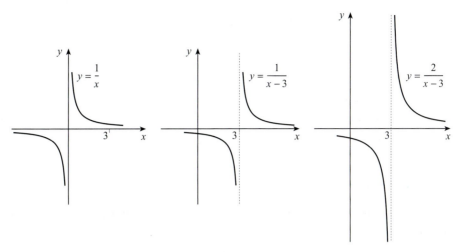

Fig. 1.1

Example 1.1.2

The graph $y = f(x)$ is transformed by a translation of -2 in the y-direction and reflection in the x-axis. Find the equation which results from doing

(a) the translation before the reflection,

(b) the reflection before the translation.

(a) After the y-translation of -2, $y = f(x)$ becomes $y - (-2) = f(x)$, which is $y = f(x) - 2$.

After the y-reflection, $y = f(x) - 2$ becomes $-y = f(x) - 2$, which is $y = 2 - f(x)$.

(b) After the y-reflection, $y = f(x)$ becomes $-y = f(x)$, which is $y = -f(x)$.

After the y-translation, $y = -f(x)$ becomes $y - (-2) = -f(x)$, which is $y = -2 - f(x)$.

Sometimes you want to ask the question the other way round: what transformations will convert a known simple graph into a graph with a more complicated equation?

Example 1.1.3

Find a translation and a stretch which transform the graph $y = \sin x$ to the graph $y = \sin\left(\frac{1}{2}x - \frac{1}{6}\pi\right)$, beginning with

(a) the translation,   (b) the stretch.

In each case you should look for a link equation, which is the equation of the graph after the first transformation and before the second.

(a) One possible link equation is $y = \sin\left(x - \frac{1}{6}\pi\right)$.

To get from $y = \sin x$ to $y = \sin\left(x - \frac{1}{6}\pi\right)$, x-translate by $\frac{1}{6}\pi$.

To get from $y = \sin\left(x - \frac{1}{6}\pi\right)$ to $y = \sin\left(\frac{1}{2}x - \frac{1}{6}\pi\right)$, x-stretch with factor 2.

(b) Begin by noting that $\sin\left(\frac{1}{2}x - \frac{1}{6}\pi\right)$ can be written as $\sin\frac{1}{2}\left(x - \frac{1}{3}\pi\right)$, and take $y = \sin\frac{1}{2}x$ as the link equation.

To get from $y = \sin x$ to $y = \sin\frac{1}{2}x$, x-stretch with factor 2.

To get from $y = \sin\frac{1}{2}x$ to $y = \sin\frac{1}{2}\left(x - \frac{1}{3}\pi\right)$, x-translate by $\frac{1}{3}\pi$.

Both methods are illustrated in Fig. 1.2. The left chain shows method (a), the right chain method (b).

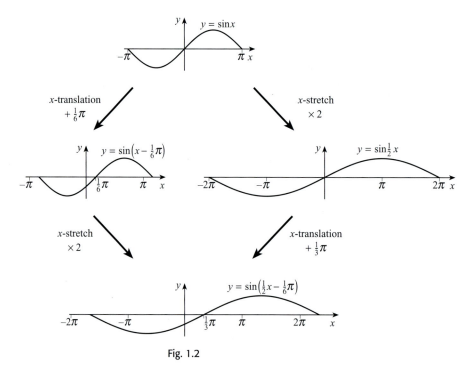

Fig. 1.2

By combining transformations it is possible to obtain the graph of any quadratic from that of $y = x^2$.

Example 1.1.4

Find a chain of transformations to obtain the graph of $y = 4 + 12x - 2x^2$ from that of $y = x^2$.

Begin by expressing the quadratic in completed square form:

$$4 + 12x - 2x^2 = 4 - 2(x^2 - 6x) = 4 - 2(x^2 - 6x + 9) + 18 = 22 - 2(x - 3)^2.$$

To transform $y = x^2$ to $y = 22 - 2(x - 3)^2$ requires four steps in some order:

- an x-translation of 3
- a y-reflection
- a y-stretch with factor 2
- a y-translation.

Only one of these is in the x-direction, and this can be carried out at any stage. You may as well do it first, so that the first link equation is $y = (x - 3)^2$.

After that there are several solutions to the problem, depending on the order in which you carry out the y-reflection, the y-stretch and the y-translation. Here are two possibilities.

First solution   This uses link equations

$$y = (x - 3)^2, \quad y = -(x - 3)^2, \quad y = -2(x - 3)^2.$$

An x-translation of 3 transforms $y = x^2$ to $y = (x - 3)^2$.

A y-reflection transforms $y = (x - 3)^2$ to $y = -(x - 3)^2$.

A y-stretch with factor 2 transforms $y = -(x - 3)^2$ to $y = -2(x - 3)^2$.

A y-translation of 22 transforms $y = -2(x - 3)^2$ to $y = 22 - 2(x - 3)^2$, which is $y = 4 + 12x - 2x^2$.

Second solution $y = 4 + 12x - 2x^2$ can also be written as $y = -2((x - 3)^2 - 11)$, which suggests a different sequence of link equations:

$$y = (x - 3)^2, \quad y = (x - 3)^2 - 11, \quad y = 2((x - 3)^2 - 11).$$

An x-translation of 3 transforms $y = x^2$ to $y = (x - 3)^2$.

A y-translation of -11 transforms $y = (x - 3)^2$ to $y = (x - 3)^2 - 11$.

A y-stretch with factor 2 transforms $y = (x - 3)^2 - 11$ to $y = 2((x - 3)^2 - 11)$.

A y-reflection transforms $y = 2((x - 3)^2 - 11)$ to $y = -2((x - 3)^2 - 11)$, which is $y = 4 + 12x - 2x^2$.

Exercise 1

1 The graph of $y = x^3$ is transformed by moving it first by 1 unit in the x-direction and then by 2 units in the y-direction. Find its new equation and sketch the final graph.

2 Write down two simple transformations which will transform $y = \sin x$ into $y = 2 \sin \left(x + \frac{1}{6}\pi \right)$. Sketch the final graph.

Does the order of your transformations matter? If so, give the equation of the new graph which you get if you carry out your transformations in the other order.

3 Write down two simple transformations which will transform $y = \cos x$ into $y = \cos \left(3x + \frac{1}{2}\pi \right)$. Sketch the final graph.

Does the order of your transformations matter? If so, give the equation of the new graph which you get if you carry out your transformations in the other order.

4 Each of the following graphs is enlarged by a factor of 2 in both the x- and y-directions. Give their new equations.

    (a) $y = x^3$ (b) $y = \dfrac{1}{x}$ (c) $y = x$ (d) $y = 2^x$

5 The graph of the straight line $y = x$ is transformed as follows:

    a translation by 4 units in the positive x-direction,

    followed by stretch in the y-direction with scale factor 2,

    followed by reflection in the x-axis.

    Find the equation of the final graph.

6 The graph of $y = \dfrac{1}{x}$ is first stretched by a factor of 3 in the x-direction and then stretched by a factor of $\frac{1}{3}$ in the y-direction. What is the effect on the original curve?

7 The function $f(x)$ is defined by $f(x) = 5(x + 2)^2 - 7$ for all real values of x.

    (a) Describe clearly a sequence of transformations which will transform the graph of $y = x^2$ to the graph of $y = f(x)$.

    (b) Sketch the graph of $y = f(x)$.

    (c) Describe a sequence of transformations which will transform the graph of $y = f(x)$ to the graph of $y = x^2$.

    (d) Find $f'(x)$ and sketch the graph of $y = f'(x)$.

    (e) Describe a sequence of transformations which will transform the graph of $y = 2x$ to the graph of $y = f'(x)$.

Miscellaneous exercise 1

1 The curve with equation $y = (x - 3)^2$ is transformed as follows:

    a translation by 3 units in the negative x-direction,

    followed by stretch in the y-direction with scale factor 3,

    followed by reflection in the x-axis.

    Find the equation of the final graph.

2 (a) Give a set of simple transformations which, when applied in succession, change the graph of $y = x^2$ to the graph with equation $y = 4 - 2x + x^2$.

    (b) Find the equation of the graph such that, when the same transformations are applied to it, becomes $y = x^2$.

3 The graph of $y = x^2$ can be transformed to that of $y = 2(x + 1)^2$ by means of a translation and a stretch, in that order. State the magnitude and direction of the translation. State also the scale factor and direction of the stretch.   (OCR, adapted)

4 Show that any power function with an equation of the form $y = a^x$, where $a > 0$, has the property that for all values of b, $f(x + b) = f(x) f(b)$. Interpret this property in terms of transformations.

5 (a) Draw sketches of the graphs of $y = \sin x$, $y = \cos x$, $y = -\sin x$ and $y = -\cos x$.

   (b) In each of the following parts use transformations to decide which of the graphs of part (a) are the same as the following graphs.

   (i) $y = \sin\left(x + \frac{1}{2}\pi\right)$ (ii) $y = \cos\left(x - \frac{3}{2}\pi\right)$
   (iii) $y = -\cos\left(x + \frac{7}{2}\pi\right)$ (iv) $y = \sin\left(\frac{3}{2}\pi - x\right)$

6 (a) The graph of $y = 3\cos(2x + \alpha)$ can be obtained from the graph of $y = \cos x$ by a translation followed by two enlargements. Describe each of these three transformations, and give the number of roots of the equation $3\cos(2x + \alpha) = k$, in the interval $0 \leqslant x < 2\pi$, where $-3 < k < 3$.

   (b) Generalise your answer to give the number of roots of the equation $a\cos(nx + \alpha) = k$ in the interval $0 \leqslant x < 2\pi$, where $a > 0$, n is a positive integer and $-a < k < a$.

   (c) How does your answer to part (b) change if n is a negative integer?

7 The straight line $y = ax + b$ is transformed by two translations. One translation is by 4 units in the positive x-direction and the other is by 7 units in the positive y-direction. Given that the equation of the transformed line is $y = 6x - 27$, find the values of a and b.

8 The curve $y = cx^2 + d$ is transformed by a translation, a stretch and a reflection in that order. The translation is by 2 units in the negative x-direction, the stretch is in the y-direction with factor 4 and the reflection is in the y-axis. The equation of the final curve is $y = 12x^2 - 48x + 20$. Find the equation of the graph

   (a) before the reflection,   (b) before the stretch.

   Hence find the values of c and d.

9 If the graph of $y = f(x)$ is reflected in the x-axis and then in the y-axis, what is its new equation? If the graph is the same as the original, what type of function is $f(x)$?

10 Find the transformed equation when the graph of $y = x^2$ is transformed by the given three transformations one after the other. Give the equation of the graph which results after each transformation, in the form $y = f(x)$. In each case, a translation is denoted by T, a stretch by S and a reflection by R.

1st transformation	2nd transformation	3rd transformation
(a) T, 2, x-direction	S, factor 3, x-direction	R, x-axis
(b) S, factor $\frac{1}{2}$, x-direction	R, y-axis	T, -3, x-direction
(c) R, y-axis	T, 4, y-direction	S, factor 2, y-direction

11 The graph of $y = -3(x + 1)^4$ has been produced from the graph of $y = x^4$ by three successive transformations: a translation, a stretch and then a reflection. Define each of the transformations clearly, and state the equation of the graph after each of the first two transformations. Sketch the graph of $y = -3(x + 1)^4$.

2 Functions

This chapter develops the idea of a function further, and more theoretically, than in earlier parts of the course. It introduces a kind of algebra of functions, by showing how to find a composite function. When you have completed it, you should

- understand the terms 'domain' and 'range', and appreciate the importance of defining the domain of a function
- be able to use correct language and notation associated with functions
- know when functions can be combined by the operation of composition, and be able to form the composite function
- know the 'one–one' condition for a function to have an inverse, and be able to form the inverse function
- know the relationship between the graph of a one–one function and the graph of its inverse function.

2.1 The domain of a function

When you produce a graph of $y = mx + c$ or $y = x^2$ you are aware that you cannot show the whole graph. However small the scale, and however large the screen or the paper, the graph will eventually spill over the edge. This is because x can be any real number, as large as you like in both positive and negative directions.

You have met functions which cannot be defined for all real numbers. Examples are $\frac{1}{x}$, which has no meaning when x is 0; and $\sqrt{x}$, which has no meaning when x is negative.

Example 2.1.1
For what values of x does $\sqrt{x(6-x)}$ have a meaning?

Since a negative number does not have a real square root, $\sqrt{x(6-x)}$ exists only if $x(6-x) \geq 0$, that is if $0 \leq x \leq 6$.

There are also times when you use a function which has a meaning for all real numbers x, but you are interested in it only when x is restricted in some way. For example, the formula for the volume of a cube is $V = x^3$. Although you can calculate x^3 for any real number x, you would only use this formula for $x > 0$.

Example 2.1.2
One pair of sides of a rectangle is 1 metre longer than the other pair. If the length of one of the shorter sides is x metres, find a formula for the area of the rectangle in square metres.

The sides have lengths x metres and $(x + 1)$ metres, so the area in square metres is $x(x + 1)$.

Example 2.1.3

Find a formula for the sum of the first x even numbers.

> You know from C2 Section 2.2 that the sum of all the natural numbers from 1 to r is $\frac{1}{2}r(r+1)$. So the sum of the first x even numbers is
>
> $$2 + 4 + 6 + \cdots + 2x = 2(1 + 2 + 3 + \cdots + x) = 2 \times \tfrac{1}{2}x(x+1) = x(x+1).$$

In these two examples the function is given by the same expression, but the variable x is understood in different ways. In Example 2.1.2 the question makes sense if x is any positive real number. In Example 2.1.3, x can only be a positive integer.

You could therefore distinguish three different functions:

> $f(x) = x(x+1)$, where x is a real number
>
> $A(x) = x(x+1)$, where x is a positive real number
>
> $S(x) = x(x+1)$, where x is a positive integer.

Although these are all given by the same expression, they have different properties. For example, $f(x)$ has a minimum value when $x = -\frac{1}{2}$, but $A(x)$ and $S(x)$ are not defined for this value of x.

So two possible reasons why a function $f(x)$ might not be defined for all real numbers x are

- the algebraic expression for $f(x)$ may only have meaning for some x
- only some x are relevant in the context in which the function is being used.

The set of numbers x for which a function $f(x)$ is defined is called the **domain** of the function. For example, the domain of the function in Example 2.1.1 is the set of real numbers such that $0 \leqslant x \leqslant 6$, because these are the only numbers for which $\sqrt{x(6-x)}$ exists. In Examples 2.1.2 and 2.1.3 the domains are the positive real numbers and the positive integers respectively, because these are the only numbers which make sense in the contexts, even though the formula $x(x+1)$ has a meaning for any real number x.

2.2 The range of a function

Once you have decided the domain of a function $f(x)$, you can ask what values $f(x)$ can take. This is called the **range** of the function.

Example 2.2.1

Find the range of the function $x(6-x)$ over its largest possible domain, and interpret this geometrically.

> The expression $x(6-x)$ can be evaluated for any real number x, so the domain can be taken as the complete set of real numbers. Completing the square, it can be written as $9 - (x-3)^2$. Since $(x-3)^2 \geqslant 0$ for all real numbers x, the range is the set of real numbers y such that $y \leqslant 9$.

The graph of $y = x(6-x)$ is a parabola with its vertex at $(3, 9)$, as shown in Fig. 2.1. This shows that, for some value of x, there is a point on the graph whose y-coordinate is any number up to and including 9.

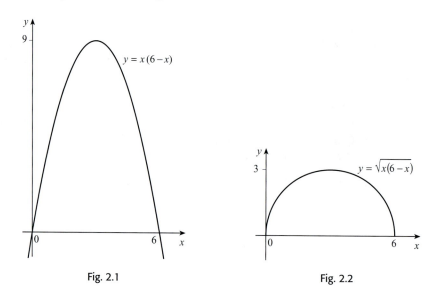

Fig. 2.1   Fig. 2.2

Example 2.2.2

Find the range of the function $\sqrt{x(6-x)}$, taking its domain to be the set of numbers $0 \leqslant x \leqslant 6$.

> Two ways of answering the question are suggested. Method 1 is based on the graphs in Fig. 2.1 and Fig. 2.2; you could show these for yourself with a graphic calculator. Method 2 is an algebraic argument, using the theory of quadratic equations. You can use whichever you prefer, but it is worth trying to understand both. In other examples only one of the two methods may work, or one may be easier than the other.

Method 1   You can use Fig. 2.1 to sketch the graph of $y = \sqrt{x(6-x)}$ in Fig. 2.2. For any value of x, the y-coordinate in Fig. 2.2 is the positive square root of the corresponding y-coordinate in Fig. 2.1. This square root only exists when $y \geqslant 0$ in Fig. 2.1, that is when $0 \leqslant x \leqslant 6$; and since the maximum value in Fig. 2.1 is 9, the maximum value in Fig. 2.2 is $\sqrt{9} = 3$. So the range of $\sqrt{x(6-x)}$ is $0 \leqslant y \leqslant 3$.

Method 2   Writing $y = \sqrt{x(6-x)}$, note first that $y \geqslant 0$ by the definition of $\sqrt{\ }$.

Also $y^2 = x(6-x)$, so $x^2 - 6x + y^2 = 0$.

Now if you give y any value, this is a quadratic equation for x. This equation has real roots provided that the discriminant is greater than or equal to 0. That is,

$$(-6)^2 - 4 \times 1 \times y^2 \geqslant 0, \text{ so } y^2 \leqslant 9.$$

Recalling that y cannot be negative, it follows that $0 \leqslant y \leqslant 3$. This is the range of the function.

You will recognise $x^2 - 6x + y^2 = 0$ as the equation of a circle, $(x - 3)^2 + y^2 = 9$, with centre $(3, 0)$ and radius 3. But since y is the positive square root, the equation $y = \sqrt{x(6 - x)}$ gives only the part of the circle for which $y \geq 0$, which is the semicircle in Fig. 2.2.

Example 2.2.3

A marching guardsman swings his arms so that their angle in front of the downward vertical varies from $-40°$ to $80°$. When this angle is x, the height of his thumbnail above the ground is y metres, where $y = 1.8 - 0.8 \cos x$. Find the range of this function as he marches.

In Fig. 2.3 the solid curve shows the graph of y in the domain $-40° \leqslant x \leqslant 80°$, and the dotted curves show how the graph continues outside the given domain. You can see that, on the solid curve, the graph takes values between $y = 1$ (when $x = 0°$) and $y = 1.661...$ (when $x = 80°$).

So the range of the function is $1 \leqslant y \leqslant 1.66$, correct to 3 significant figures.

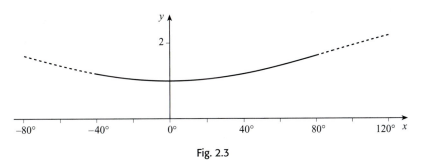

Fig. 2.3

Notice that in this example the domain is a set of angles, but the range is a set of numbers.

Exercise 2A

1 Find the largest possible domain of each of the following functions.

(a) $\sqrt{x}$ 　　　　　　(b) $\sqrt{-x}$ 　　　　　　(c) $\sqrt{x - 4}$ 　　　　　　(d) $\sqrt{4 - x}$

(e) $\sqrt{x(x - 4)}$ 　　　(f) $\sqrt{2x(x - 4)}$ 　　　(g) $\sqrt{x^2 - 7x + 12}$ 　　(h) $\sqrt{x^3 - 8}$

(i) $\dfrac{1}{x - 2}$ 　　　　(j) $\dfrac{1}{\sqrt{x - 2}}$ 　　　　(k) $\dfrac{1}{1 + \sqrt{x}}$ 　　　　(l) $\dfrac{1}{(x - 1)(x - 2)}$

2 Find the range of each of the following functions. The functions are defined for all real values of x.

(a) $f(x) = x^2 + 4$ 　　　　(b) $f(x) = 2(x^2 + 5)$ 　　　(c) $f(x) = (x - 1)^2 + 6$

(d) $f(x) = -(1 - x)^2 + 7$ 　(e) $f(x) = 3(x + 5)^2 + 2$ 　(f) $f(x) = 2(x + 2)^4 - 1$

3 Each of the following functions is defined for all real values of x. By writing them in completed-square form, find their ranges.

(a) $f(x) = x^2 - 6x + 10$ 　(b) $f(x) = x^2 + 7x + 1$ 　(c) $f(x) = x^2 - 3x + 4$

(d) $f(x) = 2x^2 + 8x + 1$ 　(e) $f(x) = 3x^2 + 5x - 12$ 　(f) $f(x) = -x^2 - 6x + 12$

4 These functions are each defined for the given domain. Sketch their graphs and find their ranges.

(a) $f(x) = 2x$ for $0 \leqslant x \leqslant 8$

(b) $f(x) = 3 - 2x$ for $-2 \leqslant x \leqslant 2$

(c) $f(x) = x^2$ for $-1 \leqslant x \leqslant 4$

(d) $f(x) = x^2$ for $-5 \leqslant x \leqslant -2$

(e) $f(x) = \sin x$ for $30° \leqslant x \leqslant 120°$

(f) $f(x) = 2 + 4\cos x$ for $-60° \leqslant x \leqslant 40°$

5 The domain of each of the following functions is the set of all positive real numbers. Find the range of each function.

(a) $f(x) = 2x + 7$

(b) $f(x) = -5x$

(c) $f(x) = 3x - 1$

(d) $f(x) = x^2 - 1$

(e) $f(x) = (x + 2)(x + 1)$

(f) $f(x) = (x - 1)(x - 2)$

(g) $f(x) = \ln(1 + x)$

(h) $f(x) = \ln(1 + e^x)$

(i) $f(x) = e^{-2x}$

6 The domain of each of the following functions is the set of values of x for which the algebraic expression has meaning. Find their ranges.

(a) $f(x) = x^8$

(b) $f(x) = x^{11}$

(c) $f(x) = \dfrac{1}{x^3}$

(d) $f(x) = \dfrac{1}{x^4}$

(e) $f(x) = x^4 + 5$

(f) $f(x) = \frac{1}{4}x + \frac{1}{8}$

(g) $f(x) = \sqrt{4 - x^2}$

(h) $f(x) = \sqrt{4 - x}$

(i) $\dfrac{1}{1 + e^x}$

(j) $e^{\sqrt{x}}$

(k) e^{-x^2}

(l) $f(x) = \sqrt{\sin x}$

7 A piece of wire 24 cm long has the shape of a rectangle. Given that the width is w cm, show that the area, A cm², of the rectangle is given by the function $A = w(12 - w)$. Find the greatest possible domain and the corresponding range of this function in this context.

8 Sketch the graph of $y = x(8 - 2x)(22 - 2x)$. Given that y cm³ is the volume of a cuboid with height x cm, length $(22 - 2x)$ cm and width $(8 - 2x)$ cm, as shown in the diagram, state an appropriate domain for the function given above.

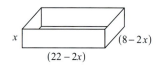

2.3 Function notation

When you use a calculator to do a calculation like $\sqrt{7.29}$, $\log_{10} 1000$ or $\sin \frac{1}{6}\pi$ (in radians) you use two different types of key:

- number keys, with which you can make up 'input numbers' such as 7.29, 1000 or $\frac{1}{6}\pi$
- function keys, such as $[\sqrt{}]$, [log] and [sin].

(There are other keys which don't come into either of these categories, but you can ignore them in this discussion.)

In the rest of this chapter sin, cos and tan stand for these functions as operated by your calculator in 'radian mode'. The symbol log stands for $\log_{10}$.

Different makes of calculator operate in different ways. Sometimes, to find $\sqrt{7.29}$, you begin by keying in the function $\sqrt{}$; the calculator 'remembers' this, and probably displays it, but can't do anything until you key in the input number 7.29.

Other calculators operate in the reverse order. You first key in 7.29, which the calculator 'remembers' and displays. Then, on keying in the function $\sqrt{}$, the calculation can proceed.

The details are not important. What matters is that you begin with an input number and a function; nothing can happen until both are keyed in. The function then operates on the input number to produce an output number. The process can be represented symbolically:

$$
\begin{array}{lll}
\text{Input} & & \text{Output} \\
7.29 & \rightarrow \quad [\sqrt{}] \quad \rightarrow & 2.7 \\
1000 & \rightarrow \quad [\log] \quad \rightarrow & 3 \\
\tfrac{1}{6}\pi & \rightarrow \quad [\sin] \quad \rightarrow & 0.5
\end{array}
$$

Not all functions can be operated with a single key. A function such as 'add 3' will use a key for the operation + and a key for 3, probably followed by a key with a label such as [=] or [ans].

But the principle is the same. The important point is that the function key sequence is the same whatever input number it is applied to. You could write

$$ 4 \quad \rightarrow \quad [\text{add 3}] \quad \rightarrow \quad 7. $$

You can think of a function as a kind of machine. Just as you can have a bread machine, put the ingredients in and take out a loaf, so a function takes in a number in the domain and turns it into a number in the range. For a general input number

$$
\begin{array}{lll}
x & \rightarrow \quad [\text{square}] \quad \rightarrow & x^2, \\
x & \rightarrow \quad [\text{add 3}] \quad \rightarrow & x + 3,
\end{array}
$$

and so on. And, for a general function,

$$ x \quad \rightarrow \quad [\text{f}] \quad \rightarrow \quad \text{f}(x). $$

This course has often used phrases like 'the function x^2', 'the function $\cos x$', or 'the function $\text{f}(x)$', and you have understood what is meant. Working mathematicians do this all the time. But it is strictly wrong; x^2, $\cos x$ and $\text{f}(x)$ are symbols for the *output* when the input is x, not for the function itself. When you need to use precise language, you should refer to 'the function square', 'the function cos' or 'the function f'.

Unfortunately only a few functions have convenient names like 'square' or 'cos'. There is no simple name for a function whose output is given by an expression such as $x^2 - 6x + 4$. The way round this is to decide for the time being to call this function f (or any other letter you like). You can then write

$$ \text{f} : x \mapsto x^2 - 6x + 4. $$

You read this as 'f is the function which turns any input number x in the domain into the output number $x^2 - 6x + 4$'. Notice the bar at the blunt end of the arrow; this avoids confusion with the arrow which has been used to stand for 'tends to' in finding gradients of tangents.

> Try to write a key sequence to represent this function. (With some calculators you may need the memory keys.)

Example 2.3.1
If $f : x \mapsto x(5 - x)$, what is $f(3)$?

The symbol $f(3)$ stands for the output when the input is 3. The function called f turns the input 3 into the output $3(5 - 3) = 6$. So $f(3) = 6$.

This idea of using an arrow to show the connection between the input and the output can also be linked to the graph of the function. Fig. 2.4 shows the graph of $y = x(5 - x)$, with the input number 3 on the x-axis. An arrow which goes up the page from this point and bends through a right angle when it hits the graph takes you to the output number 6 on the y-axis.

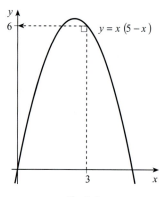

Fig. 2.4

2.4 Forming composite functions

If you want to work out the value of $(x - 3)^2$ when $x = 8$, you say to yourself something like

'8 minus 3 equals 5, and 5 squared is 25'.

That is, you use the number 5 as a staging post between the input number 8 and the output number 25. You are in fact putting two function calculations together,

$$8 \quad \rightarrow \quad [\text{subtract 3}] \quad \rightarrow \quad 5$$

and

$$5 \quad \rightarrow \quad [\text{square}] \quad \rightarrow \quad 25.$$

You could represent the whole calculation in a single chain:

$$8 \quad \rightarrow \quad [\text{subtract 3}] \quad \rightarrow \quad 5 \quad \rightarrow \quad [\text{square}] \quad \rightarrow \quad 25.$$

The output of the first function becomes the input of the second.

In this example, the complete function $x \mapsto (x - 3)^2$ is called the 'composite' of the functions 'subtract 3' and 'square'. The separate functions are called 'components' of the complete function.

Example 2.4.1

Find the output if the functions square and log act in succession on inputs of (a) 10, (b) x.

(a) 10 $\rightarrow$ [square] $\rightarrow$ 100 $\rightarrow$ [log] $\rightarrow$ 2.

(b) x $\rightarrow$ [square] $\rightarrow$ x^2 $\rightarrow$ [log] $\rightarrow$ $\log(x^2)$.

Notice that since in (b) the input to the function log is x^2, not x, the output is $\log(x^2)$, not $\log x$. For a general input, and two general functions f and g, this would become:

x $\rightarrow$ [f] $\rightarrow$ $f(x)$ $\rightarrow$ [g] $\rightarrow$ $g(f(x))$.

Since the output of the composite function is $g(f(x))$, the composite function itself is denoted by gf. Notice that gf must be read as 'first f, then g'. You must get used to reading the symbol gf from right to left. Writing fg means 'first g, then f', which is almost always a different function from gf. For instance, if you change the order of the functions in Example 2.4.1 part (a), instead of the output 2 you get

10 $\rightarrow$ [log] $\rightarrow$ 1 $\rightarrow$ [square] $\rightarrow$ 1.

> The **composite function** gf is applied by operating on an input number with the function f, then operating on the result with the function g.
>
> That is, for any input number x,
>
> $$gf(x) = g(f(x)).$$
>
> In general, the composite functions gf and fg are different functions.

Example 2.4.2

Let $f : x \mapsto x + 3$ and $g : x \mapsto x^2$. Find gf and fg. Show that there is just one number x such that $gf(x) = fg(x)$.

The composite function gf is represented by

x $\rightarrow$ [f] $\rightarrow$ $x + 3$ $\rightarrow$ [g] $\rightarrow$ $(x + 3)^2$

and fg is represented by

x $\rightarrow$ [g] $\rightarrow$ x^2 $\rightarrow$ [f] $\rightarrow$ $x^2 + 3$.

So $gf : x \mapsto (x + 3)^2$ and $fg : x \mapsto x^2 + 3$.

If $gf(x) = fg(x)$, $(x + 3)^2 = x^2 + 3$, so $x^2 + 6x + 9 = x^2 + 3$, or $x = -1$.

It is worth checking the answer to Example 2.4.2 numerically. With the input number -1, 'add 3' followed by square gives

-1 plus 3 equals 2, and 2 squared is 4;

'square' followed by 'add 3' gives

-1 squared is 1, 1 plus 3 equals 4.

The final answer is 4 in both cases, but the intermediate numbers are different.

As a further check, try taking some other input number and show that this gives a different output number for the two functions.

Example 2.4.3

If $f : x \mapsto \cos x$ and $g : x \mapsto \dfrac{1}{x}$, calculate (a) $gf(\frac{1}{3}\pi)$, (b) $gf(\frac{1}{2}\pi)$.

(a) $\frac{1}{3}\pi \quad \rightarrow \quad [\cos] \quad \rightarrow \quad 0.5 \quad \rightarrow \quad [\text{reciprocal}] \quad \rightarrow \quad 2$
   so $gf(\frac{1}{3}\pi) = 2$.

(b) $\frac{1}{2}\pi \quad \rightarrow \quad [\cos] \quad \rightarrow \quad 0 \quad \rightarrow \quad [\text{reciprocal}] \quad \rightarrow \quad !!$

The problem in part (b) is that $\cos \frac{1}{2}\pi = 0$ and $\frac{1}{0}$ is not defined.

> Try working Example 2.4.3 with a calculator. What does it give in part (b)?

What has happened in Example 2.4.3 part (b) is that the number 0 is in the range of the function f, but it is not in the domain of g. You always need to be aware that this may happen when you find the composite of two functions. It is time to look again at domains and ranges, so that you can avoid this problem.

2.5   Domain and range revisited

When the letters x and y are used in mathematics, for example in an equation such as $y = 2x - 10$, it is generally understood that they stand for real numbers. But sometimes it is important to be absolutely precise about this. The symbol $\mathbb{R}$ is used to stand for 'the set of real numbers', and the symbol $\in$ for 'belongs to'. With these symbols, you can shorten the statement 'x is a real number', or 'x belongs to the set of real numbers', to $x \in \mathbb{R}$. So you can write

$$f : x \mapsto 2x - 10, \quad x \in \mathbb{R}$$

to indicate that f is the function whose domain is the set of real numbers which turns any input x into the output $2x - 10$.

Strictly, a function is not completely defined unless you state the domain as well as the rule for obtaining the output from the input. In this case the range is also $\mathbb{R}$, although you do not need to state this in describing the function.

You know from Section 2.1 that for some functions the domain is part of $\mathbb{R}$, because the expression $f(x)$ only has meaning for some $x \in \mathbb{R}$. (Here $\in$ has to be read as 'belonging to' rather than 'belongs to'.) The set of real numbers for which $f(x)$ has a meaning will be called the **natural domain** of f. With a calculator, if you input a number which is not in the natural domain, the output will be an 'error' display.

For the square root function, for example, the natural domain is the set of positive real numbers and zero, so you write

$$\text{square root} : x \mapsto \sqrt{x}, \quad \text{where } x \in \mathbb{R} \text{ and } x \geqslant 0.$$

Example 2.5.1

Find the range of the functions

(a) sin, with natural domain $\mathbb{R}$,

(b) sin, with domain $x \in \mathbb{R}$ and $0 < x < \frac{1}{2}\pi$.

From the graph of $y = \sin x$ shown in Fig. 2.5 you can read off the ranges:

(a) For $x \in \mathbb{R}$, the range is $y \in \mathbb{R}$, $-1 \leqslant y \leqslant 1$.

(b) For $x \in \mathbb{R}$, $0 < x < \frac{1}{2}\pi$, the range is $y \in \mathbb{R}$, $0 < y < 1$.

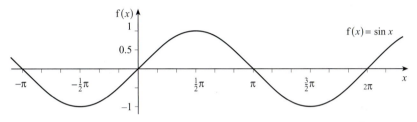

Fig. 2.5

Although the letter x is usually used in describing the domain, and y for the range, this is not essential. The set of numbers $y \in \mathbb{R}$, $0 < y < 1$ is the same set of numbers as $x \in \mathbb{R}$, $0 < x < 1$ or $t \in \mathbb{R}$, $0 < t < 1$.

It is especially important to understand this when you find composite functions. For example, in Example 2.4.3 part (a), the number 0.5 appears first as the output for the input $\frac{1}{3}\pi$ to the function $f : x \mapsto \cos x$, so you might think of this as $y = \cos \frac{1}{3}\pi = 0.5$. But for the input to the function $g : x \mapsto \dfrac{1}{x}$, it is natural to write $x = 0.5$. The number 0.5 belongs first to the range of f, then to the domain of g.

This is where Example 2.4.3 part (b) breaks down. The number 0, which appears as the output when the input to f is $\frac{1}{2}\pi$, is not in the natural domain of g. So although $\frac{1}{2}\pi$ is in the natural domain of f, it is not in the natural domain of gf.

The general rule is:

> To form the composite function gf, the domain D of f must be chosen so that the whole of the range of f is included in the domain of g. The function gf is then defined as gf : $x \mapsto g(f(x))$, $x \in D$.

For the functions in Example 2.4.3, the domain of g is the set $\mathbb{R}$ excluding 0, so the domain of f must be chosen to exclude the numbers x for which $\cos x = 0$. These are $\ldots$, $-\frac{5}{2}\pi$, $-\frac{3}{2}\pi$, $-\frac{1}{2}\pi$, $+\frac{1}{2}\pi$, $+\frac{3}{2}\pi$, $+\frac{5}{2}\pi$, $\ldots$, all of which can be summed up by the formula $\frac{1}{2}\pi + n\pi$, where n is an integer.

There is a neat way of writing this, using the standard symbol $\mathbb{Z}$ for the set of integers $\ldots$, -3, -2, -1, 0, 1, 2, 3, $\ldots$. The domain of f can then be expressed as $x \in \mathbb{R}$, $x \neq \frac{1}{2}\pi + n\pi$, $n \in \mathbb{Z}$.

Example 2.5.2

Find the natural domain and the corresponding range of the function $x \mapsto \sqrt{x(x-3)}$.

You can express the function as gf, where $f : x \mapsto x(x-3)$ and $g : x \mapsto \sqrt{x}$.

The natural domain of g is $x \in \mathbb{R}$, $x \geqslant 0$, so you want the range of f to be included in $y \in \mathbb{R}$, $y \geqslant 0$. (Switching from x to y is not essential, but you may find it easier.) The solution of the inequality $y = x(x-3) \geqslant 0$ is $x \geqslant 3$ or $x \leqslant 0$.

The natural domain of gf is therefore $x \in \mathbb{R}$, $x \geqslant 3$ or $x \leqslant 0$.

With this domain the range of f is $y \in \mathbb{R}$, $y \geqslant 0$, so the numbers input to g are given by $x \in \mathbb{R}$, $x \geqslant 0$. With this domain, the range of g is $y \in \mathbb{R}$, $y \geqslant 0$. This is therefore the range of the combined function gf.

Try using a graphic calculator to plot the graph $y = \sqrt{x(x-3)}$, using a window of $-1 \leqslant x \leqslant 4$ and $0 \leqslant y \leqslant 2$. You should find that no points are plotted for the 'illegal' values of x in the interval $0 < x < 3$. If you were to input a number in this interval, such as 1, you will get as far as $1(1-3) = -2$, but the final $\sqrt{}$ key will give you an error message or some display which does not represent a real number.

Exercise 2B

1 Given $f : x \mapsto (3x+5)^2$, where $x \in \mathbb{R}$, find the values of

(a) f(2), (b) f(−1), (c) f(7).

2 Given $g : x \mapsto 3x^2+5$, where $x \in \mathbb{R}$, find the values of

(a) g(2), (b) g(−1), (c) g(7).

3 Given $f : x \mapsto \dfrac{4}{x+5}$, where $x \in \mathbb{R}$ and $x \neq -5$, find the values of

(a) f(−1), (b) f(−4), (c) f(3).

4 Given $g : x \mapsto \dfrac{4}{x}+5$, where $x \in \mathbb{R}$ and $x \neq 0$, find the values of

(a) g(−1), (b) g(−4), (c) g(3).

5 Find the output if the functions 'square', 'subtract 4' act in succession on an input of

(a) 2, (b) −5, (c) $\frac{1}{2}$, (d) x.

6 Find the output if the functions 'cos', 'add 2', 'cube' act in succession on an input of

(a) 0, (b) $\frac{1}{2}\pi$, (c) $\frac{2}{3}\pi$, (d) x.

7 Find the output if the functions 'square root', 'multiply by 2', 'subtract 10', 'square' act in succession on an input of

(a) 9, (b) 16, (c) $\frac{1}{4}$, (d) x.

8 Break the following functions down into two or more components.

(a) $f : x \mapsto 4x+9$ (b) $f : x \mapsto 4(x+9)$ (c) $f : x \mapsto 2x^2-5$

(d) $f : x \mapsto 2(x-5)^2$ (e) $f : x \mapsto (\sqrt{x}-3)^3$, $x \geqslant 0$ (f) $f : x \mapsto \sqrt{(x-2)^2+10}$

9 Find the natural domain and corresponding range of each of the following functions.

(a) $f : x \mapsto x^2$

(b) $f : x \mapsto \cos x$

(c) $f : x \mapsto \sqrt{x - 3}$

(d) $f : x \mapsto x^2 + 5$

(e) $f : x \mapsto \dfrac{1}{\sqrt{x}}$

(f) $f : x \mapsto x(4 - x)$

(g) $f : x \mapsto \sqrt{x(4 - x)}$

(h) $f : x \mapsto x^2 + 4x + 10$

(i) $f : x \mapsto (1 - \sqrt{x - 3})^2$

10 Given that $f : x \mapsto 2x + 1$ and $g : x \mapsto 3x - 5$, where $x \in \mathbb{R}$, find the value of the following.

(a) $gf(1)$

(b) $gf(-2)$

(c) $fg(0)$

(d) $fg(7)$

(e) $ff(5)$

(f) $ff(-5)$

(g) $gg(4)$

(h) $gg(2\frac{2}{9})$

11 Given that $f : x \mapsto x^2$ and $g : x \mapsto 4x - 1$, where $x \in \mathbb{R}$, find the value of the following.

(a) $fg(2)$

(b) $gg(4)$

(c) $gf(-3)$

(d) $ff(\frac{1}{2})$

(e) $fgf(-1)$

(f) $gfgf(2)$

12 Given that $f : x \mapsto 5 - x$ and $g : x \mapsto \dfrac{4}{x}$, where $x \in \mathbb{R}$ and $x \neq 0$ or 5, find the value of the following.

(a) $ff(7)$

(b) $ff(-19)$

(c) $gg(1)$

(d) $gg(\frac{1}{2})$

(e) $gggg(\frac{1}{2})$

(f) $fffff(6)$

(g) $fgfg(2)$

(h) $fggf(2)$

13 Given that $f : x \mapsto 2x + 5$, $g : x \mapsto x^2$ and $h : x \mapsto \dfrac{1}{x}$, where $x \in \mathbb{R}$ and $x \neq 0$ or $-\dfrac{5}{2}$, find the following composite functions.

(a) fg

(b) gf

(c) fh

(d) hf

(e) ff

(f) hh

(g) gfh

(h) hgf

14 Given that $f : x \mapsto \sin x$, $g : x \mapsto x^3$ and $h : x \mapsto x - 3$, where $x \in \mathbb{R}$, find the following functions.

(a) hf

(b) fh

(c) fhg

(d) fg

(e) hhh

(f) gf

15 Given that $f : x \mapsto x + 4$, $g : x \mapsto 3x$ and $h : x \mapsto x^2$, where $x \in \mathbb{R}$, express each of the following in terms of f, g, h as appropriate.

(a) $x \mapsto x^2 + 4$

(b) $x \mapsto 3x + 4$

(c) $x \mapsto x^4$

(d) $x \mapsto 9x^2$

(e) $x \mapsto 3x + 12$

(f) $x \mapsto 3(x^2 + 8)$

(g) $x \mapsto 9x + 16$

(h) $x \mapsto x^2 + 8x + 16$

(i) $x \mapsto 9x^2 + 48x + 64$

16 In each of the following, find the natural domain and the range of the function gf.

(a) $f : x \mapsto \sqrt{x}$ $g : x \mapsto x - 5$

(b) $f : x \mapsto x + 3$ $g : x \mapsto \sqrt{x}$

(c) $f : x \mapsto x - 2$ $g : x \mapsto \dfrac{1}{x}$

(d) $f : x \mapsto \sin x$ $g : x \mapsto \sqrt{x^2}$

(e) $f : x \mapsto |x - 3|$ $g : x \mapsto \sqrt{x}$

(f) $f : x \mapsto 16 - x^2$ $g : x \mapsto \sqrt[4]{x}$

(g) $f : x \mapsto x^2 - x - 6$ $g : x \mapsto \sqrt{x}$

(h) $f : x \mapsto x + 2$ $g : x \mapsto \dfrac{1}{\sqrt{-x}}$

17 Given that $f : x \mapsto x^2$ and $g : x \mapsto 3x - 2$, where $x \in \mathbb{R}$, find a, b and c such that

(a) $fg(a) = 100$,

(b) $gg(b) = 55$,

(c) $fg(c) = gf(c)$.

18 Given that $f : x \mapsto ax + b$ and that $ff : x \mapsto 9x - 28$, find the possible values of a and b.

19 For $f : x \mapsto ax + b$, $f(2) = 19$ and $ff(0) = 55$. Find the possible values of a and b.

20 The functions $f : x \mapsto 4x + 1$ and $g : x \mapsto ax + b$ are such that $fg = gf$ for all real values of x. Show that $a = 3b + 1$.

2.6 Reversing functions

If your sister is 2 years older than you, then you are 2 years younger than her. To get her age from yours you use the 'add 2' function; to get your age from hers you 'subtract 2'. The functions 'add 2' and 'subtract 2' are said to be **inverse functions** of each other. That is, 'subtract 2' is the inverse function of 'add 2' (and vice versa).

You know many pairs of inverse functions: 'double' and 'halve', 'cube' and 'cube root' are simple examples.

There are also some functions which are their own inverses, such as 'change sign'; to undo the effect of a change of sign, you just change sign again. Another example is 'reciprocal' $\left(x \mapsto \dfrac{1}{x} \right)$. These functions are said to be **self-inverse**.

The inverse of a function f is denoted by the symbol f^{-1}. If f turns an input number x into an output number y, then f^{-1} turns y into x. You can illustrate this graphically by reversing the arrow which symbolises the function, as in Fig. 2.6. The range of f becomes the domain of f^{-1}, and the domain of f becomes the range of f^{-1}.

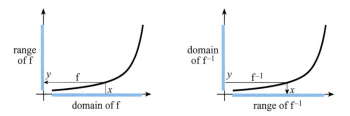

Fig. 2.6

You have used inverse functions in calculations about triangles. Often you know an angle, and calculate the length of a side by using one of the trigonometric functions such as tan. But if you know the sides and want to calculate the angle you use the inverse function, which is denoted by $\tan^{-1}$.

On many calculators you find values of $\tan^{-1}$ by using a sequence of two keys: first an 'inverse' key (which on some calculators is labelled 'shift' or '2nd function') and then 'tan'. In what follows this is referred to as 'the $\tan^{-1}$ key', and similarly for the $\sin^{-1}$ and $\cos^{-1}$ functions.

Example 2.6.1

Find the values of $\cos^{-1} y$ when (a) $y = 0.5$, (b) $y = -1$, (c) $y = 1.5$.

Using the $\cos^{-1}$ key with inputs 0.5, -1, 1.5 in turn gives outputs of 1.047...($= \frac{1}{3}\pi$), 3.141...($= \pi$), and an error message!

So, in radian mode, (a) $\cos^{-1} 0.5 = \frac{1}{3}\pi$, (b) $\cos^{-1}(-1) = \pi$, but (c) $\cos^{-1} 1.5$ has no meaning. Fig. 2.7 shows the graph of $y = \cos x$ with domain $x \in \mathbb{R}$, $0 \leqslant x \leqslant \pi$. This shows that the range of the function cos is $-1 \leqslant x \leqslant 1$. Since this is the domain of the inverse function, the answer to (c) is explained by the fact that 1.5 lies outside this interval.

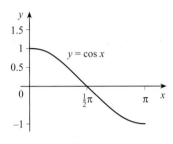

Fig. 2.7

If you try to check by finding the cosines of the answers to this example, you get

(a) $0.5 \quad \rightarrow \quad [\cos^{-1}] \quad \rightarrow \quad \frac{1}{3}\pi \quad \rightarrow \quad [\cos] \quad \rightarrow \quad 0.5,$

(b) $-1 \quad \rightarrow \quad [\cos^{-1}] \quad \rightarrow \quad \pi \quad \rightarrow \quad [\cos] \quad \rightarrow \quad -1.$

This is of course what you would expect; the function and its inverse cancel each other out. In general, if $-1 \leqslant y \leqslant 1$, then

$y \quad \rightarrow \quad [\cos^{-1}] \quad \rightarrow \quad [\cos] \quad \rightarrow \quad y.$

You may therefore be surprised by the result of the next example.

Example 2.6.2

If $f : x \mapsto \sin x$ and $g : x \mapsto \sin^{-1} x$, evaluate   (a) $gf(\frac{1}{4}\pi)$,   (b) $gf(\frac{3}{4}\pi)$.

Work this example for yourself using the calculator sequence

$x \quad \rightarrow \quad [\sin] \quad \rightarrow \quad [\sin^{-1}] \quad \rightarrow \quad gf(x).$

You should get the answers (a) 0.785...($= \frac{1}{4}\pi$, as you would expect), (b) 0.785...($= \frac{1}{4}\pi$).

The answer to part (b) calls for a more careful look at the theory of inverse functions.

2.7 One–one functions

The answers to Example 2.6.2 can be explained by Fig. 2.8, which shows the graph of $y = \sin x$ over the interval $0 \leqslant x \leqslant \pi$. The graph rises from $y = 0$ to $y = 1$ over the values for x for which the angle is acute, and then falls symmetrically back to $y = 0$ over the values for which the angle is obtuse. This is because the sine of the obtuse angle x is equal to the sine of the supplementary angle $(\pi - x)$. So $\sin \frac{1}{4}\pi = \sin \frac{3}{4}\pi$, and the calculator gives the value 0.707... for both.

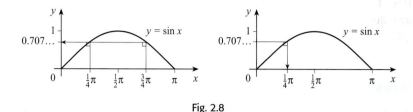

Fig. 2.8

When you use the $\sin^{-1}$ key to find $\sin^{-1}(0.707...)$, the calculator has to give the same answer in either case. It is programmed always to give the answer nearest to zero, which in this case is $\frac{1}{4}\pi$.

Exactly the same problem arises whenever you try to reverse a function which has the same output for more than one input. And in mathematics, such ambiguity is not acceptable. The solution adopted is a drastic one: to refuse to define an inverse for any function which has the same output for more than one input. That is, the only functions which have an inverse function are those for which each output in the range comes from only one input. These functions are said to be 'one–one'.

> A function f defined for some domain D is **one–one** if, for each number y in the range R of f there is only one number $x \in D$ such that $y = f(x)$. The function with domain R defined by $f^{-1} : y \mapsto x$, where $y = f(x)$, is the **inverse function** of f.

This definition was illustrated above in Fig. 2.6, which was drawn to ensure that the function f was one–one.

The way in which this is achieved in practice is to restrict the domain of f. For example, the function $x \mapsto \sin x$, $x \in \mathbb{R}$, whose graph is shown in Fig. 2.5, is not one–one, so it does not have an inverse. But the function $x \mapsto \sin x$, where $x \in \mathbb{R}$ and $-\frac{1}{2}\pi \leqslant x \leqslant \frac{1}{2}\pi$, shown in Fig. 2.9, is one–one; it is the inverse of this function which is denoted by $\sin^{-1}$, and activated by the familiar key sequence on the calculator.

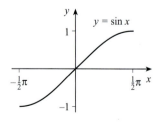

Fig. 2.9

Fig. 2.6 suggests that, if you combine a function with its inverse, you get back to the number you started with. That is,

$$f^{-1}f(x) = x, \quad \text{and} \quad ff^{-1}(y) = y.$$

The functions $f^{-1}f$ and ff^{-1} are called **identity functions** because their inputs and outputs are identical. But there is a subtle difference between these two composite functions, since their domains may not be the same; the first has domain D and the second has domain R.

2.8 Finding inverse functions

For very simple one-step functions it is easy to write down an expression for the inverse function. The inverse of 'add 2' is 'subtract 2', so

$$f : x \mapsto x + 2, x \in \mathbb{R} \qquad \text{has inverse} \qquad f^{-1} : x \mapsto x - 2, x \in \mathbb{R}.$$

Notice that the inverse could equally well be written as

$$f^{-1} : y \mapsto y - 2, y \in \mathbb{R}.$$

You can sometimes break down more complicated functions into a chain of simple steps. You can then find the inverse by going backwards through each step in reverse order. (This is sometimes called the 'shoes and socks' process: you put your socks on before your shoes, but you take off your shoes before your socks. In mathematical notation, $(gf)^{-1} = f^{-1}g^{-1}$, where f denotes putting on your socks and g your shoes.)

However, this method does not always work, particularly if x appears more than once in the expression for the function. You can then try writing $y = f(x)$, and turn the formula round into the form $x = g(y)$. Then g is the inverse of f.

Example 2.8.1
Find the inverse of $f : x \mapsto 2x + 5, \ x \in \mathbb{R}$.

Note first that f is one–one, and that the range is $\mathbb{R}$.

Method 1   You can break the function down as

$$x \quad \rightarrow \quad [\text{double}] \quad \rightarrow \quad [\text{add 5}] \quad \rightarrow \quad 2x + 5.$$

To find f^{-1}, go backwards through the chain (read from right to left):

$$\tfrac{1}{2}(x - 5) \quad \leftarrow \quad [\text{halve}] \quad \leftarrow \quad [\text{subtract 5}] \quad \leftarrow \quad x.$$

So $f^{-1} : x \mapsto \tfrac{1}{2}(x - 5), \ x \in \mathbb{R}$.

Method 2   If $y = 2x + 5$,

$$y - 5 = 2x,$$
$$x = \tfrac{1}{2}(y - 5).$$

So the inverse function is $f^{-1} : y \mapsto \tfrac{1}{2}(y - 5), \ y \in \mathbb{R}$.

The two answers are the same, even though different letters are used.

Example 2.8.2

Restrict the domain of the function f : $x \mapsto x^2 - 2x$ so that an inverse function exists, and find an expression for f^{-1}.

Fig. 2.10 shows the graph of $y = x^2 - 2x$, $x \in \mathbb{R}$, which is quadratic with its vertex at $(1, -1)$. For $y > -1$ there are two values of x for each y, so the graph does not represent a one–one function. One way of making it one–one is to chop off the part of the graph to the left of its axis of symmetry. The remainder has domain $x \in \mathbb{R}$, $x \geqslant 1$, and range $y \in \mathbb{R}$, $y \geqslant -1$.

Method 1   Completing the square, $f(x) = (x - 1)^2 - 1$, so you can break the function down as

$$x \to [\text{subtract } 1] \to [\text{square}] \to [\text{subtract } 1] \to y.$$

In reverse,

$$1 + \sqrt{y + 1} \leftarrow [\text{add } 1] \leftarrow [\sqrt{\ }] \leftarrow [\text{add } 1] \leftarrow y.$$

So the inverse function is $f^{-1} : y \mapsto 1 + \sqrt{y + 1}$, $y \in \mathbb{R}$, $y \geqslant -1$.

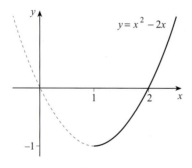

Fig. 2.10

Notice that $+\sqrt{\ }$ was chosen for the inverse of 'square', rather than $-\sqrt{\ }$. The positive square root was chosen to make $x \geqslant 1$.

Method 2   If $y = x^2 - 2x$, then $x^2 - 2x - y = 0$.

This is a quadratic equation with roots

$$x = \frac{2 \pm \sqrt{4 + 4y}}{2} = 1 \pm \sqrt{1 + y}.$$

Since $x \geqslant 1$, you must choose the positive sign, giving $x = 1 + \sqrt{1 + y}$. So the inverse function is $f^{-1} : y \mapsto 1 + \sqrt{y + 1}$, $y \in \mathbb{R}$, $y \geqslant -1$.

Example 2.8.3

Find the inverse of the function $x \mapsto \dfrac{x+2}{x-2}$, where $x \in \mathbb{R}$ and $x \neq 2$.

It is not obvious that this function is one–one, or what its range is. However, using the second method and writing $y = \dfrac{x+2}{x-2}$,

$$y(x-2) = x + 2,$$
$$yx - 2y = x + 2,$$
$$yx - x = 2y + 2,$$
$$x(y-1) = 2(y+1),$$
$$x = \frac{2(y+1)}{y-1}.$$

This shows that, unless $y = 1$, there is just one value of x for each value of y. So f must be one–one, the inverse function therefore exists, and

$$f^{-1} : y \mapsto \frac{2(y+1)}{y-1} \text{ where } y \in \mathbb{R} \text{ and } y \neq 1.$$

2.9 Graphing inverse functions

Fig. 2.11 shows the graph of $y = f(x)$, where f is a one–one function with domain D and range R. Since f^{-1} exists, with domain R and range D, you can also write the equation as $x = f^{-1}(y)$. You can regard Fig. 2.11 as the graph of both f and f^{-1}.

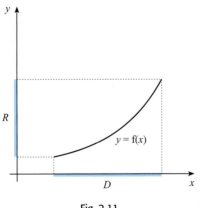

Fig. 2.11

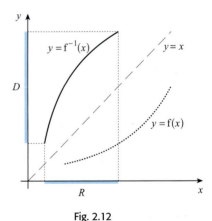

Fig. 2.12

But you sometimes want to draw the graph in the more conventional form, as $y = f^{-1}(x)$ with the domain along the x-axis. To do this you have to swap the x- and y-axes, which you do by reflecting the graph in Fig. 2.11 in the line $y = x$. (Make sure that you have the same scale on both axes!) Then the x-axis is reflected into the y-axis and vice versa, and the graph of $x = f^{-1}(y)$ is reflected into the graph of $y = f^{-1}(x)$. This is shown in Fig. 2.12.

> If f is a one–one function, the graphs of $y = f(x)$ and $y = f^{-1}(x)$ are reflections of each other in the line $y = x$.

Example 2.9.1

For the function $f : x \mapsto x^2 - 2x$ in Example 2.8.2, draw the graphs of $y = f(x)$ and $y = f^{-1}(x)$.

Example 2.8.2 showed that $f^{-1}(x) = 1 + \sqrt{x + 1}$, $x \in \mathbb{R}$, $x \geqslant -1$.

Fig. 2.13 shows the graphs of $y = f(x) = x^2 - 2x$ for $x \geqslant 1$ and $y = f^{-1}(x) = 1 + \sqrt{x + 1}$ for $x \geqslant -1$. You can see that these graphs are reflections of each other in the line $y = x$.

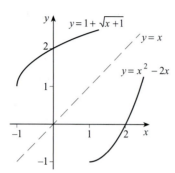

Fig. 2.13

Exercise 2C

1 Each of the following functions has domain $\mathbb{R}$. In each case use a graph to show that the function is one–one, and write down its inverse.

(a) $f : x \mapsto x + 4$ (b) $f : x \mapsto x - 5$ (c) $f : x \mapsto 2x$

(d) $f : x \mapsto \frac{1}{4}x$ (e) $f : x \mapsto x^3$ (f) $f : x \mapsto \sqrt[5]{x}$

2 Given the function $f : x \mapsto x - 6$, $x \in \mathbb{R}$, find the values of the following.

(a) $f^{-1}(4)$ (b) $f^{-1}(1)$ (c) $f^{-1}(-3)$ (d) $ff^{-1}(5)$ (e) $f^{-1}f(-4)$

3 Given the function $f : x \mapsto 5x$, $x \in \mathbb{R}$, find the values of the following.

(a) $f^{-1}(20)$ (b) $f^{-1}(100)$ (c) $f^{-1}(7)$ (d) $ff^{-1}(15)$ (e) $f^{-1}f(-6)$

4 Given the function $f : x \mapsto \sqrt[3]{x}$, $x \in \mathbb{R}$, find the values of the following.

(a) $f^{-1}(2)$ (b) $f^{-1}\left(\frac{1}{2}\right)$ (c) $f^{-1}(8)$ (d) $f^{-1}f(-27)$ (e) $ff^{-1}(5)$

5 Each of the following functions has domain $\mathbb{R}$. Determine which are one–one functions.

(a) $f : x \mapsto 3x + 4$ (b) $f : x \mapsto x^2 + 1$ (c) $f : x \mapsto x^2 - 3x$

(d) $f : x \mapsto 5 - x$ (e) $f : x \mapsto \cos x$ (f) $f : x \mapsto x^3 - 2$

(g) $f : x \mapsto \frac{1}{2}x - 7$ (h) $f : x \mapsto \sqrt{x^2}$ (i) $f : x \mapsto x(x - 4)$

(j) $f : x \mapsto x^3 - 3x$ (k) $f : x \mapsto x^9$ (l) $f : x \mapsto \sqrt{x^2 + 1}$

6 Determine which of the following functions, with the specified domains, are one–one.

(a) $f : x \mapsto x^2$, $x > 0$ (b) $f : x \mapsto \cos x$, $-\frac{1}{2}\pi \leqslant x \leqslant \frac{1}{2}\pi$

(c) $f : x \mapsto 1 - 2x$, $x < 0$ (d) $f : x \mapsto x(x - 2)$, $0 < x < 2$

(e) $f : x \mapsto x(x-2), \ x > 2$ (f) $f : x \mapsto x(x-2), \ x < 1$

(g) $f : x \mapsto \sqrt{x}, \ x > 0$ (h) $f : x \mapsto x^2 + 6x - 5, \ x > 0$

(i) $f : x \mapsto x^2 + 6x - 5, \ x < 0$ (j) $f : x \mapsto x^2 + 6x - 5, \ x > -3$

7 Each of the following functions has domain $x \geqslant k$. In each case, find the smallest possible value of k such that the function is one–one.

(a) $f : x \mapsto x^2 - 4$ (b) $f : x \mapsto (x+1)^2$ (c) $f : x \mapsto (3x-2)^2$

(d) $f : x \mapsto x^2 - 8x + 15$ (e) $f : x \mapsto x^2 + 10x + 1$ (f) $f : x \mapsto (x+4)(x-2)$

(g) $f : x \mapsto x^2 - 3x$ (h) $f : x \mapsto 6 + 2x - x^2$ (i) $f : x \mapsto (x-4)^4$

8 Use Method 1 of Example 2.8.1 to find the inverse of each of the following functions.

(a) $f : x \mapsto 3x - 1, \ x \in \mathbb{R}$ (b) $f : x \mapsto \frac{1}{2}x + 4, \ x \in \mathbb{R}$ (c) $f : x \mapsto x^3 + 5, \ x \in \mathbb{R}$

(d) $f : x \mapsto \sqrt{x} - 3, \ x > 0$ (e) $f : x \mapsto \dfrac{5x-3}{2}, \ x \in \mathbb{R}$ (f) $f : x \mapsto (x-1)^2 + 6, \ x \geqslant 1$

9 Use Method 2 of Example 2.8.1 to find the inverse of each of the following functions.

(a) $f : x \mapsto 6x + 5, \ x \in \mathbb{R}$ (b) $f : x \mapsto \dfrac{x+4}{5}, \ x \in \mathbb{R}$

(c) $f : x \mapsto 4 - 2x, \ x \in \mathbb{R}$ (d) $f : x \mapsto \dfrac{2x+7}{3}, \ x \in \mathbb{R}$

(e) $f : x \mapsto 2x^3 + 5, \ x \in \mathbb{R}$ (f) $f : x \mapsto \dfrac{1}{x} + 4, \ x \in \mathbb{R}$ and $x \neq 0$

(g) $f : x \mapsto \dfrac{5}{x-1}, \ x \in \mathbb{R}$ and $x \neq 1$ (h) $f : x \mapsto (x+2)^2 + 7, \ x \in \mathbb{R}$ and $x \geqslant -2$

(i) $f : x \mapsto (2x-3)^2 - 5, \ x \in \mathbb{R}$ and $x \geqslant \frac{3}{2}$ (j) $f : x \mapsto x^2 - 6x, \ x \in \mathbb{R}$ and $x \geqslant 3$

10 For each of the following, find the inverse function and sketch the graphs of $y = f(x)$ and $y = f^{-1}(x)$.

(a) $f : x \mapsto 4x, \ x \in \mathbb{R}$ (b) $f : x \mapsto x + 3, \ x \in \mathbb{R}$

(c) $f : x \mapsto \sqrt{x}, \ x \in \mathbb{R}$ and $x \geqslant 0$ (d) $f : x \mapsto 2x + 1, \ x \in \mathbb{R}$

(e) $f : x \mapsto (x-2)^2, \ x \in \mathbb{R}$ and $x \geqslant 2$ (f) $f : x \mapsto 1 - 3x, \ x \in \mathbb{R}$

(g) $f : x \mapsto \dfrac{3}{x}, \ x \in \mathbb{R}$ and $x \neq 0$ (h) $f : x \mapsto 7 - x, \ x \in \mathbb{R}$

11 Show that the following functions are self-inverse.

(a) $f : x \mapsto 5 - x, \ x \in \mathbb{R}$ (b) $f : x \mapsto -x, \ x \in \mathbb{R}$

(c) $f : x \mapsto \dfrac{4}{x}, \ x \in \mathbb{R}$ and $x \neq 0$ (d) $f : x \mapsto \dfrac{6}{5x}, \ x \in \mathbb{R}$ and $x \neq 0$

(e) $f : x \mapsto \dfrac{x+5}{x-1}, \ x \in \mathbb{R}$ and $x \neq 1$ (f) $f : x \mapsto \dfrac{3x-1}{2x-3}, \ x \in \mathbb{R}$ and $x \neq \frac{3}{2}$

12 Find the inverse of each of the following functions.

(a) $f : x \mapsto \dfrac{x}{x-2}, \ x \in \mathbb{R}$ and $x \neq 2$ (b) $f : x \mapsto \dfrac{2x+1}{x-4}, \ x \in \mathbb{R}$ and $x \neq 4$

(c) $f : x \mapsto \dfrac{x+2}{x-5}, \ x \in \mathbb{R}$ and $x \neq 5$ (d) $f : x \mapsto \dfrac{3x-11}{4x-3}, \ x \in \mathbb{R}$ and $x \neq \frac{3}{4}$

13 The function $f : x \mapsto x^2 - 4x + 3$ has domain $x \in \mathbb{R}$ and $x > 2$.

(a) Determine the range of f.

(b) Find the inverse function f^{-1} and state its domain and range.

(c) Sketch the graphs of $y = f(x)$ and $y = f^{-1}(x)$.

14 The function $f : x \mapsto \sqrt{x - 2} + 3$ has domain $x \in \mathbb{R}$ and $x > 2$.

(a) Determine the range of f.

(b) Find the inverse function f^{-1} and state its domain and range.

(c) Sketch the graphs of $y = f(x)$ and $y = f^{-1}(x)$.

15 The function $f : x \mapsto x^2 + 2x + 6$ has domain $x \in \mathbb{R}$ and $x \leqslant k$. Given that f is one–one, determine the greatest possible value of k. When k has this value,

(a) determine the range of f,

(b) find the inverse function f^{-1} and state its domain and range,

(c) sketch the graphs of $y = f(x)$ and $y = f^{-1}(x)$.

16 The inverse of the function $f : x \mapsto ax + b, \ x \in \mathbb{R}$ is $f^{-1} : x \mapsto 8x - 3$. Find a and b.

17 The function $f : x \mapsto px + q, \ x \in \mathbb{R}$, is such that $f^{-1}(6) = 3$ and $f^{-1}(-29) = -2$. Find $f^{-1}(27)$.

18 The function $f : x \mapsto x^2 + x + 6$ has domain $x \in \mathbb{R}$ and $x > 0$. Find the inverse function and state its domain and range.

19 The function $f : x \mapsto -2x^2 + 4x - 7$ has domain $x \in \mathbb{R}$ and $x < 1$. Find the inverse function and state its domain and range.

20 For each of the following functions, sketch the graph of $y = f^{-1}(x)$.

(a) $f : x \mapsto \sin x, \ x \in \mathbb{R}$ and $-\frac{1}{2}\pi \leqslant x \leqslant \frac{1}{2}\pi$

(b) $f : x \mapsto \cos x, \ x \in \mathbb{R}$ and $0 \leqslant x \leqslant \pi$

(c) $f : x \mapsto \tan x, \ x \in \mathbb{R}$ and $-\frac{1}{2}\pi < x < \frac{1}{2}\pi$

21 The function $f : x \mapsto \log_2 x$ has domain $x \in \mathbb{R}$ and $x > 0$. Find the inverse function. Sketch the graph of $y = f^{-1}(x)$, and hence sketch the graph of $y = \log_2 x$.

Miscellaneous exercise 2

1 The following functions are defined for all real values of x. Find their ranges.

(a) $f(x) = 9 - 2x^2$ (b) $f(x) = 5x - 7$

(c) $f(x) = x^2 + 16x - 5$ (d) $f(x) = (2x + 5)(2x - 7)$

2 The function $f(x) = 16 - 6x - x^2$ has domain all real values of x. Find the maximum value of $f(x)$ and state the range of $f(x)$.

3 The functions f and g are defined by

$$f : x \mapsto 4x + 9, x \in \mathbb{R}, \qquad g : x \mapsto x^2 + 1, x \in \mathbb{R}.$$

Find the value of each of the following.

(a) fg(2)   (b) fg(2$\sqrt{3}$)   (c) gf(−2)

(d) ff(−3)   (e) gg(−4)   (f) fgf($\frac{1}{2}$)

4 Find the natural domain and corresponding range of each of the following functions.

(a) f : $x \mapsto 4 - x^2$ (b) f : $x \mapsto (x + 3)^2 - 7$ (c) f : $x \mapsto \sqrt{x + 2}$

(d) f : $x \mapsto 5x + 6$ (e) f : $x \mapsto (2x + 3)^2$ (f) f : $x \mapsto 2 - \sqrt{x}$

5 The functions f and g are defined by

$$f : x \mapsto x^3, \ x \in \mathbb{R}, \qquad g : x \mapsto 1 - 2x, \ x \in \mathbb{R}.$$

Find the functions

(a) fg,   (b) gf,   (c) gff,   (d) gg,   (e) g^{-1}.

6 The function f is defined by f : $x \mapsto 2x^3 - 6$, $x \in \mathbb{R}$. Find the values of the following.

(a) f(3)   (b) f^{-1}(48)   (c) f^{-1}(−8)   (d) f^{-1}f(4)   (e) ff^{-1}(4)

7 The function f is defined for all real values of x by $f(x) = x^{\frac{1}{3}} + 10$. Evaluate

(a) ff(−8),   (b) f^{-1}(13).   (OCR)

8 Show that the function f : $x \mapsto (x + 3)^2 + 1$, with domain $x \in \mathbb{R}$ and $x > 0$, is one–one and find its inverse.

9 The function f is defined by f : $x \mapsto 4x^3 + 3$, $x \in \mathbb{R}$. Give the corresponding definition of f^{-1}. State a relationship between the graphs of f and f^{-1}.   (OCR)

10 Given that $f(x) = 3x^2 - 4$, $x > 0$, and $g(x) = x + 4$, $x \in \mathbb{R}$, find

(a) f^{-1}(x), $x > -4$,   (b) fg(x), $x > -4$.   (OCR)

11 The functions f, g and h are defined by

$$f : x \mapsto 2x + 1, \ x \in \mathbb{R}, \quad g : x \mapsto x^5, \ x \in \mathbb{R}, \quad h : x \mapsto \frac{1}{x}, \ x \in \mathbb{R} \text{ and } x \neq 0.$$

Express each of the following in terms of f, g, h as appropriate.

(a) $x \mapsto (2x + 1)^5$ (b) $x \mapsto 4x + 3$ (c) $x \mapsto x^{\frac{1}{5}}$ (d) $x \mapsto 2x^{-5} + 1$

(e) $x \mapsto \dfrac{1}{2x^5 + 1}$ (f) $x \mapsto \dfrac{x - 1}{2}$ (g) $x \mapsto \sqrt[5]{\dfrac{2}{x^5} + 1}$ (h) $x \mapsto \dfrac{2}{x - 1}$

12 The function f is defined by f : $x \mapsto x^2 + 1$, $x \geqslant 0$. Sketch the graph of the function f and, using your sketch or otherwise, show that f is a one–one function. Obtain an expression in terms of x for f^{-1}(x) and state the domain of f^{-1}.

The function g is defined by g : $x \mapsto x - 3$, $x \geqslant 0$. Give an expression in terms of x for gf(x) and state the range of gf.   (OCR)

13 The function $y = x^2 - 4ax$, where a is a positive constant, is defined for all real values of x. Given that the range is $y \geqslant -7$, find the exact value of a.

14 The functions f and g are defined by

$$f : x \mapsto x^2 + 6x, \ x \in \mathbb{R}, \qquad g : x \mapsto 2x - 1, \ x \in \mathbb{R}.$$

Find the two values of x such that $fg(x) = gf(x)$, giving each answer in the form $p + q\sqrt{3}$.

15 The function f is defined by $f : x \mapsto x^2 - 2x + 7$ with domain $x \leqslant k$. Given that f is a one–one function, find the greatest possible value of k and find the inverse function f^{-1}.

16 Functions f and g are defined by

$$f : x \mapsto x^2 + 2x + 3, \ x \in \mathbb{R}, \qquad g : x \mapsto ax + b, \ x \in \mathbb{R}.$$

Given that $fg(x) = 4x^2 - 48x + 146$ for all x, find the possible values of a and b.

17 The function f is defined by $f : x \mapsto 1 - x^2, \ x \leqslant 0$.

(a) Sketch the graph of f.

(b) Find an expression, in terms of x, for $f^{-1}(x)$ and state the domain of f^{-1}.

(c) The function g is defined by $g : x \mapsto 2x, \ x \leqslant 0$. Find the value of x for which $fg(x) = 0$.   (OCR)

18 Functions f and g are defined by $f : x \mapsto 4x + 5, \ x \in \mathbb{R}$ and $g : x \mapsto 3 - 2x, \ x \in \mathbb{R}$. Find

(a) f^{-1},   (b) g^{-1},   (c) $f^{-1}g^{-1}$,   (d) gf,   (e) $(gf)^{-1}$.

19 Functions f and g are defined by $f : x \mapsto 2x + 7, \ x \in \mathbb{R}$ and $g : x \mapsto x^3 - 1, \ x \in \mathbb{R}$. Find

(a) f^{-1},   (b) g^{-1},   (c) $g^{-1}f^{-1}$,   (d) $f^{-1}g^{-1}$,

(e) fg,   (f) gf,   (g) $(fg)^{-1}$,   (h) $(gf)^{-1}$.

20 Given the function $f : x \mapsto 10 - x, \ x \in \mathbb{R}$, evaluate

(a) $f(7)$,   (b) $f^2(7)$,   (c) $f^{15}(7)$,   (d) $f^{100}(7)$.

[The notation f^2 represents the composite function ff, f^3 represents fff, and so on.]

21 Given the function $f : x \mapsto \dfrac{x + 5}{2x - 1}, \ x \in \mathbb{R}$ and $x \neq \frac{1}{2}$, find

(a) $f^2(x)$,   (b) $f^3(x)$,   (c) $f^4(x)$,   (d) $f^{10}(x)$,   (e) $f^{351}(x)$.

22 Given the function $f(x) = \dfrac{2x - 4}{x}, \ x \in \mathbb{R}$ and $x \neq 0$, find

(a) $f^2(x)$,   (b) $f^{-1}(x)$,   (c) $f^3(x)$,

(d) $f^4(x)$,   (e) $f^{12}(x)$,   (f) $f^{82}(x)$.

23 Show that a function of the form $x \mapsto \dfrac{x + a}{x - 1}, \ x \in \mathbb{R}$ and $x \neq 1$, is self-inverse for all values of the constant a except one. State the exceptional value of a.

24 The function $\text{int}(x)$, sometimes called the integer part of x, is defined to be the greatest integer less than or equal to x.

Sketch the graphs of $y = \text{int}(x)$ and $y = x - \text{int}(x)$ for the domain $-2 \leqslant x \leqslant 3$. What are the ranges of $\text{int}(x)$ and $y = x - \text{int}(x)$ for this domain?

3 Exponential growth and decay

In C2 you were introduced to geometric sequences and exponential functions. In this chapter these are shown to have applications as mathematical models in everyday situations and in physical, biological and social sciences. When you have completed it, you should

- understand what is meant by exponential growth and exponential decay in both discrete and continuous models
- be able to distinguish exponential models from other models of growth and decay, and be able to calculate the constants in exponential models
- appreciate the uniformity of the exponential growth graph.

3.1 Discrete exponential growth

Geometric sequences arise in many everyday contexts. Here are two examples. The first has a common ratio greater than 1, the second has a common ratio between 0 and 1.

Example 3.1.1
A person invests £1000 in a building society account which pays interest of 6% annually. Calculate the amount in the account over the next 8 years.

The interest in any year is 0.06 times the amount in the account at the beginning of the year. This is added on to the sum of money already in the account. The amount at the end of each year, after interest has been added, is 1.06 times the amount at the beginning of the year. So

Amount after 1 year $= £1000 \times 1.06 = £1060$
Amount after 2 years $= £1060 \times 1.06 = £1124$
Amount after 3 years $= £1124 \times 1.06 = £1191$, and so on.

Continuing in this way, you get the amounts shown in Table 3.1, to the nearest whole number of pounds.

Number of years	0	1	2	3	4	5	6	7	8
Amount (£)	1000	1060	1124	1191	1262	1338	1419	1504	1594

Table 3.1

You can see a graph of these values in Fig. 3.2.

Notice that in the first year the interest is £60, but in the eighth year it is £90. This is because the amount on which the 6% is calculated has gone up from £1000 to £1504. This is characteristic of 'exponential growth', in which the increase is proportional to the current amount. As the amount goes up, the increase goes up.

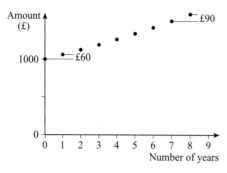

Fig. 3.2

Example 3.1.2

A car cost £15 000 when new, and each year its value decreases by 20% . Find its value on the first five anniversaries of its purchase.

The value at the end of each year is 0.8 times its value a year earlier. The results of this calculation are given in Table 3.3.

Number of years	0	1	2	3	4	5
Value (£)	15 000	12 000	9600	7680	6144	4915

Table 3.3

These values are shown in the graph in Fig. 3.4.

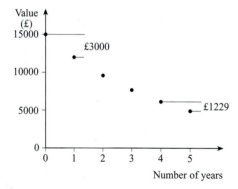

Fig. 3.4

The value goes down by £3000 in the first year, but by only £1229 in the fifth year, because by then the 20% is calculated on only £6144 rather than £15 000. This is characteristic of 'exponential decay', in which the decrease is proportional to the current value. Notice that, if the 20% rule continues, the value never becomes zero however long you keep the car.

In both these examples it is more natural to think of the first term of the sequence as u_0 rather than u_1. Also, since the values are given at regular intervals of time, it is helpful to use the letter t for the 'counting variable'. That is, $£u_t$ stands for the amount in the account, or the value of the car, after t years.

The sequence in Example 3.1.1 then has

$$u_0 = 1000 \quad \text{and} \quad u_{t+1} = 1.06u_t \quad \text{for } 0 \leqslant t \leqslant 7.$$

From this you can deduce that $u_1 = 1000 \times 1.06$, $u_2 = 1000 \times 1.06^2$, and more generally $u_t = 1000 \times 1.06^t$.

The sequence in Example 3.1.2 has

$$u_0 = 15\,000 \quad \text{and} \quad u_{t+1} = 0.8u_t \quad \text{for } 0 \leqslant t \leqslant 4.$$

In this case $u_1 = 15\,000 \times 0.8$, $u_2 = 15\,000 \times 0.8^2$ and $u_t = 15\,000 \times 0.8^t$.

These are both examples of exponential sequences. (The word 'exponential' comes from 'exponent', which is another word for index. The reason for the name is that the variable t appears in the exponent of the formula for u_t.) An exponential sequence is a special kind of geometric sequence, in which the first term a and common ratio r are both positive. If the first term is denoted by u_0, the sequence can be defined recursively by

$$u_0 = a \quad \text{and} \quad u_{t+1} = ru_t,$$

or by the formula

$$u_t = ar^t.$$

If $r > 1$ the sequence represents exponential growth; if $0 < r < 1$ it represents exponential decay.

You saw in both examples that between any term and the next the increase or decrease is proportional to the current value. This is characteristic of any exponential sequence. Thus, for any value of t,

$$u_{t+1} - u_t = ru_t - u_t,$$

which is $(r - 1)$ times u_t.

Exponential sequences

In a discrete situation, a sequence u_t represents the value of a quantity after t units of time, where t is an integer and $t \geqslant 0$. If

$$u_0 = a \text{ (where } a > 0) \text{ and } u_{t+1} = ru_t \quad \text{for } t = 0, 1, 2, 3, \ldots,$$

the sequence represents

   exponential growth if $r > 1$

or   **exponential decay** if $0 < r < 1$.

The sequence can be described by the formula

$$u_t = ar^t \quad \text{for } t = 0, 1, 2, 3, \ldots.$$

The increase or decrease in the value of the quantity between times t and $t + 1$ is $r - 1$ times the value at time t: that is,

$$u_{t+1} - u_t = (r - 1)u_t.$$

Example 3.1.3

The cost of building a conservatory is made up of the cost of labour and the cost of materials. The price quoted in a firm's 2005 catalogue is based on labour costs of £2000 and material costs of £1600. In succeeding years the labour costs increase exponentially by 10% a year, and the material costs decrease exponentially by 5% a year. Find how the total costs change over the next three years, and investigate whether they change exponentially.

If the labour costs after t years are £L_t, the material costs are £M_t, and the total costs are £C_t, then

$$L_0 = 2000 \quad \text{and} \quad L_{t+1} = 1.1L_t;$$
$$M_0 = 1600 \quad \text{and} \quad M_{t+1} = 0.95M_t;$$
and $\quad C_t = L_t + M_t.$

These equations can be used, for $t = 0, 1, 2$ in turn, to calculate the labour and material costs in Table 3.5. These are then added to give the total costs.

Year	2005	2006	2007	2008
Labour costs	£2000	£2200	£2420	£2662
Materials costs	£1600	£1520	£1444	£1371.80
Total costs	£3600	£3720	£3864	£4033.80

Table 3.5

A graph of the total costs is shown in Fig. 3.6.

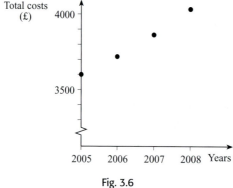

Fig. 3.6

You can see from the graph that the total costs increase each year, and also that the amount by which they increase goes up each year. But this is not in itself enough to show that they are growing exponentially. For this to be true, the ratio of the total costs in successive years should be constant. So calculate

$$\frac{C_1}{C_0} = \frac{3720}{3600} = 1.033..., \quad \frac{C_2}{C_1} = \frac{3864}{3720} = 1.038..., \quad \frac{C_3}{C_2} = \frac{4033.80}{3864} = 1.043....$$

Since these ratios are not the same, the growth in total costs is not exponential.

Although the independent variable in exponential growth and decay is usually time, this is not always the case. For example, you could construct a staircase in which the rise grows exponentially from each step to the next. In an example like this, you might choose to use a different letter for the variable instead of t.

Exercise 3A

1   There are at present 4000 houses in a town, and this number is growing exponentially by 10% every year. How many houses will there be in three years time?

   Calculate the number of new houses which will be completed in each of the next three years. Show that this number is also growing exponentially by 10% every year.

2   The attendances at the last four matches played by a football team were 4000, 3600, 3240 and 2916. Show that these are decreasing exponentially, and predict the attendances at the next two matches if this trend continues.

3   Each New Year's Eve Scrooge works out the value of his possessions. In 2004 it was £50 000, and he expects it to grow exponentially by 20% a year. Find the value in each year up to 2009 on this assumption.

   Find how much richer he becomes in each year, and show that these amounts also increase exponentially.

4   It is estimated that the population of sparrows on an island is decaying exponentially by 20% each decade, and that the population of sparrowhawks is growing by 20%. If there were 100 000 sparrows and 1000 sparrowhawks when recording began, calculate how many of each there will be after 1, 2 and 3 decades.

   Calculate how many sparrows there will be to each sparrowhawk after 1, 2 and 3 decades. How is this ratio changing?

5   A girl fills a jug with one-quarter lemon squash and three-quarters water. She fills a glass with one-tenth of the contents, drinks it and then tops up the jug with water.

   (a) What proportion of the contents of the refilled jug is lemon squash?

   (b) If she repeats this again and again, what proportion of the contents of the jug will be lemon squash after she has refilled it 2, 3 and 4 times?

   (c) Write a formula for the proportion of lemon squash in the jug after she has refilled it t times.

6   In Example 3.1.1 find an expression for the amount of interest received in the tth year. Does the amount of interest grow exponentially?

7   In Example 3.1.2 find an expression for the reduction in the value of the car in the tth year after it was purchased. Does this reduction decay exponentially?

8 The population of a town is decreasing steadily at a rate of 4% each year. The population in 2003 was 21 000. Estimate the population in

(a) 2007,   (b) 1995.

9 A man of mass 90 kg plans to diet and to reduce his mass to 72 kg in four weeks by a constant percentage reduction each week.

(a) What should his mass be 1 week after starting his diet?

(b) He forgets to stop after 4 weeks. Estimate his mass 1 week later.

10 The table gives the retail price index (to the nearest whole number) on 1 April for several consecutive years in a number of countries. In which countries could you say that the index is increasing or decreasing exponentially?

			Year		
Country	2000	2001	2002	2003	2004
Amnesia	185	200	216	233	252
Bonvivia	135	150	165	180	195
Candida	100	120	144	173	207
Declinia	180	169	159	150	141
Erewhon	80	69	59	50	41

11 In 1838 the Rev. H Moseley presented a paper to the Royal Society on his measurements of shells. One cone-shaped shell called *Turritella duplicata* grew in a series of whorls, whose successive widths, in inches, were 0.41, 0.48, 0.57, 0.67, 0.80, 0.94. Show that these measurements fit a model of exponential growth, and predict the width of the next two whorls.

12 Show that, if a sequence of data grows or decays exponentially, then the logarithms form an arithmetic sequence. Verify this from the data in Question 11, and estimate the common difference. What does this represent?

3.2 Continuous exponential growth

Exponential growth doesn't only occur in situations which increase by discrete steps. Rampant inflation, a nuclear chain reaction, the spread of an epidemic or the growth of cells are processes which take place in continuous time, and they need to be described by functions having the real numbers rather than the natural numbers for their domain.

For continuous exponential growth, the equation $u_t = ar^t$, where $t = 0, 1, 2, \ldots$, is replaced by

$$f(t) = ab^t, \quad \text{where } t \text{ is a real number and } t \geqslant 0.$$

In this equation a stands for the initial value when $t = 0$, and b is a positive constant which indicates how fast the quantity is growing. (The idea of a 'common ratio' no longer applies in the continuous case, so a different letter is used.) The graph of f(t) is shown in Fig. 3.7.

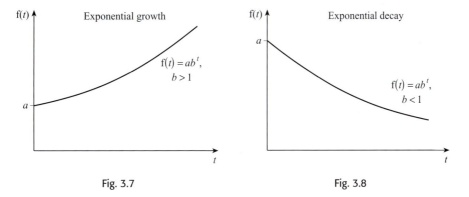

Fig. 3.7   Fig. 3.8

For exponential growth, b has to be greater than 1. If $0 < b < 1$ the graph takes the form of Fig. 3.8; for large values of t the graph gets closer to the t-axis but never reaches it. This then represents exponential decay. Examples of this are the amount of radioactive uranium in a lump of ore, and the concentration of an antibiotic in the bloodstream.

The letter t has again been used for the variable, since in most examples of exponential growth and decay the quantity you are measuring is a function of the time. If this is not the case (for example, the air pressure decays exponentially with the height above the earth's surface) you might use a different letter for the variable.

Exponential variation

In a continuous situation, a function f(t) represents the value of a quantity after t units of time, where t is a real number and $t \geqslant 0$. If

$$f(t) = ab^t \quad (\text{where } a > 0),$$

the function represents

exponential growth if $b > 1$

or   **exponential decay** if $0 < b < 1$.

Example 3.2.1

The population of the US grew exponentially from the end of the War of Independence until the Civil War. It increased from 3.9 million at the 1790 census to 31.4 million in 1860. What would the population have been in 1990 if it had continued to grow at this rate?

If the population t years after 1790 is P million, and if the growth were exactly exponential, then P and t would be related by an equation of the form

$$P = 3.9b^t,$$

where $P = 31.4$ when $t = 70$. The constant b therefore satisfies the equation

$$31.4 = 3.9b^{70},$$

so $\qquad b^{70} = \dfrac{31.4}{3.9},$

$$b = \left(\frac{31.4}{3.9}\right)^{\frac{1}{70}} = 1.030\dots.$$

At this rate the population in 1990 would have grown to about $3.9 \times 1.030\dots^{200}$ million, which is between 1.5 and 1.6 billion.

You can shorten this calculation as follows. In 70 years, the population multiplied by $\dfrac{31.4}{3.9}$.

In 200 years, it therefore multiplied by $\left(\dfrac{31.4}{3.9}\right)^{\frac{200}{70}}$. The 1990 population can then be

calculated as $3.9 \times \left(\dfrac{31.4}{3.9}\right)^{\frac{200}{70}}$ million, without working out b as an intermediate step.

Example 3.2.2
Carbon dating in archaeology is based on the decay of the isotope carbon-14, which has a half-life of 5715 years. By what percentage does carbon-14 decay in 100 years?

The half-life of a radioactive isotope is the time it would take half of any sample of the isotope to decay. After t years one unit of carbon-14 is reduced to b^t units, where

$$b^{5715} = 0.5 \qquad \text{(since 0.5 units are left after 5715 years)}$$

so $\qquad b = 0.5^{\frac{1}{5715}} = 0.999\,878\dots.$

When $t = 100$ the quantity left is $b^{100} \approx 0.988$ units, a reduction of 0.012 units, or 1.2%.

Again, you could shorten the calculation by expressing the multiplying factor as $0.5^{\frac{100}{5715}}$. The fraction $\frac{100}{5715}$ expresses the ratio of 100 years to the half-life of 5715 years. So the multiplying factor is $\frac{1}{2}$ raised to the power of the number of half-lives.

3.3 Graphs of exponential growth

In C2 Section 7.5 equations of the form $p^x = c$, where the unknown appears in the index, were solved by taking logarithms of both sides. This technique can be extended to deal with economic, social or scientific data which you think might exhibit exponential growth or decay.

Suppose that a quantity y is growing exponentially, so that its value at time t is given by

$$y = ab^t,$$

where a and b are constants. Taking logarithms of both sides of this equation, to any base,

$$\begin{aligned} \log y &= \log(ab^t) \\ &= \log a + \log b^t \\ &= \log a + t \log b. \end{aligned}$$

The expression on the right increases linearly with t. So if $\log y$ is plotted against t, the graph would be a straight line with gradient $\log b$ and intercept $\log a$.

Example 3.3.1

If $\log y = 0.322 - 0.531t$, where $\log y$ denotes $\log_{10} y$, express y in terms of t.

Equating the right side to $\log a + t \log b$, $\log a = 0.322$ and $\log b = -0.531$. So, since the logarithms are to base 10, $a = 10^{0.322} = 2.10$ and $b = 10^{-0.531} = 0.294$ (both correct to 3 significant figures). In exponential form the equation for y is therefore

$$y = 2.10 \times 0.294^t.$$

If you prefer, you can write this calculation in a different way, using the property that if $\log y = x$ then $y = 10^x$, so $y = 10^{\log y}$. Therefore

$$y = 10^{\log y} = 10^{0.322 - 0.531t} = 10^{0.322} \times (10^{-0.531})^t = 2.10 \times 0.294^t.$$

Example 3.3.2

An investment company claims that the price of its shares has grown exponentially over the past six years, and supports its claim with Fig. 3.9. Is this claim justified?

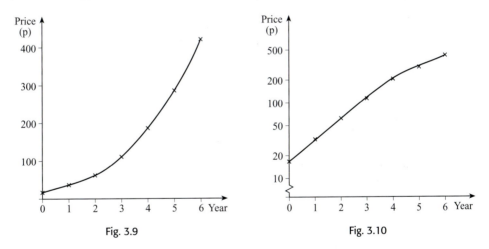

Fig. 3.9   Fig. 3.10

Fig. 3.10 shows this information with the price presented on a logarithmic scale (see C2 Section 7.4). A price of y pence is represented by a line of length proportional to $\log y$. You can recognise this by noticing that, for example, the distance on the scale from 50p to 100p is the same as the distance from 100p to 200p; this is because $\log 100 - \log 50 = \log \frac{100}{50} = \log 2$, and $\log 200 - \log 100 = \log \frac{100}{50} = \log 2$.

If the claim were true, the graph in Fig. 3.10 would be a straight line. This seems approximately true for the first three years, but in later years the graph begins to bend downwards, suggesting that the early promise of exponential growth has not been sustained.

The ideas of the last two examples can be combined, not just to investigate whether there is an exponential relationship, but also to find the numerical constants in the equation.

Example 3.3.3*

Use the census data in Table 3.11 for the US to justify the statement in Example 3.2.1, that the population grew exponentially from 1790 to 1860.

Year	1790	1800	1810	1820	1830	1840	1850	1860
Population (millions)	3.9	5.3	7.2	9.6	12.9	17.0	23.2	31.4

Table 3.11

If you plot these figures on a graph, as in Fig. 3.12, it is clear that the points lie on a smooth curve with a steadily increasing gradient, but this doesn't by itself show that the growth is exponential.

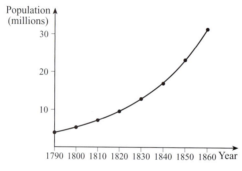

Fig. 3.12

To approach the question scientifically, the first step is to choose appropriate notation. For the population, you may as well work in millions of people, as in the table; there is no point in cluttering the data with lots of zeros, which would in any case give a false illusion of accuracy. So let P stand for the number of millions of people in the population. As for the date, since you are only interested in the period from 1790 to 1860, it is better to choose a variable t to stand for the number of years after 1790 rather than the actual year number. The theory then being investigated is that P and t are related by an equation of the form

$$P = ab^t \quad \text{for } 0 \leqslant t \leqslant 70.$$

To convert this into a linear equation, take logarithms of both sides of the equation. You can use logarithms to any base you like; if you choose 10, the equation becomes

$$\log_{10} P = \log_{10} a + t \log_{10} b,$$

in which the independent variable is t and the dependent variable is $\log_{10} P$. So Table 3.13 contains values in terms of these variables.

t	0	10	20	30	40	50	60	70
$\log_{10} P$	0.59	0.72	0.86	0.98	1.11	1.23	1.37	1.50

Table 3.13

These values are used to plot the graph in Fig. 3.14. You can see that the points very nearly lie on a straight line, though not exactly so; you wouldn't expect a population to follow a precise mathematical relationship. However, it is quite close enough to justify the claim that the growth of the population was exponential.

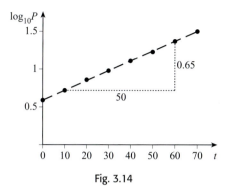

Fig. 3.14

The dashed line in Fig. 3.14 is an attempt to draw by eye a line that best fits the plotted points. By measurement, it seems that the intercept on the vertical axis is about 0.59; and, by using a suitable gradient triangle (shown with dotted lines), you can find that the gradient is about $\dfrac{0.65}{50} = 0.013$.

So the line has equation

$$\log_{10} P = 0.59 + 0.013t,$$

which is of the desired form $\log_{10} P = \log_{10} a + t \log_{10} b$ with $\log_{10} a \approx 0.59$ and $\log_{10} b \approx 0.013$.

So $a \approx 10^{0.59} \approx 3.9$ and $b \approx 10^{0.013} \approx 1.03$.

It follows that, over the period from 1790 to 1860, the growth of the population could be described to a good degree of accuracy by the law

$$P = 3.9 \times 1.03^t.$$

An equation like $P = 3.9 \times 1.03^t$ is called a **mathematical model**. It is not an exact equation giving the precise size of the population, but it is an equation of a simple form which describes the growth of the population to a very good degree of accuracy. For example, if you wanted to know the population in 1836, when $t = 46$, you could calculate $3.9 \times 1.03^{46} = 15.2...$, and assert with confidence that in that year the population of the US was between 15 and $15\frac{1}{2}$ million.

3.4 Transformations of the growth graph

The sum of a geometric series was found in C2 Section 6.2 by multiplying each term by the common ratio r. The effect of this was to produce a new series, which ran from the second term to the $(n+1)$th term of the original series. That is, the multiplication simply pushed the sequence along by one term.

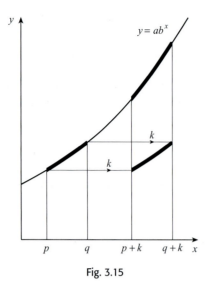

Fig. 3.15

A similar result holds for continuous exponential growth or decay. Fig. 3.15 shows part of the graph of $y = ab^x$ over an interval $p < x < q$. If you apply a translation of k in the x-direction to any graph $y = f(x)$, the equation of the translated graph is $y = f(x - k)$. In this case, the equation is

$$y = ab^{x-k},$$

and you can use the laws of indices to write this as

$$y = ab^{x-k} = (ab^{-k})b^x.$$

The translated graph covers the interval $p + k < x < q + k$.

If you now apply a stretch of factor b^k in the y-direction, you get a graph with equation

$$y = b^k(ab^{-k})b^x = ab^{k-k}b^x = ab^x.$$

So the combination of the translation and the stretch takes the graph back to itself, but over the interval $p + k < x < q + k$ rather than $p < x < q$. This means that there is a special uniformity about the exponential growth function. If you are given a part of its graph, you can construct the whole graph by means of translations and stretches.

Exercise 3B

1 A rumour spreads exponentially through a college. 100 people have heard it by noon, and 200 by 1 p.m. How many people have heard it

(a) by 3 p.m.,   (b) by 12.30 p.m.,   (c) by 1.45 p.m.?

2 A cup of coffee at 85 °C is placed in a freezer at 0 °C. The temperature of the coffee decreases exponentially, so that after 5 minutes it is 30 °C.

(a) What is its temperature after 3 minutes?

(b) Find how long it will take for the temperature to drop to 5 °C.

3 The population of Camford is increasing at a rate of 6% each year. On 1 January 1990 it was 35 200. What was its population on

(a) 1 January 2000, (b) 1 July 1990, (c) 1 January 1980?

4 The population of the United Kingdom in 1971 was 5.5615×10^7; by 1992 it was estimated to be 5.7384×10^7. Assuming a steady exponential growth estimate the population in

(a) 2003, (b) 1981.

5 The strength of a radioactive source is said to 'decay exponentially'. Explain briefly what is meant by exponential decay, and illustrate your answer by means of a sketch-graph.

After t years the strength S of a particular radioactive source, in appropriate units, is given by $S = 10\,000 \times 3^{-0.0014t}$. State the value of S when $t = 0$, and find the value of t when the source has decayed to one-half of its initial strength, giving your answer correct to 3 significant figures. (OCR, adapted)

6 An orchestra tunes to a frequency of 440, which sounds the A which is 9 semitones above middle C. Each octave higher doubles the frequency, and each of the 12 semitones in the octave increases the frequency in the same ratio.

(a) What is this ratio?

(b) Find the frequency of middle C.

(c) How many semitones above the tuning A is a note with a frequency of 600? Where is this on the scale?

7 (a) If $\log_{10} y = 0.4 + 0.6x$, express y in terms of x.

(b) If $\log_{10} y = 12 - 3x$, express y in terms of x.

(c) If $\log_{10} y = 0.7 + 1.7x$, express y in terms of x.

(d) If $\log_{10} y = 0.7 + 2\log_{10} x$, express y in terms of x.

(e) If $\log_{10} y = -0.5 - 5\log_{10} x$, express y in terms of x.

8* Population census data for the US from 1870 to 1910 were as follows.

Year	1870	1880	1890	1900	1910
Population (millions)	38.6	50.2	63.0	76.0	92.0

Investigate how well these figures can be described by an exponential model.

9 With the data of Example 3.1.3, graph the logarithm of the amount against t, and explain how your graph can be used to show that the amount does not grow exponentially.

10* For the data in Exercise 3A Question 10, use graphs of log(index) for each country to investigate whether the increase or decrease of the index is exponential. Where it is, give an expression for the index in the year $(2000 + t)$ in the form ar^t.

11 The points P and Q on the graph of $y = 3 \times 2^x$ have x-coordinates 3 and 4 respectively.

    (a) The images of P and Q after a translation of 5 units in the x-direction are P' and Q'. Write down the coordinates of P' and Q'.

    P'' and Q'' are the images of P' and Q' after a stretch of factor 2^5 in the y-direction.

    (b) Find the coordinates of P'' and Q''.

    (c) Show that P'' and Q'' both lie on the graph of $y = 3 \times 2^x$.

Miscellaneous exercise 3

1 A savings account is opened with a single payment of £2000. It attracts compound interest at a constant rate of 0.5% per month.

    (a) Find the amount in the account after two complete years.

    (b) Find after how many months the value of the investment will have doubled.

2 A radioactive substance decays at a rate of 12% per hour.

    (a) Find after how many hours half of the radioactive material will be left.

    (b) How many hours earlier did it have twice the current amount of radioactive material?

3 A biological culture contains 500 000 bacteria at 12 noon on Monday. The culture increases by 10% every hour. At what time will the culture exceed 4 million bacteria?

4 A dangerous radioactive substance has a half-life of 90 years. It will be deemed safe when its activity is down to 0.05 of its initial value. How long will it be before it is deemed safe?

5* In a spectacular experiment on cell growth the following data were obtained, where N is the number of cells at a time t minutes after the start of the growth.

t	1.5	2.7	3.4	8.1	10
N	9	19	32	820	3100

    At $t = 10$ a chemical was introduced which killed off the culture.

    The relationship between N and t was thought to be modelled by $N = ab^t$, where a and b are constants.

    (a) Use a graph to determine how these figures confirm the supposition that the relationship is of this form. Find the values of a and b, each to the nearest integer.

    (b) If the growth had not been stopped at $t = 10$ and had continued according to your model, how many cells would there have been after 20 minutes?   (MEI, adapted)

6 If you buy a 5-year National Savings Certificate of the 68th issue, its value increases by 2.35% in the first year, by 2.45% in the second year, and by 2.65%, 2.85%, 3.21% in the remaining 3 years. National Savings states that, over the full period, this is equivalent to a constant compound rate of 2.70% per year. Justify this statement.

7 The membership of a society has grown from 5000 to 7000 over a period of three years. If the growth in membership is exponential, what will it be after a further two years?

8 It is feared that the population of a species of finch on a remote island is endangered. At the beginning of the year 2000 it was estimated that there were 800 breeding pairs. By the beginning of 2005 this number had dropped to 640. If the size of the population is decreasing exponentially, in which year would you expect the number of breeding pairs to drop below 200?

9 During the five years that the Purple Party were in power, the rate of inflation increased exponentially by 20% each year, When the Grey Party took over, the rate of inflation immediately began to decrease exponentially by 10% each year. Illustrate this with a graph. How long will it take for the Grey Party to get the rate down to the level it was at when the Purple Party came in?

10 A cup of tea is poured out at a temperature of 99 °C. Two minutes later its temperature is 96 °C. The temperature in the room is 15 °C. If the difference between the temperature of the tea and the room temperature decreases exponentially with time, write an expression for the temperature of the tea in the cup t minutes after it is poured.

If you like to drink your tea at a temperature between 90 °C and 85 °C, how long after it is poured would you drink it?

4 Extending differentiation and integration

This chapter is about differentiating a certain kind of composite function of the form $f(ax + b)$. When you have completed it, you should

- be able to differentiate composite functions of the form $(ax + b)^n$
- be able to integrate composite functions of the form $(ax + b)^n$.

You may want to leave out Section 4.3 on a first reading, and you will find that the exercises are independent of it. You will, however, need the results stated at the end of Section 4.1 and in Section 4.2 (and proved in Section 4.3).

4.1 Differentiating $(ax + b)^n$

To differentiate a function like $(2x + 1)^3$, the only method available to you at present is to use the binomial theorem to multiply out the brackets, and then to differentiate term by term.

Example 4.1.1

Find $\dfrac{dy}{dx}$ for   (a) $y = (2x + 1)^3$,   (b) $y = (1 - 3x)^4$.

(a) Expanding by the binomial theorem,

$$y = (2x)^3 + 3 \times (2x)^2 \times 1 + 3 \times (2x) \times 1^2 + 1^3 = 8x^3 + 12x^2 + 6x + 1.$$

So $\dfrac{dy}{dx} = 24x^2 + 24x + 6.$

It is useful to express the result in factors, as $\dfrac{dy}{dx} = 6(4x^2 + 4x + 1) = 6(2x + 1)^2.$

(b) Expanding by the binomial theorem,

$$y = 1^4 + 4 \times 1^3 \times (-3x) + 6 \times 1^2 \times (-3x)^2 + 4 \times 1 \times (-3x)^3 + (-3x)^4$$
$$= 1 - 12x + 54x^2 - 108x^3 + 81x^4.$$

So $\dfrac{dy}{dx} = -12 + 108x - 324x^2 + 324x^3$
$$= -12(1 - 9x + 27x^2 - 27x^3)$$
$$= -12(1 - 3x)^3.$$

Exercise 4A

In Question 1, see if you can predict what the result of the differentiation will be. If you can predict the result, then check by carrying out the differentiation, and factorising your result. If you can't, differentiate and simplify and look for a pattern in your answer.

1 Find $\dfrac{dy}{dx}$ for each of the following functions. In parts (d) and (e), a and b are constants.

   (a) $(x + 3)^2$ (b) $(2x - 3)^2$ (c) $(1 - 3x)^3$ (d) $(ax + b)^3$

   (e) $(b - ax)^3$ (f) $(1 - x)^5$ (g) $(2x - 3)^4$ (h) $(3 - 2x)^4$

2 Suppose that $y = (ax + b)^n$, where a and b are constants and n is a positive integer. Make a guess at a formula for $\dfrac{dy}{dx}$.

3 Use the formula you guessed in Question 2, after checking that it is correct, to differentiate each of the following functions, where a and b are constants.

(a) $(x + 3)^{10}$ (b) $(2x - 1)^5$ (c) $(1 - 4x)^7$ (d) $(3x - 2)^5$

(e) $(4 - 2x)^6$ (f) $4(2 + 3x)^6$ (g) $(2x + 5)^5$ (h) $(2x - 3)^9$

In Exercise 4A, you were asked to predict how to differentiate a function of the form $(ax + b)^n$ where a and b are constants, and n is a positive integer. The result was

$$\text{If } y = (ax + b)^n, \text{ then } \frac{dy}{dx} = n(ax + b)^{n-1} \times a.$$

Now assume that the same formula works for all n, including fractional and negative values. There is a proof in Section 4.3, but you can skip this on a first reading. The result, however, is important, and you must be able to use it confidently.

> If a, b and n are constants, and $y = (ax + b)^n$, then $\dfrac{dy}{dx} = n(ax + b)^{n-1} \times a$.

Example 4.1.2

Find $\dfrac{dy}{dx}$ when   (a) $y = \sqrt{3x + 2}$,   (b) $y = \dfrac{1}{1 - 2x}$.

(a) Writing $\sqrt{3x + 2}$ in index form as $(3x + 2)^{\frac{1}{2}}$ and using the result in the box,

$$\frac{dy}{dx} = \tfrac{1}{2}(3x + 2)^{-\frac{1}{2}} \times 3 = \frac{3}{2} \frac{1}{(3x + 2)^{\frac{1}{2}}} = \frac{3}{2\sqrt{3x + 2}}.$$

(b) In index form $y = (1 - 2x)^{-1}$, so $\dfrac{dy}{dx} = -1(1 - 2x)^{-2} \times (-2) = \dfrac{2}{(1 - 2x)^2}$.

Example 4.1.3

Find any stationary points on the graph $y = \sqrt{2x + 1} + \dfrac{1}{\sqrt{2x + 1}}$, and determine whether they are maxima, minima or neither.

$\sqrt{2x + 1}$ is defined for $x \geqslant -\tfrac{1}{2}$, and $\dfrac{1}{\sqrt{2x + 1}}$ for $x > -\tfrac{1}{2}$. So the largest possible domain is $x > -\tfrac{1}{2}$.

$y = (2x + 1)^{\frac{1}{2}} + (2x + 1)^{-\frac{1}{2}}$, so $\dfrac{dy}{dx} = \tfrac{1}{2}(2x + 1)^{-\frac{1}{2}} \times 2 + \left(-\tfrac{1}{2}\right)(2x + 1)^{-\frac{3}{2}} \times 2$, or

$\dfrac{dy}{dx} = (2x + 1)^{-\frac{1}{2}} - (2x + 1)^{-\frac{3}{2}}$, which can be written as

$$\frac{1}{(2x + 1)^{\frac{1}{2}}} - \frac{1}{(2x + 1)^{\frac{3}{2}}} = \frac{2x + 1 - 1}{(2x + 1)^{\frac{3}{2}}} = \frac{2x}{(2x + 1)^{\frac{3}{2}}}.$$

Stationary points are those for which $\dfrac{dy}{dx} = 0$, which happens when $x = 0$.

Also $\quad \dfrac{d^2y}{dx^2} = -\frac{1}{2}(2x+1)^{-\frac{3}{2}} \times 2 - \left(-\frac{3}{2}\right)(2x+1)^{-\frac{5}{2}} \times 2$

$\qquad\qquad = -(2x+1)^{-\frac{3}{2}} + 3(2x+1)^{-\frac{5}{2}}.$

When $x = 0$, $\dfrac{d^2y}{dx^2} = -(1)^{-\frac{3}{2}} + 3(1)^{-\frac{5}{2}} = 2 > 0$, so y has a minimum at $x = 0$.

A proof of the statement 'if $y = (ax+b)^n$, then $\dfrac{dy}{dx} = n(ax+b)^{n-1} \times a$' is given in Section 4.3 in the following form.

> If a and b are constants, and if $\dfrac{d}{dx}f(x) = g(x)$,
>
> then $\dfrac{d}{dx}f(ax+b) = ag(ax+b)$.

For the special case in this section, $f(x) = x^n$ and $g(x) = nx^{n-1}$. Then

$$\frac{d}{dx}(ax+b)^n = \frac{d}{dx}f(ax+b) = ag(ax+b) = an(ax+b)^{n-1}.$$

Exercise 4B

1 Find $\dfrac{dy}{dx}$ for each of the following.

   (a) $y = (4x+5)^5$ (b) $y = (2x-7)^8$ (c) $y = (2-x)^6$ (d) $y = \left(\frac{1}{2}x+4\right)^4$

2 Find $\dfrac{dy}{dx}$ for each of the following.

   (a) $y = \dfrac{1}{3x+5}$ (b) $y = \dfrac{1}{(4-x)^2}$ (c) $y = \dfrac{1}{(2x+1)^3}$ (d) $y = \dfrac{4}{(4x-1)^4}$

3 Find $\dfrac{dy}{dx}$ for each of the following.

   (a) $y = \sqrt{2x+3}$ (b) $y = \sqrt[3]{6x-1}$ (c) $y = \dfrac{1}{\sqrt{4x+7}}$ (d) $y = 5(3x-2)^{-\frac{2}{3}}$

4 Given that $y = (2x+1)^3 + (2x-1)^3$, find the value of $\dfrac{dy}{dx}$ when $x = 1$.

5 Find the coordinates of the point on the curve $y = (1-4x)^{\frac{3}{2}}$ at which the gradient is -30.

6 Find the equation of the tangent to the curve $y = \dfrac{1}{3x+1}$ at $\left(-1, -\frac{1}{2}\right)$.

7 Find the equation of the normal to the curve $y = \sqrt{6x+3}$ at the point for which $x = 13$.

8 The curve $y = (ax+b)^4$ crosses the y-axis at $(0, 16)$ and has gradient 160 there. Find the possible values of a and b.

9 Find the coordinates of the stationary point of the curve $y = \sqrt{2x+1} - \frac{1}{3}x + 7$, and determine whether the stationary point is a maximum or a minimum.

4.2   Integrating $(ax + b)^n$

You can also use the differentiation result in reverse for integration. For example, to integrate $(3x + 1)^3$, you should recognise that it comes from differentiating $(3x + 1)^4$.

A first guess at the integral $\int (3x + 1)^3 \, dx$ is $(3x + 1)^4$. If you differentiate $(3x + 1)^4$, you find that you get $4(3x + 1)^3 \times 3 = 12(3x + 1)^3$. Therefore

$$\int (3x + 1)^3 dx = \tfrac{1}{12}(3x + 1)^4 + k.$$

You can formalise the guessing process by reversing the main results from Section 4.1.

$$\int (ax + b)^n \, dx = \frac{1}{a} \times \frac{1}{n + 1}(ax + b)^{n+1} + k.$$

For a general function $g(x)$ the corresponding result is:

$$\int g(ax + b) \, dx = \frac{1}{a} f(ax + b) + k \text{ where } f(x) \text{ is the simplest integral of } g(x).$$

Applying this to the previous example, $g(x) = x^3$, $a = 3$ and $b = 1$. Then $f(x) = \tfrac{1}{4}x^4$, so

$$\int (3x + 1)^3 dx = \int g(3x + 1) dx = \tfrac{1}{3} f(3x + 1) + k = \tfrac{1}{3} \times \tfrac{1}{4}(3x + 1)^4 + k$$

$$= \tfrac{1}{12}(3x + 1)^4 + k.$$

Example 4.2.1

Find the integrals of   (a) $\sqrt{5 - 2x}$,   (b) $\dfrac{1}{(3 - x)^2}$.

(a) **Method 1**   The first guess at $\int \sqrt{5 - 2x} \, dx = \int (5 - 2x)^{\frac{1}{2}} \, dx$ is $(5 - 2x)^{\frac{3}{2}}$.

Differentiating $(5 - 2x)^{\frac{3}{2}}$, you obtain $\tfrac{3}{2}(5 - 2x)^{\frac{1}{2}} \times (-2) = -3(5 - 2x)^{\frac{1}{2}}$. Therefore

$$\int (5 - 2x)^{\frac{1}{2}} \, dx = -\tfrac{1}{3}(5 - 2x)^{\frac{3}{2}} + k.$$

Method 2   Using the result in the box, $g(x) = \sqrt{x} = x^{\frac{1}{2}}$, $a = -2$, $b = 5$, so

$$f(x) = \frac{x^{\frac{3}{2}}}{3/2} = \tfrac{2}{3}x^{\frac{3}{2}}, \text{ and}$$

$$\int \sqrt{5 - 2x} \, dx = \tfrac{1}{-2} \times \tfrac{2}{3}(5 - 2x)^{\frac{3}{2}} + k = -\tfrac{1}{3}(5 - 2x)^{\frac{3}{2}} + k.$$

(b) First write $\dfrac{1}{(3 - x)^2}$ as $(3 - x)^{-2}$. Then

$$\int \frac{1}{(3 - x)^2} \, dx = \int (3 - x)^{-2} dx = \tfrac{1}{-1} \times \tfrac{1}{-1}(3 - x)^{-1} + k = \frac{1}{3 - x} + k.$$

Some people like to use a trial and error method of integration: guess the form of the answer, differentiate the guess, then adjust it in the light of the result. Others prefer to remember and apply a general rule. The two approaches are illustrated by Methods 1 and 2. With practice you might find that you can guess the correct integral at the first go, but you should always check your answer by differentiation, because it is easy to make a numerical mistake.

Example 4.2.2

Find the area between the curve $y = 16 - (2x + 1)^4$ and the x-axis. (See Fig. 4.1.)

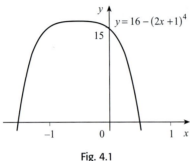

Fig. 4.1

To find where the graph cuts the x-axis, solve the equation $16 - (2x + 1)^4 = 0$. Thus $(2x + 1)^4 = 16$, so $(2x + 1) = 2$ or $(2x + 1) = -2$, leading to the limits of integration, $x = \frac{1}{2}$ and $x = -\frac{3}{2}$.

The area is given by

$$\int_{-\frac{3}{2}}^{\frac{1}{2}} (16 - (2x + 1)^4)\, dx = \left[16x - \tfrac{1}{10}(2x + 1)^5\right]_{-\frac{3}{2}}^{\frac{1}{2}}$$

$$= \left(16 \times \tfrac{1}{2} - \tfrac{1}{10}\left(2 \times \tfrac{1}{2} + 1\right)^5\right)$$

$$- \left(16 \times \left(-\tfrac{3}{2}\right) - \tfrac{1}{10}\left(2 \times \left(-\tfrac{3}{2}\right) + 1\right)^5\right)$$

$$= \left(8 - \tfrac{1}{10} \times 2^5\right) - \left(-24 - \tfrac{1}{10} \times (-2)^5\right)$$

$$= 4.8 - (-20.8) = 25.6.$$

The required area is then 25.6.

Exercise 4C

1 Integrate the following with respect to x.

   (a) $(2x + 1)^6$ (b) $(3x - 5)^4$ (c) $(1 - 7x)^3$ (d) $\left(\tfrac{1}{2}x + 1\right)^{10}$

2 Integrate the following with respect to x.

   (a) $(5x + 2)^{-3}$ (b) $2(1 - 3x)^{-2}$ (c) $\dfrac{1}{(x + 1)^5}$ (d) $\dfrac{3}{2(4x + 1)^4}$

3 Integrate the following with respect to x.

(a) $\sqrt{10x+1}$ (b) $\dfrac{1}{\sqrt{2x-1}}$ (c) $\left(\frac{1}{2}x+2\right)^{\frac{2}{3}}$ (d) $\dfrac{8}{\sqrt[4]{2+6x}}$

4 Evaluate the following integrals.

(a) $\displaystyle\int_1^5 (2x-1)^3\, dx$ (b) $\displaystyle\int_1^3 \sqrt{8x+1}\, dx$ (c) $\displaystyle\int_1^3 \dfrac{1}{(x+2)^2}\, dx$ (d) $\displaystyle\int_1^3 \dfrac{2}{(x+2)^3}\, dx$

5 Find the value of each of the following improper integrals.

(a) $\displaystyle\int_{-2}^2 \dfrac{1}{\sqrt{x+2}}\, dx$ (b) $\displaystyle\int_{\frac{1}{2}}^{\frac{9}{2}} \dfrac{6}{\sqrt[3]{2x-1}}\, dx$

6 Find the value of each of the following infinite integrals.

(a) $\displaystyle\int_0^\infty \dfrac{1}{(4x+1)^2}\, dx$ (b) $\displaystyle\int_{-\infty}^1 \dfrac{5}{(5-2x)^3}\, dx$

7 Find the area of each of the following shaded regions.

(a)
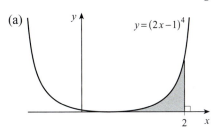

(b)
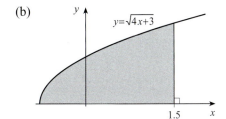

(c)
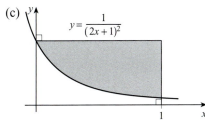

(d)
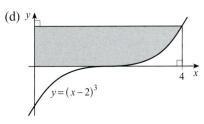

8 Given that $\displaystyle\int_{1.25}^p (4x-5)^4\, dx = 51.2$, find the value of p.

9 The diagram shows the curve $y = (2x-5)^4$. The point P has coordinates $(4, 81)$ and the tangent to the curve at P meets the x-axis at Q.

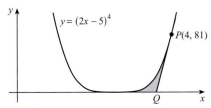

Find the area of the region (shaded in the diagram) enclosed between the curve, PQ and the x-axis.

10 Find the area of the region enclosed between the curves $y = (x-2)^4$ and $y = (x-2)^3$.

4.3*   Justifying the rule for differentiating f($ax + b$)

You may omit this section if you wish; a more general piece of theory will be developed in Chapter 9.

Suppose that you know how to differentiate $y = f(x)$; call the result g(x), so $\dfrac{dy}{dx} = g(x)$.

What can you deduce about the gradient of the graph of f($ax + b$), where a and b are constants? For example, you know how to differentiate $y = \sqrt{x} = x^{\frac{1}{2}}$; how can you use this information to differentiate $y = (3x + 1)^{\frac{1}{2}}$?

The argument is presented in two parts.

How does translation affect the gradient?

If $\dfrac{d}{dx} f(x) = g(x)$, what is $\dfrac{d}{dx} f(x - k)$?

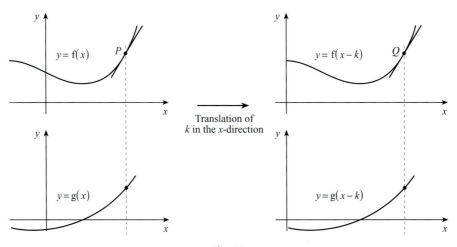

Fig. 4.2

The left side of Fig. 4.2 shows the relationship between the graphs of a function f(x) and its derived function g(x). On the right, the graphs have been translated by k units in the direction of the positive x-axis, with corresponding points shown on each graph. The vertical dashed lines show that, because the gradients at P and Q have the same value, the graph of the gradient function is also translated by k units in the same direction. (See C1 Section 10.1.)

$$\text{If } \frac{d}{dx} f(x) = g(x), \text{ then } \frac{d}{dx} f(x - k) = g(x - k).$$

How does stretching affect the gradient?

Suppose first that a is positive. In C1 Section 10.2 you saw that 'replacing x by $\dfrac{x}{c}$ in the equation $y = f(x)$ produces a stretch of factor c in the x-direction'. If you replace c by $\dfrac{1}{a}$ you will see that the effect of replacing x by ax in the equation $y = f(x)$ is to stretch the graph by a factor of $\dfrac{1}{a}$ in the x-direction.

Fig. 4.3 shows the graphs of the functions $y = f(x)$ and $y = f(ax)$ with corresponding points P and Q marked on each graph.

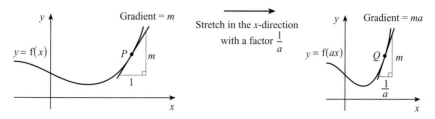

Fig. 4.3

To answer the question, 'What is the relation between the gradients at P and at Q?', consider what happens to the gradient of the tangent at P under the stretch with factor $\frac{1}{a}$. Suppose that the tangent at P has gradient m; a right-angled triangle with base 1 and height m has been drawn to illustrate this gradient. On the right, the figure has been stretched by a factor of $\frac{1}{a}$, that is, compressed by a factor of a, in the x-direction. The right-angled triangle now has a base of $\frac{1}{a}$, so the gradient of the new tangent is $\frac{m}{1/a} = am$. That is, the gradient of the tangent has been multiplied by a factor of a.

If a is negative, the transformation could be made up of two parts. The first part would be a reflection in the y-axis which would multiply the gradient by -1. The second would be a stretch of $\frac{1}{|a|}$. So the effect on the gradient would be to multiply it by $-|a|$; but, as a is negative, this is the same as multiplying by a.

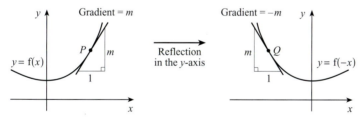

Fig. 4.4

> Stretching a graph by a factor of $\frac{1}{a}$ in the x-direction multiplies the gradient at every point by a. So if $\frac{d}{dx}f(x) = g(x)$, then $\frac{d}{dx}f(ax) = ag(ax)$.

You can combine the results in the two boxes above to find the result of differentiating $f(ax + b)$, by writing $f(ax + b)$ in the form $f\left(a\left(x + \frac{b}{a}\right)\right)$.

The result in the first box says that

$$\text{if } \frac{d}{dx}f(x) = g(x), \quad \text{then } \frac{d}{dx}f\left(x + \frac{b}{a}\right) = g\left(x + \frac{b}{a}\right).$$

Using the result in the second box then shows that

$$\frac{\mathrm{d}}{\mathrm{d}x}\mathrm{f}\left(a\left(x+\frac{b}{a}\right)\right) = a\mathrm{g}\left(a\left(x+\frac{b}{a}\right)\right) = a\mathrm{g}(ax + b).$$

This is the result in the box at the end of Section 4.1.

Miscellaneous exercise 4

1 Differentiate $(4x - 1)^{20}$ with respect to x. (OCR)

2 Differentiate $\dfrac{1}{(3 - 4x)^2}$ with respect to x. (OCR)

3 Evaluate $\displaystyle\int_0^{\frac{2}{3}} (3x - 2)^3 \, \mathrm{d}x$. (OCR)

4 Find $\displaystyle\int_0^4 \sqrt{2x + 1} \, \mathrm{d}x$. (OCR)

5 Find the equation of the tangent to the curve $y = (4x + 3)^5$ at the point $\left(-\frac{1}{2}, 1\right)$, giving your answer in the form $y = mx + c$. (OCR)

6 The diagram shows a sketch of the curve $y = \sqrt{4 - x}$ and the line $y = 2 - \frac{1}{3}x$. The coordinates of the points A and B where the curve and line intersect are $(0, 2)$ and $(3, 1)$ respectively. Calculate the area of the region between the line and the curve (shaded in the diagram), giving your answer as an exact fraction. (OCR)

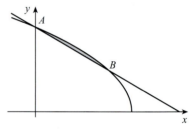

7 The diagram shows the curve $y = (2x - 3)^3$.

   (a) Find the x-coordinates of the two points on the curve which have gradient 6.

   (b) The region shaded in the diagram is bounded by part of the curve and by the two axes. Find, by integration, the area of this region. (OCR)

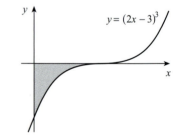

8 The diagram shows the curve with equation $y = \sqrt{4x + 1}$ and the normal to the curve at the point A with coordinates $(6, 5)$.

   (a) Show that the equation of the normal to the curve at A is $y = -\frac{5}{2}x + 20$.

   (b) Find the area of the region (shaded in the diagram) which is enclosed by the curve, the normal and the x-axis. Give your answer as a fraction in its lowest terms. (OCR)

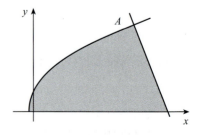

9 Find the equation of the tangent to the curve $y = \dfrac{50}{(2x-1)^2}$ at the point $(3, 2)$, giving your answer in the form $ax + by + c = 0$, where a, b and c are integers. (OCR)

10 Sketch the graph of $y = (x-2)^2 - 4$ showing clearly on your graph the coordinates of any stationary points and of the intersections with the axes.

Find the coordinates of the stationary points on the graph of $y = (x-2)^3 - 12(x-2)$ and sketch the graph, giving the exact coordinates (in surd form, where appropriate) of the intersections with the axes. (OCR)

11 The diagram shows the curve $y = \sqrt{x+4}$. The curve meets the x-axis at the point A and the y-axis at the point B. The normal at B meets the x-axis at the point C.

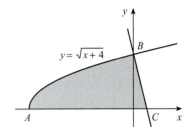

(a) Find the coordinates of A and B, and show that C has coordinates $\left(\frac{1}{2}, 0\right)$.

(b) Calculate the area of the region (shaded in the diagram) bounded by the x-axis, the line BC and the part of the curve between A and B giving your answer as an exact fraction. (OCR)

12 The diagram shows the curve

$$y = \frac{1}{\sqrt[3]{4x+3}}.$$

Find the area of the shaded region.

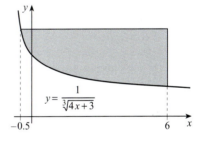

13 The diagram shows the curve

$$y = \left(\tfrac{1}{2}x - 2\right)^6 + 5.$$

Find the area of the shaded region.

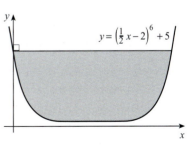

14 The diagram shows the curves

$$y = (2x-3)^3 \text{ and } y = (3-2x)^5.$$

Find the area of the region (shaded in the diagram) enclosed between the two curves and the y-axis.

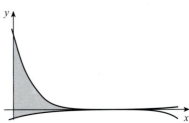

15 A curve has equation $y = \frac{1}{12}(3x + 1)^4 - 8x$.

(a) Show that there is a stationary point where $x = \frac{1}{3}$ and determine whether this stationary point is a maximum or a minimum.

(b) At a particular point of the curve, the equation of the tangent is $48x + 3y + c = 0$. Find the value of the constant c.   (OCR)

16 The diagram shows the curve $y = (1 - 4x)^5 + 20x$. The curve has a maximum point at P as shown.

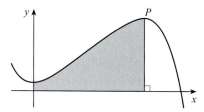

Show that the curve has a minimum point which lies on the y-axis and calculate the area of the region shaded in the diagram.

17 Find the coordinates of the stationary point of the curve $y = \dfrac{1}{2x + 1} - \dfrac{1}{(2x + 1)^2}$ and determine whether the stationary point is a maximum or a minimum.

18 Find the coordinates of the stationary point of the curve $y = \sqrt{4x - 1} + \dfrac{9}{\sqrt{4x - 1}}$ and determine whether the stationary point is a maximum or a minimum.

19 Given $y = (3x - 7)^5 + 5(3x - 7)^4$, show that $\dfrac{dy}{dx} = 45(3x - 7)^3(x - 1)$.

(a) Deduce the coordinates of the stationary points of the curve.

(b) Evaluate $\displaystyle\int_{1}^{\frac{7}{3}} (3x - 7)^3(x - 1)\,dx$.

20 The diagram shows parts of the curves

$$y = (3x - 5)^3 \text{ and } y = \frac{32}{(3x - 5)^2}.$$

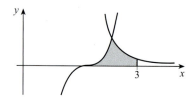

Calculate the area of the region shaded in the diagram.

21* (a) Expand $(ax + b)^3$ using the binomial theorem. Differentiate the result with respect to x and show that the derivative is $3a(ax + b)^2$.

(b) Expand $(ax + b)^4$ using the binomial theorem. Differentiate the result with respect to x and show that the derivative is $4a(ax + b)^3$.

(c) Write down the expansion of $(ax + b)^n$ where n is a positive integer. Differentiate the result with respect to x. Show that the derivative is $na(ax + b)^{n-1}$.

5 Differentiating exponentials and logarithms

This chapter deals with exponentials and logarithms as functions which can be differentiated and integrated. When you have completed it, you should

- understand how to find the derivative of b^x from the definition
- understand the reason for selecting e as the exponential base
- know the derivative and integral of e^x
- know that continuous exponential variation can be expressed either as $y = ab^t$ or as $y = ae^{ct}$ and be able to convert either form to the other
- know the derivative of $\ln x$, and how to obtain it
- know the integral of $\dfrac{1}{x}$, and be able to use it for both positive and negative x
- be able to use the extended methods from Chapter 4 to broaden the range of such functions that you can differentiate and integrate.

5.1 Differentiating exponential functions

You saw in Section 3.1 that one of the features of exponential sequences is that the increase in the value between times t and $t + 1$ is proportional to the current value at time t. There is a corresponding property for continuous exponential variation; but in this case it is the derivative, rather than the increase over a finite unit of time, which is proportional to the current value.

To investigate this, it is necessary to find out how to differentiate the general exponential function, with equation $f(x) = b^x$, which you first met in C2 Section 7.1. It will be simplest to begin with a particular value $b = 2$, and to consider $f(x) = 2^x$.

Fig. 5.1 shows a graph of $f(x) = 2^x$. You can see that the gradient is always positive, and also that the gradient increases as x increases. So the graph of the gradient function $f'(x)$ has a shape something like Fig. 5.2. The question is, what is the equation of this gradient function?

Before launching into algebra, it is worth while doing a numerical experiment. Begin by displaying the graph of $y = 2^x$ on a graphic calculator. One point on this graph is $(0, 1)$. Now try adding to the display a line through $(0, 1)$ with equation $y - 1 = mx$, and experiment with different values of m until the line looks like a tangent to the curve. What value do you get for m?

Now move to the point $(1, 2)$ on the graph and repeat the experiment. That is, find a line with equation $y - 2 = m(x - 1)$ which looks like a tangent. What value do you now get for m?

Repeat the experiment with lines through $(2, 4)$ and $(-1, 0.5)$. Can you see any pattern in the values of m at the various points?

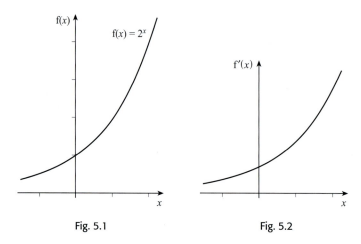

Fig. 5.1   Fig. 5.2

The numbers *m* which you have found experimentally are approximate values of f′(x) where x = 0, x = 1, x = 2 and x = −1. You can now show these in a table, which is probably something like Table 5.3.

x	−1	0	1	2
f(x)	0.5	1	2	4
approximate f′(x)	*0.35*	*0.7*	*1.4*	*2.8*

Table 5.3

Do your values agree approximately with the entries in italics in the last line of the table?

It is not difficult to spot a rule from Table 5.3. For each value of *x*, it looks as if the value of f′(x) is approximately 0.7 times the value of f(x). That is,

$$\text{if } f(x) = 2^x, \quad \text{then} \quad f'(x) \approx 0.7 \times 2^x.$$

This is illustrated in Fig. 5.4, which shows the graphs of f(x) and f′(x) plotted using the same axes. What this experimental result suggests is that the graph of f′(x) is obtained from the graph of f(x) by a stretch in the *y*-direction of factor approximately 0.7.

If you have the appropriate facilities, you could use a spreadsheet (or a ready-made package) to display the graph of the gradient function.

This can now be checked by an algebraic argument, using the definition in C1 Section 5.8, that

$$f'(x) = \lim_{h \to 0} \frac{f(x+h) - f(x)}{h}.$$

For this function, as illustrated in Fig. 5.5,

$$f(x+h) - f(x) = 2^{x+h} - 2^x = 2^x \times 2^h - 2^x$$
$$= 2^x(2^h - 1).$$

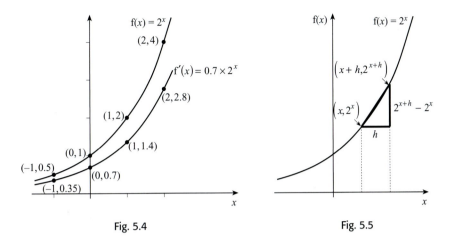

Fig. 5.4   Fig. 5.5

So the definition becomes

$$f'(x) = \lim_{h \to 0} \frac{2^x(2^h - 1)}{h}.$$

Since 2^x does not involve h, you can write

$$f'(x) = 2^x \lim_{h \to 0} \frac{2^h - 1}{h}.$$

This shows that $f'(x)$ is the product of two factors: 2^x, which is independent of h, and a limit expression which is independent of x.

This limit expression is in fact the gradient of the tangent at the point $(0, 1)$. This is because $\dfrac{2^h - 1}{h}$ is the gradient of the chord joining $(0, 1)$ to $(h, 2^h)$, and as h tends to 0 this chord tends to the tangent. So

$$f'(x) = 2^x \times \text{ gradient of the tangent at } (0, 1) = 2^x \times f'(0);$$

and since 2^x is $f(x)$, this can be written as

$$f'(x) = f(x) \times f'(0).$$

This confirms that the rate of growth of $f(x)$ is proportional to its current value.

The next step is to evaluate the limiting value $f'(0)$. You can do this, to a good level of accuracy, by adapting the numerical argument that was used in C1 Section 5.1 to find the gradient at a point of $y = x^2$. It is clear from the graph of $f(x) = 2^x$ in Fig. 5.1 that the gradient of the tangent at $(0, 1)$ is smaller than the gradient of any chord joining $(0, 1)$ to a point $(h, 2^h)$ with $h > 0$, and greater than the gradient of any such chord with $h < 0$. For example, taking h to be 0.0001 and -0.0001 in turn, you find

$$\text{gradient of chord from } (0, 1) \text{ to } (0.0001, 2^{0.0001}) \text{ is } \frac{2^{0.0001} - 1}{0.0001 - 0} = 0.69317...$$

and

$$\text{gradient of chord from } (0, 1) \text{ to } (-0.0001, 2^{-0.0001}) \text{ is } \frac{2^{-0.0001} - 1}{-0.0001 - 0} = 0.69312....$$

So $0.69312... < f'(0) < 0.69317...$.

This shows that $f'(0) = 0.6931...$.

It follows that, for the function $f(x) = 2^x$, the derived function is

$f'(x) = \text{constant} \times 2^x$, where the constant is $f'(0) = 0.6931...$.

You will see that the rule $f'(x) \approx 0.7 \times 2^x$ suggested by Table 5.3 and Fig. 5.4 fits very well with the result given by the theoretical argument.

There is nothing special about taking b to be 2. You could find the derivative for any other exponential function b^x in exactly the same way. The only difference is that the numerical value of the constant $f'(0)$ is different for different values of the base b.

> For the general exponential function $f(x) = b^x$, where $b > 0$ and $b \neq 1$, the derived function is $f'(x) = \text{constant} \times b^x$, where the value of the constant, which depends on the base b, is equal to $f'(0)$.

Example 5.1.1
Show that, for any exponential function, the graph of $y = b^x$ bends upwards.

If $y = b^x$,

$$\frac{dy}{dx} = f'(0)b^x$$

and

$$\frac{d^2y}{dx^2} = f'(0) \times f'(0)b^x = (f'(0))^2 b^x.$$

Since $b \neq 1$, $f'(0)$ is not zero, so $(f'(0))^2 > 0$. Also, for all x, $b^x > 0$.

Therefore $\dfrac{d^2y}{dx^2} > 0$ for all x, so the graph bends upwards.

If you look back to C2 Fig. 7.3, you can see that $f'(0)$ is positive for $b > 1$ and negative for $0 < b < 1$, but in either case the graph bends upwards throughout its length.

5.2   The number e

If you carry out the limit calculation $\lim\limits_{h \to 0} \dfrac{b^h - 1}{h}$ for values of b other than 2, you get values for the constant $f'(0)$ like those in Table 5.6 below. Since the values of $f'(0)$ depend on b, they have been denoted by $L(b)$.

b	2	3	4	5	6	8	9	10
$L(b)$	0.6931	1.0986	1.3863	1.6094	1.7918	2.0794	2.1972	2.3026

Table 5.6

Before reading on, you should work out one or two of these for yourself. If you are working in a group, you could share the work and verify the whole table. It is also interesting to find L(b) for a few values of b less than 1, such as 0.1, 0.2, 0.25 and 0.5. Look at the answers and keep a record of anything you notice for future reference.

None of these limits works out to a nice recognisable number; in fact they are all irrational numbers. But Table 5.6 suggests that between $b = 2$ and $b = 3$ there should be a number for which L(b) is 1. This is the number denoted by the letter e, and it turns out to be one of the most important numbers in mathematics.

You can find the value of e more precisely by calculating L(b) with b to more decimal places. For example, the limit calculation shows that $L(2.71) = 0.9969...$, which is too small, and $L(2.72) = 1.0006...$, which is too large, so $2.71 < e < 2.72$. However, this is a rather tedious process, and there are far more efficient ways of calculating e to many decimal places.

If you have facilities for constructing the graph of a gradient function, you could experiment by displaying the graphs of $y = b^x$ and the gradient function using the same axes, for different values of b. If the two graphs coincide, then b is equal to e.

Note that $L(e) = 1$, and that L(b) is the symbol used for the constant f'(0) in the statement

if $f(x) = b^x$, then $f'(x) = f'(0)b^x$.

This means that, if $f(x) = e^x$ then $f'(0) = 1$, so

if $f(x) = e^x$, then $f'(x) = e^x$.

It is this property that makes e^x so much more important than all the other exponential functions. It can be described as the 'natural' exponential function, but usually it is called 'the exponential function' (to distinguish it from b^x for any other value of b, which is simply 'an exponential function').

The function e^x is sometimes written as exp x, so that the symbol 'exp' strictly stands for the function itself, rather than the output of the function. Thus, in formal function notation,

$\exp : x \mapsto e^x$.

For the (natural) exponential function e^x, or exp x,
$$\frac{d}{dx}e^x = e^x.$$

Many calculators have a special key labelled [exp] or [e^x], for finding values of this function. If you want to know the numerical value of e, you can use this key with an input of 1, so that the output is $e^1 = e$. This gives $e = 2.718\,281\,828...$. (But do not assume that this is a recurring decimal; e is in fact an irrational number, and the single repetition of the digits 1828 is a curious accident.)

Example 5.2.1

Find the equations of the tangents to the graph $y = e^x$ at the points   (a) $(0, 1)$,   (b) $(1, e)$.

(a) Since $\dfrac{dy}{dx} = e^x$, the gradient at $(0, 1)$ is $e^0 = 1$. The equation of the tangent is therefore $y - 1 = 1(x - 0)$, which you can simplify to $y = x + 1$.

(b) The gradient at $(1, e)$ is $e^1 = e$. The equation of the tangent is $y - e = e(x - 1)$, which you can simplify to $y = e x$.

It is interesting that the tangent at $(1, e)$ passes through the origin. You can demonstrate this nicely with a graphic calculator.

Example 5.2.2

Find   (a) $\dfrac{d}{dx}e^{2x}$,   (b) $\dfrac{d}{dx}e^{-3x}$,   (c) $\dfrac{d}{dx}e^{2+x}$.

These are all of the form $\dfrac{d}{dx}f(ax + b)$, with $f(x) = e^x$. It was shown in Section 4.1 that the derivative is $ag(ax + b)$, where $g(x) = f'(x)$. In this case $g(x) = e^x$. The answers are therefore   (a) $2e^{2x}$,   (b) $-3e^{-3x}$,   (c) e^{2+x}.

For (c) you could write e^{2+x} as $e^2 e^x$. Since e^2 is constant, the derivative is $e^2 e^x$, or e^{2+x}.

Each time you meet a new result about differentiation, you should look for a corresponding result about integration. From $\dfrac{d}{dx}e^x = e^x$ it follows that:

For the (natural) exponential function e^x, or $\exp x$,

$$\int e^x \, dx = e^x + k.$$

Example 5.2.3

Find the area under the graph of $y = e^{2x}$ from $x = 0$ to $x = 1$.

$\displaystyle\int e^{2x} \, dx$ is of the form $\displaystyle\int g(ax + b) \, dx$ with $g(x) = e^x$. The indefinite integral is therefore $\dfrac{1}{a}f(ax + b) + k$, where $f(x)$ is the simplest integral of $g(x)$. In this case, $f(x) = e^x$, so that $\displaystyle\int e^{2x} \, dx = \tfrac{1}{2}e^{2x} + k$.

The area under the graph is therefore $\displaystyle\int_0^1 e^{2x} \, dx = \left[\tfrac{1}{2}e^{2x}\right]_0^1 = \tfrac{1}{2}e^2 - \tfrac{1}{2}e^0 = \tfrac{1}{2}(e^2 - 1)$.

In Examples 5.2.2 and 5.2.3 the rules for differentiating and integrating e^x are combined with the methods of extending differentiation and integration in Chapter 4. If you do this in general you get

$$\frac{d}{dx}e^{ax+b} = ae^{ax+b} \quad \text{and} \quad \int e^{ax+b} \, dx = \frac{1}{a}e^{ax+b} + k.$$

But it is probably better to learn the simpler rules in the blue boxes and to apply these using the methods in Chapter 4, rather than trying to remember these more complicated rules. After a little practice you will find that the process becomes almost automatic.

Exercise 5A

1 Differentiate each of the following functions with respect to x.

(a) e^{3x} (b) e^{-x} (c) $3e^{2x}$ (d) $-4e^{-4x}$

(e) e^{3x+4} (f) e^{3-2x} (g) e^{1-x} (h) $3e \times e^{2+4x}$

2 Find, in terms of e, the gradients of the tangents to the following curves for the given values of x.

(a) $y = 3e^x$, where $x = 2$ (b) $y = 2e^{-x}$, where $x = -1$

(c) $y = x - e^{2x}$, where $x = 0$ (d) $y = e^{6-2x}$, where $x = 3$

3 Find the equations of the tangents to the given curves for the given values of x.

(a) $y = e^x$, where $x = -1$ (b) $y = 2x - e^{-x}$, where $x = 0$

(c) $y = x^2 + 2e^{2x}$, where $x = 2$ (d) $y = e^{-2x}$, where $x = \ln 2$

4 Find any stationary points of the graph of $y = 2x - e^x$, and determine whether they are maxima or minima.

5 Find the following indefinite integrals.

(a) $\int e^{3x}\, dx$ (b) $\int e^{-x}\, dx$ (c) $\int 3e^{2x}\, dx$ (d) $\int -4e^{-4x}\, dx$

(e) $\int e^{3x+4}\, dx$ (f) $\int e^{3-2x}\, dx$ (g) $\int e^{1-x}\, dx$ (h) $\int 3e \times e^{2+4x}\, dx$

6 Find the values of each of the following definite integrals in terms of e, or give their exact values.

(a) $\int_1^2 e^{2x}\, dx$ (b) $\int_{-1}^1 e^{-x}\, dx$ (c) $\int_{-2}^0 2e^{1-2x}\, dx$ (d) $\int_4^5 2e^{2x}\, dx$

(e) $\int_{\ln 3}^{\ln 9} e^x\, dx$ (f) $\int_0^{\ln 2} 2e^{1-2x}\, dx$ (g) $\int_0^1 e^{x\ln 2}\, dx$ (h) $\int_{-3}^9 e^{x\ln 3}\, dx$

7 Find the area bounded by the graph of $y = e^{2x}$, the axes and the line $x = 2$.

8 Find $\int_0^N e^{-x}\, dx$. Deduce the value of $\int_0^\infty e^{-x}\, dx$.

9 When you apply the trapezium rule with one interval to approximate the area under the graph of $y = e^x$ for $0 \leqslant x \leqslant 1$, would you expect to get an overestimate or an underestimate? Show that this approximation to the exact area leads to $e \approx 3$.

5.3   Application to exponential growth and decay

The method of finding the constants in equations for exponential growth or decay, based on the equivalence

$$y = ab^t \quad \Leftrightarrow \quad \log y = \log a + t \log b$$

can be used with logarithms to any base. But there are some advantages in using logarithms to the base e; and a special symbol, ln, is used to denote $\log_e$. The reason for this symbol is that the letter 'n' stands for 'natural'; and the logarithm ln is called the 'natural logarithm' because the number e is based on a mathematical property (that $\dfrac{d}{dx}e^x = e^x$) rather than a physical accident (that mathematicians have 10 fingers).

Remember that the general definition of a logarithm (given in C2 Section 7.2) is that

$$y = b^x \quad \Leftrightarrow \quad x = \log_b y.$$

If this is applied with $b = e$ you get a definition of the natural logarithm:

> The **natural logarithm** function, ln, is defined by the equivalence
> $$y = e^x \quad \Leftrightarrow \quad x = \ln y.$$

Now suppose that you have an exponential equation $y = ab^t$, and that $c = \ln b$. (Remember that by definition b is positive.) Then $b = e^c$, so that

$$y = a(e^c)^t = ae^{ct},$$

using the power-on-power rule for indices. This is an alternative way of writing the exponential equation.

Since $c = \ln b$, it follows that $c > 0$ if $b > 1$ and $c < 0$ if $0 < b < 1$. So the constant c is positive for exponential growth and negative for exponential decay.

> The continuous exponential equation can be written in the form
> $$y = ae^{ct}$$
> where a is the initial value of y and c is constant.
>
> This represents exponential growth if $c > 0$ and exponential decay if $c < 0$.

Example 5.3.1 (see Example 3.2.2)
Carbon-dating in archaeology is based on the decay of the isotope carbon-14, which has a half-life of 5715 years. Express this property in exponential form.

> Since the isotope decays exponentially, a unit of carbon-14 is reduced by a factor of e^{ct} after t years, where c is a negative constant. You are given that the reduction factor is 0.5 when $t = 5715$, so
>
> $$e^{c \times 5715} = 0.5.$$

Expressing this equation in natural logarithmic form,

$$5715c = \ln 0.5 = -0.6931...,$$

$$c = \frac{-0.6931...}{5715} = -0.000121, \text{ correct to 3 significant figures.}$$

So a unit of carbon-14 is reduced by a factor of $e^{-0.000121t}$ after t years.

If you take natural logarithms of both sides of the equation $y = ae^{ct}$ you get

$$\ln y = \ln a + \ln(e^{ct}) = \ln a + ct$$

(because, for any number x, $\ln(e^x) = \log_e(e^x) = x$). So if you draw a graph of $\ln y$ against t, it will be a straight line with gradient c and y-intercept $\ln a$.

This is illustrated in Example 5.3.2, in which Example 3.3.3 is re-worked using natural logarithms instead of logarithms to base 10.

Example 5.3.2* (see Example 3.3.3)
Use the census data in Table 5.7 to model the population growth in the US from 1790 to 1860 as an equation of the form $P = ae^{ct}$.

Year	1790	1800	1810	1820	1830	1840	1850	1860
Population (millions)	3.9	5.3	7.2	9.6	12.9	17.0	23.2	31.4

Table 5.7

In Example 3.3.3 Table 5.7 was adapted to produce a table of values of $\log_{10} P$. If you take logarithms to base e instead, you get Table 5.8.

t	0	10	20	30	40	50	60	70
$\ln P$	1.36	1.67	1.97	2.26	2.56	2.83	3.14	3.45

Table 5.8

These values are plotted as a graph in Fig. 5.9, which shows that the points fit approximately on a straight line. By measurement, it seems that the intercept on the vertical axis is about 1.37; and, from the gradient triangle shown with dotted lines, the gradient is about $\frac{1.5}{50} = 0.03$. So the line has equation

$$\ln P = 1.37 + 0.03t.$$

You can finish off the calculation in one of two ways.

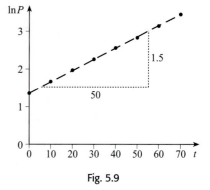

Fig. 5.9

Method 1   Comparing the equation of the line with

$$\ln P = \ln a + ct,$$

derived from $P = ae^{ct}$, you find that $\ln a = 1.37$ and $c = 0.03$. And since

$$\ln a = 1.37 \quad \Leftrightarrow \quad a = e^{1.37} \approx 3.9,$$

the population is given approximately by the equation

$$P = 3.9e^{0.03t}.$$

Method 2   Since $\ln P = 1.37 + 0.03t$ approximately,

$$P = e^{1.37+0.03t} = e^{1.37} \times e^{0.03t} \approx 3.9e^{0.03t}.$$

Example 5.3.3*

A thousand people waiting at a medical centre were asked to record how long they had to wait before they saw a doctor. Their results are summarised in Table 5.10.

Waiting time (minutes)	0 to 5	5 to 10	10 to 15	15 to 20	20 to 30	30 to 60	more than 60
Number of people	335	218	155	90	111	85	6

Table 5.10

Show that the proportion p of people who had to wait at least t minutes can be modelled by an equation of the form $p = e^{-kt}$, and find the value of k.

Obviously all of the people had to wait at least 0 minutes; all but 335, that is $1000 - 335 = 665$, had to wait at least 5 minutes; of these, $665 - 218 = 447$ had to wait at least 10 minutes; and so on. So you can make a table of p, the proportion that had to wait at least t minutes, for various values of t. This is Table 5.11.

t	0	5	10	15	20	30	60
p	1	0.665	0.447	0.292	0.202	0.091	0.006

Table 5.11

If you plot these values for yourself, you will see that they appear to fit an exponential decay graph; but to show this conclusively it is necessary to rewrite the equation so that it can be represented by a straight line.

Now if $p = e^{-kt}$ as suggested in the question, $\ln p = -kt$, so a graph of $\ln p$ against t would be a straight line through the origin with gradient $-k$. So make a table of values of $\ln p$, as in Table 5.12.

t	0	5	10	15	20	30	60
$\ln p$	0	-0.41	-0.81	-1.23	-1.60	-2.40	-5.12

Table 5.12

These values are plotted in Fig. 5.13.

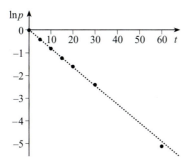

Fig. 5.13

This example differs from Example 5.3.2 in that you know that the graph must pass through the origin. So draw the best line that you can through the origin to fit the plotted points. From Fig. 5.13 the gradient of this line is about -0.082.

So the proportion who had to wait more than t minutes is modelled by the equation $p = \mathrm{e}^{-0.082t}$.

One reason for writing the exponential equation $y = ab^t$ in the alternative form $y = a\mathrm{e}^{ct}$, is that it is easy to differentiate, as

$$\frac{\mathrm{d}y}{\mathrm{d}t} = a \times c\mathrm{e}^{ct}.$$

It follows that

$$\frac{\mathrm{d}y}{\mathrm{d}t} = cy.$$

That is, the quantity y grows at a rate which is c times its current value.

For example, the equation $P = 3.9\mathrm{e}^{0.03t}$ obtained in Example 5.3.2 for the population of the US can be differentiated to show that

$$\frac{\mathrm{d}P}{\mathrm{d}t} = 0.03P.$$

The interpretation of this is that the population increased at a rate of 3% of its current value. Thus when the population was 10 million, it was increasing at a rate of 300 000 per year; by the time the population had reached 20 million, the rate of increase had doubled to 600 000 per year.

> A quantity Q growing (or decaying) exponentially according to the law $Q = a\mathrm{e}^{ct}$ has a rate of growth (or decay) equal to c (or $-c$) times its current value.

Exercise 5B

1 Write the following in the form e^{cx}, giving the constant c correct to 3 significant figures.

(a) 10^x (b) 0.1^x (c) 2.5^x (d) 0.4^x

2 Write the following in the form ae^{ct}, giving the constants a and c correct to 3 significant figures.

(a) 3.6×1.1^t (b) 0.342×5.71^t (c) 7.13×0.518^t (d) 0.161×0.0172^t

3 Write the following in the form ab^t, giving the constants a and b correct to 3 significant figures.

(a) $100e^{-3t}$ (b) $2.83e^{1.46t}$ (c) $0.326e^{-0.132t}$ (d) $0.507e^{0.0123t}$

4 (a) If $\ln y = 0.4 + 0.6x$, expess y in terms of x.

(b) If $\ln y = 12 - 3x$, express y in terms of x.

(c) If $\ln y = 0.7 + 1.7x$, express y in terms of x.

(d) If $\ln y = 0.7 + 2\ln x$, express y in terms of x.

(e) If $\ln y = -0.5 - 5\ln x$, express y in terms of x.

Compare your answers with the answers to Exercise 3B Question 7.

5 The government sets a target for the annual rate of inflation at 2% per year. This means that after t years the value of a pound, £ V, would be reduced to £ 1.02^{-t}. Express V in the form e^{ct}.

6 A sick person takes a tablet of mass 500 mg whose contents are gradually absorbed into the body. The mass not yet absorbed after t minutes is modelled by the formula $500e^{-ct}$ mg. After 30 minutes only 25 mg remains unabsorbed.

(a) Find the value of c.

(b) Find the rate at which the contents of the tablet are being absorbed

   (i) when the person first takes the tablet,

   (ii) when half of the tablet has been absorbed.

7 The speed of a skydiver in free fall is modelled by the equation $v = 50(1 - e^{-0.2t})$, where v is her speed in metres per second after t seconds.

(a) What speed is she certain not to exceed, however far she falls?

(b) Show that her acceleration decreases exponentially.

(c) Calculate her acceleration

   (i) after 10 seconds

   (ii) when her speed has reached 45 metres per second.

(d) If she continues in free fall for a minute, how far does she fall?

(e) Sketch graphs of

   (i) her acceleration,   (ii) her speed   (iii) the distance she has fallen.

(Use $v = \dfrac{dx}{dt}$, and $a = \dfrac{dv}{dt}$, where x is the distance travelled, v is the speed and a is the acceleration. See C1 Section 12.2.)

8 An epidemic is spreading exponentially through a community, so that the total number of people who have been admitted to hospital in the first t weeks (including those who have subsequently been discharged) is modelled by the equation $y = 5e^{0.3t}$.

   (a) At what rate are new patients being admitted

      (i) after 5 weeks   (ii) after 200 people have already been admitted?

   (b) Patients remain in hospital for 2 weeks and are then discharged. Find an expression for the number of patients in hospital after t weeks (for $t \geqslant 2$), and show that this number also increases exponentially.

   (c) If at a certain time there are 50 patients in hospital, at what rate per week is this number increasing?

5.4 Differentiating the natural logarithm

The equivalence

$$y = e^x \quad \Leftrightarrow \quad x = \log_e y$$

can be written, using the notation exp and ln for the exponential function and natural logarithm, as

$$y = \exp x \quad \Leftrightarrow \quad x = \ln y.$$

This shows that exp and ln are inverse functions, in the sense defined in Section 2.6. The domain of exp is the set of real numbers $\mathbb{R}$; the domain of ln is the set of positive real numbers, usually denoted by $\mathbb{R}^+$.

You are already familiar with the graphs of exponential functions of the form $y = b^x$. The graph of $y = e^x$ is the graph of this form which has gradient 1 at the point $(0, 1)$; this is shown in Fig. 5.14. It is, of course, the same as the graph of $x = \ln y$. It was explained in Section 2.9 that, to get the graph of $y = \ln x$, you reflect the graph of $y = e^x$ in the line $y = x$. This is also shown in Fig. 5.14. Notice from the graph that $\ln x$ exists only if $x > 0$, and that the graph passes through $(1, 0)$, which is the reflection of $(0, 1)$ in the line $y = x$.

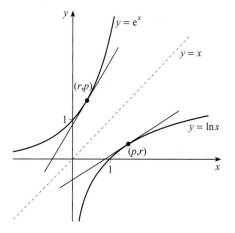

Fig. 5.14

The most important property of the natural logarithm is the derivative of $\ln x$. This can be deduced from the result $\dfrac{d}{dx} e^x = e^x$ in Section 5.2, but first we need a result from coordinate geometry.

Mini-theorem   If a line with gradient m (where $m \neq 0$) is reflected in the line $y = x$, the gradient of the reflected line is $\dfrac{1}{m}$.

Proof   The proof is much like that of the perpendicular line property given in C1 Section 1.9. Fig. 5.15 shows the line of gradient m with a 'gradient triangle' ABC. Its reflection in $y = x$ is the triangle DEF. Completing the rectangle $DEFG$, DGF is a gradient triangle for the reflected line.

$GF = DE = AB = 1$ and $DG = EF = BC = m$, so the gradient of the reflected line is

$$\frac{GF}{DG} = \frac{1}{m}.$$

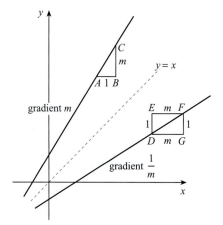

Fig. 5.15

Now consider the graphs of $y = \ln x$ and $y = e^x$ in Fig. 5.14. Since these are graphs of inverse functions, they are reflections of each other in the line $y = x$. The reflection of the tangent at the point (p, r) on $y = \ln x$ is the tangent at the point (r, p) on $y = e^x$, where $p = e^r$.

Since $\dfrac{d}{dx} e^x = e^x$, the gradient of the tangent at (r, p) is e^r, which is equal to p. It follows, by the mini-theorem, that the gradient of the tangent to $y = \ln x$ at (p, r) is $\dfrac{1}{p}$. Since this holds for any point (p, r) on $y = \ln x$, you can deduce that:

$$\text{For } x > 0, \ \frac{d}{dx} \ln x = \frac{1}{x}.$$

Example 5.4.1
Find the minimum value of the function $f(x) = 2x - \ln x$.

The natural domain of $f(x)$ is $x > 0$.

Since $f'(x) = 2 - \frac{1}{x}$, $f'(x) = 0$ when $x = \frac{1}{2}$.

Also $f''(x) = \dfrac{1}{x^2}$, so $f''\left(\frac{1}{2}\right) = 4 > 0$. So the function has a minimum when $x = \frac{1}{2}$.

The minimum value is $f\left(\frac{1}{2}\right) = 1 - \ln \frac{1}{2}$. Since $\ln \frac{1}{2} = \ln 2^{-1} = -\ln 2$, you can write the minimum value more simply as $1 + \ln 2$.

Unless you specifically need a numerical answer, it is better to leave it as $1 + \ln 2$, which is exact, than to use a calculator to convert it into decimal form.

Example 5.4.2

Find (a) $\dfrac{d}{dx} \ln(3x + 1)$, (b) $\dfrac{d}{dx} \ln 3x$, (c) $\dfrac{d}{dx} \ln x^3$.

(a) This is of the form $f(ax + b)$, with $f(x) = \ln x$, so the derivative is

$$3 \times \frac{1}{3x + 1} = \frac{3}{3x + 1}.$$

(b) **Method 1** You can find the derivative as in part (a), as

$$3 \times \frac{1}{3x} = \frac{1}{x}.$$

Method 2 You can use the multiplication rule for logarithms to write

$$\ln 3x = \ln 3 + \ln x,$$

Since $\ln 3$ is constant,

$$\frac{d}{dx} \ln 3x = \frac{d}{dx} \ln x = \frac{1}{x}.$$

(c) Begin by using the power rule to write $\ln x^3$ as $3 \ln x$. Then

$$\frac{d}{dx} \ln x^3 = \frac{d}{dx} (3 \ln x) = 3 \times \frac{1}{x} = \frac{3}{x}.$$

In Example 5.4.2(a) the rule for differentiating $\ln x$ is combined with the method of extending differentiation in Chapter 4. If you do this in general you get

$$\frac{d}{dx} \ln(ax + b) = a \times \frac{1}{ax + b} = \frac{a}{ax + b}.$$

It is probably not worthwhile to learn this as a separate rule. But it is often a good idea to begin by using one of the rules for logarithms (see C2 Section 7.3) to write the function in a form that is easier to differentiate, as illustrated by Example 5.4.2 parts (b) and (c).

Exercise 5C

1 Differentiate each of the following functions with respect to x.

(a) $\ln 2x$ (b) $\ln(2x - 1)$ (c) $\ln(1 - 2x)$ (d) $\ln x^2$

(e) $\ln(a + bx)$ (f) $\ln \dfrac{1}{x}$ (g) $\ln \dfrac{1}{3x + 1}$ (h) $\ln \dfrac{2x + 1}{3x - 1}$

(i) $3 \ln x^{-2}$ (j) $\ln(x(x + 1))$ (k) $\ln(x^2(x - 1))$ (l) $\ln(x^2 + x - 2)$

2 Find the equations of the tangents to the following graphs for the given values of x.

(a) $y = \ln x$, where $x = \tfrac{1}{2}$ (b) $y = \ln 2x$, where $x = \tfrac{1}{2}$

(c) $y = \ln ex$, where $x = 1$ (d) $y = \ln 3x$, where $x = e$

3 Find any stationary values of the following curves and determine whether they are maxima or minima. Sketch the curves.

(a) $y = x - \ln x$

(b) $y = \frac{1}{2}x^2 - \ln 2x$

(c) $y = x^2 - 2\ln x$

(d) $y = x^n - n\ln x$ for $n \geqslant 1$

4 Prove that the tangent at the point where $x = e$ to the curve with equation $y = \ln x$ passes through the origin.

5 Find the equation of the normal at $x = 2$ to the curve with equation $y = \ln(2x - 3)$.

6 Let $f(x)\ln(x - 2) + \ln(x - 6)$. Write down the natural domain of $f(x)$.
Find $f'(x)$ and hence find the intervals for which $f'(x)$ is (a) positive, (b) negative.
Without using a calculator, draw a sketch of the curve.

7 Repeat Question 6 for the functions

(i) $f(x) = \ln(x - 2) + \ln(6 - x)$,   (ii) $f(x) = \ln(2 - x) + \ln(x - 6)$.

5.5   The reciprocal integral

Now that you know that $\dfrac{d}{dx}\ln x = \dfrac{1}{x}$, you also know a new result about integration:

$$\text{For } x > 0, \int \frac{1}{x}\,dx = \ln x + k.$$

This is an important step forward. You will recall that in C2 Section 5.1, when giving the indefinite integral $\displaystyle\int x^n\,dx = \frac{1}{n+1}x^{n+1} + k$, a special exception had to be made for the case $n = -1$. You can now see why: $\displaystyle\int \frac{1}{x}\,dx$ is an entirely different kind of function, the natural logarithm.

Example 5.5.1

Find the area under the graph of $y = \dfrac{1}{x}$ from $x = 2$ to $x = 4$.

Before working out the exact answer, notice from Fig. 5.16 that the area should be less than the area of the trapezium formed by joining $(2, 0.5)$ and $(4, 0.25)$ with a chord. This area is

$$\tfrac{1}{2} \times 2 \times (0.5 + 0.25) = 0.75.$$

The exact area is given by the integral

$$\int_2^4 \frac{1}{x}\,dx = [\ln x]_2^4 = \ln 4 - \ln 2$$
$$= \ln \tfrac{4}{2} = \ln 2.$$

The calculator gives this as $0.693\,14\ldots$, which is less than 0.75, as expected.

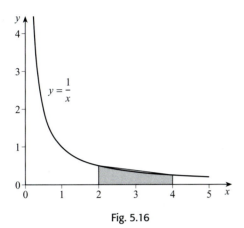

Fig. 5.16

Example 5.5.2

Find the indefinite integral $\int \dfrac{1}{3x-1}\, dx$.

This is of the form $\int g(ax+b)\, dx$, so the integral is $\dfrac{1}{a} f(ax+b)+k$, where f(x) is the simplest integral of g(x). Here, g(x) is $\dfrac{1}{x}$, so f(x) = ln x. Therefore

$$\int \frac{1}{3x-1}\, dx = \frac{1}{3}\ln(3x-1)+k.$$

Note that this integral is only valid if $x > \frac{1}{3}$, since $\ln(3x-1)$ only exists if $3x-1 > 0$.

Exercise 5D

1 Carry out the following indefinite integrations, and state the values of x for which your answer is valid.

(a) $\displaystyle\int \frac{1}{2x}\, dx$ (b) $\displaystyle\int \frac{1}{x-1}\, dx$ (c) $\displaystyle\int \frac{1}{1-x}\, dx$ (d) $\displaystyle\int \frac{1}{4x+3}\, dx$

(e) $\displaystyle\int \frac{4}{1-2x}\, dx$ (f) $\displaystyle\int \frac{4}{1+2x}\, dx$ (g) $\displaystyle\int \frac{4}{-1-2x}\, dx$ (h) $\displaystyle\int \frac{4}{2x-1}\, dx$

2 Calculate the area under the graph of $y = \dfrac{1}{x}$ from

(a) $x = 3$ to $x = 6$ (b) $x = 4$ to $x = 8$

(c) $x = \frac{1}{2}$ to $x = 1$ (d) $x = a$ to $x = 2a$,   where $a > 0$

3 Calculate the areas under the following graphs.

(a) $y = \dfrac{1}{x+2}$ from $x = -1$ to $x = 0$ (b) $y = \dfrac{1}{2x-1}$ from $x = 2$ to $x = 5$

(c) $y = \dfrac{2}{3x-5}$ from $x = 4$ to $x = 6$ (d) $y = \dfrac{e}{ex-7}$ from $x = 4$ to $x = 5$

(e) $y = \dfrac{1}{-x-1}$ from $x = -3$ to $x = -2$ (f) $y = 2 + \dfrac{1}{x-1}$ from $x = 2$ to $x = 6$

4 Draw a sketch of $y = \dfrac{2}{x+1}$, and use your sketch to make a rough estimate of the area under the graph between $x = 3$ and $x = 5$. Compare your answer with the exact answer.

5 Use the trapezium rule with three ordinates to find an approximation to the area under the graph of $y = \dfrac{6}{3x+4}$ between $x = 3$ and $x = 5$, indicating whether the approximation is an overestimate or an underestimate. Compare your answer with the exact area.

6 Given that $\dfrac{dy}{dx} = \dfrac{3}{2x+1}$ and that the graph of y against x passes through the point $(1, 0)$, find y in terms of x.

7 A curve has the property that $\dfrac{dy}{dx} = \dfrac{8}{4x-3}$, and it passes through $(1, 2)$. Find its equation.

5.6 Extending the reciprocal integral

You will have noticed that the statements of $\dfrac{d}{dx}\ln x = \dfrac{1}{x}$ and $\displaystyle\int \dfrac{1}{x}\,dx = \ln x$ both contain the condition 'for $x > 0$'. In the case of the derivative the reason is obvious, since $\ln x$ is only defined for $x > 0$. But no such restriction applies to the function $\dfrac{1}{x}$. This then raises the question, what is $\displaystyle\int \dfrac{1}{x}\,dx$ when $x < 0$?

A guess might be that it is $\ln(-x)$. This has a meaning if x is negative, and you can differentiate it as a special case of $\dfrac{d}{dx}f(ax+b)$ with $a = -1$, $b = 0$ and $f(x) = \ln x$. This gives

$$\frac{d}{dx}\ln(-x) = -1 \times \frac{1}{(-x)} = \frac{1}{x}, \text{ as required.}$$

So the full statement of the reciprocal integral is:

$$\int \frac{1}{x}\,dx = \begin{cases} \ln x + k, & \text{if } x > 0, \\ \ln(-x) + k, & \text{if } x < 0. \end{cases}$$

Notice that the possibility $x = 0$ is still excluded. You should expect this, as 0 is not in the domain of the function $\dfrac{1}{x}$.

You have seen a two-part statement like this before, in the definition of $|x|$ in Section 0.2. If you turn round the equations given there, you can see that

if $x > 0$, then $x = |x|$; but if $x < 0$, then $-x = |x|$

So the two parts of the result in the blue box above can be combined as a single statement.

$$\text{For } x \neq 0, \int \frac{1}{x}\,dx = \ln |x| + k.$$

The function $|x|$ is an even function, with a graph symmetrical about the y-axis. It follows that the graph of $\ln |x|$ is symmetrical about the y-axis; it is shown in Fig. 5.17. For positive x it is the same as that of $\ln x$; for negative x, this is reflected in the y-axis.

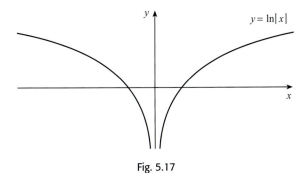

Fig. 5.17

You can see that the gradient of the graph is positive for $x > 0$ and negative for $x < 0$, which is as you would expect since $\dfrac{d}{dx} \ln |x| = \dfrac{1}{x}$.

Example 5.6.1

The graphs of $y = \dfrac{2}{x - 2}$ and $y = -x - 1$ intersect where $x = 0$ and $x = 1$. Find the area of the region between them.

You can check from a graphic calculator that the curve lies above the line, so that the area is

$$\int_0^1 \left(\frac{2}{x - 2} - (-x - 1) \right) dx = \int_0^1 \left(\frac{2}{x - 2} + x + 1 \right) dx.$$

The trap which you have to avoid is writing the integral of $\dfrac{2}{x - 2}$ as $2 \ln(x - 2)$. Over the interval $0 < x < 1$, $x - 2$ is negative, so $\ln(x - 2)$ has no meaning.

There are two ways of avoiding this. One is to write $\dfrac{2}{x - 2}$ as $\dfrac{-2}{2 - x}$. The integral of $\dfrac{1}{2 - x}$ is $-\ln(2 - x)$, so the integral of $\dfrac{-2}{2 - x}$ is $2 \ln(2 - x)$. The area is then

$$\left[2\ln(2 - x) + \tfrac{1}{2}x^2 + x \right]_0^1 = (2 \ln 1 + \tfrac{1}{2} + 1) - (2 \ln 2)$$
$$= \tfrac{3}{2} - 2 \ln 2.$$

The alternative is to use the modulus form of the integral, and to find the area as

$$\left[2\ln |x - 2| + \tfrac{1}{2}x^2 + x \right]_0^1 = (2 \ln |-1| + \tfrac{1}{2} + 1) - (2 \ln |-2|)$$
$$= \tfrac{3}{2} - 2 \ln 2.$$

You might think from this example that the modulus method has the edge. But it has to be used intelligently, as the following 'bogus' example shows.

Example 5.6.2

Find the area under the graph of $y = \dfrac{1}{x}$ from $x = -2$ to $x = +4$.

False solution

$$\int_{-2}^{4} \frac{1}{x}\,dx = [\ln |x|]_{-2}^{4}$$

$$= \ln |4| - \ln |-2|$$

$$= \ln 4 - \ln 2$$

$$= \ln \tfrac{4}{2}$$

$$= \ln 2.$$

You only have to draw the graph of $y = \dfrac{1}{x}$ to see that there is a problem here. The area does not exist for either of the intervals $-2 < x < 0$ and $0 < x < 4$, so it certainly cannot exist for $-2 < x < 4$. The interval of integration contains $x = 0$, for which the rule $\dfrac{d}{dx} \ln |x| = \dfrac{1}{x}$ breaks down.

If the result $\displaystyle\int \frac{1}{x}\,dx = \ln |x| + k$ is combined with the method of extending integration in Chapter 4, you get the more general result

$$\int \frac{1}{ax+b}\,dx = \frac{1}{a} \ln |ax+b| + k \quad \text{provided that } ax+b \neq 0.$$

This is valid both if $a > 0$ and if $a < 0$, but not of course if $a = 0$.

Example 5.6.3 uses this method for an integral with $a < 0$. Before reading the solution, show the graph of $y = \dfrac{1}{5 - 2x}$ for $1 \leqslant x \leqslant 4$ on a graphic calculator and decide which of the answers should be positive and which negative.

Example 5.6.3

Evaluate (a) $\displaystyle\int_{1}^{2} \frac{1}{5 - 2x}\,dx$, (b) $\displaystyle\int_{3}^{4} \frac{1}{5 - 2x}\,dx$.

(a) $\displaystyle\int_{1}^{2} \frac{1}{5 - 2x}\,dx = \left[\frac{1}{-2} \ln |5 - 2x| \right]_{1}^{2}$

$$= -\tfrac{1}{2} \ln |1| - \left(-\tfrac{1}{2} \ln |3| \right)$$

$$= -\tfrac{1}{2} \ln 1 + \tfrac{1}{2} \ln 3$$

$$= \tfrac{1}{2} \ln 3.$$

(b) $\displaystyle\int_{3}^{4} \frac{1}{5 - 2x}\,dx = \left[\frac{1}{-2} \ln |5 - 2x| \right]_{3}^{4}$

$$= -\tfrac{1}{2} \ln |-3| - \left(-\tfrac{1}{2} \ln |-1| \right)$$

$$= -\tfrac{1}{2} \ln 3 + \tfrac{1}{2} \ln 1$$

$$= -\tfrac{1}{2} \ln 3.$$

5.7*   The derivative of b^x

In Section 5.2 the derivative of b^x was found in the form

$$\frac{d}{dx}b^x = L(b)\,b^x,$$

where L(b) is a constant whose value depends on b.

It is now possible to find this constant. As exp and ln are inverse functions, the composite function 'exp ln' is an identity function, with domain the positive real numbers. Therefore

$$e^{\ln b} = b.$$

Raising both sides to the power x gives

$$b^x = (e^{\ln b})^x = e^{\ln b \times x},$$

by the power-on-power rule. This is of the form e^{ax}, where a is constant, so

$$\frac{d}{dx}b^x = \frac{d}{dx}(e^{\ln b \times x}) = (\ln b)\,e^{\ln b \times x} = (\ln b)\,b^x.$$

Comparing this with the earlier form of the derivative, you find that

$$L(b) = \ln b.$$

You can check this by using your calculator to compare the values of L(b) in Table 5.6 in Section 5.2 with the corresponding values of ln b. Notice also that Table 5.6 gives a number of examples of the rules for logarithms in C2 Section 7.3. For example,

$$L(4) = 2L(2), \quad L(6) = L(2) + L(3), \quad L(8) = 3L(2),$$
$$L(9) = 2L(3), \quad L(10) = L(2) + L(5).$$

You can now see why.

5.8*   Irrational indices

The equation $b^x = \exp(x \ln b)$ also provides an opportunity to tie up another loose end.

In C2 Section 7.1 it was pointed out that no meaning had yet been given to b^x when x is irrational. This gap can now be plugged.

Begin with ln b. Provided that $b > 0$, this can be calculated from the definite integral

$$\int_1^b \frac{1}{x}\,dx = [\ln x]_1^b = \ln b - \ln 1 = \ln b.$$

But with a definite integral like this it makes no odds whether b is rational or irrational. So if the definite integral is used as a *definition* of ln b, this holds when b is any real number.

Next, x and ln b are both real numbers, so the product $x \ln b$ is a real number. Call it y.

All that remains is to find exp y. Since ln is already defined, with domain $\mathbb{R}^+$ and range $\mathbb{R}$, exp can now be defined as the inverse function, with domain $\mathbb{R}$ and range $\mathbb{R}^+$. In this way $\exp(x \ln b)$ can be found for any real number x and any positive real number b.

And b^x can now be *defined* as $\exp(x \ln b)$. With this definition, it is irrelevant whether x is rational or irrational.

When x is a rational number $\dfrac{p}{q}$, this definition gives the same value as the definition $x^{\frac{p}{q}} = \sqrt[q]{x^p}$ obtained in C1 Section 7.3. But it also produces a meaning for powers such as $2^{\sqrt{3}}$ and π^{-e}.

Exercise 5E

1 Calculate the following.

(a) $\displaystyle\int_{-6}^{-3} \frac{1}{x+2}\,\mathrm{d}x$ (b) $\displaystyle\int_{-1}^{0} \frac{1}{2x-1}\,\mathrm{d}x$ (c) $\displaystyle\int_{-1}^{0} \frac{2}{5-3x}\,\mathrm{d}x$

(d) $\displaystyle\int_{1}^{2} \frac{e}{ex-7}\,\mathrm{d}x$ (e) $\displaystyle\int_{4}^{6} \frac{1}{1-x}\,\mathrm{d}x$ (f) $\displaystyle\int_{-1}^{0} \left(2 + \frac{1}{x-1}\right)\mathrm{d}x$

2 Calculate the value of $y = \ln|2x - 3|$ for $x = -2$, and find $\dfrac{\mathrm{d}y}{\mathrm{d}x}$ when $x = -2$. Sketch the graph of $y = \ln|2x - 3|$.

3* Find the derivatives with respect to x of 2^x, 3^x, 10^x and $\left(\frac{1}{2}\right)^x$.

Miscellaneous exercise 5

1 Differentiate each of the following expressions with respect to x.

(a) $\ln(3x - 4)$ (b) $\ln(4 - 3x)$ (c) $e^x \times e^{2x}$

(d) $e^x \div e^{2x}$ (e) $\ln \dfrac{2-x}{3-x}$ (f) $\ln(3 - 2x)^3$

2 Apply the trapezium rule to $\displaystyle\int_{1}^{2} \frac{1}{x}\,\mathrm{d}x$ and $\displaystyle\int_{2}^{4} \frac{1}{x}\,\mathrm{d}x$ to show that $\frac{3}{4}$ and $\frac{17}{24}$ are approximations to $\ln 2$. Determine whether they are overestimates or underestimates, and justify your answers.

3 Find the coordinates of the points of intersection of $y = \dfrac{4}{x}$ and $2x + y = 9$. Sketch both graphs for values of x such that $x > 0$. Calculate the area between the graphs.

4 A curve is given by the equation $y = \frac{2}{3}e^x + \frac{1}{3}e^{-2x}$.

(a) Evaluate a definite integral to find the area between the curve, the x-axis and the lines $x = 0$ and $x = 1$, showing your working.

(b) Use calculus to determine whether the turning point at the point where $x = 0$ is a maximum or a minimum. (OCR, adapted)

5 Find $\displaystyle\int (2 + e^{-x})\,\mathrm{d}x$. (OCR)

6 The equation of a curve is $y = 2x^2 - \ln x$, where $x > 0$. Find by differentiation the x-coordinate of the stationary point on the curve, and determine whether this point is a maximum point or a minimum point. (OCR)

7 Show that $\displaystyle\int_0^1 (e^x - e^{-x})\,dx = \dfrac{(e-1)^2}{e}$. (OCR)

8 Using differentiation, find the equation of the tangent to the curve $y = 4 + \ln(x+1)$ at the point where $x = 0$. (OCR)

9 The equation of a curve is $y = \ln(2x)$. Find the equation of the normal at the point $\left(\frac{1}{2}, 0\right)$, giving your answer in the form $y = mx + c$. (OCR)

10 (a) Express $\dfrac{x-7}{(x-4)(x-1)} + \dfrac{1}{x-4}$ as a single fraction.

(b) Use a calculator to draw a sketch of $y = \dfrac{x-7}{(x-4)(x-1)}$, and calculate the area under the graph between $x = 2$ and $x = 3$.

11 The decay of a quantity y is described by the equation $\ln y = 5.30 - 0.127t$. Express this equation in the form

(a) $y = ae^{ct}$,   (b) $y = ab^t$.

12 The diagram shows sketches of the graphs of $y = 2 - e^{-x}$ and $y = x$. These graphs intersect at $x = a$ where $a > 0$.

(a) Write down an equation satisfied by a. (Do not attempt to solve the equation.)

(b) Write down an integral which is equal to the area of the shaded region.

(c) Use integration to show that the area is equal to $1 + a - \frac{1}{2}a^2$. (OCR, adapted)

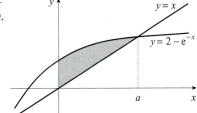

13 Find the exact value of $\displaystyle\int_0^\infty e^{1-2x}\,dx$.

14 The number of bacteria present in a culture at time t hours after the beginning of an experiment is denoted by N. The relation between N and t is modelled by $N = e^{\frac{3}{2}t}$. At what rate per hour will the number of bacteria be increasing when $t = 6$? (OCR)

15 A metal bar is heated to a certain temperature and then the heat source is removed. At time t minutes after the heat source is removed, the temperature, θ degrees Celsius, of the metal bar is given by $\theta = 280e^{-0.02t}$. At what rate is the temperature decreasing 100 minutes after the removal of the heat source? (OCR)

16 A bath is filled with water at a temperature of $40\,^\circ$C. After t minutes the temperature has fallen to $(10 + 30e^{-0.04t})\,^\circ$C.

(a) Find the rate at which the temperature is falling

(i) initially,   (ii) after 5 minutes.

(b) Find the rate at which the temperature is falling when the temperature is

(i) $38\,^\circ$C,   (ii) $24\,^\circ$C.

(c) Sketch a graph to show how the temperature decreases with time.

17 The height in metres of Jack's beanstalk t weeks after it was planted is given by the equation $h = a(e^{ct} - 1)$. Its heights at the ends of the first two weeks were 10 cm and 50 cm.

(a) Calculate the constants a and c.

(b) Find the height, and the rate at which it is increasing, after 5 weeks.

(c) Find the rate at which the height is increasing when the beanstalk is 100 metres high.

18 A hospital patient requires an injection of a certain drug once every 12 hours. Initially Q millilitres are injected. This decays exponentially so that after t hours the quantity remaining in the bloodstream is Qe^{-ct} ml, and a further injection of $\frac{3}{4}Q$ ml is given to bring the concentration up to its initial value. This process is repeated at each subsequent injection.

(a) Draw a sketch graph to illustrate the quantity in the bloodstream over a period of 2 days.

(b) Calculate the value of c.

(c) It is decided to increase the frequency of the injections to once every 8 hours. How large will the top-up injection need to be under this new regime?

19 Use your graphic calculator to draw a sketch of the curve $y = e^{-2x} - 3x$. The curve crosses the x-axis at $A(a, 0)$ and the y-axis at $B(0, 1)$. O is the origin.

(a) Write down an equation satisfied by a.

(b) Show that the tangent at A meets the y-axis at the point whose y-coordinate is $2ae^{-2a} + 3a$.

(c) Show that $\dfrac{d^2y}{dx^2} > 0$, and using the results from parts (a) and (b), deduce that $6a^2 + 3a < 1$.

(d) Find, in terms of a, the area of the region bounded by the curve and the line segments OA and OB.

(e) By comparing this area with the area of the triangle OAB, show that $3a^2 + 4a > 1$.
    Hence show that $\frac{1}{3}\sqrt{7} - \frac{2}{3} < a < \frac{1}{12}\sqrt{33} - \frac{1}{4}$.   (OCR, adapted)

20* (a) Show that e^x is an increasing function of x for all x. Deduce that $e^x \geqslant 1$ for $x \geqslant 0$.

(b) By finding the area under the graphs of $y = e^x$ and $y = 1$ between 0 and X, where $X \geqslant 0$, deduce that $e^X \geqslant 1 + X$ for $X \geqslant 0$, and that $y = e^X \geqslant 1 + X + \frac{1}{2}X^2$ for $X \geqslant 0$.

21* (a) Find the stationary value of $y = \ln x - x$, and deduce that $\ln x \leqslant x - 1$ for $x > 0$ with equality only when $x = 1$.

(b) Find the stationary value of $\ln x + \dfrac{1}{x}$, and deduce that $\dfrac{x-1}{x} \leqslant \ln x$ for $x > 0$ with equality only when $x = 1$.

(c) By putting $x = \dfrac{z}{y}$ where $0 < y < z$, deduce Napier's inequality, $\dfrac{1}{z} < \dfrac{\ln z - \ln y}{z - y} < \dfrac{1}{y}$.

[Napier was a Scottish mathematician who invented logarithms at the end of the 16th century.]

22 The Bank of Utopia offers an interest rate of 100% per annum with various options as to how the interest may be added. Gordon invests £1000 and considers the following options.

Option A   Interest added annually at the end of the year.

Option B   Interest of 50% credited at the end of each half-year.

Option C, D, E, …   The Bank is willing to add interest as often as required, subject to (interest rate) × (number of credits per year) = 100.

Investigate to find the maximum possible amount in Gordon's account after one year.

6 Trigonometry

This chapter takes further the ideas about trigonometry in C2 Chapter 1. When you have completed it, you should

- know the definitions, properties and graphs of secant, cosecant and cotangent, including the associated Pythagorean identities
- know the addition and double angle formulae for sine, cosine and tangent, and be able to use these results for calculations, solving equations and proving identities
- know how to express $a \sin \theta + b \cos \theta$ in the forms $R \sin(\theta \pm \alpha)$ and $R \cos(\theta \pm \alpha)$
- be able to use the notation for inverse functions, and know their domains and ranges, and their graphs.

6.1 Radians or degrees

All through your work in mathematics, you have probably thought of degrees as the natural unit for angle, but in C2 Chapter 9 a new unit, the radian, was introduced. This unit is important in differentiating and integrating trigonometric functions. For this reason, a new convention about angle will be adopted in this book.

If no units are given for trigonometric functions, you should assume that the units are radians, or that it doesn't matter whether the units are radians or degrees.

For example, if you see the equation $\sin x = 0.5$, then x is in radians. If you are asked for the smallest positive solution of the equation, you should give $x = \frac{1}{6}\pi$. Remember:

$$\pi \, \text{rad} = 180°.$$

Identities such as $\cos^2 A + \sin^2 A \equiv 1$ and $\dfrac{\sin \theta}{\cos \theta} \equiv \tan \theta$, or the cosine formula $a^2 = b^2 + c^2 - 2bc \cos A$, are true whatever the units of angle. Formulae such as these, for which it doesn't matter whether the unit is degrees or radians, will be shown without units for angles.

If, however, it is important that degrees are being used, you will be told. Thus one solution, in degrees, of the equation $\cos \theta = -0.5$ is $\theta = 120°$.

This may seem complicated, but the context will usually make things clear.

6.2 Secant, cosecant and cotangent

It is occasionally useful to be able to write the functions $\dfrac{1}{\cos x}, \dfrac{1}{\sin x}$ and $\dfrac{1}{\tan x}$ in shorter forms. These functions, called respectively the secant, cosecant and cotangent (written and pronounced 'sec', 'cosec' and 'cot') are not defined when the denominators are zero, so their domains contain holes.

> The definitions of **secant** and **cosecant** are
> $$\sec x = \frac{1}{\cos x}, \qquad \text{provided that } \cos x \neq 0,$$
> $$\operatorname{cosec} x = \frac{1}{\sin x}, \qquad \text{provided that } \sin x \neq 0.$$

It is a little more complicated to define the cotangent in this way, since there are values of x for which $\tan x$ is undefined. But you can use the fact that $\tan x = \dfrac{\sin x}{\cos x}$, so $\dfrac{1}{\tan x} = \dfrac{\cos x}{\sin x}$, except where the denominators are zero. This can be used as the definition of $\cot x$.

> The **cotangent** is defined by
> $$\cot x = \frac{\cos x}{\sin x}, \qquad \text{provided that } \sin x \neq 0.$$
>
> Note that $\cot x = \dfrac{1}{\tan x}$ except where $\tan x = 0$ or is undefined.

You won't find sec, cosec or cot keys on your calculator, so to find their values you have to use the sin, cos and tan keys, followed by the reciprocal key.

The graph of $y = \sec x$ is shown in Fig. 6.1, together with the graph of $y = \cos x$.

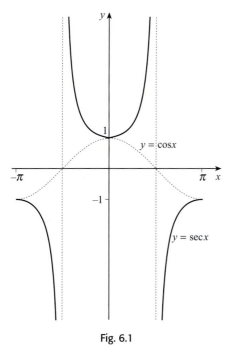

Fig. 6.1

You can see the following properties of $\sec x$ (and $\cos x$) from Fig. 6.1.

- $\sec x$ and $\cos x$ both have period 2π.

- $\sec x$ is positive when $\cos x$ is positive, between $-\frac{1}{2}\pi$ and $\frac{1}{2}\pi$; and $\sec x$ is negative when $\cos x$ is negative, for $-\pi < x < -\frac{1}{2}\pi$ and $\frac{1}{2}\pi < x < \pi$.

- $\sec x$ has a minimum value of 1 when $\cos x$ has a maximum value of 1, and a maximum value of -1 when $\cos x$ has a minimum value of -1.

- As $|\cos x| \leqslant 1$ for all x, $|\sec x| \geqslant 1$ for all x.

- $\sec x$ is undefined when $\cos x = 0$, for odd multiples of $\frac{1}{2}\pi$.

- $\sec x$ is increasing in the intervals $0 < x < \frac{1}{2}\pi$ and $\frac{1}{2}\pi < x < \pi$, where $\cos x$ is decreasing, and is decreasing in those intervals where $\cos x$ is increasing.

The graphs of $y = \operatorname{cosec} x$ (with $y = \sin x$) and $y = \cot x$ are shown in Figs. 6.2 and 6.3.

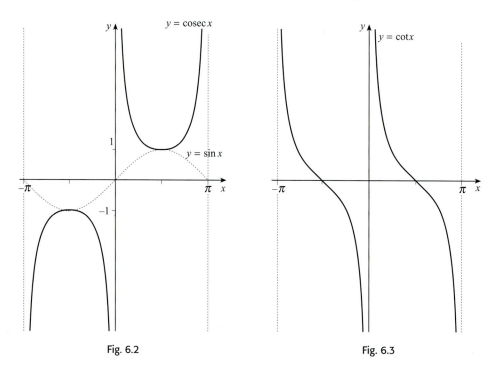

Fig. 6.2   Fig. 6.3

In Exercise 6A Question 5 you are asked to produce a list of properties of $\operatorname{cosec} x$ similar to those of $\sec x$ above.

Example 6.2.1
Find the exact values of   (a) $\sec \frac{2}{3}\pi$,   (b) $\operatorname{cosec} \frac{5}{6}\pi$,   (c) $\cot\left(-\frac{2}{3}\pi\right)$.

You need to find the values of $\cos \frac{2}{3}\pi$, $\sin \frac{5}{6}\pi$ and $\tan\left(-\frac{2}{3}\pi\right)$, using the symmetry properties in C2 Section 9.4 together with the exact values in C2 Section 1.3.

(a) $\cos \frac{2}{3}\pi = -\cos\left(\pi - \frac{2}{3}\pi\right) = -\cos \frac{1}{3}\pi = -\frac{1}{2}$, so $\sec \frac{2}{3}\pi = -2$.

(b) $\sin \frac{5}{6}\pi = \sin\left(\pi - \frac{5}{6}\pi\right) = \sin \frac{1}{6}\pi = \frac{1}{2}$, so $\operatorname{cosec} \frac{5}{6}\pi = 2$.

(c) $\tan\left(-\frac{2}{3}\pi\right) = -\tan \frac{2}{3}\pi = -(-\tan \frac{1}{3}\pi) = \sqrt{3}$, so $\cot\left(-\frac{2}{3}\pi\right) = \dfrac{1}{\sqrt{3}} = \frac{1}{3}\sqrt{3}$.

There are new forms of Pythagoras' theorem in trigonometry using these new trigonometric functions. For example, if you divide every term in the identity $\cos^2\theta + \sin^2\theta \equiv 1$ by $\cos^2\theta$, you get

$$\frac{\cos^2\theta}{\cos^2\theta} + \frac{\sin^2\theta}{\cos^2\theta} \equiv \frac{1}{\cos^2\theta}, \qquad \text{that is,} \qquad 1 + \tan^2\theta \equiv \sec^2\theta.$$

Similarly, if you divide every term of $\cos^2\theta + \sin^2\theta \equiv 1$ by $\sin^2\theta$, you get

$$\frac{\cos^2\theta}{\sin^2\theta} + \frac{\sin^2\theta}{\sin^2\theta} \equiv \frac{1}{\sin^2\theta}, \qquad \text{or} \qquad 1 + \cot^2\theta \equiv \csc^2\theta.$$

Summarising:

$$1 + \tan^2\theta \equiv \sec^2\theta,$$
$$1 + \cot^2\theta \equiv \csc^2\theta.$$

Example 6.2.2

You are given that $\cot\alpha = -\frac{15}{8}$, and that $\frac{1}{2}\pi < \alpha < \pi$. Find the values of (a) $\csc\alpha$, (b) $\cos\alpha$.

(a) As $1 + \cot^2\theta \equiv \csc^2\theta$,

$$\csc^2\alpha = 1 + \left(-\tfrac{15}{8}\right)^2 = 1 + \tfrac{225}{64} = \tfrac{289}{64},$$

giving $\csc\alpha = \pm\frac{17}{8}$.

As $\frac{1}{2}\pi < \alpha < \pi$, $\sin\alpha$ is positive, so $\csc\alpha = \dfrac{1}{\sin\alpha}$ is also positive.

So $\csc\alpha = \frac{17}{8}$.

(b) As $\cot\theta \equiv \dfrac{\cos\theta}{\sin\theta}$ and $\dfrac{1}{\sin\theta} \equiv \csc\theta$, $\cot\theta \equiv \cos\theta \times \csc\theta$. So

$$-\tfrac{15}{8} = \cos\alpha \times \tfrac{17}{8},$$

giving $\cos\alpha = -\frac{15}{17}$.

Example 6.2.3

Express $5\cot^2 x - 2\csc x + 2$ in terms of $\csc x$ and hence solve the equation $5\cot^2 x - 2\csc x + 2 = 0$ for $0 \leqslant x < 2\pi$.

Using $1 + \cot^2 x \equiv \csc^2 x$, it follows that $\cot^2 x \equiv \csc^2 x - 1$ so

$$\begin{aligned} 5\cot^2 x - 2\csc x + 2 &\equiv 5(\csc^2 x - 1) - 2\csc x + 2 \\ &\equiv 5\csc^2 x - 5 - 2\csc x + 2 \\ &\equiv 5\csc^2 x - 2\csc x - 3. \end{aligned}$$

The equation then becomes $5\csc^2 x - 2\csc x - 3 = 0$.

You could now solve this as a quadratic equation in $\csc x$, but it is probably easier to use the fact that $\csc x \equiv \dfrac{1}{\sin x}$ to turn into a quadratic equation in $\sin x$. There are two reasons for this: you are probably more comfortable working with $\sin x$ than cosec x, and calculators often do not have the values of cosec x programmed into them.

So, writing cosec $x = \dfrac{1}{\sin x}$ the equation $\dfrac{5}{\sin^2 x} - \dfrac{2}{\sin x} - 3 = 0$ becomes

$$3\sin^2 x + 2\sin x - 5 = 0$$
$$(3\sin x + 5)(\sin x - 1) = 0.$$

So $\sin x = -\frac{5}{3}$ (not possible) or $\sin x = 1$.

So $x = \frac{1}{2}\pi$.

Example 6.2.4

Prove the identity $\dfrac{1}{\sec\theta - \tan\theta} \equiv \sec\theta + \tan\theta$, provided that $\sec\theta$ and $\tan\theta$ exist.

There are four ways to approach proving identities: you can start with the left side and work towards the right; you can start with the right side and work towards the left; you can subtract one side from the other and try to show that the result is 0; or you can divide one side by the other and try to show that the result is 1. Generally you should start with the more complicated side.

Use the fourth method, and consider the right side divided by the left side.

You need to show that $(\sec\theta + \tan\theta) \div \dfrac{1}{\sec\theta - \tan\theta}$ is equal to 1.

$$
\begin{aligned}
(\sec\theta + \tan\theta) \div \dfrac{1}{\sec\theta - \tan\theta} &\equiv (\sec\theta + \tan\theta)(\sec\theta - \tan\theta) \\
&\equiv \sec^2\theta - \tan^2\theta \\
&\equiv (1 + \tan^2\theta) - \tan^2\theta \equiv 1.
\end{aligned}
$$

Therefore $\dfrac{1}{\sec\theta - \tan\theta} \equiv \sec\theta + \tan\theta$.

The condition about the existence of $\sec\theta$ and $\tan\theta$ is important, because if they don't exist the identity has no meaning.

Exercise 6A

1　Find, giving your answers to 3 decimal places,

　(a) $\cot 304°$,　　(b) $\sec(-48)°$,　　(c) $\operatorname{cosec} 62°$.

2　Simplify the following.

　(a) $\dfrac{\cos x}{\sin x}$　　(b) $\sec(-x)$　　(c) $1 + \tan^2 x$

　(d) $\sec\left(\frac{1}{2}\pi - x\right)$　(e) $\cot(\pi + x)$　　(f) $\operatorname{cosec}(\pi + x)$

3　Find the exact values of

　(a) $\sec\frac{1}{4}\pi$,　　(b) $\operatorname{cosec}\frac{1}{2}\pi$,　　(c) $\cot 150°$,　　(d) $\operatorname{cosec}(-135)°$,

　(e) $\cot\left(-\frac{1}{3}\pi\right)$,　(f) $\sec\frac{13}{6}\pi$,　　(g) $\cot(-990)°$,　　(h) $\sec 210°$.

4 Using a calculator where necessary, find the values of the following, giving any non-exact answers correct to 4 significant figures.

   (a) $\sec \frac{1}{10}\pi$ (b) $\cot \frac{1}{12}\pi$ (c) $\operatorname{cosec} 510°$ (d) $\sec(-165)°$

5 Use Fig. 6.2 to write out a list of properties of $\operatorname{cosec} x$ similar to those of $\sec x$ which follow Fig. 6.1.

6 Given that $\sin A = \frac{3}{5}$, where A is acute, and $\cos B = -\frac{1}{2}$, where B is obtuse, find the exact values of

   (a) $\sec A$,   (b) $\cot A$,   (c) $\cot B$,   (d) $\operatorname{cosec} B$.

7 Given that $\operatorname{cosec} C = 7$, $\sin^2 D = \frac{1}{2}$ and $\tan^2 E = 4$, find the possible values of $\cot C$, $\sec D$ and $\operatorname{cosec} E$, giving your answers in exact form.

8 Simplify the following.

   (a) $\dfrac{\tan \phi}{1 + \tan^2 \phi}$ (b) $\dfrac{\tan \phi}{\sec^2 \phi - 1}$ (c) $(\operatorname{cosec} \phi - 1)(\operatorname{cosec} \phi + 1)$

9 (a) Express $3 \tan^2 \phi - \sec \phi$ in terms of $\sec \phi$.

   (b) Solve the equation $3 \tan^2 \phi - \sec \phi = 1$ for $0 \leqslant \phi \leqslant 2\pi$, giving any non-exact answers to 2 decimal places.

10 Use an algebraic method to find the solution for $0 \leqslant \phi \leqslant 2\pi$ of the equation $5 \cot \phi + 2\operatorname{cosec}^2 \phi = 5$.

11 Find, in exact form, all the roots of the equation $2 \sin^2 \phi + \operatorname{cosec}^2 \phi = 3$ which lie between $0°$ and $360°$.

12 Prove that $\operatorname{cosec} A + \cot A \equiv \dfrac{1}{\operatorname{cosec} A - \cot A}$ provided that $\operatorname{cosec} A$ and $\cot A$ exist.

13 Prove that $\dfrac{\sec \theta - 1}{\tan \theta} \equiv \dfrac{\tan \theta}{\sec \theta + 1}$ provided that θ is not a multiple of $\frac{1}{2}\pi$.

6.3 The addition formulae for sine and cosine

Suppose that you know the values of $\sin A$, $\cos A$, $\sin B$ and $\cos B$. How could you calculate the values of $\sin(A + B)$, $\sin(A - B)$, $\cos(A + B)$ and $\cos(A - B)$? You could, of course, use a calculator but that would only give approximations.

There are in fact general formulae for finding expressions like $\sin(A + B)$ in terms of the sines and cosines of A and B. It is simplest to start with $\cos(A - B)$.

In Fig. 6.4, angles A and B are drawn from the x-axis. The points P and Q then have coordinates $(\cos A, \sin A)$ and $(\cos B, \sin B)$ respectively.

You can now write down the distance QP, or rather an expression for QP^2, in two ways.

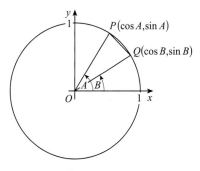

Fig. 6.4

First, you can use the distance formula in coordinate geometry (see C1 Section 1.1), which gives

$$QP^2 = (\cos A - \cos B)^2 + (\sin A - \sin B)^2$$
$$= \cos^2 A - 2\cos A \cos B + \cos^2 B + \sin^2 A - 2\sin A \sin B + \sin^2 B,$$

which can be rearranged as

$$(\cos^2 A + \sin^2 A) + (\cos^2 B + \sin^2 B) - 2(\cos A \cos B + \sin A \sin B).$$

Since, by Pythagoras' theorem in trigonometry, $\cos^2 A + \sin^2 A = 1$ and $\cos^2 B + \sin^2 B = 1$,

$$QP^2 = 2 - 2(\cos A \cos B + \sin A \sin B).$$

Secondly, you can use the cosine formula for the triangle OPQ, which gives

$$QP^2 = 1^2 + 1^2 - 2 \times 1 \times 1 \times \cos(A - B)$$
$$= 2 - 2\cos(A - B).$$

Comparing the two expressions for QP^2, you will see that

$$\cos(A - B) = \cos A \cos B + \sin A \sin B.$$

Although Fig. 6.4 is drawn with angles A and B acute and $A > B$, the proof is valid for angles A and B of any size.

Example 6.3.1
Verify the formula for $\cos(A - B)$ in the cases (a) $B = A$,   (b) $A = \frac{1}{2}\pi$, $B = \frac{1}{6}\pi$.

(a) Put $B = A$.

Then $\cos(A - A) = \cos^2 A + \sin^2 A$ and, as $\cos 0 = 1$, you get Pythagoras' theorem, $\cos^2 A + \sin^2 A = 1$.

(b) Put $A = \frac{1}{2}\pi$ and $B = \frac{1}{6}\pi$.

Then $\cos A = 0$, $\sin A = 1$, $\cos B = \frac{1}{2}\sqrt{3}$ and $\sin B = \frac{1}{2}$. The formula then gives $\cos A \cos B + \sin A \sin B = 0 \times \frac{1}{2}\sqrt{3} + 1 \times \frac{1}{2} = \frac{1}{2}$ which is consistent with

$$\cos(A - B) = \cos\left(\tfrac{1}{2}\pi - \tfrac{1}{6}\pi\right) = \cos\tfrac{1}{3}\pi = \tfrac{1}{2}.$$

If you replace B by $(-B)$ in the formula for $\cos(A - B)$ you get

$$\cos(A - (-B)) = \cos A \cos(-B) + \sin A \sin(-B).$$

Recall that cosine is an even function and that sine is an odd function (C2 Section 1.4). So $\cos(-B) = \cos B$ and $\sin(-B) = -\sin B$. Writing $\cos(A - (-B))$ as $\cos(A + B)$,

$$\begin{aligned}
\cos(A + B) &= \cos A \cos(-B) + \sin A \sin(-B) \\
&= \cos A \cos B - \sin A \sin B.
\end{aligned}$$

To find a formula for $\sin(A + B)$, first recall that $\cos\left(\frac{1}{2}\pi - \theta\right) = \sin\theta$ (see C2 Section 9.4). Using this with $\theta = A + B$,

$$\begin{aligned}
\sin(A + B) &= \cos\left(\tfrac{1}{2}\pi - (A + B)\right) = \cos\left(\left(\tfrac{1}{2}\pi - A\right) - B\right) \\
&= \cos\left(\tfrac{1}{2}\pi - A\right)\cos B + \sin\left(\tfrac{1}{2}\pi - A\right)\sin B \\
&= \sin A \cos B + \cos A \sin B.
\end{aligned}$$

You can obtain the formula for $\sin(A - B)$ in a similar way. (This is Question 6 in Exercise 6B.) The four formulae are true for all angles A and B, so they are identities.

> For all angles A and B,
> $$\sin(A + B) \equiv \sin A \cos B + \cos A \sin B,$$
> $$\sin(A - B) \equiv \sin A \cos B - \cos A \sin B,$$
> $$\cos(A + B) \equiv \cos A \cos B - \sin A \sin B,$$
> $$\cos(A - B) \equiv \cos A \cos B + \sin A \sin B.$$

These formulae are called the **addition formulae**. They are true whether the angles are measured in radians or degrees. They are also important and you should learn them, but you need not learn how to prove them.

Notice that now you have these formulae, you have a quick method of simplifying expressions such as $\cos\left(\frac{3}{2}\pi - \theta\right)$:

$$\begin{aligned}
\cos\left(\tfrac{3}{2}\pi - \theta\right) &= \cos\left(\tfrac{3}{2}\pi\right)\cos\theta + \sin\left(\tfrac{3}{2}\pi\right)\sin\theta \\
&= 0 \times \cos\theta + (-1) \times \sin\theta = -\sin\theta.
\end{aligned}$$

Example 6.3.2

Use the formulae for $\cos(A \pm B)$ to find exact values of $\cos 75°$ and $\cos 15°$.

$$\begin{aligned}
\cos 75° = \cos(45 + 30)° &= \cos 45° \cos 30° - \sin 45° \sin 30° \\
&= \tfrac{1}{2}\sqrt{2} \times \tfrac{1}{2}\sqrt{3} - \tfrac{1}{2}\sqrt{2} \times \tfrac{1}{2} = \tfrac{1}{4}(\sqrt{6} - \sqrt{2}).
\end{aligned}$$

$$\begin{aligned}
\cos 15° = \cos(45 - 30)° &= \cos 45° \cos 30° + \sin 45° \sin 30° \\
&= \tfrac{1}{2}\sqrt{2} \times \tfrac{1}{2}\sqrt{3} + \tfrac{1}{2}\sqrt{2} \times \tfrac{1}{2} = \tfrac{1}{4}(\sqrt{6} + \sqrt{2}).
\end{aligned}$$

Check these results for yourself with a calculator.

Example 6.3.3

You are given that $\sin A = \frac{8}{17}$, that $\sin B = \frac{12}{13}$, and that $0 < B < \frac{1}{2}\pi < A < \pi$. Find the exact values of $\sin(A + B)$ and $\cos(A + B)$.

From the Pythagoras identity, $\cos^2 A + \left(\frac{8}{17}\right)^2 = 1$, $\cos^2 A = 1 - \frac{64}{289} = \frac{225}{289}$, so $\cos A = \pm\frac{15}{17}$. As $\frac{1}{2}\pi < A < \pi$, $\cos A$ is negative, so $\cos A = -\frac{15}{17}$.

Similarly, $\cos^2 B + \left(\frac{12}{13}\right)^2 = 1$, so $\cos B = \pm\frac{5}{13}$. As $0 < B < \frac{1}{2}\pi$, $\cos B$ is positive, so $\cos B = \frac{5}{13}$. Then

$$\sin(A + B) = \frac{8}{17} \times \frac{5}{13} + \left(-\frac{15}{17}\right) \times \frac{12}{13} = \frac{40 - 180}{17 \times 13} = -\frac{140}{221},$$

and

$$\cos(A + B) = \left(-\frac{15}{17}\right) \times \frac{5}{13} - \frac{8}{17} \times \frac{12}{13} = \frac{-75 - 96}{17 \times 13} = -\frac{171}{221}.$$

Example 6.3.4

Prove that $\sin(A + B) + \sin(A - B) \equiv 2\sin A \cos B$.

Starting from the left side, and 'expanding' both terms,

$$\sin(A+B)+\sin(A-B) \equiv (\sin A\cos B + \cos A\sin B)+(\sin A\cos B - \cos A\sin B)$$
$$\equiv \sin A\cos B + \cos A\sin B + \sin A\cos B - \cos A\sin B$$
$$\equiv 2\sin A\cos B.$$

Hence $\sin(A + B) + \sin(A - B) \equiv 2\sin A \cos B$.

Example 6.3.5

Find the value of $\tan x$, given that $\sin(x + 30°) = 2\cos(x - 30°)$.

Use the addition formulae to write the equation as

$$\sin x \cos 30° + \cos x \sin 30° = 2\cos x \cos 30° + 2\sin x \sin 30°.$$

Collect the terms involving $\sin x$ on the left, and those involving $\cos x$ on the right, substituting the values of $\sin 30°$ and $\cos 30°$:

$$\sin x \times \tfrac{1}{2}\sqrt{3} - 2\sin x \times \tfrac{1}{2} = 2\cos x \times \tfrac{1}{2}\sqrt{3} - \cos x \times \tfrac{1}{2},$$

which can be rearranged as

$$(\tfrac{1}{2}\sqrt{3} - 1)\sin x = (\sqrt{3} - \tfrac{1}{2})\cos x.$$

Hence $\tan x = \dfrac{\sin x}{\cos x} = \dfrac{\sqrt{3} - \frac{1}{2}}{\frac{1}{2}\sqrt{3} - 1} = \dfrac{2\sqrt{3} - 1}{\sqrt{3} - 2}.$

6.4   The addition formulae for tangents

To find a formula for $\tan(A + B)$, use $\tan(A + B) = \dfrac{\sin(A + B)}{\cos(A + B)}$ together with the identities for $\cos(A + B)$ and $\sin(A + B)$. Thus

$$\tan(A + B) \equiv \frac{\sin(A + B)}{\cos(A + B)} \equiv \frac{\sin A\cos B + \cos A\sin B}{\cos A\cos B - \sin A\sin B}.$$

You can get a neater formula by dividing the top and the bottom of the fraction on the right by $\cos A \cos B$. The numerator then becomes

$$\frac{\sin A \cos B + \cos A \sin B}{\cos A \cos B} = \frac{\sin A \cos B}{\cos A \cos B} + \frac{\cos A \sin B}{\cos A \cos B} = \tan A + \tan B,$$

and the denominator becomes

$$\frac{\cos A \cos B - \sin A \sin B}{\cos A \cos B} = \frac{\cos A \cos B}{\cos A \cos B} - \frac{\sin A \sin B}{\cos A \cos B} = 1 - \tan A \tan B.$$

Therefore, putting the fraction together, $\tan(A + B) \equiv \dfrac{\tan A + \tan B}{1 - \tan A \tan B}$.

A similar derivation, or the fact that $\tan(-B) = -\tan(B)$, yields a formula for $\tan(A - B)$.

$$\tan(A + B) \equiv \frac{\tan A + \tan B}{1 - \tan A \tan B}, \quad \tan(A - B) \equiv \frac{\tan A - \tan B}{1 + \tan A \tan B}.$$

Note that these identities have no meaning if $\tan A$ or $\tan B$ is undefined, or if either denominator is zero.

Example 6.4.1
Given that $\tan(x + y) = 1$ and that $\tan x = \frac{1}{2}$, find $\tan y$.

Method 1 The most direct approach is to use the $\tan(A + B)$ formula, setting $\tan x = \frac{1}{2}$ to get an equation for $\tan y$.

$$1 = \frac{\frac{1}{2} + \tan y}{1 - \frac{1}{2}\tan y}$$

so $\qquad 1 - \frac{1}{2}\tan y = \frac{1}{2} + \tan y,$

which leads to $\tan y = \frac{1}{3}$.

Method 2 A neater method is to use the $\tan(A - B)$ formula, writing y as $(x + y) - x$.

$$\tan y = \tan((x + y) - x)$$
$$= \frac{\tan(x + y) - \tan x}{1 + \tan(x + y) \tan x}$$
$$= \frac{1 - \frac{1}{2}}{1 + 1 \times \frac{1}{2}} = \frac{1/2}{3/2} = \frac{1}{3}.$$

Example 6.4.2
Find the tangent of the angle between the lines $7y = x + 2$ and $x + y = 3$.

The gradients of the lines are $\frac{1}{7}$ and -1, so if they make angles A and B with the x-axis respectively, $\tan A = \frac{1}{7}$ and $\tan B = -1$. Then

$$\tan(A - B) = \frac{\tan A - \tan B}{1 + \tan A \tan B}$$
$$= \frac{\frac{1}{7} - (-1)}{1 + \frac{1}{7} \times (-1)} = \frac{8/7}{6/7} = \frac{4}{3}.$$

Exercise 6B

1 By writing 75 as $30 + 45$, find the exact values of $\sin 75°$ and $\tan 75°$.

2 Find the exact values of $\cos 105°$ and $\sin 105°$.

3 Express $\cos\left(x + \frac{1}{3}\pi\right)$ in terms of $\cos x$ and $\sin x$.

4 Use the expansions for $\sin(A + B)$ and $\cos(A + B)$ to simplify $\sin\left(\frac{3}{2}\pi + \phi\right)$ and $\cos\left(\frac{1}{2}\pi + \phi\right)$.

5 Express $\tan\left(\frac{1}{3}\pi + x\right)$ and $\tan\left(\frac{5}{6}\pi - x\right)$ in terms of $\tan x$.

6 Use $\sin(A - B) \equiv \cos\left(\frac{1}{2}\pi - (A - B)\right) \equiv \cos\left(\left(\frac{1}{2}\pi - A\right) + B\right)$ to derive the formula for $\sin(A - B)$.

7 Given that $\cos A = \frac{3}{5}$ and $\cos B = \frac{24}{25}$, where A and B are acute, find the exact values of
(a) $\tan A$,   (b) $\sin B$,   (c) $\cos(A - B)$,   (d) $\tan(A + B)$.

8 Given that $\sin A = \frac{3}{5}$ and $\cos B = \frac{12}{13}$, where A is obtuse and B is acute, find the exact values of $\cos(A + B)$ and $\cot(A - B)$.

9 Prove that $\cos(A + B) - \cos(A - B) \equiv -2\sin A \sin B$.

10 Prove that $\cot(A + B) \equiv \dfrac{\cot A \cot B - 1}{\cot A + \cot B}$.

11 Prove that $\tan A + \tan B \equiv \dfrac{\sin(A + B)}{\cos A \cos B}$.

12 Prove that $4\sin\left(x + \frac{1}{6}\pi\right)\sin\left(x - \frac{1}{6}\pi\right) \equiv 3 - 4\cos^2 x$.

6.5 Double angle formulae

If you put $B = A$ in the addition formulae, you obtain identities for the sine, cosine and tangent of $2A$. The first comes from $\sin(A + B) \equiv \sin A \cos B + \cos A \sin B$, which gives

$$\sin(A + A) \equiv \sin A \cos A + \cos A \sin A, \quad \text{that is} \quad \sin 2A \equiv 2\sin A \cos A.$$

From $\cos(A + B) \equiv \cos A \cos B - \sin A \sin B$ you get $\cos 2A \equiv \cos^2 A - \sin^2 A$.

Finally, the formula $\tan(A + B) \equiv \dfrac{\tan A + \tan B}{1 - \tan A \tan B}$ becomes $\tan 2A \equiv \dfrac{2\tan A}{1 - \tan^2 A}$.

These formulae are called the **double angle formulae**. You should learn them.

$$\sin 2A \equiv 2\sin A \cos A,$$
$$\cos 2A \equiv \cos^2 A - \sin^2 A,$$
$$\tan 2A \equiv \frac{2\tan A}{1 - \tan^2 A}.$$

The Pythagoras' identity can be used to produce two other forms for the identity for $\cos 2A$. If $\cos^2 A$ is replaced by $1 - \sin^2 A$, you get

$$\cos 2A \equiv (1 - \sin^2 A) - \sin^2 A,$$

that is $\cos 2A \equiv 1 - 2\sin^2 A$.

Alternatively, replace $\sin^2 A$ by $1 - \cos^2 A$, to get

$$\cos 2A \equiv \cos^2 A - (1 - \cos^2 A),$$

that is $\cos 2A \equiv 2\cos^2 A - 1$.

These identities are particularly useful in rearranged forms:

$$1 + \cos 2A \equiv 2\cos^2 A,$$
$$1 - \cos 2A \equiv 2\sin^2 A.$$

Example 6.5.1

Given that $\cos A = \frac{1}{3}$, find the exact value of $\cos 2A$.

$$\cos 2A = 2\cos^2 A - 1 = 2 \times \left(\tfrac{1}{3}\right)^2 - 1 = 2 \times \tfrac{1}{9} - 1 = -\tfrac{7}{9}.$$

Example 6.5.2

Given that $\cos A = \frac{1}{3}$, find the possible values of $\cos \frac{1}{2} A$.

Using $\cos 2A \equiv 2\cos^2 A - 1$, with $\frac{1}{2}A$ written in place of A, gives $\cos A \equiv 2\cos^2 \frac{1}{2}A - 1$.
In this case, $\frac{1}{3} = 2\cos^2 \frac{1}{2}A - 1$, giving $2\cos^2 \frac{1}{2}A = \frac{4}{3}$. This simplifies to $\cos^2 \frac{1}{2}A = \frac{2}{3}$, so
$\cos \frac{1}{2}A = \pm\sqrt{\frac{2}{3}} = \pm\frac{1}{3}\sqrt{6}$.

Example 6.5.3

Solve the equation $2\sin 2\theta = \sin \theta$, such that $0° \leqslant \theta \leqslant 360°$, giving non-exact values of θ correct to one decimal place.

Using the identity $\sin 2\theta \equiv 2\sin \theta \cos \theta$,

$$2 \times 2\sin \theta \cos \theta = \sin \theta$$
$$4\sin \theta \cos \theta = \sin \theta$$
$$\sin \theta (4\cos \theta - 1) = 0.$$

At least one of these factors must be 0. Therefore either

$$\sin \theta = 0, \quad \text{giving} \quad \theta = 0°, 180°, 360°$$

or $\quad 4\cos \theta - 1 = 0, \quad$ giving $\quad \cos \theta = 0.25$, so $\theta = 75.52...°$ or $284.47...°$.

Therefore the required roots are $\theta = 0°, 75.5°, 180°, 284.5°, 360°$.

Note that if you go straight from $4 \sin \theta \cos \theta = \sin \theta$ to $4 \cos \theta = 1$ by dividing both sides by $\sin \theta$ you may be dividing by 0, which is not allowed. You would then miss the solutions corresponding to $\sin \theta = 0$.

Example 6.5.4
Prove the identity $\cot A - \tan A \equiv 2 \cot 2A$.

Method 1   Put everything in terms of $\tan A$. Starting with the left side,

$$\cot A - \tan A \equiv \frac{1}{\tan A} - \tan A \equiv \frac{1 - \tan^2 A}{\tan A}$$

$$\equiv 2 \times \left(\frac{1 - \tan^2 A}{2 \tan A} \right) \equiv 2 \times \frac{1}{\tan 2A} \equiv 2 \cot 2A.$$

Method 2   Put everything in terms of $\sin A$ and $\cos A$. Starting with the left side,

$$\cot A - \tan A \equiv \frac{\cos A}{\sin A} - \frac{\sin A}{\cos A} \equiv \frac{\cos^2 A - \sin^2 A}{\sin A \cos A} \equiv \frac{\cos 2A}{\frac{1}{2} \sin 2A} \equiv 2 \cot 2A.$$

Example 6.5.5
Prove that $\operatorname{cosec} x + \cot x \equiv \cot \frac{1}{2}x$.

Starting with the left side, and putting everything in terms of sines and cosines,

$$\operatorname{cosec} x + \cot x \equiv \frac{1}{\sin x} + \frac{\cos x}{\sin x} \equiv \frac{1 + \cos x}{\sin x}$$

$$\equiv \frac{1 + (2\cos^2 \frac{1}{2}x - 1)}{2 \sin \frac{1}{2}x \cos \frac{1}{2}x} \equiv \frac{2 \cos^2 \frac{1}{2}x}{2 \sin \frac{1}{2}x \cos \frac{1}{2}x}$$

$$\equiv \frac{\cos \frac{1}{2}x}{\sin \frac{1}{2}x} \equiv \cot \frac{1}{2}x.$$

Exercise 6C

1   If $\sin A = \frac{2}{3}$ and A is obtuse, find the exact values of $\cos A$, $\sin 2A$ and $\tan 2A$.

2   If $\cos B = \frac{3}{4}$, find the exact values of $\cos 2B$ and $\cos \frac{1}{2}B$.

3   By expressing $\sin 3A$ as $\sin(2A + A)$, find an expression for $\sin 3A$ in terms of $\sin A$.

4   Express $\cos 3A$ in terms of $\cos A$.

5   By writing $\cos x$ in terms of $\frac{1}{2}x$, show that $\dfrac{1 - \cos x}{1 + \cos x} = \tan^2 \frac{1}{2}x$.

6   If $\cos 2A = \frac{7}{18}$, find the possible values of $\cos A$ and $\sin A$.

7   If $\tan 2A = \frac{12}{5}$, find the possible values of $\tan A$.

8   If $\tan 2A = 1$, find the possible values of $\tan A$. Hence state the exact value of $\tan 22\frac{1}{2}°$.

9 Solve these equations for values of A between 0 and 2π inclusive, giving non-exact answers correct to 2 decimal places. In each case use trigonometric identities and then check your results using a graphic calculator and its 'intersect' facility.

(a) $\cos 2A + 3 + 4\cos A = 0$

(b) $2\cos 2A + 1 + \sin A = 0$

(c) $\tan 2A + 5\tan A = 0$

10 Prove the identity $\tan 2x - \tan x \equiv \tan x \sec 2x$.

11 Prove that $(\cos A + \sin A)(\cos 2A + \sin 2A) \equiv \cos A + \sin 3A$.

6.6 The form $a \sin x + b \cos x$

Draw the graph of $y = 3\sin x + 2\cos x$ on your calculator, using a window of either 2π or $360°$, depending on whether you are in radian or degree mode. What you see may surprise you: it shows that this graph is either a cosine or a sine graph, first translated in the x-direction, and then enlarged in the y-direction.

Try this with other functions of the form $a \sin x + b \cos x$ with various values of the coefficients a and b, positive and negative.

This suggests that you can write $y = 3\sin x + 2\cos x$ in the form $y = R\sin(x + \alpha)$, where the graph $y = \sin x$ has been translated by α in the negative x-direction, and then enlarged in the y-direction by the factor R, where $R > 0$. The question is how to find the values of R and α.

If you equate the two expressions $y = 3\sin x + 2\cos x$ and $y = R\sin(x + \alpha)$, you find that

$$3\sin x + 2\cos x \equiv R\sin x \cos \alpha + R\cos x \sin \alpha.$$

Since these are to be identical, they certainly agree for $x = \frac{1}{2}\pi$ and $x = 0$. Substituting gives

$$3 = R\cos \alpha \quad \text{and} \quad 2 = R\sin \alpha.$$

You can find R and α from these equations. Imagine a right-angled triangle, which you might think of as a set square, with adjacent sides 2 units and 3 units, and hypotenuse R units. Then α is the angle shown in Fig. 6.5.

Therefore $\tan \alpha = \frac{2}{3}$, and $R = \sqrt{2^2 + 3^2} = \sqrt{13}$. It is important to remember that $R > 0$. The equations $2 = R\sin \alpha$ and $3 = R\cos \alpha$ then show that $\cos \alpha$ and $\sin \alpha$ are positive, so that the angle α is acute; in radians $\alpha = 0.58...$. Then

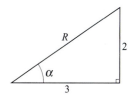

Fig. 6.5

$$3\sin x + 2\cos x \equiv (\sqrt{13}\cos 0.58...)\sin x + (\sqrt{13}\sin 0.58...)\cos x$$
$$\equiv \sqrt{13}\sin x \cos 0.58... + \sqrt{13}\cos x \sin 0.58...$$
$$\equiv \sqrt{13}\sin(x + 0.58...).$$

The form $\sqrt{13}\sin(x + 0.58...)$, while it may look less friendly than $3\sin x + 2\cos x$, is in many ways more convenient. Example 6.6.1 shows two applications.

Example 6.6.1

(a) Find the maximum and minimum values of $3 \sin x + 2 \cos x$, and find in radians to two decimal places the smallest positive values of x at which they occur.

(b) Solve the equation $3 \sin x + 2 \cos x = 1$, for $-\pi \leqslant x \leqslant \pi$, to two decimal places.

(c) Draw a sketch of the graph $y = 3 \sin x + 2 \cos x$.

(a) The maximum value of a sine function is 1. Since

$$3 \sin x + 2 \cos x \equiv \sqrt{13} \sin(x + 0.58...),$$

the maximum value of $3 \sin x + 2 \cos x$ is $\sqrt{13} \times 1 = \sqrt{13}$. And since the maximum value of the sine function occurs at $\frac{1}{2}\pi$, the relevant value of x is given by $x + 0.58... = \frac{1}{2}\pi$. Therefore the maximum $\sqrt{13}$ occurs when $x = \frac{1}{2}\pi - 0.58... = 0.98$, correct to two decimal places.

A similar argument works for the minimum value, which is $-\sqrt{13}$. And since the minimum value of the sine function occurs at $\frac{3}{2}\pi$, the relevant value of x is given by $x + 0.58... = \frac{3}{2}\pi$, that is when $x = \frac{3}{2}\pi - 0.58... = 4.12$, correct to two decimal places.

(b) $3 \sin x + 2 \cos x = 1 \quad \Leftrightarrow \quad \sqrt{13} \sin(x + 0.58...) = 1 \quad \Leftrightarrow \quad \sin(x + 0.58...) = \dfrac{1}{\sqrt{13}}.$

Using the methods of C2 Section 9.5, the solutions (between $-\pi$ and π) are

$$x + 0.58... = 0.28... \quad \text{or} \quad x + 0.58... = 2.86...,$$

so $x = -0.31$ or 2.27, correct to two decimal places.

(c) To sketch the graph, see Fig. 6.6, of $y = 3 \sin x + 2 \cos x$ it is easier to look at the alternative form $y = \sqrt{13} \sin(x + 0.58...)$ This has the shape of the sine graph, translated by -0.58 in the x-direction, and stretched in the y-direction by a factor of $\sqrt{13}$.

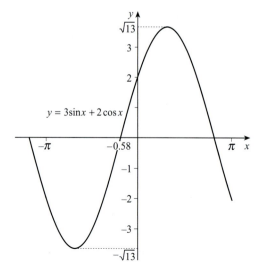

Fig. 6.6

In the general case, you can write $a \sin x + b \cos x$ in the form $R \sin(x + \alpha)$ where $R = \sqrt{a^2 + b^2}$ and α is given by the equations $R \cos \alpha = a$ and $R \sin \alpha = b$.

There is nothing special about using the form $R \sin(x + \alpha)$. It is often more convenient to use $R \cos(x + \alpha)$, $R \sin(x - \alpha)$ or $R \cos(x - \alpha)$. Thus, with the values of R and α in Example 6.6.1,

$$3 \cos x + 2 \sin x \equiv (R \cos \alpha) \cos x + (R \sin \alpha) \sin x \equiv R \cos(x - \alpha).$$

Always try to choose the form which produces the terms in the right order with the correct sign. For example, write $3 \cos x - 2 \sin x$ in the form $R \cos(x + \alpha)$, and $3 \sin x - 2 \cos x$ in the form $R \sin(x - \alpha)$. If you do this, the angle α can always be acute.

Summarising all this:

> If a and b are positive,
>
> $$a \sin x \pm b \cos x \text{ can be written in the form } R \sin(x \pm \alpha),$$
>
> $$a \cos x \pm b \sin x \text{ can be written in the form } R \cos(x \mp \alpha),$$
>
> where $R = \sqrt{a^2 + b^2}$ and $R \cos \alpha = a$, $R \sin \alpha = b$, with $0 < \alpha < \tfrac{1}{2}\pi$.

> It is better not to learn the detail of the result in the box except for $R = \sqrt{a^2 + b^2}$. Learn how to find α and work it out each time you come to it.

Example 6.6.2

Express $\sin \theta - 4 \cos \theta$ in the form $R \sin(\theta - \alpha)$ giving the values of R and α. Explain why the equation $\sin \theta - 4 \cos \theta = 5$ has no roots.

Identifying $\sin \theta - 4 \cos \theta$ with $R \sin(\theta - \alpha)$ gives

$$\sin \theta - 4 \cos \theta \equiv R \sin \theta \cos \alpha - R \cos \theta \sin \alpha,$$

so $\qquad R \cos \alpha = 1 \qquad$ and $\qquad R \sin \alpha = 4.$

Therefore $R = \sqrt{1^2 + 4^2} = \sqrt{17}$, with $\cos \alpha = \dfrac{1}{\sqrt{17}}$ and $\sin \alpha = \dfrac{4}{\sqrt{17}}$, giving $\tan \alpha = 4$ and $\alpha = 1.32...$.

Then $\sin \theta - 4 \cos \theta \equiv \sqrt{17} \sin(\theta - \alpha)$, where $\alpha = 1.32...$.

As $\sqrt{17} \sin(\theta - \alpha)$ lies between $-\sqrt{17}$ and $\sqrt{17}$, and $5 > \sqrt{17}$, the equation $\sin \theta - 4 \cos \theta = 5$ has no roots.

Exercise 6D

1 Find the value of α between $0°$ and $90°$ for which $3 \sin x + \cos x \equiv \sqrt{10} \sin(x + \alpha)$

2 Find the value of ϕ between $0°$ and $90°$ for which $3 \cos x - 4 \sin x \equiv 5 \cos(x + \phi)$.

3 Find the positive value of R and the value of $\tan \beta$, such that $5 \sin \theta + 3 \cos \theta \equiv R \sin(\theta + \beta)$.

4 Find the value of R and the value of β (correct to 3 decimal places) between 0 and $\frac{1}{2}\pi$ such that $6\cos x + \sin x \equiv R\cos(x - \beta)$.

5 Find the value of R and the value of α between 0 and $\frac{1}{2}\pi$ in each of the following cases, where the given expression is written in the given form. Give α correct to 2 decimal places.

(a) $\sin x + 2\cos x$; $R\sin(x + \alpha)$ (b) $\sin x + 2\cos x$; $R\cos(x - \alpha)$

(c) $\sin x - 2\cos x$; $R\sin(x - \alpha)$ (d) $2\cos x - \sin x$; $R\cos(x + \alpha)$

6 Express $5\cos\theta + 6\sin\theta$ in the form $R\cos(\theta - \beta)$ where $R > 0$ and $0 < \beta < \frac{1}{2}\pi$. State

(a) the maximum value of $5\cos\theta + 6\sin\theta$ and the least positive value of θ which gives this maximum,

(b) the minimum value of $5\cos\theta + 6\sin\theta$ and the least positive value of θ which gives this minimum.

7 Describe fully a combination of two single transformations that will transform the graph of $y = \cos x$ to the graph of $y = 6\cos\left(x - \frac{1}{3}\pi\right)$.

8 By expressing $6\cos x - 4\sin x$ in the form $R\cos(x + \beta)$ where $R > 0$ and $0 < \beta < \frac{1}{2}\pi$, describe a combination of two single transformations that will transform the graph of $y = \cos x$ to the graph of $y = 6\cos x - 4\sin x$.

9 Express $8\sin x + 6\cos x$ in the form $R\sin(x + \phi)$, where $R > 0$ and $0° < \phi < 90°$. Deduce the number of roots for $0° < x < 180°$ of the following equations.

(a) $8\sin x + 6\cos x = 5$ (b) $8\sin x + 6\cos x = 12$

10 Solve $7\sin x - 8\cos x = 9$ for values of x between 0 and 2π by

(a) expressing $7\sin x - 8\cos x$ in the form $R\sin(x - \beta)$,

(b) using a graphical method.

11 Solve the following equations for x in the interval $0° \leqslant x \leqslant 360°$. Give your answers to 1 decimal place.

(a) $4\sin x + 7\cos x = 6$ (b) $2\sin x - 5\cos x = 3$ (c) $9\cos x - 4\sin x = 5$

12 Solve the following equations for x in the interval $-\pi \leqslant x \leqslant \pi$. Give your answers to 2 decimal places.

(a) $7\sin x + 3\cos x = 6$ (b) $8\sin x - \cos x = 6$ (c) $8\cos x - 5\sin x = 2$

6.7   Inverse trigonometric functions

You have often used the notation $\cos^{-1}$, and the corresponding keys on the calculator, to convert a number into the angle (in either degrees or radians) which has this number for its cosine. Similarly with $\sin^{-1}$ and $\tan^{-1}$.

But now that you have used the notation f^{-1} to stand for the inverse of a function f, it seems natural to apply this to the trigonometric functions, and to think of $\cos^{-1}$, $\sin^{-1}$ and $\tan^{-1}$ as functions.

In this case $\cos^{-1}$, $\sin^{-1}$ and $\tan^{-1}$ always stand for the angle in radians.

There is one snag. For a function to have an inverse, it must be one-one. It is obvious from their graphs that cos, sin and tan are not one-one.

You know from Section 2.8 that the way round this is to define $\cos^{-1}$, $\sin^{-1}$ and $\tan^{-1}$ as the inverses of cos, sin and tan with restricted domains.

There are many possible ways of restricting the domains. The method which has been chosen is to take the domain for each function which is closest to 0; and in the case of the cosine, where there are two intervals equally close to 0, to take the positive one. This is illustrated in Figs. 6.7, 6.8 and 6.9.

Fig. 6.7 shows how the domain of the cosine function is restricted to $0 \leqslant x \leqslant \pi$ to define the function $\cos^{-1}$.

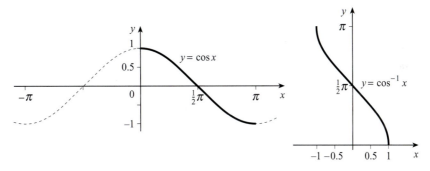

Fig. 6.7

Since cos has domain $0 \leqslant x \leqslant \pi$ and range $-1 \leqslant y \leqslant 1$, $\cos^{-1}$ has domain $-1 \leqslant x \leqslant 1$ and range $0 \leqslant y \leqslant \pi$.

Recall from Section 2.9 that if the graph of a function and its inverse are plotted on the same axes, then one is the reflection of the other in $y = x$. You can see that if the two graphs in Fig. 6.7 were superimposed, then the thicker part of the graph of $y = \cos x$ would be the reflection of $y = \cos^{-1} x$ in $y = x$, and vice versa.

Similarly Fig. 6.8 shows how the domain of the sine function is restricted to $-\frac{1}{2}\pi \leqslant x \leqslant \frac{1}{2}\pi$ to define the function $\sin^{-1}$.

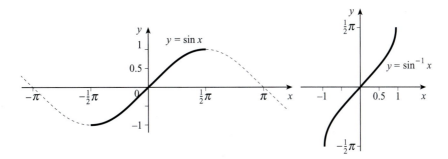

Fig. 6.8

Since sin has domain $-\frac{1}{2}\pi \leqslant x \leqslant \frac{1}{2}\pi$ and range $-1 \leqslant y \leqslant 1$, $\sin^{-1}$ has domain $-1 \leqslant x \leqslant 1$ and range $-\frac{1}{2}\pi \leqslant y \leqslant \frac{1}{2}\pi$.

Once again, the thicker part of the graph of $y = \sin x$ is the reflection of $y = \sin^{-1} x$ in the line $y = x$, and vice versa.

Fig. 6.9 shows the graph of the function $\tan^{-1}$, obtained by restricting the domain of the tangent function to $-\frac{1}{2}\pi < x < \frac{1}{2}\pi$.

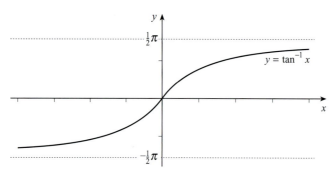

Fig. 6.9

Since tan has domain $-\frac{1}{2}\pi < x < \frac{1}{2}\pi$ and range $\mathbb{R}$, $\tan^{-1}$ has domain $\mathbb{R}$ and range $-\frac{1}{2}\pi < y < \frac{1}{2}\pi$.

Example 6.7.1 shows some of the issues you need to think about when dealing with inverse trigonometric functions. Although all the parts deal with the functions sin and $\sin^{-1}$, similar questions arise with the other trigonometric functions.

Example 6.7.1
Without using a calculator, find

(a) $\sin^{-1}\frac{1}{2}$,   (b) $\sin^{-1}\left(\sin\frac{1}{6}\pi\right)$,   (c) $\sin^{-1}\left(\sin\frac{7}{6}\pi\right)$,

(d) $\sin^{-1}(\sin 8)$,   (e) $\sin^{-1}(\sin(-2.4\pi))$.

(a) As the range of $\sin^{-1}$ is $-\frac{1}{2}\pi \leqslant x \leqslant \frac{1}{2}\pi$, you have to find the angle between $-\frac{1}{2}\pi$ and $\frac{1}{2}\pi$ whose sine is $\frac{1}{2}$. This is $\frac{1}{6}\pi$.

(b) It is very tempting to see the function sin followed by the function $\sin^{-1}$ and to say that the result is simply $\frac{1}{6}\pi$. In this case it is correct, but the reasoning is incomplete.

It is safer to say $\sin^{-1}\left(\sin\frac{1}{6}\pi\right) = \sin^{-1}\frac{1}{2} = \frac{1}{6}\pi$.

An alternative way of thinking which does not involve the calculation $\sin\frac{1}{6}\pi = \frac{1}{2}$ in the process is to ask yourself, 'What angle between $-\frac{1}{2}\pi$ and $\frac{1}{2}\pi$ has the same sine as $\frac{1}{6}\pi$?'. The only such angle is $\frac{1}{6}\pi$, so $\sin^{-1}\left(\sin\frac{1}{6}\pi\right) = \frac{1}{6}\pi$.

(c) It would be wrong in this case to say that $\sin^{-1}\left(\sin\frac{7}{6}\pi\right) = \frac{7}{6}\pi$ because $\frac{7}{6}\pi$ is not in the range of the function $\sin^{-1}$.

However, using the supplementary property $\sin\theta \equiv \sin(\pi - \theta)$,
$\sin\frac{7}{6}\pi = \sin\left(\pi - \frac{7}{6}\pi\right) = \sin\left(-\frac{1}{6}\pi\right)$, and $-\frac{1}{6}\pi$ is in the range of the function $\sin^{-1}$.
So $\sin^{-1}\left(\sin\frac{7}{6}\pi\right) = \sin^{-1}\left(\sin\frac{1}{6}\pi\right) = -\frac{1}{6}\pi$.

(d) 8 is not in the range of $\sin^{-1}$, but $8 - 2\pi = 1.71...$ has the same sine as 8.
Unfortunately $1.71...$ is still not in the range of $\sin^{-1}$, but you can use the
supplementary property, $\sin\theta \equiv \sin(\pi - \theta)$, to get $\pi - (8 - 2\pi) = 3\pi - 8 = 1.42...$.
This is in the range of $\sin^{-1}$, so $\sin^{-1}(\sin 8) = 3\pi - 8$.

(e) -2.4π is not in the range of $\sin^{-1}$, but
$$\sin^{-1}(\sin(-2.4\pi)) = \sin^{-1}(\sin(-2.4\pi + 2\pi)) = \sin^{-1}(\sin(-0.4\pi))$$
and -0.4π is in the range of $\sin^{-1}$.

Therefore $\sin^{-1}(\sin(-2.4\pi)) = -0.4\pi$.

Fig. 6.10 shows what is happening for parts (c) and (d). You may wish to draw a similar
diagram for part (e) for yourself.

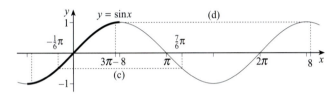

Fig. 6.10

You might find it helpful to check your answers with a calculator.

In Example 6.7.2, sine and cosine functions are mixed.

Example 6.7.2
Without using a calculator, find the exact values of

(a) $\sin^{-1}\left(\cos\frac{1}{6}\pi\right)$, (b) $\sin^{-1}(\cos 2.9\pi)$

(a) One way is simply to say that $\sin^{-1}\left(\cos\frac{1}{6}\pi\right) = \sin^{-1}\left(\frac{1}{2}\sqrt{3}\right) = \frac{1}{3}\pi$.

An alternative is to use the identity $\cos\theta \equiv \sin\left(\frac{1}{2}\pi - \theta\right)$. Then
$$\sin^{-1}\left(\cos\frac{1}{6}\pi\right) = \sin^{-1}\left(\sin\left(\frac{1}{2}\pi - \frac{1}{6}\pi\right)\right) = \sin^{-1}\left(\sin\frac{1}{3}\pi\right),$$
and since $\frac{1}{3}\pi$ is in the range of $\sin^{-1}$, $\sin^{-1}\left(\cos\frac{1}{6}\pi\right) = \frac{1}{3}\pi$.

(b) You can't find the exact numerical value of $\cos 2.9\pi$.

However, using the identity $\cos\theta \equiv \sin\left(\frac{1}{2}\pi - \theta\right)$,
$$\cos 2.9\pi = \sin(0.5\pi - 2.9\pi) = \sin(-2.4\pi),$$
so you must find $\sin^{-1}(\sin(-2.4\pi))$.

This is the same as Example 6.7.1(e), so $\sin^{-1}(\cos 2.9\pi) = -0.4\pi$.

Exercise 6E

Do not use a calculator in Questions 1 to 5.

1 Find

(a) $\cos^{-1} \frac{1}{2}\sqrt{3}$,   (b) $\tan^{-1} 1$,   (c) $\cos^{-1} 0$,   (d) $\sin^{-1} \frac{1}{2}\sqrt{3}$,

(e) $\tan^{-1}(-\sqrt{3})$,   (f) $\sin^{-1}(-1)$,   (g) $\cot^{-1} 0$,   (h) $\sec^{-1}(-1)$.

2 Find

(a) $\cos^{-1} \dfrac{1}{\sqrt{2}}$,   (b) $\sin^{-1}(-0.5)$,   (c) $\cos^{-1}(-0.5)$,   (d) $\tan^{-1}\left(\dfrac{1}{\sqrt{3}}\right)$.

3 Find

(a) $\sin(\sin^{-1} 0.5)$,   (b) $\cos(\cos^{-1}(-1))$,   (c) $\tan(\tan^{-1}\sqrt{3})$,   (d) $\cos(\cos^{-1} 0)$.

4 Find

(a) $\cos^{-1}\left(\cos \frac{3}{2}\pi\right)$,   (b) $\sin^{-1}\left(\sin \frac{13}{6}\pi\right)$,   (c) $\tan^{-1}\left(\tan \frac{1}{6}\pi\right)$,   (d) $\cos^{-1}(\cos 2\pi)$.

5 Find

(a) $\sin\left(\cos^{-1}\frac{1}{2}\sqrt{3}\right)$ (b) $\cot(\tan^{-1} 2)$ (c) $\cos(\sin^{-1}(-0.5))$ (d) $\tan(\sec^{-1}\sqrt{2})$

6 Use a graphical method to solve, correct to 3 decimal places, the equation $\cos x = \cos^{-1} x$. What simpler equation has this as its only root?

Miscellaneous exercise 6

1 (a) Starting from the identity $\sin^2 \phi + \cos^2 \phi \equiv 1$, prove that $\sec^2 \phi \equiv 1 + \tan^2 \phi$.

(b) Given that $180° < \phi < 270°$ and that $\tan \phi = \frac{7}{24}$, find the exact value of $\sec \phi$.   (OCR)

2 Solve the equation $\tan x = 3 \cot x$, giving all solutions between $0°$ and $360°$.   (OCR)

3 (a) State the value of $\sec^2 x - \tan^2 x$.

(b) The angle A is such that $\sec A + \tan A = 2$. Show that $\sec A - \tan A = \frac{1}{2}$, and hence find the exact value of $\cos A$.   (OCR)

4 Let $f(A) = \dfrac{\cos A}{1 + \sin A} + \dfrac{1 + \sin A}{\cos A}$.

(a) Prove that $f(A) = 2 \sec A$.

(b) Solve the equation $f(A) = 4$, giving your answers for A, in degrees, in the interval $0° < A < 360°$.   (OCR)

5 You are given that $\cos 30° = \dfrac{\sqrt{3}}{2}$ and $\cos 45° = \dfrac{1}{\sqrt{2}}$. Determine the exact value of $\cos 75°$.   (OCR)

6 Prove that $\sin\left(\theta + \frac{1}{2}\pi\right) \equiv \cos\theta$.   (OCR)

7 The angle α is obtuse, and $\sin\alpha = \frac{3}{5}$.

(a) Find the value of $\cos\alpha$.

(b) Find the values of $\sin 2\alpha$ and $\cos 2\alpha$, giving your answers as fractions in their lowest terms.   (OCR, adapted)

8 Given that $\sin\theta = 4\sin(\theta - 60°)$, show that $2\sqrt{3}\cos\theta = \sin\theta$. Hence find the value of θ such that $0° < \theta < 180°$. (OCR)

9 Solve the equation $\sin 2\theta - \cos^2\theta = 0$, giving values of θ in the interval $0° < \theta < 360°$. (OCR, adapted)

10 (a) Prove the identity $\cot\frac{1}{2}A - \tan\frac{1}{2}A \equiv 2\cot A$.

   (b) By choosing a suitable numerical value for A, show that $\tan 15°$ is a root of the quadratic equation $t^2 + 2\sqrt{3}t - 1 = 0$. (OCR)

11 (a) By using the substitution $t = \tan\frac{1}{2}x$, prove that $\csc x - \cot x = \tan\frac{1}{2}x$.

   (b) Use this result to show that $\tan 15° = 2 - \sqrt{3}$. (OCR)

12 Express $\sin\theta + \sqrt{3}\cos\theta$ in the form $R\sin(\theta + \alpha)$, where $R > 0$ and $0° < \alpha < 90°$. Hence find all values of θ, for $0° < \theta < 360°$, which satisfy the equation $\sin\theta + \sqrt{3}\cos\theta = 1$. (OCR)

13 (a) Express $12\cos x + 9\sin x$ in the form $R\cos(x - \alpha)$, where $R > 0$ and $0 < \theta < \frac{1}{2}\pi$.

   (b) Use the method of part (a) to find the smallest positive root α of the equation $12\cos x + 9\sin x = 14$, giving your answer correct to three decimal places. (OCR)

14 Express $2\cos x + \sin x$ in the form $R\cos(x - \alpha)$, where $R > 0$ and $0° < \alpha < 90°$. Hence

   (a) solve the equation $2\cos x + \sin x = 1$, giving all solutions between $0°$ and $360°$,

   (b) find the exact range of values of the constant k for which the equation $2\cos x + \sin x = k$ has real solutions for x. (OCR)

15 (a) Express $5\sin x + 12\cos x$ in the form $R\sin(x + \theta)$ where $R > 0$, and $0° < \theta < 90°$.

   (b) Hence, or otherwise, find the maximum and minimum values of f(x) where
   $$f(x) = \frac{30}{5\sin x + 12\cos x + 17}.$$ State also the values of x, in the range $0° < x < 360°$, at which they occur. (OCR)

16 Express $3\cos x - 4\sin x$ in the form $R\cos(x + \alpha)$ where $R > 0$, and $0° < \alpha < 90°$. Hence

   (a) solve the equation $3\cos x - 4\sin x = 2$, giving all solutions between $0°$ and $360°$,

   (b) find the greatest and least values, as x varies, of the expression $\dfrac{1}{3\cos x - 4\sin x + 8}$. (OCR)

17 (a) Find the value of $\tan^{-1}\sqrt{3} + \tan^{-1}\left(-\frac{1}{\sqrt{3}}\right)$.

   (b) If $A = \tan^{-1}x$ and $B = \tan^{-1}y$, find $\tan(A + B)$ in terms of x and y.

   (c) Show that $\tan^{-1}x + \tan^{-1}y = \tan^{-1}\dfrac{x+y}{1-xy}$ when $x = \frac{1}{2}$ and $y = \frac{1}{3}$, but not when $x = 2$ and $y = 3$.

18 If $\cos^{-1}(3x + 2) = \frac{1}{3}\pi$, find the value of x.

19 If $A = \sin^{-1}x$, where $x > 0$,

   (a) show that $\cos A = \sqrt{1 - x^2}$,

   (b) find expressions in terms of x for $\csc A$ and $\cos 2A$.

20 (a) Find the equation of the straight line joining the points $A(0, 1.5)$ and $B(3, 0)$.

   (b) Express $\sin\theta + 2\cos\theta$ in the form $r\sin(\theta + \alpha)$, where r is a positive number and θ is an acute angle.

   (c) The figure shows a map of a moor-land. The units of the coordinates are kilometres, and the y-axis points due north. A walker leaves her car somewhere on the straight road between A and B. She walks in a straight line for a distance of 2 km to a monument at the origin O. While she is looking at it the fog comes down, so that she cannot see the way back to her car. She needs to work out the bearing on which she should walk.

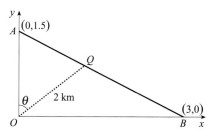

   Write down the coordinates of a point Q which is 2 km from O on a bearing of θ. Show that, for Q to be on the road between A and B, θ must satisfy the equation $2\sin\theta + 4\cos\theta = 3$. Calculate the value of θ between $0°$ and $90°$ which satisfies this equation.   (OCR)

21 The figure shows the graphs $\{1\}$ $y = 5\cos 2x + 2$ and $\{2\}$ $y = \cos x$ for $0° \leqslant x \leqslant 180°$.

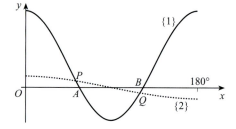

   (a) Find the coordinates of the points A and B where the graph $\{1\}$ meets the x-axis.

   (b) By solving a suitable trigonometric equation, find the x-coordinates of the two points P and Q where the graphs $\{1\}$ and $\{2\}$ intersect. Hence find the coordinates of the points P and Q.

22 Let a and b be the straight lines with equations $y = m_1 x + c_1$ and $y = m_2 x + c_2$ where $m_1 m_2 \neq 0$. Use appropriate trigonometric formulae to prove that a and b are perpendicular if and only if $m_1 m_2 = -1$.

7 The modulus function

This chapter is about the modulus function, written as $|x|$. When you have completed it, you should

- know the definition of modulus, and recognise $|x|$ as a function
- know how to draw graphs of functions involving modulus
- know how to use modulus algebraically and geometrically
- be able to solve simple equations and inequalities involving modulus.

7.1 The modulus function and its graph

In the preliminary chapter to this book, you were introduced briefly to modulus notation. But it should not surprise you that $|x|$ is actually a function.

> The **modulus** of x, written $|x|$ and pronounced 'mod x', is defined by
>
> $$|x| = x \qquad \text{if } x \geqslant 0,$$
> $$|x| = -x \qquad \text{if } x < 0.$$

The modulus of x is defined for all real numbers x. It is therefore another example of a function of x. Its domain is $\mathbb{R}$, and its range is $\mathbb{R}$, $y \geqslant 0$.

Some calculators have a key which converts any number in the display to its modulus. This key is often labelled [abs], which stands for 'absolute value'.

Fig. 7.1 shows the graph of $y = |x|$. The graph has a 'V' shape, with both branches making an angle of $45°$ with the x-axis, provided that the scales are the same on both axes.

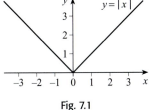

Fig. 7.1

So the graph of $y = |x|$ consists of two half-lines, with equations $y = x$ when $x \geqslant 0$ and $y = -x$ when $x < 0$.

7.2   Graphs of functions involving modulus

Example 7.2.1

Draw the graph of $y = |x - 2|$.

The graph of $y = |x - 2|$ is the same as that of $y = |x|$ translated by two units in the positive x-direction. The graph is shown in Fig. 7.2.

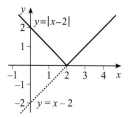

Fig. 7.2

So the graph of $y = |x - 2|$ consists of two half-lines, with equations $y = x - 2$ when $x \geqslant 2$, and $y = -(x - 2)$ when $x < 2$.

Another way of dealing with the case $x < 2$ is to note that the graph of $y = -(x - 2)$ is the reflection of $y = x - 2$ in the x-axis. (See C1 Section 10.3.) So you can draw the graph of $y = |x - 2|$ by first drawing the graph of $y = x - 2$ and then reflecting in the x-axis that part of the line which is below the x-axis. This is also illustrated in Fig. 7.2.

This method can always be used to get the graph of $y = |f(x)|$ from the graph of $y = f(x)$. In the definition of $|x|$ in the blue box on page 113, you can write any expression in place of x. So, replacing x by $f(x)$,

$$|f(x)| = f(x) \text{ if } f(x) \geqslant 0, \quad \text{and} \quad |f(x)| = -f(x) \text{ if } f(x) < 0.$$

It follows that, for the parts of the graph $y = f(x)$ which are on or above the x-axis, the graphs of $y = f(x)$ and $y = |f(x)|$ coincide. But for the parts of $y = f(x)$ below the x-axis, $y = |f(x)| = -f(x)$ is obtained from $y = f(x)$ by reflection in the x-axis.

A nice way of showing this is to draw the graph of $y = f(x)$ on a transparent sheet. You can then get the graph of $y = |f(x)|$ by folding the sheet along the x-axis so that the negative part of the sheet lies on top of the positive part.

To sketch $y = |f(x)|$:

- sketch $y = f(x)$

- then reflect any part of the graph of $y = f(x)$ which lies below the x-axis in the x-axis.

Example 7.2.2

Sketch the graphs of   (a) $y = |2x - 3|$,   (b) $y = |(x - 1)(x - 3)|$.

Figs. 7.3 and 7.4 show the graphs of (a) $y = 2x - 3$ and (b) $y = (x - 1)(x - 3)$ with the part below the x-axis (drawn dotted) reflected in the x-axis to give the graphs required.

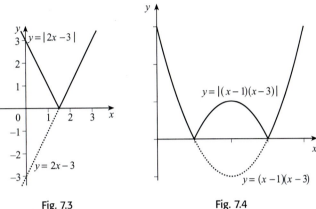

Fig. 7.3   Fig. 7.4

Try to produce these graphs on a graphic calculator. Graphs which involve the modulus function often have sharp corners. At these points the graph doesn't have a tangent, and the derivative $\dfrac{dy}{dx}$ doesn't exist. But notice that in Fig. 7.3 the point $(1\frac{1}{2}, 0)$ is a minimum point. This illustrates the point made in C1 Section 11.6 that turning points on the graph of $y = f(x)$ may occur at values of x where $f'(x)$ is either 0 or undefined.

In Fig. 7.4 you have a maximum point at $(2, 1)$ where $f'(x) = 0$, and minimum points at $(1, 0)$ and $(3, 0)$ where $f'(x)$ is undefined.

You may sometimes also want to get the graph of $y = f(|x|)$ from the graph of $y = f(x)$.

From the definition, $f(|x|)$ is the same as $f(x)$ when $x \geq 0$, but $f(|x|) = f(-x)$ when $x < 0$.

So the graph of $y = f(|x|)$ is the same as the graph of $y = f(x)$ to the right of the y-axis, but to the left of the y-axis it is the reflection in the y-axis of $y = f(x)$ for $x > 0$. (See C1 Section 10.3.)

Example 7.2.3

Sketch the graph of $y = \sin |x|$.

To the right of the y-axis the graph is the same as the graph of $y = \sin x$. The graph is completed for $x < 0$ by reflecting the graph of $y = \sin x$ to the right of the y-axis ($x > 0$) in the y-axis, to get Fig. 7.5.

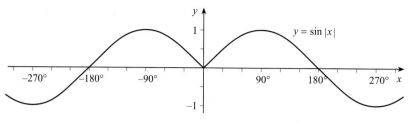

Fig. 7.5

7.3   Some algebraic properties

Let a and b be two real numbers. Since $|a|$ is always equal to either $-a$ or a, it follows that a is always equal to $-|a|$ or $|a|$. Similarly, b is always equal to $-|b|$ or $|b|$. So $a \times b$ is always equal to $|a| \times |b|$ or $-|a| \times |b|$. And since $|a| \times |b|$ is positive or zero, you can deduce that $|a \times b| = |a| \times |b|$.

A similar argument holds for division.

> If a and b are real numbers,
> $$|a \times b| = |a| \times |b|$$
> and
> $$\left|\frac{a}{b}\right| = \frac{|a|}{|b|} \quad \text{(provided that } b \neq 0\text{).}$$

Example 7.3.1

Show that   (a) $|4x + 6| = 2 \times |2x + 3|$,   (b) $|3 - x| = |x - 3|$

(a) Using the rule $|a \times b| = |a| \times |b|$,

$$|4x + 6| = |2(2x + 3)|$$
$$= |2| \times |2x + 3|$$
$$= 2 \times |2x + 3|.$$

(b) Using the rule $|a \times b| = |a| \times |b|$,

$$|3 - x| = |(-1) \times (x - 3)|$$
$$= |-1| \times |x - 3|$$
$$= 1 \times |x - 3|$$
$$= |x - 3|.$$

But beware! Similar rules don't hold for addition and subtraction.

For example, if $a = 2$ and $b = -3$, $|a + b| = |2 + (-3)| = |-1| = 1$, but $|a| + |b| = 2 + 3 = 5$. So, for these values of a and b, $|a + b|$ does not equal $|a| + |b|$. See Exercise 7A Question 3.

Exercise 7A

1 Sketch the following graphs.

(a) $y = |x + 3|$ (b) $y = |3x - 1|$ (c) $y = |x - 5|$

(d) $y = |3 - 2x|$ (e) $y = 2|x + 1|$ (f) $y = 3|x - 2|$

(g) $y = -2|2x - 1|$ (h) $y = 3|2 - 3x|$ (i) $y = |-|x||$

2 Draw sketches of each of the following sets of graphs.

(a) $y = (x - 1)(x - 3)$ and $y = |(x - 1)(x - 3)|$

(b) $y = 4 - 3x - x^2$ and $y = |4 - 3x - x^2|$

(c) $y = x^2 - 2$ and $y = |x^2 - 2|$

(d) $y = \sin x$ and $y = |\sin x|$

(e) $y = (x - 1)(x - 2)(x - 3)$ and $y = |(x - 1)(x - 2)(x - 3)|$

(f) $y = \cos 2x$ and $y = |\cos 2x|$ and $y = \cos |2x|$

(g) $y = |x - 2|$ and $y = ||x| - 2|$

3 Investigate the value of $|a + b|$ for various positive and negative choices for the real numbers a and b, and make a conjecture about the largest possible value for $|a + b|$. See also if you can make a conjecture about the smallest possible value of $|a + b|$.

4 Construct an argument like that in Section 7.3 to show that $\left|\dfrac{a}{b}\right| = \dfrac{|a|}{|b|}$, provided that $b \neq 0$.

7.4 Modulus on the number line

In Fig. 7.6 A and B are points on a number line with coordinates a and b. How can you express the distance AB in terms of a and b?

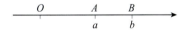

Fig. 7.6

- If B is to the right of A, then $b > a$, so $b - a > 0$ and the distance is $b - a$.
- If B is to the left of A, then $b < a$, so $b - a < 0$ and the distance is $a - b = -(b - a)$.
- If B and A coincide, then $b = a$, so $b - a = 0$ and the distance is 0.

You will recognise this as the definition of $|b - a|$.

> The distance between points on the number line with coordinates a and b is $|b - a|$.

As a special case, if a point X has coordinate x, then $|x|$ is the distance of X from the origin.

Now suppose that $|x| = 3$. What can you say about X?

Since the distance $OX = 3$, X is either 3 units to the right of O so that $x = 3$, or 3 units to the left of O so that $x = -3$.

This is also true in reverse. If $x = 3$ or $x = -3$, then X is 3 units from O, so $|x| = 3$.

A convenient way of summarising this is to write

$$|x| = 3 \quad \Leftrightarrow \quad x = 3 \text{ or } x = -3.$$

Similarly you can write

$$|x| \leqslant 3 \quad \Leftrightarrow \quad -3 \leqslant x \leqslant 3$$

since these are two different ways of saying that X is within 3 units of O on the number line.

Most people find it easier to understand these statements with the help of a number line. But you can if you prefer use a purely algebraic argument based on the definition of modulus without reference to geometry. This is illustrated in the following example.

Example 7.4.1
Use an algebraic argument to prove that $|x| \leqslant 3 \quad \Leftrightarrow \quad -3 \leqslant x \leqslant 3.$

There are two parts to the argument: both directions, $\Rightarrow$ and $\Leftarrow$, need to be proved.

(a) Proving $|x| \leqslant 3 \quad \Rightarrow \quad -3 \leqslant x \leqslant 3$

Suppose that $|x| \leqslant 3$.

Then

either $x \geqslant 0$, in which case $x = |x| \leqslant 3$, so $0 \leqslant x \leqslant 3$

or $x < 0$, in which case $x = -|x| \geqslant -3$, so $-3 \leqslant x < 0$.

In either case, $-3 \leqslant x \leqslant 3$.

So $|x| \leqslant 3 \quad \Rightarrow \quad -3 \leqslant x \leqslant 3$

(b) Proving $|x| \leqslant 3 \quad \Leftarrow \quad -3 \leqslant x \leqslant 3$

Suppose that $-3 \leqslant x \leqslant 3$.

This is a combination of two statements, $x \leqslant 3$ and $-3 \leqslant x$. The second of these can be written as $-x \leqslant 3$, so $-3 \leqslant x \leqslant 3$ means $x \leqslant 3$ and $-x \leqslant 3$.

Since $|x|$ is always equal to one or other of x and $-x$, it follows that $|x| \leqslant 3$.

So $|x| \leqslant 3 \quad \Leftarrow \quad -3 \leqslant x \leqslant 3$

Putting the results from parts (a) and (b) of the proof together gives

$$|x| \leqslant 3 \quad \Leftrightarrow \quad -3 \leqslant x \leqslant 3.$$

In this example there is nothing special about the number 3. You could use the same argument with 3 replaced by any positive number a to show that

$$|x| \leqslant a \quad \Leftrightarrow \quad -a \leqslant x \leqslant a.$$

What happens if $a = 0$?

In that case the left side of the equivalence is $|x| \leqslant 0$; but since $|x|$ is never negative, this is the same as saying that $|x| = 0$, that is $x = 0$.

And the right side is $-0 \leqslant x \leqslant 0$, that is $0 \leqslant x \leqslant 0$, and again $x = 0$.

So, in a rather trivial way, $\quad |x| \leqslant a \quad \Leftrightarrow \quad -a \leqslant x \leqslant a \quad$ when $a = 0$.

The two results can be combined in a single statement:

> If $a \geqslant 0$, $\quad |x| \leqslant a \quad \Leftrightarrow \quad -a \leqslant x \leqslant a.$

You can get a useful generalisation by replacing x in this statement by $x - k$, where k is a constant:

$$\text{If } a \geqslant 0, \quad |x - k| \leqslant a \quad \Leftrightarrow \quad -a \leqslant x - k \leqslant a.$$

If you add k to each side of the inequalities $-a \leqslant x - k \leqslant a$ you get $k - a \leqslant x \leqslant k + a$.

The equivalence then becomes:

> If $a \geqslant 0$, $\quad |x - k| \leqslant a \quad \Leftrightarrow \quad k - a \leqslant x \leqslant k + a.$

This result is used when you give a number correct to a certain number of decimal places. For example, to say that $x = 3.87$ 'correct to two decimal places' is in effect saying that $|x - 3.87| \leqslant 0.005$.

However, $|x - 3.87| \leqslant 0.005$ is equivalent to

$$3.87 - 0.005 \leqslant x \leqslant 3.87 + 0.005,$$

or $\quad 3.865 \leqslant x \leqslant 3.875.$

This is illustrated in Fig. 7.7.

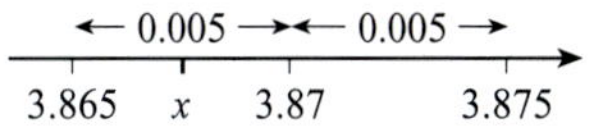

Fig. 7.7

Exercise 7B

1 Write the given inequalities in an equivalent form of the type $a < x < b$ or $a \leqslant x \leqslant b$.

(a) $|x - 3| < 1$ (b) $|x + 2| \leqslant 0.1$ (c) $|2x - 3| \leqslant 0.001$ (d) $|4x - 3| \leqslant 8$

2 Rewrite the given inequalities using modulus notation.

(a) $1 \leqslant x \leqslant 2$ (b) $-1 < x < 3$ (c) $-3.8 \leqslant x \leqslant -3.5$ (d) $2.3 < x < 3.4$

7.5   Equations involving modulus

There is no standard way of solving equations and inequalities which involve the modulus function. In most of the examples which follow various methods are used.

- Method 1 is based on graphs.
- Method 2 uses critical values.

Sometimes a third method is given, based on a geometric interpretation or applying a standard result. It is worth learning all these methods. You can then choose the one you are most comfortable with.

Example 7.5.1
Solve the equation $|x - 2| = 3$.

Method 1   Using graphs

First draw the graphs of $y = |x - 2|$ (see Example 7.2.1) and $y = 3$. These are shown in Fig. 7.8.

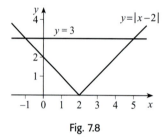

Fig. 7.8

There is one intersection to the left of $x = 2$. This is where $y = 2 - x$ meets $y = 3$, giving $x = -1$.

For the intersection to the right of $x = 2$, $y = x - 2$ meets $y = 3$ where $x = 5$.

The solution is therefore $x = 5$ or $x = -1$.

Method 2   Using critical values

The critical values method is shown in Table 7.9.

	$x < 2$	$x \geqslant 2$
$|x - 2|$	$-(x - 2)$	$x - 2$

Table 7.9

If $x < 2$, the equation $|x - 2| = 3$ reduces to $-(x - 2) = 3$ giving $x = -1$.

If $x \geqslant 2$, the equation reduces to $x - 2 = 3$ giving $x = 5$.

The solution is therefore $x = 5$ or $x = -1$.

Method 3   Using geometry

$|x - 2|$ is the distance of x from 2. If this distance is 3, then, thinking geometrically, $x = 2 + 3 = 5$ or $x = 2 - 3 = -1$.

Example 7.5.2
Solve the equation $|x - 2| = |2x - 1|$.

Method 1   Using graphs

The graphs of $y = |x - 2|$ and $y = |2x - 1|$ are drawn in Fig. 7.10.

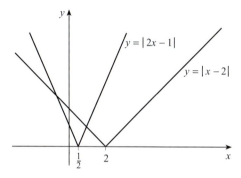

Fig. 7.10

From the graphs, you can see that there is an intersection to the left of $x = \frac{1}{2}$, when $y = -(x - 2)$ meets $y = -(2x - 1)$.

This gives $-(x - 2) = -(2x - 1)$, leading to $x = -1$.

There is another intersection in the interval $\frac{1}{2} \leqslant x \leqslant 2$, where $y = -(x - 2)$ meets $y = 2x - 1$.

This gives $-(x - 2) = 2x - 1$, leading to $x = 1$.

The solution is therefore $x = -1$ or $x = 1$.

Method 2   Using critical values

The critical values method is shown in Table 7.11.

	$x < \frac{1}{2}$	$\frac{1}{2} \leqslant x \leqslant 2$	$x > 2$
$|x - 2|$	$-(x - 2)$	$-(x - 2)$	$x - 2$
$|2x - 1|$	$-(2x - 1)$	$2x - 1$	$2x - 1$

Table 7.11

If $x < \frac{1}{2}$, the equation $|x - 2| = |2x - 1|$ reduces to $-(x - 2) = -(2x - 1)$, giving $x = -1$.

If $\frac{1}{2} \leqslant x \leqslant 2$, the equation reduces to $-(x - 2) = 2x - 1$, giving $x = 1$.

If $x > 2$, the equation reduces to $x - 2 = 2x - 1$, giving $x = -1$, which is not consistent with $x > 2$.

The solution is therefore $x = -1$ or $x = 1$.

Method 3   Using geometry

Since $|2x - 1| = \left|2\left(x - \frac{1}{2}\right)\right| = |2| \times \left|x - \frac{1}{2}\right|$, the equation can be written as $|x - 2| = 2 \times \left|x - \frac{1}{2}\right|$. This means that you want the points x on the number line such that the distance of x from 2 is twice the distance of x from $\frac{1}{2}$ (see Fig. 7.12). It is easy to see that, if x is between $\frac{1}{2}$ and 2 then $x = 1$; and if x is to the left of $\frac{1}{2}$, then $x = -1$.

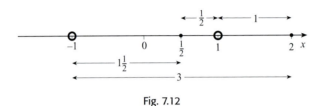

Fig. 7.12

7.6   Inequalities involving modulus

The methods for solving equations involving modulus can be modified to solve inequalities.

Example 7.6.1
Solve the inequality $|x - 2| < 3$.

Method 1   Using graphs

The graphs of $y = |x - 2|$ and $y = 3$ are shown in Fig. 7.13.

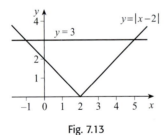

Fig. 7.13

From Example 7.5.1, the graphs intersect at $x = -1$ and $x = 5$. Then, using the graph, $|x - 2| < 3$ when $-1 < x < 5$.

Method 2   Using critical values

The critical values method is shown in Table 7.14.

	$x < 2$	$x \geqslant 2$
$|x - 2|$	$-(x - 2)$	$x - 2$

Table 7.14

(i) If $x < 2$, the inequality $|x - 2| < 3$ reduces to $-(2x - 1) < 3$ giving $x > -1$.

   $x > -1$ is the same as $-1 < x$, so this case becomes $-1 < x < 2$.

(ii) If $x \geqslant 2$, the inequality reduces to $x - 2 < 3$ giving $x < 5$.

   $x \geqslant 2$ is the same as $2 \leqslant x$, so this case becomes $2 \leqslant x < 5$.

Combining cases (i) and (ii), the solution is $-1 < x < 5$.

Method 3   Using a proved result

From the result 'If $a \geqslant 0$, the inequalities $|x - k| \leqslant a$ and $k - a \leqslant x \leqslant k + a$ are equivalent', the solution is $2 - 3 < x < 2 + 3$, which is $-1 < x < 5$.

Example 7.6.2
Solve the inequality $|x - 2| \geqslant |2x - 3|$.

Method 1   Using graphs

Consider the graphs of $y = |x - 2|$ and $y = |2x - 3|$. These were drawn in Figs. 7.2 and 7.3. They are reproduced together in Fig. 7.15.

You can see from this that $|x - 2| \geqslant |2x - 3|$ between the points of intersection of the graphs.

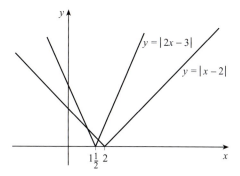

Fig. 7.15

The intersection to the left of $x = 1\frac{1}{2}$ is given by $-(x - 2) = -(2x - 3)$, leading to $x = 1$.

The intersection between $x = 1\frac{1}{2}$ and $x = 2$ is given by $-(x - 2) = 2x - 3$, leading to $x = 1\frac{2}{3}$.

So $|x - 2| \geqslant |2x - 3|$ when $1 \leqslant x \leqslant 1\frac{2}{3}$.

Method 2   The critical values method is shown in Table 7.16.

	$x < 1\frac{1}{2}$	$1\frac{1}{2} \leqslant x \leqslant 2$	$x > 2$
$|x - 2|$	$-(x - 2)$	$-(x - 2)$	$x - 2$
$|2x - 3|$	$-(2x - 3)$	$2x - 3$	$2x - 3$

Table 7.16

If $x < 1\frac{1}{2}$, the inequality $|x - 2| \geqslant |2x - 3|$ becomes $-(x - 2) \geqslant -(2x - 3)$ which gives $x \geqslant 1$. As $x \geqslant 1$ is the same as $1 \leqslant x$, so, combining this with $x < 1\frac{1}{2}$, you get $1 \leqslant x < 1\frac{1}{2}$.

If $1\frac{1}{2} \leqslant x \leqslant 2$, the inequality becomes $-(x - 2) \geqslant 2x - 3$ which gives $3x \leqslant 5$ or $x \leqslant 1\frac{2}{3}$. Combining this with $1\frac{1}{2} \leqslant x \leqslant 2$ gives $1\frac{1}{2} \leqslant x \leqslant 1\frac{2}{3}$.

If $x > 2$, the inequality becomes $x - 2 \geqslant 2x - 3$, giving $x \leqslant 1$. This is inconsistent with $x > 2$.

Since the inequality is satisfied when $1 \leqslant x < 1\frac{1}{2}$ and when $1\frac{1}{2} \leqslant x \leqslant 1\frac{2}{3}$, combining these gives the complete solution as $1 \leqslant x \leqslant 1\frac{2}{3}$.

Example 7.6.3
Solve the inequality $|x - 2| \geqslant 2x + 1$.

Method 1 Using graphs

The graphs of $y = |x - 2|$ and $y = 2x + 1$ are shown in Fig. 7.17.

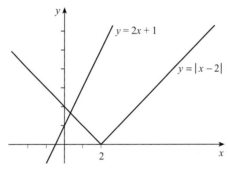

Fig. 7.17

The point of intersection of the graphs is to the left of $x = 2$, that is when $-(x - 2) = 2x + 1$, giving $x = \frac{1}{3}$.

From the graphs $|x - 2| \geqslant 2x + 1$ when $x \leqslant \frac{1}{3}$.

Method 2 Using critical values

The critical values are shown in Table 7.18.

	$x < 2$	$x \geqslant 2$
$|x - 2|$	$-(x - 2)$	$x - 2$

Table 7.18

If $x < 2$, then $|x - 2| = -(2 - x)$, so the inequality $|x - 2| \geqslant 2x + 1$ becomes $-(x - 2) \geqslant 2x + 1$, giving $x \leqslant \frac{1}{3}$. Combining this with $x < 2$ the original inequality is satisfied when $x \leqslant \frac{1}{3}$.

If $x \geqslant 2$, then $|x - 2| = x - 2$, so the inequality becomes $x - 2 \geqslant 2x + 1$, giving $x \leqslant -3$.
This is inconsistent with $x \geqslant 2$.

So the complete solution is $x \leqslant \frac{1}{3}$.

7.7 Squares, square roots and moduli

You know that, if x is any real number, then $x^2 \geqslant 0$. It follows that $|x^2| = x^2$. Also, from the rule
$|a \times b| = |a| \times |b|$, $|x^2| = |x| \times |x| = |x|^2$.

> If x is any real number, $|x^2| = |x|^2 = x^2$.

Now since $|x|^2 = x^2$, and $|x|$ is positive or zero, it follows that $|x|$ is the square root of x^2. You
can verify this by evaluating the composite function

$$x \quad \rightarrow \quad [\text{square}] \quad \rightarrow \quad x^2 \quad \rightarrow \quad [\sqrt{}] \quad \rightarrow \quad \sqrt{x^2}$$

on your calculator with various inputs for x, positive or negative. If you put $x = 3$, say, then
you will get the display sequence $3, 9, 3$. But if you put $x = -3$, you will get $-3, 9, 3$, because $\sqrt{}$
always gives the positive square root. That is, $\sqrt{x^2}$ is equal to x when $x \geqslant 0$, but equal to $-x$
when $x < 0$. This is just the definition of $|x|$. It follows that:

> If x is any real number, $\sqrt{x^2} = |x|$.

> Verify this by displaying the graphs of $y = \sqrt{x^2}$ and $y = |x|$ on a graphic calculator.

Example 7.7.1
Find the distance between the points with coordinates (a, k) and (b, k).

> **Method 1** Both points have the same y-coordinate, so the distance is the same as
> the distance between points with coordinates a and b on the number line, which is
> $|b - a|$.

> **Method 2** By the formula for the distance between two points in C1 Section 1.1,
> the distance is

$$\sqrt{(b - a)^2 + (k - k)^2} = \sqrt{(b - a)^2 + 0} = \sqrt{(b - a)^2} = |b - a|,$$

using $\sqrt{x^2} = |x|$ with $x = b - a$.

Useful results connecting squares with moduli can be got from the identity

$$x^2 - a^2 \equiv |x|^2 - |a|^2 \equiv (|x| - |a|)(|x| + |a|).$$

Suppose first that $a \neq 0$. Then $|a| > 0$, so $|x| + |a| > 0$. It then follows that

$$x^2 - a^2 = 0 \quad \Leftrightarrow \quad |x| - |a| = 0,$$
$$x^2 - a^2 > 0 \quad \Leftrightarrow \quad |x| - |a| > 0,$$
$$x^2 - a^2 < 0 \quad \Leftrightarrow \quad |x| - |a| < 0.$$

You can easily check that the first two of these are also true when $a = 0$; but the third is impossible if $a = 0$, since it gives $x^2 < 0$, which can never occur for any real number x.

$$|x| = |a| \quad \Leftrightarrow \quad x^2 = a^2,$$
$$|x| > |a| \quad \Leftrightarrow \quad x^2 > a^2, \quad \text{and}$$
$$\text{if } a \neq 0, \quad |x| < |a| \quad \Leftrightarrow \quad x^2 < a^2.$$

These relations are sometimes useful in solving equations and inequalities. They are effective because, although squaring is involved, the two sides are logically equivalent. The usual warning that squaring may introduce extra roots which don't satisfy the original equation doesn't apply.

It may be helpful to look at Example 0.3.1 where squaring led to extra roots.

Example 7.7.2 (see Example 7.5.2)
Solve the equation $|x - 2| = |2x - 1|$.

$$
\begin{aligned}
|x - 2| = |2x - 1| \quad &\Leftrightarrow \quad (x - 2)^2 = (2x - 1)^2 \\
&\Leftrightarrow \quad x^2 - 4x + 4 = 4x^2 - 4x + 1 \\
&\Leftrightarrow \quad 3x^2 - 3 = 0 \\
&\Leftrightarrow \quad 3(x + 1)(x - 1) = 0 \\
&\Leftrightarrow \quad x = -1 \quad \text{or} \quad x = 1.
\end{aligned}
$$

Example 7.7.3 (see Example 7.6.2)
Solve the inequality $|x - 2| \geqslant |2x - 3|$.

$$
\begin{aligned}
|x - 2| \geqslant |2x - 3| \quad &\Leftrightarrow \quad (x - 2)^2 \geqslant (2x - 3)^2 \\
&\Leftrightarrow \quad x^2 - 4x + 4 \geqslant 4x^2 - 12x + 9 \\
&\Leftrightarrow \quad 3x^2 - 8x + 5 \leqslant 0 \\
&\Leftrightarrow \quad (x - 1)(3x - 5) \leqslant 0 \\
&\Leftrightarrow \quad 1 \leqslant x \leqslant 1\tfrac{2}{3}.
\end{aligned}
$$

This method is very quick when it works, but there is a drawback. It can only be used for a very specific type of equation or inequality. It is easy to fall into the trap of assuming it can be applied to equations and inequalities of forms other than $|f(x)| = |g(x)|$ or $|f(x)| < |g(x)|$, which can have disastrous consequences.

Example 7.7.4
Solve the equation $|x - 2| + |1 - x| = 0$.

If you write the equation in the from $|x - 2| = -|1 - x|$, it should be obvious that the equation has no solution, because the left side is nearly always positive and the right side is nearly always negative.

False solution

$$|x - 2| + |1 - x| = 0 \iff |x - 2| = -|1 - x|$$
$$\iff (!)(x - 2)^2 = (1 - x)^2$$
$$\iff x^2 - 4x + 4 = 1 - 2x + x^2$$
$$\iff 2x = 3$$
$$\iff x = 1\tfrac{1}{2}.$$

There is no justification for the step marked (!). The previous line has the form $|x| = -|a|$, not $|x| = |a|$, so the result in the box can't be used.

Exercise 7C

1 Solve the following equations, using at least two methods for each case.

(a) $|x + 2| = 5$ (b) $|x - 1| = 7$

(c) $|2x - 3| = 3$ (d) $|3x + 1| = 10$

(e) $|x + 1| = |2x - 3|$ (f) $|x - 3| = |3x + 1|$

(g) $|2x + 1| = |3x + 9|$ (h) $|5x + 1| = |11 - 2x|$

2 Solve the following inequalities, using at least two methods for each case.

(a) $|x + 2| < 1$ (b) $|x - 3| > 5$

(c) $|2x + 7| \leqslant 3$ (d) $|3x + 2| \geqslant 8$

(e) $|x + 2| < |3x + 1|$ (f) $|2x + 5| > |x + 2|$

(g) $|x| > |2x - 3|$ (h) $|4x + 1| \leqslant |4x - 1|$

3 Solve the inequalities

(a) $|x - 2| > 2 - 2x,$ (b) $3 - 2x > |1 - 3x|,$ (c) $|2 - x| \leqslant |x + 2|.$

4 Are the following statements true or false? Give a counterexample where appropriate.

(a) The graph of $y = |f(x)|$ never has negative values for y.

(b) The graph of $y = f(|x|)$ never has negative values for y.

Miscellaneous exercise 7

1 Solve the inequality $|x + 1| < |x - 2|$.   (OCR)

2 Find the greatest and least values of x satisfying the inequality $|2x - 1| \leqslant 5$.   (OCR)

3 Sketch, on a single diagram, the graphs of $x + 2y = 6$ and $y = |x + 2|$. Hence, or otherwise, solve the inequality $|x + 2| < \tfrac{1}{2}(6 - x)$.   (OCR)

4 Solve the equation $|x| = |2x + 1|$.   (OCR)

5 Sketch the graph of $y = |x + 2|$ and hence, or otherwise, solve the inequality $|x + 2| > 2x + 1$.   (OCR)

6 Solve the equation $4|x| = |x - 1|$.

On the same diagram sketch the graphs of $y = 4|x|$ and $y = |x - 1|$ and, hence or otherwise, solve the inequality $4|x| > |x - 1|$.

7 The functions f and g are defined on the set of real numbers as follows:

$$\text{f: } x \mapsto |2 \sin x|, \qquad \text{g: } x \mapsto \sin |2x|.$$

(a) (i) Make clearly labelled sketches of the graphs of $y = \text{f}(x)$ and $y = \text{g}(x)$ in the interval $-270° \leq x \leq 270°$.

   (ii) State the range of each function.

(b) Decide whether or not each function is periodic and, if so, state its period.   (OCR)

8 Solve the inequality $|x| < 4|x - 3|$.

9 Solve the equations   (a) $x + |2x - 1| = 3$,   (b) $3 + |2x - 1| = x$.

10 A graph has equation $y = x + |2x - 1|$. Express y as a linear function of x (that is, in the form $y = mx + c$ for constants m and c) in each of the following intervals for x.

(a) $x > \frac{1}{2}$ (b) $x < \frac{1}{2}$ (OCR)

11 Draw sketches of the graphs of the following functions, where the angles are in degrees.

(a) $y = \sin 3x$ (b) $y = |\sin 3x|$ (c) $y = \sin |3x|$

12 Simplify the following.

(a) $\sqrt{\sec^2 \phi - 1}$ (b) $\dfrac{1}{\sqrt{1 + \cot^2 \phi}}$ (c) $\dfrac{1}{\sqrt{\csc^2 \phi - 1}}$

13* Rewrite the function $\text{k}(x)$ defined by $\text{k}(x) = |x + 3| + |4 - x|$ for the following three cases, without using the modulus in your answer.

(a) $x > 4$ (b) $-3 \leq x \leq 4$ (c) $x < -3$

Hence sketch the graph of $y = \text{k}(x)$.

14* Sketch, on separate diagrams, the graphs of $y = |x|$, $y = |x - 3|$ and $y = |x - 3| + |x + 3|$. Find the solution set of the equation $|x - 3| + |x + 3| = 6$.   (OCR)

15* Sketch the graph of $y = |2x - 3| + |5 - x|$.

(a) Calculate the y-coordinate of the point where the graph cuts the y-axis.

(b) Determine the gradient of the graph where $x < -5$.   (OCR, adapted)

Revision exercise 1

1 The graph of $y = e^x$ can be transformed to that of $y = e^{x+1}$ either by means of a stretch or by means of a translation. State the scale factor and the directions of the stretch and the magnitude and direction of the translation.

   Describe the transformation which maps the graph of $y = e^x$ onto the graph of $y = \ln x$.

   (OCR)

2 Show that $\displaystyle\int_3^{12} \frac{2}{x}\,dx = \ln 16$.

   (OCR)

3 Find $\displaystyle\int (4x + 3)^{10}\,dx$.

   (OCR)

4 A radioactive substance is decaying exponentially. Initially its mass is 480 grams. Its mass, M grams, at a time t years after the initial observation is given by $M = 480e^{kt}$, where k is a constant. When $t = 330$, the mass of the substance will be 240 grams.

   (a) State the value of the mass when $t = 660$.

   (b) Determine the value of k.

   (c) Find the rate at which the mass will be decreasing when $t = 200$.

   (OCR)

5 The functions f and g are defined for all real numbers by

   $$f: x \mapsto 2e^{3x}, \quad g: x \mapsto x - k.$$

   where k is a positive constant.

   (a) Evaluate $f(g(k))$.

   (b) Find an expression for $f^{-1}(x)$.

   (c) Sketch on the same diagram the graphs of $y = f(x)$ and $y = f^{-1}(x)$, indicating the relationship between the graphs.

   (d) The diagram shows the graph of $y = |g(f(x))|$, which meets the x-axis at A and the y-axis at $(0, 6)$.

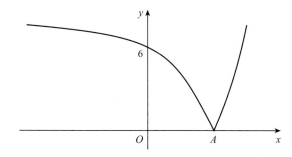

   Find k and determine the exact value of the x-coordinate of A.

6 Differentiate with respect to x

   (a) $(3 - 2x)^5$,   (b) $\ln(4x + 7)$.   (OCR)

7 Each of the functions f and g has domain $-3 \leqslant x \leqslant 3$. The left diagram shows the curve $y = f(x)$, which meets the x-axis at $(-2, 0)$ and the y-axis at $(0, 4)$. The right diagram shows the curve $y = g(x)$, which meets the x-axis at $(2, 0)$ and the y-axis at $(0, 3)$.

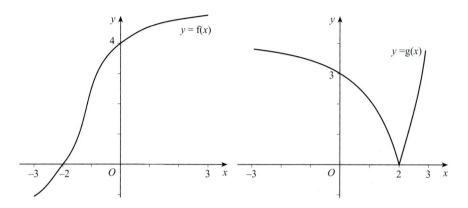

   (a) Determine the value of $g(f(-2))$.

   (b) State which one of the functions f and g is one-one and sketch the graph of its inverse. You should indicate on your sketch the coordinates of intersections with the axes.

   (c) Given that $g(x) = |h(x)|$, where $g(x) \neq h(x)$, sketch the graph of a possible curve $y = h(x)$.   (OCR)

8 (a) A quantity N is growing exponentially. The table shows values of N at different times t. Determine the values of P and q.

t	20	30	40	q
N	50	100	P	800

   (b) A radioactive substance is decaying exponentially. Its mass, m grams, after t years is given by $m = 600e^{-0.0035t}$.

      (i) Find the value of t for which $m = 300$.

      (ii) Find, correct to 2 significant figures, the rate at which the mass is decreasing when $t = 80$.   (OCR)

9 (a) Use the trapezium rule, with two intervals each of width 5, to show that
   $$\int_5^{15} \frac{3}{x+5}\, dx \approx \tfrac{17}{8}.$$

   (b) Show that the exact value of $\int_5^{15} \frac{3}{x+5}\, dx$ is $\ln 8$.

   (c) Use a sketch graph to show how you can deduce from parts (a) and (b) that $\ln 8 < \tfrac{17}{8}$.   (OCR)

10 (a) Find the gradient of the curve $y = 5e^{3x}$ at the point for which $x = \ln a$, giving your answer in simplified form in terms of the constant a.

(b) Prove that $\displaystyle\int_{A}^{A^3} \frac{1}{x-1}\, dx = \ln(A^2 + A + 1)$ for values of the constant A such that $A > 1$.

(OCR)

11 The function f is defined for all real values of x by $f(x) = |2x - 1| + 4$.

(a) Sketch the graph of $y = f(x)$ and state the range of f.

(b) Evaluate ff(0).

(c) Solve the equation $f(x) = 100$.

(d) The function g is defined by $g(x) = |2x - 1| + 4$, $x < 0$. Find an expression for $g^{-1}(x)$.

(OCR)

12 (a) Given that $\sin(\theta + 45°) = 2\sin\theta$, show that $\tan\theta = \dfrac{1}{2\sqrt{2} - 1}$.

(b) Hence solve the equation $\sin(\theta + 45°) = 2\sin\theta$, for values of θ between $0°$ and $360°$, giving your answers correct to the nearest degree.

(OCR)

13 Without using a calculator, find the exact value of $\left(\sin 22\tfrac{1}{2}° + \cos 22\tfrac{1}{2}°\right)^2$.

(OCR)

14 (a) In the diagram, $ABCD$ represents a rectangular table with sides 3.5 m and 1.5 m. It has been turned so that it wedges in a passsage of width 2.5 m.

Given that θ is the acute angle between the longer side and the passage, as shown in the diagram, show clearly why $7\sin\theta + 3\cos\theta = 5$.

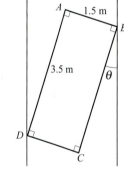

(b) Express $7\sin\theta + 3\cos\theta$ in the form $R\sin(\theta + \alpha)$ where $R > 0$ and $0° < \alpha < 90°$.

(c) Find θ.

(OCR)

15 (a) Write down the formula for $\tan 2x$ in terms of $\tan x$.

(b) By letting $\tan x = t$, show that the equation $4\tan 2x + 3\cot x \sec^2 x = 0$ becomes $3t^4 - 8t^2 - 3 = 0$.

(c) Find all the solutions of the equation $4\tan 2x + 3\cot x \sec^2 x = 0$ which lie in the range $0 \leqslant x \leqslant 2\pi$.

(OCR)

16 The function $x \mapsto \dfrac{1-x}{1+2x}$, $x \in \mathbb{R}$, $x \neq -\tfrac{1}{2}$ has an inverse. Find the inverse function, giving your answer in similar language to the original.

17 Differentiate $y = \dfrac{1}{\sqrt{2x+3}}$ with respect to x. Draw a sketch of the curve.

18 (a) The function f is defined by $f(x) = x^2 - 2x - 1$ for the domain $-2 \leqslant x \leqslant 5$. Write $f(x)$ in completed square form. Hence find the range of f. Explain why f does not have an inverse.

   (b) A function g is defined by $g(x) = 2x^2 - 4x - 3$. Write down a domain for g such that g^{-1} exists.   (OCR, adapted)

19 Calculate the area of the region in the first quadrant bounded by the curve with equation $y = \sqrt{9 - x}$ and the axes.

20 The function f is defined for the domain $x \geqslant 0$ by $f: x \mapsto 4 - x^2$.

   (a) Sketch the graph of f and state the range of f.

   (b) Describe a simple transformation whereby the graph of $y = f(x)$ may be obtained from the graph of $y = x^2$ for $x \geqslant 0$.

   (c) The inverse of f is denoted by f^{-1}. Find an expression for $f^{-1}(x)$ and state the domain of f^{-1}.

   (d) Show, by reference to a sketch, or otherwise, that the solution to the equation $f(x) = f^{-1}(x)$ can be obtained from the quadratic equation $x^2 + x - 4 = 0$. Determine the solution of $f(x) = f^{-1}(x)$, giving your value to two decimal places.

21 You are given that the equation $f(x) = 0$ has a solution at $x = 3$. Using this information, write down as many solutions as you can to each of the following equations.

   (a) $2f(x + 5) = 0$ (b) $f(3x) = 0$

   (c) $|f(x)| = 0$ (d) $f(|x|) = 0$ (OCR)

22 The number of bacteria in a culture increases exponentially with time. When observation started there were 1000 bacteria, and five hours later there were 10 000 bacteria. Find, correct to 3 significant figures,

   (a) when there were 5000 bacteria,

   (b) when the number of bacteria would exceed one million,

   (c) how may bacteria there would be 12 hours after the first observation.

23 Use the addition formulae to find an expression for $\cos^2(A + B) + \sin^2(A + B)$. Verify that your expression reduces to 1.

   Use a similar method to find an expression for $\cos^2(A + B) - \sin^2(A + B)$. Verify that this reduces to $\cos(2A + 2B)$.

24 In the figure A, B, C are the points on the graph of $y = \sin x$ for which $x = \alpha - \frac{1}{3}\pi, \alpha, \alpha + \frac{1}{3}\pi$ respectively. D is the point $(\alpha, 0)$.

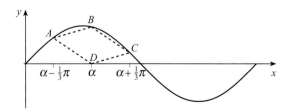

   (a) Sketch separate diagrams showing $ABCD$ in the special cases where $\alpha = \frac{1}{3}\pi, \alpha = \frac{1}{2}\pi, \alpha = \frac{2}{3}\pi$.

(b) Use addition formulae to simplify $\sin\left(\alpha - \frac{1}{3}\pi\right) + \sin\left(\alpha + \frac{1}{3}\pi\right)$.

(c) Write down the coordinates of the mid-point of AC.

(d) Show that $ABCD$ is a parallelogram. (OCR)

25 Solve the equation $3\cos 2x + 4\sin 2x = 2$, for values of x between 0 and 2π, giving your answers correct to two decimal places.

26 ABC is a right-angled triangle as shown in the diagram. A rectangle $AXYZ$ is drawn around the triangle, with angle $XAB = \theta$.

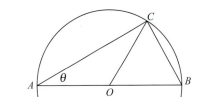

By expressing the perimeter of the rectangle in the form $R\cos(\theta - \alpha)$, find

(a) the maximum perimeter of the rectangle as θ varies,

(b) the corresponding value of θ, giving your answer to the nearest 0.1 of a degree. (OCR, adapted)

27 The figure shows part of a circle with centre O and radius r. Points A, B and C lie on the circle such that AB is a diameter. Angle $BAC = \theta$ radians.

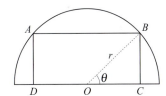

(a) Find angle AOC in terms of θ, and use the cosine rule in triangle AOC to express AC^2 in terms of r and θ.

(b) By considering triangle ABC, write down the length of AC in terms of r and θ, and deduce that $\cos 2\theta = 2\cos^2\theta - 1$. (OCR)

28 The diagram shows a fixed semicircle, with centre O and radius r, and an inscribed rectangle $ABCD$. The vertices A and B of the rectangle lie on the circumference of the semicircle, and C and D lie on the diameter. The size of angle BOC is θ radians.

(a) Express the perimeter, p, of the rectangle in terms of r and θ, and show that the area, a, may be expressed as $a = r^2\sin 2\theta$.

(b) Find the maximum value of a as θ varies, and show that when a has its maximum value, $p = 3r\sqrt{2}$.

(c) Find, in terms of r, the area of the rectangle which has maximum perimeter. (OCR, adapted)

29 The number of bacteria present in a culture at time t hours after the beginning of an experiment is denoted by N. The relation between N and t is modelled by $N = 100e^{\frac{3}{2}t}$.

(a) After how many hours will the number of bacteria be 9000?

(b) At what rate per hour will the number of bacteria be increasing when $t = 6$? (OCR)

30 By using a graphical method, or otherwise, establish the identities

   (a) $\sin^{-1} x + \cos^{-1} x \equiv \frac{1}{2}\pi$,   (b) $\tan^{-1} x + \tan^{-1}\left(\dfrac{1}{x}\right) \equiv \frac{1}{2}\pi$ or $-\frac{1}{2}\pi$.

31 Give the domains and the ranges of the following functions.

   (a) $2\sin^{-1} x - 4$ (b) $2\sin^{-1}(x-4)$

32 The curve with equation $y = 2x^2 - 3x + 7$ is translated by p units in the negative y-direction, then stretched in the x-direction by the positive scale factor q and finally translated in the positive x-direction by r units. If the final curve has equation $y = \frac{1}{2}x^2 - \frac{19}{2}x + 46$ find the values of p, q and r.

33 (a) Express $2x^2 + 4x - 1$ in the form $a[(x + p)^2 + q]$, stating the values of the constants a, p and q.

   (b) Sketch the graph of $y = 2x^2 + 4x - 1$, stating the coordinates of the vertex.

   (c) The graph of $2x^2 + 4x - 1$ is obtained from the graph of $y = x^2$ by a series of transformations. Describe such a sequence, specifying each transformation fully, and stating the order in which they are applied.   (OCR)

34 The functions f and g are defined as follows:

$$\text{f}: x \mapsto 5e^{\frac{1}{2}x} - 6, \quad x \in \mathbb{R}, \qquad \text{g}: x \mapsto |x - 2|, \quad x \in \mathbb{R}.$$

   (a) Determine the range of f and the range of g.

   (b) Find an expression for $\text{f}^{-1}(x)$.

   (c) Find the solutions of the equation $\text{gf}(x) = 7$, giving each in an exact form.

35 The function f is defined for all real x by $\text{f}(x) = \cos x - \sqrt{3}\sin x$.

   (a) Express $\text{f}(x)$ in the form $R\cos(x + \phi)$, where $R > 0$ and $0° < \phi < 90°$.

   (b) Solve the equation $|\text{f}(x)| = 1$, giving your answers in the interval $0° \leqslant x \leqslant 360°$.   (OCR)

8 Solving equations numerically

This chapter is about numerical methods for equations which cannot be solved exactly. When you have completed it, you should

- be able to use the sign-change rule to find approximate solutions by decimal search
- know how to use a chord approximation to improve the efficiency of decimal search
- be able to use an iterative method to produce a sequence which converges to a root
- understand that the choice of iterative method affects whether a sequence converges or not, and know what determines its behaviour
- appreciate that it is possible to modify an iterative method to speed up convergence
- appreciate that decisions about choice of method may depend on what sort of calculator or computer software you are using.

How you use this chapter will depend on what calculating aids you have available. It has been written to emphasise the underlying mathematical principles, so that you can follow the procedures with a simple calculator. But if you have a programmable or graphic calculator, if you like to write your own computer programs, or if you have access to a spreadsheet, you will be able to carry out some of the calculations far more quickly.

8.1 Some basic principles

In mathematical problems the final step is often to solve an equation. If this is a linear or a quadratic equation, or if it is an equation which can be reduced to one of these forms, then you have a method for solving it. But for equations of any other form you usually have to resort to some kind of solution by successive approximation, either numerical or algebraic.

Any equation in x can be rearranged so that it takes the form $f(x) = 0$. A value of x for which $f(x)$ takes the value 0 is called a **root** of the equation. The **solution** of the equation is the set of all the roots.

A useful way of representing the solution of $f(x) = 0$ is to draw the graph of $y = f(x)$. The roots are the x-coordinates of the points of the graph on the x-axis.

This leads at once to a result which is very useful for locating roots.

> **The sign-change rule**
> If the function $f(x)$ is continuous for an interval $p \leqslant x \leqslant q$ of its domain, and if $f(p)$ and $f(q)$ have opposite signs, then there is at least one root of $f(x) = 0$ between p and q.

This is illustrated in Fig. 8.1. The condition that $f(x)$ is continuous means that the graph cannot jump across the x-axis without meeting it.

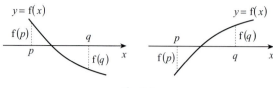

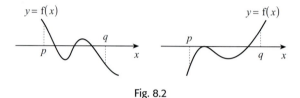

Fig. 8.1

The words 'at least one' are important. Fig. 8.2 shows that there may be more than one root between p and q.

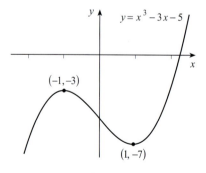

Fig. 8.2

When you have an equation to solve, it usually helps to begin by finding the shape of the graph of $y = f(x)$.

Suppose that you want to solve the cubic equation

$$x^3 - 3x - 5 = 0.$$

Writing $f(x) = x^3 - 3x - 5$, you can find

$$f'(x) = 3x^2 - 3 = 3(x + 1)(x - 1) \text{ and } f''(x) = 6x.$$

It follows that $f(x)$ has a maximum where $x = -1$ and a minimum where $x = 1$. The coordinates of the maximum and minimum points are $(-1, -3)$ and $(1, -7)$. From this you can draw a sketch of the graph, as in Fig. 8.3.

Fig. 8.3

The graph shows that this equation has only one root, and that it is greater than 1. Also, $f(x)$ is negative for values of x below the root, and positive above the root. This suggests where to start looking for it.

8.2   Decimal search

This section describes how you can use the sign-change rule to find a sequence of approximations to the root, improving the accuracy by one decimal place at a time.

Continuing with the equation $x^3 - 3x - 5 = 0$, the graph in Fig. 8.3 suggests calculating $f(2) = -3$ and $f(3) = 13$. It follows from the sign-change rule that the root is between 2 and 3.

You could now start calculating $f(2.1)$, $f(2.2)$, ... until you reach a value of x for which $f(x)$ is positive. But it is worth spending a moment to ask if this is a sensible strategy.

Fig. 8.4 is a sketch of the graph of $f(x)$ between $x = 2$ and $x = 3$. Does this help to suggest roughly where X is?

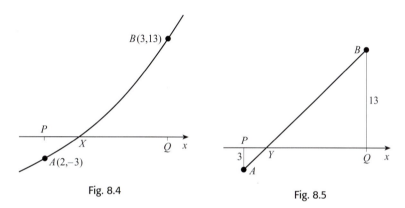

Fig. 8.4   Fig. 8.5

Suppose that you replace the curve by the straight line segment joining A and B, as in Fig. 8.5. Then the point Y where the chord AB cuts the x-axis is probably not far from X. Since $\frac{13}{3} = 4.3\ldots$, the length of QB is about 4 times that of PA, so YQ is about 4 times PY. It follows that PQ is about 5 times PY; that is,

$$PY \approx \tfrac{1}{5} \times PQ = \tfrac{1}{5} \times 1 = 0.2.$$

This calculation is called 'linear interpolation', because you are finding a point between two known values by replacing the curve with a straight line. For this purpose a very rough estimate to one significant figure is enough.

This suggests that, to locate X, it might be best to begin by calculating $f(2.2) = -0.952$. Since this is negative, Fig. 8.4 shows that 2.2 is between P and X. So go on to calculate $f(2.3) = 0.267$.

There is no need to go further. Since $f(2.2)$ is negative and $f(2.3)$ is positive, the root is between 2.2 and 2.3.

If you use a graphic calculator, the equivalent procedure would be to zoom in on the interval $2 \leqslant x \leqslant 3$. You will then see that the graph cuts the x-axis between 2.2 and 2.3.

The process is now repeated to get the second decimal place.

As $f(2.2) = -0.952$ and $f(2.3) = 0.267$ it looks as though the root is closer to 2.3 than 2.2. A linear interpolation argument suggests that it might be worth starting with 2.27 or 2.28.

So start by calculating $f(2.28) = 0.012\ldots$. Since this is positive, 2.28 is too large. Now try $f(2.27) = -0.112\ldots$, which is negative. So the root is between 2.27 and 2.28; the values of $f(2.27)$ and $f(2.28)$ suggest that the root is nearer to 2.28.

> The sign-change rule means that you do not need to draw or sketch the graph to be sure that the root lies between 2.27 and 2.28.
>
> It doesn't matter if your first tries do not include the root. In that case, you must keep searching until one value of the function is positive and a neighbouring one is negative.
>
> With a graphic calculator you would zoom in on the interval $2.2 \leqslant x \leqslant 2.3$, and see that the graph cuts the x-axis between 2.27 and 2.28.

Notice that, if you wanted to check that the root is 2.28 correct to 2 decimal places, you would need to know whether it is nearer to 2.28 than 2.27, so you would need to find $f(2.275)$, which is $-0.050\ldots$. Since this is negative, and you already know that $f(2.28)$ is positive, the root lies between 2.275 and 2.28. That is, its value is 2.28 correct to 2 decimal places.

What you are finding by this method are the terms in two sequences; one sequence of numbers above the root

$$a_0 = 3, \quad a_1 = 2.3, \quad a_2 = 2.28, \; \ldots ,$$

and one sequence of numbers below the root

$$b_0 = 2, \quad b_1 = 2.2, \quad b_2 = 2.27, \; \ldots .$$

Both sequences converge on the root as a limit; the difference between a_r and b_r is 10^{-r}, which tends to 0 as r increases.

Example 8.2.1

Solve the equation $x\,e^x = 1$, giving the root correct to 2 decimal places.

Begin by investigating the equation graphically, using the idea that a root of an equation $f(x) = g(x)$ is the x-coordinate of a point of intersection of the graphs of $y = f(x)$ and $y = g(x)$. Fig. 8.6 shows four different ways of doing this, based on the equation as stated and the three rearrangements

$$e^x = \frac{1}{x}, \quad x = e^{-x}, \quad x = -\ln x.$$

All the graphs show that there is just one root, but the third graph is probably the most informative. The tangent to $y = e^{-x}$ at $(0, 1)$ has gradient -1, and so meets $y = x$ at $\left(\frac{1}{2}, \frac{1}{2}\right)$. Since the curve bends upwards, the root is slightly greater than 0.5.

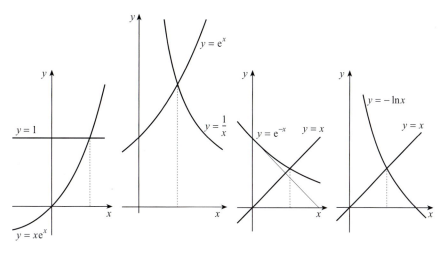

Fig. 8.6

To use the sign-change method you need to write the equation as $f(x) = 0$. There are again several possibilities:

$$x e^x - 1 = 0, \quad e^x - \frac{1}{x} = 0, \quad x - e^{-x} = 0, \quad x + \ln x = 0.$$

If you have a calculator with graphic or programming facilities it makes little difference which you use. But with a basic calculator it pays to use the form whose calculation involves the fewest key steps. This is probably the last, so take $f(x) = x + \ln x$.

The calculation then proceeds as follows.

$$f(0.5) = -0.193...,$$
$$f(0.6) = 0.089....$$

The root is between 0.5 and 0.6.

Since 0.193 is bigger than 0.089, the root is probably nearer to 0.6 rather than 0.5. Linear interpolation suggests trying 0.57.

So calculate

$$f(0.57) = 0.0078... \qquad (0.57 \text{ is too large}),$$
$$f(0.56) = -0.0198....$$

The root is between 0.56 and 0.57, and it is probably nearer to 0.57 than 0.56.

To confirm this, calculate $f(0.565) = -0.000\,59...$. Since this is negative, there is a sign change between 0.565 and 0.57. This shows that the root is 0.57, correct to 2 decimal places.

You can actually speed up the process a little by altering the procedure just before the end. Example 8.2.2, which is almost the same as Example 8.2.1, shows the speeded-up procedure.

Example 8.2.2

Solve the equation $x\,e^x = 1$ in the form $x + \ln x = 0$, giving the root correct to 3 decimal places.

Proceed in the same way as in Example 8.2.1, up to the point at which you find that the root lies between 0.56 and 0.57, and seems to be nearer to 0.57 than 0.56.

Now you might be tempted to try 0.567, but see what happens if you try 0.5675.

$f(0.5675) = 0.000\,985...$ (0.5675 is too big).

Now try 0.5665.

$f(0.5665) = -0.001\,778...$ (0.5665 is too small).

This shows directly that the root is 0.567, correct to 3 decimal places.

Exercise 8A

1 Show that there is a root of the equation $2x^3 - 3x^2 - 2x + 5 = 0$ between -1.5 and -1.

2 The equation $e^{-x} - x + 2 = 0$ has one root, α. Find an integer N such that $N < \alpha < N + 1$.

3 Given $f(x) = 3x + 13 - e^x$, evaluate $f(3)$ and $f(4)$, correct to three significant figures. Explain the significance of the answers in relation to the equation $3x + 13 = e^x$.

4 For each of parts (a) to (f),

   (i) use the sign-change rule to determine the integer N such that the equation $f(x) = 0$ has a root in the interval $N < x < N + 1$;

   (ii) use decimal search to find each root correct to two decimal places.

   (a) $f(x) = x^5 - 5x + 6$ (b) $f(x) = x + \sqrt{x^3 + 1} - 7$

   (c) $f(x) = e^x - \dfrac{5}{x}$ (d) $f(x) = 1000 - e^x \ln x$

   (e) $f(x) = \ln(x^2 + 1) - 12 - x$ (f) $f(x) = x^5 + x^3 - 1999$

5 The function $f(x)$ is such that $f(a)f(b) < 0$ for real constants a and b with $a < b$, yet $f(x) = 0$ for no value of x such that $a < x < b$. Explain the feature of the function which allows this situation to arise, and illustrate your answer with a suitable example.

8.3 Finding roots by iteration

Example 8.3.1

Find the terms of the sequence defined by the inductive definition $x_0 = 0$, $x_{r+1} = e^{-x_r}$.

The terms of the sequence are shown in Table 8.7. In the calculation all the available figures have been retained in the calculator, but the answers are tabulated correct to 5 decimal places.

From $r = 22$ onwards it seems that the values correct to 5 decimal places are all 0.567 14. This is especially convincing in this example, since you can notice that the terms are alternately below and above 0.567 14; so once you have two successive terms with this value, the same

r	x_r	r	x_r	r	x_r
0	0	9	0.571 14	18	0.567 12
1	1	10	0.564 88	19	0.567 16
2	0.367 88	11	0.568 43	20	0.567 14
3	0.692 20	12	0.566 41	21	0.567 15
4	0.500 47	13	0.567 56	22	0.567 14
5	0.606 24	14	0.566 91	23	0.567 14
6	0.545 40	15	0.567 28	24	0.567 14
7	0.579 61	16	0.567 07	. . .	. . .
8	0.560 12	17	0.567 19	. . .	. . .

Table 8.7

value will continue indefinitely. (You met a similar sequence in C2 Section 6.3. The sum sequence for a geometric series with common ratio -0.2 had terms alternately above and below 0.8333... .)

Notice also that the limit towards which these terms are converging appears to be the same (to the accuracy available) as the root of the equation $x = e^{-x}$ found in Examples 8.2.1 and 8.2.2. This is an example of a process called **iteration**, which can often be used to solve equations of the form $x = F(x)$.

> If the sequence given by the recursive definition $x_{r+1} = F(x_r)$, with some initial value x_0, converges to a limit l, then l is a root of the equation $x = F(x)$.

It is quite easy to see why. Since the sequence is given to be convergent, the left side x_{r+1} tends to l as $r \to \infty$, and the right side $F(x_r)$ tends to $F(l)$. (To be sure of this, the function $F(x)$ must be continuous.)

So $l = F(l)$; that is, l is a root of $x = F(x)$.

For another illustration take the equation $x^3 - 3x - 5 = 0$, for which the root was found earlier by the sign-change method. This can be rearranged as

$$x^3 = 3x + 5, \quad \text{or} \quad x = \sqrt[3]{3x + 5}.$$

This is of the form $x = F(x)$, so you can try to find the root by iteration, using a sequence defined by

$$x_{r+1} = \sqrt[3]{3x_r + 5}.$$

Fig. 8.3 suggests that the root is close to 2, so take $x_0 = 2$. Successive terms, correct to 5 decimal places, are then as shown in Table 8.8.

This suggests that the limit is 2.279 02, but this time you cannot be quite sure. Since the terms get steadily larger, rather than being alternately too large and too small, it is just possible that if you go on longer there might be another change in the final digit. So for a final check go back to the sign-change method. Writing $f(x) = x^3 - 3x - 5$, calculate

r	x_r	r	x_r	r	x_r
0	2	4	2.278 62	8	2.279 02
1	2.223 98	5	2.278 94	9	2.279 02
2	2.268 37	6	2.279 00	. . .	. . .
3	2.276 97	7	2.279 02	. . .	. . .

Table 8.8

$f(2.279\,015) = -0.000\,047...$ and $f(2.279\,025) = 0.000\,078....$. This shows that the root is indeed $2.279\,02$ correct to 5 decimal places.

At each step of this iteration you have to use the key sequence $\times$, 3, $+$, 5, $=$, $\sqrt[3]{}$ to get from one term to the next. If you have a calculator with an [ans] key, or if you set the process up as a small computer program or a spreadsheet, you can get the answer much more quickly.

8.4   Iterations which go wrong

There is more than one way of rearranging an equation $f(x) = 0$ as $x = F(x)$. For example, $x^3 - 3x - 5 = 0$ could be written as

$$3x = x^3 - 5, \quad \text{or} \quad x = \tfrac{1}{3}(x^3 - 5).$$

But if you perform the iteration

$$x_{r+1} = \tfrac{1}{3}(x_r^3 - 5), \quad \text{with } x_0 = 2,$$

the first few terms are

$$2, \ 1, \ -1.333\,33, \ -2.456\,79, \ -6.609\,58, \ -97.916\,54, \ \dots .$$

Clearly this is never going to converge to a limit.

The same can happen with the equation $xe^x = 1$. If, instead of constructing an iteration from $x = e^{-x}$, you write it as

$$\ln x = -x, \quad \text{or} \quad x = -\ln x,$$

then the corresponding iteration is

$$x_{r+1} = -\ln x_r.$$

You can't start with $x_0 = 0$ this time, so take x_0 to be 0.5. Then you get

$$0.5, \ 0.693\,15, \ 0.366\,51, \ 1.003\,72, \ -0.003\,71, \ \text{ERROR!}$$

The terms are alternately above and below the root, as they were in Example 8.3.1, but they get further away from it each time until you eventually get a term which is outside the domain of $\ln x$.

So if you have an equation $f(x) = 0$, and rearrange it as $x = F(x)$, then the sequence $x_{r+1} = F(x_r)$ may or may not converge to a limit. If it does, then the limit is a root of the equation. If not, you should try rearranging the equation another way.

Exercise 8B

1 For each of parts (a) to (c), find three possible rearrangements of the equation $f(x) = 0$ into the form $x = F(x)$.

(a) $f(x) = x^5 - 5x + 6$ (b) $f(x) = e^x - \dfrac{5}{x}$ (c) $f(x) = x^5 + x^3 - 1999$

2 A sequence is defined by the iteration $x_0 = 0$, $x_{r+1} = F(x_r)$ where $F(x) = \sqrt[11]{x^7 - 6}$.

(a) Rearrange the equation $x = F(x)$ into the form $f(x) = 0$, where f is a polynomial function.

(b) Use the iteration, with the given initial approximation x_0, to find the terms of the sequence $x_0, x_1, \ldots$ as far as x_5.

(c) Describe the behaviour of the sequence.

(d) If the sequence converges, investigate whether x_5 is an approximate root of $f(x) = 0$.

3 Repeat Question 2 for the sequences defined by

(i) $x_0 = 3$, $x_{r+1} = F(x_r)$ where $F(x) = \left(\dfrac{17 - x^2}{x}\right)^2$;

(ii) $x_0 = 7$, $x_{r+1} = F(x_r)$ where $F(x) = \sqrt[3]{500 + \dfrac{10}{x}}$

4 Show that the equation $x^5 + x - 19 = 0$ can be arranged into the form $x = \sqrt[3]{\dfrac{19 - x}{x^2}}$ and that the equation has a root α between $x = 1$ and $x = 2$.

Use an iteration based on this arrangement, with initial approximation $x_0 = 2$, to find the values of $x_1, x_2, \ldots, x_6$. Investigate whether this sequence is converging to α.

5 (a) Show that the equation $x^2 + 2x - e^x = 0$ has a root in the interval $2 < x < 3$.

(b) Use an iterative method based on the re-arrangement $x = \sqrt{e^x - 2x}$, with initial approximation $x_0 = 2$, to find the value of x_{10} to four decimal places. Describe what is happening to the terms of this sequence of approximations.

6 Show that the equation $e^x = x^3 - 2$ can be arranged into the form $x = \ln(x^3 - 2)$. Show also that it has a root between 2 and 3.

Use the iteration $x_{r+1} = \ln\left(x_r^3 - 2\right)$, commencing with $x_0 = 2$ as an initial approximation to the root, to show that this arrangement is not a suitable one for finding this root.

Find an alternative arrangement of $e^x = x^3 - 2$ which can be used to find this root, and use it to calculate the root correct to two decimal places.

7 (a) Determine the value of the positive integer N such that the equation $12 - x - \ln x = 0$ has a root α such that $N < \alpha < N + 1$.

(b) Define the sequence $x_0, x_1, \ldots$ of approximations to α iteratively by $x_0 = N + \frac{1}{2}$, $x_{r+1} = 12 - \ln x_r$.

Find the number of steps required before two consecutive terms of this sequence are the same when rounded to 4 significant figures. Show that this common value is equal to α to this degree of accuracy.

8.5*   Choosing convergent iterations

The rest of this chapter is about how to rearrange an equation to ensure that the iterative sequence converges. You may if you like omit it and go on to Miscellaneous Exercise 8. The issue of convergence will be explored in more detail in FP2 Chapter 8.

The solution of $x = F(x)$ can be represented graphically by the intersection of the graph of $y = F(x)$ with the line $y = x$. Fig. 8.9 shows this for the equations in the last two sections, each with two alternative forms.

(a) $xe^x = 1$ (b) $x^3 - 3x - 5 = 0$

(i) $x = e^{-x}$ (ii) $x = -\ln x$ (i) $x = \sqrt[3]{3x + 5}$ (ii) $x = \dfrac{x^3 - 5}{3}$

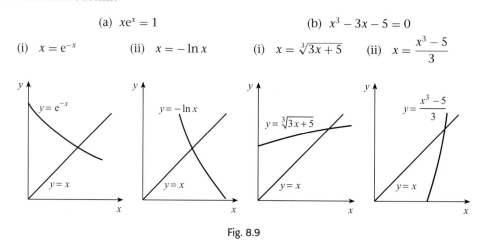

Fig. 8.9

In both cases the sequence converged in version (i), but not in version (ii).

Inspection of the graphs suggests that it is the gradient of the graph of $y = F(x)$ at or near the root which governs the nature of the iteration.

In (a)(i) the gradient is negative, but numerically quite small (about -0.5). The sequence converges, though quite slowly; it takes 22 steps to reach the root correct to 5 decimal places. The terms alternate above and below the root.

In (a)(ii) the gradient is negative, but numerically much larger (about -2). The sequence does not converge, but the terms again alternate above and below the root.

In (b)(i) the gradient is positive, and numerically small (about 0.2). The sequence converges quite fast, taking only 7 steps to reach the root correct to 5 decimal places. The terms get steadily larger, approaching the root from below.

In (b)(ii) the gradient is positive and numerically large (about 5). The sequence does not converge, and the terms get steadily smaller.

This points to the following conclusions, which are generally true. You can test these further for yourself from the sequences which you produced in Exercise 8B.

- If the equation $x = F(x)$ has a root, then a sequence defined by $x_{r+1} = F(x_r)$ with a starting value close to the root will converge if the gradient of the graph of $y = F(x)$ at and around the root is not too large (roughly between -1 and 1).

- The smaller the modulus of the gradient, the fewer steps will be needed to reach the root to a given accuracy.

- If the gradient is negative the terms will be alternately above and below the root; if it is positive, the terms will approach the root steadily from one side.

There is one further point to notice about these examples. The pairs of functions used for $F(x)$ are in fact inverses.

(a) $x \to$ [change sign] $\to$ [exp] $\to$ has output e^{-x},
    $\leftarrow$ [change sign] $\leftarrow$ [ln] $\leftarrow x$ (read right to left) has output $- \ln x$

(b) $x \to$ [×3] $\to$ [+5] $\to$ [$\sqrt[3]{}$] $\to$ has output $\sqrt[3]{3x + 5}$,
    $\leftarrow$ [÷3] $\leftarrow$ [-5] $\leftarrow$ [( )^3] $\leftarrow x$ has output $\frac{1}{3}(x^3 - 5)$.

Their graphs are therefore reflections of each other in the line $y = x$ (see Section 2.9). This is why, if the gradient of one graph is numerically small, the gradient of the other is large. This leads to a useful rule for deciding how to rearrange an equation.

If the function F is one-one, and if $x = F(x)$ has a root, then usually one of the sequences $x_{r+1} = F(x_r)$ and $x_{r+1} = F^{-1}(x_r)$ converges to the root, but the other does not.

Example 8.5.1
Show that the equation $x^3 - 3x - 1 = 0$ has three roots, and find them correct to 4 decimal places.

The graph of $y = x^3 - 3x - 1$ is shown in Fig. 8.10. It is in fact the graph in Fig. 8.3 translated by $+4$ in the y-direction. You can see that it cuts the x-axis in three places: between -2 and -1, -1 and 0, and 1 and 2.

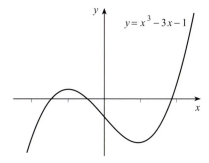

Fig. 8.10

You could use iterations based on a rearrangement $x = F(x)$, where $F(x)$ is either $\frac{1}{3}(x^3 - 1)$ or $\sqrt[3]{3x+1}$. These are illustrated in Fig. 8.11; again, they are inverse functions. To get a small gradient at the intersection, you should use $F(x) = \sqrt[3]{3x+1}$ for the first and last of the roots, and $F(x) = \frac{1}{3}(x^3 - 1)$ for the middle root.

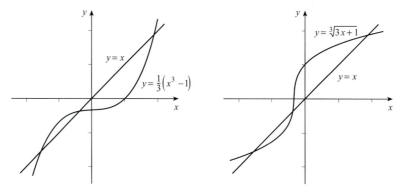

Fig. 8.11

You can check for yourself that:

$x_{r+1} = \sqrt[3]{3x_r + 1}$ with $x_0 = -2$ reaches the root -1.5321 in 11 steps,

$x_{r+1} = \frac{1}{3}(x_r^3 - 1)$ with $x_0 = 0$ reaches the root -0.3473 in 4 steps,

$x_{r+1} = \sqrt[3]{3x_r + 1}$ with $x_0 = 0$ reaches the root 1.8794 in 6 steps.

The next example shows a trick which you can use to reduce the number of steps needed to reach the root, or even to produce a convergent iteration from one which does not converge.

Example 8.5.2
For each of the equations (a) $x = e^{-x}$, (b) $x = -\ln x$, add an extra term kx to both sides, and choose k so that, near the root, the function on the right has a small gradient. Use this to produce a sequence which converges rapidly to the root.

(a) Write $kx + x = kx + e^{-x}$. You saw earlier that near the root the graph of e^{-x} has a gradient of about -0.5, so $kx + e^{-x}$ has a gradient of about $k - 0.5$. To make this small, choose $k = 0.5$. Then the equation becomes

$$1.5x = 0.5x + e^{-x}, \quad \text{or} \quad x = \tfrac{1}{3}(x + 2e^{-x}).$$

The iteration $x_{r+1} = \frac{1}{3}(x_r + 2e^{-x_r})$ with $x_0 = 1$ reaches the root $0.567\,14$, correct to 5 decimal places, in 4 steps. (In Example 8.3.1 it took 22 steps of the iteration $x_{r+1} = e^{-x_r}$ to achieve the same accuracy.)

(b) Write $kx + x = kx - \ln x$. Near the root the graph of $-\ln x$ has a gradient of about -2, so $kx - \ln x$ has a gradient of about $k - 2$. Choose $k = 2$, so that the equation becomes

$$3x = 2x - \ln x, \quad \text{or} \quad x = \tfrac{1}{3}(2x - \ln x).$$

The iteration $x_{r+1} = \frac{1}{3}(2x_r - \ln x_r)$ with $x_0 = 1$ reaches the root in 6 steps. (You saw in Section 8.4 that the iteration $x_{r+1} = -\ln x_r$ does not even converge.)

Exercise 8C*

1 In parts (a) to (f), use a graphic calculator to display the graph of $y = F(x)$, and hence decide whether the iteration $x_{r+1} = F(x_r)$, with initial approximation x_0, is suitable for finding the root of the equation $x = F(x)$ near to $x = x_0$.

Where the process leads to a convergent sequence of approximations to the required root, find this root. Where the process is unsuitable, find $F^{-1}(x)$ and use it to find the root.

Give your answers correct to 3 decimal places.

(a) $F(x) = \dfrac{3}{x} - 1$, $x_0 = 1$

(b) $F(x) = 5 - e^{3x}$, $x_0 = 0$

(c) $F(x) = \sqrt[3]{17 - x^2}$, $x_0 = 3$

(d) $F(x) = 30 - \frac{1}{10}x^6$, $x_0 = -2$

(e) $F(x) = 8 + \ln(x^2 + 7)$, $x_0 = 10$

(f) $F(x) = \dfrac{3}{20 - x^2}$, $x_0 = 4$

2 In each of parts (a) to (d) find a constant k for which

$$kx_{r+1} + x_{r+1} = kx_r + F(x_r)$$

is a better form than $x_{r+1} = F(x_r)$ to use to find the root of the equation $x = F(x)$ near x_0. In each case, find this root correct to 4 significant figures.

(a) $F(x) = 2 - 5\ln x$, $x_0 = 1$

(b) $F(x) = x^2 + 6\ln x - 50$, $x_0 = 6$

(c) $F(x) = \frac{1}{48}(x^4 - x^7 - 192)$, $x_0 = -2$

(d) $F(x) = e^x - x^2 - 2$, $x_0 = 2$

Miscellaneous exercise 8

1 Given that $f(x) = 2^x + 3^x$, evaluate $f(1)$ and $f(2)$. Using these values,

(a) state what this tells you about the root of the equation $f(x) = 10$,

(b) suggest a suitable initial approximation to this root.

2 Find the positive integer N such that $40e^{-x} = x^2$ has a root between N and $N + 1$.

3 Show that there exists a root, $x = \alpha$, of the equation $x^3 - 6x + 3 = 0$ such that $2 < \alpha < 3$. Use decimal search to find this root correct to two decimal places.

4 Show that the equation $2x - \ln(x^2 + 2) = 0$ has a root in the interval $0.3 < x < 0.4$. Use decimal search to find an interval of width 0.001 in which this root lies.

5 The equation $e^x = 50\sqrt{2x - 1}$ has two positive real roots. Use decimal search to find the larger root correct to one decimal place.

6 (a) On the same diagram, sketch the graphs of $y = 2^{-x}$ and $y = x^2$.

   (b) One of the points of intersection of these graphs has a positive x-coordinate. Find this x-coordinate correct to 2 decimal places and give a brief indication of your method.   (OCR)

7 (a) On a single diagram, sketch the graphs of $y = \tan x$ and $y = 4\cos x - 3$ for $0° \leqslant x \leqslant 180°$. Deduce the number of angles satisfying the equation $f(x) = 0$ for $0° \leqslant x \leqslant 180°$, where $f(x) = 3 + \tan x - 4\cos x$.

   (b) By evaluating $f(x)$ for suitably chosen values of x, show that a root of the equation $f(x) = 0$ occurs at $x = 28°$ (correct to the nearest degree).

8 Show that there is an angle α satisfying the equation $2\sin x - \cos x + 1 = 0$ such that $230° < \alpha < 240°$. Use a decimal search method to determine this angle to the nearest $0.1°$.

9 The points A and B have coordinates $(0, -2)$ and $(-30, 0)$ respectively.

   (a) Find an equation of the line which passes through A and B.

   The function f is defined by $f(x) = 1 + \tan 0.02x$, $-\frac{1}{2}\pi < x < \frac{1}{2}\pi$.

   (b) Explain why there is just one point where the line in (a) meets the graph of $y = f(x)$.

   (c) Use an appropriate method to find the value of the integer N such that the value of the x-coordinate of the point where the graph of $y = f(x)$ meets the line of part (a) satisfies $N < x < N + 1$. (OCR, adapted)

10 Find, correct to two decimal places, the x-coordinate of the turning point on the curve with equation $y = x^3 - 50x + 7e^x$, $x \geqslant 0$.

11 The region, R, of the plane enclosed by the axes, the curve $y = e^x + 4$ and the line $x = 2$ has area A. Find, correct to four significant figures, the value of m, $0 < m < 2$, such that the portion of R between the y-axis and the line $x = m$ has area $\frac{1}{2}A$.

12 Show that the equation $3.5x = 1.6^x$ has a real solution between 6 and 7. By rearranging the equation into the form $x = a + b\ln x$, determine this root correct to two decimal places.

13 (a) Given that $f(x) = e^{2x} - 6x$, find $f(0)$. Evaluate $f(1)$, giving your answer correct to three decimal places. Explain how the equation $f(x) = 0$ could still have a root in the interval $0 < x < 1$ even though $f(0)f(1) > 0$.

   (b) Rewrite the equation $f(x) = 0$ in the form $x = F(x)$, for some suitable function F. Taking $x_0 = 0.5$ as an initial approximation, use an iterative method to determine one of the roots of this equation correct to three decimal places. How could you demonstrate that this root has the required degree of accuracy?

   (c) Deduce the value, to two decimal places, of one of the roots of the equation $e^x - 3x = 0$.

14 (a) Show that the equation $x^3 - 3x^2 - 1 = 0$ has a root α between $x = 3$ and $x = 4$.

   (b) The iterative formula $x_{r+1} = 3 + \dfrac{1}{x_r^2}$ is used to calculate a sequence of approximations to this root. Taking $x_0 = 3$ as an initial approximation to α, determine the values of x_1, x_2, x_3 and x_4 correct to 5 decimal places. State the value of α to 3 decimal places and justify this degree of accuracy.

15* (a) Show that the equation $x + \ln x - 4 = 0$ has a root α in the interval $2 < x < 3$.

(b) Find which of the two iterative forms $x_{r+1} = e^{4-x_r}$ and $x_{r+1} = 4 - \ln x_r$ is more likely to give a convergent sequence of approximations to α, giving a reason for your answer. Use your chosen form to determine α correct to two decimal places.

16* (a) Find the positive integer N such that the equation $(t - 1) \ln 4 = \ln(9t)$ has a solution $t = r$ in the interval $N < t < N + 1$.

(b) Write down two possible rearrangements of this equation in the form $t = F(t)$ and $t = F^{-1}(t)$. Show which of these two arrangements is more suitable for using iteratively to determine an approximation to r to three decimal places, and find such an approximation.

17* (a) Find the coordinates of the points of intersection of the graphs with equations $y = x$ and $y = g(x)$, where $g(x) = \dfrac{5}{x}$.

(b) Show that the iterative process defined by $x_0 = 2$, $x_{r+1} = g(x_r)$ can't be used to find good approximations to the positive root of the equation $x = \dfrac{5}{x}$.

(c) Describe why the use of the inverse function $g^{-1}(x)$ is also inappropriate in this case.

(d) Use a graph to explain why the iterative process defined by

$$x_0 = 2, \ x_{r+1} = \tfrac{1}{2} \left(x_r + \frac{5}{x_r} \right)$$

leads to a convergent sequence of approximations to this root. Find this root correct to six decimal places.

18* (a) Use graphs to show that the equation $f(x) = 0$, where $f(x) = \cos x + 2x - 2$, has only one root. Denote this root by α.

(b) Show that, if $a_0 = 0.56$ and $b_0 = 0.64$ then $b_0 - a_0 = 10$ and $a_0 < \alpha < b_0$.

(c) Evaluate $f(m)$, where $m = \tfrac{1}{2}(a_0 + b_0)$. Determine whether $a_0 < \alpha < m$ or $m < \alpha < b_0$. Hence write down a pair of numbers, a_1 and b_1, such that $b_1 - a_1 = 0.04$ and $a_1 < \alpha < b_1$.

(d) Use a method similar to part (c) to find a pair of numbers, a_2 and b_2, such that $b_2 - a_2 = 0.02$ and $a_2 < \alpha < b_2$.

(e) Continuing this way, find a sequence of pairs of numbers, a_r and b_r, such that $b_r - a_r = 0.08 \times 2^{-r}$ and $a_r < \alpha < b_r$. Go on until you find two numbers of the sequence which enable you to write down the value of α correct to 3 decimal places. (This is called the 'bisection method'.)

19 Given the one–one function $F(x)$, explain why roots of the equation $F(x) = F^{-1}(x)$ are also roots of the equation $x = F(x)$.

Use this to solve the equations

(a) $x^3 - 1 = \sqrt[3]{1 + x}$,   (b) $\tfrac{1}{10} e^x = \ln(10x)$.

9 The chain rule

This chapter is about differentiating more general composite functions than those in Chapter 4. When you have completed it, you should

- be able to differentiate composite functions
- be able to apply differentiation to rates of change, and to related rates of change.

You can omit Sections 9.2 and 9.3 on a first reading. The exercises are independent of it.

9.1 The chain rule: an informal treatment

When you differentiate $(ax + b)^n$ by using the methods of Section 4.1, you are actually differentiating the composite function

$$x \rightarrow [\times, a, +, b, =] \rightarrow ax + b \rightarrow [\text{ raise to power } n] \rightarrow (ax + b)^n.$$

It is now time to generalise to composite functions such as $\ln(x^2 + 1)$, shown by

$$x \rightarrow [\text{ square}, +, 1, =] \rightarrow x^2 + 1 \rightarrow [\ln] \rightarrow \ln(x^2 + 1).$$

However, it is worth beginning with an easier example.

Example 9.1.1

Find the derivative of the composite function
$$x \rightarrow [\times, a, +, b, =] \rightarrow ax + b \rightarrow [\times, c, +, d, =] \rightarrow c(ax + b) + d.$$

If you let $y = c(ax + b) + d$, then

$$\frac{dy}{dx} = \frac{d}{dx}(c(ax + b) + d) = \frac{d}{dx}(cax + cb + d) = ca.$$

However, if you let u stand for the intermediate output $ax + b$, then $y = cu + d$.

So $\quad \dfrac{dy}{du} = c$ and $\dfrac{du}{dx} = a$, and $\dfrac{dy}{dx} = ca$. That is, $\dfrac{dy}{dx} = \dfrac{dy}{du} \times \dfrac{du}{dx}$.

You can think of this another way, by considering rates of change. Recall that:

- $\dfrac{dy}{dx}$ is the rate at which y changes with respect to x

- $\dfrac{dy}{du}$ is the rate at which y changes with respect to u

- $\dfrac{du}{dx}$ is the rate at which u changes with respect to x.

The equation $\dfrac{dy}{du} = c$ means that y is changing c times as fast as u; similarly u is changing a times as fast as x. It is natural to think that if y is changing c times as fast as u, and u is changing a times as fast as x, then y is changing $c \times a$ times as fast as x. Thus, again,

$$\frac{dy}{dx} = \frac{dy}{du} \times \frac{du}{dx}.$$

Example 9.1.2

Find $\dfrac{dy}{dx}$ when $y = (1 + x^2)^3$.

So far there has been no alternative to expanding by the binomial theorem. You have had to write

$$y = (1 + x^2)^3 = 1 + 3x^2 + 3x^4 + x^6.$$
$$\frac{dy}{dx} = 6x + 12x^3 + 6x^5 = 6x(1 + 2x^2 + x^4)$$
$$= 6x(1 + x^2)^2.$$

But now the relation $\dfrac{dy}{dx} = \dfrac{dy}{du} \times \dfrac{du}{dx}$ suggests another approach. If you substitute $u = 1 + x^2$, so that $y = u^3$, then

$$\frac{dy}{du} = 3u^2 = 3(1 + x^2)^2 \text{ and } \frac{du}{dx} = 2x.$$

So $\qquad \dfrac{dy}{du} \times \dfrac{du}{dx} = 3(1 + x^2)^2 \times 2x = 6x(1 + x^2)^2.$

So once again $\dfrac{dy}{dx} = \dfrac{dy}{du} \times \dfrac{du}{dx}.$

Assume now that this result, known as the chain rule, holds in all cases. It is also sometimes called the 'composite function' rule, or the 'function of a function' rule.

The chain rule is extremely easy to remember because the term du appears to cancel, but bear in mind that this is simply a helpful feature of the notation. Cancellation has no meaning in this context, but you can take full advantage of the notation.

> **The chain rule**
> If $y = g(f(x))$, and $u = f(x)$ so that $y = g(u)$, then $\dfrac{dy}{dx} = \dfrac{dy}{du} \times \dfrac{du}{dx}.$

A proof is given in Section 9.2, but you can omit the proof on a first reading.

Example 9.1.3

Differentiate $y = (2x + 1)^{\frac{1}{2}}$ with respect to x.

Substitute $u = 2x + 1$, so that $y = u^{\frac{1}{2}}$. Then $\dfrac{dy}{du} = \frac{1}{2}u^{-\frac{1}{2}} = \frac{1}{2}(2x + 1)^{-\frac{1}{2}}$ and $\dfrac{du}{dx} = 2.$

As $\dfrac{dy}{dx} = \dfrac{dy}{du} \times \dfrac{du}{dx}, \dfrac{dy}{dx} = \frac{1}{2}(2x + 1)^{-\frac{1}{2}} \times 2 = (2x + 1)^{-\frac{1}{2}} = \dfrac{1}{\sqrt{2x + 1}}.$

Example 9.1.4

Find $\dfrac{dy}{dx}$ when   (a) $y = \ln(1 + x^2)$,   (b) $y = e^{-x^2}$,   (c) $y = \sqrt{1 - x^2}$.

(a) Substitute $u = 1 + x^2$, so $y = \ln u$. Then $\dfrac{dy}{du} = \dfrac{1}{u} = \dfrac{1}{1 + x^2}$ and $\dfrac{du}{dx} = 2x$.

So $\dfrac{dy}{dx} = \dfrac{dy}{du} \times \dfrac{du}{dx} = \dfrac{1}{1 + x^2} \times 2x = \dfrac{2x}{1 + x^2}$.

(b) Substitute $u = -x^2$, so $y = e^u$. Then $\dfrac{dy}{du} = e^u = e^{-x^2}$ and $\dfrac{du}{dx} = -2x$.

So $\dfrac{dy}{dx} = \dfrac{dy}{du} \times \dfrac{du}{dx} = e^{-x^2} \times (-2x) = -2xe^{-x^2}$.

(c) Substitute $u = 1 - x^2$, so $y = \sqrt{u} = u^{\frac{1}{2}}$. Then $\dfrac{dy}{du} = \tfrac{1}{2}u^{-\frac{1}{2}} = \dfrac{1}{2\sqrt{u}} = \dfrac{1}{2\sqrt{1 - x^2}}$

and $\dfrac{du}{dx} = -2x$. So $\dfrac{dy}{dx} = \dfrac{dy}{du} \times \dfrac{du}{dx} = \dfrac{1}{2\sqrt{1 - x^2}} \times (-2x) = \dfrac{-x}{\sqrt{1 - x^2}}$.

Exercise 9A

1 Use the substitution $u = 5x + 3$ to differentiate

(a) $y = (5x + 3)^6$,   (b) $y = (5x + 3)^{\frac{1}{2}}$,   (c) $y = \ln(5x + 3)$,

with respect to x.

2 Use the substitution $u = 1 - 4x$ to differentiate

(a) $y = (1 - 4x)^5$,   (b) $y = (1 - 4x)^{-3}$,   (c) $y = e^{1-4x}$,

with respect to x.

3 Use the substitution $u = 1 + x^3$ to differentiate

(a) $y = (1 + x^3)^5$,   (b) $y = (1 + x^3)^{-4}$,   (c) $y = \ln(1 + x^3)$,

with respect to x.

4 Use the substitution $u = 2x^2 + 3$ to differentiate

(a) $y = (2x^2 + 3)^6$,   (b) $y = \dfrac{1}{2x^2 + 3}$,   (c) $y = \dfrac{1}{\sqrt{2x^2 + 3}}$,

with respect to x.

5 Differentiate $y = (2x^3 + 1)^3$ with respect to x

(a) by using the binomial theorem to expand $y = (2x^3 + 1)^3$ and then differentiating term by term,

(b) by using the chain rule.

Check that your answers are the same.

6 Differentiate $y = (3x^4 + 2)^2$ with respect to x by using the chain rule. Confirm your answer by expanding $(3x^4 + 2)^2$ and then differentiating.

7 Use appropriate substitutions to differentiate

(a) $y = (x^5 + 1)^4$, (b) $y = (2x^3 - 1)^8$, (c) $y = (e^{2x} + 3)^6$, (d) $y = (\sqrt{x} - 1)^5$,

with respect to x.

8 Differentiate the following with respect to x; try to do this without writing down the substitutions.

(a) $y = (x^2 + 6)^4$ (b) $y = (5x^3 + 4)^3$ (c) $y = (x^4 - 8)^7$ (d) $y = (2 - x^9)^5$

9 Differentiate the following with respect to x.

(a) $y = \sqrt{4x + 3}$ (b) $y = (x^2 + 4)^6$ (c) $y = (6x^3 - 5)^{-2}$ (d) $y = (5 - x^3)^{-1}$

10 Differentiate the following with respect to x.

(a) $y = (\ln x + 1)^6$ (b) $y = \left(\dfrac{1}{x} + 2\right)^4$ (c) $y = \frac{1}{2} \ln(2 + x^4)$ (d) $y = 3(e^{-x} + 1)^5$

11 Given that $f(x) = \dfrac{1}{1 + x^2}$, find

(a) $f'(2)$, (b) the value of x such that $f'(x) = 0$.

12 Given that $y = \sqrt[4]{x^3 + 8}$, find the value of $\dfrac{dy}{dx}$ when $x = 2$.

13 Given that $y = \dfrac{5}{1 + e^{3x}}$, find the value of $\dfrac{dy}{dx}$ when $x = 0$.

14 Differentiate with respect to x

(a) $y = (x^2 + 3x + 1)^6$, (b) $y = \ln(x^3 + 4x)$, (c) $y = \dfrac{1}{(x^2 + 5x)^3}$, (d) $y = 2e^{x^2 + x + 1}$.

15 Find the equation of the tangent to the curve $y = (x^2 - 5)^3$ at the point $(2, -1)$.

16 Find the equation of the tangent to the curve $y = \dfrac{1}{\sqrt{x} - 1}$ at the point $(4, 1)$.

17 Find the equation of the normal to the curve $y = \dfrac{8}{1 - x^3}$ at the point $(-1, 4)$.

18 Use the substitutions $u = x^2 - 1$ and $v = \sqrt{u} + 1$ with the chain rule in the form
$\dfrac{dy}{dx} = \dfrac{dy}{dv} \times \dfrac{dv}{du} \times \dfrac{du}{dx}$ to differentiate $y = (\sqrt{x^2 - 1} + 1)^6$.

19 Use two substitutions to find $\dfrac{d}{dx} e^{\sqrt{1 - x^2}}$.

20 A curve has equation $y = (x^2 + 1)^4 + 2(x^2 + 1)^3$. Show that $\dfrac{dy}{dx} = 4x(x^2 + 1)^2(2x^2 + 5)$ and hence show that the curve has just one stationary point. State the coordinates of the stationary point and, by considering the gradient of the curve either side of the stationary point, determine its nature.

9.2*   Deriving the chain rule

You may omit this section if you wish.

In C1 Sections 5.8 and 12.1 you met $\dfrac{dy}{dx}$ as $\dfrac{dy}{dx} = \lim\limits_{\delta x \to 0} \dfrac{\delta y}{\delta x}$.

Similarly, simply by changing the letters in the definition, $\dfrac{dy}{du} = \lim\limits_{\delta u \to 0} \dfrac{\delta y}{\delta u}$ and $\dfrac{du}{dx} = \lim\limits_{\delta x \to 0} \dfrac{\delta u}{\delta x}$.
Now, in these expressions, when y is a function of u, where u is a function of x, then as x changes u changes and so y changes.

Take a particular value of x, and increase x by δx with a corresponding increase of δu in the value of u, which, in turn, increases the value of y by δy. Then

$$\frac{\delta y}{\delta x} = \frac{\delta y}{\delta u} \times \frac{\delta u}{\delta x}$$

because δy, δu and δx are numbers which you can cancel, assuming that $\delta u \neq 0$.

To find $\dfrac{dy}{dx}$, you must take the limit as $\delta x \to 0$, so

$$\frac{dy}{dx} = \lim_{\delta x \to 0} \frac{\delta y}{\delta x} = \lim_{\delta x \to 0} \left(\frac{\delta y}{\delta u} \times \frac{\delta u}{\delta x} \right).$$

Assuming that as $\delta x \to 0$, $\delta u \to 0$ and that $\lim\limits_{\delta x \to 0} \left(\dfrac{\delta y}{\delta u} \times \dfrac{\delta u}{\delta x} \right) = \lim\limits_{\delta x \to 0} \left(\dfrac{\delta y}{\delta u} \right) \times \lim\limits_{\delta x \to 0} \left(\dfrac{\delta u}{\delta x} \right)$, it follows that

$$\frac{dy}{dx} = \lim_{\delta x \to 0} \frac{\delta y}{\delta x} = \lim_{\delta x \to 0} \left(\frac{\delta y}{\delta u} \times \frac{\delta u}{\delta x} \right)$$

$$= \lim_{\delta x \to 0} \left(\frac{\delta y}{\delta u} \right) \times \lim_{\delta x \to 0} \left(\frac{\delta u}{\delta x} \right) = \lim_{\delta u \to 0} \left(\frac{\delta y}{\delta u} \right) \times \lim_{\delta x \to 0} \left(\frac{\delta u}{\delta x} \right)$$

$$= \frac{dy}{du} \times \frac{du}{dx}.$$

This result, $\dfrac{dy}{dx} = \dfrac{dy}{du} \times \dfrac{du}{dx}$, is the chain rule for differentiating composite functions.

Note that the results in Section 4.1 are particular cases of the chain rule since, if $u = ax + b$, $\dfrac{du}{dx} = a$.

9.3*   An application of the chain rule

The chain rule enables you to extend the rule $\dfrac{d}{dx} x^n = nx^{n-1}$ to all real values of n.

> Note that, since C1 Section 8.4, you have been assuming this result for rational values of n without proof.
>
> The proof which follows applies only when $x > 0$, but it can be extended to negative values of x provided that x^n still has a meaning when $x < 0$. (See Miscellaneous Exercise 9 Question 19.)

Begin by writing x in the unusual form $x = e^{\ln x}$. Then you can write $x^n = (e^{\ln x})^n = e^{n \ln x}$. Letting $u = n \ln x$ and differentiating,

$$\frac{d}{dx}(e^u) = e^u \times \frac{du}{dx}$$

$$= e^{n \ln x} \times \frac{n}{x} = x^n \times \frac{n}{x}$$

$$= nx^{n-1}.$$

9.4 Related rates of change

You frequently need to be able to calculate the rate at which one quantity varies with another when one of them is time. In C1 Section 12.1 it was shown that if r is some quantity, then the rate of change of r with respect to time t is $\dfrac{dr}{dt}$.

Suppose now that there is some other quantity, s, which depends on r. Then as r changes, s will also change. If you know the rate of change of r, how can you find the rate of change of s?

The situation here is best described by a problem.

Example 9.4.1
Suppose that a spherical balloon is being inflated at a constant rate of 5 m^3 s^{-1}. At a particular moment, the radius of the balloon is 4 metres. Find how fast the radius of the balloon is increasing at that instant.

There are two rates of change in this problem: the rate at which the volume is increasing, given to be 5 m^3 s^{-1}, and the rate at which the radius is increasing. If, when the balloon has been inflating for t seconds, the radius is r metres, these rates of change would be $\dfrac{dV}{dt}$ and $\dfrac{dr}{dt}$. You are given that $\dfrac{dV}{dt} = 5$, and you are asked to find $\dfrac{dr}{dt}$ when $r = 4$.

Your other piece of information is that the balloon is spherical, so that $V = \frac{4}{3}\pi r^3$.

The key to solving the problem is to use the chain rule in the form

$$\frac{dV}{dt} = \frac{dV}{dr} \times \frac{dr}{dt}.$$

You can now use $\dfrac{dV}{dr} = 4\pi r^2$. Substituting the various values into the chain rule formula gives

$$5 = (4\pi \times 4^2) \times \frac{dr}{dt}.$$

Therefore, rearranging this equation, you find that $\dfrac{dr}{dt} = \dfrac{5}{64\pi}$, so the radius is increasing at $\dfrac{5}{64\pi}$ m s^{-1}.

In practice you do not need to write down so much detail, as you will see in the following examples.

Example 9.4.2

A cylinder has radius r and length $2r$. On each end, there is a hemisphere of radius r. Show that the volume of the whole solid is given by $V = \frac{10}{3}\pi r^3$. The value of r is increasing at $0.02\,\text{m}\,\text{s}^{-1}$. Calculate the rate of increase of the volume of the whole solid when the radius of the cylinder is 0.1 m.

The volume consists of two parts, the cylinder and the two hemispheres, so

$$V = 2r \times \pi r^2 + 2 \times \tfrac{2}{3}\pi r^3 = \tfrac{10}{3}\pi r^3.$$

As $\dfrac{\mathrm{d}V}{\mathrm{d}t} = \dfrac{\mathrm{d}V}{\mathrm{d}r} \times \dfrac{\mathrm{d}r}{\mathrm{d}t}$ and $V = \tfrac{10}{3}\pi r^3$, $\dfrac{\mathrm{d}r}{\mathrm{d}t} = 0.02$ and $r = 0.1$,

$$\begin{aligned}
\frac{\mathrm{d}V}{\mathrm{d}t} &= 10\pi r^2 \times 0.02 \\
&= 10\pi \times 0.1^2 \times 0.02 \\
&= 0.002\pi.
\end{aligned}$$

The rate of increase of volume of the solid is $0.002\pi\,\text{m}^3\,\text{s}^{-1}$, or about $6.28 \times 10^{-3}\,\text{m}^3\,\text{s}^{-1}$.

Example 9.4.3

The surface area of a cube is increasing at a constant rate of $24\,\text{cm}^2\,\text{s}^{-1}$. Find the rate at which its volume is increasing at the moment when the volume is $216\,\text{cm}^3$.

Let the side of the cube be x cm at time t seconds, the surface area be S cm^2 and the volume be V cm^3.

Then $S = 6x^2$, $V = x^3$ and $\dfrac{\mathrm{d}S}{\mathrm{d}t} = 24$, and you need to find $\dfrac{\mathrm{d}V}{\mathrm{d}t}$ when $V = 216$, which is when $x^3 = 216$, or $x = 6$.

> If you know S and want to find V you would need to go via x. Similarly, when you know $\dfrac{\mathrm{d}S}{\mathrm{d}t}$ and want to find $\dfrac{\mathrm{d}V}{\mathrm{d}t}$ you should expect to go via $\dfrac{\mathrm{d}x}{\mathrm{d}t}$.

From the chain rule, $\dfrac{\mathrm{d}S}{\mathrm{d}t} = \dfrac{\mathrm{d}S}{\mathrm{d}x} \times \dfrac{\mathrm{d}x}{\mathrm{d}t}$, and $S = 6x^2$.

Therefore $\dfrac{\mathrm{d}S}{\mathrm{d}t} = 12x\dfrac{\mathrm{d}x}{\mathrm{d}t}$. When $x = 6$, $\dfrac{\mathrm{d}S}{\mathrm{d}t} = 12 \times 6 \times \dfrac{\mathrm{d}x}{\mathrm{d}t}$.

But you are given that $\dfrac{\mathrm{d}S}{\mathrm{d}t} = 24$, so $24 = 12 \times 6 \times \dfrac{\mathrm{d}x}{\mathrm{d}t}$, giving $\dfrac{\mathrm{d}x}{\mathrm{d}t} = \tfrac{1}{3}$.

Now that you know $\dfrac{\mathrm{d}x}{\mathrm{d}t}$, you can find $\dfrac{\mathrm{d}V}{\mathrm{d}t}$ by using the chain rule again, in the form $\dfrac{\mathrm{d}V}{\mathrm{d}t} = \dfrac{\mathrm{d}V}{\mathrm{d}x} \times \dfrac{\mathrm{d}x}{\mathrm{d}t}$. As $V = x^3$, $\dfrac{\mathrm{d}V}{\mathrm{d}x} = 3x^2$, giving $\dfrac{\mathrm{d}V}{\mathrm{d}t} = 3x^2\dfrac{\mathrm{d}x}{\mathrm{d}t}$.

When $x = 6$, $\dfrac{\mathrm{d}V}{\mathrm{d}t} = 3 \times 6^2 \times \dfrac{\mathrm{d}x}{\mathrm{d}t} = 108\dfrac{\mathrm{d}x}{\mathrm{d}t}$.

Substituting $\dfrac{\mathrm{d}x}{\mathrm{d}t} = \tfrac{1}{3}$ into this equation, $\dfrac{\mathrm{d}V}{\mathrm{d}t} = 108 \times \tfrac{1}{3} = 36$.

Therefore the volume is increasing at a rate of $36\,\text{cm}^3\,\text{s}^{-1}$.

Exercise 9B

1   The length of the side of a square is increasing at a constant rate of 1.2 cm s^{-1}. At the moment when the length of the side is 10 cm, find

   (a) the rate of increase of the perimeter,   (b) the rate of increase of the area.

2   The length of the edge of a cube is increasing at a constant rate of 0.5 mm s^{-1}. At the moment when the length of the edge is 40 mm, find

   (a) the rate of increase of the surface area,   (b) the rate of increase of the volume.

3   A circular stain is spreading so that its radius is increasing at a constant rate of 3 mm s^{-1}. Find the rate at which the area is increasing when the radius is 50 mm.

4   A water tank has a rectangular base 1.5 m by 1.2 m. The sides are vertical and water is being added to the tank at a constant rate of 0.45 m^3 per minute. At what rate is the depth of water in the tank increasing?

5   Air is being lost from a spherical balloon at a constant rate of 0.6 m^3 s^{-1}. Find the rate at which the radius is decreasing at a instant when the radius is 2.5 m.

6   The volume of a spherical balloon is increasing at a constant rate of 0.25 m^3 s^{-1}. Find the rate at which the radius is increasing at a instant when the volume is 10 m^3.

7   A funnel has a circular top of diameter 20 cm and a height of 30 cm. When the depth of liquid in the funnel is 15 cm, the liquid is dripping from the funnel at a rate of 0.2 cm^3 s^{-1}. At what rate is the depth of the liquid in the funnel decreasing at this instant?

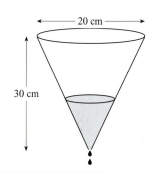

9.5   The relation between $\dfrac{dy}{dx}$ and $\dfrac{dx}{dy}$

In many applications there is little doubt which of two variables to regard as the independent variable (often denoted by x), and which as the dependent variable (y). But when a function is one-one, so that an inverse function exists, there are occasions when you can choose to treat either variable as the independent variable.

For example, you could record the progress of a journey either by noting the distance you have gone at certain fixed intervals of time, or by noting the time when you pass certain fixed landmarks. If x denotes the distance from the start and t the time, then the rate of change would be either $\dfrac{dx}{dt}$ (the speed) or $\dfrac{dt}{dx}$ (which would be measured in a unit such as minutes per mile).

Example 9.5.1

Suppose that $y = ax + b$. Find $\dfrac{dy}{dx}$ and $\dfrac{dx}{dy}$, and calculate the value of $\dfrac{dy}{dx} \times \dfrac{dx}{dy}$.

Since $y = ax + b$, $\dfrac{dy}{dx} = a$.

To find $\dfrac{dx}{dy}$, you need to rewrite the equation $y = ax + b$ in the form $x = \ldots$ to get

$$x = \frac{y - b}{a}, \text{ that is, } x = \frac{y}{a} - \frac{b}{a}.$$

Then $\dfrac{dx}{dy} = \dfrac{1}{a}$.

Finally, $\dfrac{dy}{dx} \times \dfrac{dx}{dy} = a \times \dfrac{1}{a} = 1$.

The remainder of this section is concerned with the proof that in general, $\dfrac{dy}{dx} \times \dfrac{dx}{dy} = 1$. If you wish you can omit the details of this proof, but you will need to be able to use the result.

Suppose that you are given a curve such as $y = f(x)$. You know what $\dfrac{dy}{dx}$ means, but what does $\dfrac{dx}{dy}$ mean?

From C1 Chapter 5, $\dfrac{dy}{dx} = f'(x)$ is the gradient at a point on the graph of $y = f(x)$. In Fig. 9.1, the tangent is drawn to the curve $y = f(x)$ at the point for which $x = p$. Then at this point, $\dfrac{dy}{dx} = f'(p) = \tan\theta$, where θ is the angle which the tangent makes with the x-axis. This is shown in Fig. 9.1.

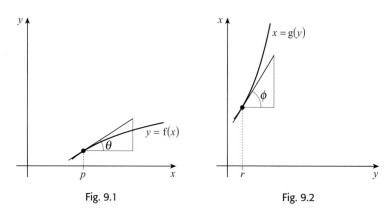

Fig. 9.1   Fig. 9.2

To find $\dfrac{dx}{dy}$, you need to write the equation $y = f(x)$ in the form $x = \ldots$. Suppose that this gives you $x = g(y)$.

When you draw this graph, you would probably draw a graph of $x = g(y)$ with the x-axis vertical and the y-axis horizontal. Then $\dfrac{dx}{dy} = g'(y)$ is the gradient at a point on the graph of

$x = \mathrm{g}(y)$. In Fig. 9.2, the tangent is drawn to the curve $x = \mathrm{g}(y)$ at the point for which $y = r$.
Then at the point $y = r$, $\dfrac{\mathrm{d}x}{\mathrm{d}y} = \mathrm{g}'(r) = \tan\phi$, where ϕ is the angle which the tangent makes
with the y-axis.

But there is no reason why the axes have to be the way that they are drawn in Fig. 9.2. If you
redraw the figure with the x-axis horizontal and the y-axis vertical you get the second diagram
in Fig. 9.3. And because $x = \mathrm{g}(y)$ is just another way of writing $y = \mathrm{f}(x)$, the curves in both
diagrams in Fig. 9.3 are the same.

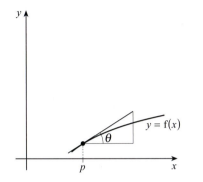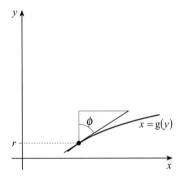

Fig. 9.3

The relationship between θ and ϕ is now clear, and is given by $\theta + \phi = \frac{1}{2}\pi$. So $\phi = \frac{1}{2}\pi - \theta$,
and

$$\tan\phi = \tan\left(\tfrac{1}{2}\pi - \theta\right)$$
$$= \cot\theta$$
$$= \frac{1}{\tan\theta}.$$

Therefore $\tan\theta \times \tan\phi = 1$.

But $\tan\theta = \mathrm{f}'(p)$ and $\tan\phi = \mathrm{g}'(r)$, so $\mathrm{f}'(p) \times \mathrm{g}'(r) = 1$, which in turn gives $\dfrac{\mathrm{d}y}{\mathrm{d}x} \times \dfrac{\mathrm{d}x}{\mathrm{d}y} = 1$.
Therefore $\dfrac{\mathrm{d}y}{\mathrm{d}x} = 1 \Big/ \dfrac{\mathrm{d}x}{\mathrm{d}y}$.

> If $y = \mathrm{f}(x)$ and $x = \mathrm{g}(y)$ are the same curve, then
> $$\frac{\mathrm{d}y}{\mathrm{d}x} = 1 \Big/ \frac{\mathrm{d}x}{\mathrm{d}y}.$$

The $\dfrac{\mathrm{d}y}{\mathrm{d}x}$ notation is very useful here, because when you see the expression
$\dfrac{\mathrm{d}y}{\mathrm{d}x} \times \dfrac{\mathrm{d}x}{\mathrm{d}y}$, it is automatic to 'cancel' to get the answer 1. It is not so obvious using
function notation that $\mathrm{f}'(p) \times \mathrm{g}'(r) = 1$.

Example 9.5.2

Verify that $\dfrac{dy}{dx} = 1 \Big/ \dfrac{dx}{dy}$ for the curves   (a) $y = e^{5x}$,   (b) $y = x^3$.

(a) If $y = e^{5x}$, then $\dfrac{dy}{dx} = 5e^{5x}$.

You can also write the relation $y = e^{5x}$ as $x = \frac{1}{5} \ln y$, so $\dfrac{dx}{dy} = \dfrac{1}{5y}$.

Since $e^{5x} = y$, $\dfrac{dy}{dx} = 5y$ and $\dfrac{dx}{dy} = \dfrac{1}{5y}$, so $\dfrac{dy}{dx} = 1 \Big/ \dfrac{dx}{dy}$.

(b) If $y = x^3$, then $\dfrac{dy}{dx} = 3x^2$.

You can also write the relation $y = x^3$ as $x = y^{\frac{1}{3}}$, so $\dfrac{dx}{dy} = \frac{1}{3} y^{-\frac{2}{3}}$.

Since $y = x^3$, $\dfrac{dx}{dy} = \frac{1}{3} y^{-\frac{2}{3}} = \frac{1}{3}(x^3)^{-\frac{2}{3}} = \frac{1}{3} x^{-2} = \dfrac{1}{3x^2}$, so $\dfrac{dy}{dx} = 1 \Big/ \dfrac{dx}{dy}$.

Example 9.5.3

Find $\dfrac{dx}{dy}$ in terms of x for the curve $y = \dfrac{1}{2x - 3}$.

If $y = \dfrac{1}{2x - 3} = (2x - 3)^{-1}$, then $\dfrac{dy}{dx} = -1 \times (2x - 3)^{-2} \times 2 = \dfrac{-2}{(2x - 3)^2}$.

Since $\dfrac{dx}{dy} = 1 \Big/ \dfrac{dy}{dx}$, $\dfrac{dx}{dy} = \dfrac{(2x - 3)^2}{-2} = -\frac{1}{2}(2x - 3)^2$.

Example 9.5.4

Find the equation of the curve which passes through the point $(1, 2)$, and for which $\dfrac{dx}{dy} = \dfrac{x}{x + 1}$.

Since $\dfrac{dx}{dy} = \dfrac{x}{x + 1}$, $\dfrac{dy}{dx} = \dfrac{x + 1}{x} = 1 + \dfrac{1}{x}$.

Therefore, integrating, $y = x + \ln x + k$.

As $(1, 2)$ lies on the curve, $2 = 1 + \ln 1 + k$, giving $k = 1$.

So the equation of the curve is $y = x + \ln x + 1$.

Exercise 9C

1 Verify that $\dfrac{dy}{dx} = 1 \Big/ \dfrac{dx}{dy}$ for the curves

(a) $y = 1 - 2x$,   (b) $y = \sqrt{1 - 2x}$,   (c) $y = e^{x^3}$.

2 Find $\dfrac{dx}{dy}$ in terms of x for the curves

(a) $y = 2x^2 + x$,   (b) $y = e^{2x - 3}$,   (c) $y = x^2 \ln x$.

3 A curve which passes through $(1, 0)$ satisfies the equation $\dfrac{dx}{dy} = x^3$. Find its equation.

Miscellaneous exercise 9

1 Differentiate $2(x^4 + 3)^5$ with respect to x.

2 Find the equation of the tangent to the curve $y = (x^2 - 5)^6$ at the point $(2, 1)$.

3 Given that $y = \sqrt{x^3 + 1}$, show that $\dfrac{dy}{dx} > 0$ for all $x > -1$.

4 Given that $y = \dfrac{1}{2x - 1} + \dfrac{1}{(2x - 1)^2}$, find the exact value of $\dfrac{dy}{dx}$ when $x = 2$.

5 Find the coordinates of the stationary point of the curve with equation $y = \dfrac{1}{x^2 + 4}$.

6 Find the equation of the normal to the curve $y = \sqrt{2x^2 + 1}$ at the point $(2, 3)$.

7 The radius of a circular disc is increasing at a constant rate of 0.003 cm s^{-1}. Find the rate at which the area is increasing when the radius is 20 cm. (OCR)

8 A viscous liquid is poured on to a flat surface. It forms a circular patch whose area grows at a steady rate of 5 cm^2 s^{-1}. Find, in terms of π,

   (a) the radius of the patch 20 seconds after pouring has commenced,

   (b) the rate of increase of the radius at this instant. (OCR)

9 The formulae for the volume of a sphere of radius r and for its surface area are $V = \frac{4}{3}\pi r^3$ and $A = 4\pi r^2$ respectively. Given that, when $r = 5$ m, V is increasing at a rate of 10 m^3 s^{-1}, find the rate of increase of A at this instant. (OCR)

10 Differentiate with respect to x

   (a) $\sqrt{x + \dfrac{1}{x}}$,   (b) $\ln(1 + \sqrt{4x})$. (OCR)

11 Using differentiation, find the equation of the tangent at the point $(2, 1)$ on the curve with equation $y = \sqrt{x^2 - 3}$. (OCR)

12 Differentiate with respect to t

   (a) $\dfrac{1}{(3t^2 + 5)^2}$,   (b) $\ln\left(\dfrac{4}{t^2}\right)$. (OCR)

13 Find the coordinates of the stationary point of the curve $y = \ln(x^2 - 6x + 10)$ and show that this stationary point is a minimum.

14 (a) Curve C_1 has equation $y = \sqrt{4x - x^2}$. Find $\dfrac{dy}{dx}$ and hence find the coordinates of the stationary point.

   (b) Show that the curve C_2 with equation $y = \sqrt{x^2 - 4x}$ has no stationary point.

15 If a hemispherical bowl of radius 6 cm contains water to a depth of x cm, the volume of the water is $\frac{1}{3}\pi x^2(18 - x)$. Water is poured into the bowl at a rate of 3 cm^3 s^{-1}. Find the rate at which the water level is rising when the depth is 2 cm.

16 Find the coordinates of the three stationary points of the curve $y = e^{x^2(x^2 - 18)}$.

17 A curve has equation $y = (x^2 - 1)^3 - 3(x^2 - 1)^2$. Find the coordinates of the stationary points and determine whether each is a minimum or a maximum. Sketch the curve.

18 An underground oil storage tank $ABCDEFGH$ is part of a square pyramid, as shown in the diagram. The complete pyramid has a square base of side 12 m and height 18 m. The tank has depth 12 m.

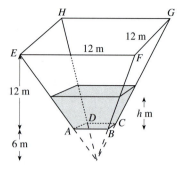

When the depth of oil in the tank is h metres, show that the volume $V\mathrm{m}^3$ is given by $V = \frac{4}{27}(h+6)^3 - 32$.

Oil is being added to the tank at the constant rate of 4.5 m³ s⁻¹. At the moment when the depth of oil is 8 m, find the rate at which the depth is increasing.

19* The expression x^n only has a meaning when $x < 0$ if n is a rational number $\dfrac{p}{q}$ and q is an odd integer. Assume that p and q have no common factors.

Make the substitution $u = -x$ so that, when $x < 0$, $u > 0$.

(a) Show that, if $x < 0$ and q is odd, then $x^{\frac{p}{q}} = -u^{\frac{p}{q}}$ if p is odd, and $x^{\frac{p}{q}} = u^{\frac{p}{q}}$ if p is even.

(b) Use the chain rule and the result in Section 9.3 to show that, if p is odd, then
$$\frac{\mathrm{d}}{\mathrm{d}x}\left(x^{\frac{p}{q}}\right) = \frac{p}{q}u^{\frac{p-q}{q}} = \frac{p}{q}x^{\frac{p}{q}-1};$$
and that, if p is even, $\dfrac{\mathrm{d}}{\mathrm{d}x}\left(x^{\frac{p}{q}}\right) = -\dfrac{p}{q}u^{\frac{p-q}{q}} = \dfrac{p}{q}x^{\frac{p}{q}-1}.$

(c) Deduce that, for all the values of n for which x^n has a meaning when x is negative,
$$\frac{\mathrm{d}}{\mathrm{d}x}(x^n) = nx^{n-1} \text{ for } x < 0.$$

10 Differentiating products

This chapter extends further the range of functions which you can differentiate. When you have completed it, you should

- know and be able to apply the product and quotient rules for differentiation.

10.1 The sum and product rules

If $f(x) = x^2 + \ln x$, then $f'(x) = 2x + \dfrac{1}{x}$. You know this, because it was proved (in C1 Chapter 5) that $\dfrac{d}{dx} x^2 = 2x$, and that $\dfrac{d}{dx} \ln x = \dfrac{1}{x}$. But the statement also depends on another property of differentiation:

> **The sum rule**
> If u and v are functions of x, and if $y = u + v$, then
> $$\frac{dy}{dx} = \frac{du}{dx} + \frac{dv}{dx}.$$

This was justified in C1 Section 5.4 by means of an example. For a general proof, it is convenient to use 'delta notation'.

Take a particular value of x, and increase x by δx. There will then be corresponding increases in u, v and y of δu, δv and δy:

$$y = u + v \quad \text{and} \quad y + \delta y = (u + \delta u) + (v + \delta v).$$

Subtracting the first equation from the second gives

$$\delta y = \delta u + \delta v; \text{ and, dividing by } \delta x, \quad \frac{\delta y}{\delta x} = \frac{\delta u}{\delta x} + \frac{\delta v}{\delta x}.$$

To find $\dfrac{dy}{dx}$, you must take the limit as $\delta x \to 0$:

$$\begin{aligned}
\frac{dy}{dx} &= \lim_{\delta x \to 0} \frac{\delta y}{\delta x} \\
&= \lim_{\delta x \to 0} \left(\frac{\delta u}{\delta x} + \frac{\delta v}{\delta x} \right) \\
&= \lim_{\delta x \to 0} \frac{\delta u}{\delta x} + \lim_{\delta x \to 0} \frac{\delta v}{\delta x} \\
&= \frac{du}{dx} + \frac{dv}{dx},
\end{aligned}$$

as required.

You might (rightly) object that the crucial assumption of the proof, that the limit of the sum of two terms is the sum of the limits, has never been justified. This can only be an assumption at this stage, because you don't yet have a mathematical definition of what is meant by a limit. But it *can* be justified, and for the time being you may quote the result with confidence. You may also assume the corresponding result for the limit of the product of two terms: this has already been assumed in Section 9.2, when proving the chain rule.

The rule for differentiating the product of two functions is rather more complicated than the rule for sums.

Example 10.1.1

Show that, if $y = uv$, then in general $\dfrac{dy}{dx}$ does *not* equal $\dfrac{du}{dx} \times \dfrac{dv}{dx}$.

The words 'in general' are put in because there might be special functions for which equality does hold. For example, if u and v are both constant functions, then y is also constant: $\dfrac{du}{dx}, \dfrac{dv}{dx}$ and $\dfrac{dy}{dx}$ are all 0, so $\dfrac{dy}{dx}$ does equal $\dfrac{du}{dx} \times \dfrac{dv}{dx}$.

To show that this is not always true, it is sufficient to find a counterexample (see Section 0.5).

For example, if $u = x^2$ and $v = x^3$, then $y = x^5$. In this case

$$\frac{dy}{dx} = 5x^4,$$

but

$$\frac{du}{dx} \times \frac{dv}{dx} = 2x \times 3x^2 = 6x^3.$$

These two expressions are not the same.

To find the correct rule, use the same notation as for the sum rule, but with $y = uv$. Then

$$y = uv \quad \text{and} \quad y + \delta y = (u + \delta u)(v + \delta v) = uv + (\delta u)v + u(\delta v) + (\delta u)(\delta v).$$

You could illustrate these equations by showing u and v as sides of a rectangle, so that y is the area. This is the unshaded region in Fig. 10.1. Then, if u increases by δu, and v by δv, the rectangle expands to include the shaded region as well. The area of the large rectangle is $y + \delta y$, so that the shaded region has area δy.

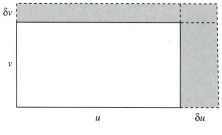

Fig. 10.1

Subtracting the equation for y from the equation for $y + \delta y$ gives

$$\delta y = (\delta u)v + u(\delta v) + (\delta u)(\delta v).$$

The three terms in the expression on the right are the areas of the three rectangles which make up the shaded region in Fig. 10.1. Notice that, if δu and δv are small, the area of the rectangle with area $(\delta u)(\delta v)$ in the top right corner is much smaller than the area of the other two shaded rectangles.

Now u and v are both functions of x, so that y is a function of x. The three increases δu, δv and δy all result from increasing x by δx. To get $\dfrac{dy}{dx}$, you have to find $\dfrac{\delta y}{\delta x}$ and then let $\delta x \to 0$. So divide the last equation by δx, to get

$$\frac{\delta y}{\delta x} = \left(\frac{\delta u}{\delta x}\right)v + u\left(\frac{\delta v}{\delta x}\right) + \left(\frac{\delta u}{\delta x}\right)(\delta v).$$

Assuming, as with the sum rule, that the limit of the sum of the terms is the sum of the limits,

$$\frac{dy}{dx} = \lim_{\delta x \to 0} \frac{\delta y}{\delta x}$$

$$= \lim_{\delta x \to 0}\left(\left(\frac{\delta u}{\delta x}\right)v\right) + \lim_{\delta x \to 0}\left(u\left(\frac{\delta v}{\delta x}\right)\right) + \lim_{\delta x \to 0}\left(\left(\frac{\delta u}{\delta x}\right)(\delta v)\right).$$

Now u and v don't depend on δx, so you can write

$$\lim_{\delta x \to 0}\left(\left(\frac{\delta u}{\delta x}\right)v\right) = \lim_{\delta x \to 0}\frac{\delta u}{\delta x} \times v = \frac{du}{dx} \times v$$

and $$\lim_{\delta x \to 0}\left(u\left(\frac{\delta v}{\delta x}\right)\right) = u \times \lim_{\delta x \to 0}\frac{\delta v}{\delta x} = u \times \frac{dv}{dx}.$$

And if you assume that the limit of the product of two factors is the product of the limits,

$$\lim_{\delta x \to 0}\left(\left(\frac{\delta u}{\delta x}\right)(\delta v)\right) = \lim_{\delta x \to 0}\left(\frac{\delta u}{\delta x}\right) \times \lim_{\delta x \to 0}\delta v;$$

and this is 0 because $\lim_{\delta x \to 0} \delta v = 0$.

Putting all this together,

$$\frac{dy}{dx} = \frac{du}{dx} \times v + u \times \frac{dv}{dx}.$$

This can be stated as:

The product rule
If u and v are functions of x, and if $y = uv$, then

$$\frac{dy}{dx} = \frac{du}{dx}v + u\frac{dv}{dx}.$$

In function notation, if $y = f(x)g(x)$, then $\dfrac{dy}{dx} = f'(x)g(x) + f(x)g'(x)$.

Example 10.1.2
Verify the product rule when $u = x^2$ and $v = x^3$.

Using the equation in the box, the right side is $2x \times x^3 + x^2 \times 3x^2 = 2x^4 + 3x^4 = 5x^4$, which is the derivative of $y = x^2 \times x^3 = x^5$.

Example 10.1.3

Find the derivatives with respect to x of   (a) $x^3 \ln x$,   (b) xe^{3x},   (c) $x^2(1+3x^2)^4$.

(a) Write $u = x^3$ and $v = \ln x$. Then $\dfrac{du}{dx} = 3x^2$ and $\dfrac{dv}{dx} = \dfrac{1}{x}$. So, using the product rule,

$$\frac{d}{dx}(x^3 \ln x) = 3x^2 \times \ln x + x^3 \times \frac{1}{x}$$
$$= 3x^2 \ln x + x^2$$
$$= x^2(3\ln x + 1).$$

You will soon find that you don't need to write this out in full. Just remember

derivative of product = derivative of first factor × second factor
+ first factor × derivative of second factor.

(b) $\dfrac{d}{dx}(xe^{3x}) = 1 \times e^{3x} + x \times (3e^{3x})$

$\qquad\qquad = e^{3x} + 3xe^{3x}$

$\qquad\qquad = (1 + 3x)e^{3x}$

(c) $\dfrac{d}{dx}(x^2(1+3x^2)^4) = 2x \times (1+3x^2)^4 + x^2(4 \times (1+3x^2)^3 \times 6x)$

$\qquad\qquad\qquad = 2x(1+3x^2)^4 + 24x^3(1+3x^2)^3$

$\qquad\qquad\qquad = (2x + 6x^3 + 24x^3)(1+3x^2)^3$

$\qquad\qquad\qquad = 2x(1+15x^2)(1+3x^2)^3.$

Notice that in part (c) the chain rule is used to find $\dfrac{dv}{dx}$.

You will often find that, after you have used the product rule, the two terms in the derivative have a common factor. If so, you should write the final answer in its factorised form. This is especially important if you want to use the derivative to find stationary points on the graph.

Example 10.1.4

Find the turning point on the graph of $y = \dfrac{1}{x}\ln x$, and determine whether it is a maximum or minimum.

Begin by noting that the graph exists only for $x > 0$.

Differentiating by the product rule,

$$\frac{dy}{dx} = \left(-\frac{1}{x^2}\right) \times \ln x + \frac{1}{x} \times \frac{1}{x}$$

$$= \frac{1}{x^2}(-\ln x + 1).$$

The turning point is where $\dfrac{dy}{dx} = 0$, which is where $\ln x = 1$, that is $x = e$.

To find whether this is a maximum or minimum you could use the product rule again to find $\dfrac{d^2y}{dx^2}$. But in this instance it is easier to investigate the change of sign of $\dfrac{dy}{dx}$.

Since the denominator x^2 is positive for $x > 0$, this depends only on the sign of $-\ln x + 1$, which is positive when $x < e$ and negative when $x > e$. So the turning point at $x = e$ is a maximum.

When $x = e$, $y = \dfrac{1}{e} \ln e = \dfrac{1}{e} \times 1 = \dfrac{1}{e}$. So the maximum point on the graph is $\left(e, \dfrac{1}{e}\right)$.

Example 10.1.5
Find the x-coordinates of the two points on the graph of $y = (1 - 4x)e^{-2x}$ at which the tangent passes through the origin.

To find where the tangent to a graph $y = f(x)$ passes through the origin, there is no need to find the equation of the tangent. In Fig. 10.2, P is the point on the curve with coordinates $(p, f(p))$. If the tangent at P passes through O, the gradient of OP is equal to the gradient of the tangent at P. That is, $\dfrac{f(p)}{p} = f'(p)$.

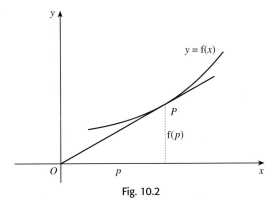

Fig. 10.2

For the graph of $y = (1 - 4x)e^{-2x}$, using the product rule gives

$$\frac{dy}{dx} = -4e^{-2x} + (1 - 4x) \times (-2e^{-2x})$$
$$= e^{-2x}(-4 - 2(1 - 4x))$$
$$= e^{-2x}(-6 + 8x).$$

The tangent at a point $P(p, (1 - 4p)e^{-2p})$ has gradient $e^{-2p}(-6 + 8p)$. This has to equal the gradient of OP, which is $\dfrac{(1 - 4p)e^{-2p}}{p}$. Therefore

$$e^{-2p}(-6 + 8p) = \frac{(1 - 4p)e^{-2p}}{p}.$$

This gives

$$-6 + 8p = \frac{1 - 4p}{p},$$

which reduces to $8p^2 - 2p - 1 = 0$.

The left side factorises as $(4p + 1)(2p - 1)$, so the roots are $-\frac{1}{4}$ and $\frac{1}{2}$.

These are the required x-coordinates.

This is illustrated in Fig. 10.3, where the two tangents passing through the origin are drawn.

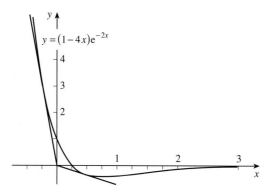

Fig. 10.3

Exercise 10A

1 Differentiate the following functions with respect to x by using the product rule. Verify your answers by multiplying out the products and then differentiating.

   (a) $(x+1)(x-1)$ (b) $x^2(x+2)$ (c) $(x^3+4)(x^2+3)$

   (d) $(3x^2+5x+2)(7x+5)$ (e) $(x^2-2x+4)(x+2)$ (f) $x^m x^n$

2 Differentiate the following with respect to x.

   (a) xe^x (b) $x^2 \ln x$ (c) $x^3(e^{-2x}+1)$

   (d) $e^x \ln x$ (e) $\sqrt{x}e^{-x}$ (f) $(1+2x)e^{-2x}$

3 Find $\dfrac{dy}{dx}$ when

   (a) $y=(x^2+3)e^x$,   (b) $y=x^2(\ln 2x+e^{2x})$,   (c) $y=(xe^x)^2$.

4 Find $f'(x)$ when

   (a) $f(x)=x^2(2+e^x)$,   (b) $f(x)=x^3 e^{2x}$,   (c) $f(x)=(4+3x^2)\ln x$.

5 Find the value of the gradient of the following curves when $x=2$. Give your answers in exact form.

   (a) $y=xe^{-2x}$ (b) $y=e^x \ln(x-1)$ (c) $y=x\ln 3x$

6 Find the equations of tangents to the following curves at the given points.

   (a) $y=x\ln(x-1)$ when $x=2$ (b) $y=x^3 \ln x$ when $x=1$

   (c) $y=x\sqrt{3x+1}$ when $x=5$ (d) $y=x^3 e^{-2x}$ when $x=0$

7 Find the coordinates of the turning points of the curve $y=x^2 e^{-x}$.

8 Differentiate the following with respect to x.

   (a) $e^x \sqrt{5x^2+2}$ (b) $(4x+1)^3 \ln 3x$ (c) $\sqrt{x}\ln 2x$

9 When $f(x)=xe^{\sqrt{x}}$, find the exact value of $f'(4)$.

10 Find the equation of the normal to the curve $y = x \ln(2x - 1)$ at the point on the curve with x-coordinate 1.

11 Find the coordinates of the stationary point on the curve $y = (x^2 - 4)\sqrt{4x - 1}$, $x \geq \frac{1}{4}$.

12 The volume, V, of a solid is given by $V = x^2\sqrt{8 - x}$. Find the maximum value of V and the value of x at which it occurs.

13 Find the x-coordinates of the stationary points on the curve $y = x^n e^{-x}$, where n is a positive integer. Determine the nature of these stationary points, distinguishing between the cases when n is odd and when n is even.

14 Use the product rule to establish the product rule, $\dfrac{d}{dx}uvw = \dfrac{du}{dx}vw + u\dfrac{dv}{dx}w + uv\dfrac{dw}{dx}$, for differentiating a 'triple' product. Use this rule to find $\dfrac{d}{dx}(x(1 + x)e^x)$.

10.2 Differentiating quotients

Functions of the form $\dfrac{u}{v}$ can often be written in a different form so that they can be differentiated by rules you know already, such as the product rule or the chain rule. Example 10.2.1 illustrates some possibilities.

Example 10.2.1

Differentiate with respect to x (a) $f(x) = \dfrac{x}{e^x}$,   (b) $g(x) = \dfrac{e^x}{x}$.

(a) Since $\dfrac{1}{e^x} = e^{-x}$, you can write $f(x)$ as xe^{-x}. Therefore

$$f'(x) = \frac{d}{dx}(xe^{-x}) = 1e^{-x} + x(-e^{-x}) = e^{-x}(1 - x).$$

(b) **Method 1**   You can write $g(x)$ as $g(x) = e^x \times \dfrac{1}{x}$, so

$$g'(x) = \frac{d}{dx}e^x \times \frac{1}{x} + e^x \times \frac{d}{dx}\left(\frac{1}{x}\right) = e^x \times \frac{1}{x} + e^x \times \left(\frac{-1}{x^2}\right),$$

using the product rule.

You can simplify this to $g'(x) = e^x\left(\dfrac{x - 1}{x^2}\right)$.

Method 2   Since $g(x) = \dfrac{1}{f(x)}$, where $f(x)$ is the same as in part (a), the chain rule gives

$$g'(x) = \left(\frac{-1}{f(x)^2}\right) \times f'(x) = -\frac{f'(x)}{f(x)^2}.$$

Therefore, using the result of part (a),

$$g'(x) = -\frac{e^{-x}(1 - x)}{\left(\frac{x}{e^x}\right)^2} = -e^{2x}e^{-x}\left(\frac{1 - x}{x^2}\right)$$

$$= -e^x\left(\frac{1 - x}{x^2}\right) = e^x\left(\frac{x - 1}{x^2}\right).$$

However, it is often useful to have a separate formula for differentiating $\dfrac{u}{v}$. This can be found by applying the product rule to $u \times \dfrac{1}{v}$, using the chain rule to differentiate $\dfrac{1}{v}$.

This gives

$$\frac{d}{dx}\left(\frac{u}{v}\right) = \frac{d}{dx}\left(u \times \frac{1}{v}\right) = \frac{du}{dx} \times \frac{1}{v} + u \times \left(-\frac{1}{v^2}\right)\frac{dv}{dx}$$

$$= \frac{du}{dx}\frac{1}{v} - \frac{u}{v^2}\frac{dv}{dx}.$$

This can be conveniently written as:

> **The quotient rule**
> If u and v are functions of x, and if $y = \dfrac{u}{v}$, then
>
> $$\frac{dy}{dx} = \frac{\dfrac{du}{dx}v - u\dfrac{dv}{dx}}{v^2}.$$
>
> In function notation, if $y = \dfrac{f(x)}{g(x)}$, then $\dfrac{dy}{dx} = \dfrac{f'(x)g(x) - f(x)g'(x)}{(g(x))^2}$.

Use this formula to get the answers to Example 10.2.1.

Example 10.2.2

Find the minimum and maximum values of $f(x) = \dfrac{x - 1}{x^2 + 3}$.

The denominator is never zero, so $f(x)$ is defined for all real numbers.

The quotient rule with $u = x - 1$ and $v = x^2 + 3$ gives

$$f'(x) = \frac{1 \times (x^2 + 3) - (x - 1) \times 2x}{(x^2 + 3)^2} = \frac{-x^2 + 2x + 3}{(x^2 + 3)^2}$$

$$= \frac{-(x^2 - 2x - 3)}{(x^2 + 3)^2} = \frac{-(x + 1)(x - 3)}{(x^2 + 3)^2}.$$

So $f'(x) = 0$ when $x = -1$ and $x = 3$.

You could use the quotient rule again to find $f''(x)$, but in this example it is much easier to note that $f'(x)$ is positive when $-1 < x < 3$ and negative when $x < -1$ and when $x > 3$. So there is a minimum at $x = -1$ and a maximum at $x = 3$.

The minimum value is $f(-1) = \frac{-2}{4} = -\frac{1}{2}$, and the maximum value is $\frac{2}{12} = \frac{1}{6}$.

Exercise 10B

1 Differentiate with respect to x

(a) $\dfrac{x}{1 + 5x}$,

(b) $\dfrac{x^2}{3x - 2}$,

(c) $\dfrac{x^2}{1 + 2x^2}$,

(d) $\dfrac{e^{3x}}{4x - 3}$,

(e) $\dfrac{x}{1 + x^3}$,

(f) $\dfrac{e^x}{x^2 + 1}$.

2 Differentiate with respect to x

(a) $\dfrac{x}{\sqrt{x+1}}$,

(b) $\dfrac{\sqrt{x-5}}{x}$,

(c) $\dfrac{\sqrt{3x+2}}{2x}$.

3 Find $\dfrac{dy}{dx}$ when

(a) $y = \dfrac{e^x}{\sqrt{x}}$,

(b) $y = \dfrac{e^x + 5x}{e^x - 2}$,

(c) $y = \dfrac{\sqrt{1-x}}{\sqrt{1+x}}$.

4 Find $\dfrac{dy}{dx}$ when

(a) $y = \dfrac{\ln x}{x}$,

(b) $y = \dfrac{\ln(x^2 + 4)}{x}$,

(c) $y = \dfrac{\ln(3x + 2)}{2x - 1}$.

5 Find the equation of the tangent at the point with coordinates $(1, 1)$ to the curve with equation $y = \dfrac{x^2 + 3}{x + 3}$. (OCR)

6 (a) If $f(x) = \dfrac{e^x}{2x + 1}$, find $f'(x)$.

(b) Find the coordinates of the turning point on the curve $y = f(x)$.

7 Find the equation of the normal to the curve $y = \dfrac{2x - 1}{x(x - 3)}$ at the point on the curve where $x = 2$.

8 Find the x-coordinates of the turning points on the curve $y = \dfrac{x^2 + 4}{2x - x^2}$.

9 (a) If $f(x) = \dfrac{x^2 - 3x}{x + 1}$, find $f'(x)$.

(b) Find the values of x for which $f(x)$ is decreasing.

Miscellaneous exercise 10

1 Differentiate $\dfrac{x}{\sqrt{x+3}}$ simplifying your answer as far as possible. (OCR)

2 Given that $y = xe^{-3x}$, find $\dfrac{dy}{dx}$.

Hence find the coordinates of the stationary point on the curve $y = xe^{-3x}$. (OCR)

3 Use differentiation to find the coordinates of the turning point on the curve whose equation is $y = \dfrac{\sqrt{x}}{4x + 2}$.

4 A curve has equation $y = \dfrac{x}{\sqrt{2x^2 + 1}}$.

(a) Show that $\dfrac{dy}{dx} = (2x^2 + 1)^{-\frac{3}{2}}$.

(b) Hence show that the curve has no turning points. (OCR)

5 For the graph of $y = x\sqrt{3 - x}$

(a) state the values of x for which y exists,

(b) find the gradient at the origin,

(c) find the coordinates of the maximum point.

Use your answers to draw a sketch of the graph.

6 Find the maximum value of $f(x) = xe^{-\frac{1}{2}x^2}$.

7 Find the maximum and minimum points on the graph of $y = x(\ln x)^2$. Find also the values of x for which the graph bends downwards. Use your answers to draw a sketch of the graph.

8 Find the turning points on the graph of $y = x^2 e^{\frac{1}{2}x}$. Use your answer to draw a sketch of the graph.

Find the equation of the tangent to the graph at the point where $x = p$.

Show that there are three points on the curve at which the tangent passes through $(3, 0)$. State their coordinates, and illustrate the property on your sketch.

9 A sketch of part of the curve $y = \dfrac{x(x+3)}{2x-2}$ is shown in the diagram.

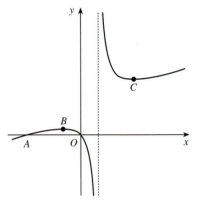

(a) Write down the coordinates of the point A and state the equation of the asymptote shown as a broken line parallel to the y-axis.

(b) Find the equation of the tangent to the curve at A.

(c) Show, by using calculus, that the coordinates of the turning point at B are $(-1, 0.5)$ and calculate the coordinates of the turning point at C.   (OCR)

10 (a) Find the value of x for which $x^2 e^{-ax}$ has its maximum value, where a is a positive constant. Denoting this by c, and the maximum value by M, deduce that

$$xe^{-ax} < \frac{M}{x} \quad \text{if } x > c.$$

Hence show that $xe^{-ax} \to 0$ as $x \to \infty$.

(b) Use a similar method to show that $x^2 e^{-ax} \to 0$ as $x \to \infty$.

11 Volumes of revolution

This chapter is about using integration to find the volume of a particular kind of solid, called a solid of revolution. When you have completed it, you should

- be able to find a volume of revolution about either the x- or the y-axis.

11.1 Solids of revolution

Let O be the origin, and let OA be a line through the origin, as shown in Fig. 11.1. Consider the region between the line OA and the x-axis, shown shaded. If you rotate this region about the x-axis through $360°$, it sweeps out a solid cone, shown in Fig. 11.2. A solid shape constructed in this way is called a **solid of revolution**. The volume of a solid of revolution is sometimes called a **volume of revolution**.

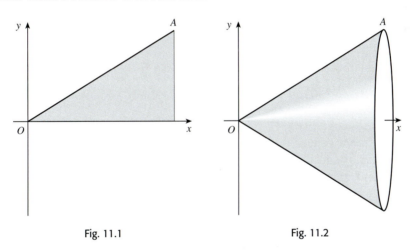

Fig. 11.1   Fig. 11.2

Calculating a volume of revolution is similar in many ways to calculating the area of a region under a curve which you saw in C2 Chapter 5, and can be illustrated by an example.

Suppose that the region between the graph of $y = \sqrt{x}$ and the x-axis from $x = 1$ to $x = 4$, shown in Fig. 11.3, is rotated about the x-axis to form the solid of revolution in Fig. 11.4.

The key is to begin by asking a more general question: what is the volume, V, of the solid of revolution from $x = 1$ as far as any value of x? This solid is shown by the light shading in Fig. 11.4.

Suppose that x is increased by δx. Since y and V are both functions of x, the corresponding increases in y and V can be written as δy and δV. The increase δV is shown by darker shading in Fig. 11.4. Examine this increase δV in the volume more closely. It is shown in more detail in the left diagram in Fig. 11.5.

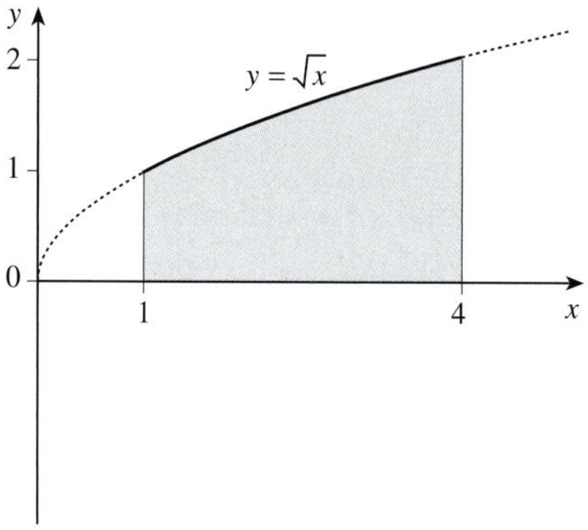

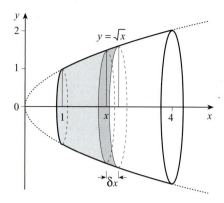

Fig. 11.3

Fig. 11.4

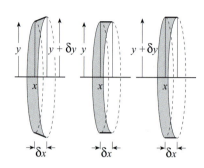

Fig. 11.5

The increase δV in the volume is between the volumes of two disc-like cylinders, each of width δx and having radii y and $y + \delta y$. (These two cylinders are shown in the centre and right diagrams in Fig. 11.5.) So

$$\delta V \text{ is between } \pi y^2 \delta x \text{ and } \pi (y + \delta y)^2 \delta x$$

from which it follows that $\dfrac{\delta V}{\delta x}$ is between πy^2 and $\pi (y + \delta y)^2$.

Now let δx tend to 0. From the definition in C1 Section 12.1, $\dfrac{\delta V}{\delta x}$ tends to the derivative $\dfrac{\mathrm{d} V}{\mathrm{d} x}$. Also, δy tends to 0, so that $y + \delta y$ tends to y. It follows that

$$\frac{\mathrm{d} V}{\mathrm{d} x} = \pi y^2.$$

So V is a function whose derivative is πy^2. In this example $y = \sqrt{x}$, so $\dfrac{\mathrm{d} V}{\mathrm{d} x} = \pi x$. Therefore

$$V = \tfrac{1}{2}\pi x^2 + k$$

for some number k.

Since the volume V is 0 when $x = 1$, $0 = \tfrac{1}{2}\pi \times 1^2 + k$, giving $k = -\tfrac{1}{2}\pi$. Thus

$$V = \tfrac{1}{2}\pi x^2 - \tfrac{1}{2}\pi.$$

To find the volume up to $x = 4$, substitute $x = 4$ in this expression for V. The volume is $\frac{1}{2}\pi \times 4^2 - \frac{1}{2}\pi = \frac{1}{2}\pi(16 - 1) = \frac{15}{2}\pi$.

You can shorten the last part of this work by noticing that you can use the integral notation introduced in C2 Section 5.5:

$$V = \int_1^4 \pi y^2 \, dx = \int_1^4 \pi x \, dx = \left[\tfrac{1}{2}\pi x^2\right]_1^4 = \tfrac{1}{2}\pi \times 16 - \tfrac{1}{2}\pi \times 1 = \tfrac{15}{2}\pi.$$

Notice that the argument used at the beginning of the example was completely general, and did not depend in any way on the equation of the original curve.

> The answer has been given without a unit, because it is not usual to attach a unit to the variables x and y when graphs are drawn. But if in a particular situation x and y each denote numbers of units, then you should attach the corresponding unit to the value of V.

> When the region under the graph of $y = f(x)$ between $x = a$ and $x = b$ (where $a < b$) is rotated about the x-axis, the volume of the solid of revolution formed is
> $$\int_a^b \pi y^2 \, dx \quad \text{or} \quad \int_a^b \pi (f(x))^2 \, dx.$$

Example 11.1.1

Find the volume generated when the region under the graph of $y = 1 + x^2$ between $x = -1$ and $x = 1$ is rotated through four right angles about the x-axis.

> The phrase 'four right angles' is sometimes used in place of $360°$ for describing the rotation about the x-axis.

The required volume is V cubic units, where

$$V = \int_{-1}^1 \pi y^2 \, dx = \int_{-1}^1 \pi (1 + x^2)^2 \, dx = \int_{-1}^1 \pi (1 + 2x^2 + x^4) \, dx$$

$$= \left[\pi \left(x + \tfrac{2}{3}x^3 + \tfrac{1}{5}x^5\right)\right]_{-1}^1$$

$$= \pi\left\{\left(1 + \tfrac{2}{3} + \tfrac{1}{5}\right) - \left((-1) + \tfrac{2}{3}(-1)^3 + \tfrac{1}{5}(-1)^5\right)\right\} = \tfrac{56}{15}\pi.$$

The volume of the solid is $\frac{56}{15}\pi$.

> It is usual to give the result as an exact multiple of π, unless you are asked for an answer correct to a given number of significant figures or decimal places.

You can also use the method to obtain the formula for the volume of a cone.

Example 11.1.2

Prove that the volume V of a cone with base radius r and height h is $V = \frac{1}{3}\pi r^2 h$.

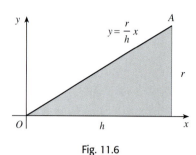

Fig. 11.6

The triangle which rotates to give the cone is shown in Fig. 11.6, where the 'height' has been drawn across the page. The gradient of OA is $\dfrac{r}{h}$, so its equation is $y = \dfrac{r}{h}x$.

Therefore, remembering that π, r and h are constants and do not depend on x,

$$V = \int_0^h \pi y^2 \, dx = \int_0^h \pi \left(\frac{r}{h}x\right)^2 dx = \int_0^h \pi \frac{r^2}{h^2} x^2 \, dx$$

$$= \pi \frac{r^2}{h^2} \int_0^h x^2 \, dx = \pi \frac{r^2}{h^2}\left[\tfrac{1}{3}x^3\right]_0^h = \pi \frac{r^2}{h^2} \times \tfrac{1}{3}h^3 = \tfrac{1}{3}\pi r^2 h.$$

11.2   Volumes of revolution about the *y*-axis

In Fig. 11.7, the region between the graph of $y = f(x)$ between $y = c$ and $y = d$ is rotated about the *y*-axis to give the solid shown in Fig. 11.8.

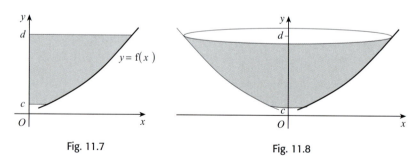

Fig. 11.7   Fig. 11.8

To find the volume of this solid of revolution about the *y*-axis, you can reverse the roles of x and y in the discussion in Section 11.1.

> When the the region bounded by the graph of $y = f(x)$, the lines $y = c$ and $y = d$ and the *y*-axis is rotated about the *y*-axis, the volume of the solid of revolution formed is
>
> $$\int_c^d \pi x^2 \, dy.$$

You can only use this result if the inverse function $x = f^{-1}(y)$ is defined for $c \leqslant y \leqslant d$ (see Section 2.7). Remember that the limits in the integral are limits for y, not for x.

Example 11.2.1

Find the volume generated when the region bounded by $y = x^3$ and the y-axis between $y = 1$ and $y = 8$ is rotated through $360°$ about the y-axis.

Since the volume is given by $\int_{1}^{8} \pi x^2 \, dy$, you need to express x^2 in terms of y.

The equation $y = x^3$ can be inverted to give $x = y^{\frac{1}{3}}$, so that $x^2 = y^{\frac{2}{3}}$. Then

$$V = \int_{1}^{8} \pi y^{\frac{2}{3}} \, dy = \pi \left[\tfrac{3}{5} y^{\frac{5}{3}} \right]_{1}^{8} = \pi \left(\tfrac{3}{5} \times 8^{\frac{5}{3}} \right) - \pi \left(\tfrac{3}{5} \times 1^{\frac{5}{3}} \right)$$
$$= \pi \left(\tfrac{3}{5} \times 32 \right) - \pi \left(\tfrac{3}{5} \times 1 \right) = \tfrac{93}{5} \pi.$$

The required volume is $\tfrac{93}{5} \pi$.

11.3 Rotating regions between curves

You can modify the methods used so far to find the volume of a region between two curves which is rotated about an axis.

Here is an example.

Example 11.3.1

Find the volume generated when the region between the curves $y = \tfrac{1}{2}x$ and $y = \sqrt{x}$ is rotated through $360°$ about the x-axis.

Fig. 11.9 shows the two curves in the first quadrant and their reflections in the x-axis.

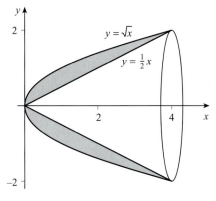

Fig. 11.9

The curves intersect when $\tfrac{1}{2}x = \sqrt{x}$, that is, when $x^2 = 4x$ or $x(x - 4) = 0$.

So the curves intersect when $x = 0$ and when $x = 4$.

You can find the required volume by finding the volume of the solid of revolution formed by rotating the curve $y = \sqrt{x}$ and then subtracting the cone formed by rotating $y = \frac{1}{2}x$. If this volume is V, then

$$V = \int_0^4 \pi (\sqrt{x})^2 \, dx - \int_0^4 \pi \left(\tfrac{1}{2}x\right)^2 \, dx$$

$$= \int_0^4 \pi x \, dx - \int_0^4 \pi \times \tfrac{1}{4}x^2 \, dx$$

$$= \pi \left[\tfrac{1}{2}x^2\right]_0^4 - \pi \left[\tfrac{1}{12}x^3\right]_0^4$$

$$= 8\pi - \tfrac{64}{12}\pi$$

$$= 8\pi - \tfrac{16}{3}\pi = \tfrac{8}{3}\pi.$$

Thus the required volume is $\frac{8}{3}\pi$ units.

You can easily generalise this argument to:

> If two graphs, $y = f(x)$ and $y = g(x)$, intersect at $x = a$ and $x = b$, and $f(x) \geqslant g(x)$ in the interval $a \leqslant x \leqslant b$, then the volume of the solid of revolution formed by rotating the region between the graphs about the x-axis is
>
> $$\int_a^b \pi (f(x))^2 \, dx - \int_a^b \pi (g(x))^2 \, dx \quad \text{or} \quad \int_a^b \pi \{(f(x))^2 - (g(x))^2\} \, dx.$$

There is no need to learn this formula because it is very easy to derive it from the $\int_a^b \pi y^2 \, dx$ result.

Example 11.3.2 deals with a similar situation when two graphs are rotated about the y-axis.

Example 11.3.2
Find the volume obtained when the minor segment between the circle $x^2 + y^2 = 25$ and the chord $x = 4$ is rotated about the y-axis.

The graphs intersect when $25 - y^2 = 16$, that is, when $y^2 = 9$, or when $y = \pm 3$.

Fig. 11.10 shows the situation with the minor segment shaded.

The required volume V is then given by

$$V = \int_{-3}^3 \pi (25 - y^2) \, dy - \int_{-3}^3 \pi 4^2 \, dy$$

$$= \pi \int_{-3}^3 (9 - y^2) \, dy$$

$$= \pi \left[9y - \tfrac{1}{3}y^3\right]_{-3}^3$$

$$= \pi \left((27 - \tfrac{1}{3} \times 27) - ((-27) - \tfrac{1}{3} \times (-27))\right)$$

$$= \pi (18) - \pi (-18) = 36\pi.$$

The required volume is 36π.

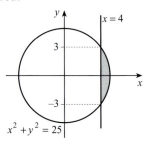

Fig. 11.10

Exercise 11

In all the questions in this exercise, leave your answers as multiples of π.

1 Find the volume generated when the region under the graph of $y = f(x)$ between $x = a$ and $x = b$ is rotated through $360°$ about the x-axis.

(a) $f(x) = x$; $a = 3$, $b = 5$ (b) $f(x) = x^2$; $a = 2$, $b = 5$

(c) $f(x) = x^3$; $a = 2$, $b = 6$ (d) $f(x) = \dfrac{1}{x}$; $a = 1$, $b = 4$

(e) $f(x) = e^x$; $a = 0$, $b = 1$ (f) $f(x) = e^{-x}$; $a = 0$, $b = 2$

2 Find the volume formed when the region under the graph of $y = f(x)$ between $x = a$ and $x = b$ is rotated through $360°$ about the x-axis.

(a) $f(x) = x + 3$; $a = 3$, $b = 9$ (b) $f(x) = x^2 + 1$; $a = 2$, $b = 5$

(c) $f(x) = \sqrt{x + 1}$; $a = 0$, $b = 3$ (d) $f(x) = x(x - 2)$; $a = 0$, $b = 2$

(e) $f(x) = e^{\frac{1}{2}x}$; $a = 1$, $b = 3$ (f) $f(x) = e^{-2x}$; $a = 0$, $b = 1$

3 Find the volume generated when the region bounded by the graph of $y = f(x)$, the y-axis and the lines $y = c$ and $y = d$ is rotated about the y-axis to form a solid of revolution.

(a) $f(x) = x^2$; $c = 1$, $d = 3$ (b) $f(x) = x + 1$; $c = 1, d = 4$

(c) $f(x) = \sqrt{x}$; $c = 2, d = 7$ (d) $f(x) = \dfrac{1}{x}$; $c = 2, d = 5$

(e) $f(x) = \sqrt{9 - x}$; $c = 0, d = 3$ (f) $f(x) = x^2 + 1$; $c = 1, d = 4$

(g) $f(x) = x^{\frac{2}{3}}$; $c = 1, d = 5$ (h) $f(x) = \dfrac{1}{x} + 2$; $c = 3, d = 5$

4 In each case the region enclosed between the following curves and the x-axis is rotated through $360°$ about the x-axis. Find the volume of the solid generated.

(a) $y = (x + 1)(x - 3)$ (b) $y = 1 - x^2$

(c) $y = x^2 - 5x + 6$ (d) $y = x^2 - 3x$

5 The region enclosed between the graphs of $y = x$ and $y = x^2$ is denoted by R. Find the volume generated when R is rotated through $360°$ about

(a) the x-axis,   (b) the y-axis.

6 The region enclosed between the graphs of $y = 4x$ and $y = x^2$ is denoted by R. Find the volume generated when R is rotated through $360°$ about

(a) the x-axis,   (b) the y-axis.

7 The region enclosed between the graphs of $y = \sqrt{x}$ and $y = x^2$ is denoted by R. Find the volume generated when R is rotated through $360°$ about

(a) the x-axis,   (b) the y-axis.

8 A glass bowl is formed by rotating about the y-axis the region between the graphs of $y = x^2$ and $y = x^3$. Find the volume of glass in the bowl.

9 The region enclosed by both axes, the line $x = 2$ and the curve $y = \frac{1}{8}x^2 + 2$ is rotated about the y-axis to form a solid. Find the volume of this solid.

10 The region between the curves $y = x^2$ and $y = x^3$ between $x = 0$ and $x = 1$ is rotated about the x-axis. Find the volume of the solid of revolution formed.

11 (a) Find the x-coordinates of the points of intersection of the graphs with equations $y = 20 - x^2$ and $y = 16 - 3x$, and sketch the graphs.

   (b) Find the volume of the solid of revolution formed when the region between the two graphs is rotated about the x-axis.

12 The region bounded by the curve $y = \frac{1}{2}(e^x - e^{-x})$, the lines $x = -1$, $x = 1$ and the x-axis is rotated through $360°$ about the x-axis. Find the volume of the solid formed.

Miscellaneous exercise 11

1 The region bounded by the curve $y = x^2 + 1$, the x-axis, the y-axis and the line $x = 2$ is rotated completely about the x-axis. Find, in terms of π, the volume of the solid formed. (OCR)

2 Explain why the coordinates (x, y) of any point on a circle, centre O, radius a satisfy the equation $x^2 + y^2 = a^2$.

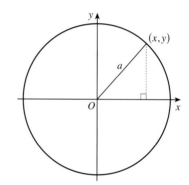

The semicircle above the x-axis is rotated about the x-axis through $360°$ to form a sphere of radius a. Explain why the volume V of this sphere is given by

$$V = 2\pi \int_0^a (a^2 - x^2)\, dx.$$

Hence show that $V = \frac{4}{3}\pi a^3$.

3 The ellipse with equation $\dfrac{x^2}{a^2} + \dfrac{y^2}{b^2} = 1$, shown in the diagram, has semi-axes a and b.

The ellipse is rotated about the x-axis to form an 'ellipsoid'. Find the volume of this ellipsoid.

Deduce the volume of the ellipsoid if, instead, the ellipse had been rotated about the y-axis.

4 The diagram shows the curve $y = x^{-\frac{2}{3}}$.

   (a) Show that the shaded area A is infinite.

   (b) Find the shaded area B.

   (c) Area A is rotated through $360°$ about the x-axis. Find the volume generated.

   (d) Area B is rotated through $360°$ about the y-axis. Find the volume generated.

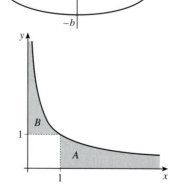

5 Investigate the equivalent areas and volumes to those in Question 4 for the equations
   (i) $y = x^{-\frac{3}{5}}$,   (ii) $y = x^{-\frac{1}{4}}$.

6 Sketch the curve $y = 9 - x^2$, stating the coordinates of the turning point and of the intersections with the axes.

The finite region bounded by the curve and the x-axis is denoted by R.

(a) Find the area of R and hence or otherwise find $\int_0^9 \sqrt{9 - y}\, dy$.

(b) Find the volume of the solid of revolution obtained when R is rotated through $360°$ about the x-axis.

(c) Find the volume of the solid of revolution obtained when R is rotated through $360°$ about the y-axis.

7 The region R is bounded by the part of the curve $y = (x - 2)^{\frac{3}{2}}$ for which $2 \leqslant x \leqslant 4$, the x-axis, and the line $x = 4$. Find, in terms of π, the volume of the solid obtained when R is rotated through four right angles about the x-axis. (OCR)

8 The diagram shows the region R, which is bounded by the axes and the part of the curve $y^2 = 4a(a - x)$ lying in the first quadrant. Find, in terms of a,

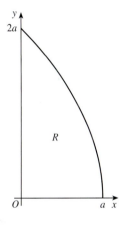

(a) the area of R,

(b) the volume, V_x, of the solid formed when R is rotated completely about the x-axis.

The volume of the solid formed when R is rotated completely about the y-axis is V_y. Show that $V_y = \frac{8}{15} V_x$.

The region S, lying in the first quadrant, is bounded by the curve $y^2 = 4a(a - x)$ and the lines $y = a$ and $y = 2a$. Find, in terms of a, the volume of the solid formed when S is rotated completely about the y-axis. (OCR, adapted)

9 The region under the curve with equation $y = \dfrac{1}{\sqrt{x}}$ is rotated through four right angles about the x-axis to form a solid. Find the volume of the solid between $x = 2$ and $x = 5$.

10 The region under the curve with equation $y = \dfrac{1}{\sqrt{2x - 1}}$ is rotated through four right angles about the x-axis to form a solid. Find the volume of the solid between $x = 3$ and $x = 8$.

11 The graph of $y = \dfrac{1}{x^2}$ between $x = 1$ and $x = 2$ is rotated about the y-axis. Find the volume of the solid formed.

12 The part of the graph between $y = e^{\frac{1}{2}x}$, the line $y = 2$ and the y-axis is rotated about the x-axis to make a solid of revolution. Find the volume of this solid, giving your answer in the form $\pi(a \ln b - c)$, where a, b and c are integers.

13 A metal napkin ring is modelled by rotating the part of the graph of $y = 5 - x^2$ cut off by the line $y = 4$ about the x-axis. Find the volume of the solid of revolution formed.

14 A sphere of radius r where $r > 2$ has a circular hole drilled completely through it so that the axis of the hole is a diameter of the sphere. The hole has length 4. Prove that the volume of the piece of the sphere which remains is independent of r.

12 Simpson's rule

This chapter gives another method, in addition to the trapezium rule, for approximating to integrals. When you have completed it, you should be able to

- carry out numerical integration of functions by Simpson's rule.

12.1 The inaccuracy of the trapezium rule

In C2 Chapter 10 you studied the trapezium rule. You saw then that the trapezium rule is a method of finding a numerical approximation to a definite integral based on the idea that the area under the curve shaded in Fig. 12.1 can be approximated by the area of the trapezium in Fig. 12.2.

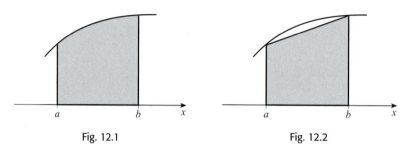

Fig. 12.1   Fig. 12.2

This method ignores the space between the trapezium and the curve, and it is natural to wonder whether there is a better way of approximating to the area in Fig. 12.1.

12.2 A geometric basis for Simpson's rule

Suppose that, instead of approximating to the curve by a straight line, you approximate to it by using a parabola with its axis vertical. This is illustrated in Fig. 12.3.

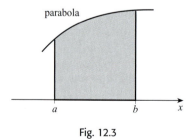

Fig. 12.3

As the equation of a parabola is quadratic it has three coefficients. To find these you need three pieces of information. This means that you can make the parabola fit the curve in Fig. 12.1 at three points. Take these to be at the two ends and at the middle of the interval.

None of the diagrams has so far shown a y-axis. The area of the shaded region under the parabola in Fig. 12.4 depends only on y_0, y_1 and y_2 and the width $b - a$. This means that you can choose the position of the y-axis wherever it is most convenient.

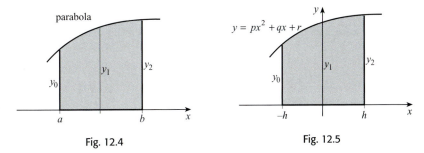

Fig. 12.4   Fig. 12.5

Choose the position of the y-axis to lie halfway between a and b, along the ordinate of height y_1, as shown in Fig. 12.5. It is also helpful to put $b - a = 2h$, so that the shaded region runs from $x = -h$ to $x = h$.

Suppose that, with the y-axis in this position, the equation of the parabola is $y = px^2 + qx + r$, where p, q and r are constants which will need to be found.

The area A under the parabola is

$$A = \int_{-h}^{h} (px^2 + qx + r)\, dx$$
$$= \left[\tfrac{1}{3} px^3 + \tfrac{1}{2} qx^2 + rx \right]_{-h}^{h}$$
$$= \left(\tfrac{1}{3} ph^3 + \tfrac{1}{2} qh^2 + rh \right) - \left(\tfrac{1}{3} p(-h)^3 + \tfrac{1}{2} q(-h)^2 + r(-h) \right)$$
$$= \tfrac{1}{3} ph^3 + \tfrac{1}{2} qh^2 + rh + \tfrac{1}{3} ph^3 - \tfrac{1}{2} qh^2 + rh$$
$$= \tfrac{2}{3} ph^3 + 2rh.$$

Notice that the result $A = \tfrac{2}{3} ph^3 + 2rh$ does not depend on q.

To find p and r you need the information that when $x = -h$, $y = y_0$, when $x = 0$, $y = y_1$ and when $x = h$, $y = y_2$.

This information leads to the equations

$$y_0 = p(-h)^2 + q(-h) + r,$$
$$y_1 = p \times 0^2 + q \times 0 + r,$$
$$y_2 = ph^2 + qh + r,$$

which reduce to

$$y_0 = ph^2 - qh + r,$$
$$y_1 = r,$$
$$y_2 = ph^2 + qh + r.$$

The second equation gives r directly, but you still need to find p. Adding the first and third equations gives

$$y_0 + y_2 = 2ph^2 + 2r$$

and since $r = y_1$,

$$y_0 + y_2 = 2ph^2 + 2y_1,$$

so $$2ph^2 = y_0 + y_2 - 2y_1.$$

Substituting these values in the expression for the area under the parabola,

$$\begin{aligned}
A &= \tfrac{2}{3}ph^3 + 2rh \\
&= \tfrac{1}{3}h \times 2ph^2 + 2h \times r \\
&= \tfrac{1}{3}h \times (y_0 + y_2 - 2y_1) + 2h \times y_1 \\
&= \tfrac{1}{3}h(y_0 + y_2 - 2y_1 + 6y_1) \\
&= \tfrac{1}{3}h(y_0 + y_2 + 4y_1) \\
&= \tfrac{1}{3}h(y_0 + 4y_1 + y_2).
\end{aligned}$$

Since the area under the parabola does not depend on the position of the y-axis, this formula also gives the area under the parabola in Fig. 12.4, between $x = a$ and $x = b$.

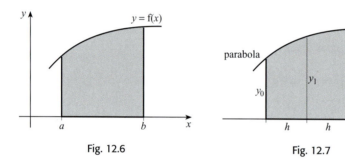

Fig. 12.6   Fig. 12.7

Returning to the original problem, the area under $y = f(x)$ between $x = a$ and $x = b$ in Fig. 12.6 is given by

$$\int_a^b f(x)\,dx.$$

As the area under the parabola in Fig. 12.7 is an approximation to the required area,

$$\int_a^b f(x)\,dx \approx \tfrac{1}{3}h(y_0 + 4y_1 + y_2),$$

where $b - a = 2h$.

This is the simplest form of **Simpson's rule**.

Thomas Simpson published this rule in 1743, although it had been used by others much earlier in 1668.

Notice that this form of Simpson's rule is based on two equal intervals of width h.

Example 12.2.1

Use the simplest form of Simpson's rule to find estimates for

(a) $\displaystyle\int_0^1 \frac{1}{1+x^2}\,dx$ and   (b) $\displaystyle\int_0^1 \sqrt{1+x^3}\,dx$.

(a) Take two intervals of width 0.5.

Then $y_0 = \dfrac{1}{1+0^2} = 1$, $y_1 = \dfrac{1}{1+0.5^2} = \dfrac{1}{1.25} = 0.8$ and $y_2 = \dfrac{1}{1+1^2} = \dfrac{1}{2} = 0.5$ so

$\displaystyle\int_0^1 \frac{1}{1+x^2}\,dx \approx \tfrac{1}{3} \times 0.5 \times (1 + 4 \times 0.8 + 0.5) = \tfrac{1}{3} \times 0.5 \times 4.7 = 0.7833\ldots$.

Hence $\displaystyle\int_0^1 \frac{1}{1+x^2}\,dx \approx 0.783$, to 3 significant figures.

(b) Take two intervals of width 0.5.

Then $y_0 = \sqrt{1+0^3} = \sqrt{1} = 1$, $y_1 = \sqrt{1+0.5^3} = \sqrt{1.125} = 1.060\ldots$ and
$y_2 = \sqrt{1+1^3} = \sqrt{2} = 1.414\ldots$, so

$\displaystyle\int_0^1 \sqrt{1+x^3}\,dx \approx \tfrac{1}{3} \times 0.5 \times (1 + 4 \times 1.060\ldots + 1.414\ldots)$

$\qquad\qquad = \tfrac{1}{3} \times 0.5 \times 6.656\ldots = 1.109\ldots$.

Hence $\displaystyle\int_0^1 \sqrt{1+x^3}\,dx \approx 1.11$, to 3 significant figures.

It is interesting to compare these results with the corresponding example in C2 Section 10.2 on the trapezium rule, where the answers were 0.75 and 1.21 respectively. The accurate answer for the first integral is $\frac{1}{4}\pi$, which is 0.785 correct to 3 significant figures. In part (b) the correct answer is 1.111 to 4 significant figures, so the Simpson approximation gives the answer correctly to 3 significant figures. In both cases the Simpson approximation is much closer than the trapezium approximation.

Exercise 12A

1 Use Simpson's rule to find approximations, to 5 decimal places, to

(a) $\displaystyle\int_0^1 e^x\,dx$,   (b) $\displaystyle\int_1^2 \frac{1}{x}\,dx$.

In each case compare your answer with the exact answer, stating the percentage error to 1 significant figure.

2 Use Simpson's rule to find an approximation, to 5 decimal places, to $\displaystyle\int_1^2 \ln x\,dx$.

3 Use Simpson's rule to estimate, to 5 decimal places, the value of $\displaystyle\int_0^{\frac{1}{2}\pi} \sin x\,dx$. Use the symmetry of the graph of $y = \sin x$ to deduce an approximation to $\displaystyle\int_0^{\pi} \sin x\,dx$.

12.3   Simpson's rule: general form

Just as with the trapezium rule, you can improve the accuracy of an estimate of area under a curve by Simpson's rule by increasing the number of intervals, and then using the simple form of Simpson's rule on each *pair* of intervals.

Divide the interval from a to b into $2n$ equal intervals, each of width h, so that $2nh = b - a$.

Call the x-coordinate of the left side of the first interval x_0, so $x_0 = a$, and then successively let $x_1 = x_0 + h$, $x_2 = x_0 + 2h$ and so on until $x_{n-1} = x_0 + (n-1)h$ and $x_{2n} = x_0 + 2nh = b$.

To shorten the amount of writing, use the shorthand $y_0 = f(x_0)$, $y_1 = f(x_1)$ and so on, as in Fig. 12.8.

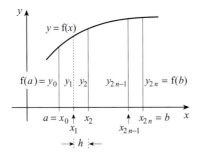

Fig. 12.8

Then, using the simple form of the Simpson's rule on each pair of intervals of width $2h$ in turn, you find that

$$\int_a^b f(x)\,dx \approx \tfrac{1}{3}h(y_0 + 4y_1 + y_2) + \tfrac{1}{3}h(y_2 + 4y_3 + y_4) + \tfrac{1}{3}h(y_4 + 4y_5 + y_6) + \cdots$$
$$+ \tfrac{1}{3}h(y_{2n-2} + 4y_{2n-1} + y_{2n})$$
$$= \tfrac{1}{3}h(y_0 + 4y_1 + y_2 + y_2 + 4y_3 + y_4 + y_4 + 4y_5 + y_6 + \cdots$$
$$+ y_{2n-2} + 4y_{2n-1} + y_{2n})$$
$$= \tfrac{1}{3}h(y_0 + 4y_1 + 2y_2 + 4y_3 + 2y_4 + \cdots + 2y_{2n-2} + 4y_{2n-1} + y_{2n}).$$

Simpson's rule with $2n$ intervals is sometimes called Simpson's rule with $2n + 1$ ordinates (y-values).

> **Simpson's rule** with $2n$ intervals (or $2n + 1$ ordinates) is
>
> $$\int_a^b f(x)\,dx \approx \tfrac{1}{3}h(y_0 + 4y_1 + 2y_2 + 4y_3 + 2y_4 + \cdots$$
> $$+ 2y_{2n-2} + 4y_{2n-1} + y_{2n}),$$
> where $h = \dfrac{b-a}{2n}$.

There are several points to notice about this form of Simpson's rule.

- With the trapezium rule you could choose any number of intervals, but with Simpson's rule it is essential that the interval $a < x < b$ is divided into an even number of subintervals.

- With the trapezium rule it is often possible to know from the shape of the graph whether the approximation is an overestimate or an underestimate, but this is not possible with Simpson's rule.

- It is often convenient to arrange the formula as

$$\tfrac{1}{3}h((y_0 + y_{2n}) + 4(y_1 + y_3 + \cdots + y_{2n-1}) + 2(y_2 + y_4 + \cdots + y_{2n-2})),$$

and to remember it as

$$\tfrac{1}{3}h((y_{\text{ends}}) + 4(y_{\text{odds}}) + 2(y_{\text{evens}})),$$

This explains the way in which the tables are laid out in Examples 12.3.1 and 12.3.2.

Example 12.3.1

Use Simpson's rule with 4 intervals to approximate to $\displaystyle\int_0^1 \frac{dx}{1 + x^2}$. Give your answer to 6 decimal places.

The values of y_n in Table 12.9 are given to 7 decimal places.

	n	x_n	y_n	Sums	Weight	Total
Ends $\{$	0	0	1			
	4	1	0.5	1.5	$\times 1 =$	1.5
Odds $\{$	1	0.25	0.941 176 5			
	3	0.75	0.64	1.581 176 5	$\times 4 =$	6.324 705 9
Evens	2	0.5	0.8	0.8	$\times 2 =$	1.6
						9.424 705 9

Table 12.9

The factor $\tfrac{1}{3}h$ is $\tfrac{1}{3} \times 0.25$. Therefore the approximation to the integral is $\tfrac{1}{3} \times 0.25 \times 9.424\ 705\ 9 = 0.785\ 392\ 2$. Thus the 4-interval approximation to 6 decimal places is 0.785 392.

The accurate value of this integral is $\tfrac{1}{4}\pi = 0.785\ 398\ 16...$, so you can see that Simpson's rule is just 6 out in the sixth decimal place.

Organising a table to find $y_0 + 4y_1 + 2y_2 + 4y_3 + 2y_4 + \cdots + 2y_{2n-2} + 4y_{2n-1} + y_{2n}$ is important, but precisely how you do it is up to you. It may well depend on the kind of software or calculator that you have. What is important, however, is that you make clear how you reach your answer.

Example 12.3.2

Use Simpson's rule with eleven ordinates to estimate the value of $\int_0^1 \sqrt{1+x^3}\,dx$. Give your answer to 5 decimal places.

The values of y_n in Table 12.10 are given to 7 decimal places.

	n	x_n	y_n	Sums	Weight	Total
Ends {	0	0	1			
	10	1	1.414 213 6	2.414 213 6	$\times 1 =$	2.414 213 6
Odds {	1	0.1	1.000 499 9			
	3	0.3	1.013 410 1			
	5	0.5	1.060 660 2			
	7	0.7	1.158 878 8			
	9	0.9	1.314 914 5	5.548 363 5	$\times 4 =$	22.193 454 0
Evens {	2	0.2	1.003 992 0			
	4		1.031 503 8			
	6		1.102 723 9			
	8		1.229 634 1	4.367 853 8	$\times 2 =$	8.735 707 6
						33.343 375 2

Table 12.10

The factor $\frac{1}{3}h$ is $\frac{1}{3} \times \frac{1}{10}$. Therefore the approximation to the integral is $\frac{1}{3} \times \frac{1}{10} \times 33.343\ 375\ 2 = 1.111\ 445\ 8$. Thus the 11-ordinate approximation to 5 decimal places is 1.111 45.

Exercise 12B

1 Use Simpson's rule with 5 ordinates to find approximations, to 5 decimal places, to

(a) $\int_0^1 e^x\,dx$ (b) $\int_1^2 \frac{1}{x}\,dx$

In each case compare your answer with the exact answer, stating the percentage error to 1 significant figure.

2 Use Simpson's rule with 4 intervals to find an approximation, to 5 decimal places, to $\int_1^2 \ln x\,dx$.

3 Use Simpson's rule with 10 intervals to find 5-decimal-place approximations to

(a) $\int_0^{0.5} \frac{6}{\sqrt{1-x^2}}\,dx$.   (b) $\int_0^{\pi} \sin x\,dx$.

4 The graph of $y = \sqrt[3]{1+x^2}$ between $x = 0$ and $x = 2$ is rotated about the x-axis to form a volume of revolution. Use Simpson's rule with 11 ordinates to find the volume of this solid, giving your answer to 3 decimal places.

Miscellaneous exercise 12

1 Use Simpson's rule with 5 ordinates to calculate $\int_0^1 x \sin \frac{1}{2}\pi x \, dx$, giving your answer to 5 decimal places.

2 Use Simpson's rule with 10 intervals to calculate $\int_0^2 x e^{-x} \, dx$, giving your answer to 5 decimal places.

3 The values of a function are given in the table.

x	0	0.25	0.5	0.75	1
$f(x)$	1.0000	0.9689	0.8776	0.7317	0.5403

Use Simpson's rule to estimate $\int_0^1 f(x) \, dx$.

4 Calculate an approximation to $\int_0^4 e^{-x^2} \, dx$, using Simpson's rule with 11 ordinates. The value of this integral is close to $\frac{1}{2}\sqrt{\pi}$. What approximation do you obtain for π from your result, and to how many figures is it correct?

5 (a) Calculate the exact value of $\int_0^1 e^x \, dx$.

   (b) Use Simpson's rule with 3 ordinates to calculate an approximate value of $\int_0^1 e^x \, dx$ giving your answer in exact form in terms of e. Denote your answer by S.

   (c) Writing $p = \sqrt{e}$, use the equation $S = \int_0^1 e^x \, dx$ to find an approximation to e. Give your answer to 3 decimal places.

6 Using Simpson's rule with 4 intervals, calculate an approximation to the volume of the solid of revolution obtained when the graph of $y = \ln 2x$ between $x = 1$ and $x = 3$ is rotated about the x-axis. Give your answer to 5 significant figures.

7 The integral $\int_{36}^{64} \sqrt{x} \, dx$ is denoted by I.

   (a) Find the exact value of I.

   (b) Use Simpson's rule with two intervals to find an estimate for I, giving your answer in terms of $\sqrt{2}$.

   Use your two answers to deduce that $\sqrt{2} \approx \frac{99}{70}$.

8 A river is 30 metres wide in a certain region and its depth, d metres, at a point x metres from one side is given by the formula $d = \frac{1}{60}\sqrt{x(30-x)(30+x)}$.

   (a) Use Simpson's rule with 6 intervals to estimate the cross-sectional area of the river in this region, giving your answer to 3 significant figures.

   (b) Given that, in this region, the river is flowing at a uniform speed of 50 metres per minute, estimate the number of cubic metres of water passing per minute.

   (OCR, adapted)

9 The speeds of an athlete on a training run were recorded at 30-second intervals:

Time after start (s)	0	30	60	90	120	150	180	210	240
Speed (m s^{-1})		3.0	4.6	4.8	5.1	5.4	5.2	4.9	4.6	3.8

The area under a speed–time graph represents the distance travelled. Use Simpson's rule to estimate the distance covered by the athlete, to the nearest 10 metres.

10 At a time t minutes after the start of a journey, the speed of a car travelling along a main road is v km h^{-1}. The table gives values of v every minute on the 10-minute journey.

t	0	1	2	3	4	5	6	7	8	9	10
v	0	31	46	42	54	57	73	70	68	48	0

Use Simpson's rule to estimate of the length of the 10-minute journey in kilometres. Give your answer to a sensible degree of approximation.

11 (a) Simpson's rule is used to approximate to $\int_0^4 x^4 \, dx$, with $2n$ intervals for $n = 1$, $n = 2$ and $n = 4$. Calculate the errors in each case. What do the answers suggest about the effect on the error of doubling the number of intervals?

(b) Carry out similar calculations with $\int_0^\pi \sin x \, dx$, given that the exact value of the integral is 2. Is the effect of doubling the number of intervals the same as in part (a)?

12* In the figure, $y = Q(x)$ is the equation of the quadratic graph through $(-h, y_0)$, $(0, y_1)$ and (h, y_2), and $y = C(x)$ is the equation of a cubic polynomial through these points. Let $f(x) = C(x) - Q(x)$.

(a) Show that $f(-h) = f(0) = f(h)$.

(b) Explain why $f(x)$ is given by an equation of the form $f(x) = a(x + h)x(x - h)$, where a is a constant.

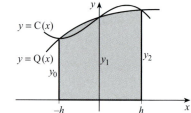

(c) Find $\int_{-h}^{h} f(x) \, dx$. Hence show that Simpson's rule gives exact answers for the area under $y = C(x)$ from $x = -h$ to $x = h$.

13* When deriving Simpson's rule, an alternative way of writing the equation of the parabola is $y = px(x - h) + q(x + h)(x - h) + rx(x + h)$. The values of y at $x = -h$, $x = 0$ and $x = h$ are y_0, y_1 and y_2 respectively.

(a) Find the values of p, q and r.

(b) Carry out the integration $\int_{-h}^{h} y \, dx$ and confirm that you get the same result for the area under the parabola as that found in Section 12.2.

14* Two methods are used to approximate to the value of $\int_a^b f(x)\,dx$. The interval $a \leqslant x \leqslant b$ is divided into $2n$ equal parts, and the values of $f(x)$ at the ends of successive intervals are $y_0, y_1, y_2, \ldots, y_{2n-1}, y_{2n}$; $h = \dfrac{b-a}{2n}$. The area under the curve is then approximated

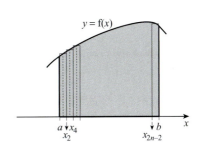

(a) as the sum of the areas of $2n$ trapezia, giving the answer T; and

(b) as the sum of the areas of n rectangles of equal width, whose heights are the values of $f(x)$ at the midpoints of each of the n intervals, as shown in the diagram, giving the answer R.

Write down expressions for T and R. If the curve bends downwards, state for each approximation whether it is an overestimate or an underestimate.

Show that the Simpson rule approximation to the area is equal to $\frac{2}{3}T + \frac{1}{3}R$.

Revision exercise 2

1 Find the coordinates of the stationary point of the curve $y = \ln(x^2 - 6x + 10)$ and show that this stationary point is a minimum.

2 Use a calculator to find a number a for which $e^x > x^5$ for all $x > a$.

3 Use appropriate rules of differentiation to find $\dfrac{dy}{dx}$ in each of the following cases.

(a) $y = \dfrac{3x^2}{\ln x}$ for $x > 1$

(b) $y = \left(1 - \dfrac{x}{5}\right)^{10}$ (OCR)

4 The diagram shows a sector of a circle with centre O and radius r, and a chord AB which subtends an angle θ radians at O, where $0 < \theta < \pi$.

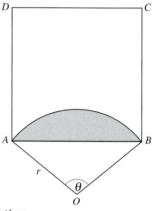

A square $ABCD$ is drawn, as shown in the diagram. It is given that the area of the shaded segment is exactly one-eighth of the area of the square. Show that

$$2\theta - 2\sin\theta + \cos\theta - 1 = 0.$$

Hence show that θ lies between 1 and 2, and use a numerical method to find θ correct to 1 decimal place.

5 (a) Use Simpson's rule with five ordinates to find an approximation to the value of the integral $\displaystyle\int_1^2 e^{\frac{1}{x}}\,dx$. Give your answer correct to 3 significant figures.

(b) Differentiate $e^{\frac{1}{x}}$.

(c) Do you expect your answer to part (a) to be an overestimate or an underestimate of the true value of $\displaystyle\int_1^2 e^{\frac{1}{x}}\,dx$? Give a reason for your answer.

6 The diagram shows the graph of $y = \sqrt{e^{2x} + 4}$. The region R, shaded in the diagram, is bounded by the curve and by the lines $y = 0$, $x = 0$ and $x = 1.5$.

The region R is rotated through four right angles about the x-axis. Find the volume of the solid formed, giving your answer in terms of π and e.   (OCR)

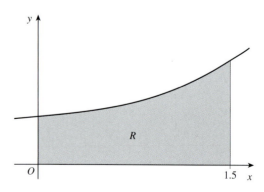

7 The number of rodents on a small remote island is recorded over a period of time. The number of rodents at time t years is denoted by P. The quantities P and t are treated as continuous variables.

   (a) One model for the number of rodents is given by $P = 280 - \dfrac{1450}{t + 10}$. Find an expression for $\dfrac{\mathrm{d}P}{\mathrm{d}t}$. Hence determine the value predicted by the model for the rate at which the number of rodents will be increasing when $t = 5$.

   (b) An alternative model for the number of rodents is given by $P = 280 - \dfrac{1450}{e^{0.2t} + 9}$.

   Determine the value predicted by the model for the rate at which the number of rodents will be increasing when $t = 5$.

   (c) For the alternative model described in part (b), state the value of P when $t = 0$ and state what the model predicts will happen to the number of rodents in the long term.   (OCR)

8 The function f is defined by

   $$\mathrm{f}{:}x \mapsto \tfrac{1}{4}\ln(3x + 6) \quad x > -2$$

   and a sketch of the graph of $y = \mathrm{f}(x)$ is shown.

   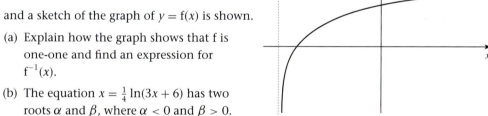

   (a) Explain how the graph shows that f is one-one and find an expression for $\mathrm{f}^{-1}(x)$.

   (b) The equation $x = \tfrac{1}{4}\ln(3x + 6)$ has two roots α and β, where $\alpha < 0$ and $\beta > 0$.

      (i) Show that $\alpha < -1.9995$, and hence state the value of α correct to 3 decimal places.

      (ii) Use an iteration process based on the equation $x = \tfrac{1}{4}\ln(3x + 6)$ to find the value of β correct to 3 decimal places. You should show the result of each iteration.

      (iii) Explain why the curves with equations $y = \mathrm{f}(x)$ and $y = \mathrm{f}^{-1}(x)$ meet at the points (α, α) and (β, β).   (OCR)

9 Find the equation of the tangent to the curve $y = (x^2 + 1)^5$ at the point $(-1, 32)$. Give your answer in the form $y = mx + c$.

10 The diagram shows a sector OAB of a circle, centre O and radius 10 cm. Angle AOB is θ radians. The point C lies on OB and is such that AC is perpendicular to OB. The region R (shaded in the diagram) is bounded by the arc AB and by the lines AC and CB. The area of R is 22 cm^2.

   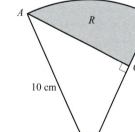

   (a) Show that $\theta = 0.44 + \sin\theta\cos\theta$.

   (b) Show that θ lies between 0.9 and 1.0.

   (c) Use an iterative process based on the equation in part (a) to find the value of θ correct to 2 decimal places. You should show the result of each iteration.   (OCR)

11 The sequence defined by the iterative formula $x_{n+1} = \sqrt[3]{17 - 5x_n}$, with $x_1 = 2$, converges to α.

(a) Use the iterative formula to find α correct to 2 decimal places. You should show the result of each iteration.

(b) Find a cubic equation of the form $x^3 + cx + d = 0$ which has α as a root.

12 The diagram shows the curve $y = \dfrac{1}{\sqrt{4x - 1}}$.
The region R (shaded in the diagram) is enclosed by part of the curve and by the lines $x = 1$, $x = 2$ and $y = 0$.

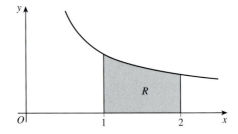

(a) Find the exact area of R.

(b) The region R is rotated through four right angles about the x-axis. Find the exact volume of the solid formed.

(c) Find the percentage errors when Simpson's rule with two intervals is used to calculate the area of R and the volume of the solid of revolution. Give your answers correct to 2 significant figures.   (OCR, adapted)

13 The mean annual temperature of the water in a certain large lake is expected to increase due to climatic change. A model giving the mean annual temperature, $\theta\,°C$, at a time t years after the first observation is $\theta = 0.0006t^2 + 0.05t + 4.3$.

The number of crustaceans in the lake depends on the water temperature. A model giving the number, N, of crustaceans is $N = 320e^{0.4\theta}$.

(a) According to the models, how many crustaceans were present in the lake when the first observation was made?

(b) By first writing down expressions for $\dfrac{d\theta}{dt}$ and $\dfrac{dN}{d\theta}$, find the rate at which the models predict that the number of crustaceans will be increasing when $t = 30$.   (OCR)

14 The diagram shows the graph of $y = \sqrt{1 + x^2}$.
The region R, shaded in the diagram, is bounded by the curve and the lines $x = 0$, $x = a$ and $y = 0$. When R is rotated through four right angles about the x-axis, the volume of the solid produced is 25 cubic units.

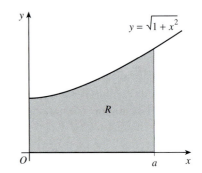

(a) Find an equation for a and show that a suitable rearrangement of the equation leads to the iterative formula

$$a_{n+1} = \sqrt[3]{\dfrac{75}{\pi} - 3a_n}.$$

(b) Use the iterative formula in part (a) with $a_1 = 2.5$ to find a_2, a_3 and a_4, giving each value correct to 3 decimal places. Hence state the value of a correct to 2 decimal places.   (OCR)

15 The volume of a sphere is increasing at a rate of 75 cm^3 s^{-1}. Find the rate at which the radius is increasing at the instant when the radius of the sphere is 15 cm. Give your answer correct to 2 significant figures. (OCR)

16 The diagram shows a circle with centre C and radius r. The chord AB is such that the angle $ACB = \theta$ radians. It is given that the area of the minor segment, shaded in the diagram, is one-fifth of the area of the whole circle.

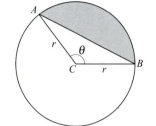

(a) Show that $\theta = \frac{2}{5}\pi + \sin\theta$.

(b) Use an iteration process based on the equation in part (a), with a starting value of 2, to find the value of θ correct to 1 decimal place. You should state the result of each iteration. (OCR)

17 The region R is bounded by the x-axis, the line $x = 16$ and the curve with equation $y = 6 - \sqrt{x}$, where $16 \leqslant x \leqslant 36$. Find, in terms of π, the volume of the solid generated when R is rotated through one revolution about the x-axis. (OCR, adapted)

18 Find $\dfrac{\mathrm{d}^2 y}{\mathrm{d}x^2}$ for each of the following functions with respect to x.

(a) $y = (x^3 + 2x - 1)^3$ (b) $y = \mathrm{e}^{3x-1}$ (c) $y = \ln(x^2 - 1)$ (d) $y = \sqrt{\dfrac{1}{x^2 + 1}}$

19 A spherical star is collapsing in size, while remaining spherical. When its radius is one million kilometres, the radius is decreasing at the rate 500 km s^{-1}. Find

(a) the rate of decrease of its volume,   (b) the rate of decrease of its surface area.

20 The region R is bounded by the x-axis, the y-axis, part of the curve with equation $y = \mathrm{e}^{2x}$ and part of the straight line with equation $x = 3$.

Calculate, giving your answers in exact form,

(a) the area of R,

(b) the volume of the solid of revolution generated when R is rotated through four right angles about the x-axis.

21 Use Simpson's rule with 6 intervals to calculate an approximation to $\displaystyle\int_0^3 \mathrm{e}^{-x^2}\, \mathrm{d}x$, giving your answer correct to 4 decimal places.

22 Use an approximate method to find all the roots of the cubic equation $x^3 - 2x^2 - 2x + 2 = 0$, giving your answers correct to 2 decimal places.

23 (a) Let $y = \mathrm{e}^{3x^2 - 6x}$. Find $\dfrac{\mathrm{d}y}{\mathrm{d}x}$.

(b) Find the coordinates of the stationary point on the curve $y = \mathrm{e}^{3x^2 - 6x}$, and decide whether it is a maximum or a minimum.

(c) Find the equation of the normal to the curve $y = \mathrm{e}^{3x^2 - 6x}$ at the point where $x = 2$.

24 The region R, bounded by the curve $y = 2x + \dfrac{1}{x^2}$, the
x-axis and the lines $x = 1$ and $x = k$ is shaded in
the figure.

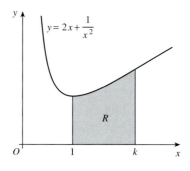

(a) Use integration to calculate the area of the region R
when $k = 2$.

For a different value of k, the area of R is 10 square units.

(b) Show that k satisfies the equation $k^3 - 10k - 1 = 0$,
and use a numerical method to find the value of
k correct to 3 significant figures.   (OCR, adapted)

25 (a) Show that the equation $9e^{-x} = x^2$, $x > 0$, has a solution, α, near to $x = 1.5$.

(b) Show that two possible rearrangements of the equation are $x = 3e^{-\frac{1}{2}x}$ and $x = \ln\left(\dfrac{9}{x^2}\right)$.

(c) Each of these rearrangements is used iteratively with starting value $x = 1.5$ in order to
find the solution, α. Show, numerically or otherwise, that one iteration converges and
the other diverges.

(d) An iteration which diverges can sometimes be used to obtain a solution as follows.

Use x_0 to find x_1 from the iterative formula.

Let $x_2 = \frac{1}{2}(x_0 + x_1)$.

Use x_2 to find x_3 from the iterative formula.

Let $x_4 = \frac{1}{2}(x_2 + x_3)$, etc.

Use this method on the diverging iteration in part (c) to discover whether it produces
the required solution, α, in this case.   (MEI)

Practice examination 1 for C3

Time 1 hour 30 minutes

Answer all the questions.

You are permitted to use a graphic calculator in this paper.

1. Solve exactly the equation $|x - 2| = |3 - 2x|$. [4]

2. (i) Show that the equation $x^3 - 3x - 10 = 0$ has a root between $x = 2$ and $x = 3$. [2]

   (ii) Find an approximation, correct to 3 decimal places, to this root using an iteration based on the equation in the form $x = (3x + 10)^{\frac{1}{3}}$. [4]

3. (i) Sketch the graph of $y = \tan^{-1} x$, and state the value to which y tends as $x \to \infty$. [2]

   (ii) Use Simpson's rule with four intervals each of width 0.25 to estimate the value of
   $$\int_0^1 \tan^{-1} x \, dx.$$ [4]

4. The region R is bounded by the curve $y = \dfrac{1}{2x + 1}$, the x-axis, and the lines $x = 1$ and $x = 4$.

   (i) Find the exact area of R, giving your answer in a simplified form. [4]

   (ii) The region R is rotated completely about the x-axis to form a solid of revolution. Show that the volume of this solid is $\frac{1}{9}\pi$. [4]

5. The angle θ (in radians) satisfies the equation $\tan 2\theta = \sin \theta$.

   (i) Show that either $\sin \theta = 0$ or $2 \cos \theta = \cos 2\theta$. [3]

   (ii) Hence show that the smallest positive value of θ is $\cos^{-1}\left(\dfrac{1 - \sqrt{3}}{2}\right)$. [5]

6. Use differentiation to find the exact coordinates of the turning point on each of the following curves.

   (i) $y = xe^x$ [4]

   (ii) $y = \dfrac{\ln x}{x}$ [5]

7. The amount, q units, of radioactivity present in a substance is given at time t seconds by the equation $q = 10e^{-\frac{1}{100}t}$.

   (i) Calculate the rate of decrease in the amount of radioactivity when $t = 5$. [3]

   The 'half-life', T seconds, of the radioactive substance is the time after which the amount of radioactivity present has halved from its value when $t = 0$.

   (ii) Calculate the half-life of the substance. [4]

   (iii) What can you say about the amounts of radioactivity present after $2T$ seconds, $3T$ seconds, $4T$ seconds, etc? [2]

8 The functions f and g are defined by

$$f : x \mapsto \frac{1}{x+1}, \qquad -1 < x \leqslant 2,$$
$$g : x \mapsto 2x - 1, \qquad x \in \mathbb{R}.$$

(i) Find the range of f.   [2]

(ii) Calculate gf(1).   [2]

(iii) Find an expression in terms of x for $g^{-1}(x)$.   [2]

(iv) Solve for x the equation $3g(x) = 5gf(x)$.   [4]

9 (i) Sketch the graphs of $y = \tan\theta$ and $y = \sec\theta$, in each case for $0 \leqslant \theta < \frac{1}{2}\pi$.   [2]

(ii) Prove that $\sec\theta - \tan\theta = \dfrac{1}{\sec\theta + \tan\theta}$.   [2]

(iii) Deduce from parts (i) and (ii) that

$$0 < \sec\theta - \tan\theta \leqslant 1,$$

for values of θ such that $0 \leqslant \theta < \frac{1}{2}\pi$. Explain your reasoning clearly.   [3]

(iv) Given that

$$\sec\theta - \tan\theta = \tfrac{1}{2},$$

find the exact value of $\cos\theta$.   [5]

Practice examination 2 for C3

Time 1 hour 30 minutes

Answer all the questions.

You are permitted to use a graphic calculator in this paper.

1 The volume of a sphere is increasing at a constant rate of 5 cm^3 s^{-1}. For an instant when the radius is 50 cm, calculate

    (i) the rate at which the radius is increasing,   [4]

    (ii) the rate at which the surface area is increasing.   [2]

    [The volume and surface area of a sphere of radius r are given by $V = \frac{4}{3}\pi r^3$ and $A = 4\pi r^2$ respectively.]

2 A solid is made by rotating the region bounded by the curve $y = (3x - 1)^{\frac{3}{2}}$, the x-axis and the lines $x = \frac{2}{3}$ and $x = \frac{4}{3}$ through four right angles about the x-axis. Find the volume of the solid, giving your answer in terms of π.   [6]

3 Differentiate the following with respect to x, simplifying the answers:

    (i) $x^2 e^{2x}$;   [3]

    (ii) $\ln\left(\dfrac{x}{x+1}\right)$.   [4]

4 (i) Write down the formula for $\tan 2\theta$ in terms of $\tan \theta$.   [1]

    (ii) Deduce that $\tan 22\frac{1}{2}°$ is a root of the equation $t^2 + 2t - 1 = 0$, and hence find the exact value of $\tan 22\frac{1}{2}°$.   [4]

    (iii) Express the other root of the quadratic equation in part (b) in trigonometrical form.   [2]

5 (i) Sketch the graph of $y = \cot x$, for values of x between 0 and 2π.   [1]

    (ii) Solve, for $0 < x < 2\pi$, each of the the inequalities

        (i) $\cot x < 1$,   [2]

        (ii) $|\cot x| < 1$.   [3]

    (iii) Explain briefly why, although $\cot x$ can be written as $\dfrac{\cos x}{\sin x}$, the solution set of the inequality $\cot x < 1$ is not the same as the solution set of the inequality $\cos x < \sin x$, and state a value of x that satisfies one of these inequalities but not the other.   [3]

6 *OAB* is a stiff bent rod, consisting of two straight parts *OA* and *OB* of lengths 6 and 4 respectively, with a right-angle bend at *A*, as shown in the diagram. The rod can rotate about *O*, and the angle that *OA* makes with the *x*-axis is θ, where $0° < \theta < 90°$. The projections of *B* on the *x*- and *y*-axes are *P* and *Q* respectively.

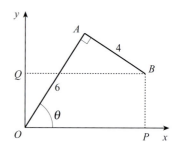

(i) Show that $OP = 6\cos\theta + 4\sin\theta$, and find a similar expression for *OQ*. [3]

(ii) Prove that the area of the rectangle *OPBQ* is $10\sin 2\theta - 24\cos 2\theta$. [3]

(iii) By writing the area of the rectangle in the form $R\sin(2\theta - \alpha)$, find the maximum value of the area as θ varies, and the value of θ for which the maximum occurs. [5]

7 The diagram shows the graph of $y = e^{-x}$. The point *P* has coordinates (a, e^{-a}), and the lines *PM* and *PN* are parallel to the axes.

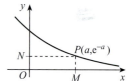

(i) Find $\displaystyle\int_0^a e^{-x}\,dx$ in terms of *a*.

The area of the rectangle *OMPN* is one quarter of the area under the curve $y = e^{-x}$ from $x = 0$ to $x = a$. [3]

(ii) Show that $e^a = 4a + 1$. [3]

(iii) Show that this equation has a root between 2 and 3, and show graphically that this is the only positive root. [4]

(iv) Use the iteration $a_{n+1} = \ln(4a_n + 1)$ to find the positive value of *a* satisfying the equation in part (ii). Give your answer correct to 2 decimal places. [3]

8 The diagram shows the graph of the function f given by
$$f : x \mapsto \frac{x+1}{x-1}, \quad x \in \mathbb{R}, \ x \neq 1.$$

(i) State the range of f. [1]

(ii) Explain how you can tell from the diagram that f has an inverse, and give a definition of the inverse function f^{-1} in a form similar to the definition of f shown above. [4]

(iii) What can you deduce from your answer to part (ii) about the graph of f in relation to the line $y = x$? [1]

The function g is given by g: $x \mapsto \dfrac{1}{x}$, $x \in \mathbb{R}$, $x \neq 0$.

(iv) Show algebraically that $f(x) \equiv 1 + 2g(x - 1)$. [3]

(v) Hence describe a sequence of geometrical transformations that transform the graph of $y = g(x)$ to that of $y = f(x)$. [4]

Module C4

Core 4

1 Differentiating trigonometric functions

This chapter shows how to differentiate the functions $\sin x$ and $\cos x$. When you have completed it, you should

- be familiar with a number of inequalities and limits involving trigonometric functions, and their geometrical interpretations
- know the derivatives and indefinite integrals of $\sin x$ and $\cos x$
- be able to differentiate a variety of trigonometric functions using the chain rule and the product and quotient rules
- be able to integrate a variety of trigonometric functions, using identities where necessary.

1.1 The advantage of using radians

In the first three modules of this course you have learnt how to differentiate a variety of functions: powers and polynomials (C1 Chapter 5), and exponentials and logarithms (C3 Chapter 5). The basic results are the derivatives of x^n, e^x and $\ln x$; once you know these, many combinations of these functions can be differentiated using techniques such as the chain rule and the product rule.

The same is true of the trigonometric functions. The only results you need to find from first principles are the derivatives of the sine and cosine functions. You can then use identities like $\tan\theta \equiv \dfrac{\sin\theta}{\cos\theta}$ and definitions such as $\sec\theta \equiv \dfrac{1}{\cos\theta}$ to differentiate the other functions. (In fact, you only need to know how to differentiate sine, since cosine can then be differentiated using $\cos\theta \equiv \sin\left(\theta + \frac{1}{2}\pi\right)$. But it is hardly worthwhile, since it is very easy to deal with sine and cosine at the same time.)

The first important point to make is that the rules for differentiating $\sin\theta$ and $\cos\theta$ are based on an angle θ measured in radians. This is not surprising. The degree is an artificial unit of angle; it is a historical accident that a revolution was divided into 360 parts. But there are good mathematical reasons for using the radian as a unit.

The graphs of $\sin\theta$ and $\cos\theta$ show the advantage of working in radians when differentiating. Look at Figs. 1.2 and 1.3 in Section 1.2, where these graphs are drawn correctly to scale. Differentiation is about finding the gradient, and you can see from both figures that the gradient where the graph crosses the horizontal axis is equal to 1. This doesn't happen if any other unit is used for θ.

> This may remind you of the reason for choosing e for the base of the exponential function, since the derivative of e^x when $x = 0$ is equal to 1.

The crucial property of radians that you need comes from looking at the function $\dfrac{\sin\theta}{\theta}$ for small values of θ. Try using your calculator to evaluate this expression for $\theta = 0.1$, $\theta = 0.01$

and $\theta = 0.001$. You should get successively $0.998\,334...$, $0.999\,983...$, and $0.999\,999....$ It is not difficult to guess that as θ tends to 0, the value of $\dfrac{\sin\theta}{\theta}$ tends to 1. This is the key to differentiating $\sin\theta$ and $\cos\theta$.

The next two sections of this chapter develop the basic theory. Section 1.2 uses the definition of radians to get some important properties of the trigonometric functions, including the result $\displaystyle\lim_{\theta\to 0}\dfrac{\sin\theta}{\theta} = 1$. In Section 1.3 these properties are used to obtain the derivatives of $\sin\theta$ and $\cos\theta$. The rest of the chapter then uses these results to find the derivatives and integrals of many other trigonometric functions and to use these for various practical applications.

1.2 Some inequalities and limits

Fig. 1.1 shows a sector OAB of a circle with radius r units and angle θ radians (where $\theta < \tfrac{1}{2}\pi$). The tangent at B meets OA produced at D. Comparing areas, you will see that

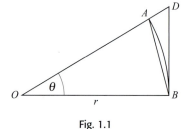

Fig. 1.1

$$\text{triangle } OAB < \text{sector } OAB < \text{triangle } ODB.$$

So using the formulae for the area of a triangle (C2 Section 4.2) and a sector (C2 Section 9.3),

$$\tfrac{1}{2}r^2\sin\theta < \tfrac{1}{2}r^2\theta < \tfrac{1}{2}r \times r\tan\theta.$$

Dividing by $\tfrac{1}{2}r^2$, it follows that, for $0 < \theta < \tfrac{1}{2}\pi$,

$$\sin\theta < \theta < \tan\theta.$$

If θ is small, Fig. 1.1 suggests that the three numbers $\sin\theta$, θ and $\tan\theta$ will be very close to each other.

Check this by setting $\theta = 0.1$ on your calculator. Remember to put it into radian mode.

So you can also write, if θ is small,

$$\sin\theta \approx \theta \quad \text{and} \quad \tan\theta \approx \theta.$$

One useful form of the inequality can be found by taking the left and right parts separately. First, since $\theta > 0$, you can divide the inequality $\sin\theta < \theta$ by θ to obtain

$$\frac{\sin\theta}{\theta} < 1.$$

Secondly, you can write $\theta < \tan\theta$ as $\theta < \dfrac{\sin\theta}{\cos\theta}$. Multiplying this by $\cos\theta$ and dividing by θ, both of which are positive since $0 < \theta < \tfrac{1}{2}\pi$, gives

$$\cos\theta < \frac{\sin\theta}{\theta}.$$

Putting these new inequalities together again gives, for $0 < \theta < \frac{1}{2}\pi$,

$$\cos\theta < \frac{\sin\theta}{\theta} < 1.$$

This is illustrated in Fig. 1.2.

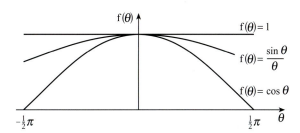

Fig. 1.2

Notice that the graphs have been extended to the left to cover the interval $-\frac{1}{2}\pi < \theta < \frac{1}{2}\pi$.

Since $\cos(-\theta) = \cos\theta$ and $\dfrac{\sin(-\theta)}{(-\theta)} = \dfrac{-\sin\theta}{-\theta} = \dfrac{\sin\theta}{\theta}$, both $\cos\theta$ and $\dfrac{\sin\theta}{\theta}$ are even functions. This means that the inequality holds also for $-\frac{1}{2}\pi < \theta < 0$.

However, Fig. 1.2 obscures an important point, that $\dfrac{\sin\theta}{\theta}$ is not defined when $\theta = 0$, since the fraction then becomes the meaningless $\dfrac{0}{0}$. But the graph does show that $\dfrac{\sin\theta}{\theta}$ approaches the limit 1 as $\theta \to 0$.

> If $0 < \theta < \frac{1}{2}\pi$, $\sin\theta < \theta < \tan\theta$.
>
> As $\theta \to 0$, $\dfrac{\sin\theta}{\theta} \to 1$.

Example 1.2.1
Show that the graph of $y = \sin x$, shown in Fig. 1.3, has gradient 1 at the origin.

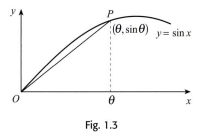

Fig. 1.3

Let the point P on the graph have coordinates $(\theta, \sin\theta)$, so $\dfrac{\sin\theta}{\theta}$ is the gradient of the chord OP. As $\theta \to 0$, this tends to the gradient of the tangent at the origin.

But as $\theta \to 0$, $\dfrac{\sin\theta}{\theta} \to 1$, so the sine graph has gradient 1 at the origin.

The inequality $\sin\theta < \theta < \tan\theta$ also says something about lengths. In Fig. 1.4, the sector in Fig. 1.1 has been reflected in the radius OB; C and E are the reflections of A and D. Then $AC = 2r\sin\theta$, arc $ABC = r(2\theta) = 2r\theta$, and $DE = 2r\tan\theta$. So the inequality states that

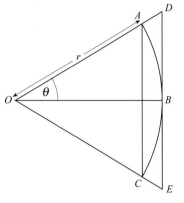

$$\text{chord } AC < \text{arc } ABC < \text{tangent } DE.$$

Note also that, in Fig. 1.4,

$$\frac{\text{chord } AC}{\text{arc } ABC} = \frac{2r\sin\theta}{2r\theta} = \frac{\sin\theta}{\theta},$$

so that the ratio of the chord to the arc tends to 1 as θ tends to 0. This result will be needed in the next section.

Fig. 1.4

> In a circular sector, as the angle at the centre tends to 0, the ratio of the chord to the arc tends to 1.

1.3 Derivatives of sine and cosine functions

This section shows how the limits established in Section 1.2 can be used to differentiate sines and cosines. You can if you like skip this for a first reading, and pick up the chapter at Section 1.4.

The proof is based on the definitions of $\cos\theta$ and $\sin\theta$ (given in C2 Sections 1.1 and 1.2) as the x- and y-coordinates of a point on a circle of radius 1 unit.

> In C2 $\cos\theta$ and $\sin\theta$ were defined with θ in degrees, but the definitions work just as well with θ in radians.

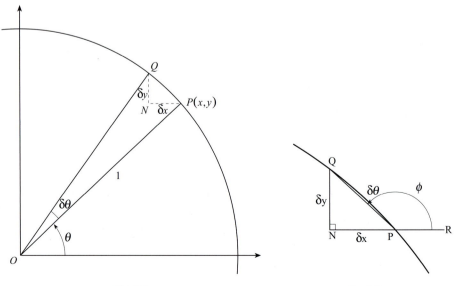

Fig. 1.5   Fig. 1.6

In Fig. 1.5, the point P has coordinates $x = \cos\theta$ and $y = \sin\theta$. If the angle is increased by $\delta\theta$, x increases by δx (which is actually a negative increase if θ is an acute angle, as shown here) and y by δy. The increases in x and y are represented in the figure by the displacements PN and NQ.

Fig. 1.6 is an enlargement of the part of Fig. 1.5 around PNQ. Because the circle has unit radius, the arc PQ has length $\delta\theta$. Extend the line NP to R, parallel to the x-axis, and let ϕ be the angle RPQ. Then

$$\delta x = PQ\cos\phi \quad \text{and} \quad \delta y = PQ\sin\phi.$$

> Note that, since ϕ is an obtuse angle, these equations make δx negative and δy positive, as you would expect from the diagrams. If P were located in another quadrant of the circle, the signs would be different, but the equations for δx and δy would still be correct.

The aim is to find $\dfrac{\mathrm{d}x}{\mathrm{d}\theta}$ and $\dfrac{\mathrm{d}y}{\mathrm{d}\theta}$, which are defined as

$$\lim_{\delta\theta\to 0}\frac{\delta x}{\delta\theta} \quad \text{and} \quad \lim_{\delta\theta\to 0}\frac{\delta y}{\delta\theta}.$$

Now $\dfrac{\delta x}{\delta\theta} = \dfrac{PQ}{\delta\theta} \times \cos\phi = \cos\phi \times \dfrac{\text{chord } PQ}{\text{arc } PQ}$,

and $\dfrac{\delta y}{\delta\theta} = \dfrac{PQ}{\delta\theta} \times \sin\phi = \sin\phi \times \dfrac{\text{chord } PQ}{\text{arc } PQ}$.

Fig. 1.7 shows that the angle ϕ tends to $\theta + \frac{1}{2}\pi$ as $\delta\theta$ tends to 0. Also it was shown in the last section that $\dfrac{\text{chord } PQ}{\text{arc } PQ}$ tends to 1.

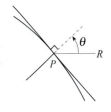

Fig. 1.7

Assuming (as is true) that the limit of the product is equal to the product of the two limits, it follows that

$$\frac{\mathrm{d}x}{\mathrm{d}\theta} = \cos\left(\theta + \tfrac{1}{2}\pi\right) \times 1 \quad \text{and} \quad \frac{\mathrm{d}y}{\mathrm{d}\theta} = \sin\left(\theta + \tfrac{1}{2}\pi\right) \times 1.$$

That is, $\dfrac{\mathrm{d}x}{\mathrm{d}\theta} = -\sin\theta \quad \text{and} \quad \dfrac{\mathrm{d}y}{\mathrm{d}\theta} = \cos\theta.$

> The relation $\phi = \theta + \frac{1}{2}\pi$ applies whichever quadrant θ is in, so these results hold for all values of $\theta \in \mathbb{R}$.

1.4 Working with trigonometric derivatives

You have seen the emphasis in trigonometry shift from calculations about triangles to properties of the sine and cosine as functions with domain the real numbers and range the interval $-1 \leqslant y \leqslant 1$. This trend is given a further boost by finding the derivatives, so you can now treat trigonometric functions much like other functions in the mathematical store-cupboard, such as polynomials, power functions, exponential functions and logarithms.

Putting the results of the last section into the usual notation, replacing θ by x:

$$\frac{d}{dx}\cos x = -\sin x, \quad \frac{d}{dx}\sin x = \cos x.$$

Fig. 1.8 shows the graph of $f(x) = \sin x$ for $0 \leqslant x \leqslant 2\pi$ and, below it, the graphs of $f'(x) = \cos x$ and $f''(x) = -\sin x$.

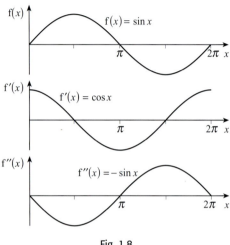

Fig. 1.8

You can see from these that the graph of $f(x)$ is increasing when $f'(x)$ is positive, and decreasing when $f'(x)$ is negative. There is a maximum at $\frac{1}{2}\pi$ where $\cos x$ is zero, and $f''\left(\frac{1}{2}\pi\right) = -\sin\left(\frac{1}{2}\pi\right) = -1 < 0$.

Also, the graph of $f(x)$ is bending downwards between 0 and π, where $f''(x) = -\sin x$ is negative. What is different in this example from other similar diagrams is that the three graphs are simply translations of each other parallel to the x-axis.

Once you know the derivatives of $\sin x$ and $\cos x$, you can use the product rule and the chain rule to find the derivatives of many other trigonometric functions.

Example 1.4.1
Use the product rule to find the derivatives with respect to x of

(a) $x^3 \sin x$,   (b) $\dfrac{1}{x}\cos x$.

(a) Writing $u = x^3$ and $v = \sin x$ in $\dfrac{d}{dx}(uv) = \dfrac{du}{dx}v + u\dfrac{dv}{dx}$ gives

$$\frac{d}{dx}(x^3 \sin x) = \left(\frac{d}{dx}x^3\right) \times \sin x + x^3 \times \left(\frac{d}{dx}\sin x\right) = 3x^2 \sin x + x^3 \cos x.$$

(b) $\dfrac{d}{dx}\left(\dfrac{1}{x}\cos x\right) = \left(-\dfrac{1}{x^2}\right) \times \cos x + \dfrac{1}{x} \times (-\sin x) = -\dfrac{1}{x^2}\cos x - \dfrac{1}{x}\sin x.$

Example 1.4.2

Use the chain rule to differentiate with respect to x

(a) $\sin\left(3x - \frac{1}{4}\pi\right)$,   (b) $\cos^4 x$,   (c) $\sec x$.

(a) $\dfrac{d}{dx}\sin\left(3x - \frac{1}{4}\pi\right) = \cos\left(3x - \frac{1}{4}\pi\right) \times 3 = 3\cos\left(3x - \frac{1}{4}\pi\right)$.

(b) Remember that $\cos^4 x$ is the conventional way of writing $(\cos x)^4$, so its derivative is $4(\cos x)^3 \times \dfrac{d}{dx}\cos x$.

$\dfrac{d}{dx}\cos^4 x = 4\cos^3 x \times (-\sin x) = -4\cos^3 x \sin x$.

(c) $\dfrac{d}{dx}\sec x = \dfrac{d}{dx}\left(\dfrac{1}{\cos x}\right) = -\dfrac{1}{\cos^2 x} \times (-\sin x) = \dfrac{\sin x}{\cos^2 x}$.

The answer to part (c) can be written in several ways. For example,

$$\frac{\sin x}{\cos^2 x} = \frac{\sin x/\cos x}{\cos x} = \frac{\tan x}{\cos x}$$

or

$$\frac{\sin x}{\cos^2 x} = \sin x \times \left(\frac{1}{\cos^2 x}\right) = \sin x \sec^2 x$$

or

$$\frac{\sin x}{\cos^2 x} = \left(\frac{1}{\cos x}\right) \times \left(\frac{\sin x}{\cos x}\right) = \sec x \tan x.$$

The most usual form is the last one, and it is a result worth remembering.

$$\frac{d}{dx}\sec x = \sec x \tan x.$$

Example 1.4.3

Find $\dfrac{d}{dx}\ln\sec x$.

$$\frac{d}{dx}\ln\sec x = \frac{1}{\sec x} \times \sec x \tan x = \tan x.$$

Of course the result of this example is only valid for those values of x for which $\ln\sec x$ exists, that is where $\sec x$ is positive. But if $\sec x$ is negative, $-\sec x$ is positive, so that $\ln(-\sec x)$ does exist, and you can differentiate this to get

$$\frac{d}{dx}\ln(-\sec x) = \frac{1}{-\sec x} \times (-\sec x \tan x) = \tan x.$$

The function which is equal to either $\sec x$ or $-\sec x$, whichever is positive, is the modulus, $|\sec x|$. So a more complete statement would be

$$\frac{d}{dx}\ln|\sec x| = \tan x.$$

This is true whether $\sec x$ is positive or negative.

Example 1.4.4

Differentiate with respect to x (a) $\sin^2 3x$,   (b) $\sin^5 x \cos^3 x$.

(a) This is a composite function which splits into three steps:

$$x \xrightarrow{\times 3} 3x \xrightarrow{\sin} \sin 3x \xrightarrow{\text{square}} \sin^2 3x.$$

Begin by dealing with the first two steps and note that

$$\frac{\mathrm{d}}{\mathrm{d}x} \sin 3x = \cos 3x \times 3 = 3\cos 3x.$$

Then differentiate $\sin^2 3x$, which is $(\sin 3x)^2$, as

$$\frac{\mathrm{d}}{\mathrm{d}x} \sin^2 3x = 2\sin 3x \times \frac{\mathrm{d}}{\mathrm{d}x} \sin 3x.$$

Putting the two steps together,

$$\frac{\mathrm{d}}{\mathrm{d}x} \sin^2 3x = 2\sin 3x \times 3\cos 3x = 6\sin 3x \cos 3x.$$

(b) This requires both the product rule and the chain rule. First use the chain rule to note that

$$\frac{\mathrm{d}}{\mathrm{d}x} \sin^5 x = 5\sin^4 x \times \cos x = 5\sin^4 x \cos x$$

and $\dfrac{\mathrm{d}}{\mathrm{d}x} \cos^3 x = 3\cos^2 x \times (-\sin x) = -3\sin x \cos^2 x.$

Then, by the product rule,

$$\frac{\mathrm{d}}{\mathrm{d}x}(\sin^5 x \cos^3 x) = \left(\frac{\mathrm{d}}{\mathrm{d}x} \sin^5 x\right) \times \cos^3 x + \sin^5 x \times \left(\frac{\mathrm{d}}{\mathrm{d}x} \cos^3 x\right)$$
$$= 5\sin^4 x \cos x \times \cos^3 x + \sin^5 x \times (-3\sin x \cos^2 x)$$
$$= 5\sin^4 x \cos^4 x - 3\sin^6 x \cos^2 x$$
$$= \sin^4 x \cos^2 x(5\cos^2 x - 3\sin^2 x).$$

In time you will find that you can leave out some of the steps in differentiations like those in Example 1.4.4, but it is easy to make mistakes so to begin with it is safer to write down the intermediate steps.

A specially important result is the derivative of $\tan x$. This can be found by writing $\tan x$ as $\dfrac{\sin x}{\cos x}$ and differentiating this by using the quotient rule.

$$\frac{\mathrm{d}}{\mathrm{d}x} \tan x = \frac{\mathrm{d}}{\mathrm{d}x}\left(\frac{\sin x}{\cos x}\right) = \frac{\left(\dfrac{\mathrm{d}}{\mathrm{d}x} \sin x\right) \times \cos x - \sin x \times \left(\dfrac{\mathrm{d}}{\mathrm{d}x} \cos x\right)}{\cos^2 x}$$

$$= \frac{\cos x \times \cos x - \sin x \times (-\sin x)}{\cos^2 x} = \frac{\cos^2 x + \sin^2 x}{\cos^2 x}.$$

You can now use the identity $\cos^2 x + \sin^2 x \equiv 1$ to simplify this as $\dfrac{\mathrm{d}}{\mathrm{d}x} \tan x = \dfrac{1}{\cos^2 x}$, which is $\sec^2 x$.

$$\frac{\mathrm{d}}{\mathrm{d}x}\tan x = \sec^2 x.$$

Although you can always work this out if you need to, it is important enough to be worth remembering.

Exercise 1A

1 Differentiate the following with respect to x.

(a) $-\sin x$

(b) $-\cos x$

(c) $\sin 4x$

(d) $2\cos 3x$

(e) $\sin \frac{1}{2}\pi x$

(f) $\cos 3\pi x$

(g) $\cos(2x - 1)$

(h) $5\sin\left(3x + \frac{1}{4}\pi\right)$

2 Differentiate the following with respect to x.

(a) $x\cos x$

(b) $\sin x \cos x$

(c) $x^3(\sin x + 1)$

(d) $e^{-x}\sin x$

(e) $x^2(\sin x + \cos x)$

(f) $e^x(\sin x - \cos x)$

3 Differentiate the following with respect to x.

(a) $\sin^2 x$

(b) $\cos^2 x$

(c) $\cos^3 x$

(d) $5\sin^2 \frac{1}{2}x$

(e) $\cos^4 2x$

(f) $\sin x^2$

(g) $7\cos 2x^3$

(h) $\cos^3 2\pi x$

(i) $e^{\sin x}$

(j) $e^{\cos 3x}$

(k) $5e^{\sin^2 x}$

(l) $\cos(e^x)$

4 Differentiate the following with respect to x.

(a) $x\sin^2 x$

(b) $\frac{1}{x}\cos^2 x$

(c) $\sin x \cos^2 x$

(d) $\sin^3 x \cos^3 x$

(e) $x^2 \sin^2 2x$

(f) $\sqrt{x}\cos^2 \frac{1}{2}x$

5 Differentiate the following with respect to x.

(a) $\sec^4 x$

(b) $\tan^4 x$

(c) $\tan^3 \frac{1}{3}x$

(d) $\sec^2 x \tan^3 x$

(e) $x\tan 2x$

(f) $\dfrac{\sin^2 x}{\cos^3 x}$

6 Prove the following.

(a) $\frac{\mathrm{d}}{\mathrm{d}x}\mathrm{cosec}\,x = -\mathrm{cosec}\,x \cot x$

(b) $\frac{\mathrm{d}}{\mathrm{d}x}\cot x = -\mathrm{cosec}^2 x$

(c) $\frac{\mathrm{d}}{\mathrm{d}x}\ln|\sin x| = \cot x$

(d) $\frac{\mathrm{d}}{\mathrm{d}x}\ln|\cos x| = -\tan x$

(e) $\frac{\mathrm{d}}{\mathrm{d}x}\ln|\tan x| = 2\mathrm{cosec}\,2x$

(f) $\frac{\mathrm{d}}{\mathrm{d}x}\ln|\cot x| = -2\mathrm{cosec}\,2x$

7 For the following equations find an expression for $\dfrac{\mathrm{d}^2 y}{\mathrm{d}x^2}$.

(a) $y = \tan x$

(b) $y = \sec x$

(c) $y = e^{\sin x}$

(d) $y = \sin^2 2x$

(e) $y = \sin^3 x$

(f) $y = x\cos \frac{1}{2}x$

8 Use the inequalities $\sin\theta < \theta < \tan\theta$ for a suitable value of θ to show that π lies between 3 and $2\sqrt{3}$.

9 Combine the facts that $\dfrac{d}{dx}\sin x = \cos x$ and that $\sin\left(x + \frac{1}{2}\pi\right) = \cos x$ to show that $\dfrac{d}{dx}\cos x = -\sin x$.

10 Find $\dfrac{d}{dx}\sin(a + x)$, first by using the chain rule, and secondly by using the addition formula to expand $\sin(a + x)$ before differentiating. Verify that you get the same answer by both methods.

11 Find $\dfrac{d}{dx}\cos\left(\frac{3}{2}\pi - x\right)$. Check your answer by simplifying $\cos\left(\frac{3}{2}\pi - x\right)$ before you differentiate, and $\sin\left(\frac{3}{2}\pi - x\right)$ after you differentiate.

12 Show that $\dfrac{d}{dx}(2\cos^2 x)$, $\dfrac{d}{dx}(-2\sin^2 x)$ and $\dfrac{d}{dx}\cos 2x$ are all the same. Explain why.

13 Find $\dfrac{d}{dx}\sin^2\left(x + \frac{1}{4}\pi\right)$, and write your answer in its simplest form.

14 Prove that $\dfrac{d}{dx}(e^x\sin(x + a)) = \sqrt{2}e^x\sin\left(x + a + \frac{1}{4}\pi\right)$. Hence show that, if $y = e^x\sin x$, then $\dfrac{d^2y}{dx^2} = 2e^x\cos x$.

15 Show that $\dfrac{d}{dx}\tan^2 x = \dfrac{d}{dx}\sec^2 x$. Explain why.

16* The chain rule suggests that $\dfrac{d}{dx}\ln\ln\sin x = \dfrac{\cot x}{\ln\sin x}$. What is wrong with this?

1.5 Some applications

In most practical applications, the independent variable for the sine and cosine functions represents time rather than angle. Just as e^x is the natural function for describing exponential growth and decay, so sine and cosine are the natural functions for describing periodic phenomena. They can be used to model situations as different as the trade cycle, variation in insect populations, seasonal variation in sea temperature, rise and fall of tides (as in C2 Example 1.1.3), motion of a piston in a car cylinder and propagation of radio waves.

Example 1.5.1
The height in metres of the water in a harbour is given approximately by the formula $h = 6 + 3\cos\frac{1}{6}\pi t$ where t is the time measured in hours from noon. Find an expression for the rate at which the water is rising at time t. When is it rising fastest?

Using the chain rule, the rate at which the water is rising is

$$\frac{dh}{dt} = \left(-3\sin\tfrac{1}{6}\pi t\right) \times \tfrac{1}{6}\pi = -\tfrac{1}{2}\pi\sin\tfrac{1}{6}\pi t.$$

The water rises fastest when $\sin\frac{1}{6}\pi t = -1$, that is when $\frac{1}{6}\pi t = \frac{3}{2}\pi, \frac{7}{2}\pi, \frac{11}{2}\pi, \dots$, so $t = 9,\ 21,\ 33,\ \dots$. The water is rising fastest at 9 p.m. and again at 9 a.m. (This is exactly half-way between low and high tide.)

Example 1.5.2

Find the minima and maxima of $f(x) = 4\cos x + \cos 2x$.

Although the domain is $\mathbb{R}$, you only need to consider the interval $0 \leqslant x < 2\pi$. Since the period of $\cos x$ is 2π, and the period of $\cos 2x$ is π, the graph of $f(x)$ repeats itself after each interval of length 2π.

$f'(x) = -4\sin x - 2\sin 2x = -4\sin x - 4\sin x\cos x = -4\sin x(1 + \cos x)$, so $f'(x) = 0$ when $\sin x = 0$ or $\cos x = -1$, that is when $x = 0$ or π.

$f''(x) = -4\cos x - 4\cos 2x$, so $f''(0) = -4 - 4 = -8$ and $f''(\pi) = 4 - 4 = 0$. There is therefore a maximum at $x = 0$, but the $f''(x)$ method does not work at $x = \pi$. You must instead consider the sign of $f'(x)$ below and above π.

The factor $1 + \cos x$ is always positive except at $x = \pi$, where it is 0; the factor $\sin x$ is positive for $0 < x < \pi$ and negative for $\pi < x < 2\pi$. So $f'(x) = -4\sin x(1 + \cos x)$ is negative for $0 < x < \pi$ and positive for $\pi < x < 2\pi$. There is therefore a minimum of $f(x)$ at π.

Over the whole domain there are maxima at 0, $\pm 2\pi$, $\pm 4\pi$, $\ldots$; the maximum value is $4 + 1 = 5$. There are minima at $\pm\pi$, $\pm 3\pi$, $\pm 5\pi$, $\ldots$, with minimum value $-4 + 1 = -3$. If you have access to a graphic calculator, use it to check these results.

Notice that, although it is periodic, the graph is not a simple transformation of a sine graph.

Example 1.5.3

Find the points on the graph of $y = x\sin x$ at which the tangent passes through the origin.

For the tangent at a point P to pass through the origin, its gradient must be equal to the gradient of the line joining O to P.

The product rule gives $\dfrac{dy}{dx} = \sin x + x\cos x$, so the tangent at a point $P(p, p\sin p)$ has gradient $\sin p + p\cos p$. This has to equal the gradient of OP, which is $\dfrac{p\sin p}{p} = \sin p$.

Therefore

$$\sin p + p\cos p = \sin p,$$

giving $p\cos p = 0$.

This equation is satisfied by $p = 0$, though in fact the geometrical argument used above breaks down when $p = 0$; can you see why? But anyway, it is obvious that the tangent at O passes through O.

The equation is also satisfied when $\cos p = 0$, that is by all odd multiples of $\frac{1}{2}\pi$. These points have coordinates $(0, 0)$, $\left(\pm\frac{1}{2}\pi, \frac{1}{2}\pi\right)$, $\left(\pm\frac{3}{2}\pi, -\frac{3}{2}\pi\right)$, $\left(\pm\frac{5}{2}\pi, \frac{5}{2}\pi\right)$, ... This is illustrated in Fig. 1.9.

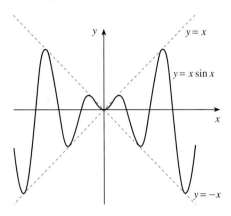

Fig. 1.9

The graph oscillates between the lines $y = x$ and $y = -x$, touching $y = x$ when $\sin|x| = 1$, and $y = -x$ when $\sin|x| = -1$.

Exercise 1B

1 The gross national product (GNP) of a country, P billion dollars, is given by the formula $P = 1 + 0.02t + 0.05\sin 0.6t$, where t is the time in years after the year 2000. At what rate is the GNP changing

(a) in the year 2000,   (b) in the year 2005?

2 A tuning fork sounding A above middle C oscillates 440 times a second. The displacement of the tip of the tuning fork is given by $0.02\cos(2\pi \times 440t)$ millimetres, where t is the time in seconds after it is activated. Find

(a) the greatest velocity,   (b) the greatest acceleration of the tip as it oscillates.

(If x is the displacement from a fixed point, the velocity is $v = \dfrac{dx}{dt}$ and the acceleration is $a = \dfrac{dv}{dt}$. See C1 Section 12.2.)

3 Show that, if $y = \sin nt$, where n is constant, then $\dfrac{d^2y}{dt^2} = -n^2 y$. What can you deduce about the shape of the graph of $y = \sin nt$? Give a more general equation which has the same property.

4 (a) Find the equation of the tangent where $x = \frac{1}{3}\pi$ on the curve $y = \sin x$.

(b) Find the equation of the normal where $x = \frac{1}{4}\pi$ on the curve $y = \cos 3x$.

(c) Find the equation of the normal where $x = \frac{1}{4}\pi$ on the curve $y = \sec x$.

(d) Find the equation of the tangent where $x = \frac{1}{4}\pi$ on the curve $y = \ln\sec x$.

(e) Find the equation of the tangent where $x = \frac{1}{2}\pi$ on the curve $y = 3\sin^2 x$.

5 Find whether the tangent to $y = \cos x$ at $x = \frac{5}{6}\pi$ cuts the y-axis above or below the origin.

6 Find the coordinates of the point of intersection of the tangents to $y = \sin x$ and $y = \tan x$ at the points where $x = \frac{1}{3}\pi$.

7 Find any stationary points in the interval $0 \leqslant x < 2\pi$ on each of the following curves, and find out whether they are maxima, minima or neither.

(a) $y = \sin x + \cos x$
(b) $y = x + \sin x$
(c) $y = \sin^2 x + 2\cos x$
(d) $y = \cos 2x + x$
(e) $y = \sec x + \operatorname{cosec} x$
(f) $y = \cos 2x - 2\sin x$

8 Find the stationary points in the interval $0 \leqslant x \leqslant \pi$ on each of the following curves, and determine whether they are maxima, minima or neither. State whether the functions are even or odd, and sketch their graphs in the interval $0 \leqslant x \leqslant \pi$.

(a) $y = \sin x \cos^3 x$
(b) $y = \sin^2 x \cos x$
(c) $y = \sin^3 x \cos^3 x$
(d) $y = \sin^6 x \cos^2 x$

9 Sketch the graphs with the following equations, and find expressions for $\dfrac{dy}{dx}$.

(a) $y = \sin \sqrt{x}$
(b) $y = \sqrt{\cos x}$
(c) $y = \sin \dfrac{1}{x}$

10* A pendulum hanging vertically is pulled aside through an angle of $10°$ and then released. The angle $\theta°$ which it makes with the vertical t seconds later is given by $\theta = 10\mathrm{e}^{-0.01\pi t}(\cos \pi t + 0.01 \sin \pi t)$. (Angles on the side opposite to the original displacement are taken to be negative.)

(a) Show that $\theta = 10$ and $\dfrac{d\theta}{dt} = 0$ when $t = 0$.

(b) The pendulum is at an extreme of its swing when $\dfrac{d\theta}{dt} = 0$. Find the times at which this occurs. Show that the values of θ at these times are in geometric progression, and find the common ratio.

(c) Find the times at which the pendulum is vertical.

(d) Sketch a graph of θ against t.

(e) Find an expression for $\dfrac{d^2\theta}{dt^2}$, and show that $\dfrac{d^2\theta}{dt^2} + 0.02\pi \dfrac{d\theta}{dt} + 1.0001\pi^2\theta = 0$.

11* A violent oscillation, called 'resonance', can be created by forcing a system to oscillate at its natural frequency. A resonating system can be described by an equation $x = t \cos \pi t$, where $t \geqslant 0$.

(a) What can you say about x if t is

(i) an even integer,   (ii) an odd integer,   (iii) an odd multiple of $\frac{1}{2}$?

(b) Find an equation for the values of t when $\dfrac{dx}{dt} = 0$. Use graphs to show that this occurs when t is slightly greater than an integer.

(c) Sketch a graph of x against t.

(d) Find an expression for $\dfrac{d^2x}{dt^2}$, and show that $\dfrac{d^2x}{dt^2} + \pi^2 x = -2\pi \sin \pi t$.

1.6   Integrating trigonometric functions

The results in Section 1.4 give you some new indefinite integrals. For example,

$$\text{from } \frac{d}{dx}\cos x = -\sin x \quad \text{it follows that} \quad \int \sin x \, dx = -\cos x + k,$$

and $$\text{from } \frac{d}{dx}\tan x = \sec^2 x \quad \text{it follows that} \quad \int \sec^2 x \, dx = \tan x + k.$$

So you now know the following integrals:

$$\int \cos x \, dx = \sin x + k, \qquad \int \sin x \, dx = -\cos x + k,$$

$$\int \tan x \, dx = \ln|\sec x| + k,$$

$$\int \sec^2 x \, dx = \tan x + k, \qquad \int \sec x \tan x \, dx = \sec x + k,$$

where x is in radians.

Be very careful to get the signs correct when you differentiate or integrate sines and cosines. The minus sign appears when you differentiate $\cos x$, and when you integrate $\sin x$. If you forget which way round the signs go, draw for yourself sketches of the $\sin x$ and $\cos x$ graphs from 0 to $\frac{1}{2}\pi$. You can easily see that it is the $\cos x$ graph which has the negative gradient.

You will often need these integrals with a multiple of x. For example, since

$$\frac{d}{dx}\sin ax = a\cos ax \quad \text{(by the chain rule)},$$

$$\int \cos ax \, dx = \frac{1}{a}\sin ax + k;$$

and similarly for the other integrals.

Example 1.6.1

Find (a) $\displaystyle\int \tan\left(2x - \tfrac{1}{4}\pi\right) dx,$ (b) $\displaystyle\int \tan^2 x \, dx.$

(a) Use the rule in C3 Section 4.2, that $\displaystyle\int g(ax+b)\,dx = \frac{1}{a}f(ax+b) + k$ where f(x) is the simplest integral of g(x).

The simplest integral of $\tan x$ is $\ln|\sec x|$, so

$$\int \tan\left(2x - \tfrac{1}{4}\pi\right) dx = \tfrac{1}{2}\ln\left|\sec\left(2x - \tfrac{1}{4}\pi\right)\right| + k.$$

(b) This is not one of the integrals in the box, but you can work it out by using the identity $1 + \tan^2 x \equiv \sec^2 x$.

$$\int \tan^2 x \, dx = \int (\sec^2 x - 1)\,dx = \int \sec^2 x \, dx - \int 1 \, dx = \tan x - x + k.$$

Example 1.6.2

Find the area under the graph of $y = \sin\left(2x + \frac{1}{3}\pi\right)$ from $x = 0$ as far as the first point at which the graph cuts the positive x-axis.

The graph cuts the x-axis where $\sin\left(2x + \frac{1}{3}\pi\right) = 0$. That is, for positive x, where $2x + \frac{1}{3}\pi = \pi,\ 2\pi,\ \ldots$. The first positive root is $x = \frac{1}{3}\pi$.

$$\int_0^{\frac{1}{3}\pi} \sin\left(2x + \frac{1}{3}\pi\right) dx = \left[\frac{1}{2} \times \left(-\cos\left(2x + \frac{1}{3}\pi\right)\right)\right]_0^{\frac{1}{3}\pi}$$
$$= \frac{1}{2} \times \left(-\cos\pi - \left(-\cos\frac{1}{3}\pi\right)\right)$$
$$= \frac{1}{2} \times \left(1 + \frac{1}{2}\right) = \frac{3}{4}.$$

So the area is $\frac{3}{4}$.

You can adapt the addition and double angle formulae found in C3 Sections 6.4 and 6.5 to integrate more complicated trigonometric functions involving sines and cosines. The most useful results are:

$$2\sin A \cos A \equiv \sin 2A.$$
$$2\cos^2 A \equiv 1 + \cos 2A, \quad 2\sin^2 A \equiv 1 - \cos 2A.$$

The equations in the second line are needed so often that it is worthwhile remembering them in this form. Other results which are occasionally useful are

$$2\sin A \cos B \equiv \sin(A - B) + \sin(A + B),$$
$$2\cos A \cos B \equiv \cos(A - B) + \cos(A + B),$$
$$2\sin A \sin B \equiv \cos(A - B) - \cos(A + B).$$

It is easy to prove all of these formulae by starting on the right side and using the addition and double angle formulae.

Example 1.6.3

Let R be the region under the graph of $y = \sin^2 x$ in the interval $0 \leqslant x \leqslant \pi$. Find

(a) the area of R,   (b) the volume of revolution formed by rotating R about the x-axis.

(a) The area is given by

$$\int_0^\pi \sin^2 x \, dx = \int_0^\pi \frac{1}{2}(1 - \cos 2x) \, dx = \left[\frac{1}{2}\left(x - \frac{1}{2}\sin 2x\right)\right]_0^\pi$$
$$= \left(\frac{1}{2}\pi - 0\right) - (0 - 0) = \frac{1}{2}\pi.$$

(b) The volume of revolution is given by $\int_0^\pi \pi \left(\sin^2 x\right)^2 dx.$

Now $\left(\sin^2 x\right)^2 \equiv \left(\frac{1}{2}(1 - \cos 2x)\right)^2 \equiv \frac{1}{4}(1 - 2\cos 2x + \cos^2 2x)$
$\equiv \frac{1}{4}\left(1 - 2\cos 2x + \frac{1}{2}(1 + \cos 4x)\right)$ using $2\cos^2 A \equiv 1 + \cos 2A$
$\equiv \frac{3}{8} - \frac{1}{2}\cos 2x + \frac{1}{8}\cos 4x.$ with $2x$ instead of A

So $\int_0^\pi \pi \left(\sin^2 x\right)^2 dx = \left[\pi\left(\frac{3}{8}x - \frac{1}{4}\sin 2x + \frac{1}{32}\sin 4x\right)\right]_0^\pi = \frac{3}{8}\pi^2.$

The area is $\frac{1}{2}\pi$ and the volume is $\frac{3}{8}\pi^2$.

Example 1.6.4*

Find   (a) $\int \sin 2x \cos 3x \, dx$,   (b) $\int \cos^3 x \, dx$.

(a) Writing $A = 2x$ and $B = 3x$ in the formula for $2 \sin A \cos B$,

$$2 \sin 2x \cos 3x \equiv \sin(2x - 3x) + \sin(2x + 3x)$$
$$\equiv \sin(-x) + \sin 5x$$
$$\equiv -\sin x + \sin 5x.$$

So $\int \sin 2x \cos 3x \, dx = \frac{1}{2}\left(\cos x - \frac{1}{5}\cos 5x\right) + k = \frac{1}{2}\cos x - \frac{1}{10}\cos 5x + k.$

(b) None of the formulae given above can be used directly, but $\cos^3 x$ can be written in other forms which can be integrated.

Method 1 $\cos^3 x \equiv \cos^2 x \cos x$

$$\equiv \tfrac{1}{2}(1 + \cos 2x)\cos x$$
$$\equiv \tfrac{1}{2}\cos x + \tfrac{1}{2}\cos 2x \cos x$$
$$\equiv \tfrac{1}{2}\cos x + \tfrac{1}{4}(\cos x + \cos 3x) \qquad \left\{ \begin{array}{l} \text{using } 2\cos A \cos B \\ \equiv \cos(A - B) + \cos(A + B) \end{array} \right.$$
$$\equiv \tfrac{3}{4}\cos x + \tfrac{1}{4}\cos 3x.$$

Therefore $\int \cos^3 x \, dx = \tfrac{3}{4}\sin x + \tfrac{1}{12}\sin 3x + k.$

Method 2 $\cos^3 x \equiv \cos^2 x \cos x$

$$\equiv (1 - \sin^2 x)\cos x$$
$$\equiv \cos x - \sin^2 x \cos x.$$

You can integrate the first term directly. To see how to integrate $\sin^2 x \cos x$, look back to Example 1.4.2(b). When $\cos^4 x$ was differentiated using the chain rule, a factor $\dfrac{d}{dx}\cos x = -\sin x$ appeared in the answer. In a similar way,

$$\frac{d}{dx}\sin^3 x = 3\sin^2 x \times \cos x = 3\sin^2 x \cos x.$$

Therefore $\int \cos^3 x \, dx = \int (\cos x - \sin^2 x \cos x)\, dx$

$$= \sin x - \tfrac{1}{3}\sin^3 x + k.$$

In (b) it is not obvious that the two methods have given the same answer, but if you work out some values, or use a calculator to draw the graphs, you will find that they are in agreement. The reason for this is that

$$\sin 3x \equiv \sin(2x + x)$$
$$\equiv \sin 2x \cos x + \cos 2x \sin x$$
$$\equiv (2 \sin x \cos x)\cos x + (1 - 2\sin^2 x)\sin x$$
$$\equiv 2 \sin x(1 - \sin^2 x) + (1 - 2\sin^2 x)\sin x$$
$$\equiv 3 \sin x - 4\sin^3 x.$$

Therefore, $\tfrac{3}{4}\sin x + \tfrac{1}{12}\sin 3x \equiv \tfrac{3}{4}\sin x + \tfrac{1}{4}\sin x - \tfrac{1}{3}\sin^3 x \equiv \sin x - \tfrac{1}{3}\sin^3 x.$

Exercise 1C

1 Integrate the following with respect to x.

    (a) $\cos 2x$

    (b) $\sin 3x$

    (c) $\cos(2x + 1)$

    (d) $\sin(3x - 1)$

    (e) $\sin(1 - x)$

    (f) $\cos\left(4 - \tfrac{1}{2}x\right)$

    (g) $\sin\left(\tfrac{1}{2}x + \tfrac{1}{3}\pi\right)$

    (h) $\cos\left(3x - \tfrac{1}{4}\pi\right)$

    (i) $-\sin\tfrac{1}{2}x$

2 Evaluate the following.

    (a) $\displaystyle\int_0^{\frac{1}{2}\pi} \sin x\, dx$

    (b) $\displaystyle\int_0^{\frac{1}{4}\pi} \cos x\, dx$

    (c) $\displaystyle\int_0^{\frac{1}{4}\pi} \sin 2x\, dx$

    (d) $\displaystyle\int_{\frac{1}{4}\pi}^{\frac{1}{3}\pi} \cos 3x\, dx$

    (e) $\displaystyle\int_{\frac{1}{6}\pi}^{\frac{1}{3}\pi} \sin\left(3x + \tfrac{1}{6}\pi\right) dx$

    (f) $\displaystyle\int_0^{\frac{1}{2}\pi} \sin\left(\tfrac{1}{4}\pi - x\right) dx$

    (g) $\displaystyle\int_0^1 \cos(1 - x)\, dx$

    (h) $\displaystyle\int_0^{\frac{1}{2}} \sin\left(\tfrac{1}{2}x + 1\right) dx$

    (i) $\displaystyle\int_0^{2\pi} \sin\tfrac{1}{2}x\, dx.$

3 Integrate the following with respect to x

    (a) $\tan 2x$

    (b) $\sec^2 3x$

    (c) $\sec 3x \tan 3x$

    (d) $\tan\left(\tfrac{1}{4}\pi - x\right)$

    (e) $\tan^2 \tfrac{1}{2}x$

    (f) $\dfrac{\sin 2x}{\cos^2 2x}$

4 Evaluate the following.

    (a) $\displaystyle\int_0^{\frac{1}{4}\pi} \tan x\, dx$

    (b) $\displaystyle\int_0^{\frac{1}{12}\pi} \tan 3x\, dx$

    (c) $\displaystyle\int_0^{\frac{1}{12}\pi} \tan^2 3x\, dx$

    (d) $\displaystyle\int_0^{\frac{1}{2}\pi} \sec^2\left(x - \tfrac{1}{3}\pi\right) dx$

5 Integrate the following with respect to x.

    (a) $\cos^2 x$

    (b) $\cos^2 \tfrac{1}{2}x$

    (c) $\sin^2 2x$

    (d) $\sin^3 x \cos x$

6* Integrate the following with respect to x.

    (a) $\sin 3x \cos 4x$

    (b) $\sin^3 x$

    (c) $\sin^5 x$ (write as $(1 - \cos^2 x)^2 \sin x$)

    (d) $\sin 2x \sin 6x$

7 Use the results from Exercise 1A Question 6 to find

    (a) $\displaystyle\int \cot x\, dx,$

    (b) $\displaystyle\int \operatorname{cosec}^2 x\, dx,$

    (c) $\displaystyle\int \operatorname{cosec} x \cot x\, dx,$

    (d) $\displaystyle\int \cot^2 x\, dx,$

    (e) $\displaystyle\int \operatorname{cosec} x\, dx,$

    (f) $\displaystyle\int \sec x\, dx \left(= \int \operatorname{cosec}\left(x + \tfrac{1}{2}\pi\right) dx\right).$

8 Find the area of the region between the curve $y = \cos x$ and the x-axis from $x = 0$ to $x = \tfrac{1}{2}\pi$.

Find also the volume generated when this region is rotated about the x-axis.

9 Find the area of the region bounded by the curve $y = 1 + \sin x$, the x-axis and the lines $x = 0$ and $x = \pi$.

Find also the volume generated when this region is rotated about the x-axis.

10 The curves $y = \sin x$, $y = \cos x$ and the x-axis enclose a region shown shaded in the sketch.

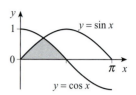

(a) Find the area of the shaded region.

(b) Find the volume generated when this region is rotated about the x-axis.

11 In the interval $0 \le x \le \pi$ the curve $y = \sin x + \cos x$ meets the y-axis at P and the x-axis at Q.

(a) Find the coordinates of P and Q.

(b) Calculate the area of the region enclosed between the curve and the axes bounded by P and Q.

(c) Calculate also the volume generated when this region is rotated about the x-axis.

12 The region bounded by parts of the x-axis, the line $x = \frac{1}{3}\pi$ and the curve $y = \tan x$ is denoted by R.

(a) Find the area of R.

(b) Find the volume of the solid formed by rotating R through a complete revolution about the x-axis.

Miscellaneous exercise 1

1 (a) Differentiate $\ln \sin 2x$ with respect to x, simplifying your answer.

(b) Given that $y = \cos^2 x$, find $\dfrac{dy}{dx}$.

(c) Differentiate $\sin(t^3 + 4)$ with respect to t.

(d) Find $\displaystyle\int \cos^2 3x \, dx$.

(e) Differentiate $\cos \sqrt{x}$ with respect to x.

(f) Find $\displaystyle\int \sin^2 \frac{1}{3}x \, dx$.

(g)* Find $\displaystyle\int \sin \frac{3}{2}x \cos \frac{1}{2}x \, dx$.

2 (a) Express $\sin^2 x$ in terms of $\cos 2x$.

(b) The region R is bounded by the part of the curve $y = \sin x$ between $x = 0$ and $x = \pi$ and the x-axis. Show that the volume of the solid formed when R is rotated completely about the x-axis is $\frac{1}{2}\pi^2$.   (OCR)

3 (a) Use the addition formulae to find expressions involving surds for $\sin \frac{1}{12}\pi$ and $\tan \frac{1}{12}\pi$. If necessary, rationalise the denominators.

(b) Show that π lies between $3\sqrt{2}(\sqrt{3} - 1)$ and $12(2 - \sqrt{3})$. Use a calculator to evaluate these expressions correct to 3 decimal places.

4 A function f is defined by $f(x) = e^x \cos x$, for $0 \leqslant x \leqslant 2\pi$.

(a) Find $f'(x)$.

(b) State the values of x between 0 and 2π for which $f'(x) < 0$.

(c) What does the fact that $f'(x) < 0$ in this interval tell you about the shape of the graph of $y = f(x)$? (OCR)

5 P, Q and R are the points on the graph of $y = \cos x$ for which $x = 0$, $x = \frac{1}{4}\pi$ and $x = \frac{1}{2}\pi$ respectively. Find the point S where the normal at Q meets the y-axis. Compare the distances SP, SQ and SR. Use your answers to draw a sketch showing how the curve $y = \cos x$ over the interval $-\frac{1}{2}\pi < x < \frac{1}{2}\pi$ is related to the circle with centre S and radius SQ.

6* By writing $\cos\theta$ as $\cos 2(\frac{1}{2}\theta)$, and using the approximation $\sin\theta \approx \theta$ when θ is small, show that $\cos\theta \approx 1 - \frac{1}{2}\theta^2$ when θ is small.

Since sine is an odd function, it is suggested that a better approximation for sine might have the form $\sin\theta \approx \theta - k\theta^3$ when θ is small. By writing $\sin\theta$ as $\sin 2(\frac{1}{2}\theta)$, using the approximation $\cos\theta \approx 1 - \frac{1}{2}\theta^2$ and equating the coefficients of θ^3, find an appropriate numerical value for k.

Investigate whether this approximation is in fact better, by evaluating θ and $\theta - k\theta^3$ numerically when $\theta = \frac{1}{6}\pi$.

7 The motion of an electric train on the straight stretch of track between two stations is given by $x = 11\left(t - \dfrac{45}{\pi}\sin\left(\dfrac{\pi}{45}t\right)\right)$, where x metres is the distance covered t seconds after leaving the first station. The train stops at these two stations and nowhere between them.

(a) Find the velocity, $v\,\text{m s}^{-1}$ in terms of t. Hence find the time taken for the journey between the two stations.

(b) Calculate the distance between the two stations. Hence find the average velocity of the train.

(c) Find the acceleration of the train 30 seconds after leaving the first station. (OCR)

(If x is the displacement from a fixed point, the velocity is $v = \dfrac{dx}{dt}$ and the acceleration is $a = \dfrac{dv}{dt}$. See C1 Section 12.2.)

8 A mobile consists of a bird with flapping wings suspended from the ceiling by two elastic strings. A small weight A hangs below it. A is pulled down and then released. After t seconds, the distance, y cm, of A below its equilibrium position is modelled by the periodic function $y = 5\cos 2t + 10\sin t$.

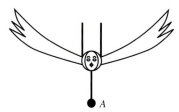

(a) Verify that the (t, y) graph has a stationary point where $t = \frac{1}{6}\pi$.

(b) Show that all the stationary points of the graph correspond to solutions of the equation $\cos t(2\sin t - 1) = 0$. Find the other two solutions in the interval $0 \leqslant t \leqslant \pi$.

(c) State one limitation of the model. Explain why $y = e^{-kt}(5\cos 2t + 10\sin t)$, where k is a small constant, might give a better model. (OCR)

9 (a) By first expressing $\cos 4x$ in terms of $\cos 2x$, show that

$$\cos 4x = 8\cos^4 x - 8\cos^2 x + 1,$$

and hence show that

$$8\cos^4 x = \cos 4x + 4\cos 2x + 3.$$

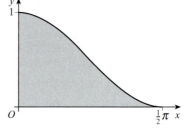

(b) The region R, shown shaded in the diagram, is bounded by the part of the curve $y = \cos^2 x$ between $x = 0$ and $x = \frac{1}{2}\pi$ and by the x- and y-axes. Show that the volume of the solid formed when R is rotated completely about the x-axis is $\frac{3}{16}\pi^2$. (OCR)

10 In this question $f(x) = \sin\frac{1}{2}x + \cos\frac{1}{3}x$.

(a) Find $f'(x)$.

(b) Find the values of $f(0)$ and $f'(0)$.

(c) State the periods of $\sin\frac{1}{2}x$ and $\cos\frac{1}{3}x$.

(d) Write down another value of x (not 0) for which $f(x) = f(0)$ and $f'(x) = f'(0)$. (OCR)

11 The diagram shows a sketch, not to scale, of part of the graph of $y = f(x)$, where $f(x) = \sin x + \sin 2x$ and where x is measured in radians.

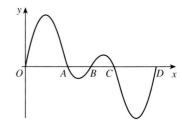

(a) Find, in terms of π, the x-coordinates of the points A, B, C and D, shown in the diagram, where the graph of f meets the positive x-axis.

(b) Show that $f(\pi - \theta)$ may be expressed as $\sin\theta - \sin 2\theta$, and show also that $f(\pi - \theta) + f(\pi + \theta) = 0$ for all values of θ.

(c) Differentiate $f(x)$, and hence show that the greatest value of $f(x)$, for $0 \leqslant x \leqslant 2\pi$, occurs when $\cos x = \dfrac{-1+\sqrt{33}}{8}$. (OCR)

12 Find the gradient of the curve $y = \dfrac{\sin x}{x^2}$ at the point where $x = \pi$, leaving your answer in terms of π. (OCR)

13 A curve C has equation $y = \dfrac{\sin x}{x}$, where $x > 0$.

Find $\dfrac{dy}{dx}$, and hence show that the x-coordinate of any stationary point of C satisfies the equation $x = \tan x$. (OCR)

14 The region R, shown shaded in the diagram, is bounded by the x- and y-axes, the line $x = \frac{1}{3}\pi$ and the curve $y = \sec \frac{1}{2}x$. Show that the volume of the solid formed when R is rotated completely about the x-axis is $\dfrac{2\pi}{\sqrt{3}}$.

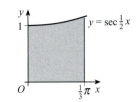

15 A length of channel of given depth d is to be made from a rectangular sheet of metal of width $2a$. The metal is to be bent in such a way that the cross-section $ABCD$ is as shown in the figure, with $AB + BC + CD = 2a$ and with AB and CD each inclined to the line BC at an angle θ. Show that $BC = 2(a - d \operatorname{cosec} \theta)$ and that the area of the cross-section $ABCD$ is

$$2ad + d^2(\cot \theta - 2 \operatorname{cosec} \theta).$$

Show that the maximum value of $2ad + d^2(\cot \theta - 2 \operatorname{cosec} \theta)$, as θ varies, is $d(2a - d\sqrt{3})$.

By considering the length of BC, show that the cross-sectional area can only be made equal to this maximum value if $2d \leqslant a\sqrt{3}$.   (OCR)

2 Integration

This chapter is about two methods of integration, one derived from the rule for differentiating a product, and the other derived from the chain rule for differentiation. When you have completed it, you should

- know and be able to apply the method of integration by parts
- understand and be able to find integrals using both direct and reverse substitution
- be able to find new limits of integration when a definite integral is evaluated by substitution
- recognise the form $\int \dfrac{f'(x)}{f(x)}\, dx$, and be able to write down the integral at sight.

2.1 Integration by parts

Each time you learn a new technique for differentiation, you also increase the number of functions you can integrate. Integration by parts depends on the product rule for differentiation.

For example, from

$$\frac{d}{dx}(x \sin x) = \sin x + x \cos x$$

you can deduce that

$$x \sin x = \int \sin x \, dx + \int x \cos x \, dx = -\cos x + k + \int x \cos x \, dx.$$

You can rearrange this to give the new result

$$\int x \cos x \, dx = x \sin x + \cos x - k.$$

But if you were asked to find $\int x \cos x \, dx$, how would you begin? You would not immediately guess that the answer comes from differentiating $x \sin x$. You can get round this difficulty by applying the same argument to the general product rule.

From $\dfrac{d}{dx}(uv) = \dfrac{du}{dx}v + u\dfrac{dv}{dx}$ you can deduce that

$$uv = \int \frac{du}{dx} v \, dx + \int u \frac{dv}{dx}\, dx.$$

If you can find one of the integrals on the right, this equation tells you the other. It can be rearranged to give the rule:

> **Integration by parts**
>
> $$\int u \frac{dv}{dx}\, dx = uv - \int \frac{du}{dx} v \, dx.$$

For example, if you want to integrate $x \cos x$, you write $u = x$ and find a function v such that $\dfrac{dv}{dx} = \cos x$. The simplest function is $v = \sin x$. The rule gives

$$\int x \cos x \, dx = x \sin x - \int 1 \times \sin x \, dx$$
$$= x \sin x + \cos x + k.$$

Notice that the result on the previous page has a constant $-k$, and the same integral here has a constant $+k$. It is not difficult to see that the two forms are equivalent.

Example 2.1.1

Find $\displaystyle\int x e^{3x} \, dx$.

Take $u = x$ and find v such that $\dfrac{dv}{dx} = e^{3x}$. The simplest function for v is $\frac{1}{3}e^{3x}$. The rule gives

$$\int x e^{3x} \, dx = x \times \tfrac{1}{3}e^{3x} - \int 1 \times \tfrac{1}{3}e^{3x} \, dx$$
$$= \tfrac{1}{3}x e^{3x} - \tfrac{1}{9}e^{3x} + k$$
$$= \tfrac{1}{9}(3x - 1)e^{3x} + k.$$

The next example applies the method to a definite integral. The rule then takes the form:

$$\int_a^b u \frac{dv}{dx} \, dx = [uv]_a^b - \int_a^b \frac{du}{dx} v \, dx.$$

Example 2.1.2

Find $\displaystyle\int_2^8 x \ln x \, dx$.

If you write $u = x$, you need v to satisfy $\dfrac{dv}{dx} = \ln x$. But although you know the derivative of $\ln x$, you do not yet know its integral. (See Example 2.1.3.)

When this occurs, try writing the product the other way round. Take $u = \ln x$, and find a v such that $\dfrac{dv}{dx} = x$, which is $v = \frac{1}{2}x^2$. The rule then gives

$$\int_2^8 x \ln x \, dx = \left[\ln x \times \tfrac{1}{2}x^2 \right]_2^8 - \int_2^8 \frac{1}{x} \times \tfrac{1}{2}x^2 \, dx$$
$$= 32 \ln 8 - 2 \ln 2 - \int_2^8 \tfrac{1}{2}x \, dx$$
$$= 32 \ln 2^3 - 2 \ln 2 - \left[\tfrac{1}{4}x^2 \right]_2^8$$
$$= 32(3 \ln 2) - 2 \ln 2 - (16 - 1)$$
$$= 94 \ln 2 - 15.$$

It is usually best to leave the answer in a simple exact form, as in Example 2.1.2. If you need a numerical value, it is easy enough to calculate it.

Example 2.1.3

Find $\int \ln x \, dx$.

You wouldn't at first expect to use integration by parts for this, since it doesn't look like a product. But taking u as $u = \ln x$ and $\dfrac{dv}{dx} = 1$, so that $v = x$, the rule gives

$$\int \ln x \, dx = \ln x \times x - \int \frac{1}{x} \times x \, dx = x \ln x - \int 1 \, dx$$
$$= x \ln x - x + k.$$

The integral of $\ln x$ is an important result. You need not remember the answer, but you should remember how to get it.

The next example concerns two integrals which are used in probability.

Example 2.1.4

Find $\displaystyle\int_0^\infty x e^{-ax} \, dx$ and $\displaystyle\int_0^\infty x^2 e^{-ax} \, dx$, where a is positive.

Begin by finding the integrals from 0 to s, and then consider their limits as $s \to \infty$.

For both integrals take $\dfrac{dv}{dx} = e^{-ax}$, so $v = -\dfrac{1}{a} e^{-ax}$.

$$\int_0^s x e^{-ax} \, dx = \left[x \times \left(-\frac{1}{a} \right) e^{-ax} \right]_0^s - \int_0^s 1 \times \left(-\frac{1}{a} \right) e^{-ax} \, dx$$

$$= -\frac{1}{a} s e^{-as} - \left[\frac{1}{a^2} e^{-ax} \right]_0^s$$

$$= -\frac{1}{a} s e^{-as} - \frac{1}{a^2} e^{-as} + \frac{1}{a^2}.$$

$$\int_0^s x^2 e^{-ax} \, dx = \left[x^2 \times \left(-\frac{1}{a} \right) e^{-ax} \right]_0^s - \int_0^s 2x \times \left(-\frac{1}{a} \right) e^{-ax} \, dx$$

$$= -\frac{1}{a} s^2 e^{-as} + \frac{2}{a} \int_0^s x e^{-ax} \, dx.$$

The integral in the last line here is the integral that has just been found, so you could now use the first answer to complete the evaluation of $\displaystyle\int_0^s x^2 e^{-ax} \, dx$.

For the infinite integral, you need to know the limits of e^{-as}, $s e^{-as}$ and $s^2 e^{-as}$ as $s \to \infty$. You know that $e^{-as} \to 0$, and C3 Miscellaneous exercise 10 Question 10 shows that also $s e^{-as} \to 0$ and $s^2 e^{-as} \to 0$.

It follows that $\displaystyle\int_0^\infty x e^{-ax} \, dx = \frac{1}{a^2}$, and that $\displaystyle\int_0^\infty x^2 e^{-ax} \, dx = \frac{2}{a} \int_0^\infty x e^{-ax} \, dx = \frac{2}{a^3}$.

Exercise 2A

1 Use integration by parts to integrate the following functions with respect to x.

(a) $x \sin x$ (b) $3x e^x$ (c) $(x+4)e^x$

2 Use integration by parts to integrate the following functions with respect to x.

(a) $x e^{2x}$ (b) $x \cos 4x$ (c) $x \ln 2x$

3 Find

(a) $\displaystyle\int x^5 \ln 3x \, dx,$ (b) $\displaystyle\int x e^{2x+1} \, dx,$ (c) $\displaystyle\int \ln 2x \, dx.$

4 Find the exact values of

(a) $\displaystyle\int_1^e x \ln x \, dx,$ (b) $\displaystyle\int_0^{\frac{1}{2}\pi} x \sin \tfrac{1}{2}x \, dx,$ (c) $\displaystyle\int_1^e x^n \ln x \, dx \quad (n > 0).$

5 Prove that $\displaystyle\int x^2 \sin x \, dx = -x^2 \cos x + 2 \int x \cos x \, dx$. Hence, by using integration by parts a second time, find $\displaystyle\int x^2 \sin x \, dx$. Use a similar method to integrate the following functions with respect to x.

(a) $x^2 e^{2x}$ (b) $x^2 \cos \tfrac{1}{2}x$

6 Find the area bounded by the curve $y = x e^{-x}$, the x-axis and the lines $x = 0$ and $x = 2$. Find also the volume of the solid of revolution obtained by rotating this region about the x-axis.

7 Find the area between the x-axis and the curve $y = x \sin 3x$ for $0 \leqslant x \leqslant \tfrac{1}{3}\pi$. Leave your answer in terms of π. Find also the volume of the solid of revolution obtained by rotating this region about the x-axis.

8* By using integration by parts twice in succession, find

(a) $\displaystyle\int_0^\pi e^x \cos x \, dx,$ (b) $\displaystyle\int_{-\pi}^\pi e^{-4x} \sin 2x \, dx,$ (c) $\displaystyle\int_0^1 e^{-ax} \cos bx \, dx.$

9* Find

(a) $\displaystyle\int_0^\infty e^{-x} \sin x \, dx,$ (b) $\displaystyle\int_0^1 \frac{x}{\sqrt{1-x}} \, dx.$

Draw diagrams to illustrate the areas measured by these definite integrals.

2.2 Direct substitution

None of the methods of integration you have met so far could be used to find

$$\int \frac{1}{x + \sqrt{x}} \, dx.$$

However, by expressing x in terms of a new variable, integrals like this can be put into a form which you know how to integrate.

Denote the integral by I, so that

$$\frac{dI}{dx} = \frac{1}{x + \sqrt{x}}.$$

The difficulty in solving this equation for I lies in the square root, so write $x = u^2$. Then, by the chain rule,

$$\frac{dI}{du} = \frac{dI}{dx} \times \frac{dx}{du} = \frac{1}{u^2 + u} \times 2u = \frac{2}{u + 1}.$$

From this you can integrate to find I in terms of u, as

$$I = 2\ln|u + 1| + k.$$

The solution to the original equation is then found by replacing u by $\sqrt{x}$, so that

$$I = 2\ln(\sqrt{x} + 1) + k.$$

> You do not need the modulus sign, since $\sqrt{x} + 1$ is always positive.

You can easily check by differentiation that this integral is correct.

This method is called **integration by substitution**. It is the equivalent for integrals of the chain rule for differentiation.

In general, to find $I = \int f(x)\,dx$, the equation $\dfrac{dI}{dx} = f(x)$ is changed by writing x as some function $s(u)$. Then $\dfrac{dI}{du} = f(x) \times \dfrac{dx}{du} = g(u) \times \dfrac{dx}{du}$, where $g(u) = f(s(u))$. If you can find $\int g(u) \times \dfrac{dx}{du}\,du$, then you can find the original integral by replacing u by $s^{-1}(x)$.

> If $x = s(u)$ and $g(u) = f(s(u))$, then $\int f(x)\,dx$ is equal to $\int g(u) \times \dfrac{dx}{du}\,du$, with u replaced by $s^{-1}(x)$.

Do not try to memorise this as a formal statement; what is important is to learn how to use the method. Notice how the notation helps; although the dx and du in the integrals have no meaning in themselves, the replacement of dx in the first integral by $\dfrac{dx}{du}\,du$ in the second makes the method easy to apply.

Applying this method to the example above you would write, with $x = u^2$,

$$\int \frac{1}{x + \sqrt{x}}\,dx = \int \frac{1}{u^2 + u} \times 2u\,du$$

$$= \int \frac{2}{u + 1}\,du$$

$$= 2\ln|u + 1| + k$$

$$= 2\ln(\sqrt{x} + 1) + k.$$

Example 2.2.1

Find $\int \dfrac{1}{x} \ln x \, dx$ using the substitution $x = e^u$.

The difficulty lies in the logarithm factor, which is removed by using the substitution $x = e^u$ (that is, $\ln x = u$). Then $\dfrac{dx}{du} = e^u$, and the integral becomes

$$\int \frac{1}{e^u} \ln(e^u) \times e^u \, du = \int u \, du = \tfrac{1}{2}u^2 + k.$$

Replacing u in this expression by $\ln x$, the original integral is

$$\int \frac{1}{x} \ln x \, dx = \tfrac{1}{2}(\ln x)^2 + k.$$

Example 2.2.2

Find $\int \dfrac{6x}{\sqrt{2x+1}} \, dx$ by writing $2x + 1$ as u^2.

The awkward bit of the integral is the expression $\sqrt{2x+1}$. If $2x + 1$ is written as u^2, then $\sqrt{2x+1}$ is equal to u. The equation $2x + 1 = u^2$ is equivalent to $x = \tfrac{1}{2}u^2 - \tfrac{1}{2}$. This substitution gives $\dfrac{dx}{du} = \tfrac{1}{2}(2u) = u$. So $\int \dfrac{6x}{\sqrt{2x+1}} \, dx$ becomes

$$\int \frac{6\left(\tfrac{1}{2}u^2 - \tfrac{1}{2}\right)}{u} \times u \, du = \int (3u^2 - 3) \, du = u^3 - 3u + k.$$

You want this in terms of x, so substituting $\sqrt{2x+1}$ for u gives

$$\int \frac{6x}{\sqrt{2x+1}} \, dx = (\sqrt{2x+1})^3 - 3\sqrt{2x+1} + k.$$

It is quite acceptable to leave the answer in this form, but it would be neater to note that $(\sqrt{2x+1})^3 = (2x+1)\sqrt{2x+1}$, so

$$\int \frac{6x}{\sqrt{2x+1}} \, dx = (2x+1)\sqrt{2x+1} - 3\sqrt{2x+1} + k$$

$$= (2x + 1 - 3)\sqrt{2x+1} + k$$

$$= 2(x - 1)\sqrt{2x+1} + k.$$

Since this is quite a complicated piece of algebra, it is worth checking it by using the product rule to differentiate $2(x - 1)\sqrt{2x+1}$, and showing that the result is $\dfrac{6x}{\sqrt{2x+1}}$.

The method used in this example is sometimes described as 'substituting $u = \sqrt{2x+1}$' and sometimes as 'substituting $x = \tfrac{1}{2}(u^2 - 1)$'. In the course of the calculation you use the relation both ways round, so either description is equally appropriate.

Example 2.2.3

Use the substitution $x = 2 \sin u$ to find $\displaystyle\int \sqrt{4 - x^2} \, dx$.

The reason for substituting $x = 2 \sin u$ is that

$$4 - x^2 = 4 - 4\sin^2 u = 4(1 - \sin^2 u) = 4\cos^2 u.$$

Therefore $\sqrt{4 - x^2} = 2\cos u$. Also $\dfrac{dx}{du} = 2\cos u$. The integral then becomes

$$\int 2\cos u \times 2\cos u \, du = \int 4\cos^2 u \, du$$
$$= \int 2(1 + \cos 2u) \, du$$
$$= 2u + \sin 2u + k.$$

To get the original integral, note that $\sin u = \frac{1}{2}x$, so that $2u = 2\sin^{-1}\frac{1}{2}x$. But rather than using this form in the second term, it is simpler to expand $\sin 2u$ as $2\sin u \cos u$, which is $x \times \frac{1}{2}\sqrt{4 - x^2}$. Therefore

$$\int \sqrt{4 - x^2} \, dx = 2\sin^{-1}\frac{1}{2}x + \frac{1}{2}x\sqrt{4 - x^2} + k.$$

Notice one further detail. The reference in the general statement (just before Example 2.2.1) to the inverse function s^{-1} should alert you to the need for the substitution function s to be one–one. This is arranged in the usual way, by restricting the domain of s.

In the example which introduced this section, for $x = u^2$ to have an inverse you can restrict u to be non-negative. This justifies writing $\sqrt{x}$ as u (since by definition $\sqrt{x} \geqslant 0$) when the variable was changed from x to u, and then replacing u by $\sqrt{x}$ (rather than $-\sqrt{x}$) at the final stage.

In Example 2.2.3, the domain of u is restricted to the interval $-\frac{1}{2}\pi \leqslant u \leqslant \frac{1}{2}\pi$, so that the substitution function $x = 2\sin u$ has inverse $u = \sin^{-1}\frac{1}{2}x$, with $\sin^{-1}$ defined as in C3 Section 6.7. Over this interval $\cos u \geqslant 0$, which justifies taking $2\cos u$ to be the positive square root of $4 - x^2$.

Exercise 2B

1 Use the given substitutions to find the following integrals.

(a) $\displaystyle\int \frac{1}{x - 2\sqrt{x}} \, dx$ $x = u^2$

(b) $\displaystyle\int \frac{1}{(3x + 4)^2} \, dx$ $x = \frac{1}{3}(u - 4)$

(c) $\displaystyle\int \sin\left(\frac{1}{3}\pi - \frac{1}{2}x\right) dx$ $x = \frac{2}{3}\pi - 2u$

(d) $\displaystyle\int x(x - 1)^5 \, dx$ $x = 1 + u$

(e) $\displaystyle\int \frac{e^x}{1 + e^x} \, dx$ $x = \ln u$

(f) $\displaystyle\int \frac{1}{3\sqrt{x} + 4x} \, dx$ $x = u^2$

(g) $\displaystyle\int 3x\sqrt{x + 2} \, dx$ $x = u^2 - 2$

(h) $\displaystyle\int \frac{x}{\sqrt{x - 3}} \, dx$ $x = 3 + u^2$

(i) $\displaystyle\int \frac{1}{x \ln x} \, dx$ $x = e^u$

(j) $\displaystyle\int \frac{1}{\sqrt{4 - x^2}} \, dx$ $x = 2\sin u$

2 Use a substitution of the form $ax + b = u$, that is $x = \dfrac{1}{a}(u - b)$, to find the following integrals.

(a) $\displaystyle\int x(2x + 1)^3 \, dx$

(b) $\displaystyle\int (x + 2)(2x - 3)^5 \, dx$

(c) $\displaystyle\int x\sqrt{2x - 1} \, dx$

(d) $\displaystyle\int \dfrac{x - 2}{\sqrt{x - 4}} \, dx$

(e) $\displaystyle\int \dfrac{x}{(x + 1)^2} \, dx$

(f) $\displaystyle\int \dfrac{x}{2x + 3} \, dx$

3 (a) Use the substitution $x = \tan u$ to show that $\displaystyle\int \dfrac{1}{1 + x^2} \, dx = \tan^{-1} x + k$.

(b) Use the substitution $x = \ln u$ to find $\displaystyle\int \dfrac{e^x}{1 + e^{2x}} \, dx$.

2.3 Definite integrals

The most difficult part in Example 2.2.3 was not the integration, but getting the result back from an expression in u to an expression in x. If you have a definite integral to find, this last step is not necessary. Instead you can use the substitution equation to change the interval of integration from values of x to values of u.

$$\text{If } x = s(u), \text{ then } \int_a^b f(x) \, dx = \int_p^q g(u) \times \dfrac{dx}{du} \, du,$$

$$\text{where } g(u) = f(s(u)), \text{ and } p = s^{-1}(a), \, q = s^{-1}(b).$$

Once again, it is more important to be able to use the result than to remember it in this form.

Example 2.3.1

Find $\displaystyle\int_0^1 \sqrt{4 - x^2} \, dx$,

(a) using the substitution $x = 2 \sin u$,

(b) by relating it to an area.

(a) Follow Example 2.2.3 as far as the form of the integral in terms of u, and note that the new limits of integration are $\sin^{-1}\left(\frac{1}{2} \times 0\right) = 0$ and $\sin^{-1}\left(\frac{1}{2} \times 1\right) = \frac{1}{6}\pi$. Therefore

$$\int_0^1 \sqrt{4 - x^2} \, dx = \int_0^{\frac{1}{6}\pi} 4\cos^2 u \, du$$

$$= \left[2u + \sin 2u\right]_0^{\frac{1}{6}\pi}$$

$$= \tfrac{1}{3}\pi + \sin \tfrac{1}{3}\pi$$

$$= \tfrac{1}{3}\pi + \tfrac{1}{2}\sqrt{3}.$$

(b) If $y = \sqrt{4 - x^2}$, then $x^2 + y^2 = 4$, which is the equation of a circle with centre the origin and radius 2. The integral therefore represents the area of the region under the upper semicircle from $x = 0$ to $x = 1$, shown shaded in Fig. 2.1.

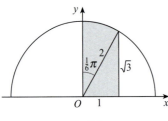

Fig. 2.1

This region consists of a sector with angle $\frac{1}{6}\pi$ and a triangle with base 1 and height $\sqrt{3}$. The value of the integral is therefore

$$\tfrac{1}{2} \times 2^2 \times \left(\tfrac{1}{6}\pi\right) + \tfrac{1}{2} \times 1 \times \sqrt{3} = \tfrac{1}{3}\pi + \tfrac{1}{2}\sqrt{3}.$$

Example 2.3.2

Find $\displaystyle\int_0^1 \frac{1}{1+x^2}\, dx$ using the substitution $x = \tan u$.

The substitution $x = \tan u$ makes $1 + x^2 = 1 + \tan^2 u = \sec^2 u$. Also $\dfrac{dx}{du} = \sec^2 u$, $\tan^{-1} 0 = 0$ and $\tan^{-1} 1 = \frac{1}{4}\pi$. Therefore

$$\int_0^1 \frac{1}{1+x^2}\, dx = \int_0^{\frac{1}{4}\pi} \frac{1}{\sec^2 u} \times \sec^2 u\, du$$

$$= \int_0^{\frac{1}{4}\pi} 1\, du$$

$$= [u]_0^{\frac{1}{4}\pi}$$

$$= \tfrac{1}{4}\pi.$$

Exercise 2C

1 Use the given substitutions to find the following integrals.

(a) $\displaystyle\int_0^1 \frac{e^x}{1+e^x}\, dx$ $x = \ln u$ (b) $\displaystyle\int_9^{16} \frac{1}{x - 2\sqrt{x}}\, dx$ $x = u^2$

(c) $\displaystyle\int_1^2 x(x-1)^5\, dx$ $x = 1 + u$ (d) $\displaystyle\int_1^2 x\sqrt{x-1}\, dx$ $x = 1 + u$

(e) $\displaystyle\int_0^1 \frac{1}{\sqrt{4-x^2}}\, dx$ $x = 2\sin u$ (f) $\displaystyle\int_6^9 \frac{x^2}{\sqrt{x-5}}\, dx$ $x = 5 + u$

(g) $\displaystyle\int_{-4}^4 \sqrt{16 - x^2}\, dx$ $x = 4\sin u$ (h) $\displaystyle\int_1^6 \frac{1}{4+x^2}\, dx$ $x = 2\tan u$

(i) $\displaystyle\int_e^{e^2} \frac{1}{x(\ln x)^2}\, dx$ $x = e^u$ (j) $\displaystyle\int_0^{\frac{1}{2}} \frac{1}{(1-x^2)^{\frac{3}{2}}}\, dx$ $x = \sin u$

2 Use the substitution $x = \sin^2 u$ to calculate $\displaystyle\int_0^{\frac{1}{2}} \sqrt{\frac{x}{1-x}}\, dx$.

3 Use the given trigonometric substitutions to evaluate the following infinite and improper integrals.

(a) $\displaystyle\int_0^\infty \frac{1}{x^2+4}\,\mathrm{d}x$ $x = 2\tan u$ (b) $\displaystyle\int_0^3 \frac{1}{\sqrt{9-x^2}}\,\mathrm{d}x$ $x = 3\sin u$

(c) $\displaystyle\int_{-\infty}^\infty \frac{1}{9x^2+4}\,\mathrm{d}x$ $x = \tfrac{2}{3}\tan u$ (d) $\displaystyle\int_0^1 \frac{1}{\sqrt{x(1-x)}}\,\mathrm{d}x$ $x = \sin^2 u$

(e) $\displaystyle\int_1^\infty \frac{1}{(1+x^2)^{\frac{3}{2}}}\,\mathrm{d}x$ $x = \tan u$ (f) $\displaystyle\int_1^\infty \frac{1}{x\sqrt{x^2-1}}\,\mathrm{d}x$ $x = \sec u$

4 Evaluate the following infinite integrals by using the given substitutions.

(a) $\displaystyle\int_2^\infty \frac{1}{x(\ln x)^3}\,\mathrm{d}x$ $x = e^u$ (b) $\displaystyle\int_0^\infty xe^{-\frac{1}{2}x^2}\,\mathrm{d}x$ $x = \sqrt{u}$

5* Use the substitution $x = \sigma u$, followed by a change of letter in the integrand, to show that, if $\sigma > 0$,

$$\int_{-\infty}^\infty e^{-\frac{x^2}{2\sigma^2}}\,\mathrm{d}x = \sigma \int_{-\infty}^\infty e^{-\frac{1}{2}x^2}\,\mathrm{d}x.$$

6* Use the substitution $x = \dfrac{a^2}{u}$, where $a > 0$, to show that

$$\int_0^a \frac{1}{a^2+x^2}\,\mathrm{d}x = \int_a^\infty \frac{1}{a^2+x^2}\,\mathrm{d}x.$$

7* Use the substitution $x = \pi - u$, followed by a change of letter, to prove that $\displaystyle\int_0^\pi x\sin x\,\mathrm{d}x = \int_0^\pi (\pi - x)\sin x\,\mathrm{d}x$. Hence show that $\displaystyle\int_0^\pi x\sin x\,\mathrm{d}x = \tfrac{1}{2}\pi \int_0^\pi \sin x\,\mathrm{d}x$, and evaluate this integral.

2.4 Reverse substitution

If $y = \sqrt{1+\ln x}$, then the chain rule gives $\dfrac{\mathrm{d}y}{\mathrm{d}x} = \dfrac{1}{2\sqrt{1+\ln x}} \times \dfrac{1}{x}$. So, Turning this into integral form,

$$\int \frac{1}{\sqrt{1+\ln x}} \times \frac{1}{x}\,\mathrm{d}x = 2\sqrt{1+\ln x} + k.$$

But how could you find this integral if you didn't know the answer to start with? You can see that the integrand is the product of two factors. The first of these has the form of a composite function of x; you could write it as $\dfrac{1}{\sqrt{u}}$, where $u = 1 + \ln x$. The lucky break is that the second factor, $\dfrac{1}{x}$, is the derivative $\dfrac{\mathrm{d}u}{\mathrm{d}x}$. So the integral can be written as

$$\int \frac{1}{\sqrt{u}} \times \frac{\mathrm{d}u}{\mathrm{d}x}\,\mathrm{d}x,$$

which can be worked out as

$$\int \frac{1}{\sqrt{u}}\,\mathrm{d}u = 2\sqrt{u} + k = 2\sqrt{1+\ln x} + k.$$

This seems to be a different form of integration by substitution, in which you can already see the derivative $\dfrac{du}{dx}$ as part of the integrand.

To describe it in general terms, write $\dfrac{1}{\sqrt{1+\ln x}}$ as f(x), $u = 1 + \ln x$ as r(x) and $\dfrac{1}{\sqrt{u}}$ as g(u), so f(x) = g(r(x)) and $\dfrac{du}{dx} = \dfrac{1}{x}$. You then get:

If $u = $ r(x), and if g(r(x)) = f(x), then $\displaystyle\int f(x) \times \dfrac{du}{dx}\,dx$ is equal to $\displaystyle\int g(u)\,du$, with u replaced by r(x).

You can check that this is in effect the same as the statement in Section 2.2 with f and g, x and u interchanged, and r written in place of s. But the method of applying it is different, because you need to begin by identifying the derivative $\dfrac{du}{dx}$ as a factor in the integrand.

As before, do not memorise the general statement, but learn to use the method by studying some examples.

Example 2.4.1

Find $\displaystyle\int x^2\sqrt{1+x^3}\,dx$ by writing $1 + x^3$ as u.

Begin by noticing that the derivative of $1 + x^3$ is $3x^2$, so that if the integral is written as

$$\int \tfrac{1}{3}\sqrt{1+x^3} \times 3x^2\,dx,$$

then it can be changed into the form

$$\int \tfrac{1}{3}(1+x^3)^{\frac{1}{2}} \times \dfrac{du}{dx}\,dx$$

with $u = 1 + x^3$. This is equal to

$$\int \tfrac{1}{3}u^{\frac{1}{2}}\,du = \tfrac{2}{9}u^{\frac{3}{2}} + k,$$

with u replaced by $1 + x^3$. That is,

$$\int x^2\sqrt{1+x^3}\,dx = \tfrac{2}{9}(1+x^3)^{\frac{3}{2}} + k.$$

Example 2.4.2

Find $\displaystyle\int_0^{\frac{1}{2}\pi} \cos^4 x \sin x\,dx$ by writing $\cos x$ as u.

If the integrand is written as $-\cos^4 x \times (-\sin x)$, then the second factor is $\dfrac{du}{dx}$ with $u = \cos x$.

$$\int_0^{\frac{1}{2}\pi} \cos^4 x \sin x\,dx = \int_0^{\frac{1}{2}\pi} -\cos^4 x \times \dfrac{du}{dx}\,dx$$

$$= \int_1^0 -u^4\,du = -\big[\tfrac{1}{5}u^5\big]_1^0 = \tfrac{1}{5}.$$

Notice that the limits of integration change from 0, $\frac{1}{2}\pi$ to 1, 0 at the step where the integral

changes from $\displaystyle\int_0^{\frac{1}{2}\pi} -\cos^4 x \times \frac{du}{dx}\,dx$ to $\displaystyle\int_1^0 -u^4\,du$. Since $\cos x$ is decreasing over the interval

$0 \leqslant x \leqslant \frac{1}{2}\pi$, the limits for u appear in reversed order.

Example 2.4.3

Find $\displaystyle\int \frac{\cos x - \sin x}{\sin x + \cos x}\,dx$ by writing $\sin x + \cos x$ as u.

Write this as $\displaystyle\int \frac{1}{\sin x + \cos x} \times (\cos x - \sin x)\,dx$. If $u = \sin x + \cos x$, this is

$\displaystyle\int \frac{1}{\sin x + \cos x} \times \frac{du}{dx}\,dx$, which is $\displaystyle\int \frac{1}{u}\,du = \ln|u| + k$.

So $\displaystyle\int \frac{\cos x - \sin x}{\sin x + \cos x}\,dx = \ln|\sin x + \cos x| + k$.

In this last example the integral has the form $\displaystyle\int \frac{f'(x)}{f(x)}\,dx$, where $f(x) = \sin x + \cos x$. This type of integral often arises, and the result is important:

$$\int \frac{f'(x)}{f(x)}\,dx = \ln|f(x)| + k.$$

Example 2.4.4

Find $\displaystyle\int_0^1 \frac{e^x - e^{-x}}{e^x + e^{-x}}\,dx$.

The integrand is $\dfrac{f'(x)}{f(x)}$ with $f(x) = e^x + e^{-x}$, so the value of the integral is

$$[\ln|e^x + e^{-x}|]_0^1 = \ln\left(e + \frac{1}{e}\right) - \ln 2 = \ln\left(\frac{e^2 + 1}{2e}\right).$$

Exercise 2D

1 Use the given substitutions to find the following integrals.

(a) $\displaystyle\int 2x(x^2 + 1)^3\,dx$ $u = x^2 + 1$ (b) $\displaystyle\int x\sqrt{4 + x^2}\,dx$ $u = 4 + x^2$

(c) $\displaystyle\int \sin^5 x \cos x\,dx$ $u = \sin x$ (d) $\displaystyle\int \tan^3 x \sec^2 x\,dx$ $u = \tan x$

(e) $\displaystyle\int \frac{2x^3}{\sqrt{1 - x^4}}\,dx$ $u = 1 - x^4$ (f) $\displaystyle\int \cos^3 2x \sin 2x\,dx$ $u = \cos 2x$

2 Without carrying out a substitution, write down the following indefinite integrals.

(a) $\displaystyle\int \frac{\cos x}{1 + \sin x}\,dx$ (b) $\displaystyle\int \frac{x^2}{1 + x^3}\,dx$ (c) $\displaystyle\int \cot x\,dx$

(d) $\displaystyle\int \frac{e^x}{4 + e^x}\,dx$ (e) $\displaystyle\int \frac{2e^{3x}}{5 - e^{3x}}\,dx$ (f) $\displaystyle\int \tan 3x\,dx$

3 Evaluate each of the following integrals, giving your answer in an exact form.

(a) $\displaystyle\int_1^2 \frac{e^x}{e^x - 1}\,dx$ (b) $\displaystyle\int_4^5 \frac{x-2}{x^2 - 4x + 5}\,dx$ (c) $\displaystyle\int_0^{\frac{1}{6}\pi} \frac{\sin 2x}{1 + \cos 2x}\,dx$

2.5* Choosing a suitable substitution

This section is optional. If you wish, you may omit it and go straight to the Miscellaneous exercise at the end of the chapter.

Although you can now differentiate almost any function made up of powers, logarithms, exponentials and trigonometric functions, integration is more of a problem. You will remember that even as simple an integral as $\displaystyle\int \frac{1}{x}\,dx$ could not be found until you had learnt about logarithms. There are many quite simple-looking integrals, such as $\displaystyle\int \sqrt{\sin x}\,dx$, $\displaystyle\int \sqrt{1 + x^3}\,dx$ and $\displaystyle\int e^x \ln x\,dx$, which can't be found in terms of the functions you know.

Integration by substitution greatly enlarges the number of functions you can integrate, but the problem is how to choose a substitution which works. There is no complete answer to this, and sometimes a very unexpected substitution produces an answer. However, here are a few simple guidelines.

If the integral includes

$(ax + b)^n$,	try $ax + b = u$, that is $x = \dfrac{1}{a}u - \dfrac{b}{a}$
$\sqrt[n]{ax + b}$,	try $ax + b = u^n$, that is $x = \dfrac{1}{a}u^n - \dfrac{b}{a}$
$a - bx^2$,	try $x = \sqrt{\dfrac{a}{b}}\,\sin u$
$a + bx^2$,	try $x = \sqrt{\dfrac{a}{b}}\,\tan u$
$bx^2 - a$,	try $x = \sqrt{\dfrac{a}{b}}\,\sec u$
e^x,	try $e^x = u$, that is $x = \ln u$
$x = \ln(ax + b)$,	try $ax + b = e^u$, that is $x = \dfrac{1}{a}e^u - \dfrac{b}{a}$.

Occasionally you will find that you still can't do the integration after the first substitution, but that a second substitution will do the trick.

Example 2.5.1

Find $\displaystyle\int \frac{1}{\sqrt{e^{2x} - 1}}\,dx$, where $x \geqslant 0$.

The condition $x \geqslant 0$ is needed because, if x is negative, e^{2x} is less than 1, and $\sqrt{e^{2x} - 1}$ doesn't exist.

The integral includes e^x, so try $e^x = u$, that is $x = \ln u$. Then $\dfrac{dx}{du} = \dfrac{1}{u}$ and $e^{2x} = (e^x)^2 = u^2$, so the integral becomes

$$\int \frac{1}{\sqrt{u^2 - 1}} \times \frac{1}{u}\, du.$$

This looks no better than the original integral. But since it includes $u^2 - 1$, try a second substitution $u = \sec v$. Then $\dfrac{du}{dv} = \sec v \tan v$, so the second integral becomes

$$\int \frac{1}{\sqrt{\sec^2 v - 1}} \times \frac{1}{\sec v} \times \sec v \tan v\, dv,$$

which is

$$\int \frac{1}{\tan v} \times \frac{1}{\sec v} \times \sec v \tan v\, dv, \quad \text{or more simply} \int 1\, dv.$$

This integral you can do! Working backwards, since $\displaystyle\int 1\, dv = v + k$,

$$\int \frac{1}{\sqrt{u^2 - 1}} \times \frac{1}{u}\, du = \sec^{-1} u + k,$$

and finally

$$\int \frac{1}{\sqrt{e^{2x} - 1}}\, dx = \sec^{-1}(e^x) + k.$$

Exercise 2E*

1 Use substitutions of the form suggested in Section 2.5 to find the following integrals.

(a) $\displaystyle\int \frac{1}{\sqrt{1 - 9x^2}}\, dx$
(b) $\displaystyle\int \sqrt{16 - 9x^2}\, dx$
(c) $\displaystyle\int \frac{1}{2 + e^{-x}}\, dx$

(d) $\displaystyle\int \frac{x}{\sqrt[3]{1 + x}}\, dx$
(e) $\displaystyle\int (1 - x^2)^{-\frac{3}{2}}\, dx$
(f) $\displaystyle\int \frac{1}{2 - \sqrt{x}}\, dx$

In part (f), you may need to use two substitutions, one after the other.

2 Find the following integrals by using suitable substitutions.

(a) $\displaystyle\int 2x(1 + x^2)^5\, dx$
(b) $\displaystyle\int 4x\sqrt{3 + 2x^2}\, dx$

(c) $\displaystyle\int x^2(5 - 3x^3)^6\, dx$
(d) $\displaystyle\int \frac{3x^2}{\sqrt{1 + x^3}}\, dx$

(e) $\displaystyle\int \sec^4 x \tan x\, dx$
(f) $\displaystyle\int \sin^3 4x \cos 4x\, dx$

3 Evaluate each of the following integrals, giving your answer in an exact form.

(a) $\displaystyle\int_0^{\frac{1}{2}\pi} \frac{\cos x}{\sqrt{1 + 3\sin x}}\, dx$
(b) $\displaystyle\int_0^2 x(x^2 + 1)^3\, dx$
(c) $\displaystyle\int_0^{\frac{1}{4}\pi} \sin x \cos^2 x\, dx$

(d) $\displaystyle\int_1^8 (1 + 2x)\sqrt{x + x^2}\, dx$
(e) $\displaystyle\int_0^{\frac{1}{3}\pi} \frac{\sin x}{(1 + \cos x)^2}\, dx$
(f) $\displaystyle\int_0^3 2x\sqrt{1 + x^2}\, dx$

(g) $\displaystyle\int_0^{\frac{1}{4}\pi} \sec^2 x \tan^2 x\, dx$
(h) $\displaystyle\int_1^e \frac{(\ln x)^n}{x}\, dx$
(i) $\displaystyle\int_0^{\frac{1}{3}\pi} \sec^3 x \tan x\, dx$

4 Find an expression, in terms of n and a, for $\int_0^a \dfrac{x}{(1+x^2)^n}\,dx$. For what values of n does

$\int_0^\infty \dfrac{x}{(1+x^2)^n}\,dx$ exist? State its value in terms of n.

Miscellaneous exercise 2

1 By using the substitution $u = 2x - 1$, or otherwise, find $\displaystyle\int \dfrac{2x}{(2x-1)^2}\,dx$.   (OCR)

2 Use integration by parts to determine $\displaystyle\int 3x\sqrt{x-1}\,dx$.   (OCR)

3 Use the trapezium rule with subdivisions at $x = 3$ and $x = 5$ to obtain an approximation to
$\displaystyle\int_1^7 \dfrac{x^3}{1+x^4}\,dx$, giving your answer correct to three places of decimals.

By evaluating the integral exactly, show that the error in the approximation is about 4.1%
    (OCR)

4 Use integration by parts to determine the exact value of $\displaystyle\int_0^{\frac{1}{2}\pi} 3x \sin 2x\,dx$.   (OCR)

5 Use integration by parts to determine $\displaystyle\int_0^{\frac{1}{3}} xe^{2x}\,dx$.   (OCR)

6 Use the given substitution and then use integration by parts to complete the integration.

(a) $\displaystyle\int \cos^{-1} x\,dx \quad x = \cos u$ (b) $\displaystyle\int \tan^{-1} x\,dx \quad x = \tan u$ (c) $\displaystyle\int (\ln x)^2\,dx \quad x = e^u$

7 Use the substitution $x = \sin u$ to find $\displaystyle\int_0^1 \sin^{-1} x\,dx$.

8 Find $\displaystyle\int \dfrac{1}{e^x + 4e^{-x}}\,dx$, by means of the substitution $u = e^x$, followed by the substitution
$u = 2\tan v$.   (OCR, adapted)

9 Find $\displaystyle\int \dfrac{6x}{1+3x^2}\,dx$.   (OCR)

10 Calculate the exact value of $\displaystyle\int_0^3 \dfrac{x}{1+x^2}\,dx$.   (OCR)

11 By using the substitution $u = \sin x$, or otherwise, find $\displaystyle\int \sin^3 x \sin 2x\,dx$, giving your
answer in terms of x.   (OCR)

12 By means of the substitution $u = 1 + \sqrt{x}$, or otherwise, find $\displaystyle\int \dfrac{1}{1+\sqrt{x}}\,dx$, giving your
answer in terms of x.   (OCR)

13 Integrate with respect to x, (i) by using a substitution of the form $ax + b = u$, and (ii) by
parts, and show that your answers are equivalent.

(a) $x\sqrt{4x-1}$,   (b) $x\sqrt{2-x}$,   (c) $x\sqrt{2x+3}$.

14 Use the substitution $u = \ln x$ to show that $\displaystyle\int_e^{e^2} \frac{1}{x\sqrt{\ln x}}\, dx = 2\sqrt{2} - 2.$ (OCR)

15 Use the substitution $u = 4 + x^2$ to show that $\displaystyle\int_0^1 \frac{x^3}{\sqrt{4 + x^2}}\, dx = \tfrac{1}{3}(16 - 7\sqrt{5}).$ (OCR)

16 Use the substitution $u = 3x - 1$ to express $\displaystyle\int x(3x - 1)^4\, dx$ as an integral in terms of u.

Hence, or otherwise, find $\displaystyle\int x(3x - 1)^4\, dx$, giving your answer in terms of x.   (OCR)

17 Show, by means of the substitution $x = \tan\theta$, that $\displaystyle\int_0^1 \frac{1}{(x^2 + 1)^2}\, dx = \int_0^{\frac{1}{4}\pi} \cos^2\theta\, d\theta.$

Hence find the exact value of $\displaystyle\int_0^1 \frac{1}{(x^2 + 1)^2}\, dx.$

18 Find

(a) $\displaystyle\int x(1 + x)^6\, dx,$ (b) $\displaystyle\int x(3x - 1)^4\, dx,$ (c) $\displaystyle\int x(ax + b)^{12}\, dx.$

19 Evaluate $\displaystyle\int_0^1 xe^{-x}\, dx$, showing all your working.   (OCR)

20 Showing your working clearly, use integration by parts to evaluate $\displaystyle\int_0^\pi 4x\sin\tfrac{1}{2}x\, dx.$ (OCR)

21 The diagram (not to scale) shows the region R bounded by the axes, the curve $y = (x^2 + 1)^{-\frac{3}{2}}$ and the line $x = 1$. The integral

$$\int_0^1 (x^2 + 1)^{-\frac{3}{2}}\, dx$$

is denoted by I.

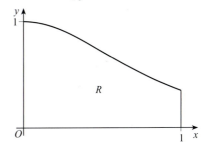

(a) Use the trapezium rule, with ordinates at $x = 0$, $x = \tfrac{1}{2}$ and $x = 1$, to estimate the value of I, giving your answer to 3 significant figures.

(b) Use the substitution $x = \tan\theta$ to show that $I = \tfrac{1}{2}\sqrt{2}.$

(c) By using the trapezium rule, with the same ordinates as in part (a), or otherwise, estimate the volume of the solid formed when R is rotated completely about the x-axis, giving your answer correct to 3 significant figures.

(d) Find the exact value of the volume in part (c), and compare your answers to parts (c) and (d).

(e) Re-work parts (a) and (c) using Simpson's rule instead of the trapezium rule. Are the answers you get more accurate or less?   (OCR, adapted)

22 By using the substitution $u = 3x + 1$, or otherwise, show that

$$\int_0^1 \frac{x}{(3x+1)^2}\, dx = \tfrac{2}{9}\ln 2 - \tfrac{1}{12}.$$

The diagram shows the finite region R in the first quadrant which is bounded by the curve $y = \dfrac{6\sqrt{x}}{3x+1}$, the x-axis and the line $x = 1$. Find the volume of the solid formed when R is rotated completely about the x-axis, giving your answer in terms of π and $\ln 2$.

(OCR)

3 Parametric equations

This chapter is about a method of describing curves using parameters. When you have completed it, you should

- know how to describe a curve using a parameter
- be able, in simple cases, to convert from a parametric equation of a curve to the cartesian equation of the curve
- be able to use parametric methods to establish properties of curves.

3.1 Introduction

Imagine that, at a funfair, a person P is going round on a roundabout, centre the origin O and radius 1 unit, at a constant speed (see Fig. 3.1). Suppose that P starts at the x-axis and moves anticlockwise in such a way that the angle at the centre t seconds after starting is t radians.

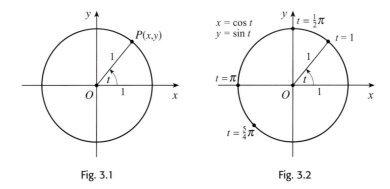

Fig. 3.1   Fig. 3.2

Where is P after t seconds? You can see from Fig. 3.1 that the coordinates of P are given by

$$x = \cos t, \quad y = \sin t.$$

These equations allow you to find the position of P at any time, and they describe the path of P completely.

Fig. 3.2 shows the values of t at various points on the first revolution of the roundabout. Notice that for each value of t there is a unique point on the curve.

During the first revolution, each point on the curve has a t-value corresponding to the time that the person is at that point. However, for each further revolution there will be another t-value associated with the point.

Example 3.1.1

Find the t-value of the starting point, the first time that P returns to it.

> The starting point is $(1, 0)$. Since $x = \cos t$, $y = \sin t$, you find that $1 = \cos t$ and $0 = \sin t$. These equations are simultaneously satisfied by $t = 0, \pm 2\pi, \pm 4\pi, \dots$. The smallest positive solution is $t = 2\pi$.

The equations $x = \cos t$, $y = \sin t$ are an example of **parametric equations**, and the variable t is an example of a **parameter**. In this case the variable t represents time, but in other cases it may not, as you will see in Example 3.1.2.

You may be able to draw curves from parametric equations on your graphic calculator. Put your calculator into parametric mode. You then have to enter the parametric equations into the calculator, and you may have to give an interval of values of t. For example, if you gave an interval of 0 to π for t in Example 3.1.1, you would get only the upper semicircle of the path. If you use the trace key, your calculator will also give you the t-value for any point.

> Recall that the curve looks like a circle only if you use the same scale on each axis.

You could also plot the curve using a spreadsheet with graph-plotting facilities or other graph-plotting software.

Here are other examples of parametric curves.

Example 3.1.2

A curve has parametric equations $x = t^2$, $y = 2t$. Sketch the curve for values of t from -3 to 3.

> Draw up a table of values, Table 3.3.

t	-3	-2	-1	0	1	2	3
x	9	4	1	0	1	4	9
y	-6	-4	-2	0	2	4	6

Table 3.3

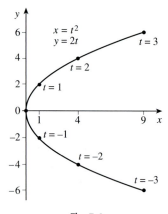

Fig. 3.4

> The points $(9, -6)$, $(4, -4)$, $(1, -2)$, $(0, 0)$, $(1, 2)$, $(4, 4)$ and $(9, 6)$ lie on the curve shown in Fig. 3.4. The points which are plotted are labelled with the t-values of the parameter.

The idea that a point is defined by the value of its parameter is an important one. Thus, for the curve $x = t^2$, $y = 2t$ you can talk about the point $t = -2$, which means the point $(4, -4)$.

The curve looks like a parabola on its side, and you will, in the next section, be able to prove that it is.

Example 3.1.3

A curve has parametric equations $x = \sin t$, $y = \sin 2t$, for values of t from 0 to 2π. Plot the curve, and indicate the points corresponding to values of t which are multiples of $\frac{1}{6}\pi$.

Draw up a table of values, Table 3.5.

t	0	$\frac{1}{6}\pi$	$\frac{1}{3}\pi$	$\frac{1}{2}\pi$	$\frac{2}{3}\pi$	$\frac{5}{6}\pi$	
x	0	0.5	0.866	1	0.866	0.5	
y	0	0.866	0.866	0	−0.866	−0.866	
t	π	$\frac{7}{6}\pi$	$\frac{4}{3}\pi$	$\frac{3}{2}\pi$	$\frac{5}{3}\pi$	$\frac{11}{6}\pi$	2π
x	0	−0.5	−0.866	−1	−0.866	−0.5	0
y	0	0.866	0.866	0	−0.866	−0.866	0

Table 3.5

Fig. 3.6 illustrates this curve, with the points from the table labelled with their t-values, except for the origin, which is the point for which $t = 0$, $t = \pi$ and $t = 2\pi$.

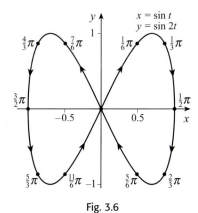

Fig. 3.6

Notice the arrows, which show the way that the values of t are increasing. These are not essential, but you should put them in if you want to show the direction in which the parameter is increasing.

If you use values of t outside the interval from 0 to 2π, the curve will repeat itself.

Finally, you should notice that parametric equations enable you to produce curves whose equations can't be written in the form $y = f(x)$. Neither the circle in Fig. 3.2 nor the curves in Fig. 3.4 or Fig. 3.6 can be drawn using a function equation, because none of them have just one value of y for each value of x.

It is time to give a definition of a parameter.

> If $x = f(t)$ and $y = g(t)$, where f and g are functions of a variable t defined for some domain of values of t, then the equations $x = f(t)$ and $y = g(t)$ are called **parametric equations**, and the variable t is a **parameter**.

Exercise 3A

1 Find the coordinates of the point on the curve $x = 5t^2$, $y = 10t$
   (a) when $t = 6$,   (b) when $t = -1$.

2 Find the coordinates of the point on the curve $x = 1 - \dfrac{1}{t}$, $y = 1 + \dfrac{1}{t}$
   (a) when $t = 3$,   (b) when $t = -1$.

3 The parametric equations of a curve are $x = 2\cos t$, $y = 2\sin t$ for $0 \leqslant t < 2\pi$. What is the value of t at the point $(0, 2)$?

4 A curve is given by $x = 5\cos t$, $y = 2\sin t$ for $0 \leqslant t < 2\pi$. Find the value of t at the point $\left(-2\tfrac{1}{2}, \sqrt{3}\right)$.

5 Sketch the curve given by $x = t^2$, $y = \dfrac{1}{t}$ for $t > 0$.

6 Sketch the curve given by $x = 3\cos t$, $y = 2\sin t$ for $0 \leqslant t < 2\pi$.

7 Sketch the graph of $x = 3t^2$, $y = 6t$ for $-4 \leqslant t \leqslant 4$.

8 Sketch the locus given by $x = \cos^2 t$, $y = \sin^2 t$ for $0 \leqslant t < 2\pi$.

3.2   From parametric to cartesian equations

Suppose that you have a curve C given parametrically by the equations $x = f(t)$ and $y = g(t)$ where f and g are functions defined for some domain of values of t. If you eliminate the parameter t between the two equations, then every point of C lies on the curve with the resulting cartesian equation.

For example, in Example 3.1.2 the curve is given parametrically by $x = t^2$, $y = 2t$. In this case, you can write $t = \tfrac{1}{2}y$, so that $x = \left(\tfrac{1}{2}y\right)^2 = \tfrac{1}{4}y^2$, which you can rewrite as $y^2 = 4x$. The parameter t has been eliminated between the two equations $x = t^2$, $y = 2t$. You can see from Fig. 3.4 that $y^2 = 4x$ is simply $y = \tfrac{1}{4}x^2$ 'on its side'.

> If $x = f(t)$ and $y = g(t)$ are parametric equations of a curve C, and you eliminate the parameter between the two equations, each point of the curve C lies on the curve represented by the resulting cartesian equation.

Example 3.2.1

A curve is given parametrically by the equations $x = 2t + 1$, $y = 3t - 2$. Show that the 'curve' is a straight line and find its gradient.

From the first equation $t = \tfrac{1}{2}(x - 1)$, so $y = 3\left(\tfrac{1}{2}(x - 1)\right) - 2$, that is, $2y = 3x - 7$. This is the equation of a straight line. Its gradient is $\tfrac{3}{2}$.

Example 3.2.2

Let E be the curve given parametrically by $x = a\cos t$, $y = b\sin t$, where a and b are constants and t is a parameter which takes values from 0 to 2π. Find the cartesian equation of E.

Since $x = a\cos t$ and $y = b\sin t$, $\cos t = \dfrac{x}{a}$ and $\sin t = \dfrac{y}{b}$. Then, using $\cos^2 t + \sin^2 t \equiv 1$,

$\left(\dfrac{x}{a}\right)^2 + \left(\dfrac{y}{b}\right)^2 = 1$. Fig. 3.7 shows the curve $\dfrac{x^2}{a^2} + \dfrac{y^2}{b^2} = 1$, which is an ellipse. If b is

equal to a, it is a circle of radius a.

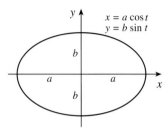

Fig. 3.7

Exercise 3B

1 Find cartesian equations for curves with these parametric equations.

(a) $x = t^2$, $y = \dfrac{1}{t}$ (b) $x = 3t^2$, $y = 6t$ (c) $x = 2\cos t$, $y = 2\sin t$

2 Find cartesian equations for curves with these parametric equations.

(a) $x = \cos^2 t$, $y = \sin^2 t$ (b) $x = \cos^3 t$, $y = \sin^3 t$

(c) $x = 1 - \dfrac{1}{t}$, $y = 1 + \dfrac{1}{t}$ (d) $x = 3t^2$, $y = 2t^3$

3 Show that parametric equations for a circle with centre (p, q) and radius r are $x = p + r\cos t$, $y = q + r\sin t$. Eliminate the parameter t to obtain the cartesian equation of the circle in the form $(x - p)^2 + (y - q)^2 = r^2$.

3.3 Differentiation and parametric form

Suppose that C is a curve with its equation given parametrically. How can you find the gradient at a point on the curve without first finding the cartesian equation of the curve?

Consider a point P with parameter t on the curve. The coordinates (x, y) of P are both functions of t, so as t changes, x and y also change. You can use the result in the blue box, but if you need to know why the result is true, read the rest of the section.

> If a curve is given parametrically by equations for x and y in terms of a parameter t, then
> $$\frac{dy}{dx} = \frac{dy}{dt} \bigg/ \frac{dx}{dt}.$$

To establish the result in the blue box, increase the value of t by δt; then there are corresponding increases of δx in x and δy in y.

Then, provided that $\delta x \neq 0$, $\dfrac{\delta y}{\delta x} = \dfrac{\delta y}{\delta t} \bigg/ \dfrac{\delta x}{\delta t}$.

As $\delta t \to 0$, both $\delta x \to 0$ and $\delta y \to 0$, so $\lim\limits_{\delta x \to 0} \dfrac{\delta y}{\delta x} = \lim\limits_{\delta t \to 0} \dfrac{\delta y}{\delta x}$.

Therefore, assuming that $\lim\limits_{\delta t \to 0} \left(\dfrac{\delta y}{\delta t} \bigg/ \dfrac{\delta x}{\delta t} \right) = \left(\lim\limits_{\delta t \to 0} \dfrac{\delta y}{\delta t} \right) \bigg/ \left(\lim\limits_{\delta t \to 0} \dfrac{\delta x}{\delta t} \right)$,

$$\dfrac{dy}{dx} = \lim\limits_{\delta x \to 0} \dfrac{\delta y}{\delta x} = \lim\limits_{\delta t \to 0} \dfrac{\delta y}{\delta x} = \lim\limits_{\delta t \to 0} \left(\dfrac{\delta y}{\delta t} \bigg/ \dfrac{\delta x}{\delta t} \right) = \left(\lim\limits_{\delta t \to 0} \dfrac{\delta y}{\delta t} \right) \bigg/ \left(\lim\limits_{\delta t \to 0} \dfrac{\delta x}{\delta t} \right)$$

$$= \dfrac{dy}{dt} \bigg/ \dfrac{dx}{dt}.$$

Therefore $\dfrac{dy}{dx} = \dfrac{dy}{dt} \bigg/ \dfrac{dx}{dt}$.

> Notice that, just as the chain rule for differentiation is easy to remember because of 'cancelling', so is this rule. However, you should remember that this is a helpful feature of the notation, and cancellation has no meaning in this context.

Example 3.3.1
Find the gradient at $t = 3$ on the parabola $x = t^2$, $y = 2t$.

$\dfrac{dy}{dt} = 2$ and $\dfrac{dx}{dt} = 2t$, so $\dfrac{dy}{dx} = \dfrac{dy}{dt} \bigg/ \dfrac{dx}{dt} = \dfrac{2}{2t} = \dfrac{1}{t}$.

When $t = 3$, the gradient is $\frac{1}{3}$.

Example 3.3.2
Find the equation of the normal at $(-8, 4)$ to the curve which is given parametrically by $x = t^3$, $y = t^2$. Sketch the curve, showing the normal.

For the point $(-8, 4)$, $t^3 = -8$ and $t^2 = 4$. These are both satisfied by $t = -2$.

As $\dfrac{dy}{dt} = 2t$ and $\dfrac{dx}{dt} = 3t^2$, $\dfrac{dy}{dx} = \dfrac{dy}{dt} \bigg/ \dfrac{dx}{dt} = \dfrac{2t}{3t^2} = \dfrac{2}{3t}$.

When $t = -2$ the gradient is $\dfrac{2}{3 \times (-2)} = -\frac{1}{3}$, so the gradient of the normal is $-\dfrac{1}{-\frac{1}{3}} = 3$.

Therefore the equation of the normal is $y - 4 = 3(x - (-8))$ or $y = 3x + 28$.

Notice with this curve that the gradient is not defined when $t = 0$, because the tangent at the origin is the y-axis.

A point on a curve where the curve changes direction suddenly, like the point on this curve at $t = 0$, is called a **cusp**.

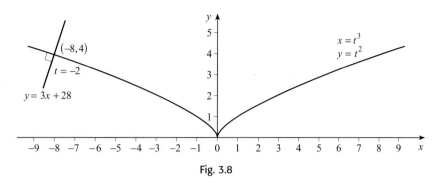

Fig. 3.8

You can now sketch the curve, shown in Fig. 3.8, but recall that the normal will look perpendicular to the curve only if the scales on both axes are the same.

Exercise 3C

1 Find $\dfrac{dy}{dx}$ in terms of t for the following curves.

(a) $x = t^3, y = 2t$

(b) $x = \sin t, y = \cos t$

(c) $x = 2\cos t, y = 3\sin t$

(d) $x = t^3 + t, y = t^2 - t$

2 Find the gradient of the tangent on the following curves, at the specified values of t.

(a) $x = 3t^2, y = 6t$ when $t = 0.5$

(b) $x = t^3, y = t^2$ when $t = 2$

(c) $x = 1 - \dfrac{1}{t}, y = 1 + \dfrac{1}{t}$ when $t = 2$

(d) $x = t^2, y = \dfrac{1}{t}$ when $t = 3$

3 Find the gradient of the normal on the following curves, at the specified values of t.

(a) $x = 5t^2, y = 10t$ when $t = 3$

(b) $x = \cos^2 t, y = \sin^2 t$ when $t = \frac{1}{3}\pi$

(c) $x = \cos^3 t, y = \sin^3 t$ when $t = \frac{1}{6}\pi$

(d) $x = t^2 + 2, y = t - 2$ when $t = 4$

4 Show that the equation of the tangent to the curve $x = 3\cos t, y = 2\sin t$ when $t = \frac{3}{4}\pi$ is $3y = 2x + 6\sqrt{2}$.

5 (a) Find the gradient of the curve $x = t^3, y = t^2 - t$ at the point $(1, 0)$.

(b) Hence find the equation of the tangent to the curve at this point.

6 A curve has parametric equations $x = t - \cos t, y = \sin t$. Find the equation of the tangent to the curve when $t = \pi$.

7 Find the equations of the tangents to these curves at the specified values.

(a) $x = t^2, y = 2t$ when $t = 3$

(b) $x = 5\cos t, y = 3\sin t$ when $t = \frac{11}{6}\pi$

8 Find the equations of the normals to these curves at the specified values.

   (a) $x = 5t^2$, $y = 10t$ when $t = 3$

   (b) $x = \cos t$, $y = \sin t$ when $t = \frac{2}{3}\pi$

9 (a) Find the equation of the normal to the hyperbola $x = 4t$, $y = \dfrac{4}{t}$ at the point $(8, 2)$.

   (b) Find the coordinates of the point where this normal crosses the curve again.

10 (a) Find the equation of the normal to the parabola $x = 3t^2$, $y = 6t$ at the point where $t = -2$.

   (b) Find the coordinates of the point where this normal crosses the curve again.

3.4 Proving properties of curves

Parameters are a very powerful tool for proving properties about curves. Here are two examples which show a general method.

Example 3.4.1
A parabola is given by $x = at^2$, $y = 2at$. The tangent at a point P on the parabola meets the x-axis at T. Prove that PT is bisected by the tangent at the vertex of the parabola.

> There is no good reason why this parabola is on its side, but it is conventional to think of the parabola parametrically as $x = at^2$, $y = 2at$ rather than $x = 2at$, $y = at^2$. In this case, the vertex is still the point where the axis of symmetry meets the parabola, which is the origin, and the tangent at the vertex is the y-axis.

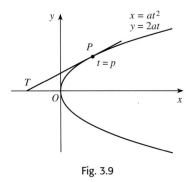

Fig. 3.9

Let P be the point on the parabola, shown in Fig. 3.9, with coordinates $(at^2, 2at)$. Since

$$\frac{dy}{dx} = \frac{dy}{dt} \Big/ \frac{dx}{dt} = \frac{2a}{2at} = \frac{1}{t},$$

the gradient at P is $\dfrac{1}{t}$. The equation of the tangent at P is therefore

$$y - 2at = \frac{1}{t}(x - at^2), \text{ which can be simplified to } ty = x + at^2.$$

This tangent meets the x-axis at the point where $y = 0$, so $x = -at^2$ and T is the point with coordinates $(-at^2, 0)$.

The mid-point of PT is $\left(\frac{1}{2}(at^2 + (-at^2)), \frac{1}{2}(2at + 0)\right)$ which is $(0, at)$. Since the tangent at the vertex has equation $x = 0$, the point $(0, at)$ lies on it. Therefore PT is bisected by the tangent at the vertex.

Example 3.4.2

A curve is given parametrically by $x = a\cos^3 t$, $y = a\sin^3 t$, where a is a positive constant, for $0 \leqslant t < 2\pi$. The tangent at any point P meets the x-axis at A and the y-axis at B. Prove that the length of AB is constant.

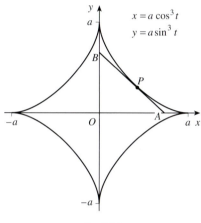

Fig. 3.10

Let P be the point on the curve, shown in Fig. 3.10, with parameter t. P has coordinates $(a\cos^3 t, a\sin^3 t)$.

To find the gradient at P, calculate

$$\frac{dy}{dx} = \frac{dy}{dt} \bigg/ \frac{dx}{dt}$$

$$= \frac{3a\sin^2 t \cos t}{-3a\sin t \cos^2 t} = -\frac{\sin t}{\cos t}.$$

The gradient at P is $-\dfrac{\sin t}{\cos t}$.

The equation of the tangent at P is $y - a\sin^3 t = -\dfrac{\sin t}{\cos t}(x - a\cos^3 t)$.

This can be simplified to

$$y\cos t + x\sin t = a\sin^3 t \cos t + a\sin t \cos^3 t$$

$$= a\sin t \cos t(\sin^2 t + \cos^2 t)$$

$$= a\sin t \cos t.$$

The points A and B have coordinates $(a \cos t, 0)$ and $(0, a \sin t)$. The length AB is

$$\sqrt{(0 - a \cos t)^2 + (a \sin t - 0)^2} = \sqrt{a^2 \cos^2 t + a^2 \sin^2 t} = a.$$

The length AB is therefore constant.

The curve $x = a \cos^3 t$, $y = a \sin^3 t$ is called an *astroid*. If you think of the tangent as a ladder of length a sliding down the 'wall and floor' made by the y-axis and the x-axis, then the ladder always touches the astroid.

Exercise 3D

1 A curve is given parametrically by the equations $x = t^2$, $y = t + 1$.

   (a) Find $\dfrac{dy}{dx}$ in terms of t and find the equation of the tangent at the point with parameter t.

   (b) Find the cartesian equation of the curve.

2 A curve is given parametrically by the equations $x = t^2 + t$, $y = t^2 - t$.

   (a) Find $\dfrac{dy}{dx}$ in terms of t and find the equation of the normal at the point with parameter t.

   (b) Find the cartesian equation of the curve.

3 (a) Find the equation of the tangent at $(-8, 4)$ to the curve which is given parametrically by $x = t^3$, $y = t^2$.

   (b) Show that this tangent meets the curve again at the point with parameter 1.

   (c) Find the cartesian equation of the curve.

4 Let P be the point on the curve $x = t^2$, $y = \dfrac{1}{t}$ with coordinates $\left(p^2, \dfrac{1}{p}\right)$.

   (a) Find the equation of the tangent at P.

   (b) This tangent meets the x- and y-axes at A and B respectively. Find the coordinates of A and B.

   (c) Prove that $PA = 2BP$.

5 A parabola is given parametrically by $x = at^2$, $y = 2at$. P is the point $(ap^2, 2ap)$.

   (a) The foot of the perpendicular from P onto the axis of symmetry is F. Find the coordinates of F.

   (b) Find the equation of the normal to the parabola at P.

   (c) G is the point where the normal from P crosses the axis of symmetry. Find the coordinates of G.

   (d) Prove that $FG = 2a$.

6 P, Q, R and S are four points on the hyperbola $x = ct$, $y = \dfrac{c}{t}$ with parameters p, q, r and s respectively.

   (a) Find the gradients of the chords PQ and RS.

   (b) Prove that if the chord PQ is perpendicular to the chord RS, then $pqrs = -1$.

7 Let H be the curve with parametric equations $x = t$, $y = \dfrac{1}{t}$, and let P be the point on H with parameter p.

(a) Find the equation of the tangent at P.

(b) The tangent at P meets the x-axis at T. Find the coordinates of T.

(c) Prove that $OP = PT$, where O is the origin.

8 P is a point on the parabola given parametrically by $x = at^2$, $y = 2at$, where a is a constant. Let S be the point $(a, 0)$, Q be the point $(-a, 2at)$ and T be the point where the tangent at P to the parabola crosses the axis of symmetry of the parabola.

(a) Find the equation of the tangent to the parabola at P and use it to find the coordinates of T.

(b) Show that $SP = PQ = QT = ST = at^2 + a$.

(c) Prove that angle QPT is equal to angle SPT.

(d) If PM is parallel to the axis of the parabola, with M to the right of P, and PN is the normal to the parabola at P, show that angle MPN is equal to angle NPS.

9 P is a point on the ellipse with parametric equations $x = 5\cos t$, $y = 3\sin t$ for $0 \leqslant t < 2\pi$, and F and G are the points $(-4,0)$ and $(4,0)$ respectively. Prove that

(a) $FP = 5 + 4\cos t$, (b) $FP + PG = 10$.

Let the normal at P make angles θ and ϕ with FP and GP respectively. Prove that

(c) $\tan\theta = \dfrac{4}{3}\sin t$, (d) $\theta = \phi$.

10* Let P and Q be the points with parameters t and $t + \pi$ on the curve, called a *cardioid*, with parametric equations $x = 2\cos t - \cos 2t$, $y = 2\sin t - \sin 2t$. Let A be the point $(1, 0)$. Prove that

(a) the gradient of AP is $\tan t$,

(b) PAQ is a straight line,

(c) the length of the line segment PQ is constant.

Miscellaneous exercise 3

1 The parametric equations of a curve are $x = \cos t$, $y = 2\sin t$ where the parameter t takes all values such that $0 \leqslant t \leqslant \pi$.

(a) Find the value of t at the point A where the line $y = 2x$ intersects the curve.

(b) Show that the tangent to the curve at A has gradient -2 and find the equation of this tangent in the form $ax + by = c$, where a and b are integers. (OCR)

2 The parametric equations of a curve are $x = 2\cos t$, $y = 5 + 3\cos 2t$, where $0 < t < \pi$. Express $\dfrac{dy}{dx}$ in terms of t, and hence show that the gradient at any point of the curve is less than 6. (OCR)

3 A curve is defined by the parametric equations $x = t - \dfrac{1}{t}$, $y = t + \dfrac{1}{t}$, $t \neq 0$.

    (a) Use parametric differentiation to determine $\dfrac{dy}{dx}$ as a function of the parameter t.

    (b) Show that the equation of the normal to the curve at the point where $t = 2$ may be written as $3y + 5x = 15$.

    (c) Determine the cartesian equation of the curve.   (OCR)

4 A curve is defined parametrically by $x = t^3 + t$, $y = t^2 + 1$.

    (a) Find $\dfrac{dy}{dx}$ in terms of t.

    (b) Find the equation of the normal to this curve at the point where $t = 1$.   (OCR)

5 A curve is defined by the parametric equations $x = \sin t$, $y = \sqrt{3} \cos t$.

    (a) Determine $\dfrac{dy}{dx}$ in terms of t for points on the curve where t is not an odd multiple of $\frac{1}{2}\pi$.

    (b) Find an equation for the tangent to the curve at the point where $t = \frac{1}{6}\pi$.

    (c) Show that all points on the curve satisfy the equation $x^2 + \frac{1}{3}y^2 = 1$.   (OCR)

6 The parametric equations of a curve are $x = t + e^{-t}$, $y = 1 - e^{-t}$, where t takes all real values. Express $\dfrac{dy}{dx}$ in terms of t, and hence find the value of t for which the gradient of the curve is 1, giving your answer in logarithmic form.   (OCR)

7 A curve is defined by the parametric equations $x = 3 \sin t$, $y = 2 \cos t$.

    (a) Show that the cartesian equation of the curve is $4x^2 + 9y^2 = 36$.

    (b) Determine an equation of the normal to the curve at the point with parameter $t = \alpha$ where $\sin \alpha = 0.6$ and $\cos \alpha = 0.8$.

    (c) Find the cartesian coordinates of the point where the normal in part (b) meets the curve again.   (OCR)

8 A curve is defined parametrically for $0 \leqslant t \leqslant \pi$ by $x = 2(1 + \cos t)$, $y = 4 \sin^2 t$.

    (a) Determine the equation of the tangent to the curve at the point where $t = \frac{1}{3}\pi$.

    (b) Obtain the cartesian equation of the curve in simplified form.   (OCR)

9 Sketch, with the help of a calculator, curves with the following parametric equations, for $0 \leqslant t < 2\pi$. Indicate on your sketches, with arrows, the direction on each curve in which t is increasing.

    (a) $x = \cos t$, $y = \cos 2t$ (b) $x = \sin t$, $y = \cos 2t$

    (c) $x = \sin t$, $y = \sin 3t$ (d) $x = \sin t$, $y = \cos 3t$

    (e) $x = \cos 2t$, $y = \sin 3t$ (f) $x = \cos 2t$, $y = \cos 3t$

    (g) $x = \sin 2t$, $y = \sin 3t$ (h) $x = \sin 2t$, $y = \cos 3t$

    (These are examples of *Lissajous figures*.)

10 A curve is defined parametrically by $x = t^2$, $y = t^2$ where t is real.

  (a) Describe the curve.

  (b) Eliminate the parameter to find the cartesian equation of the curve. Describe the curve resulting from the cartesian equation.

  (c) Reconcile what you find with the result in the blue box in Section 3.2.

4 Vectors

This chapter introduces the idea of vectors as a way of doing geometry in two or three dimensions. When you have completed it, you should

- understand the idea of a translation, and how it can be expressed either in column form or in terms of basic unit vectors
- know and be able to use the rules of vector algebra
- understand the idea of displacement and position vectors, and use these to prove geometrical results
- know the form of the vector equation of a line, and use this to solve problems involving intersecting, parallel and skew lines
- appreciate similarities and differences between the geometries of two and three dimensions.

4.1 Translations of a plane

In C1 Section 10.1 you saw how to translate a graph through distance k in the x- or y-direction: $y = f(x)$ becomes respectively $y = f(x - k)$ or $y = f(x) + k$. A practical way of doing this is to draw the graph on a transparent sheet placed over a coordinate grid, and then to move this sheet across or up the grid by k units.

The essential feature of a translation is that the sheet moves over the grid without turning. A more general translation would move the sheet k units across and l units up the grid. This is shown in Fig. 4.1, where several points move in the same direction through the same distance. Such a translation is called a **vector** and is written $\begin{pmatrix} k \\ l \end{pmatrix}$.

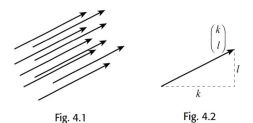

Fig. 4.1   Fig. 4.2

For example, the translations of $y = f(x)$ described above would be performed by the vectors $\begin{pmatrix} k \\ 0 \end{pmatrix}$ and $\begin{pmatrix} 0 \\ k \end{pmatrix}$ respectively.

In practice, drawing several arrows, as in Fig. 4.1, is not a convenient way of representing a vector. It is usual to draw just a single arrow, as in Fig. 4.2. But you must understand that the position of the arrow in the (x, y)-plane is of no significance. This arrow is just one of infinitely many that could be drawn to represent the vector.

Later you may meet other uses of vectors. For example, mechanics uses velocity vectors, momentum vectors, force vectors, and so on. When you need to make the distinction, the vectors described here are called **translation vectors**. These are the only vectors used in this book.

4.2 Vector algebra

It is often convenient to use a single letter to stand for a vector. In print, bold type is used to distinguish vectors from numbers. For example, in $\mathbf{p} = \begin{pmatrix} k \\ l \end{pmatrix}$, $\mathbf{p}$ is a vector but k and l are numbers, called the **components** of the vector $\mathbf{p}$ in the x- and y-directions.

> In handwriting vectors are indicated by a wavy line underneath the letter: $\underset{\sim}{p} = \begin{pmatrix} k \\ l \end{pmatrix}$. It is important to get into the habit of writing vectors in this way, so that it is quite clear in your work which letters stand for vectors and which for numbers.

If s is any number and $\mathbf{p}$ is any vector, then $s\mathbf{p}$ is another vector. If $s > 0$, the vector $s\mathbf{p}$ is a translation in the same direction as $\mathbf{p}$ but s times as large; if $s < 0$ it is in the opposite direction and $|s|$ times as large. A number such as s is often called a **scalar**, because it usually changes the scale of the vector.

The similar triangles in Fig. 4.3 show that $s\mathbf{p} = \begin{pmatrix} sk \\ sl \end{pmatrix}$. In particular, $(-1)\mathbf{p} = \begin{pmatrix} -k \\ -l \end{pmatrix}$, which is a translation of the same magnitude as $\mathbf{p}$ but in the opposite direction. It is denoted by $-\mathbf{p}$.

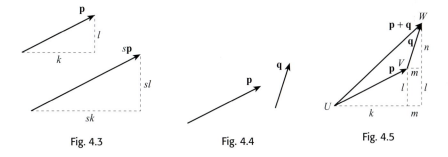

Fig. 4.3   Fig. 4.4   Fig. 4.5

Vectors are added by performing one translation after another. In Fig. 4.4, $\mathbf{p}$ and $\mathbf{q}$ are two vectors. To form their sum, you want to represent them as a pair of arrows by which you can trace the path of a particular point of the moving sheet. In Fig. 4.5, $\mathbf{p}$ is shown by an arrow from U to V, and $\mathbf{q}$ by an arrow from V to W. Then when the translations are combined, the point of the sheet which was originally at U would move first to V and then to W. So the sum $\mathbf{p} + \mathbf{q}$ is represented by an arrow from U to W.

Fig. 4.5 also shows that:

$$\text{If } \mathbf{p} = \begin{pmatrix} k \\ l \end{pmatrix} \text{ and } \mathbf{q} = \begin{pmatrix} m \\ n \end{pmatrix}, \text{ then } \mathbf{p} + \mathbf{q} = \begin{pmatrix} k + m \\ l + n \end{pmatrix}.$$

To form the sum $\mathbf{q}+\mathbf{p}$ the translations are performed in the reverse order. In Fig. 4.6, $\mathbf{q}$ is now represented by the arrow from U to Z; and since $UVWZ$ is a parallelogram, $\mathbf{p}$ is represented by the arrow from Z to W. This shows that

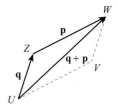

$$\mathbf{p}+\mathbf{q}=\mathbf{q}+\mathbf{p}.$$

This is called the **commutative rule for addition** of vectors.

Fig. 4.6

Example 4.2.1

If $\mathbf{p}=\begin{pmatrix}3\\-1\end{pmatrix}$ and $\mathbf{q}=\begin{pmatrix}2\\3\end{pmatrix}$, calculate   (a) $\mathbf{p}+\mathbf{p}$,   (b) $\mathbf{p}+\mathbf{q}$.

(a) $\mathbf{p}+\mathbf{p}=\begin{pmatrix}3\\-1\end{pmatrix}+\begin{pmatrix}3\\-1\end{pmatrix}=\begin{pmatrix}3+3\\(-1)+(-1)\end{pmatrix}=\begin{pmatrix}6\\-2\end{pmatrix}.$

(b) $\mathbf{p}+\mathbf{q}=\begin{pmatrix}3\\-1\end{pmatrix}+\begin{pmatrix}2\\3\end{pmatrix}=\begin{pmatrix}3+2\\(-1)+3\end{pmatrix}=\begin{pmatrix}5\\2\end{pmatrix}.$

Example 4.2.2

If $\mathbf{p}=\begin{pmatrix}2\\-3\end{pmatrix}$, $\mathbf{q}=\begin{pmatrix}1\\2\end{pmatrix}$ and $\mathbf{r}=\begin{pmatrix}5\\3\end{pmatrix}$, show that there is a number s such that $\mathbf{p}+s\mathbf{q}=\mathbf{r}$.

You can write $\mathbf{p}+s\mathbf{q}$ in column vector form as

$$\begin{pmatrix}2\\-3\end{pmatrix}+s\begin{pmatrix}1\\2\end{pmatrix}=\begin{pmatrix}2\\-3\end{pmatrix}+\begin{pmatrix}s\\2s\end{pmatrix}=\begin{pmatrix}2+s\\-3+2s\end{pmatrix}.$$

If this is equal to $\mathbf{r}$, then both the x- and y-components of the two vectors must be equal. This gives the two equations

$$2+s=5 \ \text{ and } \ -3+2s=3.$$

Both these equations are satisfied by $s=3$, so it follows that $\mathbf{p}+3\mathbf{q}=\mathbf{r}$. You can check this for yourself using squared paper or a screen display, showing arrows representing $\mathbf{p}$, $\mathbf{q}$, $\mathbf{p}+3\mathbf{q}$ and $\mathbf{r}$.

The idea of addition can be extended to three or more vectors. But when you write $\mathbf{p}+\mathbf{q}+\mathbf{r}$ it is not clear whether you first add $\mathbf{p}$ and $\mathbf{q}$ and then add $\mathbf{r}$ to the result, or whether you add $\mathbf{p}$ to the result of adding $\mathbf{q}$ and $\mathbf{r}$. Fig. 4.7 shows that it doesn't matter, since the outcome is the same either way. That is,

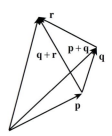

$$(\mathbf{p}+\mathbf{q})+\mathbf{r}=\mathbf{p}+(\mathbf{q}+\mathbf{r}).$$

This is called the **associative rule for addition** of vectors.

Fig. 4.7

To complete the algebra of vector addition, the symbol $\mathbf{0}$ is needed for the **zero vector**, the 'stay-still' translation, which has the properties that, for any vector $\mathbf{p}$,

$$0\mathbf{p}=\mathbf{0}, \ \mathbf{p}+\mathbf{0}=\mathbf{p}, \ \text{and} \ \mathbf{p}+(-\mathbf{p})=\mathbf{0}.$$

Vector addition and multiplication by a scalar can be combined according to the two **distributive rules** for vectors:

$$s(\mathbf{p} + \mathbf{q}) = s\mathbf{p} + s\mathbf{q} \qquad \text{(from the similar triangles in Fig. 4.8)}$$

and $\quad (s + t)\mathbf{p} = s\mathbf{p} + t\mathbf{p} \qquad$ (see Fig. 4.9)

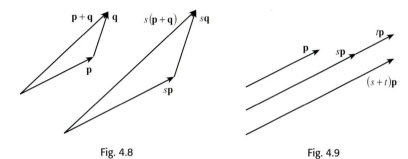

Fig. 4.8 　　　　　　　　　　Fig. 4.9

Subtraction of vectors is defined by

$$\mathbf{p} + \mathbf{x} = \mathbf{q} \iff \mathbf{x} = \mathbf{q} - \mathbf{p}.$$

This is illustrated in Fig. 4.10. Notice that to show $\mathbf{q} - \mathbf{p}$ you represent $\mathbf{p}$ and $\mathbf{q}$ by arrows which both start at the same point; this is different from addition, where the arrow representing $\mathbf{q}$ starts where the $\mathbf{p}$ arrow ends. Comparing Fig. 4.10 with Fig. 4.11 shows that

$$\mathbf{q} - \mathbf{p} = \mathbf{q} + (-\mathbf{p}).$$

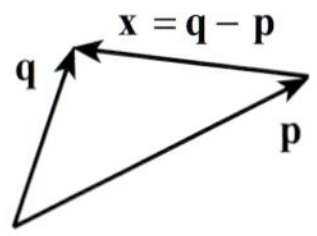

Fig. 4.10 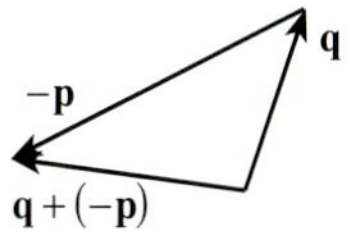 　　　　　　Fig. 4.11

In summary, the rules of vector addition, subtraction and multiplication by scalars look very similar to the rules of number addition, subtraction and multiplication. But the diagrams show that the rules for vectors are interpreted differently from the rules for numbers.

4.3　Basic unit vectors

If you apply the rules of vector algebra to a vector in column form, you can see that

$$\mathbf{p} = \begin{pmatrix} k \\ l \end{pmatrix} = \begin{pmatrix} k + 0 \\ 0 + l \end{pmatrix} = \begin{pmatrix} k \\ 0 \end{pmatrix} + \begin{pmatrix} 0 \\ l \end{pmatrix} = k\begin{pmatrix} 1 \\ 0 \end{pmatrix} + l\begin{pmatrix} 0 \\ 1 \end{pmatrix}.$$

The vectors $\begin{pmatrix} 1 \\ 0 \end{pmatrix}$ and $\begin{pmatrix} 0 \\ 1 \end{pmatrix}$ which appear in this last expression are called **basic unit vectors** in the x- and y-directions. They are denoted by the letters $\mathbf{i}$ and $\mathbf{j}$, so

$$\mathbf{p} = k\mathbf{i} + l\mathbf{j}.$$

This is illustrated by Fig. 4.12. The equation shows that any vector in the plane can be constructed as the sum of multiples of the two basic vectors **i** and **j**.

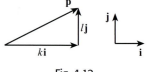

Fig. 4.12

The vectors $k\mathbf{i}$ and $l\mathbf{j}$ are called the **component vectors** of **p** in the x- and y-directions.

You now have two alternative notations for doing algebra with vectors. For example, if you want to find $3\mathbf{p} - 2\mathbf{q}$, where **p** is $\begin{pmatrix} 2 \\ 5 \end{pmatrix}$ and **q** is $\begin{pmatrix} 1 \\ -3 \end{pmatrix}$, you can write either

$$3\begin{pmatrix} 2 \\ 5 \end{pmatrix} - 2\begin{pmatrix} 1 \\ -3 \end{pmatrix} = \begin{pmatrix} 6 \\ 15 \end{pmatrix} - \begin{pmatrix} 2 \\ -6 \end{pmatrix} = \begin{pmatrix} 6-2 \\ 15-(-6) \end{pmatrix} = \begin{pmatrix} 4 \\ 21 \end{pmatrix}$$

or $3(2\mathbf{i} + 5\mathbf{j}) - 2(\mathbf{i} - 3\mathbf{j}) = (6\mathbf{i} + 15\mathbf{j}) - (2\mathbf{i} - 6\mathbf{j}) = 6\mathbf{i} + 15\mathbf{j} - 2\mathbf{i} + 6\mathbf{j} = 4\mathbf{i} + 21\mathbf{j}.$

You will find that sometimes one of these forms is more convenient than the other, but more often it makes no difference which you use.

Exercise 4A

When you are asked to illustrate a vector equation geometrically, you should show vectors as arrows on a grid of squares, either on paper or on screen.

1   Illustrate the following equations geometrically.

(a) $\begin{pmatrix} 4 \\ 1 \end{pmatrix} + \begin{pmatrix} -3 \\ 2 \end{pmatrix} = \begin{pmatrix} 1 \\ 3 \end{pmatrix}$

(b) $3\begin{pmatrix} 1 \\ -2 \end{pmatrix} = \begin{pmatrix} 3 \\ -6 \end{pmatrix}$

(c) $\begin{pmatrix} 0 \\ 4 \end{pmatrix} + 2\begin{pmatrix} 1 \\ -2 \end{pmatrix} = \begin{pmatrix} 2 \\ 0 \end{pmatrix}$

(d) $\begin{pmatrix} 3 \\ 1 \end{pmatrix} - \begin{pmatrix} 5 \\ 1 \end{pmatrix} = \begin{pmatrix} -2 \\ 0 \end{pmatrix}$

(e) $3\begin{pmatrix} -1 \\ 2 \end{pmatrix} - \begin{pmatrix} -4 \\ 3 \end{pmatrix} = \begin{pmatrix} 1 \\ 3 \end{pmatrix}$

(f) $4\begin{pmatrix} 2 \\ 3 \end{pmatrix} - 3\begin{pmatrix} 3 \\ 2 \end{pmatrix} = \begin{pmatrix} -1 \\ 6 \end{pmatrix}$

(g) $\begin{pmatrix} 2 \\ -3 \end{pmatrix} + \begin{pmatrix} 4 \\ 5 \end{pmatrix} + \begin{pmatrix} -6 \\ -2 \end{pmatrix} = \begin{pmatrix} 0 \\ 0 \end{pmatrix}$

(h) $2\begin{pmatrix} 3 \\ -1 \end{pmatrix} + 3\begin{pmatrix} -2 \\ 3 \end{pmatrix} + \begin{pmatrix} 0 \\ -7 \end{pmatrix} = \begin{pmatrix} 0 \\ 0 \end{pmatrix}$

2   Rewrite each of the equations in Question 1 using unit vector notation.

3   Express each of the following vectors as column vectors, and illustrate your answers geometrically.

(a) $\mathbf{i} + 2\mathbf{j}$ (b) $3\mathbf{i}$ (c) $\mathbf{j} - \mathbf{i}$ (d) $4\mathbf{i} - 3\mathbf{j}$

4   Show that there is a number s such that $s\begin{pmatrix} 1 \\ 2 \end{pmatrix} + \begin{pmatrix} -3 \\ 1 \end{pmatrix} = \begin{pmatrix} -1 \\ 5 \end{pmatrix}$. Illustrate your answer geometrically.

5   If $\mathbf{p} = 5\mathbf{i} - 3\mathbf{j}$, $\mathbf{q} = 2\mathbf{j} - \mathbf{i}$ and $\mathbf{r} = \mathbf{i} + 5\mathbf{j}$, show that there is a number s such that $\mathbf{p} + s\mathbf{q} = \mathbf{r}$. Illustrate your answer geometrically.

Rearrange this equation so as to express **q** in terms of **p** and **r**. Illustrate the rearranged equation geometrically.

6   Find numbers s and t such that $s\begin{pmatrix} 5 \\ 4 \end{pmatrix} + t\begin{pmatrix} -3 \\ -2 \end{pmatrix} = \begin{pmatrix} 1 \\ 2 \end{pmatrix}$. Illustrate your answer geometrically.

7 If $\mathbf{p} = 4\mathbf{i} + \mathbf{j}$, $\mathbf{q} = 6\mathbf{i} - 5\mathbf{j}$ and $\mathbf{r} = 3\mathbf{i} + 4\mathbf{j}$, find numbers s and t such that $s\mathbf{p} + t\mathbf{q} = \mathbf{r}$. Illustrate your answer geometrically.

8 Show that it isn't possible to find numbers s and t such that $\begin{pmatrix} 4 \\ -2 \end{pmatrix} + s\begin{pmatrix} 3 \\ 1 \end{pmatrix} = \begin{pmatrix} -6 \\ 3 \end{pmatrix}$ and $\begin{pmatrix} 3 \\ 4 \end{pmatrix} + t\begin{pmatrix} -1 \\ 2 \end{pmatrix} = \begin{pmatrix} 1 \\ 1 \end{pmatrix}$. Give geometrical reasons.

9 If $\mathbf{p} = 2\mathbf{i} + 3\mathbf{j}$, $\mathbf{q} = 4\mathbf{i} - 5\mathbf{j}$ and $\mathbf{r} = \mathbf{i} - 4\mathbf{j}$, find a set of numbers f, g and h such that $f\mathbf{p} + g\mathbf{q} + h\mathbf{r} = \mathbf{0}$. Illustrate your answer geometrically. Give a reason why there is more than one possible answer to this question.

10 If $\mathbf{p} = 3\mathbf{i} - \mathbf{j}$, $\mathbf{q} = 4\mathbf{i} + 5\mathbf{j}$ and $\mathbf{r} = 2\mathbf{j} - 6\mathbf{i}$,

    (a) can you find numbers s and t such that $\mathbf{q} = s\mathbf{p} + t\mathbf{r}$,

    (b) can you find numbers u and v such that $\mathbf{r} = u\mathbf{p} + v\mathbf{q}$?

    Give a geometrical reason for your answers.

4.4   Position vectors

If E and F are two points on a grid, there is a unique translation which takes you from E to F. This translation can be represented by the arrow which starts at E and ends at F, and it is denoted by the symbol $\overrightarrow{EF}$.

(Some books use **EF** in bold type rather than $\overrightarrow{EF}$ to emphasise that it is a vector.)

However, although this translation is unique, its name is not. If G and H are two other points on the grid such that the lines EF and GH are parallel and equal in length (so that $EFHG$ is a parallelogram, see Fig. 4.13), then the translation $\overrightarrow{EF}$ also takes you from G to H, so that it could also be denoted by $\overrightarrow{GH}$. In a vector equation $\overrightarrow{EF}$ could be replaced by $\overrightarrow{GH}$ without affecting the truth of the statement.

Vectors written like this are sometimes called **displacement vectors**. But they are not a different kind of vector, just translation vectors written in a different way.

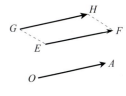

There is, however, one displacement vector which is especially important. This is the translation that starts at the origin O and ends at a point A where (in Fig. 4.13) $\overrightarrow{OA} = \overrightarrow{EF} = \overrightarrow{GH}$. The translation which takes you from O to A is called the **position vector** of A.

Fig. 4.13

There is a close link between the coordinates of A and the component form of its position vector. If A has coordinates (u, v), then to get from O to A you must move u units in the x-direction and v units in the y-direction, so that the vector $\overrightarrow{OA}$ has components u and v.

> The position vector of the point A with coordinates (u, v) is
> $$\overrightarrow{OA} = \begin{pmatrix} u \\ v \end{pmatrix} = u\mathbf{i} + v\mathbf{j}.$$

A useful convention is to use the same letter for a point and its position vector. For example, the position vector of the point A can be denoted by $\mathbf{a}$. This 'alphabet convention' will be used wherever possible in this book. It has the advantages that it economises on letters of the alphabet and avoids the need for repetitive definitions.

4.5   Algebra with position vectors

Multiplication by a scalar has a simple interpretation in terms of position vectors. If the vector $s\mathbf{a}$ is the position vector of a point D, then:

- If $s > 0$, D lies on the directed line OA (produced if necessary) such that $OD = sOA$.

- If $s < 0$, D lies on the directed line AO produced such that $OD = |s|OA$.

This is shown in Fig. 4.14 for $s = \frac{3}{2}$ and $s = -\frac{1}{2}$.

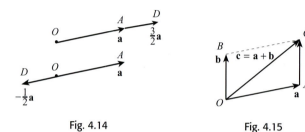

Fig. 4.14   Fig. 4.15

To identify the point with position vector $\mathbf{a} + \mathbf{b}$ is not quite so easy, because the arrows from O to A and from O to B are not related in the way needed for addition (see Fig. 4.5). It is therefore necessary to complete the parallelogram $OACB$, as in Fig. 4.15.

Then

$$\mathbf{a} + \mathbf{b} = \overrightarrow{OA} + \overrightarrow{OB} = \overrightarrow{OA} + \overrightarrow{AC} = \overrightarrow{OC}.$$

This is called the **parallelogram rule of addition** for position vectors.

Subtraction can be shown in either of two ways. If you compare Fig. 4.16 with Fig. 4.10, you will see that $\mathbf{b} - \mathbf{a}$ is the displacement vector $\overrightarrow{AB}$. To interpret this as a position vector, draw a line OE equal and parallel to AB, so that $\overrightarrow{OE} = \overrightarrow{AB}$. Then E is the point with position vector $\mathbf{b} - \mathbf{a}$.

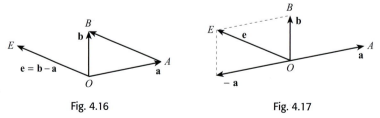

Fig. 4.16   Fig. 4.17

Alternatively, you can write $\mathbf{b} - \mathbf{a}$ as $\mathbf{b} + (-\mathbf{a})$, and then apply the parallelogram rule of addition to the points with position vectors $\mathbf{b}$ and $-\mathbf{a}$. By comparing Figs. 4.16 and 4.17 you can see that this leads to the same point E.

You will use the following relation often: it is worth remembering.

> The displacement vector $\overrightarrow{AB}$ is given by
> $$\overrightarrow{AB} = \overrightarrow{OB} - \overrightarrow{OA} = \mathbf{b} - \mathbf{a}.$$

Example 4.5.1

Points A and B have position vectors $\mathbf{a}$ and $\mathbf{b}$. Find the position vectors of

(a) the mid-point M of AB,   (b) the point of trisection T such that $AT = \frac{2}{3}AB$.

(a) **Method 1**   The displacement vector $\overrightarrow{AB} = \mathbf{b} - \mathbf{a}$, so $\overrightarrow{AM} = \frac{1}{2}(\mathbf{b} - \mathbf{a})$.

Therefore $\mathbf{m} = \overrightarrow{OM} = \overrightarrow{OA} + \overrightarrow{AM} = \mathbf{a} + \frac{1}{2}(\mathbf{b} - \mathbf{a}) = \frac{1}{2}\mathbf{a} + \frac{1}{2}\mathbf{b}$.

Method 2   If the parallelogram $OACB$ is completed (see Fig. 4.15) then $\mathbf{c} = \mathbf{a} + \mathbf{b}$. Since the diagonals of $OACB$ bisect each other, the mid-point M of AB is also the midpoint of OC. Therefore

$$\mathbf{m} = \tfrac{1}{2}\mathbf{c} = \tfrac{1}{2}(\mathbf{a} + \mathbf{b}) = \tfrac{1}{2}\mathbf{a} + \tfrac{1}{2}\mathbf{b}.$$

(b) The first method of (a) can be modified. $\overrightarrow{AT} = \frac{2}{3}\overrightarrow{AB} = \frac{2}{3}(\mathbf{b} - \mathbf{a})$, so

$$\mathbf{t} = \mathbf{a} + \tfrac{2}{3}(\mathbf{b} - \mathbf{a}) = \tfrac{1}{3}\mathbf{a} + \tfrac{2}{3}\mathbf{b}.$$

> The displacement vector of the mid-point M of AB is given by
> $$\mathbf{m} = \tfrac{1}{2}(\mathbf{a} + \mathbf{b}).$$

The results of Example 4.5.1 can be used to prove an important theorem about triangles.

Example 4.5.2

In triangle ABC the mid-points of BC, CA and AB are D, E and F. Prove that the lines AD, BE and CF (called the **medians**) meet at a point G, which is a point of trisection of each of the medians (see Fig. 4.18).

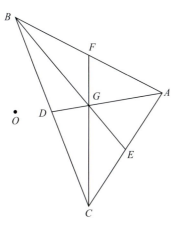

Fig. 4.18

From Example 4.5.1, $\mathbf{d} = \frac{1}{2}\mathbf{b} + \frac{1}{2}\mathbf{c}$, and the point of trisection on the median AD closer to D has position vector

$$\tfrac{1}{3}\mathbf{a} + \tfrac{2}{3}\mathbf{d} = \tfrac{1}{3}\mathbf{a} + \tfrac{2}{3}\left(\tfrac{1}{2}\mathbf{b} + \tfrac{1}{2}\mathbf{c}\right)$$
$$= \tfrac{1}{3}\mathbf{a} + \tfrac{1}{3}\mathbf{b} + \tfrac{1}{3}\mathbf{c}.$$

This last expression is symmetrical in $\mathbf{a}$, $\mathbf{b}$ and $\mathbf{c}$. It therefore also represents the point of trisection on the median BE closer to E, and the point of trisection on CF closer to F.

Therefore the three medians meet each other at a point G, with position vector $\mathbf{g} = \frac{1}{3}(\mathbf{a} + \mathbf{b} + \mathbf{c})$. This point is called the **centroid** of the triangle.

Exercise 4B

In this exercise the alphabet convention is used, that $\mathbf{a}$ stands for the position vector of the point A, and so on.

1 The points A and B have coordinates $(3, 1)$ and $(1, 2)$. Plot on squared paper the points C, $D, \ldots, H$ defined by the following vector equations, and state their coordinates.

   (a) $\mathbf{c} = 3\mathbf{a}$ (b) $\mathbf{d} = -\mathbf{b}$ (c) $\mathbf{e} = \mathbf{a} - \mathbf{b}$

   (d) $\mathbf{f} = \mathbf{b} - 3\mathbf{a}$ (e) $\mathbf{g} = \mathbf{b} + 3\mathbf{a}$ (f) $\mathbf{h} = \frac{1}{2}(\mathbf{b} + 3\mathbf{a})$

2 Points A and B have coordinates $(2, 7)$ and $(-3, -3)$ respectively. Use a vector method to find the coordinates of C and D, where

   (a) C is the point such that $\overrightarrow{AC} = 3\,\overrightarrow{AB}$,

   (b) D is the point such that $\overrightarrow{AD} = \frac{3}{5}\,\overrightarrow{AB}$.

3 C is the point on AB produced such that $\overrightarrow{AB} = \overrightarrow{BC}$. Express $\mathbf{c}$ in terms of $\mathbf{a}$ and $\mathbf{b}$. Check your answer by using the result of Example 4.5.1(a) to find the position vector of the mid-point of AC.

4 C is the point on AB such that $AC : CB = 4 : 3$. Express $\mathbf{c}$ in terms of $\mathbf{a}$ and $\mathbf{b}$.

5 If C is the point on AB such that $\overrightarrow{AC} = t\,\overrightarrow{AB}$, prove that $\mathbf{c} = t\mathbf{b} + (1 - t)\mathbf{a}$.

6 Write a vector equation connecting $\mathbf{a}$, $\mathbf{b}$, $\mathbf{c}$ and $\mathbf{d}$ to express the fact that $\overrightarrow{AB} = \overrightarrow{DC}$. Deduce from your equation that

   (a) $\overrightarrow{DA} = \overrightarrow{CB}$,

   (b) if E is the point such that $OAEC$ is a parallelogram, then $OBED$ is a parallelogram.

7 ABC is a triangle. D is the mid-point of BC, E is the mid-point of AC, F is the mid-point of AB and G is the mid-point of EF. Express the displacement vectors $\overrightarrow{AD}$ and $\overrightarrow{AG}$ in terms of $\mathbf{a}$, $\mathbf{b}$ and $\mathbf{c}$. What can you deduce about the points A, D and G?

8 $OABC$ is a parallelogram, M is the mid-point of BC, and P is the point of trisection of AC closer to C. Express $\mathbf{b}$, $\mathbf{m}$ and $\mathbf{p}$ in terms of $\mathbf{a}$ and $\mathbf{c}$. Deduce that $\mathbf{p} = \frac{2}{3}\mathbf{m}$, and interpret this equation geometrically.

9* *ABC* is a triangle. *D* is the mid-point of *BC*, *E* is the mid-point of *AD* and *F* is the point of trisection of *AC* closer to *A*. *G* is the point on *FB* such that $\overrightarrow{FG} = \frac{1}{4}\overrightarrow{FB}$. Express **d**, **e**, **f** and **g** in terms of **a**, **b** and **c**, and deduce that *G* is the same point as *E*. Draw a figure to illustrate this result.

10* *OAB* is a triangle, *Q* is the point of trisection of *AB* closer to *B* and *P* is the point on *OQ* such that $\overrightarrow{OP} = \frac{2}{5}\overrightarrow{OQ}$. *AP* produced meets *OB* at *R*. Express $\overrightarrow{AP}$ in terms of **a** and **b**, and hence find the number *k* such that $\overrightarrow{OA} + k\overrightarrow{AP}$ does not depend on **a**. Use your answer to express **r** in terms of **b**, and interpret this geometrically.

Use a similar method to identify the point *S* where *BP* produced meets *OA*.

4.6 The vector equation of a line

Fig. 4.19 shows a line through a point *A* in the direction of a non-zero vector **p**.

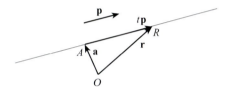

Fig. 4.19

If *R* is any point on the line, the displacement vector $\overrightarrow{AR}$ is a multiple of **p**, so that

$$\mathbf{r} = \overrightarrow{OR} = \overrightarrow{OA} + \overrightarrow{AR} = \mathbf{a} + t\mathbf{p},$$

where *t* is a scalar. The value of *t* measures the ratio of the displacement $\overrightarrow{AR}$ to **p**, and so takes a different value for each point *R* on the line.

> Points on a line through *A* in the direction of **p** have position vectors $\mathbf{r} = \mathbf{a} + t\mathbf{p}$, where *t* is a variable scalar. This is called the **vector equation** of the line.

The following examples show how vector equations can be used as an alternative to the cartesian equations with which you are familiar.

To illustrate alternative techniques the first will be solved by using vectors in column form, and the second by using the basic unit vectors.

Example 4.6.1

Find a vector equation for the line through $(2, -1)$ with gradient $\frac{3}{4}$, and deduce its cartesian equation.

This question will be solved using vectors in column form.

The position vector of the point $(2, -1)$ is $\begin{pmatrix} 2 \\ -1 \end{pmatrix}$. There are many vectors with gradient $\frac{3}{4}$, but the simplest is the vector which goes 4 units across the grid and 3 units up, that is, $\begin{pmatrix} 4 \\ 3 \end{pmatrix}$. So the equation of the line is

$$\mathbf{r} = \begin{pmatrix} 2 \\ -1 \end{pmatrix} + t\begin{pmatrix} 4 \\ 3 \end{pmatrix}.$$

If R has coordinates (x, y), the position vector $\mathbf{r}$ is $\begin{pmatrix} x \\ y \end{pmatrix}$, so this can be written

$$\begin{pmatrix} x \\ y \end{pmatrix} = \begin{pmatrix} 2 + 4t \\ -1 + 3t \end{pmatrix}.$$

This is equivalent to the two equations

$$x = 2 + 4t, \ y = -1 + 3t,$$

which you will recognise as parametric equations for the line.

The cartesian equation is found by eliminating t. Multiplying the first equation by 3 and the second by 4 and subtracting gives

$$3x - 4y = 3(2 + 4t) - 4(-1 + 3t) = 10.$$

You can check that $3x - 4y = 10$ has gradient $\frac{3}{4}$ and contains the point $(2, -1)$.

Example 4.6.2
Find a vector equation for the line through $(3, 1)$ parallel to the y-axis, and deduce its cartesian equation.

This question will be solved using the basic unit vectors.

A vector parallel to the y-axis is $\mathbf{j}$, and the position vector of $(3, 1)$ is $3\mathbf{i} + \mathbf{j}$, so the vector equation of the line is

$$\mathbf{r} = (3\mathbf{i} + \mathbf{j}) + t\mathbf{j}.$$

Writing $\mathbf{r}$ as $x\mathbf{i} + y\mathbf{j}$, this is

$$x\mathbf{i} + y\mathbf{j} = (3\mathbf{i} + \mathbf{j}) + t\mathbf{j}.$$

This is equivalent to the two equations $x = 3$, $y = 1 + t$.

No elimination is necessary this time: the first equation does not involve t, so the cartesian equation is just $x = 3$.

Example 4.6.3
Find the points common to the pairs of lines

(a) $\mathbf{r} = \begin{pmatrix} 1 \\ 2 \end{pmatrix} + s\begin{pmatrix} 1 \\ 1 \end{pmatrix}$ and $\mathbf{r} = \begin{pmatrix} 3 \\ -2 \end{pmatrix} + t\begin{pmatrix} 1 \\ 4 \end{pmatrix}$,   (b) $\mathbf{r} = \begin{pmatrix} 3 \\ 1 \end{pmatrix} + s\begin{pmatrix} 4 \\ -2 \end{pmatrix}$ and $\mathbf{r} = \begin{pmatrix} 1 \\ 2 \end{pmatrix} + t\begin{pmatrix} -6 \\ 3 \end{pmatrix}$.

Notice that different letters are used for the variable scalars on the two lines.

(a) Position vectors of points on the two lines can be written as

$$\mathbf{r} = \begin{pmatrix} 1+s \\ 2+s \end{pmatrix} \quad \text{and} \quad \mathbf{r} = \begin{pmatrix} 3+t \\ -2+4t \end{pmatrix}.$$

If these are the same point,

$$1+s = 3+t \quad \text{and} \quad 2+s = -2+4t,$$
$$\text{that is} \quad s - t = 2 \quad \text{and} \quad s - 4t = -4.$$

This is a pair of simultaneous equations for s and t, with solution $s = 4$, $t = 2$.

Substituting these values into the equation of one of the lines gives $\mathbf{r} = \begin{pmatrix} 5 \\ 6 \end{pmatrix}$. So the point common to the two lines has coordinates $(5, 6)$.

(b) You can check for yourself that the procedure used in (a) leads to the equations

$$3 + 4s = 1 - 6t \quad \text{and} \quad 1 - 2s = 2 + 3t,$$
$$\text{that is} \quad 2s + 3t = -1 \quad \text{and} \quad 2s + 3t = -1.$$

The two equations are the same! So there is really only one equation to solve, and this has infinitely many solutions in s and t. If you take any value for s, say $s = 7$, and calculate the corresponding value $t = -5$, then you have a solution of both vector equations. You can easily check that $s = 7$, $t = -5$ gives the position vector $\begin{pmatrix} 31 \\ -13 \end{pmatrix}$ in both lines. (Try some other pairs of values for yourself.)

The reason for this is that the direction vectors of the two lines are $\begin{pmatrix} 4 \\ -2 \end{pmatrix} = 2\begin{pmatrix} 2 \\ -1 \end{pmatrix}$ and $\begin{pmatrix} -6 \\ 3 \end{pmatrix} = -3\begin{pmatrix} 2 \\ -1 \end{pmatrix}$. This means that the lines have the same direction, so they are either parallel or the same line. Also the position vectors of the given points on the two lines are $\begin{pmatrix} 3 \\ 1 \end{pmatrix}$ and $\begin{pmatrix} 1 \\ 2 \end{pmatrix}$, and $\begin{pmatrix} 3 \\ 1 \end{pmatrix} - \begin{pmatrix} 1 \\ 2 \end{pmatrix} = \begin{pmatrix} 2 \\ -1 \end{pmatrix}$; so the line joining these points is also in the same direction. The lines are therefore identical. This is illustrated in Fig. 4.20.

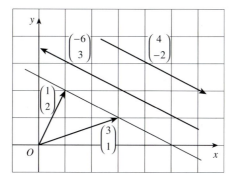

Fig. 4.20

The general result demonstrated in Example 4.6.3(b) is:

> The lines with vector equations $\mathbf{r} = \mathbf{a} + s\mathbf{p}$ and $\mathbf{r} = \mathbf{b} + s\mathbf{q}$ have the same direction if $\mathbf{p}$ is a multiple of $\mathbf{q}$. If in addition $\mathbf{b} - \mathbf{a}$ is a multiple of $\mathbf{q}$, the lines are the same; otherwise the lines are parallel.

This also shows that lines do not have unique vector equations. Two equations may represent the same line even though the vectors $\mathbf{a}$ and $\mathbf{b}$, and the vectors $\mathbf{p}$ and $\mathbf{q}$, are different.

Example 4.6.4

Show that the lines with vector equations $\mathbf{r} = 2\mathbf{i} - 3\mathbf{j} + s(-\mathbf{i} + 3\mathbf{j})$ and $\mathbf{r} = 4\mathbf{i} + t(2\mathbf{i} - 6\mathbf{j})$ are parallel, and find a vector equation for the parallel line through $(1, 1)$.

The direction vectors of the two lines are $-\mathbf{i} + 3\mathbf{j}$ and $2\mathbf{i} - 6\mathbf{j}$.

As $2\mathbf{i} - 6\mathbf{j} = -2(-\mathbf{i} + 3\mathbf{j})$, $2\mathbf{i} - 6\mathbf{j}$ is a scalar multiple of $-\mathbf{i} + 3\mathbf{j}$, so the lines are in the same or, in this case, opposite directions. The lines are therefore parallel.

The position vector of $(1, 1)$ is $\mathbf{i} + \mathbf{j}$, so an equation for the parallel line through $(1, 1)$ is $\mathbf{r} = \mathbf{i} + \mathbf{j} + s(-\mathbf{i} + 3\mathbf{j})$. Or, alternatively, you could use $\mathbf{r} = \mathbf{i} + \mathbf{j} + t(2\mathbf{i} - 6\mathbf{j})$.

Example 4.6.5

Find a vector equation for the line with cartesian equation $2x + 5y = 1$.

The gradient of the line is $-\frac{2}{5}$, so the direction vector could be taken as $\begin{pmatrix} 5 \\ -2 \end{pmatrix}$.

A point on the line is $(-2, 1)$, with position vector $\begin{pmatrix} -2 \\ 1 \end{pmatrix}$. So a possible vector equation is $\mathbf{r} = \begin{pmatrix} -2 \\ 1 \end{pmatrix} + t\begin{pmatrix} 5 \\ -2 \end{pmatrix}$.

Note that in this example the direction vector could have been taken as $\begin{pmatrix} 10 \\ -4 \end{pmatrix}$ and the point on the line as $(3, -1)$, giving $\mathbf{r} = \begin{pmatrix} 3 \\ -1 \end{pmatrix} + t\begin{pmatrix} 10 \\ -4 \end{pmatrix}$. It is not obvious from these two equations that they represent the same line.

Exercise 4C

1   Write down vector equations for the line through the given point in the specified direction. Then eliminate t to obtain the cartesian equation.

(a) $(2, -3)$, $\begin{pmatrix} 1 \\ 2 \end{pmatrix}$

(b) $(4, 1)$, $\begin{pmatrix} -3 \\ 2 \end{pmatrix}$

(c) $(5, 7)$, parallel to the x-axis

(d) $(0, 0)$, $\begin{pmatrix} 2 \\ -1 \end{pmatrix}$

(e) (a, b), $\begin{pmatrix} 0 \\ 1 \end{pmatrix}$

(f) $(\cos \alpha, \sin \alpha)$, $\begin{pmatrix} -\sin \alpha \\ \cos \alpha \end{pmatrix}$

2 Find vector equations for lines with the following cartesian equations.

   (a) $x = 2$ (b) $x + 3y = 7$ (c) $2x - 5y = 3$

3 Find the coordinates of the points common to the following pairs of lines, if any.

   (a) $\mathbf{r} = \begin{pmatrix} 2 \\ 0 \end{pmatrix} + s\begin{pmatrix} 5 \\ 3 \end{pmatrix}$, $\mathbf{r} = \begin{pmatrix} 3 \\ -1 \end{pmatrix} + t\begin{pmatrix} 1 \\ 1 \end{pmatrix}$ (b) $\mathbf{r} = \begin{pmatrix} 5 \\ 1 \end{pmatrix} + s\begin{pmatrix} -1 \\ 2 \end{pmatrix}$, $\mathbf{r} = \begin{pmatrix} 3 \\ -5 \end{pmatrix} + t\begin{pmatrix} 1 \\ 0 \end{pmatrix}$

   (c) $\mathbf{r} = \begin{pmatrix} 2 \\ -1 \end{pmatrix} + s\begin{pmatrix} 1 \\ -3 \end{pmatrix}$, $\mathbf{r} = \begin{pmatrix} 4 \\ 0 \end{pmatrix} + t\begin{pmatrix} -2 \\ 6 \end{pmatrix}$ (d) $\mathbf{r} = \begin{pmatrix} -1 \\ -4 \end{pmatrix} + s\begin{pmatrix} 3 \\ 4 \end{pmatrix}$, $\mathbf{r} = \begin{pmatrix} 11 \\ -1 \end{pmatrix} + t\begin{pmatrix} -4 \\ 3 \end{pmatrix}$

   (e) $\mathbf{r} = \begin{pmatrix} 7 \\ 1 \end{pmatrix} + s\begin{pmatrix} 6 \\ -4 \end{pmatrix}$, $\mathbf{r} = \begin{pmatrix} 10 \\ -1 \end{pmatrix} + t\begin{pmatrix} -9 \\ 6 \end{pmatrix}$ (f) $\mathbf{r} = \begin{pmatrix} 2 \\ 1 \end{pmatrix} + s\begin{pmatrix} 3 \\ 0 \end{pmatrix}$, $\mathbf{r} = \begin{pmatrix} -1 \\ 3 \end{pmatrix} + t\begin{pmatrix} 0 \\ -2 \end{pmatrix}$

4 Write down in parametric form the coordinates of any point on the line through $(2, -1)$ in the direction $\begin{pmatrix} 1 \\ 3 \end{pmatrix}$. Use these to find the point where this line intersects the line $5y - 6x = 1$.

5 Find the coordinates of the point where the line with vector equation $\mathbf{r} = \begin{pmatrix} -3 \\ 4 \end{pmatrix} + t\begin{pmatrix} 2 \\ -1 \end{pmatrix}$ intersects the line with cartesian equation $2x + y = 7$.

6 Which of the following points lie on the line joining $(2, 0)$ to $(4, 3)$?

   (a) $(8, 9)$ (b) $(12, 13)$ (c) $(-4, -1)$ (d) $(-6, -12)$ (e) $\left(3\tfrac{1}{3}, 2\right)$

7 Find vector equations for the lines joining the following pairs of points.

   (a) $(3, 7), (5, 4)$ (b) $(2, 3), (2, 8)$ (c) $(-1, 2), (5, -1)$

   (d) $(-3, -4), (5, 8)$ (e) $(-2, 7), (4, 7)$ (f) $(1, 3), (-4, -2)$

8 A quadrilateral $ABCD$ has vertices $A(4, -1)$, $B(-3, 2)$, $C(-8, -5)$ and $D(4, -5)$.

   (a) Find vector equations for the diagonals AC, BD and find their point of intersection.

   (b) Find the points of intersection of BA produced and CD produced, and of CB produced and DA produced.

9 Show that the vectors $\begin{pmatrix} a \\ b \end{pmatrix}$ and $\begin{pmatrix} -b \\ a \end{pmatrix}$ are perpendicular to each other. Is this still true

   (a) if a is zero but b is not,

   (b) if b is zero but a is not,

   (c) if both a and b are zero?

   Find a vector equation for the line through $(1, 2)$ perpendicular to the line with vector equation $\mathbf{r} = \begin{pmatrix} 7 \\ 2 \end{pmatrix} + t\begin{pmatrix} 3 \\ 4 \end{pmatrix}$.

10 Find a vector in the direction of the line l with cartesian equation $3x - y = 8$. Write down a vector equation for the line through $P(1, 5)$ which is perpendicular to l. Hence find the coordinates of the foot of the perpendicular from P to l.

11 Use the method of Question 10 to find the coordinates of the foot of the perpendicular from $(-3, -2)$ to $5x + 2y = 10$.

12 Find a vector equation for the line joining the points $(-1, 1)$ and $(4, 11)$. Use this to write parametric equations for any point on the line. Hence find the coordinates of the points where the line meets the parabola $y = x^2$.

13 Find the coordinates of the points where the line through $(-5, -1)$ in the direction $\begin{pmatrix} 2 \\ 3 \end{pmatrix}$ meets the circle $x^2 + y^2 = 65$.

4.7 Vectors in three dimensions

The power of vector methods is best appreciated when they are used to do geometry in three dimensions. This requires setting up axes in three directions, as in Fig. 4.21. The usual convention is to take x- and y-axes in a horizontal plane (shown shaded), and to add a z-axis pointing vertically upwards.

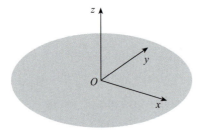

Fig. 4.21

These axes are said to be 'right-handed': if the outstretched index finger of your right hand points in the x-direction, and you bend your middle finger to point in the y-direction, then your thumb can naturally point up in the z-direction.

A vector $\mathbf{p}$ in three dimensions is a translation of the whole of space relative to a fixed coordinate framework. (You could imagine Fig. 4.1 as a blizzard, with the arrows showing the translations of the individual snowflakes.)

It is written as $\begin{pmatrix} l \\ m \\ n \end{pmatrix}$, which is a translation of l, m and n units in the x-, y- and z-directions. It can also be written in the form $l\mathbf{i} + m\mathbf{j} + n\mathbf{k}$, where $\mathbf{i} = \begin{pmatrix} 1 \\ 0 \\ 0 \end{pmatrix}$, $\mathbf{j} = \begin{pmatrix} 0 \\ 1 \\ 0 \end{pmatrix}$, $\mathbf{k} = \begin{pmatrix} 0 \\ 0 \\ 1 \end{pmatrix}$ are basic unit vectors in the x-, y- and z-directions.

Almost everything that you know about coordinates in two dimensions carries over into three dimensions in an obvious way, but you need to notice a few differences:

• The axes can be taken in pairs to define coordinate planes. For example, the x- and y-axes define the horizontal plane, called the xy-plane. All points in this plane have z-coordinate zero, so the equation of the plane is $z = 0$. Similarly the xz-plane and the yz-plane have equations $y = 0$ and $x = 0$; these are both vertical planes.

- The idea of the gradient of a line does not carry over into three dimensions. However, you can still use a vector to describe the direction of a line. This is one of the main reasons why vectors are especially useful in three dimensions.

- In three dimensions lines which are not parallel may or may not meet. (Think of a railway crossing a road. They may either intersect, at a level crossing, or not intersect, where there is a viaduct or railway bridge.) Non-parallel lines which do not meet are said to be **skew**.

Example 4.7.1
Points A and B have coordinates $(-5, 3, 4)$ and $(-2, 9, 1)$. The line AB meets the xy-plane at C. Find the coordinates of C.

The displacement vector $\overrightarrow{AB}$ is

$$\mathbf{b} - \mathbf{a} = \begin{pmatrix} -2 \\ 9 \\ 1 \end{pmatrix} - \begin{pmatrix} -5 \\ 3 \\ 4 \end{pmatrix} = \begin{pmatrix} 3 \\ 6 \\ -3 \end{pmatrix} = 3 \begin{pmatrix} 1 \\ 2 \\ -1 \end{pmatrix}.$$

So $\begin{pmatrix} 1 \\ 2 \\ -1 \end{pmatrix}$ can be taken as a direction vector for the line. A vector equation for the line is therefore

$$\mathbf{r} = \begin{pmatrix} -5 \\ 3 \\ 4 \end{pmatrix} + t \begin{pmatrix} 1 \\ 2 \\ -1 \end{pmatrix}, \quad \text{or} \quad \mathbf{r} = \begin{pmatrix} -5 + t \\ 3 + 2t \\ 4 - t \end{pmatrix}.$$

C is the point on the line at which $z = 0$, so that $4 - t = 0$, giving $t = 4$. It therefore has position vector $\mathbf{c} = \begin{pmatrix} -1 \\ 11 \\ 0 \end{pmatrix}$ and coordinates $(-1, 11, 0)$.

Example 4.7.2
Find the point of intersection (if there is one) of the lines $\mathbf{r} = \begin{pmatrix} 1 \\ 4 \\ -2 \end{pmatrix} + s \begin{pmatrix} 2 \\ -3 \\ 1 \end{pmatrix}$ and $\mathbf{r} = \begin{pmatrix} 4 \\ 2 \\ 4 \end{pmatrix} + t \begin{pmatrix} -1 \\ 4 \\ 5 \end{pmatrix}.$

If the point with parameter s on the first line is the same as the point with parameter t on the second, then

$$\begin{pmatrix} 1 \\ 4 \\ -2 \end{pmatrix} + s \begin{pmatrix} 2 \\ -3 \\ 1 \end{pmatrix} = \begin{pmatrix} 4 \\ 2 \\ 4 \end{pmatrix} + t \begin{pmatrix} -1 \\ 4 \\ 5 \end{pmatrix}.$$

Equating the components gives

$$\begin{array}{ccc} 1 + 2s = 4 - t & & 2s + t = 3 \\ 4 - 3s = 2 + 4t & \text{or} & 3s + 4t = 2 \\ -2 + s = 4 + 5t & & s - 5t = 6 \end{array}$$

Solving the first two equations simultaneously gives $s = 2$ and $t = -1$.

It is important to check whether these values satisfy the third equation, $s - 5t = 6$: substituting $s = 2$ and $t = -1$ gives

$$\text{left side} = 2 - 5 \times (-1) = 7,$$

so there is no solution to the set of equations. The lines do not intersect.

Example 4.7.3
Find the value of u for which the lines $\mathbf{r} = (\mathbf{j} - \mathbf{k}) + s(\mathbf{i} + 2\mathbf{j} + \mathbf{k})$ and $\mathbf{r} = (\mathbf{i} + 7\mathbf{j} - 4\mathbf{k}) + t(\mathbf{i} + u\mathbf{k})$ intersect.

Points on the lines can be written as $s\mathbf{i} + (1 + 2s)\mathbf{j} + (-1 + s)\mathbf{k}$ and $(1 + t)\mathbf{i} + 7\mathbf{j} + (-4 + ut)\mathbf{k}$. If these are the same point, then

$$s = 1 + t, \quad 1 + 2s = 7, \quad \text{and} \quad -1 + s = -4 + ut.$$

The first two equations give $s = 3$ and $t = 2$. Putting these values into the third equation gives $-1 + 3 = -4 + 2u$, so $u = 3$.

You can easily check that, with these values, both equations give $\mathbf{r} = 3\mathbf{i} + 7\mathbf{j} + 2\mathbf{k}$, so the point of intersection has coordinates $(3, 7, 2)$. For every other value of u the lines are skew.

Exercise 4D

1 Write down vector equations for the line through the given point in the specified direction.

(a) $(2, -3, 5)$, $\begin{pmatrix} 1 \\ 2 \\ -6 \end{pmatrix}$
    (b) $(4, -1, 1)$, $\begin{pmatrix} 4 \\ -2 \\ -3 \end{pmatrix}$

(c) $(5, 7, 4)$, parallel to the x-axis
    (d) $(0, 0, 0)$, $\begin{pmatrix} 2 \\ -3 \\ 1 \end{pmatrix}$

2 Investigate whether or not it is possible to find numbers s and t which satisfy the following vector equations.

(a) $s\begin{pmatrix} 3 \\ 4 \\ 1 \end{pmatrix} + t\begin{pmatrix} 2 \\ -1 \\ 0 \end{pmatrix} = \begin{pmatrix} 0 \\ 11 \\ 2 \end{pmatrix}$

(b) $\begin{pmatrix} -1 \\ -2 \\ 3 \end{pmatrix} + s\begin{pmatrix} 1 \\ 2 \\ -1 \end{pmatrix} + t\begin{pmatrix} 3 \\ -1 \\ 1 \end{pmatrix} = \begin{pmatrix} 5 \\ 3 \\ 1 \end{pmatrix}$

(c) $s\begin{pmatrix} 1 \\ 2 \\ -3 \end{pmatrix} + t\begin{pmatrix} 5 \\ 1 \\ 1 \end{pmatrix} = \begin{pmatrix} 1 \\ -7 \\ 11 \end{pmatrix}$

3 Find if the following pairs of lines intersect. If they do, give the point of intersection.

(a) $\mathbf{r} = \mathbf{i} + s\,(\mathbf{i} + \mathbf{j} + \mathbf{k})$ and $\mathbf{r} = 8\mathbf{i} + 3\mathbf{j} + 3\mathbf{k} + t\,(\mathbf{i})$

(b) $\mathbf{r} = 3\mathbf{i} - 2\mathbf{j} - \mathbf{k} + s\,(-2\mathbf{i} + 3\mathbf{j} - 5\mathbf{k})$ and $\mathbf{r} = 8\mathbf{i} + 4\mathbf{j} + \mathbf{k} + t\,(-\mathbf{i} - 3\mathbf{j} + \mathbf{k})$

(c) $\mathbf{r} = -3\mathbf{i} + 5\mathbf{j} + 2\mathbf{k} + s\,(-\mathbf{i} - 2\mathbf{j} - 4\mathbf{k})$ and $\mathbf{r} = 8\mathbf{i} + 5\mathbf{j} + \mathbf{k} + t\,(-\mathbf{i} - 3\mathbf{j} + 3\mathbf{k})$

4 Find vector equations for the lines joining the following pairs of points.

(a) $(8, 7, 5)$, $(-1, 2, -1)$ (b) $(2, -2, 0)$, $(2, -1, 0)$ (c) $(4, 5, -2)$, $(-2, -3, 4)$

5 If $\mathbf{p} = 2\mathbf{i} - \mathbf{j} + 3\mathbf{k}$, $\mathbf{q} = 5\mathbf{i} + 2\mathbf{j}$ and $\mathbf{r} = 4\mathbf{i} + \mathbf{j} + \mathbf{k}$, find a set of numbers f, g and h such that $f\mathbf{p} + g\mathbf{q} + h\mathbf{r} = \mathbf{0}$. What does this tell you about the translations represented by $\mathbf{p}$, $\mathbf{q}$ and $\mathbf{r}$?

6 A and B are points with coordinates $(2, 1, 4)$ and $(5, -5, -2)$. Find the coordinates of the point C such that $\overrightarrow{AC} = \frac{2}{3}\,\overrightarrow{AB}$.

7 For each of the following sets of points A, B, C and D, determine whether the lines AB and CD are parallel, intersect each other, or are skew.

(a) $A(3, 2, 4)$, $B(-3, -7, -8)$, $C(0, 1, 3)$, $D(-2, 5, 9)$

(b) $A(3, 1, 0)$, $B(-3, 1, 3)$, $C(5, 0, -1)$, $D(1, 0, 1)$

(c) $A(-5, -4, -3)$, $B(5, 1, 2)$, $C(-1, -3, 0)$, $D(8, 0, 6)$

(d) $A(2, 0, 3)$, $B(-1, 2, 1)$, $C(4, -1, 5)$, $D(10, -5, 1)$

8 Find a vector equation for the line l through $(3, 2, 6)$ parallel to the line with vector equation $\mathbf{r} = \begin{pmatrix} 4 \\ 0 \\ 5 \end{pmatrix} + t \begin{pmatrix} -3 \\ 1 \\ 2 \end{pmatrix}$. Find also the coordinates of the points where l meets the xy-plane and the xz-plane.

9 A line cuts the yz-plane at the point $(0, 4, 3)$ and the xz-plane at the point $(6, 0, 5)$. Find the coordinates of the point where it cuts the xy-plane.

10 A student displays her birthday cards on strings which she has pinned to opposite walls of her room, whose floor measures 3 metres by 4 metres. Relative to one corner of the room, the coordinates of the ends of the first string are $(0, 3.3, 2.4)$ and $(3, 1.3, 1.9)$ in metre units. The coordinates of the ends of the second string are $(0.7, 0, 2.3)$ and $(1.5, 4, 1.5)$. Find the difference in the heights of the two strings where one passes over the other.

11 Four points A, B, C and D with position vectors $\mathbf{a}$, $\mathbf{b}$, $\mathbf{c}$ and $\mathbf{d}$ are vertices of a tetrahedron. The mid-points of BC, CA, AB, AD, BD, CD are denoted by P, Q, R, U, V, W. Find the position vectors of the mid-points of PU, QV and RW.

What do you notice about the answer? State your conclusion as a geometrical theorem.

12 If E and F are two points with position vectors $\mathbf{e}$ and $\mathbf{f}$, find the position vector of the point H such that $\overrightarrow{EH} = \frac{3}{4}\,\overrightarrow{EF}$.

With the notation of Question 11, express in terms of $\mathbf{a}$, $\mathbf{b}$, $\mathbf{c}$ and $\mathbf{d}$ the position vectors of G, the centroid of triangle ABC, and of H, the point on DG such that $DH : HG = 3 : 1$.

Miscellaneous exercise 4

1 Two lines have equations $\mathbf{r} = \begin{pmatrix} 1 \\ 3 \\ 2 \end{pmatrix} + \lambda \begin{pmatrix} 4 \\ -2 \\ 1 \end{pmatrix}$ and $\mathbf{r} = \begin{pmatrix} 3 \\ 8 \\ 7 \end{pmatrix} + \mu \begin{pmatrix} 2 \\ -3 \\ -1 \end{pmatrix}$. Show that the lines
   intersect, and find the position vector of the point of intersection.   (OCR)

2 (a) A straight line, l_1, has vector equation $\mathbf{r} = \begin{pmatrix} 4 \\ 2 \end{pmatrix} + t \begin{pmatrix} 1 \\ 4 \end{pmatrix}$ where $\mathbf{r} = \begin{pmatrix} x \\ y \end{pmatrix}$. Find the cartesian
        equation of this line.

   (b) Another straight line, l_2, has equation $2x - 3y + 3 = 0$. Find a vector equation for it.

   (c) Find, in either cartesian or vector form, an equation of the line through $(-1, 5)$ parallel
        to l_2.   (OCR)

3 Investigate the intersection of the following pairs of lines, one given by a vector equation
   and the other by a cartesian equation.

   (a) $\mathbf{r} = \begin{pmatrix} 2 \\ 0 \end{pmatrix} + t \begin{pmatrix} 1 \\ -3 \end{pmatrix}$, $3x + y = 8$

   (b) $\mathbf{r} = \begin{pmatrix} -1 \\ 4 \end{pmatrix} + t \begin{pmatrix} 2 \\ 5 \end{pmatrix}$, $x - 4y = 1$

   (c) $\mathbf{r} = \begin{pmatrix} 0 \\ 3 \end{pmatrix} + t \begin{pmatrix} 2 \\ -1 \end{pmatrix}$, $2y + x = 6$

4 Show that the two lines with equations $\mathbf{r} = -2\mathbf{i} + 3\mathbf{j} - \mathbf{k} + s(4\mathbf{i} - 2\mathbf{j} + \mathbf{k})$ and
   $\mathbf{r} = 2\mathbf{i} + 4\mathbf{j} + 3\mathbf{k} + t(-4\mathbf{i} + \mathbf{j} - 2\mathbf{k})$ intersect, and find the position vector of the point of
   intersection.

5 Find whether or not the line passing through the points $(1, 5, 1)$ and $(3, 7, -2)$ meets the
   line $\mathbf{r} = \begin{pmatrix} 6 \\ -2 \\ 1 \end{pmatrix} + t \begin{pmatrix} -3 \\ 5 \\ 1 \end{pmatrix}$.

6 (a) Find a vector equation for the line with cartesian equation $2x + 3y = 7$.

   (b) Find the cartesian equation of the line with vector equation $\mathbf{r} = \begin{pmatrix} 3 \\ 4 \end{pmatrix} + t \begin{pmatrix} 1 \\ 3 \end{pmatrix}$.

   (c) Find the point of intersection of the two lines
        (i) by using both cartesian equations,
        (ii) by using both vector equations,
        (iii) by using the equations in the forms given in parts (a) and (b).

7 $ABCD$ is a parallelogram. The coordinates of A, B, D are $(4, 2, 3)$, $(18, 4, 8)$ and $(-1, 12, 13)$
   respectively. The origin of coordinates is O.

   (a) Find the vectors $\overrightarrow{AB}$ and $\overrightarrow{AD}$. Find the coordinates of C.

   (b) Show that $\overrightarrow{OA}$ can be expressed in the form $\lambda \overrightarrow{AB} + \mu \overrightarrow{AD}$, stating the values of λ and μ.
        What does this tell you about the plane $ABCD$?   (MEI)

8 A tunnel is to be excavated through a hill. In order to define position, coordinates (x, y, z) are taken relative to an origin O such that x is the distance east from O, y is the distance north and z is the vertical distance upwards, with one unit equal to 100 m. The tunnel starts at point $A(2, 3, 5)$ and runs in the direction $\begin{pmatrix} 1 \\ 1 \\ -0.5 \end{pmatrix}$.

(a) Write down the equation of the tunnel in the form $\mathbf{r} = \mathbf{u} + \lambda \mathbf{t}$.

(b) An old tunnel through the hill has equation $\mathbf{r} = \begin{pmatrix} 4 \\ 1 \\ 2 \end{pmatrix} + \mu \begin{pmatrix} 7 \\ 15 \\ 0 \end{pmatrix}$. Show that the point P on the new tunnel where $x = 7\frac{1}{2}$ is directly above a point Q in the old tunnel. Find the vertical separation PQ of the tunnels at this point. (MEI)

9 Find the intersection of the lines $\mathbf{r} = \begin{pmatrix} -1 \\ 0 \end{pmatrix} + s \begin{pmatrix} \cos \alpha \\ \sin \alpha \end{pmatrix}$ and $\mathbf{r} = \begin{pmatrix} 1 \\ 0 \end{pmatrix} + t \begin{pmatrix} -\sin \alpha \\ \cos \alpha \end{pmatrix}$, giving your answer in a simplified form. Interpret your answer geometrically.

10 A balloon flying over flat fenland reports its position at 7.40 a.m. as $(7.8, 5.4, 1.2)$, the coordinates being given in kilometres relative to a checkpoint on the ground. By 7.50 a.m. its position has changed to $(9.3, 4.4, 0.7)$. Assuming that it continues to descend at the same speed along the same line, find the coordinates of the point where it would be expected to land, and the time when this would occur.

11 An airliner climbs so that its position relative to the airport control tower t minutes after take-off is given by the vector $\mathbf{r} = \begin{pmatrix} 1 \\ 2 \\ 0 \end{pmatrix} + t \begin{pmatrix} 4 \\ 5 \\ 0.6 \end{pmatrix}$, the units being kilometres. The x- and y-axes point towards the east and the north respectively.

(a) Find the position of the airliner when it reaches its cruising height of 9000 m.

(b) With reference to (x, y) coordinates on the ground, the coastline has equation $x + 3y = 140$. How high is the aircraft flying as it crosses the coast?

(c) Calculate the speed of the airliner over the ground in kilometres per hour, and the bearing on which it is flying.

(d) Calculate the speed of the airliner through the air, and the angle to the horizontal at which it is climbing.

12 Two airliners take off simultaneously from different airports. As they climb, their positions relative to an air traffic control centre t minutes later are given by the vectors

$\mathbf{r}_1 = \begin{pmatrix} 5 \\ -30 \\ 0 \end{pmatrix} + t \begin{pmatrix} 8 \\ 2 \\ 0.5 \end{pmatrix}$ and $\mathbf{r}_2 = \begin{pmatrix} 13 \\ 26 \\ 0 \end{pmatrix} + t \begin{pmatrix} 6 \\ -3 \\ 0.6 \end{pmatrix}$, the units being kilometres. Find the coordinates of the point on the ground over which both airliners pass. Find also the difference in heights, and the difference in the times, when they pass over that point.

13 The centre line of an underground railway tunnel follows a line given by $\mathbf{r} = t\begin{pmatrix} 10 \\ 8 \\ -1 \end{pmatrix}$ for

$0 \leqslant t \leqslant 40$, the units being metres. The centre line of another tunnel at present stops at

the point with position vector $\begin{pmatrix} 200 \\ 100 \\ -25 \end{pmatrix}$ and it is proposed to extend this in a direction

$\begin{pmatrix} 5 \\ 7 \\ u \end{pmatrix}$. The constant u has to be chosen so that, at the point where one tunnel passes over

the other, there is at least 15 metres difference in depth between the centre lines of the
two tunnels. What restriction does this impose on the value of u?

Another requirement is that the tunnel must not be inclined at more than 5° to the
horizontal. What values of u satisfy both requirements?

14* A mathematical market trader packages fruit in three sizes. An Individual bag holds 1
apple and 2 bananas; a Jumbo bag holds 4 apples and 3 bananas; and a King-size bag
holds 8 apples and 7 bananas. She draws two vector arrows $\mathbf{a}$ and $\mathbf{b}$ to represent an apple
and a banana respectively, and then represents the three sizes of bag by vectors
$\mathbf{I} = \mathbf{a} + 2\mathbf{b}$, $\mathbf{J} = 4\mathbf{a} + 3\mathbf{b}$ and $\mathbf{K} = 8\mathbf{a} + 7\mathbf{b}$. Find numbers s and t such that $\mathbf{K} = s\mathbf{I} + t\mathbf{J}$.

By midday she has sold all her King-size bags, but she has plenty of Individual and Jumbo
bags left. She decides to make up some more King-size bags by using the contents of the
other bags. How can she do this so that she has no loose fruit left over?

15* A curve is given by parametric equations $x = f(\theta)$, $y = g(\theta)$. Show that the direction of the

tangent at the point with parameter θ is given by $\begin{pmatrix} f'(\theta) \\ g'(\theta) \end{pmatrix}$. Write down a vector equation

for the tangent to the curve at this point.

Hence find a vector equation for the tangent at the point with parameter θ for the curves
with the following equations, and deduce the cartesian equation.

(a) $x = \theta^2$, $y = \theta^3$ (b) $x = 3\cos\theta$, $y = 2\sin\theta$

5 The binomial expansion

The binomial theorem tells you how to expand $(1 + x)^n$ when n is a positive integer. This chapter extends this result to all rational values of n. When you have completed it, you should

- be able to expand $(1 + x)^n$ in ascending powers of x
- know that the expansion is valid for $|x| < 1$
- understand how to use expansions to find approximations
- know how to extend the method to expand powers of more general expressions.

5.1 Generalising the binomial theorem

You learnt in C2 Chapter 3 how to expand $(x + y)^n$ by the binomial theorem, when n is a positive integer. If you replace x by 1 and y by x, this expansion becomes

$$(1 + x)^n = 1^n + \frac{n}{1} \times 1^{n-1}x + \frac{n(n-1)}{1 \times 2} \times 1^{n-2}x^2 + \frac{n(n-1)(n-2)}{1 \times 2 \times 3} \times 1^{n-3}x^3 + \dots .$$

You can remove all the powers of 1, and write this more simply as

$$(1 + x)^n = 1 + \frac{n}{1}x + \frac{n(n-1)}{1 \times 2}x^2 + \frac{n(n-1)(n-2)}{1 \times 2 \times 3}x^3 + \dots . \qquad \text{Equation A}$$

Notice that in this form the terms are written in ascending powers of x (see C1 Section 9.1).

This chapter tackles the question 'Can you still use this expansion when n is not a positive integer?'

Before trying to answer this, you should notice something important about the terms. If n is a positive integer, then the form of the coefficients ensures that no terms have powers higher than x^n. For example, if $n = 5$ the coefficient of x^6 is

$$\frac{5 \times 4 \times 3 \times 2 \times 1 \times 0}{1 \times 2 \times 3 \times 4 \times 5 \times 6} = 0,$$

and all the coefficients which follow it are zero. But this only happens when n is a positive integer. For example, if $n = 4\frac{1}{2}$ the coefficients of x^4, x^5 and x^6 are

$$\frac{4\frac{1}{2} \times 3\frac{1}{2} \times 2\frac{1}{2} \times 1\frac{1}{2}}{1 \times 2 \times 3 \times 4}, \quad \frac{4\frac{1}{2} \times 3\frac{1}{2} \times 2\frac{1}{2} \times 1\frac{1}{2} \times \frac{1}{2}}{1 \times 2 \times 3 \times 4 \times 5} \quad \text{and} \quad \frac{4\frac{1}{2} \times 3\frac{1}{2} \times 2\frac{1}{2} \times 1\frac{1}{2} \times \frac{1}{2} \times \left(-\frac{1}{2}\right)}{1 \times 2 \times 3 \times 4 \times 5 \times 6}.$$

Whichever coefficient you consider, you never get a factor of 0. So, if n is not a positive integer, the expansion never stops.

The case $n = -1$

You know from C2 Section 6.3 that the sum to infinity of the geometric series

$1 + r + r^2 + r^3 + \dots$ is $\dfrac{1}{1 - r}$, provided that $|r| < 1$.

Replacing *r* by −*x* now gives

$$\frac{1}{1-(-x)} = (1+x)^{-1} = 1 - x + x^2 - x^3 + \dots .$$

Now try using Equation A with *n* = −1. This gives

$$(1+x)^{-1} = 1 + \frac{(-1)}{1}x + \frac{(-1)\times(-2)}{1\times 2}x^2 + \frac{(-1)\times(-2)\times(-3)}{1\times 2\times 3}x^3 + \dots,$$

which simplifies to

$$(1+x)^{-1} = 1 - x + x^2 - x^3 + \dots .$$

So far so good: Equation A works when *n* = −1.

The case $n = \frac{1}{2}$

If $(1+x)^{\frac{1}{2}}$ can be expanded in the form $A + Bx + Cx^2 + Dx^3 + \dots$, then you want to find $A, B, C, D, \dots$ so that

$$(A + Bx + Cx^2 + Dx^3 + \dots)^2 \equiv 1 + x.$$

This needs to be true for *x* = 0, so $A^2 = 1$. Since $(1+x)^{\frac{1}{2}}$ is the positive square root, this means that $A = 1$.

Then

$$(1 + Bx + Cx^2 + Dx^3 + \dots)^2 \equiv (1 + Bx + Cx^2 + Dx^3 + \dots)(1 + Bx + Cx^2 + Dx^3 + \dots)$$
$$\equiv 1 + (B + B)x + (C + B^2 + C)x^2$$
$$+ (D + BC + CB + D)x^3 + \dots$$
$$\equiv 1 + (2B)x + (2C + B^2)x^2 + (2D + 2BC)x^3 + \dots .$$

So $1 + x \equiv 1 + (2B)x + (2C + B^2)x^2 + (2D + 2BC)x^3 + \dots .$

Since this is an identity, you can equate coefficients of each power of *x* in turn:

$$2B = 1, \qquad \text{so } B = \tfrac{1}{2},$$
$$2C + B^2 = 0, \qquad \text{so } C = -\tfrac{1}{8},$$
$$2D + 2BC = 0, \qquad \text{so } D = \tfrac{1}{16}.$$

So it appears that $\left(1 + \tfrac{1}{2}x - \tfrac{1}{8}x^2 + \tfrac{1}{16}x^3 + \dots\right)^2 \equiv 1 + x$, and

$$(1+x)^{\frac{1}{2}} = 1 + \tfrac{1}{2}x - \tfrac{1}{8}x^2 + \tfrac{1}{16}x^3 + \dots .$$

Using Equation A with $n = \tfrac{1}{2}$ gives

$$(1+x)^{\frac{1}{2}} = 1 + \frac{\tfrac{1}{2}}{1}x + \frac{\tfrac{1}{2}\times\left(-\tfrac{1}{2}\right)}{1\times 2}x^2 + \frac{\tfrac{1}{2}\times\left(-\tfrac{1}{2}\right)\times\left(-\tfrac{3}{2}\right)}{1\times 2\times 3}x^3 + \dots$$
$$= 1 + \tfrac{1}{2}x - \tfrac{1}{8}x^2 + \tfrac{1}{16}x^3 + \dots .$$

So Equation A seems to work when $n = \tfrac{1}{2}$, at least for the first few terms.

The general case

In fact Equation A works for all rational powers of n, positive or negative. There is, however, an important restriction. You will remember, from C2 Section 6.3, that the series

$1 + r + r^2 + r^3 + \ldots$ only converges to $\dfrac{1}{1-r}$ if $|r| < 1$. A similar condition applies to the binomial expansion of $(1+x)^n$ for any value of n which is not a positive integer.

> **Binomial expansion**
> When n is rational, but not a positive integer, and $|x| < 1$,
> $$(1+x)^n = 1 + \frac{n}{1}x + \frac{n(n-1)}{1 \times 2}x^2 + \frac{n(n-1)(n-2)}{1 \times 2 \times 3}x^3 + \ldots .$$

This is sometimes called the **binomial series**. It is usual to leave out the multiplication signs when brackets are used; this will be done in the remainder of the chapter.

Example 5.1.1
Find the expansion of $(1+x)^{-2}$ in ascending powers of x up to the term in x^4.

Putting $n = -2$ in the formula for $(1+x)^n$,

$$(1+x)^{-2} = 1 + \frac{(-2)}{1}x + \frac{(-2)(-3)}{1 \times 2}x^2 + \frac{(-2)(-3)(-4)}{1 \times 2 \times 3}x^3$$
$$+ \frac{(-2)(-3)(-4)(-5)}{1 \times 2 \times 3 \times 4}x^4 + \ldots$$
$$= 1 - 2x + 3x^2 - 4x^3 + 5x^4 + \ldots .$$

The required expansion is $1 - 2x + 3x^2 - 4x^3 + 5x^4$.

Example 5.1.2
Find the expansion of $(1+3x)^{\frac{3}{2}}$ in ascending powers of x up to and including the term in x^3. For what values of x is the expansion valid?

Putting $n = \frac{3}{2}$ in the formula for $(1+x)^n$, and writing $3x$ in place of x,

$$(1+3x)^{\frac{3}{2}} = 1 + \frac{\frac{3}{2}}{1}(3x) + \frac{\left(\frac{3}{2}\right)\left(\frac{1}{2}\right)}{1 \times 2}(3x)^2 + \frac{\left(\frac{3}{2}\right)\left(\frac{1}{2}\right)\left(-\frac{1}{2}\right)}{1 \times 2 \times 3}(3x)^3 + \ldots$$
$$= 1 + \frac{9}{2}x + \frac{27}{8}x^2 - \frac{27}{16}x^3 + \ldots .$$

The required expansion is $1 + \frac{9}{2}x + \frac{27}{8}x^2 - \frac{27}{16}x^3$.

The expansion $(1+x)^n$ is valid for $|x| < 1$, so this expansion is valid for $|3x| < 1$, that is for $|x| < \frac{1}{3}$.

You should notice one other point. When n is a positive integer, the coefficient $\dfrac{n(n-1)\ldots(n-(r-1))}{1 \times 2 \times \ldots \times r}$ can be written more concisely using factorials, as $\dfrac{n!}{r!(n-r)!}$. You can't use this notation when n is not a positive integer, since $n!$ is only defined when n is a positive integer or zero. However, r is always an integer, so you can still if you like write the coefficient as $\dfrac{n(n-1)\ldots(n-(r-1))}{r!}$.

5.2   Approximations

One use of binomial expansions is to find numerical approximations to square roots, cube roots and other calculations. If $|x|$ is much smaller than 1, the power $|x^2|$ is very small, $|x^3|$ is smaller still, and you soon reach a power which, for all intents and purposes, can be neglected. So the sum of the first few terms of the expansion is a very close approximation to $(1 + x)^n$.

Example 5.2.1

Find the expansion of $(1 - 2x)^{\frac{1}{2}}$ in ascending powers of x up to and including the term in x^3. By choosing a suitable value for x, find an approximation for $\sqrt{2}$.

$$(1 - 2x)^{\frac{1}{2}} = 1 + \frac{\frac{1}{2}}{1}(-2x) + \frac{\frac{1}{2}\left(-\frac{1}{2}\right)}{1 \times 2}(-2x)^2 + \frac{\frac{1}{2}\left(-\frac{1}{2}\right)\left(-\frac{3}{2}\right)}{1 \times 2 \times 3}(-2x)^3 + \dots$$

$$= 1 - x - \tfrac{1}{2}x^2 - \tfrac{1}{2}x^3 + \dots .$$

Choosing a suitable value for x needs a bit of ingenuity. It is no use simply taking x so that $1 - 2x = 2$, which would give $x = -\tfrac{1}{2}$, since this is not nearly small enough for the terms in x^4, x^5, $\dots$ to be neglected. The trick is to find a value of x so that $1 - 2x$ has the form $2 \times$ a perfect square. A good choice is to take $x = 0.01$, so that $1 - 2 \times 0.01 = 0.98$, which is 2×0.7^2.

So put $x = 0.01$ in the expansion. This gives

$$0.98^{\frac{1}{2}} = 1 + 0.01 - \tfrac{1}{2} \times 0.01^2 - \tfrac{1}{2} \times 0.01^3 - \dots,$$

so $0.7\sqrt{2} \approx 1 - 0.01 - 0.000\,05 - 0.000\,000\,5 = 0.989\,949\,5.$

Therefore $\tfrac{7}{10}\sqrt{2} \approx 0.989\,949\,5$, giving $\sqrt{2} \approx 1.414\,214.$

5.3   Expanding other expressions

The binomial series can also be used to expand powers of expressions more complicated than $1 + x$ or $1 + ax$. If you can rewrite an expression as $Y(1 + Z)^n$ where Y and Z are expressions involving x, then you can expand $(1 + Z)^n$, substitute the appropriate expression for Z in the result and then multiply through by the expression for Y.

Example 5.3.1

Find the binomial expansion of $(4 - 3x^2)^{\frac{1}{2}}$ up to and including the term in x^4.

4 − 3x² is not of the required form, but you can write it as $4\left(1 - \tfrac{3}{4}x^2\right)$. So, using the factor rule for indices,

$$(4 - 3x^2)^{\frac{1}{2}} = 4^{\frac{1}{2}}\left(1 - \tfrac{3}{4}x^2\right)^{\frac{1}{2}} = 2\left(1 - \tfrac{3}{4}x^2\right)^{\frac{1}{2}}.$$

Then $\left(1 - \tfrac{3}{4}x^2\right)^{\frac{1}{2}} = 1 + \dfrac{\frac{1}{2}}{1}\left(-\tfrac{3}{4}x^2\right) + \dfrac{\left(\frac{1}{2}\right)\left(-\frac{1}{2}\right)}{1 \times 2}\left(-\tfrac{3}{4}x^2\right)^2 + \dots .$

Therefore $(4 - 3x^2)^{\frac{1}{2}} = 2\left(1 - \tfrac{3}{4}x^2\right)^{\frac{1}{2}} = 2 - \tfrac{3}{4}x^2 - \tfrac{9}{64}x^4 + \dots$ and the required expansion is $2 - \tfrac{3}{4}x^2 - \tfrac{9}{64}x^4.$

Example 5.3.2

Expand $\dfrac{5+x}{2-x+x^2}$ in ascending powers of x up to the term in x^3.

Write $\dfrac{5+x}{2-x+x^2} = \dfrac{5+x}{2\left(1-\frac{1}{2}x+\frac{1}{2}x^2\right)} = \frac{1}{2}(5+x)\left(1-\frac{1}{2}(x-x^2)\right)^{-1}$.

Now $(1-u)^{-1} = 1 + \dfrac{(-1)}{1}(-u) + \dfrac{(-1)(-2)}{1\times 2}(-u)^2 + \dfrac{(-1)(-2)(-3)}{1\times 2\times 3}(-u)^3 + \cdots$

$$= 1 + u + u^2 + u^3 + \cdots .$$

Writing $\frac{1}{2}(x-x^2)$ in place of u,

$$\left(1-\tfrac{1}{2}(x-x^2)\right)^{-1} = 1 + \tfrac{1}{2}(x-x^2) + \left(\tfrac{1}{2}(x-x^2)\right)^2 + \left(\tfrac{1}{2}(x-x^2)\right)^3 + \cdots .$$

Collecting together the terms on the right, and ignoring any powers higher than x^3,

$$\left(1-\tfrac{1}{2}(x-x^2)\right)^{-1} = 1 + \tfrac{1}{2}(x-x^2) + \tfrac{1}{4}(x^2 - 2x^3 + \ldots) + \tfrac{1}{8}(x^3 + \ldots) + \cdots$$

$$= 1 + \tfrac{1}{2}x - \tfrac{1}{4}x^2 - \tfrac{3}{8}x^3 + \cdots .$$

Therefore, multiplying by $\frac{1}{2}(5+x)$,

$$\dfrac{5+x}{2-x+x^2} = \tfrac{1}{2}(5+x)\left(1+\tfrac{1}{2}x - \tfrac{1}{4}x^2 - \tfrac{3}{8}x^3 + \cdots\right)$$

$$= \tfrac{1}{2}\left(5 + \tfrac{5}{2}x - \tfrac{5}{4}x^2 - \tfrac{15}{8}x^3 + \cdots + x + \tfrac{1}{2}x^2 - \tfrac{1}{4}x^3 + \cdots\right)$$

$$= \tfrac{1}{2}\left(5 + \tfrac{7}{2}x - \tfrac{3}{4}x^2 - \tfrac{17}{8}x^3 + \cdots\right)$$

$$= \tfrac{5}{2} + \tfrac{7}{4}x - \tfrac{3}{8}x^2 - \tfrac{17}{16}x^3 + \cdots .$$

The required expansion is $\frac{5}{2} + \frac{7}{4}x - \frac{3}{8}x^2 - \frac{17}{16}x^3$.

If an algebraic expression has a denominator which factorises, like

$$\dfrac{5+x}{2-x-x^2} = \dfrac{5+x}{(2+x)(1-x)},$$

there is a simpler way of expanding it, by first splitting it into partial fractions. This technique is explained in Chapter 6.

Exercise 5

1 Expand the following in ascending powers of x up to and including the term in x^2.

   (a) $(1+x)^{-3}$ (b) $(1+x)^{-5}$ (c) $(1-x)^{-4}$ (d) $(1-x)^{-6}$

2 Find the expansion of the following in ascending powers of x up to and including the term in x^2.

   (a) $(1+4x)^{-1}$ (b) $(1-2x)^{-3}$ (c) $(1-3x)^{-4}$ (d) $\left(1+\tfrac{1}{2}x\right)^{-2}$

3 Find the coefficient of x^3 in the expansion of the following.

   (a) $(1-x)^{-7}$ (b) $(1+2x)^{-1}$ (c) $(1+3x)^{-3}$ (d) $(1-4x)^{-2}$

   (e) $\left(1-\tfrac{1}{3}x\right)^{-6}$ (f) $(1+ax)^{-4}$ (g) $(1-bx)^{-4}$ (h) $(1-cx)^{-n}$

4 Find the expansion of the following in ascending powers of x up to and including the term in x^2.

(a) $(1+x)^{\frac{1}{3}}$ (b) $(1+x)^{\frac{3}{4}}$ (c) $(1-x)^{\frac{3}{2}}$ (d) $(1-x)^{-\frac{1}{2}}$

5 Find the expansion of the following in ascending powers of x up to and including the term in x^2.

(a) $(1+4x)^{\frac{1}{2}}$ (b) $(1+3x)^{-\frac{1}{3}}$ (c) $(1-6x)^{\frac{4}{3}}$ (d) $\left(1-\frac{1}{2}x\right)^{-\frac{1}{4}}$

6 Find the coefficient of x^3 in the expansions of the following.

(a) $(1+2x)^{\frac{3}{2}}$ (b) $(1-5x)^{-\frac{1}{2}}$ (c) $\left(1+\frac{3}{2}x\right)^{\frac{1}{3}}$ (d) $(1-4x)^{\frac{3}{4}}$

(e) $(1-7x)^{-\frac{1}{7}}$ (f) $(1+\sqrt{2}x)^{\frac{1}{2}}$ (g) $(1+ax)^{\frac{3}{2}}$ (h) $(1-bx)^{-\frac{1}{2}n}$

7 Show that, for small x, $\sqrt{1+\frac{1}{4}x} \approx 1+\frac{1}{8}x - \frac{1}{128}x^2$. Deduce the first three terms in the expansions of the following.

(a) $\sqrt{1-\frac{1}{4}x}$ (b) $\sqrt{1+\frac{1}{4}x^2}$ (c) $\sqrt{4+x}$ (d) $\sqrt{36+9x}$

8 Show that $\dfrac{1}{\left(1-\frac{3}{2}x\right)^2} \approx 1+3x+\frac{27}{4}x^2+\frac{27}{2}x^3$ and state the interval of values of x for which the expansion is valid. Deduce the first four terms in the expansions of the following.

(a) $\dfrac{4}{\left(1-\frac{3}{2}x\right)^2}$ (b) $\dfrac{1}{(2-3x)^2}$

9 Find the first four terms in the expansion of each of the following in ascending powers of x. State the interval of values of x for which each expansion is valid.

(a) $\sqrt{1-6x}$ (b) $\dfrac{1}{1+5x}$ (c) $\dfrac{1}{\sqrt[3]{1+9x}}$ (d) $\dfrac{1}{(1-2x)^4}$

(e) $\sqrt{1+2x^2}$ (f) $\sqrt[3]{8-16x}$ (g) $\dfrac{10}{\left(1+\frac{1}{5}x\right)^2}$ (h) $\dfrac{2}{2-x}$

(i) $\dfrac{1}{(2+x)^3}$ (j) $\dfrac{4x}{\sqrt{4+x^3}}$ (k) $\sqrt[4]{1+8x}$ (l) $\dfrac{12}{(\sqrt{3}-x)^4}$

10 Expand $\sqrt{1+8x}$ in ascending powers of x up to and including the term in x^3. By giving a suitable value to x, find an approximation for $\sqrt{1.08}$. Deduce approximations for

(a) $\sqrt{108}$,   (b) $\sqrt{3}$.

11 Expand $\sqrt[3]{1+4x}$ in ascending powers of x up to and including the term in x^2.

(a) By putting $x = 0.01$, determine an approximation for $\sqrt[3]{130}$.

(b) By putting $x = -0.000\,25$, determine an approximation for $\sqrt[3]{999}$.

12 Given that the coefficient of x^3 in the expansion of $\dfrac{1}{(1+ax)^3}$ is -2160, find a.

13 Find the coefficient of x^2 in the expansion of $\dfrac{(1-2x)^2}{(1+x)^2}$.

14 Find the first three terms in the expansion of $\dfrac{\sqrt{1+2x}}{\sqrt{1-4x}}$ in ascending powers of x. State the values of x for which the expansion is valid. By substituting $x = 0.01$ in your expansion, find an approximation for $\sqrt{17}$.

15 Given that terms involving x^4 and higher powers may be ignored and that
$$\frac{1}{(1+ax)^3} - \frac{1}{(1+3x)^4} = bx^2 + cx^3,$$ find the values of a, b and c.

16 Find the expansion of $\dfrac{1}{1-(x+x^2)}$ in ascending powers of x up to and including the term in x^4. By substitution of a suitable value of x, find the approximation, correct to 12 decimal places, of $\dfrac{1}{0.998\,999}$.

17 Find the first three terms in the expansion in ascending powers of x of
   (a) $\dfrac{8}{(2+x-x^2)^2}$,
   (b) $\dfrac{1+2x}{(1-x+2x^2)^3}$.

18 Given that the expansion of $(1+ax)^n$ is $1 - 2x + \frac{7}{3}x^2 + kx^3 + \ldots$, find the value of k.

19 Show that the expansion of $(1+4x)^{-2}$ in ascending powers of x is $1 - 8x + 48x^2 - \ldots$ and state the set of values of x for which the expansion is valid. Compare, for suitable values of x, the graphs of $y = (1+4x)^{-2}$, $y = 1 - 8x$ and $y = 1 - 8x + 48x^2$.

20 Given that $1 \equiv (1+x)^2(A + Bx + Cx^2 + Dx^3 + \ldots)$, equate coefficients of powers of x to find the values of A, B, C and D. Hence state the first four terms of the expansions in ascending powers of x of
   (a) $(1+x)^{-2}$,
   (b) $(1-x^2)^{-2}$,
   (c) $(1+2x^2)^{-2}$.

Miscellaneous exercise 5

1 Find the series expansion of $(1+2x)^{\frac{5}{2}}$ up to and including the term in x^3, simplifying the coefficients. (OCR)

2 Expand $(1-4x)^{\frac{1}{2}}$ as a series of ascending powers of x, where $|x| < \frac{1}{4}$, up to and including the term in x^3, expressing the coefficients in their simplest form. (OCR)

3 Expand $(1+2x)^{-3}$ as a series of ascending powers of x, where $|x| < \frac{1}{2}$, up to and including the term in x^3, expressing the coefficients in their simplest form. (OCR)

4 Expand $\dfrac{1}{(1+2x^2)^2}$ as a series in ascending powers of x, up to and including the term in x^6, giving the coefficients in their simplest form. (OCR)

5 Obtain the first three terms in the expansion, in ascending powers of x, of $(4+x)^{\frac{1}{2}}$. State the set of values of x for which the expansion is valid. (OCR)

6 If x is small compared with a, expand $\dfrac{a^3}{(a^2+x^2)^{\frac{3}{2}}}$ in ascending powers of $\dfrac{x}{a}$ up to and including the term in $\dfrac{x^4}{a^4}$. (OCR)

7 Given that $|x| < 1$, expand $\sqrt{1+x}$ as a series of ascending powers of x, up to and including the term in x^2. Show that, if x is small, then $(2-x)\sqrt{1+x} \approx a + bx^2$, where the values of a and b are to be stated. (OCR)

8 Expand $(1 - x)^{-2}$ as a series of ascending powers of x, given that $|x| < 1$. Hence express $\dfrac{1 + x}{(1 - x)^2}$ in the form $1 + 3x + ax^2 + bx^3 + \ldots$, where the values of a and b are to be stated. (OCR)

9 Obtain the first three terms in the expansion, in ascending powers of x, of $(8 + 3x)^{\frac{2}{3}}$, stating the set of values of x for which the expansion is valid. (OCR)

10 Write down the first four terms of the series expansion in ascending powers of x of $(1 - x)^{\frac{1}{3}}$, simplifying the coefficients. By taking $x = 0.1$, use your answer to show that $\sqrt[3]{900} \approx \frac{15\,641}{1620}$. (OCR)

11 Give the binomial expansion, for small x, of $(1 + x)^{\frac{1}{4}}$ up to and including the term in x^2, and simplify the coefficients. By putting $x = \frac{1}{16}$ in your expression, show that $\sqrt[4]{17} \approx \frac{8317}{4096}$. (OCR)

12 Expand $\dfrac{2 + \left(1 + \frac{1}{2}x\right)^6}{2 + 3x}$ in ascending powers of x up to and including the term in x^2. (OCR)

13 Show that $26\left(1 - \dfrac{1}{26^2}\right)^{\frac{1}{2}} = n\sqrt{3}$, where n is an integer whose value is to be found. Given that $|x| < 1$, expand $(1 - x)^{\frac{1}{2}}$ as a series of ascending powers of x, up to and including the term in x^2, simplifying the coefficients. By using the first *two* terms of the expansion of $26\left(1 - \dfrac{1}{26^2}\right)^{\frac{1}{2}}$, obtain an approximate value for $\sqrt{3}$ in the form $\dfrac{p}{q}$, where p and q are integers. (OCR)

14* Show that, for small values of x, $(1 + x)^{\frac{1}{3}} \approx 1 + \frac{1}{3}x - \frac{1}{9}x^2$. Sketch on the same axes (with the aid of a graphic calculator if possible) the graphs of $y = (1 + x)^{\frac{1}{3}}$, $y = 1 + \frac{1}{3}x$ and $y = 1 + \frac{1}{3}x - \frac{1}{9}x^2$.

Compare the graphs for values of x such that

(a) $-3 < x < 3$,   (b) $-1 < x < 1$,   (c) $-0.2 < x < 0.2$.

15* Given that $1 \equiv (1 + x + x^2)(A + Bx + Cx^2 + Dx^3 + Ex^4 + \ldots)$, equate coefficients of powers of x to find the values of A, B, C, D and E. Hence

(a) find the value of $\dfrac{1}{1.000\,300\,09}$ correct to 16 decimal places;

(b) show that $\dfrac{1}{(1 + x + x^2)(1 + 2x + 4x^2)} \approx 1 - 3x + 2x^2 + 9x^3 - 27x^4$ for small values of x.

16 Expand $\dfrac{1}{(1 - x)^2}$, where $|x| < 1$, in ascending powers of x up to and including the term in x^3. You should simplify the coefficients. By putting $x = 10^{-4}$ in your expansion, find $\dfrac{1}{0.9999^2}$ correct to twelve decimal places. (OCR)

17 Expand $(1 + x)^{-\frac{1}{4}}$ in ascending powers of x as far as the term in x^2, simplifying the coefficients. Prove that $\frac{3}{2}\left(1 + \dfrac{1}{80}\right)^{-\frac{1}{4}} = 5^{\frac{1}{4}}$ and, using your expansion of $(1 + x)^{-\frac{1}{4}}$ with $x = \frac{1}{80}$, find an approximate value for $5^{\frac{1}{4}}$, giving five places of decimals in your answer. (OCR)

18 Write down and simplify the series expansion of $\dfrac{1}{\sqrt{1+x}}$, where $|x| < 1$, up to and including the term in x^3. Show that using just these terms of the series with $x = 0.4$ gives a value for $\dfrac{1}{\sqrt{1.4}}$ which differs from the true value by less than 0.7%. By replacing x by z^2 in your series and then integrating, show that $\displaystyle\int_0^{0.2} \dfrac{1}{\sqrt{1+z^2}}\,dz \approx 0.1987.$ (OCR, adapted)

19* Show that the coefficient of x^n in the series expansion of $(1+2x)^{-2}$ is $(-1)^n(n+1)2^n$.

20* Show that the coefficient of x^n in the series expansion of $(1-x)^{-\frac{1}{2}}$ is $\dfrac{(2n)!}{2^{2n}(n!)^2}$.

21 Find the first three terms in the expansion in ascending powers of x of $\sqrt{\dfrac{1+2x}{1-x}}$. By putting $x = 0.02$ in your expansion, find an approximation for $\sqrt{13}$.

22 Find the first five terms in the series expansion of $\dfrac{1}{1+2x}$. Use the expansion to find an approximation to $\displaystyle\int_{-0.2}^{0.1} \dfrac{1}{1+2x}\,dx$. By also evaluating the integral exactly, find an approximation for $\ln 2$.

23 Find the first three terms in the expansion in ascending powers of x of $\dfrac{3+4x+x^2}{\sqrt[3]{1+\frac{1}{2}x}}$. Hence find an approximation to $\displaystyle\int_{-0.5}^{0.5} \dfrac{3+4x+x^2}{\sqrt[3]{1+\frac{1}{2}x}}\,dx.$

24 Find the first three terms in the expansion in ascending powers of x of

$$\frac{1}{(1-2x^2)^2(1+3x^2)^2}.$$

The diagram shows the graph of $y = 3 - 52x^2$ and part of the graph of

$$y = \frac{1}{(1-2x^2)^2(1+3x^2)^2}.$$

Use your expansion to find an approximation to the area of the region shaded in the diagram.

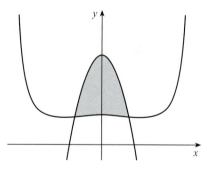

Revision exercise 3

1 Find in the form $ax + by + c = 0$ the equation of the tangent to each of the following curves at the point $x = \pi$.

(a) $y = \cos x$ (b) $y = \sin x$ (c) $y = \tan x$

(d) $y = 3\cos \frac{1}{2}x + 2\sin \frac{1}{2}x$ (e) $y = 2\sec x$ (f) $y = 3\tan \frac{1}{4}x$

2 Differentiate xe^x with respect to x. Hence integrate xe^x.   (OCR, adapted)

3 A curve has parametric equations $x = 3t^2 + 2t$, $y = 2t^2 + 3t$. Find the coordinates of the point where the tangent has gradient $\frac{3}{4}$.

4 Determine whether or not the point $(1, 2, -1)$ lies on the line passing through $(3, 1, 2)$ and $(5, 0, 5)$.

5 Find the gradient of the curve with equation $y = \cos \frac{1}{2}\pi x$ at the point for which $x = 1$. Hence find the equation of the normal at this point, giving your answer in the form $ax + by = c$.

6 Find $\displaystyle\int x\sec^2 x \, dx$.   (OCR)

7 A curve is defined parametrically by $x = \sqrt{3}\tan\theta$, $y = \sqrt{3}\cos\theta$, $0 \leqslant \theta \leqslant \pi$.

(a) Find $\dfrac{dy}{dx}$ in terms of θ.

(b) Find the equation of the tangent to the curve at the point where $\theta = \frac{1}{6}\pi$.   (OCR)

8 (a) Expand $(1 + 4x)^{\frac{1}{2}}$ in ascending powers of x, up to and including the term in x^2, simplifying the coefficients.

(b) State the set of values of x for which the expansion is valid.

(c) In the expansion of $(1 + kx)(1 + 4x)^{\frac{1}{2}}$, the coefficient of x is 7. Find the constant k and hence the coefficient of x^2.   (OCR)

9 Find the coordinates of the mid-point M of the line segment joining $A(8, 1, -1)$ and $B(2, -3, 5)$.

C is the point with coordinates $(2, 3, -4)$. Find the vector equation of the line through M parallel to the line AC.

10 (a) Use the derivative of $\cos x$ to prove that $\dfrac{d}{dx}(\sec x) = \sec x \tan x$.

(b) Use the substitution $u = \sec x$ to find the exact value of $\displaystyle\int_0^{\frac{1}{3}\pi} \sec^3 x \tan^3 x \, dx$.

11 (a) Differentiate $x\sqrt{2-x}$ with respect to x.

(b) Find $\displaystyle\int x\sqrt{2-x} \, dx$

    (i) by using the substitution $2 - x = u$,   (ii) by integration by parts.

12 The diagram shows points O, A and B, with $\overrightarrow{OA} = \mathbf{a}$ and $\overrightarrow{OB} = \mathbf{b}$.

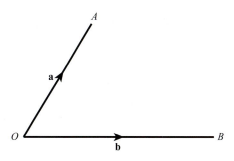

(a) Make a sketch of the diagram and mark the points C and D such that $\overrightarrow{OC} = \mathbf{a} + 2\mathbf{b}$ and $\overrightarrow{OD} = 2\mathbf{a} + \mathbf{b}$.

(b) Express $\overrightarrow{DC}$ in terms of $\mathbf{a}$ and $\mathbf{b}$, simplifying your answer.

(c) Prove that $ABCD$ is a parallelogram.   (OCR)

13 A curve is given parametrically by the equations $x = \sin t$, $y = t \cos t$, for $0 \leqslant t \leqslant \frac{1}{2}\pi$. Find an expression for $\dfrac{dy}{dx}$ terms of t, and find the cartesian equation of the curve. Check your answer by drawing the curve on your calculator from the parametric equations and from your cartesian equation, and comparing the results.

14 (a) Show that $\dfrac{d}{dx}\{e^{3x}(\cos 2x + k \sin 2x)\} = e^{3x}\{(3k - 2) \sin 2x + (2k + 3) \cos 2x\}$, where k is a constant.

(b) By letting $k = \frac{2}{3}$, find $\displaystyle\int e^{3x} \cos 2x \, dx$.

(c) Find $\displaystyle\int e^{3x} \sin 2x \, dx$.   (OCR)

15 A curve has parametric equations $x = 2 \cos^2 \theta$, $y = 3 \sin 2\theta$. Find the value of $\dfrac{dy}{dx}$ at the point on this curve where $\theta = \frac{1}{8}\pi$. Express y^2 as a function of x.   (OCR)

16 Find the following integrals.

(a) $\displaystyle\int \sin\left(2x + \frac{1}{6}\pi\right) dx$ (b) $\displaystyle\int \sin^2 3x \, dx$ (c) $\displaystyle\int \sin^2 2x \cos 2x \, dx$

17 (a) Obtain the expansion of $(8 + y)^{\frac{1}{3}}$ in ascending powers of y, up to and including the term in y^2.

(b) State the set of values for which the expansion is valid.

(c) Show that, if k^3 and higher powers of k are neglected, $(8 + 2k + k^2)^{\frac{1}{3}} = 2 + \frac{1}{6}k + \frac{5}{72}k^2$.

(d) Write down the expansion of $(8 - 2k + k^2)^{\frac{1}{3}}$ in ascending powers of k, up to and including the term in k^2.   (OCR)

18 Find the equation of the tangent at the point P with parameter t to the curve with parametric equations $x = ct$, $y = \dfrac{c}{t}$, where c is a constant. Show that, if this tangent meets the x- and y-axes at X and Y, then P is the mid-point of XY.

19 A straight line has vector equation $\mathbf{r} = \begin{pmatrix} 1 \\ 2 \end{pmatrix} + t\begin{pmatrix} 3 \\ 4 \end{pmatrix}$. Find its cartesian equation.

20 The angle made by a wasp's wings with the horizontal is given by the equation $\theta = 0.4 \sin 600t$ radians, where t is the time in seconds. How many times a second do its wings oscillate? Find an expression for $\dfrac{d\theta}{dt}$, the angular velocity, in radians per second. What is the value of θ when the angular velocity has

(a) its greatest magnitude,   (b) its smallest magnitude?

21 (a) By using the substitution $x = a \sin \theta$, show that

$$\int_{\frac{1}{2}a}^{a} \sqrt{a^2 - x^2} \, dx = \tfrac{1}{2}a^2\left(\tfrac{1}{3}\pi - \tfrac{1}{4}\sqrt{3}\right).$$

(b) The diagram shows a circle $x^2 + y^2 = a^2$ and the line $x = \tfrac{1}{2}a$. Find the area of the shaded region giving your answer in an exact form.   (OCR)

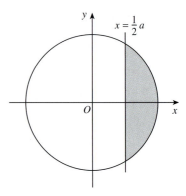

22 A curve is given parametrically by the equations $x = t(1 + t)$, $y = t^2(1 + t)$.

(a) Find $\dfrac{dy}{dx}$ in terms of t.

(b) Find the equation of the tangent to the curve at the point where $t = 2$, giving your answer in the form $ax + by + c = 0$.

(c) By first simplifying $\dfrac{y}{x}$, show that the curve has cartesian equation $x^3 = xy + y^2$.   (OCR)

23 Expand $(1 - x + x^2)^{\frac{1}{2}}$ as a series in ascending powers of x up to and including the term in x^3.

24 Find the vector equation of the straight line parallel to $\mathbf{r} = \begin{pmatrix} -2 \\ 1 \\ 3 \end{pmatrix} + s \begin{pmatrix} 1 \\ -1 \\ 1 \end{pmatrix}$ through the point $(2, -1, 4)$.

25 Find

(a) $\displaystyle\int_{\frac{1}{4}\pi}^{\frac{1}{3}\pi} \cot^4 x \, dx,$

(b) $\displaystyle\int_{0}^{\frac{1}{2}\pi} \frac{\cos x}{\sqrt{1 + \sin x}} \, dx,$

(c) $\displaystyle\int_{0}^{\frac{1}{4}\pi} x \tan^2 x \, dx,$

(d) $\displaystyle\int_{0}^{\frac{1}{2}\pi} e^{3x} \cos 4x \, dx.$

26 Sketch the graph of $y = \sec x$ between $x = -\tfrac{1}{2}\pi$ and $x = \tfrac{1}{2}\pi$. The part of the curve between $x = -\tfrac{1}{4}\pi$ and $x = \tfrac{1}{4}\pi$ is rotated about the x-axis to form a solid of revolution. Find the volume of this solid, giving your answer as a multiple of π.

27 The parametric equations of a curve are $x = t^2$, $y = 2t$.

(a) Prove that the equation of the tangent at the point with parameter t is $ty = x + t^2$.

(b) The tangent at the point $P(16, 8)$ meets the tangent at the point $Q(9, -6)$ at the point R. Find the coordinates of the point R.

(c) Prove that the line $2y - 4x - 1 = 0$ is a tangent to the curve, and find the parameter at the point of contact.   (OCR)

28 By squaring both sides of the expansion $(1 + x)^{-1} = 1 - x + x^2 - x^3 + \dots$, obtain
    the expansion of $(1 + x)^{-2}$ up to and including the term in x^3. Then use
    $(1 + x)^{-2}(1 + x)^{-1} \equiv (1 + x)^{-3}$ to obtain the expansion of $(1 + x)^{-3}$ up to and including
    the term in x^3.

29 Find the vector equation of the line which passes through $(1, 4, 2)$ and $(-2, 3, 3)$,
    and find the coordinates of its point of intersection with the line with vector equation

$$\mathbf{r} = \begin{pmatrix} 1 \\ 0 \\ 2 \end{pmatrix} + t \begin{pmatrix} 3 \\ -1 \\ -1 \end{pmatrix}.$$

30 (a) Find the area of the region enclosed between $y = \tan x$ and the x-axis from $x = 0$ to
        $x = \frac{1}{3}\pi$.

    (b) Find the volume generated when this area is rotated about the x-axis.

31 The parametric equations of a curve C are $x = a \sin \theta$, $y = 2a \cos \theta$, where a is a positive
    constant and $-\pi < \theta \le \pi$.

    (a) Show that the equation of the tangent to C at the point with parameter θ is
        $2x \sin \theta + y \cos \theta = 2a$.

    (b) This tangent passes through the point $(2a, 3a)$.

        (i) Show that θ satisfies an equation of the form $5 \sin(\theta + \alpha) = 2$, and state the value
            of $\tan \alpha$.

        (ii) Hence find the two possible values of θ.   (OCR)

32 (a) Use the substitution $y = \frac{1}{2}\pi - x$ to show that $\displaystyle\int_0^{\frac{1}{2}\pi} \sin^2 x \, dx = \int_0^{\frac{1}{2}\pi} \cos^2 y \, dy.$

    (b) Show that $\displaystyle\int_0^{\frac{1}{2}\pi} \cos^2 y \, dy = \int_0^{\frac{1}{2}\pi} \cos^2 x \, dx$, and $\displaystyle\int_0^{\frac{1}{2}\pi} \sin^2 x \, dx = \int_0^{\frac{1}{2}\pi} \cos^2 x \, dx.$

    (c) Find $\displaystyle\int_0^{\frac{1}{2}\pi} (\sin^2 x + \cos^2 x) \, dx$ and hence show that $\displaystyle\int_0^{\frac{1}{2}\pi} \sin^2 x \, dx = \frac{1}{4}\pi.$

33 Write down the first five terms in the expansion of $(1 + 2x)^{\frac{1}{2}}$. Show that, when
    differentiated, the result is zero plus the first four terms in the expansion of $(1 + 2x)^{-\frac{1}{2}}$.
    Investigate similarly the effect of differentiation on the terms of $(1 + 3x)^{\frac{1}{3}}$ and $(1 + x)^{-3}$.

34 A curve has parametric equations $x = 2 + t$, $y = 1 + mt$, where m is a constant. Find the
    cartesian equation of the curve. Interpret the geometric meaning of m.

35 Use the substitution $x = u^2$ to calculate the value of $\displaystyle\int_0^1 e^{\sqrt{x}} \, dx.$

36 Determine whether or not the straight line with vector equation $\mathbf{r} = \begin{pmatrix} -5 \\ 1 \\ -2 \end{pmatrix} + t \begin{pmatrix} 4 \\ -3 \\ 4 \end{pmatrix}$

    meets the line segment joining $(1, -1, 2)$ and $(4, -7, 8)$.

37* *A* is the point (a, b). The parametric equations of a straight line *l* passing through *A* are $x = a + t\cos\theta$, $y = b + t\sin\theta$, where θ is fixed and *t* is a parameter.

(a) Find the gradient of this line, and interpret geometrically the meaning of *t*.

(b) Write down the equation of a circle *C* whose centre is the origin and whose radius is *R*.

(c) Find a quadratic equation in *t* for the parameters of the points on *l* where *l* meets *C*.

(d) Deduce from your answer to part (c) that the roots are coincident if
$R^2 = (a\sin\theta - b\cos\theta)^2$.

(e) If θ is now allowed to vary, find the maximum value of $a\sin\theta - b\cos\theta$, and deduce that, for the equation in part (d) to be satisfied, $a^2 + b^2 \geqslant R^2$. Interpret this condition geometrically.

6 Rational functions

This chapter is about rational functions, which are fractions in which the numerator and the denominator are both polynomials. When you have completed the chapter, you should

- be able to simplify rational functions by cancelling
- be able to add, subtract, multiply and divide rational functions
- be able to split simple rational functions into their partial fractions
- be able to use partial fractions to integrate some rational functions and to find binomial expansions
- know the terms 'quotient' and 'remainder', and be able to find them when a quartic polynomial is divided by a quadratic polynomial.

6.1 Simplifying rational functions

In C1 Chapter 9 you saw that in many ways polynomials behave like integers. You can add integers or polynomials, subtract them and multiply them, and the result is another integer or polynomial. Similarly rational functions (also called 'algebraic fractions') have many properties in common with ordinary fractions. For example, just as you can cancel a fraction like $\frac{10}{15}$ to get $\frac{2}{3}$, you can cancel a rational function, but it is a little more complicated. Since you cancel $\frac{10}{15}$ in your head, it is worth looking to see what is actually happening:

$$\frac{10}{15} = \frac{2 \times 5}{3 \times 5} = \frac{2}{3}.$$

Start by factorising the numerator and denominator. Then you can divide the numerator and denominator by any common factor (5 in the example) to get the simplified fraction.

The same process is used to simplify rational functions. However, you need to realise that you cannot cancel common factors of single terms. For example, you can't cancel the 2s which appear in the numerator and denominator of $\frac{x-2}{2x-1}$. A fraction bar acts like a bracket, so $\frac{x-2}{2x-1}$ must be thought of as $\frac{(x-2)}{(2x-1)}$. Since $x-2$ and $2x-1$ have no common factor, no cancellation is possible.

Example 6.1.1

Simplify (a) $\dfrac{x-2}{2x-4}$, (b) $\dfrac{2x-3}{6x^2-x-12}$, (c) $\dfrac{3x^2-8x+4}{6x^2-7x+2}$.

(a) $\dfrac{x-2}{2x-4} = \dfrac{(x-2)}{2(x-2)} = \dfrac{1}{2}$.

(b) $\dfrac{2x-3}{6x^2-x-12} = \dfrac{(2x-3)}{(2x-3)(3x+4)} = \dfrac{1}{3x+4}$.

(c) $\dfrac{3x^2-8x+4}{6x^2-7x+2} = \dfrac{(x-2)(3x-2)}{(2x-1)(3x-2)} = \dfrac{x-2}{2x-1}$.

You cannot cancel the last answer any further. If you have factorised fully, you can only cancel factors if they are exactly the same, or if one is the negative of the other. For example, you could cancel $\dfrac{2x-3}{3-2x}$ as $\dfrac{-(3-2x)}{3-2x} = -1$.

You can check these simplifications by putting x equal to a particular value, say $x = 0$ (provided your chosen value of x does not make the denominator equal to 0). In part (a), putting $x = 0$ in the original expression gives $\frac{-2}{-4} = \frac{1}{2}$, which is the same as the simplified version. In part (b), the original becomes $\frac{-3}{-12} = \frac{1}{4}$ and the answer becomes $\frac{1}{4}$. In part (c), the original is $\frac{4}{2} = 2$ and the answer is $\frac{-2}{-1} = 2$.

Exercise 6A

1 Simplify

   (a) $\dfrac{4x-8}{2}$,

   (b) $\dfrac{9x+6}{3}$,

   (c) $\dfrac{2x^2-6x+12}{2}$,

   (d) $\dfrac{6}{18x+12}$,

   (e) $\dfrac{(2x+6)(2x-4)}{4}$,

   (f) $\dfrac{x}{x^3+x^2+x}$.

2 Simplify

   (a) $\dfrac{5x+15}{x+3}$,

   (b) $\dfrac{x+1}{4x+4}$,

   (c) $\dfrac{2x+5}{5+2x}$,

   (d) $\dfrac{3x-7}{7-3x}$,

   (e) $\dfrac{(2x+8)(3x+6)}{(2x+4)(3x+12)}$,

   (f) $\dfrac{2x^2-6x+10}{3x^2-9x+15}$.

3 Simplify

   (a) $\dfrac{x^2+5x+4}{x+1}$,

   (b) $\dfrac{x-2}{x^2+5x-14}$,

   (c) $\dfrac{6x^2+4x}{4x^2+2x}$,

   (d) $\dfrac{x^2+5x-6}{x^2-4x+3}$,

   (e) $\dfrac{2x^2+5x-12}{2x^2-11x+12}$,

   (f) $\dfrac{8x^2-6x-20}{2+5x-3x^2}$.

6.2 Multiplying and dividing rational functions

Multiplying and dividing rational functions is just like multiplying and dividing fractions in arithmetic.

Example 6.2.1

Simplify $\dfrac{91}{30} \times \dfrac{65}{49} \times \dfrac{12}{169}$.

For this example two 'methods' are shown: but the first is really not a practical method and involves hard work – it is the second method which is recommended.

Method 1   You could proceed by brute force and say that

$$\dfrac{91}{30} \times \dfrac{65}{49} \times \dfrac{12}{169} = \dfrac{91 \times 65 \times 12}{30 \times 49 \times 169}$$

$$= \dfrac{70\,980}{248\,430}.$$

If you want to get this fraction into its lowest terms, you now have to find factors which divide into the numerator and denominator, which is time consuming.

Eventually you would find that $70\,980 = 2 \times 35\,490$ and $248\,430 = 7 \times 35\,490$, so

$$\frac{91}{30} \times \frac{65}{49} \times \frac{12}{169} = \frac{70\,980}{248\,430}$$

$$= \frac{2}{7}.$$

Method 2 Start by expressing the numerators and denominators as products of factors.

As $91 = 7 \times 13$, $65 = 5 \times 13$, $12 = 2^2 \times 3$ and $30 = 2 \times 3 \times 5$, $49 = 7^2$, $169 = 13^2$, the fraction can be written as

$$\frac{7 \times 13}{2 \times 3 \times 5} \times \frac{5 \times 13}{7^2} \times \frac{2^2 \times 3}{13^2} = \frac{7 \times 13 \times 5 \times 13 \times 2^2 \times 3}{2 \times 3 \times 5 \times 7^2 \times 13^2}$$

$$= \frac{2^2 \times 3 \times 5 \times 7 \times 13^2}{2 \times 3 \times 5 \times 7^2 \times 13^2}$$

$$= \frac{2}{7}.$$

Expressing the numerator and denominator as products of factors is also profitable when dealing with algebraic fractions.

Example 6.2.2

Simplify (a) $\dfrac{2}{x} \times \dfrac{x^2 - 2x}{x - 2}$, (b) $\dfrac{x^2 - 4x + 3}{3x^2 - 13x + 12} \times \dfrac{6x^2 - 23x + 20}{x^2 - x}$.

(a) Start by expressing the numerators and denominators as products of factors. The numerators are 2 and $x(x - 2)$, and the denominators are x and $x - 2$.

Then

$$\frac{2}{x} \times \frac{x^2 - 2x}{x - 2} = \frac{2}{x} \times \frac{x(x - 2)}{x - 2}$$

$$= \frac{2x(x - 2)}{x(x - 2)}.$$

You can now divide both the numerator and denominator by $x(x - 2)$, to get

$$\frac{2}{x} \times \frac{x^2 - 2x}{x - 2} = 2.$$

(b) Using the same method as for part (a),

$$\frac{x^2 - 4x + 3}{3x^2 - 13x + 12} \times \frac{6x^2 - 23x + 20}{x^2 - x} = \frac{(x - 1)(x - 3)}{(3x - 4)(x - 3)} \times \frac{(2x - 5)(3x - 4)}{x(x - 1)}$$

$$= \frac{(x - 1)(x - 3)(2x - 5)(3x - 4)}{(3x - 4)(x - 3)x(x - 1)}$$

$$= \frac{(2x - 5)}{x}.$$

Division is defined as the reverse of multiplication in the sense that

$$a \times k = b \quad \Leftrightarrow \quad b \div k = a \quad \text{(provided that } k \neq 0\text{)}.$$

Thus $\dfrac{4}{15} \div \dfrac{3}{20}$ is the number (or fraction) x, such that $\dfrac{3}{20}x = \dfrac{4}{15}$.

Multiply both sides of the equation by the inverse (reciprocal) of $\dfrac{3}{20}$, which is $\dfrac{20}{3}$:

$$\frac{20}{3} \times \left(\frac{3}{20}x\right) = \frac{20}{3} \times \frac{4}{15} \quad \Leftrightarrow \quad \left(\frac{20}{3} \times \frac{3}{20}\right)x = \frac{20}{3} \times \frac{4}{15} \quad \Leftrightarrow \quad 1x = \frac{20}{3} \times \frac{4}{15}$$

$$\Leftrightarrow \quad x = \frac{20}{3} \times \frac{4}{15}.$$

This justifies the method for dividing by fractions in arithmetic ('turn it upside down and multiply'), which you may have used before. Then

$$x = \frac{20}{3} \times \frac{4}{15} = \frac{2 \times 2 \times 5}{3} \times \frac{2 \times 2}{3 \times 5} = \frac{16}{9}.$$

In general, if a, b, c and d are integers, and $x = \dfrac{c}{d} \div \dfrac{a}{b}$, then $\dfrac{a}{b}x = \dfrac{c}{d}$.

Multiplying by the inverse of $\dfrac{a}{b}$, which is $\dfrac{b}{a}$, gives $\dfrac{b}{a} \times \dfrac{a}{b}x = \dfrac{b}{a} \times \dfrac{c}{d} \quad \Leftrightarrow \quad x = \dfrac{b}{a} \times \dfrac{c}{d}$.

The same is true when a, b, c and d are polynomials, so

$$\frac{c(x)}{d(x)} \div \frac{a(x)}{b(x)} = \frac{c(x)}{d(x)} \times \frac{b(x)}{a(x)}.$$

Example 6.2.3
Simplify   (a) $\dfrac{3x}{x^2} \div \dfrac{x+1}{2x}$,   (b) $\dfrac{x-2}{x^2-4x+3} \div \dfrac{x}{2x^2-7x+3}$.

(a) $\dfrac{3x}{x^2} \div \dfrac{x+1}{2x} = \dfrac{3x}{x^2} \times \dfrac{2x}{x+1}$

$$= \frac{3x \times 2x}{x^2 \times (x+1)}$$

$$= \frac{6x^2}{x^2(x+1)}$$

$$= \frac{6}{x+1}.$$

(b) $\dfrac{x-2}{x^2-4x+3} \div \dfrac{x}{2x^2-7x+3} = \dfrac{x-2}{x^2-4x+3} \times \dfrac{2x^2-7x+3}{x}$

$$= \frac{x-2}{(x-1)(x-3)} \times \frac{(2x-1)(x-3)}{x}$$

$$= \frac{(x-2)(2x-1)(x-3)}{(x-1)(x-3)x}$$

$$= \frac{(x-2)(2x-1)}{x(x-1)}.$$

Remember that you can always check by putting x equal to a number and checking that your answer and the original expression simplify to the same value. For example, if you put $x = 6$ in part (b), you get

$$\frac{x-2}{x^2-4x+3} \div \frac{x}{2x^2-7x+3} = \frac{4}{15} \div \frac{6}{33}$$

which is $\dfrac{22}{15}$.

Putting $x = 6$ in the answer $\dfrac{(x-2)(2x-1)}{x(x-1)}$ gives

$$\frac{(x-2)(2x-1)}{x(x-1)} = \frac{4 \times 11}{6 \times 5} = \frac{22}{15}.$$

The fact that both answers are the same ($\frac{22}{15}$) does not prove that $\dfrac{(x-2)(2x-1)}{x(x-1)}$ is correct; but if the answers were different it would certainly be incorrect.

Exercise 6B

1 Simplify

(a) $\dfrac{1}{x} \times \dfrac{x^2}{2}$,

(b) $\dfrac{3}{2x^2} \times \dfrac{5x}{6}$,

(c) $\dfrac{3}{2x^2} \times \dfrac{5x}{6} \times \dfrac{4x^3}{15}$,

(d) $\dfrac{(x-1)}{21x^2} \times \dfrac{7x}{6} \times \dfrac{12x^3}{(x-1)^2}$.

2 Simplify

(a) $\dfrac{2x+4}{10x^2} \times \dfrac{5x}{3x+6}$,

(b) $\dfrac{5x}{3x+15} \times \dfrac{2x+10}{4}$,

(c) $\dfrac{2x^2}{x+2} \times \dfrac{x^3+2x^2}{x^4}$,

(d) $\dfrac{4x+6}{x-4} \times \dfrac{3x-12}{2x+3}$.

3 Simplify

(a) $\dfrac{x^2-x}{x+1} \times \dfrac{x^2-1}{x-1}$,

(b) $\dfrac{x^2-4}{x+2} \times \dfrac{3x}{x-2}$,

(c) $\dfrac{x^2+9x+20}{x+3} \times \dfrac{3}{x+4}$,

(d) $\dfrac{x^2+3x+2}{x^2+4x+4} \times \dfrac{x^2+5x+6}{x^2+2x+1}$,

(e) $\dfrac{4x+12}{2x+2} \times \dfrac{x^2+2x+1}{x^2+6x+9}$,

(f) $\dfrac{4x^2-9}{9x^2-4} \times \dfrac{9x^2-12x+4}{4x^2-12x+9}$.

4 Simplify

(a) $\dfrac{3}{x^2} \div \dfrac{2}{3x}$,

(b) $\dfrac{x^2}{2} \div \dfrac{2}{x}$,

(c) $\dfrac{x}{x+1} \div \dfrac{2}{x(x+1)}$,

(d) $\dfrac{x+2}{x-1} \div \dfrac{2(x+2)}{x^2}$.

5 Simplify

(a) $\dfrac{x+2}{2x+3} \div \dfrac{2x+4}{8x+12}$,

(b) $\dfrac{x}{5-2x} \div \dfrac{3x}{2x-5}$,

(c) $\dfrac{1}{x^2+6x+8} \div \dfrac{1}{x^2+8x+16}$,

(d) $\dfrac{5x-1}{2x^2+x-3} \div \dfrac{1}{2x^2+7x+6}$,

(e) $\dfrac{x^2+5x-6}{x^2-5x+4} \div \dfrac{x^2+9x+18}{x^2-x-12}$,

(f) $\dfrac{-2x^2+7x-6}{8x^2-10x-3} \div \dfrac{7x-x^2-10}{5+19x-4x^2}$.

6.3 Adding and subtracting rational functions

In cancelling and simplifying rational functions, and in multiplying and dividing them, you worked in the same way as in normal arithmetic. To add and subtract rational functions you also follow the same principles as in arithmetic, but you need to take special care of signs.

In arithmetic, to calculate $\frac{11}{15} - \frac{7}{20}$ you start by finding the lowest common multiple (LCM) of 15 and 20. You can easily see that the LCM is 60. But if you couldn't spot it, you would factorise the denominators,

$$\frac{11}{15} - \frac{7}{20} = \frac{11}{3 \times 5} - \frac{7}{2 \times 2 \times 5},$$

from which you can work out that the LCM is $2 \times 2 \times 3 \times 5 = 60$. Now

$$\frac{11}{15} - \frac{7}{20} = \frac{11 \times 4}{15 \times 4} - \frac{7 \times 3}{20 \times 3} = \frac{44}{60} - \frac{21}{60} = \frac{44-21}{60} = \frac{23}{60}.$$

Example 6.3.1

Express as single fractions in their simplest forms

(a) $\dfrac{1}{x} - \dfrac{2}{3}$,   (b) $\dfrac{3}{x+2} - \dfrac{6}{2x-1}$,   (c) $x - \dfrac{1}{x+1}$.

(a) The LCM of x and 3 is $3x$. So $\dfrac{1}{x} - \dfrac{2}{3} = \dfrac{1 \times 3}{3x} - \dfrac{2 \times x}{3x} = \dfrac{3}{3x} - \dfrac{2x}{3x} = \dfrac{3-2x}{3x}$.

(b) The LCM of $x+2$ and $2x-1$ is $(x+2)(2x-1)$. Subtracting in the usual way,

$$\frac{3}{x+2} - \frac{6}{2x-1} = \frac{3(2x-1)}{(x+2)(2x-1)} - \frac{6(x+2)}{(x+2)(2x-1)}$$

$$= \frac{3(2x-1) - 6(x+2)}{(x+2)(2x-1)}$$

$$= \frac{6x-3-6x-12}{(x+2)(2x-1)}$$

$$= \frac{-15}{(x+2)(2x-1)}.$$

Notice the sign change which gives $-6x - 12$ in the third step.

(c) A problem which sometimes arises is the failure to recognise that x is the same as $\frac{x}{1}$. Then

$$x - \frac{1}{x+1} = \frac{x}{1} - \frac{1}{x+1}$$
$$= \frac{x(x+1) - 1}{x+1}$$
$$= \frac{x^2 + x - 1}{x+1}.$$

Don't forget to check mentally by substituting a numerical value for x which makes the calculations easy. Try $x = 1$ for part (a) and $x = 0$ for part (b).

Example 6.3.2

Express $\dfrac{31x - 8}{2x^2 + 3x - 2} - \dfrac{14}{x+2}$ as a single fraction in its lowest terms.

The first step, as before, is to find the LCM of the denominators. To do this, express the denominators as products of factors.

$2x^2 + 3x - 2 = (2x - 1)(x + 2)$ and $x + 2$ does not factorise further. So the lowest common multiple is $(2x - 1)(x + 2)$.

The solution then proceeds

$$\frac{31x - 8}{2x^2 + 3x - 2} - \frac{14}{x+2} = \frac{31x - 8}{(2x - 1)(x + 2)} - \frac{14}{x+2} = \frac{31x - 8 - 14(2x - 1)}{(2x - 1)(x + 2)}$$
$$= \frac{31x - 8 - 28x + 14}{(2x - 1)(x + 2)} = \frac{3x + 6}{(2x - 1)(x + 2)}$$
$$= \frac{3(x + 2)}{(2x - 1)(x + 2)} = \frac{3}{2x - 1}.$$

Example 6.3.3

Express $\dfrac{2x}{(x + 1)(x - 2)} - \dfrac{3x - 4}{(x - 2)(x + 3)}$ as a single fraction in its lowest terms.

The lowest common multiple is $(x + 1)(x - 2)(x + 3)$. Then

$$\frac{2x}{(x + 1)(x - 2)} - \frac{3x - 4}{(x - 2)(x + 3)} = \frac{2x \times (x + 3) - (3x - 4)(x + 1)}{(x + 1)(x - 2)(x + 3)}$$
$$= \frac{2x^2 + 6x - (3x^2 - x - 4)}{(x + 1)(x - 2)(x + 3)}$$
$$= \frac{2x^2 + 6x - 3x^2 + x + 4}{(x + 1)(x - 2)(x + 3)}$$
$$= \frac{-x^2 + 7x + 4}{(x + 1)(x - 2)(x + 3)}.$$

Since the numerator does not factorise, this is in its lowest terms.

Notice how the minus sign between the fractions was handled in this example. If you had decided, incorrectly, that the LCM was $(x + 1)(x - 2)^2(x + 3)$, you would have obtained the answer $\dfrac{-x^3 + 9x^2 - 10x - 8}{(x + 1)(x - 2)^2(x + 3)}$. It is now much harder to proceed because you would have to show that $x - 2$ is a factor of the numerator, and cancel it.

Exercise 6C

1 Simplify

(a) $\dfrac{2x}{3} - \dfrac{x}{4}$,

(b) $\dfrac{5x}{2} + \dfrac{x}{3} - \dfrac{3x}{4}$,

(c) $\dfrac{x + 2}{3} + \dfrac{x + 1}{4}$,

(d) $\dfrac{2x + 1}{5} - \dfrac{x + 2}{3}$,

(e) $\dfrac{(x + 1)(x + 3)}{2} + \dfrac{(x + 2)^2}{4}$,

(f) $3x + 4 - \dfrac{2(x + 3)}{5}$.

2 Simplify

(a) $\dfrac{2}{x} + \dfrac{3}{4}$,

(b) $\dfrac{1}{2x} + \dfrac{2}{x}$,

(c) $\dfrac{5}{4x} - \dfrac{2}{3x}$,

(d) $\dfrac{x + 3}{2x} + \dfrac{x - 4}{x}$,

(e) $\dfrac{3x - 1}{x} - \dfrac{x + 1}{2}$,

(f) $\dfrac{x + 1}{x} + \dfrac{x + 1}{x^2}$.

3 Simplify

(a) $\dfrac{2}{x + 1} + \dfrac{4}{x + 3}$,

(b) $\dfrac{5}{x - 2} + \dfrac{3}{2x + 1}$,

(c) $\dfrac{4}{x + 3} - \dfrac{2}{x + 4}$,

(d) $\dfrac{7}{x - 3} - \dfrac{2}{x + 1}$,

(e) $\dfrac{4}{2x + 3} + \dfrac{5}{3x + 1}$,

(f) $\dfrac{6}{2x + 1} - \dfrac{2}{5x - 3}$.

4 Simplify

(a) $\dfrac{5}{3x - 1} - \dfrac{2}{2x + 1}$,

(b) $\dfrac{6}{4x + 1} - \dfrac{3}{2x}$,

(c) $\dfrac{3x}{x + 2} + \dfrac{5x}{x + 1}$,

(d) $\dfrac{8x}{2x - 1} - \dfrac{x}{x + 2}$,

(e) $\dfrac{x + 1}{x + 2} + \dfrac{x + 2}{x + 1}$,

(f) $\dfrac{2x + 1}{x + 4} - \dfrac{x - 5}{x - 2}$.

5 Simplify

(a) $\dfrac{2x + 3}{(x + 1)(x + 3)} + \dfrac{2}{x + 3}$,

(b) $\dfrac{5x}{x^2 + x - 2} + \dfrac{1}{x + 2}$,

(c) $\dfrac{5}{x - 3} + \dfrac{x + 2}{x^2 - 3x}$,

(d) $\dfrac{8}{x^2 - 4} - \dfrac{4}{x - 2}$,

(e) $\dfrac{13 - 3x}{x^2 - 2x - 3} + \dfrac{4}{x + 1}$,

(f) $\dfrac{11x + 27}{2x^2 + 11x - 6} - \dfrac{3}{x + 6}$.

6 Given that $\dfrac{(x + 2)f(x)}{(x + 3)(x^2 - x - 6)} \equiv 1$, find $f(x)$ in its simplest form.

7 Given that $P(x) \equiv \dfrac{5}{x + 4}$ and $Q(x) \equiv \dfrac{2}{x - 3}$,

(a) find $2P(x) + 3Q(x)$ in simplified form,

(b) find $R(x)$, where $R(x) + 4Q(x) \equiv 3P(x)$.

8 Simplify

(a) $\dfrac{2}{x^3 - 3x^2 + 2x} + \dfrac{1}{x^3 - 6x^2 + 11x - 6}$,

(b) $\dfrac{5}{2x + 1} - \dfrac{4}{3x - 1} - \dfrac{7x - 10}{6x^2 + x - 1}$.

6.4 Partial fractions with simple denominators

Sometimes you need to reverse the process of adding or subtracting rational functions. For example, instead of adding $\dfrac{3}{2x-1}$ and $\dfrac{2}{x-2}$ to get $\dfrac{7x-8}{(2x-1)(x-2)}$, you might need to find

the fractions which, when added together, give $\dfrac{7x-8}{(2x-1)(x-2)}$.

This process is called **splitting into partial fractions**.

Suppose you need to calculate

$$\int \frac{7x-8}{(2x-1)(x-2)}\,dx.$$

You cannot do this as it stands. However, if you rewrite the integrand using partial fractions, you can integrate it, as follows:

$$\int \frac{7x-8}{(2x-1)(x-2)}\,dx = \int \left(\frac{3}{2x-1}+\frac{2}{x-2}\right)dx = \int \frac{3}{2x-1}\,dx + \int \frac{2}{x-2}\,dx$$

$$= \tfrac{3}{2}\ln|2x-1| + 2\ln|x-2| + k.$$

> You may find it helpful to look up C3 Sections 5.5 and 5.6 on definite integrals involving logarithms.

In this case, to split $\dfrac{7x-8}{(2x-1)(x-2)}$ into partial fractions, start by supposing that you can write it in the form

$$\frac{7x-8}{(2x-1)(x-2)} \equiv \frac{A}{2x-1}+\frac{B}{x-2},$$

where the identity sign $\equiv$ means that the two sides are equal for all values of x for which they are defined: here, all values except $x = \tfrac{1}{2}$ and $x = 2$, where the denominators become 0.

From this point, there are two methods you can use.

Equating coefficients method

Expressing the right side as a single fraction,

$$\frac{7x-8}{(2x-1)(x-2)} \equiv \frac{A(x-2)+B(2x-1)}{(2x-1)(x-2)}.$$

Multiplying both sides of the identity by $(2x-1)(x-2)$,

$$7x-8 \equiv A(x-2)+B(2x-1).$$

You can now find A and B by the method of equating coefficients (C2 Section 8.3).

Equating coefficients of x^1: $7 = A + 2B$.
Equating coefficients of x^0: $-8 = -2A - B$.

Solving these two equations simultaneously gives $A = 3$, $B = 2$.

Substitution method

To find A, multiply both sides of the identity $\dfrac{7x-8}{(2x-1)(x-2)} \equiv \dfrac{A}{2x-1} + \dfrac{B}{x-2}$ by $2x-1$ to obtain

$$\frac{7x-8}{x-2} \equiv A + B\frac{2x-1}{x-2}.$$

Putting $x = \frac{1}{2}$ gives $A = \dfrac{\frac{7}{2}-8}{\frac{1}{2}-2} = \dfrac{-\frac{9}{2}}{-\frac{3}{2}} = 3.$

Similarly, to find B, multiply the identity by $x - 2$ to get $\dfrac{7x-8}{2x-1} \equiv A\dfrac{x-2}{2x-1} + B.$

Putting $x = 2$ gives $B = \dfrac{7 \times 2 - 8}{2 \times 2 - 1} = \dfrac{6}{3} = 2.$

By either method $\dfrac{7x-8}{(2x-1)(x-2)} \equiv \dfrac{3}{2x-1} + \dfrac{2}{x-2}.$

There are three important points to make about these solutions.

- Always check your answer by testing it with a simple value of x. For example, putting $x = 0$ gives -4 for the left side, and $-3 - 1 = -4$ for the right.

- In the substitution method, the values $x = \frac{1}{2}$ and $x = 2$ are chosen because they give simple equations for A and B. You could have chosen other values for x, but the equations for A and B would have been more complicated. Try it and see!

- You may be worried that, at the beginning of the example, the values $x = \frac{1}{2}$ and $x = 2$ were excluded, but they are then used in the substitution method. The fact is that $\dfrac{7x-8}{x-2} \equiv 3 + 2\dfrac{2x-1}{x-2}$ is true for all x except $x = 2$, including $x = \frac{1}{2}$. So it is all right to use $x = \frac{1}{2}$ to find A, since there is no need to exclude $x = \frac{1}{2}$ in the identity $\dfrac{7x-8}{x-2} \equiv A + B\dfrac{2x-1}{x-2}$. But the partial fraction form $\dfrac{A}{2x-1} + \dfrac{B}{x-2} \equiv \dfrac{7x-8}{(2x-1)(x-2)}$ has no meaning when $x = \frac{1}{2}$ (or when $x = 2$).

> An expression of the form $\dfrac{ax+b}{(px+q)(rx+s)}$ can be split into partial
>
> fractions of the form $\dfrac{A}{px+q} + \dfrac{B}{rx+s}.$

Example 6.4.1

Split $\dfrac{13x-6}{3x^2-2x}$ into partial fractions.

Rewrite $\dfrac{13x-6}{3x^2-2x}$ in the form $\dfrac{13x-6}{x(3x-2)}$, and then put $\dfrac{13x-6}{x(3x-2)} \equiv \dfrac{A}{x} + \dfrac{B}{3x-2}.$

Using the equating coefficients method, $\dfrac{13x - 6}{x(3x - 2)} \equiv \dfrac{A(3x - 2) + Bx}{x(3x - 2)}$, so

$A(3x - 2) + Bx \equiv 13x - 6$.

Equating coefficients of x^1: $3A + B = 13$.
Equating coefficients of x^0: $-2A$ $= -6$.

Solving these two equations simultaneously gives $A = 3$, $B = 4$.

Therefore $\dfrac{13x - 6}{x(3x - 2)} \equiv \dfrac{3}{x} + \dfrac{4}{3x - 2}$.

Example 6.4.2

Split $\dfrac{12x}{(x + 1)(2x + 3)(x - 3)}$ into partial fractions.

Put $\dfrac{12x}{(x + 1)(2x + 3)(x - 3)} \equiv \dfrac{A}{x + 1} + \dfrac{B}{2x + 3} + \dfrac{C}{x - 3}$.

Use the substitution method: multiplying by $x + 1$ gives

$$\dfrac{12x}{(2x + 3)(x - 3)} \equiv A + B\dfrac{x + 1}{2x + 3} + C\dfrac{x + 1}{x - 3}.$$

Putting $x = -1$, $A = \dfrac{12 \times (-1)}{(2 \times (-1) + 3)((-1) - 3)} = \dfrac{-12}{1 \times (-4)} = 3$.

Similarly, after multiplying by $2x + 3$ and putting $x = -\frac{3}{2}$, you get $B = -8$; multiplying by $x - 3$ and putting $x = 3$ gives $C = 1$.

Therefore $\dfrac{12x}{(x + 1)(2x + 3)(x - 3)} \equiv \dfrac{3}{x + 1} - \dfrac{8}{2x + 3} + \dfrac{1}{x - 3}$.

If you try to use the equating coefficients method in this example, you get three simultaneous equations, with three unknowns, to solve. In this case, the substitution method is easier.

Example 6.4.3

Calculate the value of $\displaystyle\int_1^4 \dfrac{1}{x(x - 5)}\, dx$.

Write $\dfrac{1}{x(x - 5)}$ in partial fraction form, as $\dfrac{1}{x(x - 5)} \equiv \dfrac{A}{x} + \dfrac{B}{x - 5}$.

Either method gives $A = -\frac{1}{5}$ and $B = \frac{1}{5}$, so $\dfrac{1}{x(x - 5)} \equiv \dfrac{-\frac{1}{5}}{x} + \dfrac{\frac{1}{5}}{x - 5}$.

Therefore $\displaystyle\int_1^4 \dfrac{1}{x(x - 5)}\, dx = \int_1^4 \left(-\dfrac{\frac{1}{5}}{x} + \dfrac{\frac{1}{5}}{x - 5} \right) dx$

$= \left[-\tfrac{1}{5} \ln |x| + \tfrac{1}{5} \ln |x - 5| \right]_1^4$

$= \left(-\tfrac{1}{5} \ln 4 + \tfrac{1}{5} \ln 1 \right) - \left(-\tfrac{1}{5} \ln 1 + \tfrac{1}{5} \ln 4 \right)$

$= -\tfrac{1}{5} \ln 4 + \tfrac{1}{5} \ln 1 + \tfrac{1}{5} \ln 1 - \tfrac{1}{5} \ln 4$

$= \tfrac{2}{5} \ln 1 - \tfrac{2}{5} \ln 4 = -\tfrac{2}{5} \ln 4$.

Example 6.4.4

Find $\displaystyle\int_0^\infty \frac{1}{(x+1)(2x+3)}\,dx$

You will remember from C2 Section 5.8 that $\displaystyle\int_a^\infty f(x)\,dx$ means the limit as $s \to \infty$ of $\displaystyle\int_a^s f(x)\,dx$, provided that the limit exists. So begin by finding $\displaystyle\int_0^s \frac{1}{(x+1)(2x+3)}\,dx$.

In partial fractions,

$$\frac{1}{(x+1)(2x+3)} \equiv \frac{1}{x+1} - \frac{2}{2x+3},$$

so

$$\int_0^s \frac{1}{(x+1)(2x+3)}\,dx = \int_0^s \frac{1}{x+1}\,dx - \int_0^s \frac{2}{2x+3}\,dx$$

$$= [\ln(x+1) - \ln(2x+3)]_0^s$$

$$= (\ln(s+1) - \ln(2s+3)) - (\ln 1 - \ln 3)$$

$$= (\ln(s+1) - \ln(2s+3)) + \ln 3.$$

You now have to decide what happens to the expression in the brackets as $s \to \infty$. You know that $\ln x$ becomes large when x becomes large, so as $s \to \infty$ both $\ln(s+1) \to \infty$ and $\ln(2s+3) \to \infty$. But what about their difference? Does this also tend to infinity, or does it have a finite limit?

To answer this question, the key is to write the expression in the brackets as $\ln\left(\dfrac{s+1}{2s+3}\right)$. Now when s is large, $2s+3$ is just over twice $s+1$; in fact,

$$2s + 3 = 2(s+1) + 1.$$

So $\dfrac{s+1}{2s+3}$ is just under $\frac{1}{2}$, and the expression tends to $\frac{1}{2}$ as $s \to \infty$. It follows that

$$\ln\left(\frac{s+1}{2s+3}\right) \to \ln\tfrac{1}{2} = -\ln 2.$$

Therefore

$$\int_0^\infty \frac{1}{(x+1)(2x+3)}\,dx = -\ln 2 + \ln 3 = \ln\tfrac{3}{2}.$$

Exercise 6D

1 Given that $\dfrac{a}{x-2} + \dfrac{b}{x+c} \equiv \dfrac{15x}{x^2+2x-8}$, find the values of the constants a, b and c.

2 Split the following into partial fractions.

(a) $\dfrac{2x+8}{(x+5)(x+3)}$ (b) $\dfrac{10x+8}{(x-1)(x+5)}$ (c) $\dfrac{x}{(x-4)(x-5)}$ (d) $\dfrac{28}{(2x-1)(x+3)}$

3 Split the following into partial fractions.

(a) $\dfrac{8x+1}{x^2+x-2}$ (b) $\dfrac{25}{x^2-3x-4}$ (c) $\dfrac{10x-6}{x^2-9}$ (d) $\dfrac{3}{2x^2+x}$

4 Split into partial fractions

(a) $\dfrac{35-5x}{(x+2)(x-1)(x-3)}$,   (b) $\dfrac{8x^2}{(x+1)(x-1)(x+3)}$,   (c) $\dfrac{15x^2-28x-72}{x^3-2x^2-24x}$.

5 Find

(a) $\displaystyle\int \dfrac{7x-1}{(x-1)(x-3)}\,dx$,   (b) $\displaystyle\int \dfrac{4}{x^2-4}\,dx$,

(c) $\displaystyle\int \dfrac{15x+35}{2x^2+5x}\,dx$,   (d) $\displaystyle\int \dfrac{x-8}{6x^2-x-1}\,dx$.

6 Evaluate the following, expressing each answer in a form involving a single logarithm.

(a) $\displaystyle\int_2^{10} \dfrac{2x+5}{(x-1)(x+6)}\,dx$ (b) $\displaystyle\int_0^3 \dfrac{3x+5}{(x+1)(x+2)}\,dx$

(c) $\displaystyle\int_4^5 \dfrac{6x}{x^2-9}\,dx$ (d) $\displaystyle\int_1^{\frac{3}{2}} \dfrac{4x-18}{4x^2+4x-3}\,dx$

7 Split $\dfrac{2-x}{(1+x)(1-2x)}$ into partial fractions and hence find the binomial expansion of

$\dfrac{2-x}{(1+x)(1-2x)}$ up to and including the term in x^3.

8 Split $\dfrac{3}{8x^2+6x+1}$ into partial fractions and hence find the binomial expansion of

$\dfrac{3}{8x^2+6x+1}$ up to and including the term in x^3. State the values of x for which the

expansion is valid.

9 Split $\dfrac{4ax-a^2}{x^2+ax-2a^2}$ into partial fractions.

10 Find the exact value of $\displaystyle\int_{2\sqrt5}^{3\sqrt5} \dfrac{4\sqrt5}{x^2-5}\,dx$.

11 Find $\displaystyle\int_0^\infty \dfrac{13}{(4x+1)(3x+4)}\,dx$.

6.5 Partial fractions with a repeated factor

You will have noticed in the examples of the last section that when the denominator has two
factors there are two partial fractions, with unknowns A and B. When the denominator has
three factors, there are three fractions, with unknowns A, B and C. The equating coefficients
method shows why, since you can find two unknowns by equating coefficients of x^0 and x^1,
and three unknowns by equating coefficients of x^0, x^1 and x^2.

So you would expect $\dfrac{x}{(x+1)(x+2)^2}$ to split into three fractions. Two of these must be

$\dfrac{A}{x+1}$ and $\dfrac{B}{(x+2)^2}$. What is the third?

Begin with the simpler fraction $\dfrac{x}{(x+1)(x+2)}$. You can easily check that this splits into partial fractions

$$\frac{x}{(x+1)(x+2)} \equiv \frac{2}{x+2} - \frac{1}{x+1}.$$

So

$$\frac{x}{(x+1)(x+2)^2} \equiv \frac{x}{(x+1)(x+2)} \times \frac{1}{x+2}$$

$$\equiv \left(\frac{2}{x+2} - \frac{1}{x+1}\right) \times \frac{1}{x+2}$$

$$\equiv \frac{2}{(x+2)^2} - \frac{1}{(x+1)(x+2)}.$$

This is not yet in partial fractions, since the second fraction on the right still has two factors in the denominator. But this can be put into partial fractions as

$$\frac{1}{(x+1)(x+2)} \equiv \frac{1}{x+1} - \frac{1}{x+2}.$$

It follows that

$$\frac{x}{(x+1)(x+2)^2} \equiv \frac{2}{(x+2)^2} - \left(\frac{1}{x+1} - \frac{1}{x+2}\right).$$

$$\equiv \frac{2}{(x+2)^2} - \frac{1}{x+1} + \frac{1}{x+2}$$

$$\equiv -\frac{1}{x+1} + \frac{2}{(x+2)^2} + \frac{1}{x+2}.$$

So, as well as fractions of the form $\dfrac{A}{x+1}$ and $\dfrac{B}{(x+2)^2}$ there is a fraction $\dfrac{C}{x+2}$.

The same thing happens whenever you have a repeated factor in the denominator. For example, suppose that you want to split $\dfrac{3x^2+6x+2}{(2x+3)(x+1)^2}$ into partial fractions. Two of these must be $\dfrac{A}{2x+3}$ and $\dfrac{B}{(x+1)^2}$. The third is $\dfrac{C}{x+1}$. So write

$$\frac{3x^2+6x+2}{(2x+3)(x+1)^2} \equiv \frac{A}{2x+3} + \frac{B}{(x+1)^2} + \frac{C}{x+1}.$$

Then multiplying the identity by $2x+3$ gives $\dfrac{3x^2+6x+2}{(x+1)^2} \equiv A + \dfrac{B(2x+3)}{(x+1)^2} + \dfrac{C(2x+3)}{x+1}$.

Putting $x = -\frac{3}{2}$ gives $A = \dfrac{3 \times \left(-\frac{3}{2}\right)^2 + 6 \times \left(-\frac{3}{2}\right) + 2}{\left(-\frac{3}{2}+1\right)^2} = \dfrac{\frac{27}{4} - 9 + 2}{\left(-\frac{1}{2}\right)^2} = \dfrac{-\frac{1}{4}}{\frac{1}{4}} = -1.$

You might next try multiplying the identity by $x+1$, which gives

$$\frac{3x^2+6x+2}{(2x+3)(x+1)} \equiv \frac{A(x+1)}{2x+3} + \frac{B}{x+1} + C.$$

But you cannot put $x = -1$ because neither side of the identity is defined for $x = -1$.

However, you can multiply the original identity by $(x+1)^2$ to get

$$\frac{3x^2+6x+2}{2x+3} \equiv \frac{A(x+1)^2}{2x+3} + B + C(x+1).$$

Putting $x = -1$ now gives $B = \dfrac{3 \times (-1)^2 + 6 \times (-1) + 2}{(2 \times (-1) + 3)} = \dfrac{3 - 6 + 2}{1} = -1.$

Thus $\dfrac{3x^2 + 6x + 2}{(2x + 3)(x + 1)^2} \equiv \dfrac{-1}{2x + 3} + \dfrac{-1}{(x + 1)^2} + \dfrac{C}{x + 1}.$

Here are two ways to find C. The first uses substitution and the second uses algebra.

Substitution method

There is no other especially convenient value to give x, but putting $x = 0$ in the original identity gives $\dfrac{3 \times (0)^2 + 6 \times 0 + 2}{(2 \times 0 + 3)(0 + 1)^2} = \dfrac{A}{2 \times 0 + 3} + \dfrac{B}{(0 + 1)^2} + \dfrac{C}{0 + 1},$ or $\frac{2}{3} = \frac{1}{3}A + B + C.$

Using the values $A = -1$ and $B = -1$, which you know, leads to $C = 2$.

Thus $\dfrac{3x^2 + 6x + 2}{(2x + 3)(x + 1)^2} \equiv \dfrac{-1}{2x + 3} + \dfrac{-1}{(x + 1)^2} + \dfrac{2}{x + 1}.$

Algebraic method

Write $\dfrac{3x^2 + 6x + 2}{(2x + 3)(x + 1)^2} \equiv \dfrac{-1}{2x + 3} + \dfrac{-1}{(x + 1)^2} + \dfrac{C}{x + 1}$ as

$$
\begin{aligned}
\frac{C}{x + 1} &\equiv \frac{3x^2 + 6x + 2}{(2x + 3)(x + 1)^2} + \frac{1}{2x + 3} + \frac{1}{(x + 1)^2} \\
&\equiv \frac{3x^2 + 6x + 2 + (x + 1)^2 + 2x + 3}{(2x + 3)(x + 1)^2} \\
&\equiv \frac{3x^2 + 6x + 2 + x^2 + 2x + 1 + 2x + 3}{(2x + 3)(x + 1)^2} \\
&\equiv \frac{4x^2 + 10x + 6}{(2x + 3)(x + 1)^2} \\
&\equiv \frac{2(2x + 3)(x + 1)}{(2x + 3)(x + 1)^2} \\
&\equiv \frac{2}{x + 1}.
\end{aligned}
$$

Therefore $C = 2$, as before, and $\dfrac{3x^2 + 6x + 2}{(2x + 3)(x + 1)^2} \equiv \dfrac{-1}{2x + 3} + \dfrac{-1}{(x + 1)^2} + \dfrac{2}{x + 1}.$

> You may think that the algebraic method is long-winded compared with the other methods, but it has the advantage that it is self-checking. If the factorising in the next-to-last line does not take place, then there is a mistake.

The key to finding partial fractions is to start with the correct form involving A, B and C. If you do not have that form, you will not be able to find the partial fractions.

> An expression of the form $\dfrac{ax^2 + bx + c}{(px + q)(rx + s)^2}$ can be split into partial fractions of the form $\dfrac{A}{px + q} + \dfrac{B}{(rx + s)^2} + \dfrac{C}{rx + s}.$

Example 6.5.1

Express $\dfrac{x^2 - 7x - 6}{x^2(x - 3)}$ in partial fractions.

Write $\dfrac{x^2 - 7x - 6}{x^2(x - 3)}$ in the form $\dfrac{x^2 - 7x - 6}{x^2(x - 3)} \equiv \dfrac{A}{x^2} + \dfrac{B}{x} + \dfrac{C}{x - 3}$.

You are advised to work through the details of this example for yourself.

Multiplying by x^2 gives $\dfrac{x^2 - 7x - 6}{x - 3} \equiv A + Bx + \dfrac{Cx^2}{x - 3}$; putting $x = 0$ leads to $A = 2$.

Multiplying by $x - 3$ gives $\dfrac{x^2 - 7x - 6}{x^2} \equiv \dfrac{A(x - 3)}{x^2} + \dfrac{B(x - 3)}{x} + C$; putting $x = 3$ leads to $C = -2$.

Therefore $\dfrac{x^2 - 7x - 6}{x^2(x - 3)} \equiv \dfrac{2}{x^2} + \dfrac{B}{x} - \dfrac{2}{x - 3}$.

Using the substitution method, putting $x = 1$ leads to $B = 3$.

Thus $\dfrac{x^2 - 7x - 6}{x^2(x - 3)} \equiv \dfrac{2}{x^2} + \dfrac{3}{x} - \dfrac{2}{x - 3}$.

Example 6.5.2

Express $\dfrac{9 + 4x^2}{(1 - 2x)^2(2 + x)}$ in partial fractions, and hence find the binomial expansion of

$\dfrac{9 + 4x^2}{(1 - 2x)^2(2 + x)}$ up to and including the term in x^3. State the values of x for which the

expansion is valid.

Write $\dfrac{9 + 4x^2}{(1 - 2x)^2(2 + x)} \equiv \dfrac{A}{(1 - 2x)^2} + \dfrac{B}{1 - 2x} + \dfrac{C}{2 + x}$.

Multiplying both sides by $(1 - 2x)^2$ gives $\dfrac{9 + 4x^2}{2 + x} \equiv A + B(1 - 2x) + \dfrac{C(1 - 2x)^2}{2 + x}$.

Putting $x = \frac{1}{2}$ leads to $A = 4$.

Multiplying both sides by $2 + x$ gives $\dfrac{9 + 4x^2}{(1 - 2x)^2} \equiv \dfrac{A(2 + x)}{(1 - 2x)^2} + \dfrac{B(2 + x)}{1 - 2x} + C$.

Putting $x = -2$ leads to $C = 1$.

Therefore $\dfrac{9 + 4x^2}{(1 - 2x)^2(2 + x)} \equiv \dfrac{4}{(1 - 2x)^2} + \dfrac{B}{1 - 2x} + \dfrac{1}{2 + x}$.

Using the algebraic method,

$$\dfrac{B}{1 - 2x} \equiv \dfrac{9 + 4x^2}{(1 - 2x)^2(2 + x)} - \dfrac{4}{(1 - 2x)^2} - \dfrac{1}{2 + x} \equiv \dfrac{9 + 4x^2 - 4(2 + x) - (1 - 2x)^2}{(1 - 2x)^2(2 + x)}$$

$$\equiv \dfrac{9 + 4x^2 - 8 - 4x - 1 + 4x - 4x^2}{(1 - 2x)^2(2 + x)} \equiv \dfrac{0}{(1 - 2x)^2(2 + x)} \equiv 0.$$

Thus $\dfrac{9 + 4x^2}{(1 - 2x)^2(2 + x)} \equiv \dfrac{4}{(1 - 2x)^2} + \dfrac{1}{2 + x} \equiv 4(1 - 2x)^{-2} + (2 + x)^{-1}$.

Using the binomial expansion,

$$4(1 - 2x)^{-2} = 4\left(1 + \frac{(-2)}{1}(-2x) + \frac{(-2)(-3)}{1 \times 2}(-2x)^2 \right.$$
$$\left. + \frac{(-2)(-3)(-4)}{1 \times 2 \times 3}(-2x)^3 + \dots\right)$$
$$= 4(1 + 4x + 12x^2 + 32x^3 + \dots) = 4 + 16x + 48x^2 + 128x^3 + \dots,$$

$$(2 + x)^{-1} = 2^{-1}\left(1 + \tfrac{1}{2}x\right)^{-1} = \tfrac{1}{2}\left(1 + \tfrac{1}{2}x\right)^{-1}$$
$$= \tfrac{1}{2}\left(1 + \frac{(-1)}{1}\left(\tfrac{1}{2}x\right) + \frac{(-1)(-2)}{1 \times 2}\left(\tfrac{1}{2}x\right)^2 + \frac{(-1)(-2)(-3)}{1 \times 2 \times 3}\left(\tfrac{1}{2}x\right)^3 + \dots\right)$$
$$= \tfrac{1}{2}\left(1 - \tfrac{1}{2}x + \tfrac{1}{4}x^2 - \tfrac{1}{8}x^3 + \dots\right) = \tfrac{1}{2} - \tfrac{1}{4}x + \tfrac{1}{8}x^2 - \tfrac{1}{16}x^3 + \dots.$$

Therefore

$$4(1 - 2x)^{-2} + (2 + x)^{-1}$$
$$= 4 + 16x + 48x^2 + 128x^3 + \dots + \tfrac{1}{2} - \tfrac{1}{4}x + \tfrac{1}{8}x^2 - \tfrac{1}{16}x^3 + \dots$$
$$= \tfrac{9}{2} + \tfrac{63}{4}x + \tfrac{385}{8}x^2 + \tfrac{2047}{16}x^3 + \dots,$$

so the required expansion is $\tfrac{9}{2} + \tfrac{63}{4}x + \tfrac{385}{8}x^2 + \tfrac{2047}{16}x^3$.

The expansion of $(1 - 2x)^{-2}$ is valid when $|2x| < 1$, that is when $|x| < \tfrac{1}{2}$.

The expansion of $\left(1 + \tfrac{1}{2}x\right)^{-1}$ is valid when $\left|\tfrac{1}{2}x\right| < 1$, that is when $|x| < 2$.

For the final result to hold you require both $|x| < \tfrac{1}{2}$ and $|x| < 2$, that is $|x| < \tfrac{1}{2}$.

Exercise 6E

1 Split into partial fractions

(a) $\dfrac{4}{(x - 1)(x - 3)^2}$,

(b) $\dfrac{6x^2 + 11x - 8}{(x + 2)^2(x - 1)}$,

(c) $\dfrac{4}{x^3 - 4x^2 + 4x}$,

(d) $\dfrac{8 - 7x}{2x^3 + 3x^2 - 1}$.

2 Find

(a) $\displaystyle\int \frac{6x^2 + 27x + 25}{(x + 2)^2(x + 1)}\, dx$,

(b) $\displaystyle\int \frac{97x + 35}{(2x - 3)(5x + 2)^2}\, dx$.

3 Show that $\displaystyle\int_1^6 \frac{16}{x^2(x + 4)}\, dx = \tfrac{10}{3} - \ln 3$.

4 Find the exact value of $\displaystyle\int_2^3 \frac{x(x + 14)}{2x^3 - 3x^2 + 1}\, dx$.

5 Obtain the series expansion of $\dfrac{1}{(1 + 2x)^2(1 - x)}$ up to and including the term in x^2 by

(a) multiplying the expansion of $(1 + 2x)^{-2}$ by the expansion of $(1 - x)^{-1}$,

(b) splitting $\dfrac{1}{(1 + 2x)^2(1 - x)}$ into partial fractions and finding the expansion of each fraction.

6.6   Division of polynomials

You first saw division of polynomials in C2 Example 8.4.2, where you found that if you divide the polynomial $20x^3 - x^2 - 4x - 7$ by $4x + 3$ you get

$$20x^3 - x^2 - 4x - 7 \equiv (4x + 3)(5x^2 - 4x + 2) + (-13)$$

giving a quotient of $5x^2 - 4x + 2$ and a remainder of -13.

If you write the identity above with the two factors on the right side the other way round you can see that

$$20x^3 - x^2 - 4x - 7 \equiv (5x^2 - 4x + 2)(4x + 3) + (-13).$$

This shows that if you divide $20x^3 - x^2 - 4x - 7$ by $5x^2 - 4x + 2$ you get a quotient of $4x + 3$ and a remainder of -13.

But how can you find the quotient and remainder when you divide a polynomial such as $x^4 + x^3 + x^2 + 2x - 6$ by $x^2 + x + 2$?

If you write $x^4 + x^3 + x^2 + 2x - 6$ in the form

$$x^4 + x^3 + x^2 + 2x - 6 \equiv (x^2 + x + 2)q(x) + r(x)$$

where $q(x)$ and $r(x)$ are polynomials in x, what can you deduce about $q(x)$ and $r(x)$, which are the quotient and remainder respectively?

First, notice that you cannot find $q(x)$ and $r(x)$ uniquely from this identity. For example, you could say that $q(x) = 0$ and $r(x) = x^4 + x^3 + x^2 + 2x - 6$, or you could say that $q(x) = 1$ and $r(x) = x^4 + x^3 + x^2 + 2x - 6 - (x^2 + x + 2) = x^4 + x^3 + x - 8$. You need some more information.

So, as so often with polynomials, it is worth thinking about the equivalent situation with integers. If you want to find the quotient and remainder when 100 is divided by 7, you write $100 = 14 \times 7 + 2$, but in this calculation there is an understanding that the remainder can only be $0, 1, 2, \ldots, 6$.

A similar restriction for polynomials is that the degree of the remainder should be less than that of the dividing polynomial. It turns out, but won't be proved here, that this is enough to determine the quotient and remainder polynomials $q(x)$ and $r(x)$ uniquely.

> When a polynomial $p(x)$ is divided by a polynomial $a(x)$, called the **divisor**, there is a **quotient** $q(x)$ and a **remainder** $r(x)$ such that
>
> $$p(x) \equiv a(x)\,q(x) + r(x),$$
>
> where the degree of the remainder $r(x)$ is less than that of $a(x)$. The degree of $q(x)$ is the difference of the degrees of $p(x)$ and $a(x)$.

This is a generalisation of the result stated at the end of C2 Section 8.4, where $p(x)$ was divided by a linear polynomial $sx - t$, so that the remainder was simply a constant R.

Example 6.6.1

Find the quotient and remainder when $2x^3 + 2x^2 - 5x + 5$ is divided by $x^2 - x + 2$.

From the statement in the box, the remainder has degree less than the degree of $x^2 - x + 2$, and is therefore linear, of the form $Rx + S$, where R and S are constants.

The degree of the quotient is the difference of the degrees of $2x^3 + 2x^2 - 5x + 5$ and $x^2 - x + 2$, which is $3 - 2 = 1$. The quotient is therefore linear, and can be written in the form $Ax + B$, where A and B are constants.

So

$$2x^3 + 2x^2 - 5x + 5 \equiv (x^2 - x + 2)(Ax + B) + Rx + S,$$

where you need to find the coefficients A, B, R and S.

Equating coefficients of x^3: $2 = A$.
Equating coefficients of x^2: $2 = -A + B$, so $B = 2 + A$, giving $B = 4$.
Equating coefficients of x: $-5 = 2A - B + R$, so $R = -5 - 2A + B$,
  giving $R = -5$.
Equating coefficients of x^0: $5 = 2B + S$, so $S = 5 - 2B$, giving $S = -3$.

The quotient is $2x + 4$, and the remainder is $-5x - 3$.

Example 6.6.2

Find the quotient and the remainder when $x^4 + 2x^3 + 2x^2 + 4x - 3$ is divided by $x^2 + x - 2$.

From the statement in the box, the remainder has degree less than the degree of $x^2 + x - 2$, and is therefore linear, of the form $Rx + S$, where R and S are constants.

The degree of the quotient is the difference of the degrees of $x^4 + 2x^3 + 2x^2 + 4x - 3$ and $x^2 + x - 2$, which is $4 - 2 = 2$. The quotient is therefore a quadratic, and can be written in the form $Ax^2 + Bx + C$, where A, B and C are constants.

So

$$x^4 + 2x^3 + 2x^2 + 4x - 3 \equiv (x^2 + x - 2)(Ax^2 + Bx + C) + Rx + S,$$

where you need to find the constants A, B, C, R and S.

Equating coefficients of x^4: $1 = A$.
Equating coefficients of x^3: $2 = A + B$, so $B = 2 - A$, giving $B = 1$.
Equating coefficients of x^2: $2 = -2A + B + C$, so $C = 2 + 2A - B$,
  giving $C = 3$.
Equating coefficients of x: $4 = -2B + C + R$, so $R = 4 + 2B - C$,
  giving $R = 3$.
Equating coefficients of x^0: $-3 = -2C + S$, so $S = -3 + 2C$, giving $S = 3$.

The quotient is $x^2 + x + 3$, and the remainder is $3x + 3$.

Finding the quotient and remainder can often be useful in rewriting a fraction in a different form which enables you to do other things.

For example, from Example 6.6.2, you know that

$$x^4 + 2x^3 + 2x^2 + 4x - 3 \equiv (x^2 + x - 2)(x^2 + x + 3) + 3x + 3.$$

If you divide both sides by $x^2 + x - 2$ you get

$$\frac{x^4 + 2x^3 + 2x^2 + 4x - 3}{x^2 + x - 2} \equiv x^2 + x + 3 + \frac{3x + 3}{x^2 + x - 2}.$$

You can now use partial fractions to integrate $\dfrac{3x + 3}{x^2 + x - 2}$, or to find its binomial expansion for small values of x.

Or you can say that for large values of x, $|3x + 3|$ is small compared with $|x^2 + x - 2|$, so the graph of $y = \dfrac{x^4 + 2x^3 + 2x^2 + 4x - 3}{x^2 + x - 2}$ is very close to the graph of $y = x^2 + x + 3$.

Fig. 6.1 shows the graphs of $y = \dfrac{x^4 + 2x^3 + 2x^2 + 4x - 3}{x^2 + x - 2}$ (solid lines) and $y = x^2 + x + 3$ (dotted). The scales on the axes are different: the x-axis goes from -5 to 5, while the y-axis goes from -40 to 40. This has the efect of reducing the visual distance between the graphs. But you can see for large values of $|x|$ that the dotted graph of $y = x^2 + x + 3$ is getting ever closer to the graph of $y = \dfrac{x^4 + 2x^3 + 2x^2 + 4x - 3}{x^2 + x - 2}$.

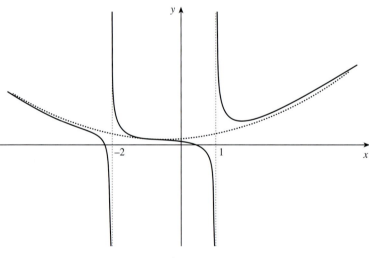

Fig. 6.1

Example 6.6.3

(a) Find the quotient and remainder when $3x^3 + 7x^2 + 8x - 5$ is divided by $x^2 + 3x + 4$.

(b) Use your result to express $\dfrac{3x^3 + 7x^2 + 8x - 5}{x^2 + 3x + 4}$ in the form $Ax + B + \dfrac{Rx + S}{x^2 + 3x + 4}$.

(c) Hence calculate $\displaystyle\int_0^1 \dfrac{3x^3 + 7x^2 + 8x - 5}{x^2 + 3x + 4}\, dx$.

(d) Use your answer to part (b) to determine how the graph of $y = \dfrac{3x^3 + 7x^2 + 8x - 5}{x^2 + 3x + 4}$ behaves for large values of $|x|$.

(a) Write $3x^3 + 7x^2 + 8x - 5 \equiv (x^2 + 3x + 4)(Ax + B) + Rx + S$, and equate coefficients to find the values of the constants A, B, R and S.

> Equating coefficients of x^3: $3 = A$.
> Equating coefficients of x^2: $7 = 3A + B$, so $B = 7 - 3A$, giving $B = -2$.
> Equating coefficients of x: $8 = 4A + 3B + R$, so $R = 8 - 4A - 3B$,
> giving $R = 2$.
> Equating coefficients of x^0: $-5 = 4B + S$, so $S = -5 - 4B$, giving $S = 3$.

So the quotient is $3x - 2$ and the remainder is $2x + 3$.

(b) Dividing the identity $3x^3 + 7x^2 + 8x - 5 \equiv (x^2 + 3x + 4)(3x - 2) + 2x + 3$ by $x^2 + 3x + 4$ gives

$$\frac{3x^3 + 7x^2 + 8x - 5}{x^2 + 3x + 4} \equiv 3x - 2 + \frac{2x + 3}{x^2 + 3x + 4}.$$

(c) Using the alternative form of $\dfrac{3x^3 + 7x^2 + 8x - 5}{x^2 + 3x + 4}$ enables you to integrate. Then

$$\int_0^1 \frac{3x^3 + 7x^2 + 8x - 5}{x^2 + 3x + 4}\, dx = \int_0^1 \left(3x - 2 + \frac{2x + 3}{x^2 + 3x + 4}\right) dx$$

$$= \left[3 \times \tfrac{1}{2}x^2 - 2x + \ln(x^2 + 3x + 4)\right]_0^1 \qquad \text{(Section 2.4)}$$

$$= \tfrac{3}{2} - 2 + \ln 8 - \ln 4$$

$$= \ln 2 - \tfrac{1}{2}.$$

(d) When $|x|$ is large, $|2x + 3|$ is small compared with $|x^2 + 3x + 4|$, so $\left|\dfrac{2x + 3}{x^2 + 3x + 4}\right|$ is small compared with $|3x - 2|$.

Since $\dfrac{3x^3 + 7x^2 + 8x - 5}{x^2 + 3x + 4} \equiv 3x - 2 + \dfrac{2x + 3}{x^2 + 3x + 4}$, for large values of x, the graph of $y = \dfrac{3x^3 + 7x^2 + 8x - 5}{x^2 + 3x + 4}$ is close to that of $y = 3x - 2$.

Fig. 6.2 illustrates this.

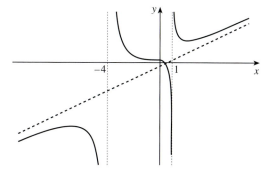

Fig. 6.2

Exercise 6F

1 Find the quotient and the remainder when

(a) x^2 is divided by $x - 1$,

(b) $12x^2$ is divided by $2x - 3$,

(c) $6x^2 - 4x - 3$ is divided by $3x - 5$,

(d) $6x^3 - 3x^2 + x - 1$ is divided by $2x^2 - x + 4$,

(e) $x^3 - 3x^2 + 5x - 7$ is divided by $x^2 + 2x - 5$,

(f) $2x^3$ is divided by $x^2 - 2x + 3$.

2 Find the quotient and the remainder when

(a) $x^4 - 2x^3 - 7x^2 + 7x + 5$ is divided by $x^2 + 2x - 1$,

(b) $x^4 - x^3 + 7x + 2$ is divided by $x^2 + x - 1$,

(c) $2x^4 - 4x^3 + 3x^2 + 6x + 5$ is divided by $x^2 + x + 1$,

(d) $6x^4 + x^3 + 13x + 10$ is divided by $2x^2 - x + 4$,

(e) x^4 is divided by $x^2 + 2x - 5$,

(f) $6x^4 - 17x^3 + 14x^2 - 4x - 8$ is divided by $2x^2 - 3x - 2$.

3 (a) Find the quotient and the remainder when x^4 is divided by $x^2 + 1$.

(b) Show that your result in part (a) leads to the identity $\dfrac{x^4}{x^2 + 1} \equiv x^2 - 1 + \dfrac{1}{x^2 + 1}$.

(c) Use the result in part (b), together with the substitution $x = \tan u$ to find $\displaystyle\int_0^1 \dfrac{x^4}{x^2 + 1}\,dx$.

4 (a) Find the quotient and the remainder when x^3 is divided by $x^2 - 1$.

(b) Show that $\dfrac{x^3}{x^2 - 1} \equiv x + \dfrac{Ax + B}{x^2 - 1}$, where A and B are constants whose values are to be found.

(c) Find $\displaystyle\int_2^7 \dfrac{x^3}{x^2 - 1}\,dx$.

5 (a) Find the quotient and remainder when $x^3 - 5x^2 + 11x - 8$ is divided by $(x - 1)(x - 2)$.

(b) Hence express $\dfrac{x^3 - 5x^2 + 11x - 8}{(x - 1)(x - 2)}$ in the form $Ax + B + \dfrac{Rx + S}{(x - 1)(x - 2)}$, where A, B, R and S are constants to be found.

(c) For your values of R and S express $\dfrac{Rx + S}{(x - 1)(x - 2)}$ in partial fractions.

(d) Calculate the value of $\displaystyle\int_3^4 \dfrac{x^3 - 5x^2 + 11x - 8}{(x - 1)(x - 2)}\,dx$.

(e) Find the binomial expansion of $\dfrac{x^3 - 5x^2 + 11x - 8}{(x - 1)(x - 2)}$ up to the term in x^2.

Miscellaneous exercise 6

1 Express $\dfrac{4}{(x-3)(x+1)}$ in partial fractions. (OCR)

2 Express $\dfrac{2}{x(x-1)(x+1)}$ in partial fractions. (OCR)

3 Express $\dfrac{2x^2+1}{x(x-1)^2}$ in partial fractions. (OCR)

4 Express $\dfrac{x^2-11}{(x+2)^2(3x-1)}$ in partial fractions. (OCR)

5 Find the quotient and remainder when x^4-4x^2+8 is divided by x^2-2x+2.

6 Find $\displaystyle\int \dfrac{1}{x(x+1)}\,dx$. (OCR)

7 Express $\dfrac{3+2x}{x^2(3-x)}$ in partial fractions.

8 Find $\displaystyle\int \dfrac{x}{(x+1)(x+2)}\,dx$. (OCR)

9 Express $\dfrac{1}{x^2(x-1)}$ in the form $\dfrac{A}{x}+\dfrac{B}{x^2}+\dfrac{C}{x-1}$, where A, B and C are constants. Hence find
$\displaystyle\int \dfrac{1}{x^2(x-1)}\,dx$. (OCR)

10 Simplify $\sqrt{\dfrac{3x^2+5x-2}{4x-3}\div\dfrac{4x^3+13x^2+4x-12}{2x(x+3)-(2-x)(1+x)}}$.

11 Find the quotient and remainder when x^4+4 is divided by x^2+2x+2. Hence find the prime factors of 10 004.

12 Simplify $\dfrac{x-21}{x^2-9}-\dfrac{3}{x+3}+\dfrac{4}{x-3}$.

13 Express $\dfrac{3}{(2x+1)(x-1)}$ in partial fractions. Hence find the exact value of
$\displaystyle\int_2^3 \dfrac{3}{(2x+1)(x-1)}\,dx$, giving your answer as a single logarithm. (OCR)

14 Express $\dfrac{1}{(x+3)(4-x)}$ in partial fractions. Hence find the exact value of
$\displaystyle\int_0^2 \dfrac{1}{(x+3)(4-x)}\,dx$, giving your answer as a single logarithm. (OCR)

15 Evaluate the following infinite integrals by using the given substitutions.

(a) $\displaystyle\int_{\ln 2}^{\infty} \dfrac{1}{e^x-1}\,dx,\qquad e^x=u$
(b) $\displaystyle\int_1^{\infty} \dfrac{1}{x(x+\sqrt{x})}\,dx,\qquad \sqrt{x}=u$

16 Express $f(x)\equiv\dfrac{2}{2-3x+x^2}$ in partial fractions and hence, or otherwise, obtain $f(x)$ as a series of ascending powers of x, giving the first four non-zero terms of this expansion. State the set of values of x for which this expansion is valid. (OCR)

17 Express $\dfrac{3-x}{(2+x)(1-2x)}$ in partial fractions and hence, or otherwise, obtain the first three terms in the expansion of this expression in ascending powers of x. State the range of values of x for which the expansion is valid. (OCR)

18 (a) Find the quotient and the remainder when $x^4 - 2x^3 + x - 1$ is divided by $x^2 + x + 1$.

(b) Hence show that, when x is large, the curve with equation $y = \dfrac{x^4 - 2x^3 + x - 1}{x^2 + x + 1}$ is closely approximated by a quadratic curve, and state the equation of this quadratic.

19 Given that $\dfrac{18 - 4x - x^2}{(4-3x)(1+x)^2} \equiv \dfrac{A}{4-3x} + \dfrac{B}{1+x} + \dfrac{C}{(1+x)^2}$, show that $A = 2$, and obtain the values of B and C. Hence show that $\displaystyle\int_0^1 \dfrac{18 - 4x - x^2}{(4-3x)(1+x)^2}\, dx = \tfrac{7}{3}\ln 2 + \tfrac{3}{2}$. (OCR)

20 Let $y = \dfrac{4 + 7x}{(2-x)(1+x)^2}$. Express y in the form $\dfrac{A}{2-x} + \dfrac{B}{1+x} + \dfrac{C}{(1+x)^2}$, where the numerical values of A, B and C are to be found. Hence, or otherwise, expand y in a series of ascending powers of x up to and including the term in x^3, simplifying the coefficients. Use your result to find the value of $\dfrac{dy}{dx}$ when $x = 0$.

21 Express $\dfrac{15 - 13x + 4x^2}{(1-x)^2(4-x)}$ in partial fractions. Hence evaluate $\displaystyle\int_2^3 \dfrac{15 - 13x + 4x^2}{(1-x)^2(4-x)}\, dx$ giving the exact value in terms of logarithms. (OCR)

22 (a) Find the quotient and the remainder when $2x^4 + x^3 - 7x^2 + 6x - 3$ is divided by $x^2 - x$.

(b) Hence write $\dfrac{2x^4 + x^3 - 7x^2 + 6x - 3}{x^2 - x}$ in the form $Ax^2 + Bx + C + \dfrac{Rx + S}{x^2 - x}$, where the constants A, B, C, R and S are to be determined.

(c) With these values of R and S, split $\dfrac{Rx + S}{x^2 - x}$ into partial fractions.

(d) Hence find the value of the integral $\displaystyle\int_3^4 \dfrac{2x^4 + x^3 - 7x^2 + 6x - 3}{x^2 - x}\, dx$.

23 Split $\dfrac{1}{x^4 - 13x^2 + 36}$ into partial fractions.

24* Let $f(x) = \dfrac{x^2 + 5x}{(1+x)(1-x)^2}$. Express $f(x)$ in the form $\dfrac{A}{1+x} + \dfrac{B}{1-x} + \dfrac{C}{(1-x)^2}$ where A, B and C are constants. The expansion of $f(x)$, in ascending powers of x, is $c_0 + c_1 x + c_2 x^2 + c_3 x^3 + \cdots + c_r x^r + \ldots$. Find c_0, c_1, c_2 and show that $c_3 = 11$. Express c_r in terms of r. (OCR)

25 It is given that $g(x) = (2x - 1)(x + 2)(x - 3)$.

(a) Express $g(x)$ in the form $Ax^3 + Bx^2 + Cx + D$, giving the values of the constants A, B, C and D.

(b) Find the value of the constant a, given that $x + 3$ is a factor of $g(x) + ax$.

(c) Express $\dfrac{x-3}{g(x)}$ in partial fractions. (OCR)

26 The diagram shows part of the graph of
$y = \dfrac{3}{\sqrt{x}(x-3)}$. The shaded region is bounded by
the curve and the lines $y = 0$, $x = 4$ and $x = 6$.
Find the volume of the solid formed when the
shaded region is rotated through four right angles
about the x-axis.

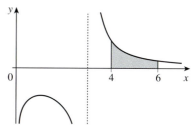

27 (a) Express $\dfrac{2}{(x-1)(x-3)}$ in partial fractions, and use the result to express $\dfrac{4}{(x-1)^2(x-3)^2}$
in partial fractions.

The finite region bounded by the curve with equation $y = \dfrac{2}{(x-1)(x-3)}$ and the lines
$x = 4$ and $y = \frac{1}{4}$ is denoted by R.

(b) Show that the area of R is $\ln \frac{3}{2} - \frac{1}{4}$.

(c) Calculate the volume of the solid formed when R is rotated through 2π radians about
the x-axis.   (OCR)

28 For the following integrals, use the given substitution to produce an integrand which is a
rational function of u, then use partial fractions to complete the integration.

(a) $\displaystyle\int \frac{1}{e^x - e^{-x}}\, dx,$ $e^x = u$ (b) $\displaystyle\int \frac{1}{x(\sqrt{x}+1)}\, dx,$ $\sqrt{x} = u$

7 Differential equations

This chapter is about differential equations of the form $\dfrac{dy}{dx} = f(x)$ or $\dfrac{dy}{dx} = f(y)$. When you have completed it, you should

- be able to find general solutions of these equations, or particular solutions satisfying given initial conditions
- know the relation connecting the derivatives $\dfrac{dy}{dx}$ and $\dfrac{dx}{dy}$, and understand its significance
- be able to formulate differential equations as models, and interpret the solutions.

Other differential equations, of the form $\dfrac{dy}{dx} = \dfrac{f(x)}{g(y)}$, appear in Chapter 8.

7.1 Forming and solving equations

Many applications of mathematics involve two variables, and you want to find a relation between them. Often this relation is expressed in terms of the rate of change of one variable with respect to the other. This then leads to a **differential equation**. Its **solution** will be an algebraic equation connecting the two variables.

Example 7.1.1
At each point P of a curve for which $x > 0$ the tangent cuts the y-axis at T, and N is the foot of the perpendicular from P to the y-axis (see Fig. 7.1). If T is always 1 unit below N, find the equation of the curve.

Since $NP = x$, the gradient of the tangent is $\dfrac{1}{x}$, so that

$$\frac{dy}{dx} = \frac{1}{x}.$$

This can be integrated directly to give

$$y = \ln x + k.$$

The modulus sign is not needed, since $x > 0$.

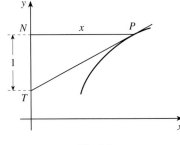

Fig. 7.1

The equation $y = \ln x + k$ is called the **general solution** of the differential equation $\dfrac{dy}{dx} = \dfrac{1}{x}$ for $x > 0$. It can be represented by a family of graphs, one for each value of k. Fig. 7.2 shows just a few typical graphs, but there are in fact infinitely many graphs with the property described. A differential equation often originates from a scientific law, or hypothesis. The equation is then called a **mathematical model** of the real-world situation.

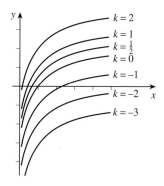

Fig. 7.2

Example 7.1.2

A rodent has mass 30 grams at birth. It reaches maturity in 3 months. The rate of growth is modelled by the differential equation $\dfrac{dm}{dt} = 120(t-3)^2$, where m grams is the mass of the rodent t months after birth. Find the mass of the rodent when fully grown.

The differential equation has general solution

$$m = 40(t-3)^3 + k.$$

However, only one equation from this family of solutions is right for this problem. It is given that, when $t = 0$ (at birth), $m = 30$. So k must satisfy the equation

$$30 = 40(0-3)^3 + k,$$

giving $30 = -1080 + k$, so $k = 1110$.

The mass of the rodent after t months is therefore

$$m = 40(t-3)^3 + 1110.$$

The mass when fully grown is found by putting $t = 3$ in this formula, giving $m = 0 + 1110 = 1110$. So the mass of the rodent at maturity is 1110 grams.

In this example the variables have to satisfy an **initial condition**, or **boundary condition**, that $m = 30$ when $t = 0$. The equation $m = 40(t-3)^3 + 1110$ is the **particular solution** of the differential equation which satisfies the initial condition.

Example 7.1.3

A botanist makes a hypothesis that the rate of growth of hothouse plants is proportional to the amount of daylight they receive. If t is the time in years after the shortest day of the year, the length of effective daylight is given by the formula $12 - 4\cos 2\pi t$ hours. On the shortest day in the December of one year the height of one plant is measured to be 123.0 cm; 55 days later the height is 128.0 cm. What will its height be on the longest day of the year in the following June?

If h is the height in centimetres, the rate of growth is given by

$$\frac{dh}{dt} = c(12 - 4\cos 2\pi t),$$

but c, the constant of proportionality, is not known. Nor can it be found directly from the data. However, integration gives

$$h = c\left(12t - \frac{2}{\pi}\sin 2\pi t\right) + k.$$

The initial condition is that $h = 123.0$ when $t = 0$, so

$$123.0 = c(0 - 0) + k,$$

giving $k = 123.0$. Therefore

$$h = c\left(12t - \frac{2}{\pi}\sin 2\pi t\right) + 123.0.$$

After 55 days the value of t is $\frac{55}{365} = 0.150...$, and it is given that at this time $h = 128.0$. So

$$128.0 = c\left(12 \times 0.150... - \frac{2}{\pi}\sin(2\pi \times 0.150...)\right) + 123.0$$

$$= c(1.80... - 0.51...) + 123.0,$$

which gives $c = 3.87...$.

Substituting this in the equation for h,

$$h = 3.87... \times \left(12t - \frac{2}{\pi}\sin 2\pi t\right) + 123.0.$$

The longest day occurs when $t = \frac{1}{2}$, and then

$$h = 3.87...(6 - 0) + 123.0 = 146, \text{ correct to 3 significant figures.}$$

According to the botanist's hypothesis, the height of the plant on the longest day will be 146 cm.

This last example is typical of many applications of differential equations. Often the form of a hypothetical law is known, but the values of the numerical constants are not. But once the differential equation has been solved, experimental data can be used to find values for the constants.

Exercise 7A

1 Find general solutions of the following differential equations.

(a) $\dfrac{dy}{dx} = (3x - 1)(x - 3)$ (b) $\dfrac{dx}{dt} = \sin^2 3t$

(c) $\dfrac{dP}{dt} = 50e^{0.1t}$ (d) $e^{2t}\dfrac{du}{dt} = 100$

(e) $\sqrt{x}\,\dfrac{dy}{dx} = x + 1$, for $x > 0$ (f) $\sin t\dfrac{dx}{dt} = \cos t + \sin 2t$, for $0 < t < \pi$

2 Solve the following differential equations with the given initial conditions. Display graphs to illustrate your answers.

(a) $\dfrac{dx}{dt} = 2e^{0.4t}$, $x = 1$ when $t = 0$

(b) $\dfrac{dv}{dt} = 6(\sin 2t - \cos 3t)$, $v = 0$ when $t = 0$

(c) $(1 - t^2)\dfrac{dy}{dt} = 2t$, $y = 0$ when $t = 0$, for $-1 < t < 1$

3 Find the solution curves of the following differential equations which pass through the given points. Display graphs to illustrate your answers.

(a) $\dfrac{dy}{dx} = \dfrac{x-1}{x^2}$, through $(1, 0)$, for $x > 0$

(b) $\dfrac{dy}{dx} = \dfrac{1}{\sqrt{x}}$, through $(4, 0)$, for $x > 0$

(c) $(x + 1)\dfrac{dy}{dx} = x - 1$, through the origin, for $x > -1$ (To integrate, substitute $x = u - 1$.)

4 In starting from rest, the driver of an electric car depresses the throttle gradually. If the speed of the car after t seconds is $v\,\mathrm{m\,s^{-1}}$, the acceleration $\dfrac{dv}{dt}$ (in m s^{-2}) is given by $0.2t$. How long does it take for the car to reach a speed of $20\,\mathrm{m\,s^{-1}}$?

5 The solution curve for a differential equation of the form $\dfrac{dy}{dx} = x - \dfrac{a}{x^2}$, for $x > 0$, passes through the points $(1, 0)$ and $(2, 0)$. Find the value of y when $x = 3$.

6 A point moves on the x-axis so that its coordinate at time t satisfies the differential equation $\dfrac{dx}{dt} = 5 + a\cos 2t$ for some value of a. It is observed that $x = 3$ when $t = 0$, and $x = 0$ when $t = \frac{1}{4}\pi$. Find the value of a, and the value of x when $t = \frac{1}{3}\pi$.

7 The normal to a curve at a point P cuts the y-axis at T, and N is the foot of the perpendicular from P to the y-axis. If, for all P, T is always 1 unit below N, find the equation of the curve.

8 Four theories are proposed about the growth of an organism:

(a) It grows at a constant rate of k units per year.

(b) It only grows when there is enough daylight, so that its rate of growth at time t years is $k(1 - \frac{1}{2}\cos 2\pi t)$ units per year.

(c) Its growth is controlled by the 10-year sunspot cycle, so that its rate of growth at time t years is $k(1 + \frac{1}{4}\cos \frac{1}{5}\pi t)$ units per year.

(d) Both (b) and (c) are true, so that its rate of growth is $k(1 - \frac{1}{2}\cos 2\pi t)(1 + \frac{1}{4}\cos \frac{1}{5}\pi t)$ units per year.

The size of the organism at time $t = 0$ is A units. For each model, find an expression for the size of the organism at time t years. Display graphs to compare the size given by the four models for $0 < t < 10$. Do they all give the same value for the size of the organism after 10 years? (In part (d), use $2\cos A\cos B \equiv \cos(A + B) + \cos(A - B)$.)

9 Water is leaking slowly out of a tank. The depth of the water after t hours is h metres, and these variables are related by a differential equation of the form $\dfrac{dh}{dt} = -ae^{-0.1t}$. Initially the depth of water is 6 metres, and after 2 hours it has fallen to 5 metres. At what depth will the level eventually settle down?

Find an expression for $\dfrac{dh}{dt}$ in terms of h.

7.2 Switching variables in differential equations

If you write a function equation in the form $y = f(x)$, then x is called the independent variable and y the dependent variable. But it was pointed out in C3 Section 9.5 that in many applications this distinction is not absolutely fixed, and that you might sometimes want to reverse the roles of x and y. That is, you might rewrite the relation in the form $x = g(y)$, and think of y as the independent variable and x as the dependent variable. In that case the derivative $\dfrac{dy}{dx}$ would be replaced by $1 \Big/ \dfrac{dx}{dy}$.

This has applications to differential equations. In all the differential equations in Section 7.1 the derivative was given as a formula involving the independent variable, which was x in Example 7.1.1 and t in Examples 7.1.2 and 7.1.3.

Often, however, the derivative is known in terms of the dependent variable. When this occurs, you can use the relation $\dfrac{dy}{dx} \times \dfrac{dx}{dy} = 1$ to turn the differential equation into a form which you know how to solve. That is,

$$\frac{dy}{dx} = f(y) \quad \Leftrightarrow \quad \frac{dx}{dy} = \frac{1}{f(y)} \quad \Leftrightarrow \quad x = \int \frac{1}{f(y)} dy.$$

Example 7.2.1

Gardeners are concerned about the spread of a species of beetle. All the specimens detected so far lie within a circular region of radius 25 kilometres, and it is suggested that the increase of the radius r kilometres might be modelled by a differential equation $\dfrac{dr}{dt} = \frac{1}{6}\sqrt{r}$, where t denotes the time in months. What does this model predict for the radius of the region colonised by the beetle after t months?

The given differential equation suggests a relationship in which t is the independent variable and r the dependent variable. But you could just as well think of it the other way round, to ask the question 'how many months will it take for the radius to reach a certain value?'.

Treating r as the independent variable, you can write

$$\frac{dt}{dr} = 1 \div \frac{dr}{dt} = \frac{6}{\sqrt{r}}.$$

This differential equation can be solved by direct integration, as

$$t = 12\sqrt{r} + k,$$

where k is a constant. It is given that, when $t = 0$, $r = 25$, so k must satisfy the equation

$$0 = 12\sqrt{25} + k, \quad \text{which gives } k = -60.$$

The solution of the differential equation is therefore

$$t = 12\sqrt{r} - 60.$$

You could leave the answer in this form. For example, if you wanted to know how many months the model predicts it would take for the radius to reach 50 kilometres, the answer would be $(12\sqrt{50} - 60)$, which is 25 months to the nearest month.

But since the question is asked the other way round, it would be better to complete the solution by expressing r in terms of t:

$$\sqrt{r} = \frac{t + 60}{12}, \quad \text{so} \quad r = \frac{(t + 60)^2}{144}.$$

The model predicts that after t months the beetle will have spread to a region of radius $\frac{1}{144}(t + 60)^2$ kilometres.

Example 7.2.2

A hot-air balloon can reach a maximum height of 1.25 km, and the rate at which it gains height decreases as it climbs, according to the formula

$$\frac{dh}{dt} = 20 - 16h,$$

where h is the height in km and t is the time in hours after lift-off. How long does the balloon take to reach a height of 1 km?

You can invert the differential equation to give

$$\frac{dt}{dh} = 1 \bigg/ \frac{dh}{dt} = \frac{1}{20 - 16h},$$

so that $t = \displaystyle\int \frac{1}{20 - 16h}\, dh.$

The solution can be completed in either of two ways. You can find the precise equation connecting h and t with an indefinite integral and the initial conditions. Alternatively you can use a definite integral to get the required numerical answer directly.

Method 1 The indefinite integral is

$$t = \int \frac{1}{20 - 16h}\, dh = -\frac{1}{16}\ln(20 - 16h) + k.$$

(Notice that $20 - 16h$ is always positive when $0 \leqslant h \leqslant 1$.) Since t is measured from the instant of lift-off, $h = 0$ when $t = 0$. The particular solution with this initial condition must therefore satisfy

$$0 = -\tfrac{1}{16}\ln 20 + k, \quad \text{so } k = \tfrac{1}{16}\ln 20.$$

The equation connecting the variables h and t is therefore

$$t = -\tfrac{1}{16}\ln(20 - 16h) + \tfrac{1}{16}\ln 20 = \tfrac{1}{16}\ln\left(\frac{20}{20 - 16h}\right) = \tfrac{1}{16}\ln\left(\frac{5}{5 - 4h}\right).$$

When $h = 1$, $t = \tfrac{1}{16}\ln\left(\dfrac{5}{5 - 4}\right) = \tfrac{1}{16}\ln 5 \approx 0.10.$

Method 2   Since only the time at $h = 1$ is required, you need not find the general equation connecting h and t. Instead, you can find the time as a definite integral, from $h = 0$ to $h = 1$:

$$\int_0^1 \frac{1}{20 - 16h}\,dh = \left[-\tfrac{1}{16}\ln(20 - 16h)\right]_0^1 = -\tfrac{1}{16}(\ln 4 - \ln 20)$$
$$= -\tfrac{1}{16}\ln\left(\tfrac{4}{20}\right) = -\tfrac{1}{16}\ln\left(\tfrac{1}{5}\right) = \tfrac{1}{16}\ln 5 \approx 0.10.$$

The balloon takes 0.1 hours, or 6 minutes, to reach a height of 1 km.

Example 7.2.3

When a ball is dropped from the roof of a tall building, the greatest speed that it can reach (called the terminal speed) is u. One model for its speed v when it has fallen a distance x is given by the differential equation

$$\frac{dv}{dx} = c\frac{u^2 - v^2}{v},$$

where c is a positive constant.

Find an expression for v in terms of x.

No units are given, but the constants u and c will depend on the units in which v and x are measured.

Since $\dfrac{dv}{dx}$ is given in terms of v rather than x, invert the equation to give

$$\frac{dx}{dv} = \frac{1}{c}\frac{v}{(u^2 - v^2)}, \quad \text{so that } x = \int \frac{1}{c}\frac{v}{(u^2 - v^2)}\,dv.$$

The integral can be found by writing the integrand as $-\dfrac{1}{2c} \times \dfrac{-2v}{u^2 - v^2}.$

Note that v must be less than u, so $u^2 - v^2 > 0$. The second factor has the form $\dfrac{f'(v)}{f(v)}$, where $f(v) = u^2 - v^2$. It can therefore be integrated using the result in Section 2.4, as

$$x = -\frac{1}{2c}\ln(u^2 - v^2) + k.$$

The ball is not moving at the instant when it is dropped, so $v = 0$ when $x = 0$. This initial condition gives an equation for k:

$$0 = -\frac{1}{2c}\ln(u^2) + k, \quad \text{so} \quad k = \frac{\ln u^2}{2c}.$$

The equation connecting v and x is therefore

$$x = \frac{1}{2c}(\ln u^2 - \ln(u^2 - v^2)) = \frac{1}{2c}\ln\left(\frac{u^2}{u^2 - v^2}\right).$$

You must now turn this equation round to get v in terms of x:

$$2cx = \ln\left(\frac{u^2}{u^2 - v^2}\right),$$

$$\frac{u^2}{u^2 - v^2} = e^{2cx},$$

$$u^2 = (u^2 - v^2)e^{2cx},$$

$$v^2 e^{2cx} = u^2(e^{2cx} - 1),$$

$$v^2 = u^2(1 - e^{-2cx}).$$

Therefore, since $v > 0$, the required expression is $v = u\sqrt{1 - e^{-2cx}}$.

Example 7.2.4

A steel ball is heated to a temperature of 700 degrees Celsius and dropped into a drum of powdered ice. The temperature falls to 500 degrees in 30 seconds. Two models are suggested for the temperature, T degrees, after t seconds:

(a) the rate of cooling is proportional to T,   (b) the rate of cooling is proportional to $T^{1.2}$.

It is found that it takes a further 3 minutes for the temperature to fall from 500 to 100 degrees. Which model fits this information better?

The rate of cooling is measured by $\dfrac{\mathrm{d}T}{\mathrm{d}t}$, and this is negative.

(a) This model is described by the differential equation

$$\frac{\mathrm{d}T}{\mathrm{d}t} = -aT, \text{ where } a \text{ is a positive constant.}$$

Inverting, $\dfrac{\mathrm{d}t}{\mathrm{d}T} = -\dfrac{1}{aT}$, which has solution $t = -\dfrac{1}{a}\ln T + k$.

Since $T = 700$ when $t = 0$, $0 = -\dfrac{1}{a}\ln 700 + k$, so $k = \dfrac{1}{a}\ln 700$.

The equation connecting T and t is therefore

$$t = \frac{1}{a}(\ln 700 - \ln T) = \frac{1}{a}\ln\frac{700}{T}.$$

The value of a can be found from the fact that $T = 500$ when $t = 30$:

$$30 = \frac{1}{a}\ln\frac{700}{500}, \text{ which gives } a = \frac{\ln 1.4}{30} \approx 0.0112.$$

(b) For this model

$$\frac{\mathrm{d}T}{\mathrm{d}t} = -bT^{1.2}, \text{ so } \frac{\mathrm{d}t}{\mathrm{d}T} = -\frac{1}{b}T^{-1.2}, \text{ and } t = \frac{1}{0.2b}T^{-0.2} + k.$$

From the initial condition, that $T = 700$ when $t = 0$,

$$0 = \frac{5}{b}700^{-0.2} + k, \text{ so } t = \frac{5}{b}(T^{-0.2} - 700^{-0.2}).$$

From the other boundary condition, that $T = 500$ when $t = 30$,

$$30 = \frac{5}{b}(500^{-0.2} - 700^{-0.2}), \text{ so } b = \frac{500^{-0.2} - 700^{-0.2}}{6} \approx 0.00313.$$

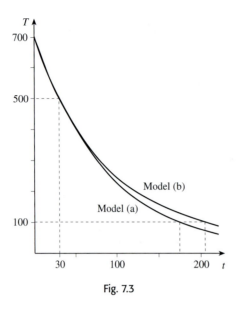

Fig. 7.3

Fig. 7.3 shows the two models to be compared, whose equations are

(a) $t = \dfrac{1}{0.0112} \ln \dfrac{700}{T}$, and

(b) $t = \dfrac{5}{0.00313}(T^{-0.2} - 700^{-0.2})$.

That is, (a) $T = 700\mathrm{e}^{-0.0112t}$, and

(b) $T = \dfrac{1}{(0.000\,626t + 0.270)^5}$.

To choose between the models, use the other piece of data, that $T = 100$ after a further 3 minutes, which is when $t = 30 + 180 = 210$. Try putting $T = 100$ in the two equations: model (a) gives $t = 174$, and model (b) gives $t = 205$.

This suggests that (b) is the better model.

7.3 The equation for exponential growth

In C3 Section 3.2 it was shown that the continuous exponential equation can be written as $y = a\mathrm{e}^{ct}$. It represents exponential growth if $c > 0$, and exponential decay if $c < 0$.

From this it follows that $\dfrac{\mathrm{d}y}{\mathrm{d}t} = ac\mathrm{e}^{ct} = cy$. That is, a quantity growing exponentially has a rate of growth equal to c times its current value.

But in many applications you want to argue the other way, to show that a quantity increasing at a rate proportional to its current value is described by an exponential equation. Denoting the quantity by Q, this is expressed mathematically by the differential equation $\dfrac{\mathrm{d}Q}{\mathrm{d}t} = cQ$, where t stands for the time and c is a constant. The sign of c is positive for exponential growth, and negative for exponential decay.

You can solve this equation by writing $\dfrac{dt}{dQ} = \dfrac{1}{cQ}$ and integrating:

$$t = \int \dfrac{1}{cQ} dQ = \dfrac{1}{c} \ln |Q| + k.$$

Suppose that Q has the value Q_0 when $t = 0$. Then $0 = \dfrac{1}{c} \ln |Q_0| + k$, so that

$$t = \dfrac{1}{c} \ln |Q| - \dfrac{1}{c} \ln |Q_0|, \text{ giving } \left| \dfrac{Q}{Q_0} \right| = e^{ct}.$$

Now Q must have the same sign as Q_0. In the equation $\dfrac{dt}{dQ} = \dfrac{1}{cQ}$ the value $Q = 0$ has to be excluded, since $\dfrac{1}{c \times 0}$ has no meaning. So if a solution begins at a positive value Q_0, Q remains positive; and if a solution begins at a negative value Q_0, Q remains negative. So $\dfrac{Q}{Q_0}$ is always positive, and you can replace $\left| \dfrac{Q}{Q_0} \right|$ in the above equation by $\dfrac{Q}{Q_0}$.

It follows that:

> If $\dfrac{dQ}{dt} = cQ$, where c is a non-zero constant, and $Q = Q_0$ when $t = 0$, then
> $Q = Q_0 e^{ct}$.

You will meet this differential equation so often that it is worthwhile learning this result. In a particular application, you can then write down the solution without going through the theory each time.

If e^c is written as b, then $b > 0$ whether c is positive or negative. The equation $Q = Q_0 e^{ct}$ can then be written as $Q = Q_0(e^c)^t = Q_0 b^t$, which has the form of the definition of exponential growth given in C3 Section 3.2.

Exercise 7B

1 Find general solutions of the following differential equations, expressing the dependent variable as a function of the independent variable. Display graphs of a number of typical solutions.

(a) $\dfrac{dy}{dx} = y^2$

(b) $\dfrac{dy}{dx} = \tan y$, for $0 < y < \tfrac{1}{2}\pi$

(c) $\dfrac{dx}{dt} = 4x$

(d) $\dfrac{dz}{dt} = \dfrac{1}{z}$, for $z > 0$

(e) $\dfrac{dx}{dt} = \operatorname{cosec} x$, for $0 < x < \pi$

(f) $u^2 \dfrac{du}{dx} = a$, for $u > 0$

2 A curve passes through the origin and satisfies the differential equation $\dfrac{dy}{dx} = a + y$, where $a > 0$. Find an expression for y in terms of x.

3 Solve the following differential equations with the given initial conditions. Display graphs to illustrate your answers.

(a) $\dfrac{dx}{dt} = -2x$, $x = 3$ when $t = 0$

(b) $\dfrac{du}{dt} = u^3$, $u = 1$ when $t = 0$

4 Find the solution curves of the following differential equations which pass through the given points. Display graphs to illustrate your answer, and suggest any restrictions which should be placed on the values of x.

  (a) $\dfrac{dy}{dx} = y + y^2$, through $(0, 1)$ (b) $\dfrac{dy}{dx} = e^y$, through $(2, 0)$

5 Given that $y = 1$ when $x = 0$, and that $\dfrac{dy}{dx} = y^3$, find an expression for y in terms of x.

  Show that, for all points on the solution curve, $x < \frac{1}{2}$ and $y > 0$. Draw a sketch of the solution curve.

6 A girl lives 500 metres from school. She sets out walking at $2\,\mathrm{m\,s^{-1}}$, but when she has walked a distance of x metres her speed has dropped to $\left(2 - \frac{1}{400}x\right)\mathrm{m\,s^{-1}}$. How long does she take to get to school?

7 A boy is eating a 250 gram hamburger. When he has eaten a mass m grams, his rate of consumption is $100 - \frac{1}{900}m^2$ grams per minute. How long does he take to finish his meal?

8 A quantity Q varies with the time t for $t > 0$, and satisfies the differential equation $\dfrac{dQ}{dt} = 2(1 - Q)$. Given that $Q = 0$ when $t = 0$, find how long it takes for Q to reach the value $\frac{1}{2}$. Show that Q is always less than 1, and that $Q \to 1$ as $t \to \infty$.

9 A sculler is rowing a 2 kilometre course. She starts rowing at $5\,\mathrm{m\,s^{-1}}$, but gradually tires, so that when she has rowed x metres her speed has dropped to $5e^{-0.0001x}\,\mathrm{m\,s^{-1}}$. How long will she take to complete the course?

10 A tree is planted as a seedling of negligible height. The rate of increase in its height, in metres per year, is given by the formula $0.2\sqrt{25 - h}$, where h is the height of the tree, in metres, t years after it is planted.

  (a) Explain why the height of the tree can never exceed 25 metres.

  (b) Write down a differential equation connecting h and t, and solve it to find an expression for t as a function of h.

  (c) How long does it take for the tree to put on

      (i) its first metre of growth,   (ii) its last metre of growth?

  (d) Find an expression for the height of the tree after t years. Over what interval of values of t is this model valid?

11 Astronomers observe a luminous cloud of stellar gas which appears to be expanding. When it is observed a month later, its radius is estimated to be 5 times the original radius. After a further 3 months, the radius appears to be 5 times as large again.

  It is thought that the expansion is described by a differential equation of the form $\dfrac{dr}{dt} = cr^m$ where c and m are constants. There is, however, a difference of opinion about the appropriate value to take for m. Two hypotheses are proposed, that $m = \frac{1}{3}$ and $m = \frac{1}{2}$. Investigate which of these models gives the best fit to the observed data.

Miscellaneous exercise 7

1 Find the solution of the differential equation $x\dfrac{dy}{dx} = 2x^2 + 7x + 3$ for which $y = 10$ when $x = 1$. (OCR)

2 In a chemical reaction, the amount z grams of a substance after t hours is modelled by the differential equation $\dfrac{dz}{dt} = 0.005(20 - z)^2$. Initially $z = 0$. Find an expression for t in terms of z, and show that $t = 15$ when $z = 12$. (OCR)

3 The gradient of a curve is given by $\dfrac{dy}{dx} = 3x^2 - 8x + 5$. The curve passes through the point $(0, 3)$. Find the equation of the curve. Find the coordinates of the two stationary points. State, with a reason, the nature of each stationary point. (MEI)

4 A quantity x grows with time according to the law $\dfrac{dx}{dt} = \dfrac{e^{-x}}{x}$. Given that $x = 1$ when $t = 0$, find how long it takes for x to reach the value 2.

5 The area of a circle of radius r metres is $A\,\text{m}^2$.
   (a) Find $\dfrac{dA}{dr}$ and write down an expression, in terms of r, for $\dfrac{dr}{dA}$.
   (b) The area increases with time t seconds in such a way that $\dfrac{dA}{dt} = \dfrac{2}{(t+1)^3}$. Find an expression, in terms of r and t, for $\dfrac{dr}{dt}$.
   (c) Solve the differential equation $\dfrac{dA}{dt} = \dfrac{2}{(t+1)^3}$ to obtain A in terms of t, given that $A = 0$ when $t = 0$.
   (d) Show that, when $t = 1$, $\dfrac{dr}{dt} = 0.081$ correct to 2 significant figures. (OCR)

6 Given that $y = 1$ when $x = 0$, and that $\dfrac{dy}{dx} = \cos^2 y$, find the value of x when $y = 0$. Show that, for all values of x, the values of y always lie between bounds $-a$ and $+a$. State the value of a.

7 At time $t = 0$ there are 8000 fish in a lake. At time t days the birth-rate of fish is equal to one-fiftieth of the number N of fish present. Fish are taken from the lake at the rate of 100 per day. Modelling N as a continuous variable, show that $50\dfrac{dN}{dt} = N - 5000$.

Solve the differential equation to find N in terms of t. Find the time taken for the population of fish in the lake to increase to 11 000.

When the population of fish has reached 11 000, it is decided to increase the number of fish taken from the lake from 100 per day to F per day. Write down, in terms of F, the new differential equation satisfied by N. Show that if $F > 220$, then $\dfrac{dN}{dt} < 0$ when $N = 11\,000$. For this range of values of F, give a reason why the population of fish in the lake continues to decrease. (OCR)

8 (a) The number of people, x, in a queue at a travel centre t minutes after it opens is modelled by the differential equation $\dfrac{dx}{dt} = 1.4t - 4$ for values of t up to 10. Interpret the term '-4' on the right side of the equation. Solve the differential equation, given that $x = 8$ when $t = 0$.

   (b) An alternative model gives the differential equation $\dfrac{dx}{dt} = 1.4t - 0.5x$ for the same values of t. Verify that $x = 13.6e^{-0.5t} + 2.8t - 5.6$ satisfies this differential equation. Verify also that when $t = 0$ this function takes the value 8.   (OCR)

9 Solve the differential equation $\dfrac{dy}{dt} = \dfrac{1 - y^2}{y}$, given that $y = a$ when $t = 0$, where $0 < a < 1$. Show that $y \to 1$ as $t \to \infty$.

10 A metal rod is 60 cm long and is heated at one end. The temperature at a point on the rod at distance x cm from the heated end is denoted by T °C. At a point halfway along the rod, $T = 290$ and $\dfrac{dT}{dx} = -6$.

   (a) In a simple model for the temperature of the rod, it is assumed that $\dfrac{dT}{dx}$ has the same value at all points on the rod. For this model, express T in terms of x and hence determine the temperature difference between the ends of the rod.

   (b) In a more refined model, the rate of change of T with respect to x is taken to be proportional to x. Set up a differential equation for T, involving a constant of proportionality k. Solve the differential equation and hence show that, in this refined model, the temperature along the rod is predicted to vary from 380 °C to 20 °C.   (OCR)

11* A battery is being charged. The charging rate is modelled by, $\dfrac{dq}{dt} = k(Q - q)$, where q is the charge in the battery (measured in ampere-hours) at time t (measured in hours), Q is the maximum charge the battery can store and k is a constant of proportionality. The model is valid for $q \geq 0.4Q$.

   (a) It is given that $q = \lambda Q$ when $t = 0$, where λ is a constant such that $0.4 \leq \lambda < 1$. Solve the differential equation to find q in terms of t. Sketch the graph of the solution.

   (b) It is noticed that the charging rate halves every 40 minutes. Show that $k = \frac{3}{2}\ln 2$.

   (c) Charging is always stopped when $q = 0.95Q$. If T is the time until charging is stopped, show that $T = \dfrac{2\ln(20(1 - \lambda))}{3\ln 2}$ for $0.4 \leq \lambda \leq 0.95$.   (MEI)

12 The rate at which the water level in a cylindrical barrel goes down is modelled by the equation $\dfrac{dh}{dt} = -\sqrt{h}$, where h is the height in metres of the level above the tap and t is the time in minutes. When $t = 0$, $h = 1$. Show by integration that $h = \left(1 - \frac{1}{2}t\right)^2$. How long does it take for the water flow to stop?

An alternative model would be to use a sine function, such as $h = 1 - \sin kt$. Find the value of k which gives the same time before the water flow stops as the previous model. Show that this model satisfies the differential equation $\dfrac{dh}{dt} = -k\sqrt{2h - h^2}$.

     (OCR, adapted)

13 A curve satisfies the differential equation $\dfrac{dy}{dx} = \dfrac{\sec y}{y}$, and $y = \frac{1}{6}\pi$ when $x = 0$. Find the value of x when $y = \frac{1}{3}\pi$.

14 A tropical island is being set up as a nature reserve. Initially there are 100 nesting pairs of fancy terns on the island. In the first year this increases by 8. In one theory being tested, the number N of nesting pairs after t years is assumed to satisfy the differential equation $\dfrac{dN}{dt} = \frac{1}{5000} N(500 - N)$.

   (a) Show that, according to this model, the rate of increase of N is 8 per year when $N = 100$. Find the rate of increase when $N = 300$ and when $N = 450$. Describe what happens as N approaches 500, and interpret your answer.

   (b) Use your answers to part (a) to sketch the solution curve of the differential equation for which $N = 100$ when $t = 0$.

   (c) Obtain the general solution of the differential equation, and the solution for which $N = 100$ when $t = 0$. Use your answer to predict after how many years the number of pairs of nesting fancy terns on the island will first exceed 300.   (OCR)

15 (a) If $\dfrac{dy}{dx} = \sqrt{y}$ and $y = 1$ when $x = 1$, show that the standard method of solution leads to the equation $y = \frac{1}{4}(x + 1)^2$.

   (b) Check by direct substitution that $y = \frac{1}{4}(x + 1)^2$ is a solution for values of x greater than -1.

   (c) Explain why $y = \frac{1}{4}(x + 1)^2$ cannot be a solution if $x < -1$. Investigate what goes wrong with the standard method of solution when $x = -1$.

   (d) Draw a graph to illustrate the solution of the differential equation.

16* A biologist is researching the population of a species. She tries a number of different models for the rate of growth of the population and solves them to compare with observed data. Her first model is $\dfrac{dp}{dt} = kp\left(1 - \dfrac{p}{m}\right)$ where p is the population at time t years, k is a constant and m is the maximum population sustainable by the environment. Find the general solution of the differential equation.

   Her observations suggest that $k = 0.2$ and $m = 100\,000$. If the initial population is $30\,000$, estimate the population after 5 years to 2 significant figures.

   She decides that the model needs to be refined. She proposes a model $\dfrac{dp}{dt} = kp\left(1 - \left(\dfrac{p}{m}\right)^{\alpha}\right)$ and investigates suitable values of α. Her observations lead her to the conclusion that the maximum growth rate occurs when the population is 70% of its maximum. Show that $(\alpha + 1)0.7^{\alpha} = 1$, and that an approximate solution of this equation is $\alpha \approx 5$. Express the time that it will take the population to reach $54\,000$ according to this model as a definite integral, and use Simpson's rule with two intervals to find this time approximately.   (MEI, adapted)

8 Curves defined implicitly

This chapter shows how to find gradients of curves which are described by implicit equations. When you have completed it, you should

- understand the nature of implicit equations, and be able to differentiate them
- be able to integrate differential equations with separable variables.

8.1 Equations of curves

In this course you have used coordinates and graphs in two ways: for understanding functions, and for obtaining geometrical results.

The graph of a function provides a visual representation of an equation $y = f(x)$. The variables x and y play different roles: for each x there is a unique y, but the reverse need not be true. The graph shows properties of the function such as whether it is increasing or decreasing, and where it has its maximum value. It is usually unnecessary to have equal scales in the x- and y-directions. Indeed, in applications, the two variables may represent quite different kinds of quantity, measured in different units.

When you use coordinates in geometry, the x- and y-coordinates have equal status. You must use the same scales in both directions, otherwise circles will not look circular and perpendicular lines will not appear perpendicular. Equations are often written not as $y = f(x)$, but in forms such as $ax + by + c = 0$ or $x^2 + y^2 + 2gx + 2fy + c = 0$, which emphasise that x and y are equal partners. These are **implicit equations** which define the relation between x and y.

Sometimes you can put such equations into the $y = f(x)$ form: for example, you can write $3x - 2y + 6 = 0$ as $y = \frac{3}{2}x + 3$.

However, the circle $(x - 2)^2 + (y - 3)^2 = 16$ has two values of y for each x between -2 and 6, given by $y = 3 \pm \sqrt{16 - (x - 2)^2}$. So the equation of the circle cannot be written as an equation of the form $y = f(x)$.

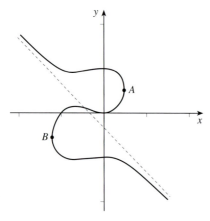

Fig. 8.1

Similarly, the curve in Fig. 8.1, whose equation is

$$x^3 + y^3 + x^2 - y = 0,$$

cannot be put into either of the forms $y = f(x)$ or $x = f(y)$. If you take a particular value for x, it gives a cubic equation for y, and if you take a particular value for y, it gives a cubic equation for x. For some values of y there are three values of x, and for some values of x there are three values of y, so the equation cannot be expressed in function form, either as $y = f(x)$ or as $x = f(y)$.

You can easily find a few features of the curve from the equation:

- The equation is satisfied by $x = 0$, $y = 0$, so the curve contains the origin.
- The curve cuts the x-axis, $y = 0$, where $x^3 + x^2 = 0$ so $x = 0$ or -1.
- The curve cuts the y-axis, $x = 0$, where $y^3 - y = 0$ so $y = -1$, 0 or 1.

The broken line in Fig. 8.1 has equation $x + y = \frac{1}{3}$. This line cuts the curve only once, at the point $\left(-\frac{4}{9}, \frac{1}{9}\right)$. The curve approaches this line as $|x|$ or $|y|$ take large values.

8.2 Finding gradients from implicit equations

When differentiation was first introduced in C1 Chapter 5, the method used was to take two points P and Q close together on the graph of $y = f(x)$, and to find the gradient of the chord joining them. Denoting their coordinates by (x, y) and $(x + \delta x, y + \delta y)$, you can write $y = f(x)$ and $y + \delta y = f(x + \delta x)$, so the gradient is

$$\frac{\delta y}{\delta x} = \frac{f(x + \delta x) - f(x)}{\delta x}.$$

Then, letting Q move round the curve towards P, you get the limiting value

$$\frac{dy}{dx} = \lim_{\delta x \to 0} \frac{\delta y}{\delta x} = \lim_{\delta x \to 0} \frac{f(x + \delta x) - f(x)}{\delta x}.$$

If you want to find $\dfrac{dy}{dx}$ for a curve like the one in Section 8.1, the same principles apply, but the algebra is different because you don't have an equation in the form $y = f(x)$. The coordinates therefore have to be substituted into the implicit equation, giving (for this example) the two equations

$$x^3 + y^3 + x^2 - y = 0, \qquad\qquad \text{Equation P}$$

and $\quad (x + \delta x)^3 + (y + \delta y)^3 + (x + \delta x)^2 - (y + \delta y) = 0. \qquad \text{Equation Q}$

Using the binomial theorem, the terms of Equation Q can be expanded to give

$$(x^3 + 3x^2(\delta x) + 3x(\delta x)^2 + (\delta x)^3) + (y^3 + 3y^2(\delta y) + 3y(\delta y)^2 + (\delta y)^3)$$
$$+ (x^2 + 2x(\delta x) + (\delta x)^2) - (y + \delta y) = 0.$$

To make this look less complicated, rearrange the terms according to the degree to which δx and δy appear, as

$$\overbrace{(x^3 + y^3 + x^2 - y)}^{\text{degree 0}} + \overbrace{(3x^2(\delta x) + 3y^2(\delta y) + 2x(\delta x) - \delta y)}^{\text{degree 1}}$$

$$+ \overbrace{(3x(\delta x)^2 + 3y(\delta y)^2 + (\delta x)^2)}^{\text{degree 2}} + \overbrace{((\delta x)^3 + (\delta y)^3)}^{\text{degree 3}} = 0.$$

The first group of terms is just the left side of Equation P, so it is zero. Since you want to find the gradient of the chord, $\dfrac{\delta y}{\delta x}$, rewrite the other groups to show this fraction:

$$(0) + \left(3x^2 + 3y^2\frac{\delta y}{\delta x} + 2x - \frac{\delta y}{\delta x}\right)\delta x + \left(3x + 3y\left(\frac{\delta y}{\delta x}\right) + 1\right)(\delta x)^2 + \left(1 + \left(\frac{\delta y}{\delta x}\right)^3\right)(\delta x)^3 = 0.$$

There is now a common factor δx (which is non-zero), so divide by it to get

$$\left(3x^2 + 3y^2\frac{\delta y}{\delta x} + 2x - \frac{\delta y}{\delta x}\right) + \left(3x + 3y\left(\frac{\delta y}{\delta x}\right)^2 + 1\right)\delta x + \left(1 + \left(\frac{\delta y}{\delta x}\right)^3\right)(\delta x)^2 = 0.$$

There is one last step, to see what happens as Q approaches P, when δx tends to 0. Then $\dfrac{\delta y}{\delta x}$ becomes $\dfrac{dy}{dx}$, so the equation becomes

$$\left(3x^2 + 3y^2\frac{dy}{dx} + 2x - \frac{dy}{dx}\right) + \left(3x + 3y\left(\frac{dy}{dx}\right)^2 + 1\right) \times 0 + \left(1 + \left(\frac{dy}{dx}\right)^3\right) \times 0^2 = 0,$$

which is simply $3x^2 + 3y^2\dfrac{dy}{dx} + 2x - \dfrac{dy}{dx} = 0$.

Now compare this with the original equation, Equation P. You can see that each term has been replaced by its derivative with respect to x. Thus x^3 has become $3x^2$, x^2 has become $2x$ and y has become $\dfrac{dy}{dx}$. The only term which calls for comment is the second, which is an application of the chain rule:

$$\frac{d}{dx}(y^3) = \frac{d}{dy}(y^3) \times \frac{dy}{dx} = 3y^2\frac{dy}{dx}.$$

This is an example of a general rule:

> To find $\dfrac{dy}{dx}$ from an implicit equation, differentiate each term with respect to x, using the chain rule to differentiate any function f(y) as
> $$f'(y)\frac{dy}{dx}.$$

For the curve in Fig. 8.1, you can find the gradient by rearranging the differentiated equation as $(3x^2 + 2x) = (1 - 3y^2)\dfrac{dy}{dx}$, so

$$\frac{dy}{dx} = \frac{3x^2 + 2x}{1 - 3y^2}.$$

It is interesting to notice that $\dfrac{dy}{dx} = 0$ when $x = 0$ or $x = -\frac{2}{3}$. Fig. 8.1 shows that each of these values of x corresponds to three points on the curve: $x = 0$ at $(0, 1)$, $(0, 0)$ and $(0, -1)$, and $x = -\frac{2}{3}$ where $y^3 - y = -\frac{4}{27}$. This is a cubic equation whose roots can be found by numerical methods of the kind described in C3 Chapter 8; they are 0.92, 0.15 and -1.07, correct to 2 decimal places.

Since when using equations in implicit form the x- and y-coordinates are regarded equally, you might also want to find $\dfrac{dx}{dy}$, which is $1 \left/ \dfrac{dy}{dx}\right.$.

$$\frac{dx}{dy} = \frac{1 - 3y^2}{3x^2 + 2x}.$$

The tangent to the curve is parallel to the y-axis when $\dfrac{dx}{dy} = 0$, which is when $y = \dfrac{1}{\sqrt{3}}$ or $-\dfrac{1}{\sqrt{3}}$. These points are labelled A and B in Fig. 8.1

If you imagine the curve split into three pieces by making cuts at A and B, then each of these pieces defines y as a function of x (since for each x there is a unique y).

On each piece $\dfrac{dy}{dx}$ can then be defined as the limit of $\dfrac{\delta y}{\delta x}$ in the usual way. If the curve is then stitched up again, you have a definition of $\dfrac{dy}{dx}$ at every point of the curve except at A and B, which are the points where the gradient of the tangent is not defined.

This makes it possible to justify the rule in the blue box. Although the algebraic expression for y in terms of x is not known, the implicit equation defines y in terms of x on each piece of the curve; and when this y is substituted, the equation becomes an identity which is true for all relevant values of x. Any identity in x can be differentiated to give another identity. This produces an equation in which each term is differentiated with respect to x, as described by the rule.

In Examples 8.2.1 and 8.2.2 two methods of solution are given. The first method uses the rule for finding $\dfrac{dy}{dx}$ from an implicit equation; the second method is one you are already familiar with. You will see that both give the same answer. But the first method requires fewer steps and can be applied to a much wider range of curves.

Example 8.2.1
Show that $(1, 2)$ is on the circle $x^2 + y^2 - 6x + 2y - 3 = 0$, and find the gradient there.

Substituting $x = 1$, $y = 2$ in the left side of the equation gives $1 + 4 - 6 + 4 - 3$, which is equal to 0.

Method 1   Differentiating term by term with respect to x,

$$2x + 2y\frac{dy}{dx} - 6 + 2\frac{dy}{dx} - 0 = 0,$$

that is,

$$x + y\frac{dy}{dx} - 3 + \frac{dy}{dx} = 0.$$

Setting $x = 1$, $y = 2$ gives

$$1 + 2\frac{dy}{dx} - 3 + \frac{dy}{dx} = 0,$$

so $\dfrac{dy}{dx} = \frac{2}{3}$ at this point.

Method 2   The centre of the circle is $(3, -1)$, so the gradient of the radius to $(1, 2)$ is
$\dfrac{2 - (-1)}{1 - 3} = -\frac{3}{2}$.

The gradient of the tangent at $(1, 2)$ is therefore $-\dfrac{1}{-\frac{3}{2}} = \frac{2}{3}$.

Example 8.2.2

Find an expression for $\dfrac{dy}{dx}$ on the curve $3x^2 - 2y^3 = 1$.

Method 1   Differentiating term by term,

$$6x - 6y^2\frac{dy}{dx} = 0, \text{ so that } \frac{dy}{dx} = \frac{x}{y^2}.$$

Method 2   This equation can be written explicitly as $y = \left(\frac{3}{2}x^2 - \frac{1}{2}\right)^{\frac{1}{3}}$, and by the
chain rule $\dfrac{dy}{dx} = \frac{1}{3}\left(\frac{3}{2}x^2 - \frac{1}{2}\right)^{-\frac{2}{3}} \times 3x = x(y^3)^{-\frac{2}{3}} = \dfrac{x}{y^2}.$

Example 8.2.3

Sketch the graph of $\cos x + \cos y = \frac{1}{2}$, and find the equation of the tangent at the point
$\left(\frac{1}{2}\pi, \frac{1}{3}\pi\right)$.

Fig. 8.2 shows the part of the graph for which the values of both of x and y are
between $-\pi$ and π. Since $\cos y \leqslant 1$, $\cos x \geqslant -\frac{1}{2}$, so $-\frac{2}{3}\pi \leqslant x \leqslant \frac{2}{3}\pi$. Similarly
$-\frac{2}{3}\pi \leqslant y \leqslant \frac{2}{3}\pi$.

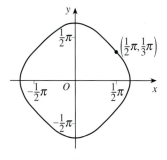

Fig. 8.2

Because cos is an even function, the graph is symmetrical about both axes; and
because the equation is unaltered by interchanging x and y, the graph is also
symmetrical about $y = x$, and hence about $y = -x$. Also, because the function cos has
period 2π, this shape is repeated over the whole plane at intervals of 2π in both
directions like a wallpaper pattern.

Differentiating,

$$- \sin x + (- \sin y)\frac{dy}{dx} = 0,$$

so

$$\frac{dy}{dx} = -\frac{\sin x}{\sin y}.$$

At $\left(\frac{1}{2}\pi, \frac{1}{3}\pi\right)$ the gradient is $-\dfrac{1}{\frac{1}{2}\sqrt{3}} = -\dfrac{2}{\sqrt{3}}$, so the equation of the tangent is

$$y - \tfrac{1}{3}\pi = -\tfrac{2}{\sqrt{3}}\left(x - \tfrac{1}{2}\pi\right), \text{ or } \quad y + \tfrac{2}{\sqrt{3}}x = \tfrac{1}{3}\pi\left(1 + \sqrt{3}\right).$$

Exercise 8A

1 Each of the following equations represents a circle. Find the gradient of the tangent at the given point (i) by finding the coordinates of the centre as in Method 2 of Example 8.2.1, and (ii) by differentiating the implicit equations.

(a) $x^2 + y^2 = 25$, $(-3, 4)$ (b) $x^2 + y^2 + 4x - 6y = 24$, $(4, 2)$

(c) $x^2 + y^2 - 6x + 8y = 0$, $(6, -8)$ (d) $x^2 + y^2 - 2x - 4y = 0$, $(0, 0)$

2 For the curves with the following equations, find expressions for $\dfrac{dy}{dx}$ in terms of x and y.

(a) $x^3 + 4y^3 - 2x^2 + y - 5 = 0$ (b) $3y^2 + 4x^3 + 2x + 1 = 0$

(c) $\sqrt{x} + \sqrt{y} = 1$ (d) $\dfrac{2}{x^2} - \dfrac{3}{y^3} = 6$

(e) $\ln(x^2 + 1) + \ln(y + 1) = x + y$

3 Find the gradients of the following curves at the given points.

(a) $x^2 + y^3 = 3$ at $(2, -1)$ (b) $3 \sin x + \cos y = 1$ at $\left(\frac{1}{6}\pi, \frac{2}{3}\pi\right)$

(c) $\dfrac{1}{\sqrt[3]{x}} + \dfrac{2}{\sqrt[3]{y^2}} = 1$ at $(8, 8)$

4 Find the points on the curve with equation $3x^2 + y^2 - 2y = 20$ at which the gradient is 2.

5 Differentiate the implicit equation $y^2 = 4x$ to find the gradient at $(9, -6)$ on the curve.

6 Differentiate the implicit equation of the ellipse $3x^2 + 4y^2 = 16$ to find the equation of the tangent at the point $(2, -1)$.

7 Differentiate the implicit equation of the hyperbola $4x^2 - 3y^2 = 24$ to find the equation of the normal at the point $(3, -2)$. Find the y-coordinate of the point where the normal meets the curve again.

8 (a) Show that the origin lies on the curve $e^x + e^y = 2$.

  (b) Differentiate the equation with respect to x, and explain why the gradient is always negative.

  (c) Find any restrictions that you can on the values of x and y, and sketch the curve.

9 Consider the curve with equation $x^2 + y^4 = 1$.

   (a) Find the coordinates of the points where the curve cuts the coordinate axes.

   (b) Show that the curve is symmetrical about both the x- and y-axes.

   (c) Show that the equation of the curve can be written in the form $y = \pm\sqrt[4]{1 - 4x^2}$ and use the first two terms of the binomial expansion to get approximations for y in terms of x.

   (d) Use your approximations to draw the shape of the curve for small values of x near the points where the curve crosses the y-axis.

   (e) Repeat parts (c) and (d) with the roles of x and y reversed.

   (f) Join up the pieces and make a sketch of the curve.

10 (a) Show that if (a, b) lies on the curve $x^2 + y^3 = 2$, then so does $(-a, b)$. What can you deduce from this about the shape of the curve?

   (b) Differentiate $x^2 + y^3 = 2$ with respect to x, and deduce what you can about the gradient for negative and for positive values of x.

   (c) Show that there is a stationary point at $(0, \sqrt[3]{2})$, and deduce its nature.

   (d) Sketch the curve.

11 Find the coordinates of the points at which the curve $y^5 + y = x^3 + x^2$ meets the coordinate axes, and find the gradients of the curve at each of these points.

12 Find the gradient of the curve $y^3 - 3y^2 + 2y = e^x + x - 1$ at the points where it crosses the y-axis.

8.3   An application to differential equations

All the differential equations in Chapter 7 had $\dfrac{dy}{dx}$ expressed as a function of either x or y; for example, $\dfrac{dy}{dx} = \sin x$ or $\dfrac{dy}{dx} = \dfrac{1}{y^2}$. Another common type of equation has the form

$$\frac{dy}{dx} = \frac{f(x)}{g(y)};$$

for example, $\dfrac{dy}{dx} = \dfrac{\sin x}{y^2}$.

Equations like $\dfrac{dy}{dx} = \dfrac{\sin x}{y^2}$ can be solved by reversing the process described in Section 8.2. Such an equation is said to have **separable variables**, because it can be rearranged to get just y on the left side and just x on the right.

Multiplying by $g(y)$ gives

$$g(y)\frac{dy}{dx} = f(x).$$

You will recognise this as the kind of equation you get when you differentiate an implicit equation.

For example, if you multiply $\dfrac{dy}{dx} = \dfrac{\sin x}{y^2}$ by y^2 you get

$$y^2 \frac{dy}{dx} = \sin x.$$

This is what you get if you differentiate with respect to x the equation

$$\tfrac{1}{3}y^3 = -\cos x + k,$$

where k is a constant.

In the general case, if you can find functions $G(y)$ and $F(x)$ such that $G'(y) = g(y)$ and $F'(x) = f(x)$, then the equation $g(y)\dfrac{dy}{dx} = f(x)$ can be written as

$$G'(y)\frac{dy}{dx} = F'(x).$$

The term on the left is $\dfrac{d}{dx}G(y)$, so you can integrate with respect to x to obtain the implicit equation

$$G(y) = F(x) + k.$$

This last step is based on $\displaystyle\int G'(y)\frac{dy}{dx}\,dx = \int G'(y)\,dy$, which you use when doing integration by substitution.

Example 8.3.1

The gradient of the tangent at each point P of a curve is equal to the square of the gradient of OP. Find the equation of the curve.

If (x, y) is a point on the curve, the gradient of OP is $\dfrac{y}{x}$, so the gradient of the tangent at P will be $\left(\dfrac{y}{x}\right)^2$. Therefore y and x satisfy the differential equation

$$\frac{dy}{dx} = \frac{y^2}{x^2}.$$

The variables can be separated by dividing by y^2, which gives

$$\frac{1}{y^2}\frac{dy}{dx} = \frac{1}{x^2}.$$

Now note that $\dfrac{1}{y^2}\dfrac{dy}{dx} = \dfrac{d}{dx}\left(-\dfrac{1}{y}\right)$ and $\dfrac{1}{x^2} = \dfrac{d}{dx}\left(-\dfrac{1}{x}\right)$.

So, integrating with respect to x gives the general solution

$$-\frac{1}{y} = -\frac{1}{x} + k.$$

Note that $\displaystyle\int \frac{1}{y^2}\frac{dy}{dx}\,dx = \int \frac{1}{y^2}\,dy = -\frac{1}{y} + \text{constant}.$

This can be written as $-\dfrac{1}{y} = -\dfrac{1 - kx}{x}$, so $y = \dfrac{x}{1 - kx}$.

It is interesting to see what happens when you take different values of k. All the curves in Fig. 8.3 have the property described above. But you have to exclude the origin, since the property has no meaning if P coincides with O.

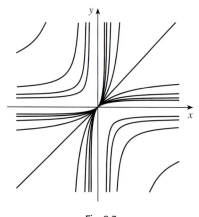

Fig. 8.3

Notice that all the curves have positive gradients at all points. This is expected, since at each point P the gradient is the square of the gradient of OP.

Notice also that if you draw a line $y = mx$ through the origin ($m \neq 0$ or 1), it will cut a lot of the curves. At every point P of intersection the gradient of OP is m, so the gradient of the curve will be m^2. So the tangents to the curves at the points where the line cuts them are all parallel.

Example 8.3.2

For the differential equation $\dfrac{dy}{dx} = \dfrac{xy}{x^2 + 1}$, find

(a) the equation of the solution curve which passes through $(1, 2)$,

(b) the general solution.

You can separate the variables by dividing by y, giving $\dfrac{1}{y}\dfrac{dy}{dx} = \dfrac{x}{x^2 + 1}$. Integrating with respect to x gives $\displaystyle\int \dfrac{1}{y}\dfrac{dy}{dx}\,dx = \int \dfrac{x}{x^2 + 1}\,dx$.

The left side can be expressed as $\displaystyle\int \dfrac{1}{y}\,dy$, and the right side has the form $\dfrac{1}{2}\displaystyle\int \dfrac{f'(x)}{f(x)}\,dx$ with $f(x) = x^2 + 1$ (see Section 2.4). So

$$\ln|y| = \tfrac{1}{2}\ln(x^2 + 1) + k.$$

(a) Substituting $x = 1$, $y = 2$ in this equation gives $\ln 2 = \tfrac{1}{2}\ln 2 + k$, so the required solution has $k = \tfrac{1}{2}\ln 2$, and is

$$\ln|y| = \tfrac{1}{2}\ln(x^2 + 1) + \tfrac{1}{2}\ln 2.$$

This equation can be written without logarithms, as

$$|y| = \sqrt{2(x^2 + 1)}.$$

In this form the equation represents not one, but two solution curves, with equations $y = \pm\sqrt{2(x^2 + 1)}$. Since the square root on the right is positive, the curve which passes through $(1, 2)$ has the equation with the positive sign, $y = \sqrt{2(x^2 + 1)}$.

(b) You already have one form of the general solution in the equation found above, but you should try to rearrange it in a simpler form. Notice that, for the particular solution through $(1, 2)$, the constant k came out as a logarithm. Similarly, in the general solution it helps to write the arbitrary constant k as $\ln A$, where A is a positive number. Then

$$\ln |y| = \tfrac{1}{2} \ln(x^2 + 1) + \ln A,$$

which can be written without logarithms as

$$|y| = A\sqrt{x^2 + 1}.$$

Now $|y|$ is positive, and so is $A\sqrt{x^2 + 1}$. But y might be negative, so

$$y = \pm A\sqrt{x^2 + 1}.$$

Finally, instead of writing the constant as $\pm A$, where A is positive, it is simpler to write it as c, where c can be positive or negative. The solution can then be expressed as

$$y = c\sqrt{x^2 + 1}.$$

There are a number of points to notice about the solution to the last example.

- Although when integrating you need to put the modulus sign in $\ln |y|$, it is not needed in $\ln(x^2 + 1)$, because $x^2 + 1$ is always positive.

- When integration introduces logarithms into the equation for the general solution, it is often worth adding the arbitrary constant in the form $+ \ln A$, rather than $+k$.

- What about the value $c = 0$? You can't include $A = 0$ in the solution because $\ln 0$ has no meaning. But obviously $y = 0$ (the x-axis) is a solution of the original differential equation, since $\dfrac{dy}{dx} = 0$ at every point. This solution in fact got lost at the very first step, dividing by y to separate the variables; you can't do this if $y = 0$. But now that this special case has been checked, you can say that the general solution of the differential equation is $y = c\sqrt{x^2 + 1}$, where the constant c can be any number, positive, negative or zero.

Check this solution for yourself by finding $\dfrac{dy}{dx}$ and showing that it does satisfy the differential equation for any value of c.

Example 8.3.3

For a certain period of about 12 years, the rate of growth of a country's gross national product (GNP) is predicted to vary between $+5\%$ and -1%. This variation is modelled by the formula $(2 + 3\cos \tfrac{1}{2}t)\%$, where t is the time in years. Find a formula for the GNP during the cycle.

Denote the GNP after t years by P. The rate of growth $\dfrac{\mathrm{d}P}{\mathrm{d}t}$ is given as a percentage of its current value, so

$$\frac{\mathrm{d}P}{\mathrm{d}t} = \frac{2 + 3\cos\frac{1}{2}t}{100}P.$$

The variables can be separated by dividing by P:

$$\frac{1}{P}\frac{\mathrm{d}P}{\mathrm{d}t} = \frac{2 + 3\cos\frac{1}{2}t}{100}.$$

Integrating,

$$\ln P = \frac{2t + 6\sin\frac{1}{2}t}{100} + k.$$

(Note that the GNP is always positive, so by definition $P > 0$.)

If P has the value P_0 when $t = 0$, then

$$\ln P_0 = 0 + k,$$

and the equation can be written

$$\ln P = \frac{2t + 6\sin\frac{1}{2}t}{100} + \ln P_0, \quad \text{or} \quad P = P_0 e^{\frac{1}{100}\left(2t + 6\sin\frac{1}{2}t\right)}.$$

Exercise 8B

1 Find the general solution of each of the following differential equations.

  (a) $\dfrac{\mathrm{d}y}{\mathrm{d}x} = \dfrac{x^2}{y^2}$ (b) $\dfrac{\mathrm{d}y}{\mathrm{d}x} = \dfrac{x}{y}$ (c) $\dfrac{\mathrm{d}y}{\mathrm{d}x} = xy$ (d) $\dfrac{\mathrm{d}y}{\mathrm{d}x} = \dfrac{1}{xy}$

2 Find the equation of the curve which satisfies the differential equation $\dfrac{\mathrm{d}y}{\mathrm{d}x} = \dfrac{y}{x(x+1)}$ and passes through the point $(1, 2)$.

3 Find the general solution of the differential equation $\dfrac{\mathrm{d}y}{\mathrm{d}x} = -\dfrac{x}{y}$. Describe the solution curves, and find the equation of the curve which passes through $(-4, 3)$.

4 Solve the differential equation $\dfrac{\mathrm{d}y}{\mathrm{d}x} = \dfrac{x+1}{2-y}$, and describe the solution curves.

5 Find the equations of the curves which satisfy the given differential equations, and pass through the given points.

  (a) $\dfrac{\mathrm{d}y}{\mathrm{d}x} = \dfrac{3y}{2x}$, $(2, 4)$ (b) $\dfrac{\mathrm{d}y}{\mathrm{d}x} = -\dfrac{3y}{2x}$, $(2, 4)$

  (c) $\dfrac{\mathrm{d}y}{\mathrm{d}x} = \dfrac{\sin x}{\cos y}$, $\left(\frac{1}{3}\pi, 0\right)$ (d) $\dfrac{\mathrm{d}y}{\mathrm{d}x} = \dfrac{\tan x}{\tan y}$, $\left(\frac{1}{3}\pi, 0\right)$

6 Solve the equation $v\dfrac{\mathrm{d}v}{\mathrm{d}x} = -\omega^2 x$, where ω is a constant. Find the particular solution for which $v = 0$ when $x = a$.

7 Find the general solution of the equations

(a) $\dfrac{dy}{dx} = \dfrac{2x(y^2 + 1)}{y(x^2 + 1)}$,

(b) $\dfrac{dy}{dx} = \tan x \cot y$.

8 Find the equations of the curves which satisfy the following differential equations and pass through the given points.

(a) $\dfrac{dy}{dx} = \dfrac{y(y - 1)}{x}$, $(1, 2)$

(b) $\dfrac{dy}{dx} = \cot x \cot y$, $\left(\tfrac{1}{6}\pi, 0\right)$

(c) $\dfrac{dy}{dx} = \dfrac{1 + y^2}{y(1 - x^2)}$, $\left(\tfrac{3}{2}, 2\right)$

(d) $\dfrac{dy}{dx} = y \tan x$, $(0, 2)$

9 Find the general solution of the differential equations

(a) $4 + x\dfrac{dy}{dx} = y^2$,

(b) $e^y \dfrac{dy}{dx} - 1 = \ln x$,

(c) $y \cos x \dfrac{dy}{dx} = 2 - y\dfrac{dy}{dx}$.

10 The gradient at each point of a curve is n times the gradient of the line joining the origin to that point. Find the general equation of the curve.

11 The size of an insect population n, which fluctuates during the year, is modelled by the equation $\dfrac{dn}{dt} = 0.01n(0.05 - \cos 0.02t)$, where t is the number of days from the start of observations. The initial number of insects is 5000.

(a) Solve the differential equation to find n in terms of t.

(b) Show that the model predicts that the number of insects will fall to a minimum after about 76 days, and find this minimum value.

12 The velocity v m s^{-1} of a spacecraft moving vertically x metres above the centre of the earth can be modelled by the equation $v\dfrac{dv}{dx} = -\dfrac{10R^2}{x^2}$, where R metres is the radius of the earth. The initial velocity at blast-off, when $x = R$, is V m s^{-1}.

Find an expression for v^2 in terms of V, x and R, and show that, according to this model, if the spacecraft is to be able to escape from the earth, then $V^2 \geqslant 20R$.

8.4 Implicit equations including products

The implicit equations in Section 8.2 contained terms in x and terms in y, but there were no terms which involved both x and y. Equations with more complicated terms can be differentiated using the product or quotient rule, sometimes in conjunction with the chain rule.

Example 8.4.1
Find the derivatives with respect to x of

(a) $y \sin x$,

(b) $y^3 \ln x$,

(c) $e^{x^2 y}$,

(d) $\cos \dfrac{x}{y}$.

(a) By the product rule,

$$\frac{d}{dx}(y \sin x) = \frac{d}{dx}y \times \sin x + y \times \frac{d}{dx}\sin x = \frac{dy}{dx}\sin x + y \cos x.$$

(b) $\dfrac{d}{dx}(y^3 \ln x) = \dfrac{d}{dx}y^3 \times \ln x + y^3 \times \dfrac{d}{dx}\ln x = 3y^2 \dfrac{dy}{dx}\ln x + \dfrac{y^3}{x}.$

(c) Using the chain rule followed by the product rule,

$$\dfrac{d}{dx}e^{x^2 y} = e^{x^2 y} \times \dfrac{d}{dx}(x^2 y) = e^{x^2 y}\left(2xy + x^2 \dfrac{dy}{dx}\right).$$

(d) $\dfrac{d}{dx}\cos\dfrac{x}{y} = -\sin\dfrac{x}{y} \times \dfrac{1 \times y - x \times \dfrac{dy}{dx}}{y^2} = \dfrac{x\dfrac{dy}{dx} - y}{y^2}\sin\dfrac{x}{y}.$

Example 8.4.2
Find the gradient of $x^2 y^3 = 72$ at the point $(3, 2)$.

Two methods are given: the first is direct; the second begins by taking logarithms. This makes expressions involving products of powers easier to handle.

Method 1 Differentiating with respect to x, using the product rule,

$$2xy^3 + x^2\left(3y^2 \dfrac{dy}{dx}\right) = 0.$$

At $(3, 2)$, $2 \times 3 \times 8 + 9 \times 3 \times 4\dfrac{dy}{dx} = 0$, so $\dfrac{dy}{dx} = -\frac{4}{9}$.

Method 2 Write the equation as $\ln(x^2 y^3) = \ln 72$. By the laws of logarithms, $\ln(x^2 y^3) = \ln x^2 + \ln y^3 = 2\ln x + 3\ln y$, so the equation is $2\ln x + 3\ln y = \ln 72$.

Differentiating, $\dfrac{2}{x} + \dfrac{3}{y}\dfrac{dy}{dx} = 0$, so $\dfrac{dy}{dx} = -\dfrac{2y}{3x}$. At $(3, 2)$, $\dfrac{dy}{dx} = -\frac{4}{9}$.

Method 2 is sometimes called 'logarithmic differentiation'.

Example 8.4.3
The equation $x^2 - 6xy + 25y^2 = 16$ represents an ellipse with its centre at the origin. What ranges of values of x and y would you need in order to plot the whole of the curve on a computer screen?

Two methods are given. The first, which uses the method of differentiation described in this chapter, can be applied to a large number of curves, although it sometimes leads to quite complicated algebra. The second method is an algebraic one; it gives the answer more quickly, but it can only be used for curves with a special type of equation.

Method 1 Fig. 8.4 shows the print-out of an ellipse set in a rectangle with sides parallel to the axes. You can see that the sides of the rectangle are tangents to the ellipse. So another way of asking the question is to find the tangents to the ellipse which are parallel to the axes; that is, to find the points at which $\dfrac{dy}{dx} = 0$ or $\dfrac{dx}{dy} = 0$.

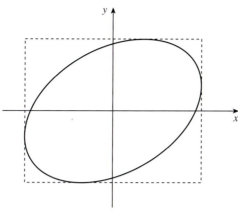

Fig. 8.4

Differentiating with respect to x,

$$2x - 6\left(1 \times y + x\frac{dy}{dx}\right) + 50y\frac{dy}{dx} = 0, \quad \text{that is,} \quad (x - 3y) + (25y - 3x)\frac{dy}{dx} = 0.$$

The tangent is parallel to the x-axis when $\dfrac{dy}{dx} = 0$, which is when $x = 3y$.

Substituting this into the equation of the ellipse gives

$$(3y)^2 - 6(3y)y + 25y^2 = 16, \quad 16y^2 = 16, \quad y = -1 \text{ or } 1.$$

The tangents are therefore parallel to the x-axis at $(-3, -1)$ and $(3, 1)$.

If the equation is differentiated with respect to y rather than x, you get

$$2x\frac{dx}{dy} - 6\frac{dx}{dy}y - 6x + 50y = 0, \quad \text{that is} \quad (x - 3y)\frac{dx}{dy} + (25y - 3x) = 0.$$

The tangent is parallel to the y-axis when $\dfrac{dx}{dy} = 0$, which occurs when $25y = 3x$.

Substituting $y = \frac{3}{25}x$ gives

$$x^2 - 6x\left(\tfrac{3}{25}x\right) + 25\left(\tfrac{3}{25}x\right)^2 = 16, \quad \tfrac{16}{25}x^2 = 16, \quad x = -5 \text{ or } 5.$$

The points of contact are $\left(-5, -\frac{3}{5}\right)$ and $\left(5, \frac{3}{5}\right)$.

To fit the curve on the screen you need $-5 \leqslant x \leqslant 5$ and $-1 \leqslant y \leqslant 1$. This is illustrated in Fig. 8.5.

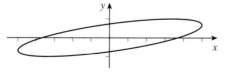

Fig. 8.5

Method 2 The question can also be answered by an algebraic method which finds the bounds for x and y without drawing the tangents.

The equation can be written as a quadratic in x:

$$x^2 - 6yx + (25y^2 - 16) = 0.$$

The condition for this to give real values of x is

$$(6y)^2 - 4(25y^2 - 16) \geqslant 0, \text{ that is, } 64 - 64y^2 \geqslant 0, \text{ so } -1 \leqslant y \leqslant 1.$$

Similarly, from the quadratic in y, which is

$$25y^2 - 6xy + (x^2 - 16) = 0,$$

you get the condition

$$(6x)^2 - 4 \times 25\,(x^2 - 16) \geqslant 0, \text{ that is, } 1600 - 64x^2 \geqslant 0, \text{ so } -5 \leqslant x \leqslant 5.$$

It is interesting to compare the two methods. The algebraic technique in Method 2 is shorter, but only works for quadratics, whereas the method which involves differentiating implicit functions is longer but works more generally.

Exercise 8C

1 Find the derivatives with respect to x of

(a) xy,
(b) xy^2,
(c) x^2y^2,
(d) $\dfrac{x^2}{y}$.

2 Find the derivatives with respect to x of

(a) $\sqrt{xy}$,
(b) $\sin(x^2y)$,
(c) $\ln(xy)$,
(d) e^{xy+y}.

3 Differentiate the implicit equations of the following curves to find the gradients at the point $(3, 4)$.

(a) $xy = 12$
(b) $4x^2 - xy - y^2 = 8$

4 Find the gradient of each of the following curves at the point given.

(a) $x \sin y = \frac{1}{2}$, $\left(1, \frac{1}{6}\pi\right)$
(b) $ye^x = xy + y^2$, $(0, 1)$
(c) $\ln(x + y) = -x$, $(0, 1)$
(d) $\cos(xy) = \frac{1}{2}$, $\left(1, \frac{1}{3}\pi\right)$

5 Find the equation of the tangent to the curve $x^2 - 2xy + 2y^2 = 5$ at the point $(1, 2)$.

6 Find the equation of the normal to the curve $2xy^2 - x^2y^3 = 1$ at the point $(1, 1)$.

7 Find the points on the curve $4x^2 + 2xy - 3y^2 = 39$ at which the tangent is parallel to one of the axes.

8* (a) Show that the curve $x^3 + y^3 = 3xy$ is symmetrical about the line $y = x$, and find the gradient of the curve at the point other than the origin for which $y = x$.

(b) Show that, close to the origin, if y is very small compared with x, then the curve is approximately given by the equation $y = kx^2$. Give the value of k.

(c) Find the coordinates of the points on the graph of $x^3 + y^3 = 3xy$ at which the tangent is parallel to one or other of the axes.

(d) Suppose now that $|x|$ and $|y|$ are both very large. Explain why $x + y \approx k$, where k is a constant, and substitute $y = k - x$ into the equation of the curve. Show that, if this equation is to be approximately satisfied by a large value of $|x|$, then $k = -1$.

(e) Draw a sketch of the curve.

9* (a) Explain why all the points on the curve $(x^2 + y^2)^2 = x^2 - y^2$ lie in the region $x^2 \geqslant y^2$.

(b) Find the coordinates of the points at which the tangent is either parallel to the x-axis or parallel to the y-axis.

(c) By considering where the curve meets the circle $x^2 + y^2 = r^2$, show that $r^2 \leqslant 1$, so the curve is bounded.

(d) Sketch the curve, which is called the *lemniscate of Bernoulli*.

Miscellaneous exercise 8

1 (a) Two quantities x and y are related to each other by the differential equation $y\dfrac{dy}{dx} = -16x$. Solve this equation to get an implicit equation of the solution curve for which $y = 0$ when $x = 0.1$.

(b) Sketch your solution curve from part (a), showing the values of x and y at which the curve cuts the coordinate axes. (OCR)

2 Find the equation of the normal at the point $(2, 1)$ on the curve $x^3 + xy + y^3 = 11$, giving your answer in the form $ax + by + c = 0$. (OCR)

3 A curve has implicit equation $x^2 - 2xy + 4y^2 = 12$.

(a) Find an expression for $\dfrac{dy}{dx}$ in terms of y and x. Hence determine the coordinates of the points where the tangents to the curve are parallel to the x-axis.

(b) Find the equation of the normal to the curve at the point $(2\sqrt{3}, \sqrt{3})$. (OCR)

4 Find the general solution of the differential equation $\dfrac{dy}{dx} = \dfrac{x(y^2 + 1)}{(x - 1)y}$, expressing y in terms of x. (OCR, adapted)

5 Solve the differential equation $\dfrac{dy}{dx} = xye^{2x}$, given that $y = 1$ when $x = 0$.

6 A curve has equation $y^3 + 3xy + 2x^3 = 9$. Obtain the equation of the normal at the point $(2, -1)$. (OCR)

7 Obtain the general solution of the differential equation $y\dfrac{dy}{dx}\tan 2x = 1 - y^2$. (OCR, adapted)

8 Find the general solution of the differential equation $\dfrac{dy}{dx} = \dfrac{y^2}{x^2 - x - 2}$ in the region $x > 2$.

Find also the particular solution which satisfies $y = 1$ when $x = 5$.   (OCR)

9 Find the solution of the differential equation $\dfrac{dy}{dx} = \dfrac{\sin^2 x}{y^2}$ which also satisfies $y = 1$ when $x = 0$.   (OCR)

10 Solve the differential equation $\dfrac{dy}{dx} = \dfrac{x}{y}e^{x+y}$, in the form $f(y) = g(x)$, given that $y = 0$ when $x = 0$.

11 A curve is defined implicitly by the equation $4y - x^2 + 2x^2y = 4x$.

   (a) Use implicit differentiation to find $\dfrac{dy}{dx}$.

   (b) Find the coordinates of the turning points on the curve.   (OCR, adapted)

12* Show that the tangent to the ellipse $\dfrac{x^2}{a^2} + \dfrac{y^2}{b^2} = 1$ at the point $P(a\cos\theta, b\sin\theta)$ has equation $bx\cos\theta + ay\sin\theta = ab$.

   (a) The tangent to the ellipse at P meets the x-axis at Q and the y-axis at R. The mid-point of QR is M. Find a cartesian equation for the locus of M as θ varies.

   (b) The tangent to the ellipse at P meets the line $x = a$ at T. The origin is at O and A is the point $(-a, 0)$. Prove that OT is parallel to AP.   (OCR)

13 To control the pests inside a large greenhouse, 600 ladybirds were introduced. After t days there are P ladybirds in the greenhouse. In a simple model, P is assumed to be a continuous variable satisfying the differential equation $\dfrac{dP}{dt} = kP$, where k is a constant. Solve the differential equation, with initial condition $P = 600$ when $t = 0$, to express P in terms of k and t.

Observations of the number of ladybirds (estimated to the nearest hundred) were made as follows:

t	0	150	250
P	600	1200	3100

Show that $P = 1200$ when $t = 150$ implies that $k \approx 0.004\,62$. Show that this is not consistent with the observed value when $t = 250$.

In a refined model, allowing for seasonal variations, it is assumed that P satisfies the differential equation $\dfrac{dP}{dt} = P(0.005 - 0.008\cos 0.02t)$ with initial condition $P = 600$ when $t = 0$. Solve this differential equation to express P in terms of t, and comment on how well this fits with the data given above.

Show that, according to the refined model, the number of ladybirds will decrease initially, and find the smallest number of ladybirds in the greenhouse.   (MEI)

14 The equation of a curve is $x^2 + 4xy + 5y^2 = 9$. Show by differentiation that the maximum and minimum values of y occur at the intersections of $x + 2y = 0$ with the curve. Find the maximum and minimum values of y. (OCR)

15 A biologist studying fluctuations in the size of a particular population decides to investigate a model for which $\dfrac{\mathrm{d}P}{\mathrm{d}t} = kP\cos kt$, where P is the size of the population at time t days and k is a positive constant.

(a) Given that $P = P_0$ when $t = 0$, express P in terms of k, t and P_0.

(b) Find the ratio of the maximum size of the population to the minimum size. (OCR)

16 The organiser of a sale, which lasted for 3 hours and raised a total of £1000, attempted to create a model to represent the relationship between s and t, where £ s is the amount which had been raised at time t hours after the start of the sale. In the model s and t were taken to be continuous variables. The organiser assumed that the rate of raising money varied directly as the time remaining and inversely as the amount already raised. Show that, for this model, $\dfrac{\mathrm{d}s}{\mathrm{d}t} = k\dfrac{3-t}{s}$, where k is a constant. Solve the differential equation, and show that the solution can be written in the form $\dfrac{s^2}{1000^2} + \dfrac{(3-t)^2}{3^2} = 1$. Hence

(a) find the amount raised during the first hour of the sale,

(b) find the rate of raising money one hour after the start of the sale. (OCR)

17* A curve C has equation $y = x + 2y^4$.

(a) Find $\dfrac{\mathrm{d}y}{\mathrm{d}x}$ in terms of y.

(b) Show that $\dfrac{\mathrm{d}^2y}{\mathrm{d}x^2} = \dfrac{24y^2}{(1-8y^3)^3}$.

(c) Write down the value of $\dfrac{\mathrm{d}y}{\mathrm{d}x}$ at the origin. Hence, by considering the sign of $\dfrac{\mathrm{d}^2y}{\mathrm{d}x^2}$, draw a diagram to show the shape of C in the neighbourhood of the origin. (OCR)

18* The curve C, whose equation is $x^2 + y^2 = e^{x+y} - 1$, passes through the origin O. Show that $\dfrac{\mathrm{d}y}{\mathrm{d}x} = -1$ at O. Find the value of $\dfrac{\mathrm{d}^2y}{\mathrm{d}x^2}$ at O. (OCR)

19 For $x > 0$ and $0 < y < \frac{1}{2}\pi$, the variables y and x are connected by the differential equation $\dfrac{\mathrm{d}y}{\mathrm{d}x} = \dfrac{\ln x}{\cot y}$, and $y = \frac{1}{6}\pi$ when $x = e$.

Find the value of y when $x = 1$, giving your answer to 3 significant figures. Use the differential equation to show that this value of y is a stationary value, and determine its nature. (MEI)

9 Scalar products of vectors

This chapter shows how vectors can be used to find results about lengths and angles. When you have completed it, you should

- know the definition of the scalar product, and its expression in components
- be able to use the rules of vector algebra which involve scalar products
- be able to use scalar products to solve geometrical problems in two and three dimensions, using general vector algebra or components.

9.1 The magnitude of a vector

Any translation can be described by giving its magnitude and direction. The notation used for the magnitude of a vector $\mathbf{p}$, ignoring its direction, is $|\mathbf{p}|$.

If you have two vectors $\mathbf{p}$ and $\mathbf{q}$ which are not equal, but which have equal magnitudes, then you can write $|\mathbf{p}| = |\mathbf{q}|$.

If s is a scalar multiple of $\mathbf{p}$, then it follows from the definition of $s\mathbf{p}$ (see Section 4.2) that $|s\mathbf{p}| = |s|\,|\mathbf{p}|$. This is true whether s is positive or negative (or zero).

The symbol for the magnitude of a vector is the same as the one for the modulus of a real number, but this does not present a problem. In fact, a real number x behaves just like the vector $x\,\mathbf{i}$ in one dimension, where $\mathbf{i}$ is a basic unit vector. This can be used to represent a displacement on the number line, and the modulus $|x|$ then measures the magnitude of the displacement, whether it is in the positive or the negative direction.

A vector of magnitude 1 is called a **unit vector**. The basic unit vectors $\mathbf{i}$, $\mathbf{j}$, $\mathbf{k}$ defined in Chapter 4 are examples of unit vectors, but they are not the only ones: there is a unit vector in every direction.

Unit vectors are sometimes distinguished by a circumflex accent ˆ over the letter. For example, a unit vector in the direction of $\mathbf{r}$ may be denoted by $\hat{\mathbf{r}}$. You can state that '$\mathbf{r}$ is a vector of magnitude $|\mathbf{r}|$ in the direction of the unit vector $\hat{\mathbf{r}}$' by writing $\mathbf{r} = |\mathbf{r}|\,\hat{\mathbf{r}}$. (Notice that $|\mathbf{r}|$ is a scalar which multiplies the vector $\hat{\mathbf{r}}$.) This notation is especially common in mechanics, but it will not generally be used in this chapter.

9.2 Scalar products

In Chapter 4 vectors were added, subtracted and multiplied by scalars, but they were not multiplied together. The next step is to define the product of two vectors:

> The **scalar product**, or **dot product** of vectors $\mathbf{p}$ and $\mathbf{q}$ is the number (or scalar) $|\mathbf{p}|\,|\mathbf{q}|\cos\theta$, where θ is the angle between the directions of $\mathbf{p}$ and $\mathbf{q}$. It is written $\mathbf{p} \cdot \mathbf{q}$ and pronounced 'p dot q'.

The angle θ may be acute or obtuse, but it is important that it is the angle between **p** and **q**, and not (for example) the angle between **p** and $-\mathbf{q}$. It is best to show θ in a diagram in which the vectors are represented by arrows with their tails at the same point, as in Fig. 9.1.

Fig. 9.1

The reason for calling this the 'scalar product', rather than simply the product, is that mathematicians also use another product, called the 'vector product'. But it is important to distinguish the scalar product from 'multiplication by a scalar', which you met in Chapter 4. To avoid confusion, many people prefer to use the alternative name 'dot product'.

For the same reason, you must always insert the 'dot' between **p** and **q** for the scalar product, but you must *not* insert a dot between s and **p** when multiplying a vector by a scalar.

For example, you can never have a scalar product of three vectors, $\mathbf{p} \cdot \mathbf{q} \cdot \mathbf{r}$. You will remember from Section 4.2 that the sum of these three vectors can be regarded as $(\mathbf{p} + \mathbf{q}) + \mathbf{r}$ or as $\mathbf{p} + (\mathbf{q} + \mathbf{r})$, and that these expressions are equal. But $(\mathbf{p} \cdot \mathbf{q}) \cdot \mathbf{r}$ has no meaning: $\mathbf{p} \cdot \mathbf{q}$ is a scalar, and you cannot form a dot product of this scalar with the vector **r**. Similarly, $\mathbf{p} \cdot (\mathbf{q} \cdot \mathbf{r})$ has no meaning.

However, $s(\mathbf{p} \cdot \mathbf{q})$, where s is scalar, does have a meaning; as you would expect, $s(\mathbf{p} \cdot \mathbf{q})$ is equal to $(s\mathbf{p}) \cdot \mathbf{q}$. The proof depends on whether s is positive (see Fig. 9.2) or negative (see Fig. 9.3).

Fig. 9.2   Fig. 9.3

If $s > 0$, then the angle between $s\mathbf{p}$ and **q** is θ, so

$$(s\mathbf{p}) \cdot \mathbf{q} = |s\mathbf{p}||\mathbf{q}| \cos \theta = |s||\mathbf{p}||\mathbf{q}| \cos \theta = |s|(|\mathbf{p}||\mathbf{q}| \cos \theta) = s(\mathbf{p} \cdot \mathbf{q}).$$

If $s < 0$, then the angle between $s\mathbf{p}$ and **q** is $\pi - \theta$, and $s = -|s|$, so

$$(s\mathbf{p}) \cdot \mathbf{q} = |s\mathbf{p}||\mathbf{q}| \cos(\pi - \theta) = |s||\mathbf{p}||\mathbf{q}|(- \cos \theta) = -|s|(|\mathbf{p}||\mathbf{q}| \cos \theta) = s(\mathbf{p} \cdot \mathbf{q}).$$

Another property of the scalar product is that $\mathbf{p} \cdot \mathbf{q} = \mathbf{q} \cdot \mathbf{p}$, which follows immediately from the definition. This is called the **commutative rule for scalar products**.

There are two very important special cases, which you get by taking $\theta = 0$ and putting $\mathbf{p} = \mathbf{q}$, and taking $\theta = \frac{1}{2}\pi$, in the definition of scalar product.

> $\mathbf{p} \cdot \mathbf{p} = |\mathbf{p}|^2$ ($\mathbf{p} \cdot \mathbf{p}$ is sometimes written as $\mathbf{p}^2$).
>
> If neither **p** nor **q** is the zero vector,
>
> $\mathbf{p} \cdot \mathbf{q} = 0$ $\Leftrightarrow$ **p** and **q** are in perpendicular directions.

These properties provide ways of using vectors to find lengths and to identify right angles.

9.3*   The distributive rule

The rules in the last section suggest that algebra with scalar products is much like ordinary algebra, except that some expressions (such as the scalar product of three vectors) have no meaning. You need one more rule to be able to use vectors to get geometrical results. This is the **distributive rule** for multiplying out brackets:

$$(\mathbf{p} + \mathbf{q}) \cdot \mathbf{r} = \mathbf{p} \cdot \mathbf{r} + \mathbf{q} \cdot \mathbf{r}.$$

You may, if you wish, omit the proof on a first reading, and go on to Section 9.4.

The proof of this needs a preliminary result. Fig. 9.4 shows a directed line l and two points A and B (in three dimensions). If lines AD and BE are drawn perpendicular to l, then the directed length DE is called the **projection** of the displacement vector $\overrightarrow{AB}$ on l.

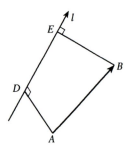

Here the word 'directed' means that a positive direction is selected on l, and that (in this diagram) DE is positive but ED would be negative.

Fig. 9.4

Theorem   If $\mathbf{p}$ is the displacement vector $\overrightarrow{AB}$, and $\mathbf{u}$ is a unit vector in the direction of l, then the projection of $\overrightarrow{AB}$ on l is $\mathbf{p} \cdot \mathbf{u}$.

> **Proof**   You will probably find the proof easiest to follow if l is drawn as a vertical line, as in Fig. 9.5. Recall that AD and BE are perpendicular to l, and so are horizontal. The shaded triangles ADM and NEB lie in the horizontal planes through D and E. The point N is such that AN is parallel to l and perpendicular to NB.

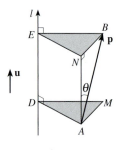

Fig. 9.5

> Then $DE = AN$, and $\mathbf{u}$ is a unit vector in the direction of AN. If the angle BAN is denoted by θ, then
>
> $$\mathbf{p} \cdot \mathbf{u} = |\mathbf{p}| \times 1 \times \cos\theta = AB\cos\theta = AN = DE,$$
>
> which is the projection of $\overrightarrow{AB}$ on l.

> Notice that, if B were below A, then the angle between $\mathbf{p}$ and $\mathbf{u}$ would be obtuse, so $\mathbf{p} \cdot \mathbf{u}$ would be negative. On l, E would be below D, so the directed length DE would also be negative.

When you have understood this proof with l vertical, you can try re-drawing Fig. 9.5 with l in some other direction, as in Fig. 9.4. If you then replace 'horizontal planes' by 'planes perpendicular to l', the proof will still hold.

Theorem For any vectors $\mathbf{p}$, $\mathbf{q}$ and $\mathbf{r}$, $(\mathbf{p} + \mathbf{q}) \cdot \mathbf{r} = \mathbf{p} \cdot \mathbf{r} + \mathbf{q} \cdot \mathbf{r}$.

Proof In Fig. 9.6 the displacement vectors $\overrightarrow{AB}$, $\overrightarrow{BC}$ and $\overrightarrow{AC}$ represent $\mathbf{p}$, $\mathbf{q}$ and $\mathbf{p} + \mathbf{q}$. The line l is in the direction of $\mathbf{r}$; this is again shown as a vertical line. The horizontal planes through A, B and C cut l at D, E and F respectively, so that AD, BE and CF are perpendicular to l.

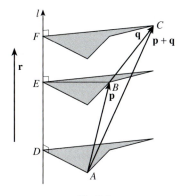

Fig. 9.6

Let $\mathbf{u}$ be a unit vector in the direction of $\mathbf{r}$, and denote $|\mathbf{r}|$ by s, so that $\mathbf{r} = s\mathbf{u}$. Then

$$\mathbf{p} \cdot \mathbf{r} = \mathbf{p} \cdot (s\mathbf{u}) = s(\mathbf{p} \cdot \mathbf{u}) = s \times DE,$$

and similarly $\mathbf{q} \cdot \mathbf{r} = s \times EF$ and $(\mathbf{p} + \mathbf{q}) \cdot \mathbf{r} = s \times DF$.

Since DE, EF and DF are directed lengths, it is always true that $DE + EF = DF$, whatever the order of the points D, E and F on l.

Therefore

$$(\mathbf{p} + \mathbf{q}) \cdot \mathbf{r} = s \times DF = s \times (DE + EF) = s \times DE + s \times EF = \mathbf{p} \cdot \mathbf{r} + \mathbf{q} \cdot \mathbf{r}.$$

As before, when you have understood this proof with l vertical, you can adapt it for any other direction of l.

9.4 Scalar products in component form

In the special cases at the end of Section 9.2, take $\mathbf{p}$ and $\mathbf{q}$ to be basic unit vectors. You then get:

> For the basic unit vectors $\mathbf{i}$, $\mathbf{j}$, $\mathbf{k}$,
>
> $$\mathbf{i} \cdot \mathbf{i} = \mathbf{j} \cdot \mathbf{j} = \mathbf{k} \cdot \mathbf{k} = 1,$$
>
> and $\quad \mathbf{j} \cdot \mathbf{k} = \mathbf{k} \cdot \mathbf{i} = \mathbf{i} \cdot \mathbf{j} = 0.$

It follows that, if vectors $\mathbf{p}$ and $\mathbf{q}$ are written in component form as $\mathbf{p} = l\,\mathbf{i} + m\,\mathbf{j} + n\,\mathbf{k}$ and $\mathbf{q} = u\,\mathbf{i} + v\,\mathbf{j} + w\,\mathbf{k}$, then

$$
\begin{aligned}
\mathbf{p} \cdot \mathbf{q} &= (l\,\mathbf{i} + m\,\mathbf{j} + n\,\mathbf{k}) \cdot (u\,\mathbf{i} + v\,\mathbf{j} + w\,\mathbf{k}) \\
&= lu\,\mathbf{i} \cdot \mathbf{i} + lv\,\mathbf{i} \cdot \mathbf{j} + lw\,\mathbf{i} \cdot \mathbf{k} + mu\,\mathbf{j} \cdot \mathbf{i} + mv\,\mathbf{j} \cdot \mathbf{j} + mw\,\mathbf{j} \cdot \mathbf{k} + nu\,\mathbf{k} \cdot \mathbf{i} + nv\,\mathbf{k} \cdot \mathbf{j} + nw\,\mathbf{k} \cdot \mathbf{k} \\
&= lu \times 1 + lv \times 0 + lw \times 0 + mu \times 0 + mv \times 1 + mw \times 0 + nu \times 0 + nv \times 0 + nw \times 1 \\
&= lu + mv + nw.
\end{aligned}
$$

In component form, the scalar product is

$$
\begin{pmatrix} l \\ m \\ n \end{pmatrix} \cdot \begin{pmatrix} u \\ v \\ w \end{pmatrix} = (l\,\mathbf{i} + m\,\mathbf{j} + n\,\mathbf{k}) \cdot (u\,\mathbf{i} + v\,\mathbf{j} + w\,\mathbf{k}) = lu + mv + nw.
$$

Combining the definition of scalar product with the component form gives:

$$
|\mathbf{p}||\mathbf{q}| \cos\theta = lu + mv + nw.
$$

These results have many applications. In particular, $\mathbf{p} \cdot \mathbf{p} = l^2 + m^2 + n^2$, showing that $\mathbf{p} \cdot \mathbf{p}$ is the square of the length of the vector $\mathbf{p}$.

Thus, $|\mathbf{p}|^2 = l^2 + m^2 + n^2$,   so that $|\mathbf{p}| = \sqrt{l^2 + m^2 + n^2}$.

Also, if you know the components of two non-zero vectors, you can easily find out if they are perpendicular by testing to see if $\cos\theta = 0$. So, using $|\mathbf{p}|\,|\mathbf{q}| \cos\theta = lu + mv + nw$, if $lu + mv + nw = 0$ then $\cos\theta = 0$ and the vectors are perpendicular.

Example 9.4.1
Prove that the vectors $3\mathbf{i} - 2\mathbf{j} + 4\mathbf{k}$ and $-4\mathbf{i} - 8\mathbf{j} - \mathbf{k}$ are perpendicular.

The scalar product of these vectors is

$$
\begin{aligned}
(3\mathbf{i} - 2\mathbf{j} + 4\mathbf{k}) \cdot (-4\mathbf{i} - 8\mathbf{j} - \mathbf{k}) &= 3 \times (-4) + (-2) \times (-8) + 4 \times (-1) \\
&= -12 + 16 - 4 = 0.
\end{aligned}
$$

As the scalar predict is 0, using the remark immediately before this example, the angle between the vectors is 90°.

Example 9.4.2
Find the angle between the vectors $\mathbf{p} = \begin{pmatrix} 1 \\ 2 \\ 3 \end{pmatrix}$ and $\mathbf{q} = \begin{pmatrix} -4 \\ 2 \\ 1 \end{pmatrix}$.

Substituting in the equation $|\mathbf{p}|\,|\mathbf{q}| \cos\theta = lu + mv + nw$ where θ is the angle between $\mathbf{p}$ and $\mathbf{q}$ requires some initial work.

$$
|\mathbf{p}| = \sqrt{1^2 + 2^2 + 3^2} = \sqrt{14} \quad \text{and} \quad |\mathbf{q}| = \sqrt{(-4)^2 + 2^2 + 1^2} = \sqrt{21}.
$$

The scalar product of **p** and **q** is

$$\mathbf{p} \cdot \mathbf{q} = 1 \times (-4) + 2 \times 2 + 3 \times 1 = 3.$$

Substituting these values in $|\mathbf{p}| |\mathbf{q}| \cos \theta = lu + mv + nw$ gives

$$\sqrt{14}\sqrt{21} \cos \theta = 3$$
$$\cos \theta = \frac{3}{\sqrt{14}\sqrt{21}}$$
$$\theta = 1.39 \text{ or } 79.9°.$$

The angle is 1.39 radians or 79.9°.

Example 9.4.3

A line has vector equation $\mathbf{r} = \begin{pmatrix} 0 \\ -4 \\ -5 \end{pmatrix} + t \begin{pmatrix} 2 \\ 3 \\ -6 \end{pmatrix}$. The point A has coordinates $(5, -10, 10)$. The foot of the perpendicular from A to the line is N.

(a) Find the coordinates of a point B on the line.

(b) For the point B find the cosine of the angle between BA and the line.

(c) Find the distance from A to the line.

It will help you to draw a sketch and to mark the data on it. The sketch (Fig. 9.7) should make no attempt to be three-dimensional.

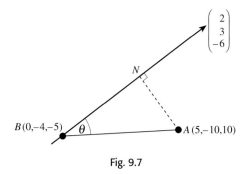

Fig. 9.7

(a) There are many choices for the coordinates of a point. One possibility is to take $t = 0$, giving the coordinates of B as $(0, -4, -5)$.

(b) Let the angle between the vectors be θ. To find θ you need to find the direction vector of the line, the vector $\overrightarrow{BA}$, and their magnitudes.

The line has direction vector $\mathbf{p} = \begin{pmatrix} 2 \\ 3 \\ -6 \end{pmatrix}$ which has magnitude $|\mathbf{p}|$, where

$$|\mathbf{p}| = \sqrt{2^2 + 3^2 + (-6)^2} = \sqrt{49} = 7$$

The vector $\overrightarrow{BA}$ is given by

$$\overrightarrow{BA} = \overrightarrow{OB} - \overrightarrow{OA} = \begin{pmatrix} 0 \\ -4 \\ -5 \end{pmatrix} - \begin{pmatrix} 5 \\ -10 \\ 10 \end{pmatrix} = \begin{pmatrix} -5 \\ 6 \\ -15 \end{pmatrix}.$$

The magnitude of $\overrightarrow{BA}$ is

$$\sqrt{(-5)^2 + 6^2 + (-15)^2} = \sqrt{286}.$$

Using $|\mathbf{p}|\,|\mathbf{q}|\cos\theta = lu + mv + nw$,

$$7\sqrt{286}\cos\theta = 2\times(-5) + 3\times 6 + (-6)\times(-15) = 98,$$

which gives $\cos\theta = \dfrac{14}{\sqrt{286}}$.

The cosine of the angle between BA and the line is $\dfrac{14}{\sqrt{286}}$.

(c) Using trigonometry, the distance from A to the line is $BA\sin\theta$.
As $\sin\theta = \sqrt{1 - \cos^2\theta}$,

$$\sin\theta = \sqrt{1 - \left(\frac{14}{\sqrt{286}}\right)^2} = \sqrt{1 - \frac{196}{286}} = \sqrt{\frac{90}{286}} = \sqrt{\frac{45}{143}}.$$

The length BA has already been found as $\sqrt{286}$.

So the required perpendicular has length $\sqrt{286} \times \sqrt{\dfrac{45}{143}} = \sqrt{90} = 3\sqrt{10}$.

The distance from A to the line is $3\sqrt{10}$.

Example 9.4.4
Use vectors to prove the addition formula for $\cos(A - B)$.

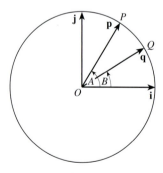

Fig. 9.8

Fig. 9.8 is a vector version of Fig. 6.4 in C3. The position vectors of P and Q are the unit vectors $\mathbf{p} = \cos A\,\mathbf{i} + \sin A\,\mathbf{j}$ and $\mathbf{q} = \cos B\,\mathbf{i} + \sin B\,\mathbf{j}$. So

$$\mathbf{p}\cdot\mathbf{q} = \cos A\cos B + \sin A\sin B.$$

The angle between **p** and **q** is $A - B$, so

$$\mathbf{p} \cdot \mathbf{q} = 1 \times 1 \times \cos(A - B).$$

Equating the two expressions for **p** · **q**,

$$\cos(A - B) = \cos A \cos B + \sin A \sin B.$$

Example 9.4.5

An aircraft flies from London Gatwick (51°N, 0°E) to Uganda Entebbe (0°N, 31°E). Taking the radius of the earth as 6370 km, find the great-circle distance between the airports.

Take the origin at the centre of the earth, the z-axis up the earth's axis, and the x-axis through the point where the Greenwich meridian meets the equator (Fig. 9.9). Taking the earth to be a sphere of radius R km, the coordinates of Gatwick are $(R \cos 51°, 0, R \sin 51°)$ and the coordinates of Entebbe are $(R \cos 31°, R \sin 31°, 0)$.

A great circle has its centre at the centre of the earth, and radius R km. If the angle between the position vectors of Gatwick and Entebbe is θ radians, then the great-circle distance is $R\theta$.

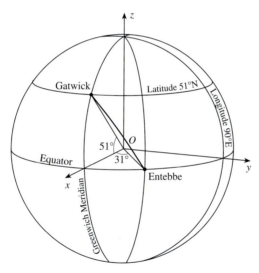

Fig. 9.9

The scalar product of the position vectors of Gatwick and Entebbe is

$$R \cos 51° \times R \cos 31° + 0 \times R \sin 31° + R \sin 51° \times 0,$$

and it is also equal to $R^2 \cos \theta$. So $\cos \theta = \cos 51° \cos 31°$, giving $\theta = 1.00...$ radians.

Taking $R = 6370$ gives $R\theta = 6370 \times 1.00...$, which is a great circle distance of slightly under 6400 km.

1 Let $\mathbf{a} = \begin{pmatrix} 3 \\ 2 \end{pmatrix}$, $\mathbf{b} = \begin{pmatrix} -4 \\ 2 \end{pmatrix}$ and $\mathbf{c} = \begin{pmatrix} 1 \\ 4 \end{pmatrix}$. Calculate $\mathbf{a} \cdot \mathbf{b}$, $\mathbf{a} \cdot \mathbf{c}$ and $\mathbf{a} \cdot (\mathbf{b} + \mathbf{c})$, and verify that
$\mathbf{a} \cdot (\mathbf{b} + \mathbf{c}) = \mathbf{a} \cdot \mathbf{b} + \mathbf{a} \cdot \mathbf{c}$.

2 Let $\mathbf{a} = 2\mathbf{i} - \mathbf{j}$, $\mathbf{b} = 4\mathbf{i} - 3\mathbf{j}$ and $\mathbf{c} = -2\mathbf{i} - \mathbf{j}$. Calculate $\mathbf{a} \cdot \mathbf{b}$, $\mathbf{a} \cdot \mathbf{c}$ and $\mathbf{a} \cdot (\mathbf{b} + \mathbf{c})$, and verify
that $\mathbf{a} \cdot (\mathbf{b} + \mathbf{c}) = \mathbf{a} \cdot \mathbf{b} + \mathbf{a} \cdot \mathbf{c}$.

3 Let $\mathbf{p} = \begin{pmatrix} 3 \\ -1 \\ 4 \end{pmatrix}$, $\mathbf{q} = \begin{pmatrix} -1 \\ -9 \\ 3 \end{pmatrix}$ and $\mathbf{r} = \begin{pmatrix} 33 \\ -13 \\ -28 \end{pmatrix}$. Calculate $\mathbf{p} \cdot \mathbf{q}$, $\mathbf{p} \cdot \mathbf{r}$ and $\mathbf{q} \cdot \mathbf{r}$. What can you
deduce about the vectors $\mathbf{p}$, $\mathbf{q}$ and $\mathbf{r}$?

4 Which of the following vectors are perpendicular to each other?

$$\mathbf{a} = 2\mathbf{i} - 3\mathbf{j} + 6\mathbf{k} \qquad \mathbf{b} = 2\mathbf{i} - 3\mathbf{j} - 6\mathbf{k} \qquad \mathbf{c} = -3\mathbf{i} - 6\mathbf{j} + 2\mathbf{k} \qquad \mathbf{d} = 6\mathbf{i} - 2\mathbf{j} - 3\mathbf{k}$$

5 Let $\mathbf{p} = \mathbf{i} - 2\mathbf{k}$, $\mathbf{q} = 3\mathbf{j} + 2\mathbf{k}$ and $\mathbf{r} = 2\mathbf{i} - \mathbf{j} + 5\mathbf{k}$. Calculate $\mathbf{p} \cdot \mathbf{q}$, $\mathbf{p} \cdot \mathbf{r}$ and $\mathbf{p} \cdot (\mathbf{q} + \mathbf{r})$ and
verify that $\mathbf{p} \cdot (\mathbf{q} + \mathbf{r}) = \mathbf{p} \cdot \mathbf{q} + \mathbf{p} \cdot \mathbf{r}$.

6 Find the magnitude of each of the following vectors.

(a) $\begin{pmatrix} -3 \\ 4 \end{pmatrix}$ 　　　　(b) $\begin{pmatrix} -2 \\ 1 \end{pmatrix}$ 　　　　(c) $\begin{pmatrix} -1 \\ -2 \end{pmatrix}$ 　　　　(d) $\begin{pmatrix} 0 \\ -1 \end{pmatrix}$

(e) $\begin{pmatrix} 1 \\ -2 \\ 2 \end{pmatrix}$ 　　　　(f) $\begin{pmatrix} 4 \\ -3 \\ 12 \end{pmatrix}$ 　　　　(g) $\begin{pmatrix} 0 \\ -3 \\ 4 \end{pmatrix}$ 　　　　(h) $\begin{pmatrix} 2 \\ -1 \\ 1 \end{pmatrix}$

(i) $\mathbf{i} - 2\mathbf{k}$ 　　　　(j) $3\mathbf{j} + 2\mathbf{k}$ 　　　　(k) $2\mathbf{i} - \mathbf{j} + 5\mathbf{k}$ 　　　　(l) $2\mathbf{k}$

7 Let $\mathbf{a} = \begin{pmatrix} 4 \\ -3 \end{pmatrix}$. Find the magnitude of $\mathbf{a}$, and find a unit vector in the same direction as $\mathbf{a}$.

8 Find unit vectors in the same directions as $\begin{pmatrix} 1 \\ -2 \\ 2 \end{pmatrix}$ and $2\mathbf{i} - \mathbf{j} + 2\mathbf{k}$.

9 Let A and B be points with position vectors $\mathbf{a} = \begin{pmatrix} 3 \\ 1 \end{pmatrix}$ and $\mathbf{b} = \begin{pmatrix} 3 \\ 2 \end{pmatrix}$ respectively. Draw a
diagram showing the points O, A and B. Calculate the angle AOB

(a) by finding the tangents of the angles α and β between $\mathbf{a}$ and the x-axis, and $\mathbf{b}$ and the
x-axis, and using the formula for $\tan(\alpha - \beta)$,

(b) by using a method based on scalar products.

10 Use a vector method to calculate the angles between the following pairs of vectors, giving
your answers in degrees to one place of decimals, where appropriate.

(a) $\begin{pmatrix} 2 \\ 1 \end{pmatrix}$ and $\begin{pmatrix} 1 \\ 3 \end{pmatrix}$ 　　(b) $\begin{pmatrix} 4 \\ -5 \end{pmatrix}$ and $\begin{pmatrix} -5 \\ 4 \end{pmatrix}$ 　　(c) $\begin{pmatrix} 4 \\ -6 \end{pmatrix}$ and $\begin{pmatrix} -6 \\ 9 \end{pmatrix}$

(d) $\begin{pmatrix} -1 \\ 4 \\ 5 \end{pmatrix}$ and $\begin{pmatrix} 2 \\ 0 \\ -3 \end{pmatrix}$ 　　(e) $\begin{pmatrix} 1 \\ 2 \\ -3 \end{pmatrix}$ and $\begin{pmatrix} 2 \\ 3 \\ -4 \end{pmatrix}$ 　　(f) $\begin{pmatrix} 2 \\ -1 \\ 3 \end{pmatrix}$ and $\begin{pmatrix} 5 \\ -2 \\ -4 \end{pmatrix}$

11 Let $\mathbf{r}_1 = \begin{pmatrix} x_1 \\ y_1 \end{pmatrix}$ and $\mathbf{r}_2 = \begin{pmatrix} x_2 \\ y_2 \end{pmatrix}$. Calculate $|\mathbf{r}_2 - \mathbf{r}_1|$ and interpret your result geometrically.

12 Find the cosine of the angle between the lines $\mathbf{r} = \begin{pmatrix} 4 \\ 2 \end{pmatrix} + s\begin{pmatrix} -2 \\ 3 \end{pmatrix}$ and $\mathbf{r} = \begin{pmatrix} 2 \\ -3 \end{pmatrix} + t\begin{pmatrix} 1 \\ 2 \end{pmatrix}$.

13 Find the cosine of the angle between the lines $\mathbf{r} = \begin{pmatrix} -1 \\ 2 \\ 3 \end{pmatrix} + s\begin{pmatrix} 4 \\ 1 \\ -1 \end{pmatrix}$ and

$$\mathbf{r} = \begin{pmatrix} 2 \\ -3 \\ 4 \end{pmatrix} + t\begin{pmatrix} -1 \\ 6 \\ 2 \end{pmatrix}.$$

14 Find the angle between the line joining $(1, 2)$ and $(3, -5)$ and the line joining $(2, -3)$ to $(1, 4)$.

15 Find the angle between the line joining $(1, 3, -2)$ and $(2, 5, -1)$ and the line joining $(-1, 4, 3)$ to $(3, 2, 1)$.

16 Find the angle between the diagonals of a cube.

17 $ABCD$ is the base of a square pyramid of side 2 units, and V is the vertex. The pyramid is symmetrical, and of height 4 units. Calculate the acute angle between AV and BC, giving your answer in degrees correct to one decimal place.

18 Two aeroplanes are flying in directions given by the vectors $300\mathbf{i} + 400\mathbf{j} + 2\mathbf{k}$ and $-100\mathbf{i} + 500\mathbf{j} - \mathbf{k}$. A person from the flight control centre is plotting their paths on a map. Find the acute angle between their paths on the map.

19 The roof of a house has a rectangular base of side 4 metres by 8 metres. The ridge line of the roof is 6 metres long, and 1 metre above the base of the roof. Calculate the acute angle between two opposite slanting edges of the roof.

20 Let P be the point (p, q) and let l be the straight line $ax + by + c = 0$.

  (a) Find a vector in the direction of l.

  (b) Find a unit vector $\mathbf{v}$ which is perpendicular to l.

  (c) Write down in the form $\mathbf{r} = \mathbf{u} + t\mathbf{v}$ the equation of the line from P perpendicular to l.

  (d) Calculate the value of the parameter t for the point where this perpendicular meets l, and hence find a formula for the perpendicular distance of P from l.

9.5 Some geometrical proofs

The algebra of vectors provides an effective and economical method for proving geometrical results. There were a few examples in Chapter 4, but with scalar products you can prove many more results, involving lengths and angles.

Example 9.5.1

Prove that the angle in a semicircle is a right angle.

This means: if AB is the diameter of a circle, and C is any other point on the circle, then angle ACB is a right angle (see Fig. 9.10).

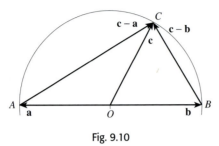

Fig. 9.10

Take an origin at the centre of the circle (radius r). If the position vector of A is $\mathbf{a}$, then the position vector $\mathbf{b}$ of B is $-\mathbf{a}$. If $\overrightarrow{OC} = \mathbf{c}$, then both $\mathbf{a} \cdot \mathbf{a}$ and $\mathbf{c} \cdot \mathbf{c}$ are equal to r^2. Therefore $\mathbf{c}^2 - \mathbf{a}^2 = 0$.

This is the difference of two squares in vector form, and it can be factorised exactly as in ordinary algebra to give

$$(\mathbf{c} - \mathbf{a}) \cdot (\mathbf{c} + \mathbf{a}) = 0, \text{ which is } (\mathbf{c} - \mathbf{a}) \cdot (\mathbf{c} - \mathbf{b}) = 0, \text{ or } \overrightarrow{AC} \cdot \overrightarrow{BC} = 0.$$

At this point vector algebra differs from ordinary algebra. Since C is not at A or B, neither $\overrightarrow{AC}$ nor $\overrightarrow{BC}$ is zero. So $\overrightarrow{AC}$ and $\overrightarrow{BC}$ are perpendicular to each other; that is, ACB is a right angle.

Example 9.5.2 (the cosine formula)

Prove that, in a triangle ABC, $a^2 = b^2 + c^2 - 2bc \cos A$.

Denote the displacement vectors $\overrightarrow{AB}$ and $\overrightarrow{AC}$ by $\mathbf{p}$ and $\mathbf{q}$ (see Fig. 9.11).

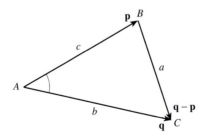

Fig. 9.11

Then $\overrightarrow{BC} = \mathbf{q} - \mathbf{p}$.

$$\begin{aligned}
a^2 &= \overrightarrow{BC} \cdot \overrightarrow{BC} = (\mathbf{q} - \mathbf{p})^2 \\
&= \mathbf{q}^2 + \mathbf{p}^2 - 2\mathbf{q} \cdot \mathbf{p} \\
&= \overrightarrow{AC} \cdot \overrightarrow{AC} + \overrightarrow{AB} \cdot \overrightarrow{AB} - 2|\mathbf{q}||\mathbf{p}| \cos A \\
&= b^2 + c^2 - 2bc \cos A.
\end{aligned}$$

Example 9.5.3

Prove that, in a triangle, the lines through the vertices perpendicular to the opposite sides (called the **altitudes**) meet at a point.

In Fig. 9.12, one vertex is taken as the origin, the other two vertices are A and B, and the altitudes through A and B meet at C.

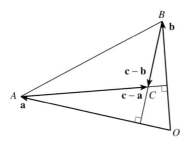

Fig. 9.12

The displacement vector $\overrightarrow{AC} = \mathbf{c} - \mathbf{a}$ is perpendicular to $\overrightarrow{OB} = \mathbf{b}$, and similarly $\mathbf{c} - \mathbf{b}$ is perpendicular to $\mathbf{a}$. So $(\mathbf{c} - \mathbf{a}) \cdot \mathbf{b} = 0$ and $(\mathbf{c} - \mathbf{b}) \cdot \mathbf{a} = 0$, which means that $\mathbf{c} \cdot \mathbf{b} = \mathbf{a} \cdot \mathbf{b}$ and $\mathbf{c} \cdot \mathbf{a} = \mathbf{b} \cdot \mathbf{a}$.

Since $\mathbf{a} \cdot \mathbf{b} = \mathbf{b} \cdot \mathbf{a}$, it follows from these two equations that $\mathbf{c} \cdot \mathbf{b} = \mathbf{c} \cdot \mathbf{a}$, so that $\mathbf{c} \cdot (\mathbf{b} - \mathbf{a}) = 0$.

The geometrical interpretation of this is that $\overrightarrow{OC}$ is perpendicular to $\overrightarrow{AB}$. So OC is the third altitude. Therefore the three altitudes meet at the point C. This point is called the **orthocentre** of the triangle.

Example 9.5.4

A tetrahedron $OABC$ has two pairs of perpendicular opposite edges. Prove that

(a) the third pair of opposite edges is perpendicular,

(b) the sums of the squares of the lengths of the three pairs of opposite edges are equal.

Fig. 9.13 shows the tetrahedron, with one vertex at the origin.

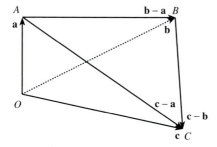

Fig. 9.13

(a) What is required is to prove that, if OA is perpendicular to BC, and OB is perpendicular to AC, then OC is perpendicular to AB. In the conventional notation for position vectors, what you have to prove is that, if $\mathbf{a} \cdot (\mathbf{c} - \mathbf{b}) = 0$ and $\mathbf{b} \cdot (\mathbf{c} - \mathbf{a}) = 0$, then $\mathbf{c} \cdot (\mathbf{b} - \mathbf{a}) = 0$.

This is algebraically identical to the proof in the previous example! The algebra has one interpretation in two dimensions, and another in three dimensions.

(b) $OA^2 + BC^2 = \mathbf{a}^2 + (\mathbf{c} - \mathbf{b})^2 = \mathbf{a}^2 + \mathbf{b}^2 + \mathbf{c}^2 - 2\mathbf{c} \cdot \mathbf{b}$.

Similarly,

$$OB^2 + CA^2 = \mathbf{a}^2 + \mathbf{b}^2 + \mathbf{c}^2 - 2\mathbf{a} \cdot \mathbf{c} \text{ and } OC^2 + AB^2 = \mathbf{a}^2 + \mathbf{b}^2 + \mathbf{c}^2 - 2\mathbf{b} \cdot \mathbf{a}.$$

From the equations in (a),

$$\mathbf{c} \cdot \mathbf{b} = \mathbf{a} \cdot \mathbf{c} = \mathbf{b} \cdot \mathbf{a}.$$

Therefore

$$OA^2 + BC^2 = OB^2 + CA^2 = OC^2 + AB^2.$$

Exercise 9B

Where appropriate, the alphabet convention (Section 4.4) has been used.

1 Draw two vectors $\mathbf{a}$ and $\mathbf{b}$ such that $|\mathbf{a}| = |\mathbf{b}|$, and complete the parallelogram $OACB$. Mark on your diagram the vectors $\mathbf{a} - \mathbf{b}$ and $\mathbf{a} + \mathbf{b}$. By considering the scalar product $(\mathbf{a} + \mathbf{b}) \cdot (\mathbf{a} - \mathbf{b})$, prove that the diagonals of a rhombus are at right angles.

2 $OACB$ is a parallelogram. Write down the vectors $\overrightarrow{OC}$ and $\overrightarrow{AB}$ in terms of $\mathbf{a}$ and $\mathbf{b}$. Use scalar products to prove that, if the parallelogram has equal diagonals, then it is a rectangle.

3 Let OAB be a triangle with $AB^2 = OA^2 + OB^2$. By considering the equation $(\mathbf{a} - \mathbf{b}) \cdot (\mathbf{a} - \mathbf{b}) = \mathbf{a} \cdot \mathbf{a} + \mathbf{b} \cdot \mathbf{b}$, prove that the triangle OAB is right-angled at O.

4 Let $OABC$ be a kite, with OB as its line of symmetry. Write down the vectors $\overrightarrow{AB}$ and $\overrightarrow{CB}$ in terms of $\mathbf{a}$, $\mathbf{b}$ and $\mathbf{c}$, and use the fact that the lengths of AB and CB are equal to write an equation involving scalar products. Use this equation, together with another equation, to prove that the diagonals of a kite are perpendicular.

5* Let OAB be a triangle. Let $\hat{\mathbf{a}}$ be a unit vector in the direction of $\mathbf{a}$ and $\hat{\mathbf{b}}$ be a unit vector in the direction of $\mathbf{b}$, and denote $|\mathbf{a}|$ and $|\mathbf{b}|$ by a and b.

(a) What can you say about the direction of $\hat{\mathbf{a}} + \hat{\mathbf{b}}$ and the directions of $\hat{\mathbf{a}}$ and $\hat{\mathbf{b}}$?

(b) Write an expression for $\hat{\mathbf{a}}$ in terms of $\mathbf{a}$ and a, and a similar one for $\hat{\mathbf{b}}$.

(c) Use the vector equation of the line AB in the form $\mathbf{r} = \mathbf{a} + t(\mathbf{b} - \mathbf{a})$ to find where the line AB intersects the line drawn from O in the direction $\hat{\mathbf{a}} + \hat{\mathbf{b}}$.

(d) Prove the angle bisector theorem, namely, that if the bisector of the angle AOB of a triangle meets the opposite side in D, then $OA : OB = AD : DB$.

6* (a) Show that, if a vector $\mathbf{p}$ is perpendicular to two vectors $\mathbf{a}$ and $\mathbf{b}$, it is also perpendicular to $s\mathbf{a} + t\mathbf{b}$ for any values of s and t which are not both zero.

   (b) Show that, if a line is perpendicular to two non-parallel lines in a plane, it is perpendicular to every line in the plane.

   (c) In a tetrahedron $OABC$, the line from C perpendicular to the plane OAB and the line from B perpendicular to the plane OAC meet at a point H. Show that $\mathbf{h} \cdot \mathbf{a} = \mathbf{c} \cdot \mathbf{a}$, and find three more equations like this connecting $\mathbf{h}$ with $\mathbf{a}$, and $\mathbf{c}$. Deduce that $\mathbf{a} \cdot (\mathbf{b} - \mathbf{c}) = 0$, and interpret this equation geometrically.

   (d) Prove also that, for this tetrahedron, $OB^2 + AC^2 = OC^2 + AB^2$.

Miscellaneous exercise 9

1 Point A has coordinates $(2, -1, 3)$ and point B has coordinates $(1, 0, 5)$.

   (a) Write down the equation of the line AB in the form $\mathbf{r} = \mathbf{a} + t\mathbf{u}$.

   (b) Find the angle between the line AB and the line $\begin{pmatrix} x \\ y \\ z \end{pmatrix} = \begin{pmatrix} 1 \\ 3 \\ 4 \end{pmatrix} + \lambda \begin{pmatrix} -4 \\ 7 \\ 6 \end{pmatrix}$, giving your answer to the nearest degree.   (MEI, adapted)

2 Find which pairs of the following vectors are perpendicular to each other.

$$\mathbf{a} = 2\mathbf{i} + \mathbf{j} - 2\mathbf{k} \qquad \mathbf{b} = 2\mathbf{i} - 2\mathbf{j} + \mathbf{k} \qquad \mathbf{c} = \mathbf{i} + 2\mathbf{j} + 2\mathbf{k} \qquad \mathbf{d} = 3\mathbf{i} + 2\mathbf{j} - 2\mathbf{k}$$

3 The vectors $\overrightarrow{AB}$ and $\overrightarrow{AC}$ are $\begin{pmatrix} -1 \\ 0 \\ 3 \end{pmatrix}$ and $\begin{pmatrix} 2 \\ 4 \\ 3 \end{pmatrix}$ respectively. The vector $\overrightarrow{AD}$ is the sum of $\overrightarrow{AB}$ and $\overrightarrow{AC}$. Determine the acute angle, in degrees correct to one decimal place, between the diagonals of the parallelogram defined by the points A, B, C and D.   (OCR)

4 The points A, B and C have position vectors $\mathbf{a} = \begin{pmatrix} 2 \\ 1 \\ 2 \end{pmatrix}$, $\mathbf{b} = \begin{pmatrix} -3 \\ 2 \\ 5 \end{pmatrix}$ and $\mathbf{c} = \begin{pmatrix} 4 \\ 5 \\ -2 \end{pmatrix}$ respectively, with respect to a fixed origin. The point D is such that $ABCD$, in that order, is a parallelogram.

   (a) Find the position vector of D.

   (b) Find the position vector of the point at which the diagonals of the parallelogram intersect.

   (c) Calculate the angle BAC, giving your answer to the nearest tenth of a degree.   (OCR)

5 The vectors $\mathbf{AB}$ and $\mathbf{AC}$ are $\begin{pmatrix} -2 \\ 6 \\ -3 \end{pmatrix}$ and $\begin{pmatrix} -2 \\ -3 \\ 6 \end{pmatrix}$ respectively.

   (a) Determine the lengths of the vectors.

   (b) Find the scalar product $\mathbf{AB} \cdot \mathbf{AC}$.

   (c) Use your result from part (b) to calculate the acute angle between the vectors. Give the angle in degrees correct to one decimal place.   (OCR)

6 A vertical aerial is supported by three straight
   cables, each attached to the aerial at a point P,
   30 metres up the aerial. The cables are attached to
   the horizontal ground at points A, B and C, each
   x metres from the foot O of the aerial, and situated
   symmetrically around it (see the diagrams).

   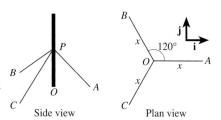
   Side view   Plan view

   Suppose that $\mathbf{i}$ is the unit vector in the direction
   $\overrightarrow{OA}$, $\mathbf{j}$ is the unit vector perpendicular to $\mathbf{i}$ in the
   plane of the ground, as shown in the plan view,
   and $\mathbf{k}$ is the unit vector in the direction $\overrightarrow{OP}$.

   (a) Write down expressions for the vectors $\overrightarrow{OA}$, $\overrightarrow{OB}$ and $\overrightarrow{OC}$ in terms of x, $\mathbf{i}$, $\mathbf{j}$ and $\mathbf{k}$.

   (b) (i) Write down an expression for the vector $\overrightarrow{AP}$ in terms of vectors $\overrightarrow{OA}$ and $\overrightarrow{OP}$.

      (ii) Hence find expressions for the vectors $\overrightarrow{AP}$ and $\overrightarrow{BP}$ in terms of x, $\mathbf{i}$, $\mathbf{j}$ and $\mathbf{k}$.

   (c) Given that $\overrightarrow{AP}$ and $\overrightarrow{BP}$ are perpendicular to each other, find the value of x.   (OCR)

7 The position vectors of three points A, B and C with respect to a fixed origin O are
   $2\mathbf{i} - 2\mathbf{j} + \mathbf{k}$, $4\mathbf{i} + 2\mathbf{j} + \mathbf{k}$ and $\mathbf{i} + \mathbf{j} + 3\mathbf{k}$ respectively. Find unit vectors in the directions of
   $\overrightarrow{CA}$ and $\overrightarrow{CB}$. Calculate angle ACB in degrees, correct to 1 decimal place.   (OCR)

8 (a) Find the angle between the vectors $2\mathbf{i} + 3\mathbf{j} + 6\mathbf{k}$ and $3\mathbf{i} + 4\mathbf{j} + 12\mathbf{k}$, giving your answer
      in radians.

   (b) The vectors $\mathbf{a}$ and $\mathbf{b}$ are non-zero.

      (i) Given that $\mathbf{a} + \mathbf{b}$ is perpendicular to $\mathbf{a} - \mathbf{b}$, prove that $|\mathbf{a}| = |\mathbf{b}|$.

      (i) Given instead that $|\mathbf{a} + \mathbf{b}| = |\mathbf{a} - \mathbf{b}|$, prove that $\mathbf{a}$ and $\mathbf{b}$ are perpendicular.   (OCR)

9 $OABCDEFG$, shown in the figure, is a cuboid.
   The position vectors of A, C and D are $4\mathbf{i}$, $2\mathbf{j}$
   and $3\mathbf{k}$ respectively.

   Calculate

   (a) $|AG|$,

   (b) the angle between AG and OB.   (OCR)

   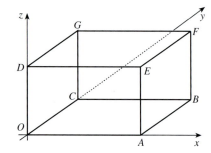

10 $\mathbf{i}$, $\mathbf{j}$ and $\mathbf{k}$ are unit vectors in the x-, y- and z-directions respectively. The three-dimensional
    vector $\mathbf{r}$ has magnitude 5, and makes angles of $\frac{1}{4}\pi$ radians with each of $\mathbf{i}$ and $\mathbf{k}$.

    (a) Write $\mathbf{r}$ as a column vector, leaving any square roots in your answer.

    (b) State the angle between $\mathbf{r}$ and the unit vector $\mathbf{j}$.   (OCR)

11 The points A, B and C have position vectors given respectively by $\mathbf{a} = 7\mathbf{i} + 4\mathbf{j} - 2\mathbf{k}$,
    $\mathbf{b} = 5\mathbf{i} + 3\mathbf{j} - 3\mathbf{k}$, $\mathbf{c} = 6\mathbf{i} + 5\mathbf{j} - 4\mathbf{k}$.

    (a) Find the angle BAC.

    (b) Find the area of the triangle ABC.   (OCR)

12 The points A, B and C have position vectors $\mathbf{a}$, $\mathbf{b}$ and $\mathbf{c}$ respectively relative to the origin O. P is the point on BC such that $\overrightarrow{PC} = \frac{1}{10}\overrightarrow{BC}$.

(a) Show that the position vector of P is $\frac{1}{10}(9\mathbf{c} + \mathbf{b})$.

(b) Given that the line AP is perpendicular to the line BC, show that
$$(9\mathbf{c} + \mathbf{b}) \cdot (\mathbf{c} - \mathbf{b}) = 10\mathbf{a} \cdot (\mathbf{c} - \mathbf{b}).$$

(c) Given also that OA, OB and OC are mutually perpendicular, prove that
$$OC = \tfrac{1}{3}OB. \hspace{4cm} \text{(OCR)}$$

13* Let $\mathbf{r} \cdot \mathbf{r} = a^2$ be the equation of a sphere, centre the origin and radius a, and let C, with position vector $\mathbf{c}$, be any other point. Let $\mathbf{u}$ be a unit vector.

(a) Write down the vector equation of the line through C in the direction $\mathbf{u}$ and write down a quadratic equation whose roots are the parameters of the points where this line meets the sphere.

(b) Find the condition that the line through C in the direction $\mathbf{u}$ is a tangent to the sphere.

(c) Deduce that, if $\mathbf{R}$ is the position vector of $\mathbf{r}$ when the line of part (a) is a tangent to the sphere, then $\mathbf{R} \cdot \mathbf{u} = 0$. Interpret this geometrically.

Revision exercise 4

1 Given that $\dfrac{dy}{dx} = (x \ln x) y^{\frac{1}{2}}$, and that $y = 1$ when $x = 1$, show that the value of y when $x = 3$ is $\left(\frac{9}{4} \ln 3\right)^2$. (OCR)

2 Let $f(x) = \dfrac{1+x}{2+x} - \dfrac{1-x}{2-x}$.

   (a) Show that $f(x)$ may be expressed as $\dfrac{2x}{4-x^2}$.

   (b) Hence or otherwise show that for small x, $f(x) = \frac{1}{2}x + \frac{1}{8}x^3 + \frac{1}{32}x^5 + \dots$. (OCR)

3 (a) Express $\dfrac{3x+7}{(x+2)(x+3)^2}$ in the form $\dfrac{A}{x+2} + \dfrac{B}{x+3} + \dfrac{C}{(x+3)^2}$, where A, B and C are constants.

   (b) When x is small, the expansion of $\dfrac{3x+7}{(x+2)(x+3)^2}$, in ascending powers of x, is

      $p + qx + rx^2 + \dots$.

      Show that $p = \frac{7}{18}$, $q = -\frac{31}{108}$ and find the value of r. (OCR)

4 (a) Express $\dfrac{1}{x(x-4)(x+4)}$ in partial fractions.

   (b) Hence find the exact value of $\displaystyle\int_1^3 \dfrac{1}{x(x-4)(x+4)}\, dx$, giving your answer in the form

      $\lambda \ln \left(\dfrac{a}{b}\right)$, where a and b are integers. (OCR)

5 The position vectors of A and B with respect to the origin O are $\begin{pmatrix} 6 \\ 2 \\ 2 \end{pmatrix}$ and $\begin{pmatrix} 2 \\ 4 \\ 3 \end{pmatrix}$ respectively. The points C and D are such that $\overrightarrow{OC} = \frac{3}{2}\overrightarrow{OA}$ and $\overrightarrow{OD} = 2\overrightarrow{OB}$.

   (a) State the position vectors of C and D.

   (b) The line through A and D is denoted by l_1 and the line through B and C is denoted by

      l_2. Show that l_1 has equation $\mathbf{r} = \begin{pmatrix} 6 \\ 2 \\ 2 \end{pmatrix} + \lambda \begin{pmatrix} -2 \\ 6 \\ 4 \end{pmatrix}$, and find an equation for l_2 in similar form.

   (c) The lines l_1 and l_2 intersect at X. Find the position vector of X.

   (d) Calculate the acute angle between l_1 and l_2, correct to the nearest degree. (OCR)

6 Find the solution of the differential equation $\dfrac{dy}{dx} = \dfrac{x^4 - 1}{x^2 y^2}$, given that $y = 2$ when $x = 1$. (OCR)

7 The position vectors of the points A and B, relative to a fixed origin O, are $6\mathbf{i} + 4\mathbf{j} - \mathbf{k}$ and $8\mathbf{i} + 5\mathbf{j} - 3\mathbf{k}$ respectively.

   (a) Find $\overrightarrow{AB}$.

   (b) Find the length AB.

   (c) Show that, for all values of the parameter λ, the point P with position vector $(8 + 2\lambda)\mathbf{i} + (5 + \lambda)\mathbf{j} - (3 + 2\lambda)\mathbf{k}$ lies on a straight line through A and B.

   (d) Determine the value of λ for which $\overrightarrow{OP}$ is perpendicular to $\overrightarrow{AB}$. (OCR)

8 (a) For the curve $2x^2 + xy + y^2 = 14$, find $\dfrac{dy}{dx}$ in terms of x and y.

   (b) Deduce that there are two points on the curve $2x^2 + xy + y^2 = 14$ at which the tangents are parallel to the x-axis, and find their coordinates.   (OCR)

9 (a) Find $\displaystyle\int x^2 \sin x \, dx$.

   (b) Find $\dfrac{d}{dx}(\tan x - x)$, giving your answer in its simplest form.

   (c) Find the general solution of the differential equation $\dfrac{dy}{dx} = x^2 \sin x \cot^2 y$.   (OCR)

10 Use the substitution $x = u^3$ to find $\displaystyle\int_{1}^{8} \dfrac{1}{x(1 + \sqrt[3]{x})} \, dx$.

11 The line L_1 passes through the point $(3, 6, 1)$ and is parallel to the vector $2\mathbf{i} + 3\mathbf{j} - \mathbf{k}$. The line L_2 passes through the point $(3, -1, 4)$ and is parallel to the vector $\mathbf{i} - 2\mathbf{j} + \mathbf{k}$.

   (a) Write down vector equations for L_1 and L_2.

   (b) Prove that L_1 and L_2 intersect, and find the coordinates of their point of intersection.

   (c) Calculate the acute angle between the lines.   (OCR)

12 The surface of a circular pond of radius a is being covered by weeds. The weeds are growing in a circular region whose centre is at the centre of the pond. At time t the region covered by the weeds has radius r and area A (see diagram). An ecologist models the growth of the weeds by assuming that the rate of increase of area covered is proportional to the area of the pond not yet covered.

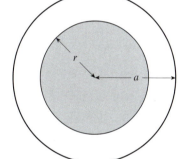

   (a) Show that $\dfrac{dA}{dt} = 2\pi r \dfrac{dr}{dt}$.

   (b) Hence show that the ecologist's model leads to the differential equation $2r \dfrac{dr}{dt} = k(a^2 - r^2)$, where k is a constant.

   (c) By solving the differential equation in part (b), express r in terms of t, a and k, given that $r = 0$ when $t = 0$.

   (d) Will the weeds ever cover the whole pond? Justify your answer.   (OCR)

13 Two lines have equations

$$\mathbf{r} = \begin{pmatrix} 3 \\ 1 \\ -2 \end{pmatrix} + s \begin{pmatrix} 1 \\ -1 \\ 4 \end{pmatrix} \quad \text{and} \quad \mathbf{r} = \begin{pmatrix} 1 \\ 0 \\ 5 \end{pmatrix} + t \begin{pmatrix} -2 \\ -3 \\ 1 \end{pmatrix}.$$

   (a) Find the acute angle between the directions of the two lines.

   (b) Prove that the lines are skew.   (OCR)

14 A curve is defined by the equation $x^2 + 4xy + 5y^2 = 4$.

   (a) Find the equation of the tangent at $(4, -2)$.

   (b) Find the equations of the tangents parallel to the y-axis.

15 An anthropologist is modelling the population of the island of A. In the model, the population at the start of the year t is P. The birth rate is 10 births per 1000 population per year. The death rate is m deaths per 1000 population per year.

(a) Show that $\dfrac{\mathrm{d}P}{\mathrm{d}t} = \dfrac{(10-m)P}{1000}$.

(b) At the start of year 0 the population was 108 000. Find an expression for P in terms of t.

(c) State one assumption about the population of A that is required for this model to be valid.

(d) If the population is to double in 100 years, find the value of m.

(e) Explain why the population cannot double in less than 69 years.   (OCR)

16 Express $\dfrac{1}{(1+x)(3-x)}$ as the sum of partial fractions. Hence express $\dfrac{1}{(1+x)^2(3-x)^2}$ as the sum of partial fractions.

A region is bounded by parts of the x- and y-axes, the curve $y = \dfrac{1}{(1+x)(3-x)}$ and the line $x = 2$. Find the area of the region, and the volume of the solid of revolution formed by rotating it about the x-axis.   (OCR)

17 The vectors **a** and **b** are shown on the grid of unit squares.

(a) Calculate $|\mathbf{a}+\mathbf{b}|$.

(b) Calculate $\mathbf{a}\cdot\mathbf{b}$.

(c) Calculate the angle between **a** and **b**.   (OCR)

18 A model for the way in which a population of animals in a closed environment varies with time is given, for $P > \frac{1}{3}$, by $\dfrac{\mathrm{d}P}{\mathrm{d}t} = \frac{1}{2}(3P^2 - P)\sin t$, where P is the size of the population in thousands at time t. Given that $P = \frac{1}{2}$ when $t = 0$, show that $\ln\dfrac{3P-1}{P} = \frac{1}{2}(1-\cos t)$.

Rearrange this equation to show that $P = \dfrac{1}{3 - \mathrm{e}^{\frac{1}{2}(1-\cos t)}}$.

Calculate the smallest positive value of t for which $P = 1$, and find the two values between which the number of animals in the population oscillates.   (MEI, adapted)

19 Two small insects A and B are crawling on the walls of a room, with A starting from the ceiling. The floor is horizontal and forms the xy-plane, and the z-axis is vertically upwards. Relative to the origin O, the position vectors of the insects at time t seconds ($0 \leqslant t \leqslant 10$) are $\overrightarrow{OA} = \mathbf{i} + 3\mathbf{j} + \left(4 - \frac{1}{10}t\right)\mathbf{k}$, $\overrightarrow{OB} = \left(\frac{1}{5}t + 1\right)\mathbf{i} - 3\mathbf{j} + 2\mathbf{k}$, where the unit of distance is the metre.

(a) Write down the height of the room.

(b) Show that the insects move in such a way that angle $BOA = 90^\circ$.

(c) For each insect, write down a vector to represent its displacement between $t = 0$ and $t = 10$, and show that these displacements are perpendicular to each other.

(d) Write down expressions for the vector $\overrightarrow{AB}$ and for $|\overrightarrow{AB}|$ and hence find the minimum distance between the insects, correct to 3 significant figures.   (OCR)

20* Consider the curve with equation $x^2 + 4y^2 = 1$.

  (a) Find the coordinates of the points where the curve cuts the coordinate axes.

  (b) Show that the curve is symmetrical about both the x- and y-axes.

  (c) Show that the equation of the curve can be written in the form $y = \pm\frac{1}{2}\sqrt{1 - x^2}$ and use the binomial expansion to get approximations for y up to and including the terms in x^2.

  (d) Use your approximations to draw the shape of the curve for small values of x near the points where the curve crosses the y-axis.

  (e) Repeat parts (c) and (d) with the roles of x and y reversed.

  (f) Join up the pieces and make a sketch of the curve.

21* By identifying the series $1 - \dfrac{1}{4} + \dfrac{1 \times 3}{4 \times 8} - \dfrac{1 \times 3 \times 5}{4 \times 8 \times 12} + \dots$ as a binomial series of the form $(1 + x)^n$ and finding the values of x and n, find the sum to infinity of the series $1 - \dfrac{1}{4} + \dfrac{1 \times 3}{4 \times 8} - \dfrac{1 \times 3 \times 5}{4 \times 8 \times 12} + \dots$.

22 The rate of destruction of a drug by the kidneys is proportional to the amount of the drug present in the body. The constant of proportionality is denoted by k. At time t the quantity of drug in the body is x. Write down a differential equation relating x and t, and show that the general solution is $x = Ae^{-kt}$, where A is an arbitrary constant.

Before $t = 0$ there is no drug in the body, but at $t = 0$ a quantity Q of the drug is administered. When $t = 1$ the amount of drug in the body is $Q\alpha$, where α is a constant such that $0 < \alpha < 1$. Show that $x = Q\alpha^t$.

When $t = 1$ and again when $t = 2$ another dose Q is administered. Show that the amount of drug in the body immediately after $t = 2$ is $Q(1 + \alpha + \alpha^2)$.

If the drug is administered at regular intervals for an indefinite period, and if the greatest amount of the drug that the body can tolerate is T, show that Q should not exceed $T(1 - \alpha)$.   (OCR, adapted)

23* Consider the curve $y^3 = (x - 1)^2$.

  (a) Find the coordinates of the points where the curve crosses the axes.

  (b) Are there any values which either x or y cannot take?

  (c) Differentiate the equation $y^3 = (x - 1)^2$ to find an expression for the gradient in terms of x and y. Find the gradient of the curve where it crosses the y-axis.

  (d) What happens to the gradient as x gets close to 1?

  (e) By making the substitution $x = 1 + X$, and examining the resulting equation between y and X, show that the curve is symmetrical about the line $x = 1$.

  (f) Make a sketch of the curve, and check your result by using your graphic calculator.

Practice examination 1 for C4

Time 1 hour 30 minutes

Answer all the questions.

You are permitted to use a graphic calculator in this paper.

1 Find the quotient and remainder when $4x^4$ is divided by $2x^2 + 1$. [4]

2 (i) Find the binomial expansion of $(1 - 3x)^{-\frac{1}{3}}$ in ascending powers of x, up to and including the term in x^3. [4]

  (ii) State the set of values of x for which the expansion is valid. [1]

3 In the diagram, OEA and OBD are straight lines. The length of OD is twice the length of OB, and the length of OE is two thirds of the length of OA. M is the mid-point of AB. The position vectors of A and B with respect to O as origin are $\mathbf{a}$ and $\mathbf{b}$ respectively.

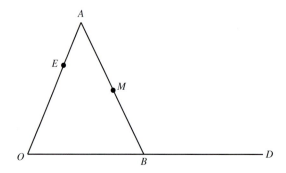

  (i) Write down the position vectors of D and M in terms of $\mathbf{a}$ and $\mathbf{b}$, and deduce that
$\overrightarrow{DM} = \frac{1}{2}\mathbf{a} - \frac{3}{2}\mathbf{b}$. [3]

  (ii) Show that $\overrightarrow{ME} = \frac{1}{6}\mathbf{a} - \frac{1}{2}\mathbf{b}$. [2]

  (iii) Explain how the results in parts (i) and (ii) show that the line joining D and E passes through M. [1]

4 The population of a community with finite resources is modelled by the differential equation $\dfrac{\mathrm{d}n}{\mathrm{d}t} = 0.01ne^{-0.01t}$, where n is the population at time t. At time $t = 0$ the population is 5000.

  (i) Solve the differential equation, expressing $\ln n$ in terms of t. [5]

  (ii) What happens to the population as t becomes large? [3]

5 (i) By writing $\cot x$ in the form $\dfrac{\cos x}{\sin x}$, show that the result of differentiating $\cot x$ with respect to x is $-\mathrm{cosec}^2 x$. [4]

  (ii) Hence find the exact value of $\displaystyle\int_{\frac{1}{4}\pi}^{\frac{1}{2}\pi} \cot^2 x \, \mathrm{d}x$. [4]

6 (i) Find $\int x \ln x \, dx$.   [4]

   (ii) Show that $\dfrac{1}{\sin x \cos x} \equiv \dfrac{\sec^2 x}{\tan x}$, and hence find the exact value of $\displaystyle\int_{\frac{1}{6}\pi}^{\frac{1}{3}\pi} \dfrac{1}{\sin x \cos x} \, dx$.   [5]

7 (i) Show that the substitution $y = e^{-x}$ transforms the integral $\displaystyle\int_0^{\ln 2} \dfrac{1}{1 + e^{-x}} \, dx$ to

   $$\int_{\frac{1}{2}}^{1} \dfrac{1}{y(1 + y)} \, dy.$$ [4]

   (ii) Hence, or otherwise, find the exact value of $\displaystyle\int_0^{\ln 2} \dfrac{1}{1 + e^{-x}} \, dx$.   [5]

8 A curve is defined parametrically by the equations $x = t + \dfrac{1}{t}$, $y = t - \dfrac{1}{t}$, where $t \neq 0$.

   (i) Find the values of the parameter for which $x = 4\frac{1}{4}$, and hence find the corresponding values of y.   [3]

   (ii) Find the gradient of the tangent at the point in the fourth quadrant for which $x = 4\frac{1}{4}$, and hence find the equation of the tangent at this point.   [4]

   (iii) Find and simplify the cartesian equation of the curve.   [4]

9 Two straight lines l_1 and l_2 have equations as follows:

   $$l_1: \quad \mathbf{r} = 2\mathbf{i} - \mathbf{j} + 3\mathbf{k} + s(\mathbf{j} - \mathbf{k}); \qquad l_2: \quad \mathbf{r} = -2\mathbf{i} + 7\mathbf{j} + 3\mathbf{k} + t(2\mathbf{i} - 3\mathbf{j} - \mathbf{k}).$$

   (i) Show that l_1 and l_2 intersect, and find the position vector of their point of intersection.   [4]

   (ii) Find the acute angle between l_1 and l_2, giving your answer correct to the nearest degree.   [4]

   (iii) The foot of the perpendicular from the point with position vector $-2\mathbf{i} + 7\mathbf{j} + 3\mathbf{k}$ to the line l_1 is P. Find the position vector of P.   [4]

Practice examination 2 for C4

Time 1 hour 30 minutes

Answer all the questions.

You are permitted to use a graphic calculator in this paper.

1 Express $\dfrac{x+1}{x(x-1)} - \dfrac{x-1}{x(x+1)}$ as a single algebraic fraction in simplified form.　　　　　[3]

2 The equation of a curve is $\sin y = x \cos 2x$. Find $\dfrac{\mathrm{d}y}{\mathrm{d}x}$ in terms of x and y, and hence find the gradient of the curve at the point $(\frac{1}{4}\pi,\ 0)$.　　　　　[5]

3 (i) Express $\dfrac{x+2}{x(x+1)^2}$ in partial fractions.　　　　　[5]

　　(ii) Find $\displaystyle\int \dfrac{x+2}{x(x+1)^2}\,\mathrm{d}x$.　　　　　[3]

4 (i) By first expressing $\sin^2 2x$ in terms of $\cos 4x$, find the exact value of $\displaystyle\int_0^{\frac{1}{6}\pi} \sin^2 2x\,\mathrm{d}x$.　　　[4]

　　(ii) Find the exact value of $\displaystyle\int_0^{\frac{1}{2}\pi} (\sin x + \cos x)^2\,\mathrm{d}x$.　　　　　[4]

5 $OABC$ is a triangular pyramid. The position vectors of A, B, C with respect to O are given by $\overrightarrow{OA} = 3\mathbf{i}$, $\overrightarrow{OB} = 4\mathbf{j}$, $\overrightarrow{OC} = 5\mathbf{k}$, where $\mathbf{i}$, $\mathbf{j}$, $\mathbf{k}$ are mutually perpendicular unit vectors. The points M and N are the feet of the perpendiculars from O to AC and BC respectively (see diagram).

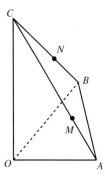

　　(i) Find $\overrightarrow{AC}$, and hence verify that the vector $\overrightarrow{OM}$ is parallel to $5\mathbf{i} + 3\mathbf{k}$.　　　　　[3]

　　(ii) Find a vector parallel to $\overrightarrow{ON}$.　　　　　[2]

　　(iii) Calculate the size of angle MON, correct to the nearest degree.　　　　　[3]

6 (i) Find the expansions of $(1 + 8x)^{\frac{1}{2}}$ and $(1 - 4x)^{-\frac{1}{2}}$ in ascending powers of x up to and including the terms in x^2. [5]

(ii) Hence find the expansion of $\sqrt{\dfrac{1 + 8x}{1 - 4x}}$ in ascending powers of x up to and including the term in x^2, and state the set of values of x for which the expansion is valid. [4]

7 Find $\displaystyle\int x(2x - 1)^5 \, dx$

(i) using the substitution $u = 2x - 1$,

(ii) using integration by parts, and show clearly that the results from the two methods agree with each other. [10]

8 (i) Find a vector equation of the line L_1 which passes through the points with position

vectors $\begin{pmatrix} 1 \\ 1 \\ -2 \end{pmatrix}$ and $\begin{pmatrix} 4 \\ -2 \\ 7 \end{pmatrix}$. [2]

(ii) Determine whether or not the point with position vector $\begin{pmatrix} -1 \\ 3 \\ 4 \end{pmatrix}$ lies on L_1, showing your reasons. [2]

The line L_2 has vector equation $\mathbf{r} = \begin{pmatrix} 0 \\ -2 \\ 1 \end{pmatrix} + t\begin{pmatrix} a \\ 1 \\ 3 \end{pmatrix}$, where a is a constant.

(iii) Find the value of a for which L_1 and L_2 intersect, and state the position vector of the point of intersection in this case. [6]

9 Water is flowing out of a small hole at the bottom of a conical container whose axis is vertical. At time t, the depth of water in the container is x and the volume of water in the container is V (see diagram). You are given that V is proportional to x^3, and that the rate at which V decreases is proportional to $\sqrt{x}$.

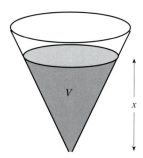

(i) Express $\dfrac{dV}{dt}$ in terms of x, $\dfrac{dx}{dt}$ and a constant. [2]

(ii) Show that x satisfies a differential equation of the form $\dfrac{dx}{dt} = -\dfrac{A}{x^{\frac{3}{2}}}$, where A is a positive constant. [2]

(iii) Find the general solution of the differential equation in part (ii) [3]

(iv) Given that the depth of water is initially 100 cm and that the depth is 25 cm after 20 minutes, find after how much longer the container will be empty. [4]

Answers to C3

1 Successive transformations

1 $y = (x - 1)^3 + 2$

2 Stretch factor 2 in the y-direction and translation of $-\frac{1}{6}\pi$ in the x-direction, in either order.

3 One possible answer is 'Translation of $-\frac{1}{2}\pi$ in the x-direction followed by a stretch with factor $\frac{1}{3}$ in the x-direction.'
Order matters:
$y = \cos\left(3\left(x + \frac{1}{2}\pi\right)\right) = \cos\left(3x + \frac{3}{2}\pi\right)$

4 (a) $4y = x^3$ (b) $y = \dfrac{4}{x}$

   (c) $y = x$ (d) $y = 2^{\frac{1}{2}x+1}$

5 $y = -2x + 8$

6 The curve remains the same.

7 (a) Translation by 2 in negative x-direction, stretch in y-direction, factor 5, translation by 7 in negative y-direction.
   (c) Translation by 7 in y-direction, stretch in y-direction, factor $\frac{1}{5}$, translation by 2 in x-direction.
   (d) $10x + 20$
   (e) Translation by 2 in negative x-direction, stretch in y-direction, factor 5.

1 $y = -3x^2$

2 (a) Translation by 3 units in the positive y direction, and translation by 1 in the positive x-direction, in either order.
   (b) $y = x^2 + 2x - 2$

3 Translation by 1 in negative x-direction, and stretch in y-direction, factor 2.

4 The result of stretching the function by a factor of $f(b)$ in the y-direction is the same as translating by b in the negative x-direction.

5 (b) (i) $y = \cos x$ (ii) $y = -\sin x$
     (iii) $y = -\sin x$ (iv) $y = -\cos x$

6 (a) Translate by α in the negative x-direction, enlarge by 3 in the y-direction and by $\frac{1}{2}$ in the x-direction; 4 roots
   (b) $2n$ roots   (c) $2|n|$ (or $-2n$) roots

7 $a = 6, b = -10$

8 (a) $y = 12x^2 + 48x + 20$
   (b) $y = 3x^2 + 12x + 5$
   $c = 3, d = -7$

9 $y = -f(-x)$, odd

10 (a) $y = (x - 2)^2$, $y = \left(\frac{1}{3}x - 2\right)^2$,
     $y = -\left(\frac{1}{3}x - 2\right)^2$
   (b) $y = 4x^2$, $y = 4x^2$, $y = 4(x + 3)^2$
   (c) $y = x^2$, $y = x^2 + 4$, $y = 2x^2 + 8$

11 A translation of -1 in the x-direction, then a stretch of factor 3 in the y-direction, finally a reflection in the x-axis:
$y = (x + 1)^4, \quad y = 3(x + 1)^4$

2 Functions

1 (a) $x \geqslant 0$ (b) $x \leqslant 0$
   (c) $x \geqslant 4$ (d) $x \leqslant 4$
   (e) $x \leqslant 0$ and $x \geqslant 4$ (f) $x \leqslant 0$ and $x \geqslant 4$
   (g) $x \leqslant 3$ and $x \geqslant 4$ (h) $x \geqslant 2$
   (i) all real numbers except 2
   (j) $x > 2$ (k) $x \geqslant 0$
   (l) all real numbers except 1 and 2

2 (a) $f(x) \geqslant 4$ (b) $f(x) \geqslant 10$
   (c) $f(x) \geqslant 6$ (d) $f(x) \leqslant 7$
   (e) $f(x) \geqslant 2$ (f) $f(x) \geqslant -1$

3 (a) $f(x) \geqslant 1$ (b) $f(x) \geqslant -\frac{45}{4}$
   (c) $f(x) \geqslant \frac{7}{4}$ (d) $f(x) \geqslant -7$
   (e) $f(x) \geqslant -\frac{169}{12}$ (f) $f(x) \leqslant 21$

4 (a) $0 \leqslant f(x) \leqslant 16$ (b) $-1 \leqslant f(x) \leqslant 7$
   (c) $0 \leqslant f(x) \leqslant 16$ (d) $4 \leqslant f(x) \leqslant 25$
   (e) $\frac{1}{2} \leqslant f(x) \leqslant 1$ (f) $4 \leqslant f(x) \leqslant 6$

5 (a) $f(x) > 7$ (b) $f(x) < 0$
   (c) $f(x) > -1$ (d) $f(x) > -1$
   (e) $f(x) > 2$ (f) $f(x) \geqslant -\frac{1}{4}$
   (g) $f(x) > 0$ (h) $f(x) > \ln 2$
   (i) $0 < f(x) < 1$

6 (a) $f(x) \geqslant 0$ (b) all real numbers
   (c) all real numbers except 0
   (d) $f(x) > 0$ (e) $f(x) \geqslant 5$
   (f) all real numbers   (g) $0 \leqslant f(x) \leqslant 2$
   (h) $f(x) \geqslant 0$ (i) $0 < f(x) < 1$
   (j) $f(x) \geqslant 1$ (k) $0 < f(x) \leqslant 1$
   (l) $0 \leqslant f(x) \leqslant 1$

7 $0 < w < 12, \ 0 < A \leqslant 36$

8 $0 < x < 4$

Exercise 2B (page 26)

1 (a) 121   (b) 4   (c) 676

2 (a) 17   (b) 8   (c) 152

3 (a) 1   (b) 4   (c) $\frac{1}{2}$

4 (a) 1   (b) 4   (c) $6\frac{1}{3}$

5 (a) 0   (b) 21
    (c) $-3\frac{3}{4}$ (d) $x^2 - 4$

6 (a) 27   (b) 8
    (c) $3\frac{3}{8}$ (d) $(\cos x + 2)^3$

7 (a) 16   (b) 4
    (c) 81   (d) $(2\sqrt{x} - 10)^2$

8 (a) qp, where $p : x \mapsto 4x$, $q : x \mapsto x + 9$
    (b) pq, with p, q as in (a)
    (c) rqp, where $p : x \mapsto x^2$, $q : x \mapsto 2x$,
      $r : x \mapsto x - 5$
    (d) qpr, with p, q, r as in (c)
    (e) rqp, where $p : x \mapsto \sqrt{x}$, $q : x \mapsto x - 3$,
      $r : x \mapsto x^3$
    (f) srqp, where $p : x \mapsto x - 2$, $q : x \mapsto x^2$,
      $r : x \mapsto x + 10$, $s : x \mapsto \sqrt{x}$

9 (a) $\mathbb{R}, \ f(x) \geqslant 0$ (b) $\mathbb{R}, \ -1 \leqslant f(x) \leqslant 1$
    (c) $x \geqslant 3, f(x) \geqslant 0$ (d) $\mathbb{R}, \ f(x) \geqslant 5$
    (e) $x > 0, \ f(x) > 0$ (f) $\mathbb{R}, \ f(x) \leqslant 4$
    (g) $0 \leqslant x \leqslant 4, \ 0 \leqslant f(x) \leqslant 2$
    (h) $\mathbb{R}, \ f(x) \geqslant 6$ (i) $x \geqslant 3, \ f(x) \geqslant 0$

10 (a) 4   (b) -14 (c) -9 (d) 33
    (e) 23   (f) -17 (g) 16   (h) 0

11 (a) 49   (b) 59   (c) 35
    (d) $\frac{1}{16}$ (e) 9   (f) 899

12 (a) 7   (b) -19 (c) 1   (d) $\frac{1}{2}$
    (e) $\frac{1}{2}$ (f) -1 (g) $3\frac{2}{3}$ (h) 2

13 (a) $x \mapsto 2x^2 + 5$ (b) $x \mapsto (2x + 5)^2$
    (c) $x \mapsto \dfrac{2}{x} + 5$ (d) $x \mapsto \dfrac{1}{2x + 5}$
    (e) $x \mapsto 4x + 15$ (f) $x \mapsto x$
    (g) $x \mapsto \left(\dfrac{2}{x} + 5\right)^2$ (h) $x \mapsto \dfrac{1}{(2x + 5)^2}$

14 (a) $x \mapsto \sin x - 3$ (b) $x \mapsto \sin(x - 3)$
    (c) $x \mapsto \sin(x^3 - 3)$ (d) $x \mapsto \sin(x^3)$
    (e) $x \mapsto x - 9$ (f) $x \mapsto (\sin x)^3$

15 (a) fh   (b) fg
    (c) hh   (d) hg or ggh
    (e) gf or fffg   (f) gffh
    (g) fgfg or ffffgg   (h) hf
    (i) hffg

16 (a) $x \geqslant 0, \ gf(x) \geqslant -5$
    (b) $x \geqslant -3, \ gf(x) \geqslant 0$
    (c) $x \neq 2, gf(x) \neq 0$
    (d) $\mathbb{R}, \ 0 \leqslant gf(x) \leqslant 1$
    (e) $\mathbb{R}, \ gf(x) \geqslant 0$
    (f) $-4 \leqslant x \leqslant 4, \ 0 \leqslant gf(x) \leqslant 2$
    (g) $x \leqslant -2$ or $x \geqslant 3, \ gf(x) \geqslant 0$
    (h) $x < -2, \ gf(x) > 0$

17 (a) $-2\frac{2}{3}$ or 4   (b) 7   (c) 1

18 $a = 3, \ b = -7$ or $a = -3, \ b = 14$

19 $a = 4, \ b = 11$ or $a = 4\frac{1}{2}, \ b = 10$

Exercise 2C (page 34)

1 (a) $x \mapsto x - 4$ (b) $x \mapsto x + 5$
    (c) $x \mapsto \frac{1}{2}x$ (d) $x \mapsto 4x$
    (e) $x \mapsto \sqrt[3]{x}$ (f) $x \mapsto x^5$

2 (a) 10   (b) 7   (c) 3   (d) 5   (e) -4

3 (a) 4   (b) 20   (c) $\frac{7}{5}$ (d) 15   (e) -6

4 (a) 8   (b) $\frac{1}{8}$ (c) 512   (d) -27 (e) 5

5 a, d, f, g, k

6 a, c, e, f, g, h, j

7 (a) 0   (b) -1 (c) $\frac{2}{3}$
    (d) 4   (e) -5 (f) -1
    (g) $1\frac{1}{2}$ (h) 1   (i) 4

8 (a) $x \mapsto \frac{1}{3}(x + 1)$ (b) $x \mapsto 2(x - 4)$
    (c) $x \mapsto \sqrt[3]{x - 5}$ (d) $x \mapsto (x + 3)^2, \ x > -3$
    (e) $x \mapsto \frac{1}{5}(2x + 3)$ (f) $x \mapsto 1 + \sqrt{x - 6}, \ x \geqslant 6$

9 (a) $y \mapsto \frac{1}{6}(y - 5)$ (b) $y \mapsto 5y - 4$
    (c) $y \mapsto \frac{1}{2}(4 - y)$ (d) $y \mapsto \frac{1}{2}(3y - 7)$
    (e) $y \mapsto \sqrt[3]{\frac{1}{2}(y - 5)}$ (f) $y \mapsto \dfrac{1}{y - 4}, \ y \neq 4$
    (g) $y \mapsto \dfrac{5}{y} + 1, \ y \neq 0$
    (h) $y \mapsto \sqrt{y - 7} - 2, \ y \geqslant 7$
    (i) $y \mapsto \frac{1}{2}(3 + \sqrt{y + 5}), \ y \geqslant -5$
    (j) $y \mapsto 3 + \sqrt{y + 9}, \ y \geqslant -9$

10 (a) $x \mapsto \frac{1}{4}x$ (b) $x \mapsto x - 3$
    (c) $x \mapsto x^2, \ x \geqslant 0$ (d) $x \mapsto \frac{1}{2}(x - 1)$
    (e) $x \mapsto \sqrt{x} + 2, \ x \geqslant 0$ (f) $x \mapsto \frac{1}{3}(1 - x)$
    (g) $x \mapsto \dfrac{3}{x}, \ x \neq 0$ (h) $x \mapsto 7 - x$

12 (a) $y \mapsto \dfrac{2y}{y - 1}, \ y \neq 1$
    (b) $y \mapsto \dfrac{4y + 1}{y - 2}, \ y \neq 2$
    (c) $y \mapsto \dfrac{5y + 2}{y - 1}, \ y \neq 1$
    (d) $y \mapsto \dfrac{3y - 11}{4y - 3}, \ y \neq \frac{3}{4}$

13 (a) $f(x) > -1$
(b) $x \mapsto 2 + \sqrt{x+1},\ x > -1,\ f^{-1}(x) > 2$

14 (a) $f(x) > 3$
(b) $x \mapsto 2 + (x-3)^2,\ x > 3,\ f^{-1}(x) > 2$

15 $k = -1$
(a) $f(x) \geqslant 5$
(b) $x \mapsto -1 - \sqrt{x-5},\ x \geqslant 5,\ f^{-1}(x) \leqslant -1$

16 $a = \frac{1}{8},\ b = \frac{3}{8}$

17 6

18 $x \mapsto \sqrt{x - 5\frac{3}{4}} - \frac{1}{2},\ x > 6,\ f^{-1}(x) > 0$

19 $x \mapsto 1 - \sqrt{-\frac{1}{2}(x+5)},\ x < -5,\ f^{-1}(x) < 1$

21 $x \mapsto 2^x$

Miscellaneous exercise 2 (page 36)

1 (a) $f(x) \leqslant 9$ (b) all real values
(c) $f(x) \geqslant -69$ (d) $f(x) \geqslant -36$

2 25; $f(x) \leqslant 25$

3 (a) 29   (b) 61   (c) 2
(d) -3 (e) 290   (f) 497

4 (a) $\mathbb{R},\ f(x) \leqslant 4$ (b) $\mathbb{R},\ f(x) \geqslant -7$
(c) $x \geqslant -2,\ f(x) \geqslant 0$ (d) $\mathbb{R},\ \mathbb{R}$
(e) $\mathbb{R},\ f(x) \geqslant 0$ (f) $x \geqslant 0,\ f(x) \leqslant 2$

5 (a) $x \mapsto (1-2x)^3$ (b) $x \mapsto 1 - 2x^3$
(c) $x \mapsto 1 - 2x^9$ (d) $x \mapsto 4x - 1$
(e) $x \mapsto \frac{1}{2}(1-x)$

6 (a) 48   (b) 3   (c) -1 (d) 4   (e) 4

7 (a) 12   (b) 27

8 $x \mapsto -3 + \sqrt{x-1},\ x > 10$

9 $x \mapsto \sqrt[3]{\frac{1}{4}(x-3)},\ x \in \mathbb{R}$; the graphs of $y = f(x)$ and $y = f^{-1}(x)$ are reflections in $y = x$

10 (a) $\sqrt{\frac{1}{3}(x+4)}$ (b) $3x^2 + 24x + 44$

11 (a) gf   (b) ff
(c) g^{-1} (d) fgh or fhg
(e) hfg   (f) f^{-1}
(g) g^{-1}fgh or g^{-1}fhg   (h) hf^{-1}

12 $f^{-1}(x) = \sqrt{x-1},\ x \geqslant 1$;
$gf(x) = x^2 - 2,\ gf(x) \geqslant -2$

13 $\frac{1}{2}\sqrt{7}$

14 $1 \pm \sqrt{3}$

15 $k = 1;\ x \mapsto 1 - \sqrt{x-6},\ x \geqslant 6$

16 $a = -2,\ b = 11$ or $a = 2,\ b = -13$

17 (b) $-\sqrt{1-x},\ x \leqslant 1$ (c) $-\frac{1}{2}$

18 (a) $x \mapsto \frac{1}{4}(x-5)$ (b) $x \mapsto \frac{1}{2}(3-x)$
(c) $x \mapsto -\frac{1}{8}(7+x)$ (d) $x \mapsto -8x - 7$
(e) $x \mapsto -\frac{1}{8}(7+x)$

19 (a) $x \mapsto \frac{1}{2}(x-7)$ (b) $x \mapsto \sqrt[3]{x+1}$
(c) $x \mapsto \sqrt[3]{\frac{1}{2}(x-5)}$ (d) $x \mapsto \frac{1}{2}(\sqrt[3]{x+1} - 7)$
(e) $x \mapsto 2x^3 + 5$ (f) $x \mapsto (2x+7)^3 - 1$
(g) $x \mapsto \sqrt[3]{\frac{1}{2}(x-5)}$ (h) $x \mapsto \frac{1}{2}(\sqrt[3]{x+1} - 7)$

20 (a) 3   (b) 7   (c) 3   (d) 7

21 (a) x (b) $\dfrac{x+5}{2x-1}$ (c) x
(d) x (e) $\dfrac{x+5}{2x-1}$

22 (a) $\dfrac{4}{2-x}$ (b) $\dfrac{4}{2-x}$ (c) x
(d) $\dfrac{2x-4}{x}$ (e) x (f) $\dfrac{2x-4}{x}$

23 -1

24 $f(x) = \{-2, -1, 0, 1, 2, 3\}$
$0 \leqslant f(x) < 1$

3 Exponential growth and decay

Exercise 3A (page 43)

1 5324; 400, 440, 484,

2 2624, 2362

3 £60 000, £72 000, £86 400, £103 680, £124 416; £10 000, £12 000, £14 400, £17 280, £20 736

4 80 000, 64 000, 51 200; 1200, 1440, 1728; 66.6..., 44.4..., 29.6...; decreases by one-third each decade

5 (a) $\frac{9}{40}$ (b) $\frac{81}{400}, \frac{729}{4000}, \frac{6561}{40\,000}$
(c) $\frac{1}{4} \times \left(\frac{9}{10}\right)^t$

6 £$\dfrac{60}{1.06} \times 1.06^t$; yes

7 £3750×0.8^t; yes

8 (a) 17 800   (b) 29 100

9 (a) 85.1 kg   (b) 68.1 kg

10 Amnesia, Candida, Declinia

11 1.11 inches, 1.31 inches

12 0.072; the $\log_{10}$ of the growth factor

Exercise 3B (page 50)

1 (a) 800   (b) 141   (c) 336

2 (a) 45.5 °C   (b) 13.6 minutes

3 (a) 63 000   (b) 36 200   (c) 19 700

4 (a) 5.83×10^7 (b) 5.65×10^7

5 10 000, 451

6 (a) $\sqrt[12]{2} \approx 1.059$ (b) 262
   (c) between 5 and 6; between D and D sharp

7 (a) $y = 2.51 \times 3.98^x$ (b) $y = 10^{12} \times 0.001^x$
   (c) $y = 5.01 \times 50.1^x$ (d) $y = 5.01x^2$
   (e) $y = \dfrac{0.316}{x^5}$

8 $p = 39.7 \times 1.022^x$ gives $p = 39.7, 49.4, 61.3,$ 76.3, 94.8. The exponential model does not fit so well in this period.

9 The points do not lie in a straight line.

10 Amnesia: 185×1.08^t
    Candida: 100×1.20^t
    Declinia: 180×0.94^t

11 (a) $(8, 24)$, $(9, 48)$
    (b) $(8, 768)$, $(9, 1536)$

Miscellaneous exercise 3 (page 52)

1 (a) £2254.32   (b) 139

2 (a) 5.42   (b) 5.42

3 9.49 a.m. Tuesday

4 389 years

5 (a) 3, 2   (b) 3.15×10^6

7 8760

8 2031

9 8.7 years

10 $(15 + 84 \times 0.982^t)$ °C; between 6.2 and 10.0 minutes

4 Extending differentiation and integration

Exercise 4A (page 54)

1 (a) $2(x + 3)$ (b) $4(2x - 3)$
   (c) $-9(1 - 3x)^2$ (d) $3a(ax + b)^2$
   (e) $-3a(b - ax)^2$ (f) $-5(1 - x)^4$
   (g) $8(2x - 3)^3$ (h) $-8(3 - 2x)^3$

2 $na(ax + b)^{n-1}$

3 (a) $10(x + 3)^9$ (b) $10(2x - 1)^4$
   (c) $-28(1 - 4x)^6$ (d) $15(3x - 2)^4$
   (e) $-12(4 - 2x)^5$ (f) $72(2 + 3x)^5$
   (g) $10(2x + 5)^4$ (h) $18(2x - 3)^8$

Exercise 4B (page 56)

1 (a) $20(4x + 5)^4$ (b) $16(2x - 7)^7$
   (c) $-6(2 - x)^5$ (d) $2\left(\tfrac{1}{2}x + 4\right)^3$

2 (a) $\dfrac{-3}{(3x + 5)^2}$ (b) $\dfrac{2}{(4 - x)^3}$
   (c) $\dfrac{-6}{(2x + 1)^4}$ (d) $\dfrac{-64}{(4x - 1)^5}$

3 (a) $\dfrac{1}{\sqrt{2x + 3}}$ (b) $\dfrac{2}{\sqrt[3]{(6x - 1)^2}}$
   (c) $\dfrac{-2}{(4x + 7)\sqrt{4x + 7}}$ (d) $\dfrac{-10}{(3x - 2)^{\frac{5}{3}}}$

4 60

5 $(-6, 125)$

6 $y = -\tfrac{3}{4}x - \tfrac{5}{4}$

7 $y = -3x + 48$

8 $a = -5, b = -2$ or $a = 5, b = 2$

9 $\left(4, 8\tfrac{2}{3}\right)$, maximum

Exercise 4C (page 58)

1 (a) $\tfrac{1}{14}(2x + 1)^7 + k$ (b) $\tfrac{1}{15}(3x - 5)^5 + k$
   (c) $-\tfrac{1}{28}(1 - 7x)^4 + k$ (d) $\tfrac{2}{11}\left(\tfrac{1}{2}x + 1\right)^{11} + k$

2 (a) $\dfrac{-1}{10(5x + 2)^2} + k$ (b) $\dfrac{2}{3(1 - 3x)} + k$
   (c) $\dfrac{-1}{4(x + 1)^4} + k$ (d) $\dfrac{-1}{8(4x + 1)^3} + k$

3 (a) $\tfrac{1}{15}(10x + 1)^{\frac{3}{2}} + k$ (b) $(2x - 1)^{\frac{1}{2}} + k$
   (c) $\tfrac{6}{5}\left(\tfrac{1}{2}x + 2\right)^{\frac{5}{3}} + k$ (d) $\tfrac{16}{9}(2 + 6x)^{\frac{3}{4}} + k$

4 (a) 820   (b) $8\tfrac{1}{6}$ (c) $\tfrac{2}{15}$ (d) $\tfrac{16}{225}$

5 (a) 4   (b) 18

6 (a) $\tfrac{1}{4}$ (b) $\tfrac{5}{36}$

7 (a) $24\tfrac{3}{10}$ (b) $4\tfrac{1}{2}$ (c) $\tfrac{2}{3}$ (d) 28

8 2.25

9 9.1125

10 $\tfrac{1}{20}$

Miscellaneous exercise 4 (page 62)

1 $80(4x - 1)^{19}$

2 $8(3 - 4x)^{-3}$

3 $-\tfrac{4}{3}$

4 $8\tfrac{2}{3}$

5 $y = 20x + 11$

6 $\tfrac{1}{6}$

7 (a) 1, 2   (b) $10\tfrac{1}{8}$

8 (b) $\tfrac{155}{6}$

9 $8x + 5y - 34 = 0$

10 $(2, -4); (0, 0), (4, 0);$
    $(0, 16), (4, -16); (2, 0),$
    $(2 \pm 2\sqrt{3}, 0), (0, 16)$

11 (a) $(-4, 0)$, $(0, 2)$ (b) $\frac{35}{6}$

12 $3\frac{1}{2}$

13 $438\frac{6}{7}$

14 $70\frac{7}{8}$

15 (a) minimum   (b) 20

16 $2\frac{1}{2}$

17 $(\frac{1}{2}, \frac{1}{4})$, maximum

18 $(2\frac{1}{2}, 6)$, minimum

19 (a) $(1, 256)$, $(2\frac{1}{3}, 0)$ (b) $-\frac{256}{45}$

20 4

5 Differentiating exponentials and logarithms

Exercise 5A (page 71)

1 (a) $3e^{3x}$ (b) $-e^{-x}$ (c) $6e^{2x}$
  (d) $16e^{-4x}$ (e) $3e^{3x+4}$ (f) $-2e^{3-2x}$
  (g) $-e^{1-x}$ (h) $12e^{3+4x}$

2 (a) $3e^2$ (b) $-2e$ (c) -1 (d) -2

3 (a) $ey = x + 2$
  (b) $y = 3x - 1$
  (c) $y = (4 + 4e^4)x - (4 + 6e^4)$
  (d) $4y = -2x + 1 + 2\ln 2$

4 $(\ln 2, 2\ln 2 - 2)$, maximum

5 (a) $\frac{1}{3}e^{3x} + k$ (b) $-e^{-x} + k$
  (c) $\frac{3}{2}e^{2x} + k$ (d) $e^{-4x} + k$
  (e) $\frac{1}{3}e^{3x+4} + k$ (f) $-\frac{1}{2}e^{3-2x} + k$
  (g) $-e^{1-x} + k$ (h) $\frac{3}{4}e^{3+4x} + k$

6 (a) $\frac{1}{2}(e^4 - e^2)$ (b) $e - \frac{1}{e}$
  (c) $e^5 - e$ (d) $e^{10} - e^8$
  (e) 6   (f) $\frac{3}{4}e$
  (g) $\frac{1}{\ln 2}$ (h) $\frac{1}{\ln 3}(3^9 - \frac{1}{27})$

7 $\frac{1}{2}(e^4 - 1)$

8 $1 - e^{-N}$; 1

9 An overestimate

Exercise 5B (page 76)

1 (a) $e^{2.30x}$ (b) $e^{-2.30x}$
  (c) $e^{0.916x}$ (d) $e^{-0.916x}$

2 (a) $3.6 \times e^{0.0953t}$ (b) $0.342 \times e^{1.74t}$
  (c) $7.13 \times e^{-0.658t}$ (d) $0.161 \times e^{-4.06t}$

3 (a) 100×0.0498^t (b) 2.83×4.31^t
  (c) 0.326×0.876^t (d) 0.507×1.01^t

4 (a) $y = 1.49e^{0.6x} = 1.49 \times 1.82^x$
  (b) $y = 1.63 \times 10^5 e^{-3x} = 1.63 \times 10^5 \times 20.1^{-x}$

(c) $y = 2.01e^{1.7x} = 2.01 \times 5.47^x$
(d) $y = 2.01x^2$
(e) $y = \dfrac{0.607}{x^5}$

5 $V = e^{-0.0198t}$

6 (a) 0.0999
  (b) (i) 49.9 mg per minute
      (ii) 25.0 mg per minute

7 (a) 50 m s^{-1}
  (c) (i) 1.35 m s^{-2} (ii) 1 m s^{-2}
  (d) 2750 m

8 (a) (i) about 7 per week   (ii) 60 per week
  (b) $2.26e^{0.3t}$ (c) 15 per week

Exercise 5C (page 79)

1 (a) $\dfrac{1}{x}$ (b) $\dfrac{2}{2x - 1}$ (c) $\dfrac{-2}{1 - 2x}$
  (d) $\dfrac{2}{x}$ (e) $\dfrac{b}{a + bx}$ (f) $-\dfrac{1}{x}$
  (g) $-\dfrac{3}{3x + 1}$ (h) $\dfrac{2}{2x + 1} - \dfrac{3}{3x - 1}$
  (i) $-\dfrac{6}{x}$ (j) $\dfrac{1}{x} + \dfrac{1}{x + 1}$
  (k) $\dfrac{2}{x} + \dfrac{1}{x - 1}$ (l) $\dfrac{1}{x - 1} + \dfrac{1}{x + 2}$

2 (a) $y = 2x - \ln 2 - 1$ (b) $y = 2x - 1$
  (c) $y = x$ (d) $ey = x + e\ln 3$

3 (a) 1, minimum   (b) $\frac{1}{2} - \ln 2$, minimum
  (c) 1, minimum   (d) 1, minimum

5 $2y = 2 - x$

6 $x > 6$, $\dfrac{1}{x - 2} + \dfrac{1}{x - 6}$ (a) $x > 6$ (b) None

7 (i) $2 < x < 6$, $\dfrac{1}{x - 2} - \dfrac{1}{6 - x}$
    (a) $2 < x < 4$ (b) $4 < x < 6$
  (ii) There are no points in the domain.

Exercise 5D (page 81)

1 (a) $y = \frac{1}{2}\ln x + k$, $\quad x > 0$
  (b) $y = \ln(x - 1) + k$, $\quad x > 1$
  (c) $y = -\ln(1 - x) + k$, $\quad x < 1$
  (d) $y = \frac{1}{4}\ln(4x + 3) + k$, $\quad x > -\frac{3}{4}$
  (e) $y = -2\ln(1 - 2x) + k$, $\quad x < \frac{1}{2}$
  (f) $y = 2\ln(1 + 2x) + k$, $\quad x > -\frac{1}{2}$
  (g) $y = -2\ln(-1 - 2x) + k$, $\quad x < -\frac{1}{2}$
  (h) $y = 2\ln(2x - 1) + k$, $\quad x > \frac{1}{2}$

2 (a) $\ln 2$ (b) $\ln 2$ (c) $\ln 2$ (d) $\ln 2$

3 (a) $\ln 2$ (b) $\frac{1}{2}\ln 3$ (c) $\frac{2}{3}\ln\frac{13}{7}$
  (d) $\ln\dfrac{5e - 7}{4e - 7}$ (e) $\ln 2$ (f) $8 + \ln 5$

4 The trapezium rule with 1 interval gives
$\frac{5}{6} = 0.833...$; exact answer $2 \ln \frac{3}{2} = 0.810...$.

5 $\frac{1509}{1976} = 0.763...$, overestimate; $2 \ln \frac{19}{13} = 0.758...$

6 $y = \frac{3}{2} \ln \left(\frac{1}{3}(2x + 1) \right)$

7 $y = 2 \ln(4x - 3) + 2$

Exercise 5E (page 86)

1 (a) $-\ln 4$ (b) $-\frac{1}{2} \ln 3$ (c) $\ln 4 - \frac{2}{3} \ln 5$

  (d) $\ln \dfrac{7 - 2e}{7 - e}$ (e) $-\ln \frac{5}{3}$ (f) $2 - \ln 2$

2 $\ln 7, -\frac{2}{7}$

3 $2^x \ln 2$, $3^x \ln 3$, $10^x \ln 10$, $-\left(\frac{1}{2}\right)^x \ln 2$

Miscellaneous exercise 5 (page 86)

1 (a) $\dfrac{3}{3x - 4}$ (b) $\dfrac{-3}{4 - 3x}$ (c) $3e^{3x}$

  (d) $-e^{-x}$ (e) $\dfrac{1}{3 - x} - \dfrac{1}{2 - x}$

  (f) $\dfrac{-6}{3 - 2x}$

2 Overestimates; the graph of $y = \dfrac{1}{x}$ lies below the straight line(s) at the top of the trapezia, with 1 and 2 intervals respectively.

3 $\left(\frac{1}{2}, 8\right)$, $(4, 1)$; $15\frac{3}{4} - 12 \ln 2$

4 (a) $\frac{2}{3}e - \frac{1}{6}e^{-2} - \frac{1}{2}$ (b) minimum

5 $2x - e^{-x} + k$

6 $x = \frac{1}{2}$, minimum

8 $y = x + 4$

9 $y = -\frac{1}{2}x + \frac{1}{4}$

10 (a) $\dfrac{2}{x - 1}$ (b) $3 \ln 2$

11 (a) $y = 200e^{-0.127t}$ (b) $y = 200 \times 0.88^t$

12 (a) $2 - e^{-a} = a$ (b) $\displaystyle\int_0^a (2 - e^{-x} - x)\,dx$

13 $\frac{1}{2}e$

14 $1.22 \times 10^4 \text{ h}^{-1}$

15 $0.76\,°C\ \text{min}^{-1}$

16 (a) (i) 1.2 °C per minute
      (ii) 0.982 °C per minute
   (b) (i) 1.12 °C per minute
      (ii) 0.56 °C per minute

17 (a) $a = 0.0333$, $c = 1.39$
   (b) 34.1 m, 47.3 m per week
   (c) 139 m per week

18 (b) 0.116 (c) about $\frac{3}{5} Q$ ml

19 (a) $e^{-2a} - 3a = 0$ (d) $\frac{1}{2} - \frac{3}{2}a^2 - \frac{1}{2}e^{-2a}$

21 (a) -1 (b) 1

22 £2718

6 Trigonometry

Exercise 6A (page 94)

1 (a) -0.675 (b) 1.494 (c) 1.133

2 (a) $\cot x$ (b) $\sec x$ (c) $\sec^2 x$
  (d) $\operatorname{cosec} x$ (e) $\cot x$ (f) $-\operatorname{cosec} x$

3 (a) $\sqrt{2}$ (b) 1 (c) $-\sqrt{3}$ (d) $-\sqrt{2}$
  (e) $-\frac{1}{3}\sqrt{3}$ (f) $\frac{2}{3}\sqrt{3}$ (g) 0 (h) $-\frac{2}{3}\sqrt{3}$

4 (a) 1.051 (b) 3.732 (c) 2 (d) -1.035

5 $\operatorname{cosec} x$ and $\sin x$ both have period 2π.
  $\operatorname{cosec} x$ is positive when $\sin x$ is positive, between 0 and π; and $\operatorname{cosec} x$ is negative when $\sin x$ is negative, between $-\pi$ and 0.
  $\operatorname{cosec} x$ has a minimum value of 1 when $\sin x$ has a maximum value of 1, and a maximum value of -1 when $\sin x$ has a minimum value of -1.
  As $|\sin x| \leqslant 1$ for all x, $|\operatorname{cosec} x| \geqslant 1$ for all x.
  $\operatorname{cosec} x$ is undefined when $\sin x = 0$, for multiples of π.
  $\operatorname{cosec} x$ is decreasing in the intervals $-\frac{1}{2}\pi < x < 0$ and $0 < x < \frac{1}{2}\pi$, where $\sin x$ is increasing, and is increasing in those intervals where $\sin x$ is decreasing.

6 (a) $\frac{5}{4}$ (b) $\frac{4}{3}$ (c) $-\frac{1}{3}\sqrt{3}$ (d) $\frac{2}{3}\sqrt{3}$

7 $\pm 4\sqrt{3}$, $\pm\sqrt{2}$, $\pm\frac{1}{2}\sqrt{5}$

8 (a) $\sin\phi\cos\phi$ (b) $\cot\phi$ (c) $\cot^2\phi$

9 (a) $3\sec^2\phi - \sec\phi - 3$
  (b) 0.72, π, 5.56

10 1.11, 2.82, 4.25, 5.96

11 $45°$, $90°$, $135°$, $225°$, $270°$, $315°$

Exercise 6B (page 100)

1 $\frac{1}{4}(\sqrt{6} + \sqrt{2})$, $2 + \sqrt{3}$

2 $\frac{1}{4}(\sqrt{2} - \sqrt{6})$, $\frac{1}{4}(\sqrt{6} + \sqrt{2})$

3 $\frac{1}{2}\cos x - \frac{1}{2}\sqrt{3}\sin x$

4 $-\cos\phi$, $-\sin\phi$

5 $\dfrac{\sqrt{3} + \tan x}{1 - \sqrt{3}\tan x}$, $\dfrac{1 + \sqrt{3}\tan x}{\tan x - \sqrt{3}}$

7 (a) $\frac{4}{3}$ (b) $\frac{7}{25}$ (c) $\frac{4}{5}$ (d) $\frac{117}{44}$

8 $-\frac{63}{65}$, $-\frac{33}{56}$

Exercise 6C (page 102)

1 $-\frac{1}{3}\sqrt{5}$, $-\frac{4}{9}\sqrt{5}$, $-4\sqrt{5}$

2 $\frac{1}{8}$, $\pm\frac{1}{4}\sqrt{14}$

3 $\sin 3A \equiv 3\sin A - 4\sin^3 A$

4 $\cos 3A \equiv 4\cos^3 A - 3\cos A$

6 $\pm\frac{5}{6}, \pm\frac{1}{6}\sqrt{11}$

7 $\frac{2}{3}, -\frac{3}{2}$

8 $\pm\sqrt{2} - 1, \sqrt{2} - 1$

9 (a) π (b) $\frac{1}{2}\pi$, 3.99, 5.44
   (c) 0, 0.87, 2.27, π, 4.01, 5.41, 2π

Exercise 6D (page 105)

1 18.4°

2 53.1°

3 $\sqrt{34}, \frac{3}{5}$

4 $\sqrt{37}, 0.165$

5 (a) $\sqrt{5}, 1.11$ (b) $\sqrt{5}, 0.46$
   (c) $\sqrt{5}, 1.11$ (d) $\sqrt{5}, 0.46$

6 $\sqrt{61}\cos(\theta - 0.876)$
   (a) $\sqrt{61}$ when $\theta = 0.876$
   (b) $-\sqrt{61}$ when $\theta = 4.018$

7 Translation of $\frac{1}{3}\pi$ in the positive x-direction and a one-way stretch parallel to the y-axis with factor 6.

8 $\sqrt{52}\cos(x + 0.588)$; translation of 0.588 in the negative x-direction and a one-way stretch parallel to the y-axis with factor $\sqrt{52}$.

9 $10\sin(x + 36.9°)$
   (a) 1   (b) 0

10 1.86 or 2.98, correct to 2 decimal places

11 (a) 71.7°, 347.8°   (b) 102.1°, 214.3°
   (c) 35.5°, 276.5°

12 (a) 0.50, 1.83   (b) 0.96, 2.43
   (c) −1.92, 0.80

Exercise 6E (page 110)

1 (a) $\frac{1}{6}\pi$ (b) $\frac{1}{4}\pi$ (c) $\frac{1}{2}\pi$ (d) $\frac{1}{3}\pi$
   (e) $-\frac{1}{3}\pi$ (f) $-\frac{1}{2}\pi$ (g) $\frac{1}{2}\pi$ (h) π

2 (a) $\frac{1}{4}\pi$ (b) $-\frac{1}{6}\pi$ (c) $\frac{2}{3}\pi$ (d) $\frac{1}{6}\pi$

3 (a) 0.5   (b) −1   (c) $\sqrt{3}$ (d) 0

4 (a) $\frac{1}{2}\pi$ (b) $\frac{1}{6}\pi$ (c) $\frac{1}{6}\pi$ (d) 0

5 (a) $\frac{1}{2}$ (b) $\frac{1}{2}$ (c) $\frac{1}{2}\sqrt{3}$ (d) 1

6 0.739; $\cos x = x$

Miscellaneous exercise 6 (page 110)

1 (b) $-\frac{25}{24}$

2 60°, 120°, 240°, 300°

3 (a) 1   (b) $\frac{4}{5}$

4 (b) 60°, 300°

5 $\frac{1}{4}(\sqrt{6} - \sqrt{2})$

7 (a) $-\frac{4}{5}$ (b) $-\frac{24}{25}, \frac{7}{25}$

8 73.9°

9 26.6°, 90°, 206.6°, 270°

12 $2\sin(\theta + 60°)$; 90°, 330°

13 (a) $15\cos(x - 0.644)$ (b) 0.276

14 $\sqrt{5}\cos(x - 26.6°)$
   (a) 90°, 323.1°   (b) $-\sqrt{5} \leq k \leq \sqrt{5}$

15 (a) $13\sin(x + 67.4°)$
   (b) 7.5 when $x = 202.6°$, 1 when $x = 22.6°$

16 $5\cos(x + 53.1°)$
   (a) 13.3°, 240.4°   (b) $\frac{1}{3}, \frac{1}{13}$

17 (a) $\frac{1}{6}\pi$ (b) $\dfrac{x + y}{1 - xy}$

18 $-\frac{1}{2}$

19 (b) $\dfrac{1}{x}, 1 - 2x^2$

20 (a) $x + 2y = 3$
   (b) $r = \sqrt{5}, \alpha = \tan^{-1} 2 = 63.4...°$
   (c) $(2\sin\theta, 2\cos\theta)$, 74.4°

21 (a) (56.8°, 0), (123.2°, 0)
   (b) 53.1°, 120°; (53.1°, 0.6), (120°, −0.5)

7 The modulus function

Exercise 7A (page 117)

3 $|a + b| \leq |a| + |b|; |a + b| \geq ||a| - |b||$

Exercise 7B (page 119)

1 (a) $2 < x < 4$ (b) $-2.1 \leq x \leq -1.9$
   (c) $1.4995 \leq x \leq 1.5005$ (d) $-1.25 \leq x \leq 2.75$

2 (a) $|x - 1.5| \leq 0.5$ (b) $|x - 1| < 2$
   (c) $|x + 3.65| \leq 0.15$ (d) $|x - 2.85| < 0.55$

Exercise 7C (page 127)

1 (a) 3, −7   (b) 8, −6   (c) 0, 3
   (d) 3, $-3\frac{2}{3}$ (e) 4, $\frac{2}{3}$ (f) $-2, \frac{1}{2}$
   (g) −2, −8   (h) $-4, 1\frac{3}{7}$

2 (a) $-3 < x < -1$ (b) $x < -2$ or $x > 8$
   (c) $-5 \leq x \leq -2$ (d) $x \leq -3\frac{1}{3}$ or $x \geq 2$
   (e) $x < -\frac{3}{4}$ or $x > \frac{1}{2}$ (f) $x < -3$ or $x > 2\frac{1}{3}$
   (g) $1 < x < 3$ (h) $x \leq 0$

3 (a) $x > 0$ (b) $-2 < x < \frac{4}{5}$ (c) $x \geq 0$

4 (a) true
   (b) false; if $f(x) = -x$, then $f(|1|) = f(1) = -1$.

Miscellaneous exercise 7 (page 127)

1 $x < \frac{1}{2}$

2 3 and −2 respectively

3 $-10 < x < \frac{2}{3}$

4 $-\frac{1}{3}$, −1

5 $x < 1$

6 $-\frac{1}{3}$, $\frac{1}{5}$; $x < -\frac{1}{3}$ or $x > \frac{1}{5}$

7 (a) (ii) $0 \leqslant f(x) \leqslant 2$, $-1 \leqslant g(x) \leqslant 1$
   (b) f(x) is periodic, with period 180°;
       g(x) is not periodic.

8 $x < 2.4$ and $x > 4$

9 (a) −2, $\frac{4}{3}$ (b) no solution

10 (a) $y = 3x - 1$ (b) $y = 1 - x$

12 (a) |tan ϕ| (b) |sin ϕ| (c) |tan ϕ|

13 (a) $2x - 1$ (b) 7   (c) $1 - 2x$

14 any value of x such that $-3 \leqslant x \leqslant 3$

15 (a) 8   (b) − 3

Revision exercise 1 (page 129)

1 Stretch factor e in the y-direction; translation
   1 in the negative x-direction.
   Reflection in the line $y = x$.

3 $\frac{1}{44}(4x + 3)^{11} + k$

4 (a) 120 g   (b) $-\frac{1}{330}\ln 2$
   (c) 0.662 grams per year

5 (a) 2   (b) $\frac{1}{3}\ln\frac{1}{2}x$
   (c) The graphs are reflections of each other in
       the line $y = x$.
   (d) 8, $\frac{1}{3}\ln 4$

6 (a) $-10(3 - 2x)^4$ (b) $\dfrac{4}{4x + 7}$

7 (a) 3
   (b) f; reflect $y = f(x)$ in the line $y = x$;
       intersections with the axes are (0, −2)
       and (4,0).
   (c) Three possibilities: reflect the part of the
       graph of g(x) to the left of $x = 2$ in the
       x-axis; reflect the part of the graph of g(x)
       to the right of $x = 2$ in the x-axis; reflect
       the whole of the graph of g(x) in the
       x-axis.

8 (a) 200, 60
   (b) (i) 198   (ii) 1.6 grams per year

9 (c) A sketch graph would show that the
       curve joining the points $x = 5$ to $x = 15$

lies wholly below the chord joining the
points $x = 5$ to $x = 15$ showing that the
integral is less than the approximation.

10 (a) $15a^3$

11 (a) $y \geqslant 4$ (b) 13   (c) $-47\frac{1}{2}, 48\frac{1}{2}$
    (d) $g^{-1}(x) = \frac{1}{2}(5 - x)$, $x > 5$

12 (b) 29°, 209°

13 $1 + \frac{1}{2}\sqrt{2}$

14 (b) $\sqrt{58}\sin(\theta + 23.2°)$ (c) 17.8°

15 (a) $\tan 2x = \dfrac{2\tan x}{1 - \tan^2 x}$
    (c) $\frac{1}{3}\pi$, $\frac{2}{3}\pi$, $\frac{4}{3}\pi$, $\frac{5}{3}\pi$

16 $x \mapsto \dfrac{1 - x}{1 + 2x}$, $x \in \mathbb{R}$, $x \neq -\frac{1}{2}$

17 $-\dfrac{1}{(2x + 3)\sqrt{2x + 3}}$

18 (a) $f(x) = (x - 1)^2 - 2$; $-2 \leqslant f(x) \leqslant 14$; f is not
        one-one since, for example,
        $f(0) = f(2) = -1$.
    (b) For example, $x \geqslant 1$.

19 18

20 (a) $y \leqslant 4$ (b) Reflect in the line $y = 2$.
    (c) $f^{-1}(x) = \sqrt{4 - x}$, $x \leqslant 4$
    (d) If $f(x) = f^{-1}(x)$, they must intersect on
        $y = x$, so $f(x) = x$. This gives the required
        equation. 1.56

21 (a) −2   (b) 1   (c) 3   (d) −3, 3

22 (a) 3.49 hours (b) 15 hours   (c) 251 000

24 (b) $\sin\alpha$ (c) $(\alpha, \frac{1}{2}\sin\alpha)$

25 1.04, 3.03, 4.18, 6.17

26 (a) $\sqrt{52}$ (b) 33.7°

27 (a) $\pi - 2\theta$, $2r^2 + 2r^2\cos 2\theta$ (b) $2r\cos\theta$

28 (a) $4r\cos\theta + 2r\sin\theta$ (b) r^2 (c) $\frac{4}{5}r^2$

29 (a) 3.00 hours (b) 1 220 000

31 (a) $-1 \leqslant x \leqslant 1$, $-\pi - 4 \leqslant y \leqslant \pi - 4$
    (b) $3 \leqslant x \leqslant 5$, $-\pi \leqslant y \leqslant \pi$

32 $p = 5$, $q = 2$, $r = 8$

33 (a) 2, 1, $-\frac{3}{2}$ (b) $(-1, -3)$
    (c) One possibility is: translate 1 in the
        negative x-direction, then translate $\frac{3}{2}$ in
        the negative y-direction, then stretch by
        a factor 2 in the y-direction.

34 (a) $-6 \leqslant f(x)$, $0 \leqslant g(x)$ (b) $2\ln\frac{1}{5}(x + 6)$
    (c) $2\ln 3$, $-2\ln 5$

35 (a) $2\cos(x + 60°)$
    (b) 0°, 60°, 180°, 240°, 360°

8 Solving equations numerically

2 2

3 1.91, −29.6; as the graph is continuous there is at least one root in the interval $3 < x < 4$.

4 (a) (i) −2   (ii) −1.71
   (b) (i) 2   (ii) 2.63
   (c) (i) 1   (ii) 1.33
   (d) (i) 6   (ii) 6.30
   (e) (i) −8   (ii) −7.86
   (f) (i) 4   (ii) 4.53

5 The graph of the function f may have a break in it. $f(x) = \dfrac{1}{x}$ has $f(-1)f(1) < 0$, but $f(x) = 0$ has no root between −1 and 1.

1 Here are three possible examples for each part.

   (a) $x = \sqrt[5]{5x - 6}$; $x = \frac{1}{5}(x^5 + 6)$; $x = \sqrt{\dfrac{5x - 6}{x^3}}$

   (b) $x = 5e^{-x}$; $x = \ln 5 - \ln x$; $x = \sqrt{5xe^{-x}}$

   (c) $x = \sqrt[5]{1999 - x^3}$; $x = \sqrt[3]{1999 - x^5}$;
   $x = \sqrt[3]{\dfrac{1999}{x^2 + 1}}$

2 (a) $f(x) = x^{11} - x^7 + 6 = 0$
   (b) −1.1769, −1.2227, −1.2338, −1.2367, −1.2375
   (c) converging to a root
   (d) x_5 is an approximate root of $f(x) = 0$

3 (i) (a) $f(x) = x^4 - x^3 - 34x^2 + 289 = 0$
      (b) 7.1111, 22.283, 463.11, 214 440, 4.598×10^{10}
      (c) diverging
   (ii) (a) $f(x) = x^4 - 500x - 10 = 0$
      (b) 7.9446, 7.9437, 7.9437, 7.9437, 7.9437
      (c) converging to a root
      (d) x_5 is an approximate root of $f(x) = 0$

4 1.6198, 1.8781, 1.6932, 1.8208, 1.7304, 1.7933; converging to $\alpha = 1.7671...$

5 (b) 0.7895 correct to 4 decimal places; terms are converging to another root.

6 $x_{r+1} = \sqrt[3]{e^{x_r} + 2}$ with $x_0 = 2$ converges to 2.27 in 11 steps;
   $x_{r+1} = \dfrac{e^{x_r} + 2}{x_r^2}$ with $x_0 = 2$ converges to 2.27 in 3 steps.

7 (a) 9   (b) 5

1 (a) no convergence; $F^{-1}(x) = \dfrac{3}{x + 1}$, 1.303
   (b) no convergence;
      $F^{-1}(x) = \frac{1}{3} \ln(5 - x)$,   0.501
   (c) converges to 2.277
   (d) no convergence;
      $F^{-1}(x) = -\sqrt[6]{300 - 10x}$, −2.624
   (e) converges to 13.200
   (f) no convergence;
      $F^{-1}(x) = \sqrt{20 - \dfrac{3}{x}}$,   4.395

2 (a) 5, 1.179   (b) −13, 6.730
   (c) 10, −1.896   (d) −3.4, 2.204

1 5, 13;
   (a) There exists a root between $x = 1$ and $x = 2$.
   (b) $1\frac{5}{8}$

2 2

3 2.15

4 $0.381 < x < 0.382$

5 5.0

6 (b) 0.77

7 (a) 2

8 233.1°

9 (a) $x + 15y + 30 = 0$
   (b) One graph is increasing from $-\infty$ to ∞, and the other decreasing, in
      $-\frac{1}{2}\pi < x < \frac{1}{2}\pi$.
      Hence there is a point of intersection, and only one.
   (c) −34

10 1.76

11 1.210

12 6.72

13 (a) 1, 1.389. There could be an even number of roots in the interval.
   (b) 0.310 or 0.756; show that f(x) changes sign between $\alpha \pm 0.0005$
   (c) 0.62 or 1.51

14 (b) 3.111 11, 3.103 32, 3.103 84, 3.103 80; 3.104

15 (b) The second, as the derivative of $4 - \ln x$ is numerically less than 1 between $x = 2$ and $x = 3$; 2.93

16 (a) 3

(b) $F(t) = 1 + \dfrac{\ln(9t)}{\ln 4}$, $F^{-1}(t) = \frac{1}{9} \times 4^{t-1}$ or vice versa; $t = F(t)$; 3.486

17 (a) $(\pm\sqrt{5}, \pm\sqrt{5})$

(c) The function g is self-inverse.

(d) 2.236 068

18 (c) $(0.56, 0.6)$ (d) $(0.58, 0.6)$

(e) $(0.58, 0.59)$, $(0.58, 0.585)$, $(0.58, 0.5825)$, $(0.581\,25, 0.5825)$, $(0.581\,875, 0.5825)$; $\alpha = 0.582$ correct to 3 decimal places.

19 Since $y = F(x)$ and $y = F^{-1}(x)$ are reflections of each other in $y = x$, any intersection of these graphs also lies on $y = x$.

(a) 1.324 72   (b) 0.111 83, 3.577 15

9   The chain rule

Exercise 9A (page 152)

1 (a) $30(5x + 3)^5$ (b) $\frac{5}{2}(5x + 3)^{-\frac{1}{2}}$

(c) $\dfrac{5}{5x + 3}$

2 (a) $-20(1 - 4x)^4$ (b) $12(1 - 4x)^{-4}$

(c) $-4e^{1-4x}$

3 (a) $15x^2(1 + x^3)^4$ (b) $-12x^2(1 + x^3)^{-5}$

(c) $\dfrac{3x^2}{1 + x^3}$

4 (a) $24x(2x^2 + 3)^5$ (b) $-4x(2x^2 + 3)^{-2}$

(c) $-2x(2x^2 + 3)^{-\frac{3}{2}}$

5 (a) $72x^8 + 72x^5 + 18x^2$

(b) $18x^2(2x^3 + 1)^2$

6 $24x^3(3x^4 + 2)$

7 (a) $20x^4(x^5 + 1)^3$ (b) $48x^2(2x^3 - 1)^7$

(c) $12e^{2x}(e^{2x} + 3)^5$ (d) $\frac{5}{2}x^{-\frac{1}{2}}(\sqrt{x} - 1)^4$

8 (a) $8x(x^2 + 6)^3$ (b) $45x^2(5x^3 + 4)^2$

(c) $28x^3(x^4 - 8)^6$ (d) $-45x^8(2 - x^9)^4$

9 (a) $2(4x + 3)^{-\frac{1}{2}}$ (b) $12x(x^2 + 4)^5$

(c) $-36x^2(6x^3 - 5)^{-3}$ (d) $3x^2(5 - x^3)^{-2}$

10 (a) $\dfrac{6}{x}(\ln x + 1)^5$ (b) $-\dfrac{4}{x^2}\left(\dfrac{1}{x} + 2\right)^3$

(c) $\dfrac{2x^3}{2 + x^4}$ (d) $-15e^{-x}(e^{-x} + 1)^4$

11 (a) $-\frac{4}{25}$ (b) 0

12 $\frac{3}{8}$

13 $-3\frac{3}{4}$

14 (a) $6(x^2 + 3x + 1)^5(2x + 3)$

(b) $\dfrac{3x^2 + 4}{x^3 + 4x}$

(c) $-3(x^2 + 5x)^{-4}(2x + 5)$

(d) $2e^{x^2+x+1}(2x + 1)$

15 $y = 12x - 25$

16 $x + 4y = 8$

17 $x + 6y = 23$

18 $6x(x^2 - 1)^{-\frac{1}{2}}(\sqrt{x^2 - 1} + 1)^5$

19 $-x(1 - x^2)^{-\frac{1}{2}}e^{\sqrt{1-x^2}}$

20 $(0, 3)$; minimum

Exercise 9B (page 157)

1 (a) 4.8 cm s^{-1} (b) 24 cm^2 s^{-1}

2 (a) 240 mm^2 s^{-1} (b) 2400 mm^3 s^{-1}

3 942 mm^2 s^{-1}

4 0.25 m min^{-1}

5 0.0076 m s^{-1}

6 0.011 m s^{-1}

7 0.0025 cm s^{-1}

Exercise 9C (page 160)

2 (a) $\dfrac{1}{4x + 1}$ (b) $\dfrac{1}{2e^{2x-3}}$ (c) $\dfrac{1}{2x\ln x + x}$

3 $y = \frac{1}{2} - \dfrac{1}{2x^2}$

Miscellaneous exercise 9 (page 161)

1 $40x^3(x^4 + 3)^4$

2 $24x + y = 49$

4 $-\frac{10}{27}$

5 $(0, \frac{1}{4})$

6 $3x + 4y = 18$

7 0.377 cm^2 s^{-1}

8 (a) $\dfrac{10}{\sqrt{\pi}}$ cm   (b) $\dfrac{1}{4\sqrt{\pi}}$ cm s^{-1}

9 4 m^2 s^{-1}

10 (a) $\frac{1}{2}\left(x + \dfrac{1}{x}\right)^{-\frac{1}{2}}\left(1 - \dfrac{1}{x^2}\right)$

(b) $\dfrac{1}{2x + \sqrt{x}}$

11 $y = 2x - 3$

12 (a) $-12t(3t^2 + 5)^{-3}$ (b) $-\dfrac{2}{t}$

13 $(3, 0)$

14 (a) $\dfrac{2 - x}{\sqrt{4x - x^2}}$, $(2, 2)$

15 $\dfrac{3}{20\pi}$ cm s^{-1}

16 $(-3, e^{-81})$, $(0, 1)$, $(3, e^{-81})$

17 $(-\sqrt{3}, -4)$ minimum; $(-1, 0)$ maximum;
$(0, -4)$ minimum; $(1, 0)$ maximum;
$(\sqrt{3}, -4)$ minimum

18 0.052 m s^{-1}

10 Differentiating products

Exercise 10A (page 168)

1 (a) $2x$
(b) $3x^2 + 4x$
(c) $5x^4 + 9x^2 + 8x$
(d) $63x^2 + 100x + 39$
(e) $3x^2$
(f) $(m+n)x^{m+n-1}$

2 (a) $(x+1)e^x$
(b) $x(2\ln x + 1)$
(c) $3x^2(e^{-2x} + 1) - 2x^3e^{-2x}$
(d) $e^x \ln x + \dfrac{e^x}{x}$
(e) $\dfrac{1}{2\sqrt{x}}e^{-x} - \sqrt{x}e^{-x} = \dfrac{(1-2x)e^{-x}}{2\sqrt{x}}$
(f) $-4xe^{-2x}$

3 (a) $(x^2 + 2x + 3)e^x$
(b) $x(2\ln 2x + 2e^{2x} + 1 + 2xe^{2x})$
(c) $2x(1+x)e^{2x}$

4 (a) $4x + (2x + x^2)e^x$ (b) $x^2(3 + 2x)e^{2x}$
(c) $6x\ln x + \dfrac{4}{x} + 3x$

5 (a) $-3e^{-4}$ (b) e^2 (c) $1 + \ln 6$

6 (a) $y = 2x - 4$
(b) $y = x - 1$
(c) $8y = 47x - 75$
(d) $y = 0$

7 $(2, 4e^{-2}), (0, 0)$

8 (a) $\dfrac{(5x^2 + 5x + 2)e^x}{\sqrt{5x^2 + 2}}$
(b) $12(4x+1)^2 \ln 3x + \dfrac{(4x+1)^3}{x}$
(c) $\dfrac{\ln 2x + 2}{2\sqrt{x}}$

9 $2e^2$

10 $x + 2y = 1$

11 $(1, -3\sqrt{3})$

12 $V \approx 51.8, x = 6.4$

13 When n is even, there is maximum at $x = n$,
and a minimum at $x = 0$. When n is odd,
there is a maximum at $x = n$; if $n > 1$, there is
also a point of inflexion at $x = 0$.

14 $(1 + 3x + x^2)e^x$

Exercise 10B (page 170)

1 (a) $\dfrac{1}{(1+5x)^2}$
(b) $\dfrac{3x^2 - 4x}{(3x-2)^2}$
(c) $\dfrac{2x}{(1+2x^2)^2}$
(d) $\dfrac{(12x - 13)e^{3x}}{(4x-3)^2}$

(e) $\dfrac{1 - 2x^3}{(1 + x^3)^2}$
(f) $\dfrac{(x-1)^2 e^x}{(x^2+1)^2}$

2 (a) $\dfrac{x+2}{2(x+1)^{\frac{3}{2}}}$
(b) $\dfrac{10 - x}{2x^2\sqrt{x-5}}$
(c) $-\dfrac{3x+4}{4x^2\sqrt{3x+2}}$

3 (a) $\dfrac{e^x(2x-1)}{2x\sqrt{x}}$
(b) $\dfrac{3e^x - 10 - 5xe^x}{(e^x - 2)^2}$
(c) $\dfrac{-1}{(1+x)^{\frac{3}{2}}(1-x)^{\frac{1}{2}}}$

4 (a) $\dfrac{1 - \ln x}{x^2}$
(b) $\dfrac{2}{x^2 + 4} - \dfrac{\ln(x^2 + 4)}{x^2}$
(c) $\dfrac{3}{(3x+2)(2x-1)} - \dfrac{2\ln(3x+2)}{(2x-1)^2}$

5 $4y = x + 3$

6 (a) $\dfrac{(2x-1)e^x}{(2x+1)^2}$
(b) $(\tfrac{1}{2}, \tfrac{1}{2}e^{\frac{1}{2}})$

7 $14y = 8x - 37$

8 $2(\sqrt{2} - 1), -2(1 + \sqrt{2})$

9 (a) $\dfrac{x^2 + 2x - 3}{(x+1)^2}$
(b) $-3 \leqslant x < -1, -1 < x \leqslant 1$

Miscellaneous exercise 10 (page 171)

1 $\dfrac{x+6}{2(x+3)^{\frac{3}{2}}}$

2 $(1 - 3x)e^{-3x}, (\tfrac{1}{3}, \tfrac{1}{3}e^{-1})$

3 $(\tfrac{1}{2}, \tfrac{1}{8}\sqrt{2})$

5 (a) $x \leqslant 3$
(b) $\sqrt{3}$
(c) $(2, 2)$

6 $\dfrac{1}{\sqrt{e}}$

7 $\left(\dfrac{1}{e^2}, \dfrac{4}{e^2}\right), (1, 0); 0 < x < \dfrac{1}{e}$

8 $(0, 0), \left(-4, \dfrac{16}{e^2}\right);$
$y - p^2 e^{\frac{1}{2}p} = (2p + \tfrac{1}{2}p^2)e^{\frac{1}{2}p}(x - p);$
$\left(-3, \dfrac{9}{e^{\frac{3}{2}}}\right), (0, 0), (4, 16e^2)$

9 (a) $(-3, 0), x = 1$
(b) $8y = 3(x+3)$
(c) $(3, 4\tfrac{1}{2})$

10 (a) $\dfrac{2}{a}$

11 Volumes of revolution

Exercise 11 (page 179)

1 (a) $\dfrac{98}{3}\pi$
(b) $\dfrac{3093}{5}\pi$
(c) $\dfrac{279\,808}{7}\pi$
(d) $\dfrac{3}{4}\pi$

(e) $\frac{1}{2}\pi(e^2-1)$ (f) $\frac{1}{2}\pi\left(1-\frac{1}{e^4}\right)$

2 (a) 504π (b) $\frac{3498}{5}\pi$

   (c) $\frac{15}{2}\pi$ (d) $\frac{16}{15}\pi$

   (e) $\pi(e^3-e)$ (f) $\frac{1}{4}\pi\left(1-\frac{1}{e^4}\right)$

3 (a) 4π (b) 9π

   (c) 3355π (d) $\frac{3}{10}\pi$

   (e) $\frac{648}{5}\pi$ (f) $\frac{9}{2}\pi$

   (g) $156\,\pi$ (h) $\frac{2}{3}\pi$

4 (a) $\frac{512}{15}\pi$ (b) $\frac{16}{15}\pi$

   (c) $\frac{1}{30}\pi$ (d) $\frac{81}{10}\pi$

5 (a) $\frac{2}{15}\pi$ (b) $\frac{1}{6}\pi$

6 (a) $\frac{2048}{15}\pi$ (b) $\frac{128}{3}\pi$

7 (a) $\frac{3}{10}\pi$ (b) $\frac{3}{10}\pi$

8 $\frac{1}{10}\pi$

9 9π

10 $\frac{2}{35}\pi$

11 (a) -1 and 4 (b) $583\frac{1}{3}\pi$

12 $\frac{1}{4}\pi\left(4+e^2-\frac{1}{e^2}\right)$

Miscellaneous exercise 11 (page 180)

1 $\frac{206}{15}\pi$

2 The distance of each point (x, y) on the circle from the origin is $\sqrt{x^2+y^2}$, and this is equal to a, so $x^2+y^2=a^2$.

3 $\frac{4}{3}\pi ab^2$; $\frac{4}{3}\pi a^2 b$

4 (b) 2

   (c) $3\,\pi$

   (d) $\frac{1}{2}\pi$

5 (i) (a) infinite   (b) $1\frac{1}{2}$

       (c) $5\,\pi$ (d) $\frac{3}{7}\pi$

   (ii) (a) infinite   (b) $\frac{1}{3}$

       (c) infinite   (d) $\frac{1}{7}\pi$

6 $(0, 9)$; $(\pm 3, 0)$, $(0, 9)$

   (a) 36; 18   (b) $\frac{1296}{5}\pi$ (c) $\frac{81}{2}\pi$

7 4π

8 (a) $\frac{4}{3}a^2$ (b) $2\pi a^3$; $\frac{53}{240}\pi a^3$

9 $\pi\ln\frac{5}{2}$

10 $\frac{1}{2}\pi\ln 3$

11 $2\pi\ln 2$

12 $\pi(8\ln 2-3)$

13 $\frac{176}{15}\pi$

12 Simpson's rule

Exercise 12A (page 185)

1 (a) 1.718 86, 0.03%   (b) 0.694 44, 0.2%

2 0.385 83

3 1.002 28, 2.004 56

Exercise 12B (page 188)

1 (a) 1.718 32, 0.002%   (b) 0.693 25, 0.02%

2 0.386 26

3 (a) 3.141 60   (b) 2.000 11

4 8.096

Miscellaneous exercise 12 (page 189)

1 0.405 12

2 0.593 97

3 0.8415

4 0.886 226 79; 3.141 591 69, 6 significant figures

5 (a) $e-1$

   (b) $\frac{1}{6}(1+4\sqrt{e}+e)$

   (c) 2.719

6 11.898

7 (a) $\frac{592}{3}$ (b) $\frac{196}{3}+\frac{280}{3}\sqrt{2}$

8 (a) 38.3 m^2 (b) 1910 m^3

9 1150 metres

10 8 km

11 (a) $\frac{128}{15}$, $\frac{8}{15}$, $\frac{1}{30}$. Doubling the number of intervals reduces the error by a factor of 16.

   (b) 0.0944, 0.004 56, 0.000 269. Approximately; the errors are reduced successively by factors of about 21 and 17.

12 (b) f(x) is a cubic polynomial, which by the factor theorem has $(x+h)$, x and $(x-h)$ as factors.

13 (a) $p=\dfrac{y_0}{2h^2}$, $q=-\dfrac{y_1}{h^2}$, $r=\dfrac{y_2}{2h^2}$

14 $T=\frac{1}{2}h\big(y_0+2y_1+2y_2+2y_3+\cdots$
$+2y_{2n-2}+2y_{2n-1}+y_{2n}\big)$,
underestimate;
$R=2h(y_1+y_3+\cdots+y_{2n-1})$, overestimate

Revision exercise 2 (page 192)

1 $(3, 0)$

2 13

3 (a) $\dfrac{6x \ln x - 3x}{(\ln x)^2}$

(b) $-2\left(1 - \dfrac{x}{5}\right)^9$

4 1.4

5 (a) 2.02   (b) $-\dfrac{1}{x^2}e^{\frac{1}{x}}$

(c) As the gradient in the interval from $x = 1$ to 2 is negative and increasing, the curve lies under the straight line segments. The answer is an overestimate.

6 $\frac{1}{2}\pi(e^3 + 11)$

7 (a) $\dfrac{1450}{(t + 10)^2}$, 6.44   (b) 5.74

(c) 135, 280; the number of rodents increases to 280.

8 (a) No value of y has more than one value of x corresponding to it; $\frac{1}{3}(e^{4x} - 6)$

(b) (i) -2.000 (ii) 0.504

(iii) $y = f(x)$ and $y = f^{-1}(x)$ are reflections of each other in $y = x$, so, if they intersect, they intersect on $y = x$.

9 $y = -160x - 128$

10 (c) 0.92

11 (a) 1.94   (b) $x^3 + 5x - 17 = 0$

12 (a) $\frac{1}{2}\sqrt{7} - \frac{1}{2}\sqrt{3}$ (b) $\frac{1}{4}\pi \ln \frac{7}{3}$

(c) 0.11%, 0.41%

13 (a) 1787

(b) $0.0012t + 0.05$, $128e^{0.4\theta}$, 139

14 (a) $\pi(a + \frac{1}{3}a^3) = 75$

(b) 2.539, 2.533, 2.534; 2.53

15 0.027

16 (b) 2.1

17 24π

18 (a) $6(x^3 + 2x - 1)(12x^4 + 18x^2 - 3x + 4)$

(b) $9e^{3x-1}$ (c) $\dfrac{2(x^2 + 1)}{(x^2 - 1)^2}$

(d) $\dfrac{2x^2 - 1}{(x^2 + 1)^2\sqrt{x^2 + 1}}$

19 (a) $2\pi \times 10^{15}$ km^3 s^{-1}

(b) $4\pi \times 10^9$ km^2 s^{-1}

20 (a) $\frac{1}{2}e^6 - \frac{1}{2}$ (b) $\frac{1}{4}\pi e^{12} - \frac{1}{4}\pi$

21 0.8862

22 -1.17, 0.69, 2.48

23 (a) $(6x - 6)e^{3x^2 - 6x}$

(b) $(1, e^{-3})$, minimum

(c) $x + 6y = 8$

24 (a) $3\frac{1}{2}$ (b) 3.21

25 (c) The first converges and the second diverges.

(d) It does converge.

Practice examinations

Practice examination 1 for C3 (page 197)

1 $1, \frac{5}{3}$

2 (ii) 2.613

3 (i)

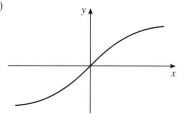

$\frac{1}{2}\pi$

(ii) 0.439

4 (i) $\frac{1}{2}\ln 3$

6 (i) $(-1, -e^{-1})$

(ii) (e, e^{-1})

7 (i) 0.0951 units per second

(ii) 69.3 seconds

(iii) Amounts are one quarter, one eighth, one sixteenth, etc. of the original.

8 (i) $f(x) \geqslant \frac{1}{3}$

(ii) 0

(iii) $\frac{1}{2}(x + 1)$

(iv) $\frac{2}{3}$

9 (i)

(iv) $\frac{4}{5}$

Practice examination 2 for C3 (page 199)

1 (i) $\dfrac{1}{2000\pi} \approx 0.000\,159\,\text{cm s}^{-1}$

(ii) $0.2\,\text{cm}^2\,\text{s}^{-1}$

2 $\dfrac{20}{3}\pi$

3 (i) $2x(1+x)\mathrm{e}^{2x}$

(ii) $\dfrac{1}{x(x+1)}$ or $\dfrac{1}{x} - \dfrac{1}{x+1}$

4 (i) $\tan 2\theta = \dfrac{2\tan\theta}{1-\tan^2\theta}$

(ii) $\sqrt{2} - 1$

(iii) $\tan 112\tfrac{1}{2}°$, for example

5 (i)

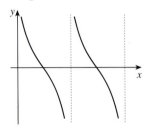

(ii) (a) $\tfrac{1}{4}\pi < x < \pi$, $\tfrac{5}{4}\pi < x < 2\pi$,

(b) $\tfrac{1}{4}\pi < x < \tfrac{3}{4}\pi$, $\tfrac{5}{4}\pi < x < \tfrac{7}{4}\pi$

(iii) Inequalities are not equivalent if $\sin x < 0$; $x = \tfrac{3}{2}\pi$, for example.

6 (i) $6\sin\theta - 4\cos\theta$

(iii) 26, when $\theta = 78.7°$

7 (i) $1 - \mathrm{e}^{-a}$ (d) 2.34

8 (i) $f(x) \in \mathbb{R}$, $f(x) \neq 1$

(ii) $f^{-1} : x \mapsto \dfrac{x+1}{x-1}$, $x \in \mathbb{R}$, $x \neq 1$

(iii) The graph is symmetrical about $y = x$, since the function is self-inverse.

(v) Translate $+1$ in the x-direction, stretch of factor 2 in the y-direction, translate $+1$ in the y-direction.

Answers to C4

1 Differentiating trigonometric functions

Exercise 1A (page 211)

1. (a) $-\cos x$ (b) $\sin x$
   (c) $4\cos 4x$ (d) $-6\sin 3x$
   (e) $\frac{1}{2}\pi\cos\frac{1}{2}\pi x$ (f) $-3\pi\sin 3\pi x$
   (g) $-2\sin(2x-1)$ (h) $15\cos\left(3x+\frac{1}{4}\pi\right)$

2. (a) $\cos x - x\sin x$
   (b) $\cos^2 x - \sin^2 x\ (=\cos 2x)$
   (c) $3x^2(\sin x + 1) + x^3\cos x$
   (d) $e^{-x}(\cos x - \sin x)$
   (e) $2x(\sin x + \cos x) + x^2(\cos x - \sin x)$
   (f) $2e^x\sin x$

3. (a) $2\sin x\cos x$ (b) $-2\cos x\sin x$
   (c) $-3\cos^2 x\sin x$ (d) $5\sin\frac{1}{2}x\cos\frac{1}{2}x$
   (e) $-8\cos^3 2x\sin 2x$ (f) $2x\cos x^2$
   (g) $-42x^2\sin 2x^3$
   (h) $-6\pi\cos^2 2\pi x\sin 2\pi x$
   (i) $\cos x\,e^{\sin x}$ (j) $-3\sin 3x\,e^{\cos 3x}$
   (k) $10\sin x\cos x\,e^{\sin^2 x}$ (l) $-e^x\sin(e^x)$

4. (a) $\sin^2 x + 2x\sin x\cos x$
   (b) $-\dfrac{1}{x^2}\cos^2 x - \dfrac{2}{x}\cos x\sin x$
   (c) $\cos^3 x - 2\sin^2 x\cos x$
   (d) $3\sin^2 x\cos^2 x(\cos^2 x - \sin^2 x)$
   (e) $2x\sin 2x(\sin 2x + 2x\cos 2x)$
   (f) $\dfrac{1}{\sqrt{x}}\cos\frac{1}{2}x\left(\frac{1}{2}\cos\frac{1}{2}x - x\sin\frac{1}{2}x\right)$

5. (a) $4\sec^4 x\tan x$
   (b) $4\tan^3 x\sec^2 x$
   (c) $\tan^2\frac{1}{3}x\sec^2\frac{1}{3}x$
   (d) $\sec^2 x\tan^2 x(2\tan^2 x + 3\sec^2 x)$
   (e) $\tan 2x + 2x\sec^2 2x$
   (f) $\dfrac{\sin x(2 + \sin^2 x)}{\cos^4 x}$

7. (a) $2\sec^2 x\tan x$
   (b) $\sec x\tan^2 x + \sec^3 x$
   (c) $e^{\sin x}(\cos^2 x - \sin x)$
   (d) $8\cos 4x$
   (e) $3\sin x(2\cos^2 x - \sin^2 x)$
   (f) $-\sin\frac{1}{2}x - \frac{1}{4}x\cos\frac{1}{2}x$

10. $\cos(a+x),\ -\sin a\sin x + \cos a\cos x$

11. $\sin(\frac{3}{2}\pi - x);\ -\sin x,\ -\cos x$

12. As $2\cos^2 x - 1 \equiv 1 - 2\sin^2 x \equiv \cos 2x$, they all differ by only a constant, and therefore have the same derivative.

13. $\cos 2x$

15. Since $\sec^2 x \equiv 1 + \tan^2 x$, $\tan^2 x$ and $\sec^2 x$ differ by only a constant, and therefore have the same derivative.

16. Since $\sin x \leqslant 1$, $\ln \sin x$ (where it exists) is always $\leqslant 0$, so $\ln \ln \sin x$ does not exist for any value of x.

Exercise 1B (page 214)

1. (a) growing at 50 million dollars per year
   (b) falling at 9.7 million dollars per year

2. (a) 55.3 mm s^{-1} (b) 153 m s^{-2}

3. The curve bends downwards when $y > 0$, and upwards when $y < 0$; $y = \sin(nt + \alpha)$.

4. (a) $2y - x = \sqrt{3} - \frac{1}{3}\pi$
   (b) $3y = \sqrt{2}\left(x - \frac{3}{2} - \frac{1}{4}\pi\right)$
   (c) $\sqrt{2}y + x = 2 + \frac{1}{4}\pi$
   (d) $y = x + \frac{1}{2}\ln 2 - \frac{1}{4}\pi$
   (e) $y = 3$

5. above, at $y = \cos\frac{5}{6}\pi + \frac{5}{12}\pi \approx 0.443$

6. $\left(\frac{1}{3}\pi - \frac{1}{7}\sqrt{3}, \frac{3}{7}\sqrt{3}\right)$

7. (a) $\left(\frac{1}{4}\pi, \sqrt{2}\right)$ maximum,
   $\left(\frac{5}{4}\pi, -\sqrt{2}\right)$ minimum
   (b) (π, π) neither
   (c) $(0, 2)$ maximum, $(\pi, -2)$ minimum
   (d) $\left(\frac{1}{12}\pi, \frac{1}{2}\sqrt{3} + \frac{1}{12}\pi\right)$ maximum,
   $\left(\frac{5}{12}\pi, -\frac{1}{2}\sqrt{3} + \frac{5}{12}\pi\right)$ minimum,
   $\left(\frac{13}{12}\pi, \frac{1}{2}\sqrt{3} + \frac{13}{12}\pi\right)$ maximum,
   $\left(\frac{17}{12}\pi, -\frac{1}{2}\sqrt{3} + \frac{17}{12}\pi\right)$ minimum
   (e) $\left(\frac{1}{4}\pi, 2\sqrt{2}\right)$ minimum,
   $\left(\frac{5}{4}\pi, -2\sqrt{2}\right)$ maximum
   (f) $\left(\frac{1}{2}\pi, -3\right)$ minimum, $\left(\frac{7}{6}\pi, \frac{3}{2}\right)$ maximum,
   $\left(\frac{3}{2}\pi, 1\right)$ minimum, $\left(\frac{11}{6}\pi, \frac{3}{2}\right)$ maximum

8. (a) $\left(\frac{1}{6}\pi, \frac{3}{16}\sqrt{3}\right)$ maximum, $\left(\frac{1}{2}\pi, 0\right)$ neither,
   $\left(\frac{5}{6}\pi, -\frac{3}{16}\sqrt{3}\right)$ minimum; odd
   (b) $(0, 0)$ minimum,
   $\left(\tan^{-1}\sqrt{2}, \frac{2}{9}\sqrt{3}\right)$ maximum,
   $\left(\pi - \tan^{-1}\sqrt{2}, -\frac{2}{9}\sqrt{3}\right)$ minimum,
   $(\pi, 0)$ maximum; even
   (c) $(0, 0)$ neither, $\left(\frac{1}{4}\pi, \frac{1}{8}\right)$ maximum,
   $\left(\frac{1}{2}\pi, 0\right)$ neither, $\left(\frac{3}{4}\pi, -\frac{1}{8}\right)$ minimum,
   $(\pi, 0)$ neither; odd

(d) $(0, 0)$ minimum, $\left(\frac{1}{3}\pi, \frac{27}{256}\right)$ maximum,
$\left(\frac{1}{2}\pi, 0\right)$ minimum, $\left(\frac{2}{3}\pi, \frac{27}{256}\right)$ maximum,
$(\pi, 0)$ minimum; even

9 (a) $\dfrac{\cos\sqrt{x}}{2\sqrt{x}}$ (b) $\dfrac{-\sin x}{2\sqrt{\cos x}}$ (c) $-\dfrac{1}{x^2}\cos\dfrac{1}{x}$

10 (b) $t = 0, 1, 2, 3, \ldots;\ -e^{-0.01\pi} \approx -0.969$
  (c) $0.503\ldots + n,\ n \in \mathbb{N}$
  (e) $10.001\pi^2 e^{-0.01\pi t}(0.01\sin\pi t - \cos\pi t)$

11 (a) (i) $x = t$ (ii) $x = -t$ (iii) $x = 0$
  (b) $\tan\pi t = \dfrac{1}{\pi t}$
  (d) $-2\pi\sin\pi t - \pi^2 t\cos\pi t$

Exercise 1C (page 219)

1 (a) $\frac{1}{2}\sin 2x + k$ (b) $-\frac{1}{3}\cos 3x + k$
  (c) $\frac{1}{2}\sin(2x + 1) + k$ (d) $-\frac{1}{3}\cos(3x - 1) + k$
  (e) $\cos(1 - x) + k$
  (f) $-2\sin\left(4 - \frac{1}{2}x\right) + k$
  (g) $-2\cos\left(\frac{1}{2}x + \frac{1}{3}\pi\right) + k$
  (h) $\frac{1}{3}\sin\left(3x - \frac{1}{4}\pi\right) + k$
  (i) $2\cos\frac{1}{2}x + k$

2 (a) 1 (b) $\frac{1}{2}\sqrt{2}$ (c) $\frac{1}{2}$
  (d) $-\frac{1}{6}\sqrt{2}$ (e) $\frac{1}{6}(\sqrt{3} - 1)$ (f) 0
  (g) $\sin 1$ (h) $2\cos 1 - 2\cos\frac{5}{4}$ (i) 4

3 (a) $\frac{1}{2}\ln|\sec 2x| + k$ (b) $\frac{1}{3}\tan 3x + k$
  (c) $\frac{1}{3}\sec 3x + k$ (d) $\ln\left|\cos\left(\frac{1}{4}\pi - x\right)\right| + k$
  (e) $2\tan\frac{1}{2}x - x + k$ (f) $\frac{1}{2}\sec 2x + k$

4 (a) $\frac{1}{2}\ln 2$ (b) $\frac{1}{6}\ln 2$
  (c) $\frac{1}{3} - \frac{1}{12}\pi$ (d) $\frac{4}{3}\sqrt{3}$

5 (a) $\frac{1}{2}\left(x + \frac{1}{2}\sin 2x\right) + k$ (b) $\frac{1}{2}(x + \sin x) + k$
  (c) $\frac{1}{2}\left(x - \frac{1}{4}\sin 4x\right) + k$ (d) $\frac{1}{4}\sin^4 x + k$

6 (a) $\frac{1}{2}\cos x - \frac{1}{14}\cos 7x + k$
  (b) $\frac{1}{3}\cos^3 x - \cos x + k$
  $\equiv \frac{1}{12}\cos 3x - \frac{3}{4}\cos x + k$
  (c) $-\cos x + \frac{2}{3}\cos^3 x - \frac{1}{5}\cos^5 x + k$
  (d) $\frac{1}{8}\sin 4x - \frac{1}{16}\sin 8x + k$

7 (a) $\ln|\sin x| + k$ (b) $-\cot x + k$
  (c) $-\operatorname{cosec} x + k$ (d) $-\cot x - x + k$
  (e) $\ln\left|\tan\frac{1}{2}x\right| + k$
  (f) $\ln\left|\tan\left(\frac{1}{2}x + \frac{1}{4}\pi\right)\right| + k$

8 $1;\ \frac{1}{4}\pi^2$

9 $\pi + 2,\ \frac{1}{2}\pi(8 + 3\pi)$

10 (a) $2 - \sqrt{2}$ (b) $\frac{1}{4}\pi(\pi - 2)$

11 (a) $(0, 1),\ \left(\frac{3}{4}\pi, 0\right)$ (b) $1 + \sqrt{2}$ (c) $\frac{1}{4}\pi(3\pi + 2)$

12 (a) $\ln 2$ (b) $\pi\left(\sqrt{3} - \frac{1}{3}\pi\right)$

Miscellaneous exercise 1 (page 220)

1 (a) $2\cot 2x$
  (b) $-2\cos x\sin x$
  (c) $3t^2\cos(t^3 + 4)$
  (d) $\frac{1}{2}x + \frac{1}{12}\sin 6x + k$
  (e) $-\dfrac{1}{2\sqrt{x}}\sin\sqrt{x}$
  (f) $\frac{1}{2}x - \frac{3}{4}\sin\frac{2}{3}x + k$
  (g) $-\frac{1}{4}(\cos 2x + 2\cos x) + k$

2 (a) $\frac{1}{2}(1 - \cos 2x)$

3 (a) $\frac{1}{4}\sqrt{2}(\sqrt{3} - 1),\ 2 - \sqrt{3}$ (b) $3.106, 3.215$

4 (a) $e^x(\cos x - \sin x)$ (b) $\frac{1}{4}\pi < x < \frac{5}{4}\pi$
  (c) The gradient is negative for these values
     of x.

5 $(0, -0.404);\ 1.404, 1.360, 1.622$

6 $\frac{1}{6}$; better, values are 0.5236 and 0.4997
  approximating to 0.5.

7 (a) $v = 11\left(1 - \cos\left(\dfrac{\pi}{45}t\right)\right)$, 90 seconds
  (b) 990 metres, 11 m s^{-1}
  (c) 0.665 m s^{-2}

8 (b) $\frac{1}{2}\pi, \frac{5}{6}\pi$
  (c) The model suggests that the motion will
     continue indefinitely, but in practice it
     will gradually die out because of friction.
     In the new model the motion will die out.

10 (a) $\frac{1}{2}\cos\frac{1}{2}x - \frac{1}{3}\sin\frac{1}{3}x$ (b) $1, \frac{1}{2}$
  (c) $4\pi, 6\pi$
  (d) any integer multiple of 12π

11 (a) $\frac{2}{3}\pi, \pi, \frac{4}{3}\pi, 2\pi$ (c) $f'(x) = \cos x + 2\cos 2x$

12 $-\dfrac{1}{\pi^2}$

13 $\dfrac{dy}{dx} = \dfrac{x\cos x - \sin x}{x^2}$

2   Integration

Exercise 2A (page 227)

1 (a) $\sin x - x\cos x + k$
  (b) $3(x - 1)e^x + k$
  (c) $(x + 3)e^x + k$

2 (a) $\frac{1}{4}(2x - 1)e^{2x} + k$
  (b) $\frac{1}{4}x\sin 4x + \frac{1}{16}\cos 4x + k$
  (c) $\frac{1}{4}x^2(2\ln 2x - 1) + k$

3 (a) $\frac{1}{36}x^6(6\ln 3x - 1) + k$
  (b) $\frac{1}{4}(2x - 1)e^{2x+1} + k$
  (c) $x(\ln 2x - 1) + k$

4 (a) $\frac{1}{4}(e^2 + 1)$

(b) $\frac{1}{2}\sqrt{2}(4-\pi)$

(c) $\dfrac{ne^{n+1}+1}{(n+1)^2}$

5 $(2-x^2)\cos x + 2x\sin x + k$

 (a) $\frac{1}{4}(2x^2 - 2x + 1)e^{2x} + k$

 (b) $2(x^2 - 8)\sin\frac{1}{2}x + 8x\cos\frac{1}{2}x + k$

6 $1 - 3e^{-2}$, $\frac{1}{4}\pi(1 - 13e^{-4})$

7 $\frac{1}{9}\pi$, $\frac{1}{324}\pi^2(2\pi^2 - 3)$

8 (a) $-\frac{1}{2}(1 + e^{\pi})$

 (b) $\frac{1}{10}e^{4\pi} - \frac{1}{10}e^{-4\pi}$

 (c) $\dfrac{a - e^{-a}(a\cos b - b\sin b)}{a^2 + b^2}$

9 (a) $\frac{1}{2}$ (b) $\frac{4}{3}$

Exercise 2B (page 230)

1 (a) $2\ln|\sqrt{x} - 2| + k$

 (b) $-\dfrac{1}{3(3x + 4)} + k$

 (c) $2\cos\left(\frac{1}{3}\pi - \frac{1}{2}x\right) + k$

 (d) $\frac{1}{6}(x-1)^6 + \frac{1}{7}(x-1)^7 + k$
  $\equiv \frac{1}{42}(6x + 1)(x-1)^6 + k$

 (e) $\ln(1 + e^x) + k$ (f) $\frac{1}{2}\ln(3 + 4\sqrt{x}) + k$

 (g) $\frac{6}{5}(x+2)^{\frac{5}{2}} - 4(x+2)^{\frac{3}{2}} + k$
  $\equiv \frac{2}{5}(3x - 4)(x+2)^{\frac{3}{2}} + k$

 (h) $6(x-3)^{\frac{1}{2}} + \frac{2}{3}(x-3)^{\frac{3}{2}} + k$
  $\equiv \frac{2}{3}(x+6)\sqrt{x-3} + k$

 (i) $\ln(|\ln x|) + k$ (j) $\sin^{-1}\frac{1}{2}x + k$

2 (a) $\frac{1}{20}(2x+1)^5 - \frac{1}{16}(2x+1)^4 + k$
  $\equiv \frac{1}{80}(8x - 1)(2x+1)^4 + k$

 (b) $\frac{1}{28}(2x-3)^7 + \frac{7}{24}(2x-3)^6 + k$
  $\equiv \frac{1}{168}(12x + 31)(2x-3)^6 + k$

 (c) $\frac{1}{6}(2x-1)^{\frac{3}{2}} + \frac{1}{10}(2x-1)^{\frac{5}{2}} + k$
  $\equiv \frac{1}{15}(3x + 1)(2x-1)^{\frac{3}{2}} + k$

 (d) $4(x-4)^{\frac{1}{2}} + \frac{2}{3}(x-4)^{\frac{3}{2}} + k$
  $\equiv \frac{2}{3}(x+2)\sqrt{x-4} + k$

 (e) $\ln|x+1| + \dfrac{1}{x+1} + k$

 (f) $\frac{1}{2}x - \frac{3}{4}\ln|2x+3| + k$

3 (b) $\tan^{-1}e^x + k$

Exercise 2C (page 232)

1 (a) $\ln\left(\frac{1}{2}(1 + e)\right)$ (b) $2\ln 2$

 (c) $\frac{13}{42}$ (d) $1\frac{1}{15}$

 (e) $\frac{1}{6}\pi$ (f) $109\frac{1}{15}$

 (g) 8π

(h) $\frac{1}{2}\left(\tan^{-1}3 - \tan^{-1}\frac{1}{2}\right) = \frac{1}{8}\pi$

(i) $\frac{1}{2}$ (j) $\frac{1}{3}\sqrt{3}$

2 $\frac{1}{4}\pi - \frac{1}{2}$

3 (a) $\frac{1}{4}\pi$ (b) $\frac{1}{2}\pi$

 (c) $\frac{1}{6}\pi$ (d) π

 (e) $1 - \frac{1}{2}\sqrt{2}$ (f) $\frac{1}{2}\pi$

4 (a) $\dfrac{1}{2(\ln 2)^2}$ (b) 1

7 π

Exercise 2D (page 235)

1 (a) $\frac{1}{4}(x^2 + 1)^4 + k$ (b) $\frac{1}{3}(4 + x^2)^{\frac{3}{2}} + k$

 (c) $\frac{1}{6}\sin^6 x + k$ (d) $\frac{1}{4}\tan^4 x + k$

 (e) $-\sqrt{1 - x^4} + k$ (f) $-\frac{1}{8}\cos^4 2x + k$

2 (a) $\ln(1 + \sin x) + k$ (b) $\frac{1}{3}\ln|1 + x^3| + k$

 (c) $\ln|\sin x| + k$ (d) $\ln(4 + e^x) + k$

 (e) $-\frac{2}{3}\ln|5 - e^{3x}| + k$ (f) $\frac{1}{3}\ln|\sec 3x| + k$

3 (a) $\ln(e + 1)$ (b) $\frac{1}{2}\ln 2$ (c) $\frac{1}{2}\ln\frac{4}{3}$

Exercise 2E (page 237)

1 (a) $\frac{1}{3}\sin^{-1}3x + k$

 (b) $\frac{8}{3}\sin^{-1}\frac{3}{4}x + \frac{1}{2}x\sqrt{16 - 9x^2} + k$

 (c) $\frac{1}{2}\ln(2e^x + 1) + k$

 (d) $\frac{3}{5}(x+1)^{\frac{5}{3}} - \frac{3}{2}(x+1)^{\frac{2}{3}} + k$
  $\equiv \frac{3}{10}(2x - 3)(x+1)^{\frac{2}{3}} + k$

 (e) $\dfrac{x}{\sqrt{1 - x^2}} + k$

 (f) $-4\ln|2 - \sqrt{x}| - 2\sqrt{x} + k$

2 (a) $\frac{1}{6}(1 + x^2)^6 + k$

 (b) $\frac{2}{3}(3 + 2x^2)^{\frac{3}{2}} + k$

 (c) $-\frac{1}{63}(5 - 3x^3)^7 + k$

 (d) $2\sqrt{1 + x^3} + k$

 (e) $\frac{1}{4}\sec^4 x + k$

 (f) $\frac{1}{16}\sin^4 4x + k$

3 (a) $\frac{2}{3}$ (b) 78

 (c) $\frac{1}{12}(4 - \sqrt{2})$

 (d) $\frac{860}{3}\sqrt{2}$

 (e) $\frac{1}{6}$

 (f) $\frac{2}{3}(10\sqrt{10} - 1)$

 (g) $\frac{1}{3}$

 (h) $\dfrac{1}{n+1}$

 (i) $\frac{7}{3}$

4 $\dfrac{1}{2(n-1)}\left(1-\dfrac{1}{(1+a^2)^{n-1}}\right)$ if $n\neq 1$,

$\frac{1}{2}\ln(1+a^2)$ if $n=1$; $n>1$; $\dfrac{1}{2(n-1)}$

Miscellaneous exercise 2 (page 238)

1 $\frac{1}{2}\ln|2x-1|-\dfrac{1}{2(2x-1)}+k$

2 $2x(x-1)^{\frac{3}{2}}-\frac{4}{5}(x-1)^{\frac{5}{2}}+k$

3 1.701; exact value is $\frac{1}{4}\ln 1201$

4 $\frac{3}{4}\pi$

5 $\frac{1}{4}-\frac{1}{12}e^{\frac{2}{3}}$

6 (a) $x\cos^{-1}x-\sqrt{1-x^2}+k$
   (b) $x\tan^{-1}x-\frac{1}{2}\ln(1+x^2)+k$
   (c) $x((\ln x)^2-2\ln x+2)+k$

7 $\frac{1}{2}\pi-1$

8 $\frac{1}{2}\tan^{-1}\frac{1}{2}e^x+k$

9 $\ln(1+3x^2)+k$

10 $\frac{1}{2}\ln 10$

11 $\frac{2}{5}\sin^5 x+k$

12 $2\sqrt{x}-2\ln(1+\sqrt{x})+k$

13 (a) $\frac{1}{60}(4x-1)^{\frac{3}{2}}(6x+1)+k$
   (b) $-\frac{2}{15}(2-x)^{\frac{3}{2}}(3x+4)+k$
   (c) $\frac{1}{5}(2x+3)^{\frac{3}{2}}(x-1)+k$

16 $\int\frac{1}{9}(u^5+u^4)\mathrm{d}u,\ \frac{1}{54}(3x-1)^6+\frac{1}{45}(3x-1)^5+k$

17 $\frac{1}{8}\pi+\frac{1}{4}$

18 (a) $\frac{1}{7}x(1+x)^7-\frac{1}{56}(1+x)^8+k$
   (b) $\frac{1}{15}x(3x-1)^5-\frac{1}{270}(3x-1)^6+k$
   (c) $\frac{1}{13}\dfrac{x(ax+b)^{13}}{a}-\frac{1}{182}\dfrac{(ax+b)^{14}}{a^2}+k$

19 $1-2e^{-1}$

20 16

21 (a) 0.696 (c) 1.69
   (d) $\pi\left(\frac{1}{4}+\frac{3}{32}\pi\right)\approx 1.71$
   (e) 0.703, 1.66; more, less

22 $\pi(8\ln 2-3)$

3 Parametric equations

Exercise 3A (page 244)

1 (a) $(180,60)$ (b) $(5,-10)$

2 (a) $(\frac{2}{3},\frac{4}{3})$ (b) $(2,0)$

3 $\frac{1}{2}\pi$

4 $\frac{2}{3}\pi$

Exercise 3B (page 245)

1 (a) $y^2=\dfrac{1}{x}$ (b) $y^2=12x$
   (c) $x^2+y^2=4$

2 (a) $x+y=1$, for $0\leqslant x\leqslant 1$
   (b) $x^{\frac{2}{3}}+y^{\frac{2}{3}}=1$
   (c) $x+y=2$, excluding $(1,1)$
   (d) $4x^3=27y^2$

Exercise 3C (page 247)

1 (a) $\dfrac{2}{3t^2}$ (b) $-\tan t$
   (c) $-\frac{3}{2}\cot t$ (d) $\dfrac{2t-1}{3t^2+1}$

2 (a) 2 (b) $\frac{1}{3}$ (c) -1 (d) $-\frac{1}{54}$

3 (a) -3 (b) 1 (c) $\sqrt{3}$ (d) -8

5 (a) $\frac{1}{3}$ (b) $3y=x-1$

6 $x+y=1+\pi$

7 (a) $3y=x+9$ (b) $5y=3\sqrt{3}x-30$

8 (a) $3x+y=165$ (b) $y=-\sqrt{3}x$

9 (a) $y=4x-30$ (b) $\left(-\frac{1}{2},-32\right)$

10 (a) $y=2x-36$ (b) $(27,18)$

Exercise 3D (page 250)

1 (a) $\dfrac{1}{2t}$, $2ty-x=t^2+2t$ (b) $x=(y-1)^2$

2 (a) $\dfrac{2t-1}{2t+1}$, $(2t-1)y+(2t+1)x=2t(2t^2+1)$
   (b) $(x-y)^2=2(x+y)$

3 (a) $x+3y=4$ (c) $x^2=y^3$

4 (a) $2p^3y+x=3p^2$ (b) $(3p^2,0)$, $\left(0,\dfrac{3}{2p}\right)$

5 (a) $(ap^2,0)$ (b) $y+px=2ap+ap^3$
   (c) $(2a+ap^2,0)$

6 (a) $\dfrac{-1}{pq}$, $\dfrac{-1}{rs}$

7 (a) $p^2y+x=2p$ (b) $(2p,0)$

8 (a) $ty-x=at^2$

Miscellaneous exercise 3 (page 251)

1 (a) $\frac{1}{4}\pi$ (b) $2x+y=2\sqrt{2}$

2 $6\cos t$

3 (a) $\dfrac{t^2-1}{t^2+1}$ (b) $y^2-x^2=4$

4 (a) $\dfrac{2t}{3t^2+1}$ (b) $2x+y=6$

5 (a) $-\sqrt{3}\tan t$ (b) $x+y=2$

6 $\dfrac{1}{e^t-1}$, $\ln 2$

7 (b) $y = 2x - 2$ (c) $(0, -2)$

8 (a) $2x + y = 9$ (b) $y = 4x - x^2$

10 (a) the half-line of gradient 1 through $(0,0)$
for which $x \geqslant 0$
   (b) $y = x$; the straight line of gradient 1
through $(0,0)$
   (c) Each point of the curve given by the
parametric equations lies on the curve
given by the cartesian equation, but the
reverse is not necessarily true, as this
example shows.

4   Vectors

Exercise 4A (page 258)

2 (a) $(4\mathbf{i} + \mathbf{j}) + (-3\mathbf{i} + 2\mathbf{j}) = \mathbf{i} + 3\mathbf{j}$
   (b) $3(\mathbf{i} - 2\mathbf{j}) = 3\mathbf{i} - 6\mathbf{j}$
   (c) $4\mathbf{j} + 2(\mathbf{i} - 2\mathbf{j}) = 2\mathbf{i}$
   (d) $(3\mathbf{i} + \mathbf{j}) - (5\mathbf{i} + \mathbf{j}) = -2\mathbf{i}$
   (e) $3(-\mathbf{i} + 2\mathbf{j}) - (-4\mathbf{i} + 3\mathbf{j}) = \mathbf{i} + 3\mathbf{j}$
   (f) $4(2\mathbf{i} + 3\mathbf{j}) - 3(3\mathbf{i} + 2\mathbf{j}) = -\mathbf{i} + 6\mathbf{j}$
   (g) $(2\mathbf{i} - 3\mathbf{j}) + (4\mathbf{i} + 5\mathbf{j}) + (-6\mathbf{i} - 2\mathbf{j}) = \mathbf{0}$
   (h) $2(3\mathbf{i} - \mathbf{j}) + 3(-2\mathbf{i} + 3\mathbf{j}) + (-7\mathbf{j}) = \mathbf{0}$

3 (a) $\begin{pmatrix} 1 \\ 2 \end{pmatrix}$ (b) $\begin{pmatrix} 3 \\ 0 \end{pmatrix}$ (c) $\begin{pmatrix} -1 \\ 1 \end{pmatrix}$ (d) $\begin{pmatrix} 4 \\ -3 \end{pmatrix}$

4 $s = 2$

5 $s = 4$; $\mathbf{q} = \frac{1}{4}(\mathbf{r} - \mathbf{p})$

6 2, 3

7 $1\frac{1}{2}, -\frac{1}{2}$

8 $\begin{pmatrix} 4 \\ -2 \end{pmatrix}$ and $\begin{pmatrix} -6 \\ 3 \end{pmatrix}$ are parallel, $\begin{pmatrix} 3 \\ 1 \end{pmatrix}$ is in a
different direction;
$\begin{pmatrix} -1 \\ 2 \end{pmatrix}$ is not parallel to $\begin{pmatrix} 1 \\ 1 \end{pmatrix} - \begin{pmatrix} 3 \\ 4 \end{pmatrix}$.

9 $1, -1, 2$; any multiple of $1, -1, 2$ will also be
fine

10 (a) no   (b) $- 2, 0$;
$\mathbf{p}$ is parallel to $\mathbf{r}$, but $\mathbf{q}$ is in a different
direction.

Exercise 4B (page 262)

1 (a) $(9, 3)$ (b) $(-1, -2)$ (c) $(2, -1)$
   (d) $(-8, -1)$ (e) $(10, 5)$ (f) $(5, 2\frac{1}{2})$

2 (a) $(-13, -23)$ (b) $(-1, 1)$

3 $2\mathbf{b} - \mathbf{a}$

4 $\frac{3}{7}\mathbf{a} + \frac{4}{7}\mathbf{b}$

6 $\mathbf{b} - \mathbf{a} = \mathbf{c} - \mathbf{d}$

7 $\frac{1}{2}(\mathbf{b} + \mathbf{c} - 2\mathbf{a}), \frac{1}{4}(\mathbf{b} + \mathbf{c} - 2\mathbf{a})$; G is the
mid-point of AD.

8 $\mathbf{b} = \mathbf{a} + \mathbf{c}$, $\mathbf{m} = \frac{1}{2}(\mathbf{a} + 2\mathbf{c})$, $\mathbf{p} = \frac{1}{3}(\mathbf{a} + 2\mathbf{c})$;
O, P and M are collinear, and $OP = \frac{2}{3}OM$.

9 $\mathbf{d} = \frac{1}{2}(\mathbf{b} + \mathbf{c})$, $\mathbf{e} = \frac{1}{4}(2\mathbf{a} + \mathbf{b} + \mathbf{c})$,
$\mathbf{f} = \frac{1}{3}(2\mathbf{a} + \mathbf{c})$, $\mathbf{g} = \frac{1}{4}(\mathbf{b} + 2\mathbf{a} + \mathbf{c})$

10 $\frac{4}{15}\mathbf{b} - \frac{13}{15}\mathbf{a}$, $k = \frac{15}{13}$, $\mathbf{r} = \frac{4}{13}\mathbf{b}$; R is on OB, with
$OR : RB = 4 : 9$ S is on OA, with $OS : SA = 2 : 9$.

Exercise 4C (page 266)

Note that, since vector equations are not unique,
other correct answers are sometimes possible.

1 (a) $\mathbf{r} = \begin{pmatrix} 2 \\ -3 \end{pmatrix} + t\begin{pmatrix} 1 \\ 2 \end{pmatrix}$, $y = 2x - 7$

   (b) $\mathbf{r} = \begin{pmatrix} 4 \\ 1 \end{pmatrix} + t\begin{pmatrix} -3 \\ 2 \end{pmatrix}$, $2x + 3y = 11$

   (c) $\mathbf{r} = \begin{pmatrix} 5 \\ 7 \end{pmatrix} + t\begin{pmatrix} 1 \\ 0 \end{pmatrix}$, $y = 7$

   (d) $\mathbf{r} = t\begin{pmatrix} 2 \\ -1 \end{pmatrix}$, $x + 2y = 0$

   (e) $\mathbf{r} = \begin{pmatrix} a \\ b \end{pmatrix} + t\begin{pmatrix} 0 \\ 1 \end{pmatrix}$, $x = a$

   (f) $\mathbf{r} = \begin{pmatrix} \cos \alpha \\ \sin \alpha \end{pmatrix} + t\begin{pmatrix} -\sin \alpha \\ \cos \alpha \end{pmatrix}$,
$x \cos \alpha + y \sin \alpha = 1$

2 (a) $\mathbf{r} = \begin{pmatrix} 2 \\ 0 \end{pmatrix} + t\begin{pmatrix} 0 \\ 1 \end{pmatrix}$

   (b) $\mathbf{r} = \begin{pmatrix} 1 \\ 2 \end{pmatrix} + t\begin{pmatrix} 3 \\ -1 \end{pmatrix}$

   (c) $\mathbf{r} = \begin{pmatrix} -1 \\ -1 \end{pmatrix} + t\begin{pmatrix} 5 \\ 2 \end{pmatrix}$

3 (a) $(7, 3)$ (b) $(8, -5)$
   (c) no common points   (d) $(4.76, 3.68)$
   (e) the lines coincide, $2x + 3y = 17$
   (f) $(-1, 1)$

4 $x = 2 + t, y = -1 + 3t$; $(4, 5)$

5 $(3, 1)$

6 (a), (d), (e)

7 (a) $\mathbf{r} = \begin{pmatrix} 3 \\ 7 \end{pmatrix} + t\begin{pmatrix} 2 \\ -3 \end{pmatrix}$

   (b) $\mathbf{r} = \begin{pmatrix} 2 \\ 3 \end{pmatrix} + t\begin{pmatrix} 0 \\ 1 \end{pmatrix}$

   (c) $\mathbf{r} = \begin{pmatrix} -1 \\ 2 \end{pmatrix} + t\begin{pmatrix} 2 \\ -1 \end{pmatrix}$

   (d) $\mathbf{r} = \begin{pmatrix} -3 \\ -4 \end{pmatrix} + t\begin{pmatrix} 2 \\ 3 \end{pmatrix}$

   (e) $\mathbf{r} = \begin{pmatrix} -2 \\ 7 \end{pmatrix} + t\begin{pmatrix} 1 \\ 0 \end{pmatrix}$

   (f) $\mathbf{r} = \begin{pmatrix} 1 \\ 3 \end{pmatrix} + t\begin{pmatrix} 1 \\ 1 \end{pmatrix}$

8 (a) $\mathbf{r} = \begin{pmatrix} 4 \\ -1 \end{pmatrix} + s\begin{pmatrix} 3 \\ 1 \end{pmatrix}$,

$\mathbf{r} = \begin{pmatrix} -3 \\ 2 \end{pmatrix} + t\begin{pmatrix} 1 \\ -1 \end{pmatrix}; (1, -2)$

(b) $(13\frac{1}{3}, -5), (4, 11\frac{4}{5})$

9 (a), (b) yes

(c) meaningless, since $\mathbf{0}$ has no direction;

$\mathbf{r} = \begin{pmatrix} 1 \\ 2 \end{pmatrix} + t\begin{pmatrix} -4 \\ 3 \end{pmatrix}$

10 $\begin{pmatrix} 1 \\ 3 \end{pmatrix}$, $\mathbf{r} = \begin{pmatrix} 1 \\ 5 \end{pmatrix} + t\begin{pmatrix} -3 \\ 1 \end{pmatrix}; (4, 4)$

11 $(2, 0)$

12 $\mathbf{r} = \begin{pmatrix} -1 \\ 1 \end{pmatrix} + t\begin{pmatrix} 1 \\ 2 \end{pmatrix}; x = -1 + t,$
$y = 1 + 2t; (-1, 1), (3, 9)$

13 $(1, 8), (-7, -4)$

Exercise 4D (page 270)

1 (a) $\mathbf{r} = \begin{pmatrix} 2 \\ -3 \\ 5 \end{pmatrix} + t\begin{pmatrix} 1 \\ 2 \\ -6 \end{pmatrix}$

(b) $\mathbf{r} = \begin{pmatrix} 4 \\ -1 \\ 1 \end{pmatrix} + t\begin{pmatrix} 4 \\ -2 \\ -3 \end{pmatrix}$

(c) $\mathbf{r} = \begin{pmatrix} 5 \\ 7 \\ 4 \end{pmatrix} + t\begin{pmatrix} 1 \\ 0 \\ 0 \end{pmatrix}$

(d) $\mathbf{r} = \begin{pmatrix} 0 \\ 0 \\ 0 \end{pmatrix} + t\begin{pmatrix} 2 \\ -3 \\ 1 \end{pmatrix}$

2 (a) $2, -3$ (b) $3, 1$
(c) no solution

3 (a) They meet at $(4, 3, 3)$.
(b) They meet at $(5, -5, 4)$.
(c) They do not intersect.

4 (a) $\mathbf{r} = \begin{pmatrix} 8 \\ 7 \\ 5 \end{pmatrix} + t\begin{pmatrix} -9 \\ -5 \\ -6 \end{pmatrix}$

(b) $\mathbf{r} = \begin{pmatrix} 2 \\ -2 \\ 0 \end{pmatrix} + t\begin{pmatrix} 0 \\ 1 \\ 0 \end{pmatrix}$

(c) $\mathbf{r} = \begin{pmatrix} 4 \\ 5 \\ -2 \end{pmatrix} + t\begin{pmatrix} -6 \\ -8 \\ 6 \end{pmatrix}$

5 Any multiple of $1, 2, -3$; the translations are
all parallel to the same plane.

6 $(4, -3, 0)$

7 (a) intersect at $(1, -1, 0)$
(b) parallel
(c) intersect at $(-7, -5, -4)$
(d) skew

8 $\mathbf{r} = \begin{pmatrix} 3 \\ 2 \\ 6 \end{pmatrix} + t\begin{pmatrix} -3 \\ 1 \\ 2 \end{pmatrix}$; $(12, -1, 0), (9, 0, 2)$

9 $(-9, 10, 0)$

10 0.4 m

11 All $\frac{1}{4}(\mathbf{a} + \mathbf{b} + \mathbf{c} + \mathbf{d})$; the lines joining
the mid-points of opposite edges of
a tetrahedron meet and bisect one
another.

12 $\frac{1}{4}\mathbf{e} + \frac{3}{4}\mathbf{f}; \frac{1}{3}(\mathbf{a} + \mathbf{b} + \mathbf{c}), \frac{1}{4}(\mathbf{a} + \mathbf{b} + \mathbf{c} + \mathbf{d})$

Miscellaneous exercise 4 (page 272)

1 $\begin{pmatrix} 9 \\ -1 \\ 4 \end{pmatrix}$

2 (a) $y = 4x - 14$ (b) $\mathbf{r} = \begin{pmatrix} 0 \\ 1 \end{pmatrix} + t\begin{pmatrix} 3 \\ 2 \end{pmatrix}$

(c) $2x - 3y + 17 = 0$, or $\mathbf{r} = \begin{pmatrix} -1 \\ 5 \end{pmatrix} + t\begin{pmatrix} 3 \\ 2 \end{pmatrix}$

3 (a) no intersection
(b) $(-3, -1)$
(c) same line

4 $-10\mathbf{i} + 7\mathbf{j} - 3\mathbf{k}$

5 The lines do not meet.

6 (a) $\mathbf{r} = \begin{pmatrix} 2 \\ 1 \end{pmatrix} + t\begin{pmatrix} 3 \\ -2 \end{pmatrix}$

(b) $y = 3x - 5$ (c) $(2, 1)$

7 (a) $\begin{pmatrix} 14 \\ 2 \\ 5 \end{pmatrix}, \begin{pmatrix} -5 \\ 10 \\ 10 \end{pmatrix}; (13, 14, 18)$

(b) $\frac{1}{3}, \frac{2}{15}$; the origin lies in the plane of the
parallelogram.

8 (a) $\mathbf{r} = \begin{pmatrix} 2 \\ 3 \\ 5 \end{pmatrix} + \lambda\begin{pmatrix} 1 \\ 1 \\ -0.5 \end{pmatrix}$ (b) 25 m

9 $(\cos 2\alpha, \sin 2\alpha)$; for all α, the intersection lies
on the circle with $(-1, 0)$ and $(1, 0)$ at ends of
a diameter.

10 $(11.4, 3, 0)$ at 8.04 a.m.

11 (a) above $(61, 77)$ on the ground
(b) 4200 m
(c) $384 \text{ km h}^{-1}, 038.7°$
(d) $386 \text{ km h}^{-1}, 5.35°$

12 $(85, -10)$; 2200 m, 2 minutes

13 $u < -1$ or $u > 0.5$; $0.5 < u < 0.753$

14 $\frac{4}{5}, \frac{9}{5}$; break up 4 Individual bags and 9 Jumbo
bags, and use the fruit to make 5 King-size
bags.

15 $\mathbf{r} = \begin{pmatrix} f(\theta) \\ g(\theta) \end{pmatrix} + t \begin{pmatrix} f'(\theta) \\ g'(\theta) \end{pmatrix}$

(a) $\mathbf{r} = \begin{pmatrix} \theta^2 \\ \theta^3 \end{pmatrix} + t \begin{pmatrix} 2\theta \\ 3\theta^2 \end{pmatrix}$, $2y = 3\theta x - \theta^3$

(b) $\mathbf{r} = \begin{pmatrix} 3\cos\theta \\ 2\sin\theta \end{pmatrix} + t \begin{pmatrix} -3\sin\theta \\ 2\cos\theta \end{pmatrix}$,
$2\cos\theta x + 3\sin\theta y = 6$

5 The binomial expansion

Exercise 5 (page 279)

1 (a) $1 - 3x + 6x^2$ (b) $1 - 5x + 15x^2$
(c) $1 + 4x + 10x^2$ (d) $1 + 6x + 21x^2$

2 (a) $1 - 4x + 16x^2$ (b) $1 + 6x + 24x^2$
(c) $1 + 12x + 90x^2$ (d) $1 - x + \frac{3}{4}x^2$

3 (a) 84   (b) -8 (c) -270 (d) 256
(e) $\frac{56}{27}$ (f) $-20a^3$ (g) $20b^3$
(h) $\frac{1}{6}n(n+1)(n+2)c^3$

4 (a) $1 + \frac{1}{3}x - \frac{1}{9}x^2$ (b) $1 + \frac{3}{4}x - \frac{3}{32}x^2$
(c) $1 - \frac{3}{2}x + \frac{3}{8}x^2$ (d) $1 + \frac{1}{2}x + \frac{3}{8}x^2$

5 (a) $1 + 2x - 2x^2$ (b) $1 - x + 2x^2$
(c) $1 - 8x + 8x^2$ (d) $1 + \frac{1}{8}x + \frac{5}{128}x^2$

6 (a) $-\frac{1}{2}$ (b) $\frac{625}{16}$ (c) $\frac{5}{24}$ (d) $-\frac{5}{2}$
(e) 20   (f) $\frac{1}{8}\sqrt{2}$ (g) $-\frac{1}{16}a^3$
(h) $\frac{1}{48}n(n+2)(n+4)b^3$

7 (a) $1 - \frac{1}{8}x - \frac{1}{128}x^2$ (b) $1 + \frac{1}{8}x^2 - \frac{1}{128}x^4$
(c) $2 + \frac{1}{4}x - \frac{1}{64}x^2$ (d) $6 + \frac{3}{4}x - \frac{3}{64}x^2$

8 $|x| < \frac{2}{3}$
(a) $4 + 12x + 27x^2 + 54x^3$
(b) $\frac{1}{4} + \frac{3}{4}x + \frac{27}{16}x^2 + \frac{27}{8}x^3$

9 (a) $1 - 3x - \frac{9}{2}x^2 - \frac{27}{2}x^3$, $|x| < \frac{1}{6}$
(b) $1 - 5x + 25x^2 - 125x^3$, $|x| < \frac{1}{5}$
(c) $1 - 3x + 18x^2 - 126x^3$, $|x| < \frac{1}{9}$
(d) $1 + 8x + 40x^2 + 160x^3$, $|x| < \frac{1}{2}$
(e) $1 + x^2 - \frac{1}{2}x^4 + \frac{1}{2}x^6$, $|x| < \frac{1}{2}\sqrt{2}$
(f) $2 - \frac{4}{3}x - \frac{8}{9}x^2 - \frac{80}{81}x^3$, $|x| < \frac{1}{2}$
(g) $10 - 4x + \frac{6}{5}x^2 - \frac{8}{25}x^3$, $|x| < 5$
(h) $1 + \frac{1}{2}x + \frac{1}{4}x^2 + \frac{1}{8}x^3$, $|x| < 2$
(i) $\frac{1}{8} - \frac{3}{16}x + \frac{3}{16}x^2 - \frac{5}{32}x^3$, $|x| < 2$
(j) $2x - \frac{1}{4}x^4 + \frac{3}{64}x^7 - \frac{5}{512}x^{10}$, $|x| < \sqrt[3]{4}$
(k) $1 + 2x - 6x^2 + 28x^3$, $|x| < \frac{1}{8}$
(l) $\frac{4}{3} + \frac{16}{9}\sqrt{3}x + \frac{40}{9}x^2 + \frac{80}{27}\sqrt{3}x^3$, $|x| < \sqrt{3}$

10 $1 + 4x - 8x^2 + 32x^3$, $1.039\,232$
(a) $10.392\,32$
(b) $1.732\,05$

11 $1 + \frac{4}{3}x - \frac{16}{9}x^2$
(a) $5.065\,78$
(b) $9.996\,67$

12 6

13 15

14 $1 + 3x + \frac{15}{2}x^2$, $|x| < \frac{1}{4}$, 4.123

15 $4, 6, -100$

16 $1 + x + 2x^2 + 3x^3 + 5x^4$, $1.001\,002\,003\,005$

17 (a) $2 - 2x + \frac{7}{2}x^2$ (b) $1 + 5x + 6x^2$

18 $-\frac{56}{27}$

19 $|x| < \frac{1}{4}$

20 (a) $1 - 2x + 3x^2 - 4x^3$
(b) $1 + 2x^2 + 3x^4 + 4x^6$
(c) $1 - 4x^2 + 12x^4 - 32x^6$

Miscellaneous exercise 5 (page 281)

1 $1 + 5x + \frac{15}{2}x^2 + \frac{5}{2}x^3$

2 $1 - 2x - 2x^2 - 4x^3$

3 $1 - 6x + 24x^2 - 80x^3$

4 $1 - 4x^2 + 12x^4 - 32x^6$

5 $2 + \frac{1}{4}x - \frac{1}{64}x^2$, $|x| < 4$

6 $1 - \frac{3x^2}{2a^2} + \frac{15x^4}{8a^4}$

7 $1 + \frac{1}{2}x - \frac{1}{8}x^2$, $a = 2, b = -\frac{3}{4}$

8 $1 + 2x + 3x^2 + 4x^3$, $a = 5, b = 7$

9 $4 + x - \frac{1}{16}x^2$, $|x| < \frac{8}{3}$

10 $1 - \frac{1}{3}x - \frac{1}{9}x^2 - \frac{5}{81}x^3$

11 $1 + \frac{1}{4}x - \frac{3}{32}x^2$

12 $\frac{3}{2} - \frac{3}{4}x + 3x^2$

13 $n = 15$, $1 - \frac{1}{2}x - \frac{1}{8}x^2$, $\frac{1351}{780}$

15 $A = 1, B = -1, C = 0, D = 1, E = -1$
(a) $0.999\,700\,000\,026\,991\,9$

16 $1 + 2x + 3x^2 + 4x^3$, $1.000\,200\,030\,004$

17 $1 - \frac{1}{4}x + \frac{5}{32}x^2$, $1.495\,35$

18 $1 - \frac{1}{2}x + \frac{3}{8}x^2 + \frac{5}{16}x^3$

21 $1 + \frac{3}{2}x + \frac{3}{8}x^2$, $3.605\,525$

22 $1 - 2x + 4x^2 - 8x^3 + 16x^4$, $0.346\,056$, 0.69

23 $3 + \frac{7}{2}x + \frac{1}{2}x^2$, $3\frac{1}{24}$

24 $1 - 2x^2 + 15x^4$, 0.531

Revision exercise 3 (page 284)

1 (a) $y + 1 = 0$
(b) $x + y - \pi = 0$

(c) $x - y - \pi = 0$

(d) $3x + 2y - 3\pi - 4 = 0$

(e) $y + 2 = 0$

(f) $3x - 2y - 3\pi + 6 = 0$

2 $xe^x + e^x$, $xe^x - e^x + k$

3 $(33, 27)$

4 The point does lie on the line.

5 $-\frac{1}{2}\pi$, $2x - \pi y = 2$

6 $x \tan x + \ln|\cos x| + k$

7 (a) $-\sin\theta \cos^2\theta$ (b) $3x + 8y = 15$

8 (a) $1 + 2x - 2x^2$ (b) $-\frac{1}{4} < x < \frac{1}{4}$

   (c) $5, 8$

9 $(5, -1, 2)$, $\mathbf{r} = \begin{pmatrix} 5 \\ -1 \\ 2 \end{pmatrix} + t \begin{pmatrix} -6 \\ 2 \\ -3 \end{pmatrix}$

10 (b) $\frac{58}{15}$

11 (a) $\dfrac{4 - 3x}{2\sqrt{2 - x}}$ (b) $\frac{-2}{15}(4 + 3x)(2 - x)^{\frac{3}{2}} + k$

12 (a)

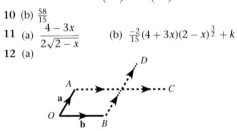

   (b) $\mathbf{b} - \mathbf{a}$

13 $1 - t \tan t$, $y = \sqrt{1 - x^2} \sin^{-1} x$

14 (b) $\frac{1}{13}e^{3x}(3 \cos 2x + 2 \sin 2x) + \text{constant}$

   (c) $\frac{1}{13}e^{3x}(3 \sin 2x - 2 \cos 2x) + \text{constant}$

15 -3, $y^2 = 9x(2 - x)$

16 (a) $-\frac{1}{2}\cos\left(2x + \frac{1}{6}\pi\right) + k$

   (b) $\frac{1}{2}x - \frac{1}{12}\sin 6x + k$

   (c) $\frac{1}{6}\sin^3 2x + k$

17 (a) $2 + \frac{1}{12}y - \frac{1}{288}y^2$ (b) $-8 < y < 8$

   (d) $2 - \frac{1}{6}k + \frac{5}{72}k^2$

18 $t^2 y + x = 2ct$

19 $3y = 4x + 2$

20 $\dfrac{300}{\pi}$, $240 \cos 600t$ (a) 0 (b) ± 0.4

21 (b) $a^2(\frac{1}{3}\pi - \frac{1}{4}\sqrt{3})$.

22 (a) $\dfrac{2t + 3t^2}{1 + 2t}$

   (b) $16x - 5y - 36 = 0$

23 $1 - \frac{1}{2}x + \frac{3}{8}x^2 + \frac{3}{16}x^3$

24 $\mathbf{r} = \begin{pmatrix} 2 \\ -1 \\ 4 \end{pmatrix} + s \begin{pmatrix} 1 \\ -1 \\ 1 \end{pmatrix}$

25 (a) $\frac{8}{27}\sqrt{3} - \frac{2}{3} + \frac{1}{12}\pi$ (b) $2(\sqrt{2} - 1)$

   (c) $\frac{1}{4}\pi - \frac{1}{32}\pi^2 - \frac{1}{2}\ln 2$ (d) $\frac{3}{25}(e^{\frac{3}{2}\pi} - 1)$

26 2π

27 (b) $(-12, 1)$ (c) $\frac{1}{2}$

28 $1 - 2x + 3x^2 - 4x^3 + \ldots$;

   $1 - 3x + 6x^2 - 10x^3 + \ldots$

29 $\mathbf{r} = \begin{pmatrix} 1 \\ 4 \\ 2 \end{pmatrix} + t \begin{pmatrix} -3 \\ -1 \\ 1 \end{pmatrix}$, $(-5, 2, 4)$

30 (a) $\ln 2$ (b) $\sqrt{3}\pi - \frac{1}{3}\pi^2$

31 (b) (i) $\frac{3}{4}$ (ii) $-0.232, 2.087$

32 (c) $\frac{1}{2}\pi$

33 $1 + x - \frac{1}{2}x^2 + \frac{1}{2}x^3 - \frac{5}{8}x^4$

34 The straight line $y - 1 = m(x - 2)$; m is the gradient.

35 2

36 They intersect at $(3, -5, 6)$.

37 (a) $\tan\theta$; t is the (signed) distance along the line measured from the point (a, b) on the line.

   (b) $x^2 + y^2 = R^2$

   (c) $t^2 + 2t(a \cos\theta + b \sin\theta) + a^2 + b^2 - R^2 = 0$

   (e) $\sqrt{a^2 + b^2}$; the right side of the equation in part (d) has a maximum value of $a^2 + b^2$ so this must be greater than (or equal to) R^2 for a solution for θ to exist. The point must lie outside or on the circle.

6 Rational functions

Exercise 6A (page 290)

1 (a) $2x - 4$ (b) $3x + 2$

   (c) $x^2 - 3x + 6$ (d) $\dfrac{1}{3x + 2}$

   (e) $(x + 3)(x - 2)$ (f) $\dfrac{1}{x^2 + x + 1}$

2 (a) 5 (b) $\frac{1}{4}$ (c) 1

   (d) -1 (e) 1 (f) $\frac{2}{3}$

3 (a) $x + 4$ (b) $\dfrac{1}{x + 7}$ (c) $\dfrac{3x + 2}{2x + 1}$

   (d) $\dfrac{x + 6}{x - 3}$ (e) $\dfrac{x + 4}{x - 4}$ (f) $\dfrac{-2(4x + 5)}{3x + 1}$

Exercise 6B (page 293)

1 (a) $\dfrac{x}{2}$ (b) $\dfrac{5}{4x}$ (c) $\dfrac{x^2}{3}$ (d) $\dfrac{2x^2}{3(x - 1)}$

2 (a) $\dfrac{1}{3x}$ (b) $\dfrac{5x}{6}$ (c) 2 (d) 6

3 (a) $x(x-1)$ (b) $3x$ (c) $\dfrac{3(x+5)}{x+3}$

(d) $\dfrac{x+3}{x+1}$ (e) $\dfrac{2(x+1)}{x+3}$

(f) $\dfrac{(2x+3)(3x-2)}{(2x-3)(3x+2)}$

4 (a) $\dfrac{9}{2x}$ (b) $\dfrac{x^3}{4}$ (c) $\dfrac{x^2}{2}$ (d) $\dfrac{x^2}{2(x-1)}$

5 (a) 2 (b) $-\frac{1}{3}$ (c) $\dfrac{x+4}{x+2}$

(d) $\dfrac{(5x-1)(x+2)}{x-1}$ (e) 1 (f) -1

Exercise 6C (page 296)

1 (a) $\dfrac{5x}{12}$ (b) $\dfrac{25x}{12}$ (c) $\dfrac{7x+11}{12}$

(d) $\dfrac{x-7}{15}$ (e) $\dfrac{3x^2+12x+10}{4}$

(f) $\dfrac{13x+14}{5}$

2 (a) $\dfrac{8+3x}{4x}$ (b) $\dfrac{5}{2x}$

(c) $\dfrac{7}{12x}$ (d) $\dfrac{3x-5}{2x}$

(e) $\dfrac{5x-2-x^2}{2x}$ (f) $\dfrac{(x+1)^2}{x^2}$

3 (a) $\dfrac{2(3x+5)}{(x+1)(x+3)}$ (b) $\dfrac{13x-1}{(x-2)(2x+1)}$

(c) $\dfrac{2(x+5)}{(x+3)(x+4)}$ (d) $\dfrac{5x+13}{(x-3)(x+1)}$

(e) $\dfrac{22x+19}{(2x+3)(3x+1)}$ (f) $\dfrac{2(13x-10)}{(2x+1)(5x-3)}$

4 (a) $\dfrac{4x+7}{(3x-1)(2x+1)}$ (b) $\dfrac{-3}{2x(4x+1)}$

(c) $\dfrac{x(8x+13)}{(x+2)(x+1)}$ (d) $\dfrac{x(6x+17)}{(2x-1)(x+2)}$

(e) $\dfrac{2x^2+6x+5}{(x+1)(x+2)}$ (f) $\dfrac{x^2-2x+18}{(x+4)(x-2)}$

5 (a) $\dfrac{4x+5}{(x+1)(x+3)}$ (b) $\dfrac{6x-1}{(x+2)(x-1)}$

(c) $\dfrac{2(3x+1)}{x(x-3)}$ (d) $\dfrac{-4x}{(x+2)(x-2)}$

(e) $\dfrac{1}{x-3}$ (f) $\dfrac{5}{2x-1}$

6 $(x-3)(x+3)$

7 (a) $\dfrac{2(8x-3)}{(x+4)(x-3)}$ (b) $\dfrac{7(x-11)}{(x+4)(x-3)}$

8 (a) $\dfrac{3}{x(x-1)(x-3)}$ (b) $\dfrac{1}{(2x+1)(3x-1)}$

Exercise 6D (page 300)

1 $a=5, b=10, c=4$

2 (a) $\dfrac{1}{x+5}+\dfrac{1}{x+3}$ (b) $\dfrac{3}{x-1}+\dfrac{7}{x+5}$

(c) $\dfrac{-4}{x-4}+\dfrac{5}{x-5}$ (d) $\dfrac{8}{2x-1}-\dfrac{4}{x+3}$

3 (a) $\dfrac{5}{x+2}+\dfrac{3}{x-1}$ (b) $\dfrac{5}{x-4}-\dfrac{5}{x+1}$

(c) $\dfrac{4}{x-3}+\dfrac{6}{x+3}$ (d) $\dfrac{3}{x}-\dfrac{6}{2x+1}$

4 (a) $\dfrac{3}{x+2}-\dfrac{5}{x-1}+\dfrac{2}{x-3}$

(b) $\dfrac{9}{x+3}-\dfrac{2}{x+1}+\dfrac{1}{x-1}$

(c) $\dfrac{3}{x}+\dfrac{5}{x-6}+\dfrac{7}{x+4}$

5 (a) $10\ln|x-3|-3\ln|x-1|+k$

(b) $\ln|x-2|-\ln|x+2|+k$

(c) $7\ln|x|+\frac{1}{2}\ln|2x+5|+k$

(d) $\frac{5}{3}\ln|3x+1|-\frac{3}{2}\ln|2x-1|+k$

6 (a) $\ln 18$ (b) $\ln 40$

(c) $3\ln\frac{16}{7}$ (d) $\ln\frac{54}{125}$

7 $\dfrac{1}{1+x}+\dfrac{1}{1-2x}$, $2+x+5x^2+7x^3$

8 $\dfrac{6}{1+4x}-\dfrac{3}{1+2x}$, $3-18x+84x^2-360x^3$; $|x|<\frac{1}{4}$

9 $\dfrac{3a}{x+2a}+\dfrac{a}{x-a}$

10 $2\ln\frac{3}{2}$

11 $2\ln 4-\ln 3$

Exercise 6E (page 305)

1 (a) $\dfrac{1}{x-1}-\dfrac{1}{x-3}+\dfrac{2}{(x-3)^2}$

(b) $\dfrac{5}{x+2}+\dfrac{2}{(x+2)^2}+\dfrac{1}{x-1}$

(c) $\dfrac{1}{x}-\dfrac{1}{(x-2)}+\dfrac{2}{(x-2)^2}$

(d) $\dfrac{2}{2x-1}-\dfrac{1}{x+1}-\dfrac{5}{(x+1)^2}$

2 (a) $4\ln|x+1|+2\ln|x+2|-\dfrac{5}{x+2}+k$

(b) $\ln|2x-3|-\ln|5x+2|-\dfrac{1}{5(5x+2)}+k$

4 $\frac{5}{2}+2\ln 2-\frac{3}{2}\ln\frac{7}{5}$

5 $1-3x+9x^2$

Exercise 6F (page 310)

1 (a) $x+1$, 1
  (b) $6x+9$, 27
  (c) $2x+2$, 7
  (d) $3x$, $-11x-1$
  (e) $x-5$, $20x-32$
  (f) $2x+4$, $2x-12$

2 (a) x^2-4x+2, $7-x$
  (b) x^2-2x+3, $2x+5$

(c) $2x^2 - 6x + 7, 5x - 2$

(d) $3x^2 + 2x - 5, 30$

(e) $x^2 - 2x + 9, 45 - 28x$

(f) $3x^2 - 4x + 4, 0$

3 (a) $x^2 - 1, 1$ (c) $\frac{1}{4}\pi - \frac{2}{3}$

4 (a) x, x (b) $A = 1, B = 0$ (c) $\frac{45}{2} + 2\ln 2$

5 (a) $x - 2, 3x - 4$

(b) $x - 2 + \dfrac{3x - 4}{(x - 1)(x - 2)}; A = 1, B = -2,$
   $R = 3, S = -4$

(c) $x - 2 + \dfrac{1}{x - 1} + \dfrac{2}{x - 2}$

(d) $\frac{3}{2} + \ln 6$ (e) $-4 - \frac{1}{2}x - \frac{5}{4}x^2$

Miscellaneous exercise 6 (page 311)

1 $\dfrac{1}{x - 3} - \dfrac{1}{x + 1}$

2 $-\dfrac{2}{x} + \dfrac{1}{x - 1} + \dfrac{1}{x + 1}$

3 $\dfrac{1}{x} + \dfrac{1}{x - 1} + \dfrac{3}{(x - 1)^2}$

4 $\dfrac{1}{x + 2} + \dfrac{1}{(x + 2)^2} - \dfrac{2}{3x - 1}$

5 $x^2 + 2x - 2, 12 - 8x$

6 $\ln|x| - \ln|x + 1| + k$

7 $\dfrac{1}{x^2} + \dfrac{1}{x} + \dfrac{1}{3 - x}$

8 $-\ln|x + 1| + 2\ln|x + 2| + k$

9 $-\dfrac{1}{x} - \dfrac{1}{x^2} + \dfrac{1}{x - 1}, -\ln|x| + \dfrac{1}{x} + \ln|x - 1| + k$

10 $\left|\dfrac{3x - 1}{4x - 3}\right|$

11 $x^2 - 2x + 2, 0; 2^2 \times 41 \times 61$

12 $\dfrac{2x}{(x - 3)(x + 3)}$

13 $-\dfrac{2}{2x + 1} + \dfrac{1}{x - 1}, \ln\frac{10}{7}$

14 $\dfrac{1}{7(x + 3)} + \dfrac{1}{7(4 - x)}, \frac{1}{7}\ln\frac{10}{3}$

15 (a) $\ln 2$ (b) $2(1 - \ln 2)$

16 $\dfrac{2}{1 - x} - \dfrac{2}{2 - x}, 1 + \frac{3}{2}x + \frac{7}{4}x^2 + \frac{15}{8}x^3; |x| < 1$

17 $\dfrac{1}{2 + x} + \dfrac{1}{1 - 2x}, \frac{3}{2} + \frac{7}{4}x + \frac{33}{8}x^2; |x| < \frac{1}{2}$

18 (a) $x^2 - 3x + 2, 2x - 3$ (b) $y = x^2 - 3x + 2$

19 $B = 1, C = 3$

20 $A = 2, B = 2, C = -1; 2 + \frac{1}{2}x - \frac{3}{4}x^2 + \frac{17}{8}x^3; \frac{1}{2}$

21 $\dfrac{1}{1 - x} + \dfrac{2}{(1 - x)^2} + \dfrac{3}{4 - x}, 2\ln 2 + 1$

22 (a) $2x^2 + 3x - 4, 2x - 3$

(b) $2x^2 + 3x - 4 + \dfrac{2x - 3}{x^2 - x}; A = 2, B = 3,$
   $C = -4, R = 2, S = -3$

(c) $\dfrac{3}{x} - \dfrac{1}{x - 1}$

(d) $\frac{187}{6} + \ln\frac{128}{81}$

23 $-\dfrac{1}{30(x + 3)} + \dfrac{1}{30(x - 3)} - \dfrac{1}{20(x - 2)} +$
   $\dfrac{1}{20(x + 2)}$

24 $-\dfrac{1}{1 + x} - \dfrac{2}{1 - x} + \dfrac{3}{(1 - x)^2},$
   $c_0 = 0, c_1 = 5, c_2 = 6; 3r + 1 - (-1)^r$

25 (a) $2x^3 - 3x^2 - 11x + 6$ (b) -14

(c) $\dfrac{2}{5(2x - 1)} - \dfrac{1}{5(x + 2)}$

26 $\pi(2 - \ln 2)$

27 (a) $\dfrac{1}{x - 3} - \dfrac{1}{x - 1}$,
   $\dfrac{1}{(x - 3)^2} - \dfrac{1}{x - 3} + \dfrac{1}{(x - 1)^2} + \dfrac{1}{x - 1}$

(c) $\left(\frac{25}{48} - \ln\frac{3}{2}\right)\pi$

28 (a) $\frac{1}{2}\ln\left|\dfrac{e^x - 1}{e^x + 1}\right| + k$

(b) $2\ln\dfrac{\sqrt{x}}{\sqrt{x} + 1} + k$

7 Differential equations

Exercise 7A (page 316)

1 (a) $y = x^3 - 5x^2 + 3x + k$

(b) $x = \frac{1}{2}t - \frac{1}{12}\sin 6t + k$

(c) $P = 500e^{0.01t} + k$

(d) $u = k - 50e^{-2t}$

(e) $y = \frac{2}{3}\sqrt{x}(x + 3) + k$

(f) $x = \ln\sin t + 2\sin t + k$

2 (a) $x = 5e^{0.4t} - 4$

(b) $v = 3 - 3\cos 2t - 2\sin 3t$

(c) $y = -\ln(1 - t^2)$

3 (a) $y = \ln x + \dfrac{1}{x} - 1$

(b) $y = 2\sqrt{x} - 4$

(c) $y = x - 2\ln(x + 1)$

4 14.1 s

5 2

6 $-6 - \frac{5}{2}\pi, 2.237$

7 $y = k - \frac{1}{2}x^2$

8 (a) $A + kt$

(b) $A + k\left(t - \dfrac{1}{4\pi}\sin 2\pi t\right)$

(c) $A + k\left(t + \dfrac{5}{4\pi}\sin\frac{1}{5}\pi t\right)$

(d) $A + k\left(\begin{array}{l} t - \dfrac{1}{4\pi}\sin 2\pi t + \dfrac{5}{4\pi}\sin\frac{1}{5}\pi t \\ -\dfrac{5}{176\pi}\sin\frac{11}{5}\pi t - \dfrac{5}{144\pi}\sin\frac{9}{5}\pi t \end{array}\right);$

all give $A + 10k$

9 $0.483\,\text{m}; -0.1h + 0.0483$

Exercise 7B (page 323)

1 (a) $y = \dfrac{1}{k - x}$ (b) $y = \sin^{-1} e^{x-k}$
   (c) $x = Ae^{4t}$ (d) $z = \sqrt{2t + c}$
   (e) $x = \cos^{-1}(k - t)$ (f) $u = \sqrt[3]{3ax + c}$

2 $y = a(e^x - 1)$

3 (a) $x = 3e^{-2t}$ (b) $u = \dfrac{1}{\sqrt{1 - 2t}}$

4 (a) $y = \dfrac{e^x}{2 - e^x}, x < \ln 2$
   (b) $y = -\ln(3 - x), x < 3$

5 $y = \dfrac{1}{\sqrt{1 - 2x}}$

6 about $6\frac{1}{2}$ minutes

7 3.6 minutes

8 $\frac{1}{2}\ln 2 \approx 0.347$ units

9 443 s

10 (a) $\dfrac{\mathrm{d}h}{\mathrm{d}t} = 0$ when $h = 25$, so the tree stops growing.
   (b) $\dfrac{\mathrm{d}h}{\mathrm{d}t} = 0.2\sqrt{25 - h}, t = -10\sqrt{25 - h} + 50$
   (c) (i) 1.0 years   (ii) 10 years
   (d) $h = t - 0.01t^2$ for $0 \leqslant t \leqslant 50$

11 $m = \frac{1}{3}$; enlargement factors over the 4 months for $m = \frac{1}{3}$ and $m = \frac{1}{2}$ are 25.6 and 35.3 respectively.

Miscellaneous exercise 7 (page 325)

1 $y = x^2 + 7x + 3\ln x + 2$

2 $t = \dfrac{10z}{20 - z}$

3 $y = x^3 - 4x^2 + 5x + 3$; $(1, 5)$ maximum, since $\dfrac{\mathrm{d}^2 y}{\mathrm{d}x^2}$ is negative at $x = 1$; $(\frac{5}{3}, 4\frac{23}{27})$ minimum, since $\dfrac{\mathrm{d}^2 y}{\mathrm{d}x^2}$ is positive at $x = \frac{5}{3}$

4 $e^2 \approx 7.39$ units

5 (a) $2\pi r, \dfrac{1}{2\pi r}$ (b) $\dfrac{1}{\pi r(t + 1)^3}$
   (c) $A = 1 - \dfrac{1}{(t + 1)^2}$

6 -1.5574; $\frac{1}{2}\pi$

7 $N = 3000e^{0.02t} + 5000$, 35 days;
   $\dfrac{\mathrm{d}N}{\mathrm{d}t} = \frac{1}{50}N - F$; since N decreases, $\dfrac{\mathrm{d}N}{\mathrm{d}t} < 0$

but $\left|\dfrac{\mathrm{d}N}{\mathrm{d}t}\right|$ gets larger, so N decreases with increasing rapidity.

8 (a) the number of people served in each minute, $x = 0.7t^2 - 4t + 8$

9 $y = \sqrt{1 - (1 - a^2)e^{-2t}}$

10 (a) $T = 470 - 6x$, $360\,°C$
   (b) $\dfrac{\mathrm{d}T}{\mathrm{d}x} = -kx$, $T = 380 - \frac{1}{10}x^2$

11 (a) $q = Q(1 - (1 - \lambda)e^{-kt})$

12 2 minutes; $\frac{1}{4}\pi$

13 $\frac{1}{12}\pi(2\sqrt{3} - 1) - \frac{1}{2}(\sqrt{3} - 1)$

14 (a) 12, $4\frac{1}{2}$, rate of increase $\to 0$, N will never exceed 500
   (c) $t = 10\ln\dfrac{N}{500 - N} + k, t = 10\ln\dfrac{4N}{500 - N}$, 18 years

15 (c) $\dfrac{\mathrm{d}y}{\mathrm{d}x} = \frac{1}{2}(x + 1) < 0$ when $x < -1$, but $\sqrt{y}$ can't be negative. $\dfrac{\mathrm{d}x}{\mathrm{d}y} = \dfrac{1}{\sqrt{y}}$ has no meaning when $y = 0$.

16 $p = \dfrac{mAe^{kt}}{1 + Ae^{kt}}$; 54 000;
   $\displaystyle\int_{30\,000}^{54\,000} \dfrac{5}{p\left(1 - \left(\frac{1}{100\,000}p\right)^5\right)}\,\mathrm{d}p$, 3.0 years

8 Curves defined implicitly

Exercise 8A (page 333)

1 (a) $\frac{3}{4}$ (b) 6   (c) $\frac{3}{4}$ (d) $-\frac{1}{2}$

2 (a) $\dfrac{4x - 3x^2}{1 + 12y^2}$ (b) $-\dfrac{6x^2 + 1}{3y}$ (c) $-\sqrt{\dfrac{y}{x}}$
   (d) $\dfrac{4y^4}{9x^3}$ (e) $-\dfrac{(y + 1)(x - 1)^2}{y(x^2 + 1)}$

3 (a) $-\frac{4}{3}$ (b) 3   (c) $-\frac{1}{2}$

4 $(-2, 4), (2, -2)$

5 $-\frac{1}{3}$

6 $3x - 2y = 8$

7 $x - 2y = 7, -\frac{86}{13}$

8 (b) $\dfrac{\mathrm{d}y}{\mathrm{d}x} = -e^{x-y}$
   (c) Both x and y are less than $\ln 2$.

9 (a) $(0, \pm 1), (\pm\frac{1}{2}, 0)$
   (c) $y \approx \pm(1 - x^2)$
   (e) $x \approx \pm(\frac{1}{2} - \frac{1}{4}y^4)$

10 (a) The curve is symmetrical about the y-axis.

(b) $\dfrac{dy}{dx} = -\dfrac{2x}{3y^2}$; when x is positive $\dfrac{dy}{dx}$ is negative, and vice versa.

(c) maximum

11 $(0, 0), (-1, 0); 0, 1$

12 $1, -2$ and 1 at $(0, 0), (0, 1)$ and $(0, 2)$ respectively

Exercise 8B (page 338)

1 (a) $y^3 = x^3 + k$ (b) $y^2 = x^2 + k$
 (c) $y = ce^{\frac{1}{2}x^2}$ (d) $y^2 = \sqrt{2\ln|x| + k}$

2 $y = \dfrac{4x}{x+1}$

3 $x^2 + y^2 = k$; a set of circles, centre $(0, 0)$,
 $x^2 + y^2 = 25$

4 $(x + 1)^2 + (y - 2)^2 = k$, circles, centre $(-1, 2)$

5 (a) $y = \sqrt{2}x^{\frac{3}{2}}$ (b) $y = 8\sqrt{2}x^{-\frac{3}{2}}$
 (c) $\sin y = \frac{1}{2} - \cos x$ (d) $\cos y = 2\cos x$

6 $v^2 = k - \omega^2 x^2$, $v^2 = \omega^2(a^2 - x^2)$

7 (a) $y^2 + 1 = k(x^2 + 1)^2$, $k > 0$
 (b) $\sec y = c \sec x$, $c \neq 0$

8 (a) $y = \dfrac{2}{2 - x}$ (b) $2\sin x \cos y = 1$
 (c) $y = \sqrt{\dfrac{2}{x - 1}}$ (d) $y = 2\sec x$

9 (a) $y = \dfrac{2(1 - kx^4)}{1 + kx^4}$ (b) $y = \ln(k + x\ln x)$
 (c) $y^2 = 4(k + \tan\frac{1}{2}x)$

10 $y = kx^n$

11 (a) $n = 5000e^{0.01(0.05t - 50\sin 0.02t)}$
 (b) 3150

12 $v^2 = \dfrac{20R^2}{x} + V^2 - 20R$

Exercise 8C (page 342)

1 (a) $y + x\dfrac{dy}{dx}$ (b) $y^2 + 2xy\dfrac{dy}{dx}$
 (c) $2xy^2 + 2x^2y\dfrac{dy}{dx}$ (d) $\dfrac{2xy - x^2\dfrac{dy}{dx}}{y^2}$

2 (a) $\dfrac{y + x\dfrac{dy}{dx}}{2\sqrt{xy}}$ (b) $\left(2xy + x^2\dfrac{dy}{dx}\right)\cos(x^2 y)$
 (c) $\dfrac{1}{x} + \dfrac{1}{y}\dfrac{dy}{dx}$ (d) $\left(y + x\dfrac{dy}{dx} + \dfrac{dy}{dx}\right)e^{xy+y}$

3 (a) $-\frac{4}{3}$ (b) $\frac{20}{11}$

4 (a) $-\frac{1}{3}\sqrt{3}$ (b) 0   (c) -2 (d) $-\frac{1}{3}\pi$

5 $3y = x + 5$

6 $x = 1$

7 $(3, 1), (-3, -1)$

8 (a) -1 (b) $\frac{1}{3}$
 (c) $(0, 0)$, there are two branches there, one parallel to each axis; $(2^{\frac{1}{3}}, 2^{\frac{2}{3}}), (2^{\frac{2}{3}}, 2^{\frac{1}{3}})$

9 (a) $(x^2 + y^2)^2 \geq 0$ so $x^2 - y^2 \geq 0$
 (b) $(\pm\frac{1}{4}\sqrt{6}, \pm\frac{1}{4}\sqrt{2}), (\pm 1, 0)$

Miscellaneous exercise 8 (page 343)

1 (a) $400x^2 + 25y^2 = 4$
 (b) $(\pm 0.1, 0), (0, \pm 0.4)$

2 $5x - 13y + 3 = 0$

3 (a) $\dfrac{x - y}{x - 4y}$, $(2, 2), (-2, -2)$
 (b) $2x - y = 3\sqrt{3}$

4 $y = \pm\sqrt{k(x - 1)^2 e^{2x} - 1}$

5 $\ln y = \frac{1}{4} + (-\frac{1}{4} + \frac{1}{2}x)e^{2x}$

6 $3x - 7y = 13$

7 $y^2 = 1 + c\,\mathrm{cosec}\,2x$

8 $y = \dfrac{3}{\ln\dfrac{x+1}{x-2} - k}$, $y = \dfrac{3}{\ln\dfrac{e^3(x+1)}{2(x-2)}}$

9 $y = \sqrt[3]{\frac{1}{4}(4 + 6x - 3\sin 2x)}$

10 $(1 + y)e^{-y} = (1 - x)e^x$

11 (a) $\dfrac{2 + x - 2xy}{2 + x^2}$
 (b) $(2, 1), (-1, -\frac{1}{2})$

12 (a) $\dfrac{a^2}{x^2} + \dfrac{b^2}{y^2} = 4$

13 $P = 600e^{kt}$, $P = 600e^{0.005t - 0.4\sin 0.02t}$; the model $P = 600e^{kt}$ is not consistent with the data; the model $P = 600e^{0.005t - 0.4\sin 0.02t}$ is consistent with the data, given to the nearest 100.
 Smallest number is 549.

14 3, maximum; -3, minimum

15 (a) $P = P_0 e^{\sin kt}$ (b) e^2

16 (a) According to the model, £745.
 (b) $£\frac{400}{3}\sqrt{5}$ per hour, which is approximately £298 per hour.

17 (a) $\dfrac{1}{1 - 8y^3}$
 (c) 1; since $\dfrac{d^2y}{dx^2}$ is zero at the origin, but positive close to the origin, the curve bends upwards.

18 4

19 0.185; minimum

9   Scalar products of vectors

Exercise 9A (page 354)

1   $-8, 11, 3$

2   $11, -3, 8$

3   $18, 0, 0$; $\mathbf{r}$ is perpendicular to both $\mathbf{p}$ and $\mathbf{q}$.

4   (a) and (d) are perpendicular; so are (b) and (c).

5   $-4, -8, -12$

6   (a) 5   (b) $\sqrt{5}$ (c) $\sqrt{5}$ (d) 1
    (e) 3   (f) 13   (g) 5   (h) $\sqrt{6}$
    (i) $\sqrt{5}$ (j) $\sqrt{13}$ (k) $\sqrt{30}$ (l) 2

7   $5, \begin{pmatrix} \frac{4}{5} \\ -\frac{3}{5} \end{pmatrix}$

8   $\begin{pmatrix} \frac{1}{3} \\ -\frac{2}{3} \\ \frac{2}{3} \end{pmatrix}, \frac{2}{3}\mathbf{i} - \frac{1}{3}\mathbf{j} + \frac{2}{3}\mathbf{k}$

9   $15.3°$

10 (a) $45°$ (b) $167.3°$ (c) $180°$
    (d) $136.7°$ (e) $7.0°$ (f) $90°$

11 $\sqrt{(x_2 - x_1)^2 + (y_2 - y_1)^2}$; the distance between the points with position vectors $\mathbf{r}_1$ and $\mathbf{r}_2$.

12 $\frac{4}{65}\sqrt{65}$

13 0

14 $172.2°$ (or $7.8°$)

15 $99.6°$ (or $80.4°$)

16 $70.5°$

17 $76.4°$

18 $48.2°$

19 $48.2°$

20 (a) $\begin{pmatrix} -b \\ a \end{pmatrix}$ or $\begin{pmatrix} b \\ -a \end{pmatrix}$ (b) $\begin{pmatrix} \dfrac{a}{\sqrt{a^2 + b^2}} \\ \dfrac{b}{\sqrt{a^2 + b^2}} \end{pmatrix}$

(c) $\mathbf{r} = \begin{pmatrix} p \\ q \end{pmatrix} + t\begin{pmatrix} \dfrac{a}{\sqrt{a^2 + b^2}} \\ \dfrac{b}{\sqrt{a^2 + b^2}} \end{pmatrix}$

(d) $-\dfrac{ap + bq + c}{\sqrt{a^2 + b^2}}, \left| \dfrac{ap + bq + c}{\sqrt{a^2 + b^2}} \right|$

Exercise 9B (page 358)

4   $\mathbf{b} - \mathbf{a}, \mathbf{b} - \mathbf{c}$;
    $(\mathbf{b} - \mathbf{a}) \cdot (\mathbf{b} - \mathbf{a}) = (\mathbf{b} - \mathbf{c}) \cdot (\mathbf{b} - \mathbf{c})$

5   (a) $\hat{\mathbf{a}} + \hat{\mathbf{b}}$ is in the direction of the bisector of the angle between the directions of $\hat{\mathbf{a}}$ and $\hat{\mathbf{b}}$.

(b) $\dfrac{1}{a}\mathbf{a}, \dfrac{1}{b}\mathbf{b}$ (c) $\dfrac{b}{a+b}\mathbf{a} + \dfrac{a}{a+b}\mathbf{b}$

6   (c) $\mathbf{h} \cdot \mathbf{b} = \mathbf{c} \cdot \mathbf{b}, \mathbf{h} \cdot \mathbf{a} = \mathbf{b} \cdot \mathbf{a}, \mathbf{h} \cdot \mathbf{c} = \mathbf{b} \cdot \mathbf{c}$; the edges OA and BC are perpendicular to each other.

Miscellaneous exercise 9 (page 359)

1   (a) $\mathbf{r} = \begin{pmatrix} 2 \\ -1 \\ 3 \end{pmatrix} + t\begin{pmatrix} -1 \\ 1 \\ 2 \end{pmatrix}$ (b) $21°$

2   $\mathbf{a}$ and $\mathbf{b}$, $\mathbf{a}$ and $\mathbf{c}$, $\mathbf{b}$ and $\mathbf{c}$, $\mathbf{b}$ and $\mathbf{d}$

3   $58.5°$

4   (a) $\mathbf{d} = \begin{pmatrix} 9 \\ 4 \\ -5 \end{pmatrix}$ (b) $\begin{pmatrix} 3 \\ 3 \\ 0 \end{pmatrix}$ (c) $120.5°$

5   (a) $7, 7$ (b) -32 (c) $130.8°$

6   (a) $x\mathbf{i}, -\frac{1}{2}x\mathbf{i} + \frac{1}{2}\sqrt{3}x\mathbf{j}, -\frac{1}{2}x\mathbf{i} - \frac{1}{2}\sqrt{3}x\mathbf{j}$
    (b) (i) $\overrightarrow{AP} = \overrightarrow{OP} - \overrightarrow{OA}$
        (ii) $-x\mathbf{i} + 30\mathbf{k}, \frac{1}{2}x\mathbf{i} - \frac{1}{2}\sqrt{3}x\mathbf{j} + 30\mathbf{k}$
    (c) $30\sqrt{2}$

7   $\dfrac{\mathbf{i} - 3\mathbf{j} - 2\mathbf{k}}{\sqrt{14}}, \dfrac{3\mathbf{i} + \mathbf{j} - 2\mathbf{k}}{\sqrt{14}}, 73.4°$

8   (a) 0.148

9   (a) $\sqrt{29}$ (b) $119.9°$ (or $60.1°$)

10 (a) (i) $\begin{pmatrix} \frac{5}{2}\sqrt{2} \\ 0 \\ \frac{5}{2}\sqrt{2} \end{pmatrix}$ (b) $90°$

11 (a) $60°$ (b) $\frac{3}{2}\sqrt{3}$

13 (a) $\mathbf{r} = \mathbf{c} + t\mathbf{u}, t^2 + 2\mathbf{c} \cdot \mathbf{u}t + (\mathbf{c} \cdot \mathbf{c} - a^2) = 0$
    (b) $(\mathbf{c} \cdot \mathbf{u})^2 = \mathbf{c} \cdot \mathbf{c} - a^2$
    (c) The radius to a sphere at the point of contact of a tangent is perpendicular to the tangent.

Revision exercise 4 (page 362)

3   (a) $A = 1, B = -1, C = 2$ (b) $\frac{35}{216}$

4   (a) $\dfrac{\frac{1}{32}}{x+4} + \dfrac{\frac{1}{32}}{x-4} - \dfrac{\frac{1}{16}}{x}$ (b) $\frac{1}{32}\ln\left(\frac{7}{135}\right)$

5   (a) $\begin{pmatrix} 9 \\ 3 \\ 3 \end{pmatrix}, \begin{pmatrix} 4 \\ 8 \\ 6 \end{pmatrix}$ (b) $\mathbf{r} = \begin{pmatrix} 2 \\ 4 \\ 3 \end{pmatrix} + \mu\begin{pmatrix} 7 \\ -1 \\ 0 \end{pmatrix}$

(c) $\frac{1}{2}\begin{pmatrix} 11 \\ 7 \\ 6 \end{pmatrix}$ (d) $68°$

6 $y^3 = x^3 + \dfrac{3}{x} + 4$

7 (a) $2\mathbf{i} + \mathbf{j} - 2\mathbf{k}$ (b) 3   (d) -3

8 (a) $-\dfrac{4x + y}{x + 2y}$ (b) $(1, -4), (-1, 4)$

9 (a) $-x^2 \cos x + 2x \sin x + 2 \cos x + k$
  (b) $\tan^2 x$
  (c) $\tan y - y = -x^2 \cos x + 2x \sin x + 2 \cos x + k$

10 $3 \ln \frac{4}{3}$

11 (a) $\mathbf{r} = 3\mathbf{i} + 6\mathbf{j} + \mathbf{k} + s(2\mathbf{i} + 3\mathbf{j} - \mathbf{k})$
    $\mathbf{r} = 3\mathbf{i} - \mathbf{j} + 4\mathbf{k} + t(\mathbf{i} - 2\mathbf{j} + \mathbf{k})$
  (b) $(1, 3, 2)$ (c) $56.9°$

12 (c) $r = a\sqrt{1 - e^{-kt}}$
  (d) The weed will not cover the whole pond
    because the expression under the square
    root, $1 - e^{-kt}$, is always less than 1,
    making $r < a$.

13 (a) $71.6°$

14 (a) $y = -2$ (b) $x = \pm 2\sqrt{5}$

15 (b) $P = 108\,000 e^{0.001(10 - m)t}$
  (c) For example, no immigration or
    emigration.
  (d) $m = 10(1 - \ln 2)$
  (e) If the death rate were zero, that is,
    the lowest possible, the population
    would take $100 \ln 2 \approx 69$ years to
    double.

16 $\dfrac{\frac{1}{4}}{1 + x} + \dfrac{\frac{1}{4}}{3 - x}$,
$\dfrac{\frac{1}{16}}{(1 + x)^2} + \dfrac{\frac{1}{16}}{(3 - x)^2} + \dfrac{\frac{1}{32}}{1 + x} + \dfrac{\frac{1}{32}}{3 - x}$;
$\frac{1}{2} \ln 3, (\frac{1}{12} + \frac{1}{16} \ln 3)\pi$

17 (a) 5   (b) 5   (c) $\frac{1}{4}\pi$

18 1.97; 500, 3550

19 (a) 4 metres
  (c) $-\mathbf{k}, 2\mathbf{i}$
  (d) $(\frac{1}{5}t)\mathbf{i} - 6\mathbf{j} + (\frac{1}{10}t - 2)\mathbf{k}, \frac{1}{20}t^2 - \frac{2}{5}t + 40$,
    6.26 m

20 (a) $(\pm 1, 0), (0, \pm\frac{1}{2})$
  (c) $y = \pm(\frac{1}{2} - \frac{1}{4}x^2)$
  (e) $x = \pm(1 - 2y^2)$

21 $\sqrt{\frac{2}{3}}$

22 $\dfrac{dx}{dt} = -kx$

23 (a) $(1,0), (0,1)$ (b) $y < 0$
  (c) $\dfrac{2(x - 1)}{3y^2}, -\frac{2}{3}$
  (d) The modulus of the gradient becomes
    very large.

Practice examinations

Practice examination 1 for C4 (page 366)

1 $2x^2 - 1$, 1

2 (a) $1 + x + 2x^2 + \frac{14}{3}x^3$ (b) $|x| < \frac{1}{3}$

3 (a) $\overrightarrow{OD} = 2\mathbf{b}$, $\overrightarrow{OM} = \frac{1}{2}(\mathbf{a} + \mathbf{b})$
  (c) $\overrightarrow{DM} = 3\,\overrightarrow{ME} \Rightarrow M$ lies on DE.

4 (a) $\ln n = 1 - e^{-0.01t} + \ln 5000$
  (b) $n \to 5000e \approx 13\,600$

5 (b) $1 - \frac{1}{4}\pi$

6 (a) $\frac{1}{2}x^2 \ln x - \frac{1}{4}x^2 + k$ (b) $\ln 3$

7 (b) $\ln \frac{3}{2}$

8 (a) $4, \frac{1}{4}; 3\frac{3}{4}, -3\frac{3}{4}$
  (b) $-\frac{17}{15}, 17x + 15y = 16$
  (c) $x^2 - y^2 = 4$

9 (a) $2\mathbf{i} + \mathbf{j} + \mathbf{k}$ (b) $68°$ (c) $2\mathbf{i} + 3\mathbf{j} - \mathbf{k}$

Practice examination 2 for C4 (page 368)

1 $\dfrac{4}{x^2 - 1}$ or $\dfrac{4}{(x - 1)(x + 1)}$

2 $\dfrac{\cos 2x - 2x \sin 2x}{\cos y}, -\frac{1}{2}\pi$

3 (a) $\dfrac{2}{x} - \dfrac{2}{x + 1} - \dfrac{1}{(x + 1)^2}$
  (b) $2 \ln \left| \dfrac{x}{x + 1} \right| + \dfrac{1}{x + 1} + k$

4 (a) $\frac{1}{12}\pi - \frac{1}{16}\sqrt{3}$ (b) $\frac{1}{2}\pi + 1$

5 (a) $-3\mathbf{i} + 5\mathbf{k}$ (b) $5\mathbf{j} + 4\mathbf{k}$ (c) $71°$

6 (a) $1 + 4x - 8x^2, 1 + 2x + 6x^2$
  (b) $1 + 6x + 6x^2, |x| < \frac{1}{8}$

7 (a) $\frac{1}{28}(2x - 1)^7 + \frac{1}{24}(2x - 1)^6 + k$
    $= \frac{1}{168}(2x - 1)^6(12x + 1) + k$
  (b) $\frac{1}{12}x(2x - 1)^6 - \frac{1}{168}(2x - 1)^7 + k$
    $= \frac{1}{168}(2x - 1)^6(12x + 1) + k$

8 (a) $\mathbf{r} = \begin{pmatrix} 1 \\ 1 \\ -2 \end{pmatrix} + \lambda \begin{pmatrix} 1 \\ -1 \\ 3 \end{pmatrix}$, or equivalent
  (b) The point does not lie on the line.
  (c) $a = 3, \begin{pmatrix} 3 \\ -1 \\ 4 \end{pmatrix}$

9 (a) $\dfrac{dV}{dt} = Cx^2 \dfrac{dx}{dt}$
  (c) $\frac{2}{5}x^{\frac{5}{2}} = -At + k$
  (d) 0.645 minutes, i.e. about 39 seconds

Index

The page numbers refer to the first mention of each term, or the box if there is one.

addition
  of fractions, 294
  of rational functions, 294
  of vectors, 255
addition formulae for cosine, 97, 352
  sine, 97
  tangent, 99
algebraic fractions, *see* rational functions
algebraic method for partial fractions,
  303
alphabet convention for position vectors,
  260
altitudes, 357
angle in a semicircle, 356
angle units, 90, 203
associative rule for addition of vectors, 256
astroid, 250
axes right-handed, 268

base, of exponential function, 68
  e, 69
basic unit vectors, 257
binomial
  approximations, 278
  expansion, 277
  series, 277
  theorem, 275
boundary condition, 315

cardiod, 251
cartesian equation
  from parametric equation, 244
  from vector equation, 264
centroid, 262
chain rule, 56, 151
coefficients, equating, 297
combining
  functions, 22
  transformations, 10

commutative rule
  for addition of vectors, 256
  for scalar products, 347
component vector, 258
components of vector, 255
composite function, 23
  rule for differentiating, 151
contradiction, proof by, 7
convergence of binomial series, 277
converting from parametric equation to
  cartesian equation, 244
converting from vector equation to cartesian
  equation, 264
cosecant, 91
cosine (cos)
  addition formulae, 97
  differentiating, 208
  double angle formulae, 100
  integrating, 216
  inverse, 107
cosine formula for a triangle, 356
cotangent, 91
counterexample, 8
critical values in modulus
  equations and inequalities, 120
curves, properties of, 248
cusp, 246

decimal search, 137
degree
  of quotient polynomial, 306
  of remainder polynomial, 306
degrees, 90
derivative
  of b^x, 69, 85
  of e^x, 69
  of $\ln x$, 78
  of $\cos x$, 208
  of product of functions, 165

derivative (*cont.*)
  of quotient of functions, 170
  of sec x, 209
  of sin x, 208
  of sum of functions, 163
  of tan x, 211
  of x^n (n real), 154
differentiating
  composite functions, 56, 151
  cosine, 208
  exponential functions, 65
  implicit equations, 330, 339
  product of functions, 165
  quotient of functions, 170
  secant, 209
  sine, 208
  tangent, 211
  with parameters, 245
differential equation, 314
  boundary condition, 315
  for exponential growth, 322
  general solution, 314
  initial condition, 315
  particular solution, 315
  separable variables, 334
  switching variables in, 318
differentiation, logarithmic, 340
displacement vector, 259
distance between two points, 117,
    125
distributive rule
  for scalar multipliers, 257
  for scalar products, 348
division
  of polynomials, 306
  of rational functions, 292
domain of a function, 17
  natural, 24
  of composite function, 25
  of identity functions, 31
  of inverse cosine, 107
  of inverse function, 30
  of inverse sine, 108
  of inverse tangent, 108
dot product, 346
double angle formulae, 100

e, 69
ellipse, 245
equating coefficients, 297, 307
equation of a line in vector form, 263
equations
  implicit, 328
  involving modulus, 120
  logic of solution, 7
  numerical solution, 135
  parametric, 242
  trigonometric, 105
exponential
  function (an), 65
  function (the), 69
  sequence, 41
  variation, 45
exponential growth and decay, 39
  continuous, 45, 75
  differential equation for, 322
  discrete, 41

function, 16
  composite, 23
  domain of, 17
  exponential (an), 65
  exponential (the), 69
  identity, 31
  inverse, 28, 30
  modulus, 113
  natural logarithm, 72
  notation, 20
  one-one, 30
  range of, 17
  self-inverse, 28

general solution
  of differential equation, 314
graph
  of cosecant, 92
  of cotangent, 92
  of growth or decay, 45
  of exponential functions, 45
  of inverse cosine, 107
  of inverse sine, 107
  of inverse tangent, 108
  of modulus function, 113

of natural logarithm, 77
of rational functions, 308
of secant, 91

identities, 94, 297
identity function, 31
implication, 4
implicit equations, 328
  differentiation of, 330
inequality
  involving modulus, 122
initial condition, 315
integral
  of $\cos x$, 216
  of e^x, 70
  of $\ln x$, 226
  of reciprocal function, 80, 82
  of $\sin x$, 216
  of $\tan x$, 216
integration
  by parts, 224
  by substitution, 228
  definite integrals, by substitution,
    231
  of e^x, 70
  of $\ln x$, 226
  of trigonometric functions, 216
  reverse substitution, 233
inverse function, 28
  graph of, 33
inverse cosine and sine, 107
  domains of, 107
inverse tangent, 108
  sum formula, 111
irrational indices, 154
iterations, 141
  convergent, 144
  which go wrong, 142

lemniscate of Bernoulli, 343
limits of integration, 231
lines
  skew, 269
  vector equation of, 263,
    268
Lissajous figures, 252

logarithm
  base, 72
  natural, 72
logarithmic differentiation, 340
logic
  counterexample, 8
  equivalence, 5, 118
  implication, 4
  in solving equations, 6
  proof by contradiction, 7

mathematical model, 315
median, in triangle, 261
mid-point, position vector of, 261
modulus, 4, 113
  equations, 120
  function, 113
  inequalities, 122
  properties of, 116
multiplication of rational functions, 290

natural
  domain, 24
  logarithm, 72
  numbers, 3
numbers
  natural, 3
  real, 3
numerical solution of equations, 135
  by decimal search, 137
  by iteration, 141

one-one function, 30
orthocentre, 357

parallelogram rule of addition for position
    vectors, 260
parameter, 242
parametric equations, 242
  relation to cartesian equations, 244
partial fractions, 297
  algebraic method, 303
  equating coefficients method, 297
  substitution method, 298, 303
  with repeated factor, 301
  with simple denominators, 297

particular solution of differential equation, 315

parts, integration by, 224

perpendicular vectors, 347

polynomials, division of, 306

position vector, 259

product rule for differentiation, 165

projection of vector, 348

proof by contradiction, 7

properties of curves, 248

Pythagoras' identities, 93

quotient polynomial, 306

quotient rule for differentiation, 170

radians, 90, 203

range of a function, 17

rate of change, 155

rational functions
   adding, 294
   dividing, 292
   multiplying, 290
   simplifying, 289
   splitting into partial fractions, 297, 301
   subtracting, 294

real numbers, 3

reflection of graph, 10, 33, 114

related rates of change, 155

remainder polynomial, 306

revolution
   solid of, 173
   volume of, 173

right-handed axes, 268

root of equation, 135

scalar, 255

scalar product, 346
   commutative rule for, 347
   component form, 350
   distributive rule for, 348

secant, 91

self-inverse function, 28

separable variables, 334

series, binomial, 277

sign-change rule, 135

Simpson's rule
   general form, 186
   simple form, 184

sine (sin)
   addition formulae, 97
   differentiating, 208
   double angle formulae, 100
   integrating, 216
   inverse, 107

solid of revolution, 173

solution of differential equation, 314

solution of equations
   bisection method, 149
   decimal search, 137
   definition, 135
   logic of, 6
   numerical, 135
   sign-change rule, 135
   using iteration, 141

stretch of graph, 10

substitution, integration by, 228
   choosing substitution, 236
   definite integrals, 231
   direct substitution, 227
   reverse substitution, 233

substitution method
   for partial fractions, 298

subtraction
   of fractions, 294
   of rational functions, 294
   of vectors, 257, 260

tangent, gradient using parameters, 246

tangent (tan)
   addition formula for, 99
   double angle formula, 100
   sum of inverse, 111

transformation of graphs, 10
   by reflection, 10
   by stretching, 10
   by translation, 10
   effect on gradient, 60

translation of graph, 10

translation vector, 255

trigonometric functions
  cosecant, 91
  cotangent, 91
  differentiating, 208
  integrating, 216
  inverse, 106
  secant, 91
trigonometric inequalities, 204
trigonometric limits, 205

unit vector, 257, 349
units for angle, 90

variables
  dependent and independent, 157, 318
  separable, 334
vectors, 254
  addition of, 255
  alphabet convention for, 260
  associative rule for addition of, 256
  basic unit vectors, 257, 349

commutative rule for addition, 256
commutative rule for scalar products,
  347
component vectors, 258
components, 255
displacement, 259
distributive rules, 257, 348
dot product, 346
equation of a line, 263, 269
in three dimensions, 268
parallel, 266
parallelogram rule of addition, 260
position, 259
projection, 348
scalar product, 346
subtraction of, 257, 260
translation, 255
zero, 256
volume of revolution, 173

zero vector, 256